THE SECOND
GREAT WAR

Photo, British Official

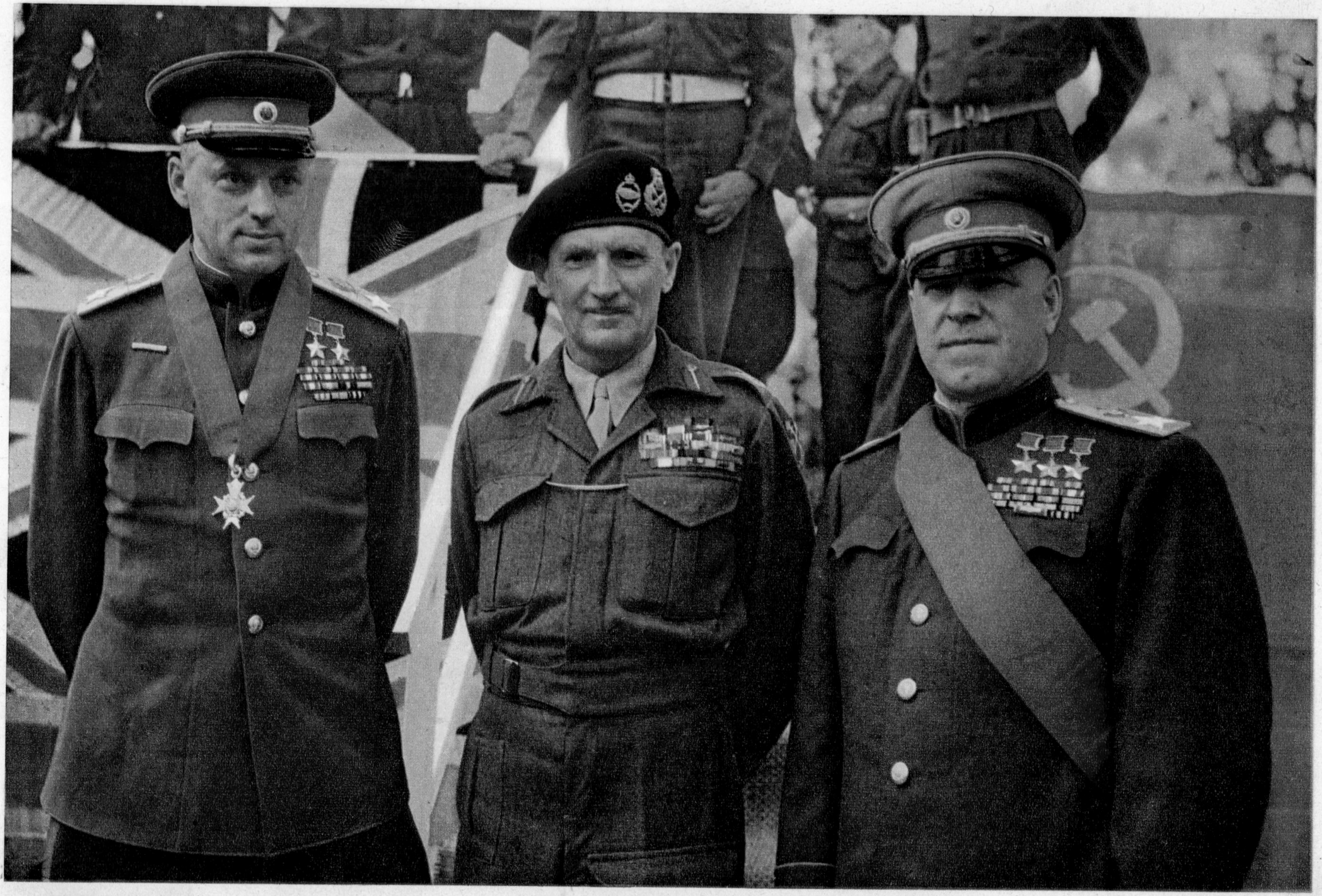

FIELD-MARSHAL MONTGOMERY INVESTS RED ARMY LEADERS WITH BRITISH HONOURS

On July 12, 1945, the Four-Power Komendatura (Military Government) assumed control in Berlin. The same day Field-Marshal Montgomery arrived to attend a ceremony at the Brandenburg Gate which was at the boundary between the British and Soviet zones. Here he invested Marshal Zhukov, Deputy Supreme Commander of the Red Army, formerly commanding the 1st White Russian Army, with the G.C.B.; and Marshal Rokossovsky, commanding the 2nd White Russian Army, with the K.C.B. He also invested with the K.B.E. Generals Malinin and Sokolovsky, respectively Chiefs of Staff to Marshal Rokossovsky and Marshal Zhukov. Field-Marshal Montgomery is seen here with Marshal Rokossovsky (left) and Marshal Zhukov after the investiture.

Frontispiece

THE SECOND GREAT WAR

A Standard History

Edited by

SIR JOHN HAMMERTON

Editor of The Great War, World War 1914-18, Europe's Fight for Freedom, etc.

Military Editor

Maj.-Gen. SIR CHARLES GWYNN, K.C.B., C.M.G., D.S.O.

Volume Nine
Pages 3577—4076

Published by

THE WAVERLEY BOOK COMPANY LTD.

in association with

THE AMALGAMATED PRESS LTD.
Farringdon Street, London, E.C.4

MADE AND PRINTED IN GREAT BRITAIN BY PURNELL AND SONS, LTD.
PAULTON (SOMERSET) AND LONDON

CONTENTS OF VOLUME NINE

LIST OF CHAPTERS

LIST OF CHAPTERS (Contd.)

HISTORIC DOCUMENTS

(The number of the page on which each document appears is given in brackets)

DIARY OF THE WAR, 1945

MAPS AND PLANS

SPECIAL PLATES IN COLOUR

CHAPTERS CLASSIFIED ACCORDING TO SUBJECT—Vols. 1 to 9

CHAPTERS CLASSIFIED ACCORDING TO SUBJECT—Vols. 1 to 9 (contd.)

NOTE. Dispatches from Allied Military Commanders and Reports on Naval Actions and Tanks are given in Appendices 1 and 2, pages 4000 and 4012

CANADIAN-SCOTTISH NEAR THE HOCHWALD

On the Rhine-Maas front, infantry of the 1st Canadian Army, with powerful tank support, captured Udem on February 27, 1945. A small town on the Goch–Wesel railway, Udem had strategic importance as a road centre. It was carried in an assault by a Canadian-Scottish battalion which later advanced into the Hochwald and surrounded Calcar next day. Here a stretcher-party trudges through ruined Udem. *Photo, British Newspaper Pool*

U.S. 1st ARMY TAKES COLOGNE AND REACHES THE RHINE

Cologne, third city of the Reich, fell to the U.S. 1st Army on March 6, 1945. Little resistance was encountered at the end. Above, a captured German Mark V tank outside the famous cathedral, which had been saved by blast walls from serious damage. Below, the devastated city after its capture, with the main railway station in the foreground, and (left) the Hohenzollern bridge : the only bridge standing across the Rhine when the Americans entered the city, it collapsed soon afterwards as a result of earlier Allied bombing. *Photos, British Official ; Associated Press*

Chapter 350

MIDDLE EAST NEUTRALS DECLARE WAR

The most significant development in the Middle East during early 1945 was perhaps the declaration of war on Germany and Japan by Turkey, Egypt, Saudi Arabia, Syria and the Lebanon. Zionist claims in Palestine, the strengthening of the Arab League and problems associated with the evacuation of Allied occupation troops were other dominating points in the 1945 history of the area. Events in the Middle East in 1944 are recorded in Chapter 303

THE defeat of the Axis Powers was, by the beginning of 1945, regarded with such certainty that the only question was when the final collapse would come. The Crimea Conference of the Three Great Powers, which took place in February (*see* page 3563), decided, among other things, that to qualify for invitation to the United Nations Conference to be held at San Francisco in April, those States which had hitherto been either neutral or not actively belligerent must declare war on the Axis, and adhere to the United Nations' declaration of January 1, 1942, before March 1. On their way home from the Crimea, Mr. Churchill and President Roosevelt had conversations in Egypt with King Farouk of Egypt, King Ibn Saud of Saudi Arabia, and Sayed Shukri al-Kawatly, President of Syria. Declarations of war on Germany and Japan followed in Egypt on February 24, in Syria on the 26th, in the Lebanon on the 27th, and in Saudi Arabia on the 28th.

EGYPT

In Egypt, this declaration led to the death of the Prime Minister, Dr. Ahmed Maher Pasha, who was assassinated on February 24 as he was crossing the Pharaonic Hall of the Parliament buildings : he had just come from a secret session of the Chamber at which he had secured the agreement of that body to the declaration of war on the Axis, and was on his way to address the Senate on the same matter. His assailant was a young lawyer, Mahmud Issawy, who had previously been under arrest for pro-Nazi sympathies. On further investigation the police found that he belonged to the Young Egypt Society, which was a definitely Fascist organization. After condemnation by a military court, he was executed on September 18.

The King immediately appointed Mahmud Fahmy el-Noukrachy Pasha, the Foreign Minister, as Prime Minister, and he carried on with the same Cabinet.

The dismissal by King Farouk in 1944 of the Prime Minister Nahas Pasha and his Government (*see* page 3056) had ended for a time at least the influence of the Wafdist Party on the direction of affairs in Egypt. Charges of corruption against that Party had been made, and appear to have influenced the action of the King in appointing Ahmed Maher Pasha Prime Minister and dissolving Parliament. Before the General Election, held on January 8, Nahas Pasha petitioned the King for the creation of a Coalition Government to conduct the elections. It must be remembered that eighty per cent of the population of Egypt is illiterate and this, coupled with the tendency of the civil service to interfere in politics, favours the Government which conducts the elections. It was because of the likelihood of electoral interference by any Government conducting elections that Nahas Pasha asked for a Coalition until the results of the election were announced. But the King refused to take any action, merely passing the request over to the new Prime Minister. As a result the Wafdist Party boycotted the elections. Since the Wafd was the only Party that had even the vaguest policy of social reform, the new Parliament consisted entirely of what might be called the Parties of the Right and Centre.

The war and the presence of considerable armed forces in the Middle East had resulted in a relative scarcity of goods, a considerable increase in note circulation, and a consequent inflation of the economy of Egypt. In the absence of direct taxation, large fortunes had been made at one end of the social scale, but even the fellaheen had felt some benefit, for the higher prices he received had enabled him to some extent to reduce his indebtedness, and Egypt's credit in sterling balances in Great Britain rose still further. The desire of Egypt to convert a portion of this into dollars to enable her to purchase on an increased scale from the United States was partly met by the Anglo-American financial agreement, provisionally signed later in the year, ratified by the British Parliament but still at the end of 1945 not sanctioned by Congress.

Financial Benefits of the War

CLEARING UP THE NAZI TRAIL IN THE DESERT

During Rommel's retreat from Egypt in 1943, the German armies left many areas thickly strewn with mines and live ammunition. In 1945 these mines and booby traps were still being detected and destroyed by experts of the Royal Army Ordnance Corps, and the loose ammunition blown up. Here a sergeant of the R.A.O.C. prepares enemy ammunition for destruction in a desert oasis in Cyrenaica.

Photo, British Official

3 z¹

REMEMBERING THE DEAD OF THE DESERT WAR

Left, plaque commemorating the British Libyan Campaign of 1940-41 and the heroism of the Western Desert Force under General Sir Archibald Wavell, unveiled on January 15, 1946, by General Sir Bernard Paget, C.-in-C., Middle East. It is in what was Marshal Graziani's palace in Benghazi. Right, memorial in All Saints' Cathedral, Cairo, unveiled by General Paget on October 17, 1945. (See illus. in pages 2007 and 2225.) *Photos, British Official*

After the adherence in January of Saudi Arabia and the Yemen to the Pan-Arab Protocol signed in Alexandria in October 1944 (*see* page 3055), King Farouk visited King Ibn Saud for informal conversation on Pan-Arab co-operation, carried an important step further when, on March 17, the Prime Ministers of Egypt, Syria, the Lebanon, Transjordan, Saudi Arabia, Iraq, together with Musa el Alami representing

EGYPT'S NEW PREMIER

On February 24, 1945, Dr. Ahmed Maher Pasha, the Premier, was assassinated in Cairo. King Farouk at once appointed as his successor Mahmud Fahmy el-Noukrachy Pasha, the Foreign Minister, here seen with Lord Killearn (formerly Sir Miles Lampson), British Ambassador to Egypt and High Commissioner for the Sudan since 1936.

the Arabs of Palestine, met in Cairo for further discussions on the proposed formation of an Arab League—a movement undoubtedly brought into being by the Zionist threat to the position of the Arabs in Palestine. Five days later they signed the Pact of the Union of the Arab States, which provided for the setting up of a League of Arab States with permanent headquarters in Cairo " by those independent Arab countries who wish to join it," with a Council on which representatives of all member States would act on an equal footing.

The objects of this League were : to foster co-operation between the States participating ; to forbid the use of force in the settlement of disputes between them ; to set up commissions to promote inter-Arab economic and cultural co-operation. This meeting of Prime Ministers also reiterated the views expressed at the meeting of October 1944 on the status of Palestine.

With the end of the war against the Axis Powers, a rise of nationalism in Egypt could be observed. The Wafdist Party, now in sullen opposition, became the centre of considerable anti-British agitation in spite of the fact that Nahas Pasha, while in office, had been markedly pro-British. The retirement by the Government of all British police officers, including Sir Thomas Russell Pasha, commandant of the Cairo police and organizer of the anti-narcotic campaign, T. Baker Pasha, commandant of the Alexandria police, and T. W. Fitzpatrick Pasha, commandant of the Suez Canal police, was announced on August 22 ; while on August 6 the Prime

Minister declared in the Senate that the time had come for the revision of the Anglo-Egyptian treaty of 1936, the abolition of all restrictions on the sovereignty of Egypt, and the withdrawal of all foreign troops. He also demanded the unity of the Nile valley (which meant the withdrawal of Britain from the Condominium of the Sudan) and the withdrawal of all British troops from the Suez Canal.

The treaty provided that if both parties were in agreement it could be revised after a period of ten years, and the British Foreign Secretary, Mr. Ernest Bevin, stated in the House

DESERT BALLOT-BOX

So that British forces overseas could vote in the General Election of July 1945, over 40 tons of ballot papers were carried to them by the R.A.F. In the Middle East, polling booths—with special precautions to ensure secrecy—were improvised in the desert. Some ballot-boxes were made from German ammunition containers. This R.A. officer deposits his vote in a desert ballot-box.

on August 22 that H.M. Government would, at the proper time, approach the question of revision " with the same friendliness and appreciation of our mutual interests as characterized the concluding part of the Egyptian Premier's speech."

Noukrachy Pasha repeated the demands for the withdrawal of foreign troops and the unification of the Nile valley in a statement he made on September 25 following a meeting in Alexandria of a Consultative Committee of Egyptian " Elder Statesmen " ; and King Farouk, opening the Egyptian Parliament on November 12, included these demands in his Speech from the Throne. A formal request for the revision of the treaty, made by the Egyptian Government in a note sent to Britain on December 20, received a reply a month later expressing Britain's readiness to review the treaty arrangements.

At the beginning of 1945 Turkey was still neutral ; but the decision of the Crimea Conference relating to invitations to San Francisco (*see* page 3579) forced the issue for her. The Turkish Parlia-

ment was summoned, and after hearing a speech from the Foreign Minister, Hasan Saka, decided unanimously on February 22 to declare war on Germany and Japan as from March 1.

On March 19 a most important development in Turkey's foreign relations took place when the Soviet Union denounced the Soviet-Turkish Treaty of Friendship and Neutrality signed in 1925. The Soviet press, commenting on this step, spoke of the different international conditions prevailing in 1945 and 1925. Then, it was said, Great Britain was hostile to the Soviet Union, and the United States was not even in diplomatic relations with her. Now the Soviet Union was in close co-operation with Britain and the United States, and the Soviet-Turkish Treaty was not of such vital importance to her.

TURKEY

The real reason for the Soviet Union's action was thought to be the desire to secure a revision of the Montreux Convention of 1936 (*see* page 719). It had been known for some time that the

Soviet Union was returning to her old demands for the right of passage for her ships through the Dardanelles and the Bosphorus into the Mediterranean, and the right to control entry of ships into the Black Sea in wartime, and on June 22, Mr. Vinogradov, Soviet Ambassador, suggested the conclusion of a new Treaty of Friendship on condition that Turkey agreed to a revision of the Montreux Convention, the cession of bases in the Straits to the U.S.S.R., and the return of Kars, Artvin and Ardahan to the Causasian Republics of the Soviet Union.

These areas had been ceded to Turkey by agreement after the First Great War, when Russia had voluntarily withdrawn from considerable areas of the Trans-Caucasus, but the suggestion made in some quarters that advantage had been taken of Russia's weakness at that time was deprecated by Mr. Sarajoglu, the Premier, when he said, " In the days when Russia could be regarded as weak, Turkey could be regarded as so weak as to be non-existent." The demand for these territories, however, was possibly a bargaining counter to secure the revision of the Montreux Convention which, after her experience in the Second Great War, the Soviet Union felt to be vital to her.

The Treaty of Friendship expired on November 7, and Soviet pressure on Turkey increased. Denunciations in the Soviet Press of the position Turkey had taken during the war grew more violent, and growing claims were made on Turkish territory. Student demonstrations in Istanbul on December 4, when left wing newspaper offices and bookshops were attacked, added to the tension. Mr. Hasan Saka continued to stress the need for friendly relations between the two countries, but declared, " We ask nothing of anyone, but at the same time we will yield nothing." The situation had not been resolved by the end of the year.

During 1945 Iraq continued to play a leading part in the movement to obtain close co-operation between the Arab States of the Middle East. Thus, Iraq **IRAQ** was represented at the discussions at Cairo in March which produced the League of Arab States (*see* page 3580). Nuri Pasha, former Iraq Prime Minister and now President of the Senate, had been largely instrumental in bringing the whole movement about and took an active part in these further developments. As in Egypt, the Zionist threat in Palestine was keenly felt also in Iraq.

During the summer, trouble developed in Iraqi Kurdistan, where Kurds under a local chief, Mullah Mustafa, caused local conflict. Mullah Mustafa finally fled across the borders into Persia where he made contact with the Russians. The trouble was largely due to tribal movements at certain times of the year. Iraq, like her neighbours, wanted to settle these nomads on cultivable land and so reduce their movements to a minimum.

With the defeat of the Axis Powers, British and American troops were in the course of the summer steadily withdrawn from the Trans-Persian road and from the railway running from Ahwaz to the Caspian. By the end of the year only a few establishments were left at the Iraqi terminals of these routes, and they were engaged in clearing up.

Rashid Ali el Gailani, leader of the 1941 revolt in Iraq (*see* Chapter 165 and page 2211) arrived at Beirut secretly as a stoker in the French steamship " Marrakesh " in June, and subsequently reached Saudi Arabia, where he sought and found sanctuary. Mr. Bevin stated in the House of Commons that he was reported to have travelled after Germany's defeat from Austria to Brussels, Paris and Marseilles ; that he was not listed as a war criminal, but was a traitor to Iraq ; and that he was satisfied Rashid Ali had entered Saudi Arabia without the permission or

previous knowledge of the government there. King Ibn Saud, questioned on the matter during a visit he paid to Egypt in January 1946, stated that he had never concealed his disapproval of the revolt, but could not refuse Rashid Ali sanctuary as a refugee. " If our sister country demands that I should hand him over," he declared, " I shall reply that he is sheltering under our protection, and I would rather give up some of my sons instead."

The state of tension existing in Syria and the Lebanon at the turn of the year (*see* page 3059) came to a head in May, involving also Franco-British relations.

TURKEY AT WAR
The Turkish National Assembly, the Kamutay, at a specially convened session on February 22, 1945, decided by a unanimous vote of all 401 representatives to declare war on Germany and Japan as from March 1. Mr. Sukru Sarajoglu, the Prime Minister, is here speaking during the brief debate which preceded the taking of the vote on the issue.
Photo, British Official

In the early part of the month, General Etienne Beynet, French Delegate-General for the Levant States, visited **SYRIA AND LEBANON** Paris to receive instructions for the negotiation of new treaties with Syria and the Lebanon designed to " settle the problems raised by the substitution of a regime of independence for the French mandate and to guarantee the cultural, economic and strategic interests of France." The French demanded the right to establish naval and air bases and to maintain troops under French command in the Republics, but proposed that the *troupes spéciales*, a gendarmerie composed of

Syrians and Lebanese under French command, and trained, equipped, paid and officered by the French, should be made over to the Syrian and Lebanese Governments.

General Beynet returned to the Levant, and while negotiations were proceeding, some French troops were landed at Beirut on May 17. Feeling became acute. The Syrian and Lebanese Foreign Ministers issued a joint statement on the 21st declaring that the landing of French troops without the consent of their Governments constituted an infringement of the sovereignty of their States, that they would not continue negotiations with the French, and that all responsibility for the situation rested with France. A demand was also made for the withdrawal of all foreign troops now that the war was over. Anti-French demonstrations started, in which French citizens were killed and injured ; and the statement by General Beynet on May 25 that the newly arrived troops were replacement troops did not lighten the tension.

Regret expressed by the British Foreign Office that the dispatch of French troops to the Levant had led to the breaking off of the negotiations that had been going forward and the statement that it was in **Britain Intervenes** consultation with all concerned and with the U.S. Government, was followed by a broadcast from Mr. Bidault, the French Foreign Minister, in which he said that " malicious propaganda and distorted information " had inferred, from the necessary relief of two French battalions serving in the Levant, that " France was resorting to intimidation and blackmail, and that she was trying to obtain by the display of force what she believed she could not obtain by negotiations."

Fierce fighting lasting several hours broke out in Damascus on the evening of May 29 between French troops and Syrians. Accusations were made by both sides as to the incidence of the outbreak. Heavy damage to property and many civilian casualties were caused by French artillery, which opened fire in many parts of Damascus. A general strike was called in Beirut on the 30th. Serious disorders were also said to have occurred in Aleppo, Homs and Hama. Next day, Mr. Eden, British Foreign Minister, stated in the House of Commons that in a message to General de Gaulle, the Prime Minister had said : " In view of the grave situation which has arisen between your troops and the Levant States and the severe fighting which has broken out, we have, with profound regret, ordered the C.-in-C. Middle East to intervene to prevent a further effusion of blood in the interests of the security of the whole Middle East, which involves communications for the war against Japan. In order to avoid collision between British and French forces we request you immediately to order the French troops to cease fire and withdraw to their barracks. Once firing has ceased and order has been restored we shall be prepared to begin tripartite talks in London."

Mr. Grew, Under-Secretary of State, said in Washington that the U.S. Government had been advised, and approved, of British intervention.

On June 1, General de Gaulle, in a broadcast, after stating that French troops in Syria had been attacked sporadically by armed bands, and had been compelled to defend themselves, went on to say that orders had been given to the French forces in the Levant to cease fire, and to stand on their positions. At a press conference he expressed the view that the difficulties in the Levant countries had arisen as a result of the British attitude, adding " to solve this unfortunate situation, France is ready for negotiations on the question as a whole, not only in connexion with Syria and the Lebanon, but the whole Arab world, for the U.S.A. and Soviet Russia are also interested in this . . . The French view is that the question might provide an opportunity for international co-operation such as is contemplated at San Francisco." Replying to questions, he recalled that during the war while all French troops except 4,000–5,000 were withdrawn from the Levant, notably to fight at Bir-Hakeim (*see* Chapter 224), 600,000 British troops (the British 9th Army) remained in that area.

General de Gaulle Replies

On June 3 the French garrison in Damascus, some 3,000 men, withdrew to a camp about five miles away, under British escort, and French civilians were evacuated next day.

On June 5 the French Cabinet proposed that the whole position in the Middle East should be submitted to a conference of the " Big Five " (Britain, Russia, U.S.A., France, China), a suggestion welcomed by the Syrian Premier. The tension between France and Britain was eased by the moderate tone of a debate held in July in the Consultative Assembly, General de Gaulle concluding his reply to the debate, " We feel profoundly the community of interests which despite everything has kept Britain and France side by

BRITISH INTERVENTION IN SYRIA

On May 31, 1945, the British Government ordered General Sir Bernard Paget, C.-in-C., Middle East, to intervene in Syria, where fighting had occurred between Syrians and the French troops in the country under the French mandate. 1. General Paget with Mr. Thomas Shone, the British Minister, leaves Beirut for Damascus. 2. British armoured car in Damascus, and 3. Wreckage in the bazaar quarter caused by French shelling. *Photos, British Official ; Keystone*

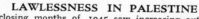

LAWLESSNESS IN PALESTINE

The closing months of 1945 saw increasing outbreaks of violence by the Jews in Palestine. On October 31-November 1 rail sabotage occurred at many places, including Lydda where the signal-box, a train and three locomotives were blown up and a British soldier and a Palestinian policeman killed. 1. Palestine Police clear the wreckage at Lydda. 2. Police patrol-boat returns to Haifa after a search for illegal immigrants. 3. Sixth Airborne Division troops examine travellers' papers. 4. Parade of mobile picket of Palestine Police Force armed with rifle, bren-gun, pick helve and metal shield to disperse rioters.

Photos, Associated Press; New York Times Photos; G.P.U.

side during these thirty years of war, but we ask that this friendship be also respected in the person of France."

Negotiations between General Beynet and Mr. Henri Pharaon, Prime Minister of the Lebanon, resulted in the handing over of more than 24,000 *troupes spéciales* without incident between July 22 and August 7 ; but continued presence of Allied troops was raised at the Security Council of the United Nations Organization when it met in London in February 1946 by the Syrian and Lebanese delegates, but in a conciliatory spirit (*see* Chapter 387). A plan for simultaneous withdrawal from Syria between March 11 and April 30 was arrived at by the French and British on March 4. On March 10, evacuation of British troops from the Lebanon by June 30, 1946, and of French troops by April 1, 1947 was announced.

The coming of peace saw no improvement in the Palestine situation. Indeed, towards the end of 1945 a sharpening of the Jewish-Arab conflict **PALESTINE** seemed in progress. The activities of the Stern Group (*see* pages 2642 and 3059) culminated in December in the blowing up of Police Headquarters in Jerusalem, while systematic outbreaks of violence all over Palestine indicated that they were organized from a centre. The aim of the extreme section of the Zionists was to break down the immigration restrictions and so create a Jewish majority in the country which would make it feasible to turn it into a Jewish State instead of simply the Jewish National Home contemplated in the Balfour Declaration. Illegal immigration along the lonely coast of Palestine continued.

The coming of the Labour Government in Great Britain during the summer aroused the hopes of the Zionists, for the Labour Party was committed by a series of conference resolutions in previous years to the extreme Zionist programme of a Jewish State. The Labour Government, however, on coming to power recognized the practical difficulties involved, and in November Mr. Bevin announced in the House of Commons that, at the suggestion of Great Britain, a joint Anglo-American commission of enquiry would be appointed to enquire into the situation resulting from the presence of destitute Jews in Europe and to make recommendations on the best method of settling them either in Palestine or in other parts of the world. This commission was a result of the situation created by a strong resolution of the United States Congress in the early autumn asking for the opening of

the doors of Palestine to Jewish immigration. The Arabs, meanwhile, fortified by the existence of the Arab League, showed every sign of determined resistance to further Jewish immigration. Mr. Bevin's announcement met with approval from the Arabs of the Middle East as showing that the new British Government was not going to be rushed into a policy at variance with the White Paper.

The association of the United States in this enquiry brought that country into direct contact with the problem of Palestine, which it had hitherto regarded from afar. The commission,

PALESTINE COMMISSIONER
The appointment was announced on November 8, 1944, as High Commissioner for Palestine and Transjordan, of Lieut.-General Sir Alan Cunningham, conqueror of Italian East Africa in the campaign of 1940–41 (see Chapters 163 and 164). Here he is arriving at Lydda airport for the swearing-in ceremony at Jerusalem on November 21. On his left (holding hat) is Mr. J. V. W. Shaw, Acting High Commissioner following Lord Gort's resignation.

appointed in December, issued a report (published as Government Blue Book Cmd. 6808, 1s. 3d.) on May 1, the chief recommendations of which were : (1) as Palestine could not alone absorb all the displaced Jews for whom homes had to be found, the whole world should share the responsibility ; (2) 100,000 certificates of admission to Palestine should be authorized during 1946 for Jewish victims of Nazi and Fascist persecution ; (3) Palestine should become neither a Jewish nor an Arab State, but a form of government should be set up which would protect the interests in the Holy Land of Christendom and of the Muslim and Jewish

faiths ; (4) as, pending the cessation of Jewish-Arab hostility, to establish an independent Palestine State (or States) would result in civil strife that might threaten the peace of the world, the government of Palestine should continue " as at present under mandate pending the execution of a trusteeship agreement under the United Nations."

Shortly after the end of fighting in Europe, Persia requested that all foreign troops be withdrawn from her soil. Dis- **PERSIA** cussions at Potsdam (*see* Chapter 380) led to an announcement in London on August 8 that British and Russian troops were to be immediately withdrawn. (By that date, the greater part of the American troops had already left.)

Under the Anglo-Soviet-Persian Treaty of 1942 (*see* page 2504), the last date for withdrawal was set at six months after the cessation of hostilities, which brought it to March 2, 1946. The British Government favoured an earlier date — December 1945 — and Anglo-Soviet discussions on the matter were continuing when the issue was complicated by a rising in Persian Azerbaijan in November, and the refusal of the Soviet occupying authorities there to allow Persian troops, sent to put down the revolt, to enter the province. The British Government sent a note to Moscow expressing the hope that the Soviet commander in Persia would be instructed not to interfere with the Persian Government's sovereignty in its own territory. The U.S. Government urged both the British and Soviet Governments to withdraw all troops from Persia by January 1946.

The Soviet Government, however, took the stand that the matter was one for purely Persian-Soviet discussion and settlement, despite the tripartite treaty, and this was still the international situation when the Persian Government presented its case for consideration to the first meeting of the Security Council of the United Nations Organization (*see* Chapter 387).

The need for reforms in Persia, and the desire for them in various sections of the population, was undoubted, but the spontaneity of the movement in Azerbaijan was in some doubt, as was the validity of the elections held in November (in which only a fraction of the population voted) which confirmed the autonomous government set up by the insurgents at Tabriz. The fact that Azerbaijan was completely shut off by the Soviet occupying authorities from outside contacts added lack of reliable information to the other difficulties of the situation.

February 1. U.S. 7th Army crossed Moder near Bischweiler; R.A.F. bombed München-Gladbach; by night attacked Mainz, Ludwigshaven and Berlin. 2nd White Russian Army stormed Torun on the Vistula; Marshal Zhukov captured Schwerin. U.S. India-based Super-Fortresses sank King George V graving-dock at Singapore.

February 2. French 1st Army liberated Colmar (Alsace). Heavy R.A.F. attacks (by night) on Karlsruhe and Wiesbaden. Red Army reached Drossen. Australians on Bougainville (Solomons) cleared enemy from lower end of Empress Augusta Bay.

February 3. U.S.A. 8th A.F. in strength attacked Berlin at noon; by night R.A.F. Lancasters bombed oil plants at Bottrop and Dortmund. Red Army captured Sternberg and Reppen, near Frankfort.

February 4. U.S. 1st Army pierced main Siegfried defences E. of Monschau; U.S. 3rd Army crossed Our, captured Bleialf. R.A.F. bombed enemy shipping in Gulf of Danzig. 1st Ukrainian Army forced Oder, S.E. of Breslau. U.S. troops of 5th Army recaptured Gallicano (Serchio Valley, Italy). Africans took Minbya (Burma); Ywathithgyi captured.

February 4-12. Three-Power Conference at Yalta, Crimea, attended by Mr. Churchill, President Roosevelt and Marshal Stalin.

February 5. U.S. 1st Army captured Hellenthal in Siegfried Line. Australians made new landing in New Britain. Announced that U.S. 1st Army had reverted to General Omar Bradley's command.

February 6. U.S. troops under French command stormed Neuf Brisach (Alsace); French troops seized Münster (Vosges). U.S.A. 8th A.F. in strength bombed Magdeburg, Leipzig and Chemnitz areas. Russians took Arnsdorf (E. Prussia). General MacArthur proclaimed fall of Manila.

February 7. R.A.F. by night and in great strength bombed Goch, Cleve, Magdeburg, Kassel, Mainz, Coblenz, Bonn, Hanover, Düsseldorf and Duisburg. Belgian Government resigned.

February 8. 1st Canadian Army renewed offensive S.E. of Nijmegen. U.S. 1st Army captured Schmidt in Hürtgen Forest. R.A.F. made major attacks on Politz (Stettin) and Wanne-Eickel (Ruhr) oil-plants. Marshal Koniev's forces crossed Oder N.W. of Breslau.

February 9. U.S. 3rd Army crossed the Prüm River. In Alsace the Colmar pocket liquidated with French and U.S. troops on the Rhine from Herlisheim to Swiss frontier opposite Basle. U.S.A. 8th A.F. heavily bombed Weimar, Magdeburg and Lutzkendorf oil-plants.

February 10-11 (night). Germans blew up floodgates and controls of Schwammenauel Dam and sluices leading to Urfttalsperre reservoir and the Rurstausee.

February 10. Canadians reached W. bank of Rhine. Announced that French 1st Army had completed destruction of German 1st Army. Heavy R.A.F. Mosquito attack on Hanover. 2nd White Russian Army captured Elbing (Baltic). XV Indian Corps took Ramree town (Arakan). Marianas-based Super-Fortresses bombed Tokyo and Yokohama areas.

February 11. 1st Ukrainian Army broke through enemy defences on W. bank of the Oder, capturing Liegnitz (Lower Silesia); 1st White Russian Army took Deutsch-Krone and Markisch-Friedland (Pomerania). India-based Super-Fortresses and "heavies" of Eastern Air Command struck at Rangoon area; other Super-Fortresses bombed Ota, near Tokyo.

February 11-12 (night). 20th Indian Division crossed Irrawaddy at Myinmu.

February 12. Scottish troops of 1st Canadian Army took Cleve; U.S. 3rd Army captured Prüm. Red Army stormed Bunzlau on Bober River; captured Bielsko (Poland). Treaty between Greek Government and E.A.M. Three-Power statement issued from Yalta.

February 13. R.A.F. by night heavily attacked Dresden twice. Last resistance ceased in Budapest. In Central Burma 19th Indian Division took Singu, 40 miles N. of Mandalay.

February 14. R.A.F. made severe double attack on Chemnitz (night). 1st White Russian Army captured Schneidemühl (Pomerania). Announced in Melbourne that over 200 R.A.A.F. Morotai-based Kittyhawks and Beaufighters had destroyed Japanese base of Tohohon (N. Celebes) in attacks over five days. Capture of Pagan (Burma). Mr. Churchill arrived in Athens with Mr. Eden and Field-Marshal Alexander.

February 15. Scottish troops established bridge-head over Niers River at Kessel. U.S.A. 8th A.F. heavily bombed Kottbus. 2nd White Russian Army captured Konitz and Tuchola (W. Poland). Tito's forces freed Mostar, capital of Herzegovina. Chinese troops took Kutkai, 48 miles N. of Lashio. U.S. forces completed capture of Bataan Peninsula.

February 16. Red Army forces under Marshals Koniev and Zhukov linked up at Grünberg (Silesia). Powerful U.S. force of carrier-based bombers attacked Tokyo and Yokohama; U.S. naval units bombarded Iwo Jima and Bonin Islands.

February 17. XV Indian Corps landed at Ru-Ywa (Arakan). U.S. carrier-based bombers kept up attacks on Tokyo region and naval forces bombardment of Iwo Jima. Corregidor (Philippines) captured by U.S. troops.

February 18. Field-Marshal Montgomery told 21st Army Group: "We stand ready for the last round." Red Army took Sagan; death in action of General I. D. Chernyakhovsky, commanding 3rd White Russian Army, Russia's youngest general.

February 18-19. 5th Army troops drove enemy from Monte Belvedere (Italy).

February 19. Marianas-based Super-Fortresses heavily bombed Tokyo. U.S. forces landed in great strength on Iwo Jima (Volcano Islands).

February 20. Nuremberg heavily bombed by U.S.A. 8th A.F.; U.S.A. 15th A.F. attacked Berchtesgaden. Soviet aircraft heavily bombed Breslau, Stettin, and Stargard. Motoyama airfield (Iwo Jima) captured.

February 21. 1st Canadian Army captured Goch. Nuremberg again heavily bombed. Russians took Czersk (N.W. Poland); Red Air Force made mass night raids on Königsberg.

February 22. U.S. 3rd Army completed liberation of Luxemburg. Over 6,000 Allied aircraft attacked some 30 rail centres in Central Germany. Soviets reached the Neisse River below Guben. Over 2,500 aircraft of the M.A.A.F. bombed communications in Bavaria, Austria, and N. Italy.

February 23. U.S. 1st and 9th Armies attacked across Roer. 1st White Russian Army captured Poznan (Poland). U.S. marines took Mt. Suribachi (Iwo Jima).

February 24. U.S. 9th Army took Jülich. R.A.F. heavily bombed Berlin (night). Brazilians took Bella Vista and La Serra (Italy). Surrender of Intramuros, last Japanese stronghold at Manila. Egypt declared war on Germany and Japan.

February 25. U.S. 1st Army completed occupation of Düren; U.S.A. 8th A.F. heavily attacked Munich; by night R.A.F. bombed Berlin. British 2nd Division crossed Irrawaddy near Myinmu (Burma). U.S. carrier-based bombers attacked Tokyo-Yokohama area.

February 26. Canadians launched offensive in Calcar–Udem sector. U.S.A. 8th A.F. heavily attacked Berlin by day; R.A.F. bombed it for the seventh successive night. Syria declared war on Germany and Japan.

February 27. R.A.F. bombed Berlin again. E. Africans captured Ywathit (Burma). With capture of Hill 382, half of Iwo Jima in U.S. hands.

February 28. U.S. 1st Army crossed Erft river; Canadians captured Calcar. Red Army took Neu-Stettin (Pomerania). Motoyama (Iwo Jima) taken by U.S. forces; last remnants of enemy garrison in Corregidor wiped out. Princess Elizabeth launched H.M.S. 'Vanguard' on the Clyde.

Chapter 351

LAST LANDINGS IN THE SOUTH-WEST PACIFIC

In this chapter, describing the final phase of the campaign in the south-west Pacific area, Miss L. E. Cheesman covers Allied operations in New Guinea, New Britain, the Solomons and Borneo. The story is taken up from the capture in June 1944 of Biak Island off New Guinea, described in Chapter 309, and the history of the campaign is followed through to its conclusion in August 1945 with the surrender of the Japanese forces in this theatre of war

VERY large concentrations of enemy forces still in mid-1944 occupied Buka and Bougainville in the Solomons, the Gazelle Peninsula of New Britain, and the Finsch Coast and part of Netherlands New Guinea. In all these areas the enemy was disabled by lack of air defences, and suffering through drastic interruption of his supply lines by air, sea and land. Even his coastal barge traffic was functioning only in a few localities. On the eve of the offensive for the American re-occupation of the Philippines, measures were taken to complete the severance of the main enemy communications, so that the isolated armies without chance of reinforcements could be dealt with singly, and U.S. forces were withdrawn from other areas to serve on the new battle front.

The capture by the Allies of the strategically important airfields of Biak (*see* page 3126) and Numfor (*see* page 3267 and illus. in page 3091) Islands had placed the remaining enemy-occupied territory of Netherlands New Guinea within reach of land-based

heavy bombers, which speedily convinced the Japanese that none of their positions was safe from an Allied invasion.

Owing to the nature of the terrain, they had few fortified positions. Their main base was Manokwari, east of the high mountain chains of the northern half of Vogelkop Peninsula. North-west of this high land was a second enemy base at Sorong on Doom Island, and the Sansapor district was at one time strongly held. On the south, Fakfak garrison had been withdrawn. Babo on McCluer Gulf, centre of a rich oil-bearing area and headquarters of the Koninklijke Petroleum Compagnie and Standard Oil Company, was also deserted because all defences and oil installations had been destroyed by Allied air attacks.

The port of Manokwari is entered by narrow, buoyed channels through high, broken land. The town is built around a conical hill on which is the Dutch Resident's house, formerly a rajah's palace. A very strong Japanese garrison held this citadel, protected by

formidable defences facing the sea, from which attack was expected.

Immediately after the occupation of Biak, U.S. pilots reported much enemy activity to the south of Manokwari, where Japanese troops were feverishly endeavouring to construct tracks across immense swamps to carry heavy traffic. Their efforts were fruitless, and no enemy routes were made serviceable for a large-scale withdrawal. Few escaped by air. General MacArthur's dispatch on June 27 mentioned that Manokwari airbase was deserted, few planes remained at Sorong, and none at Babo.

Japanese Try to Make Escape Roads

On July 30, 1944, a surprise landing was made near Cape Sansapor by U.S. troops covered by the Allied Navy and R.A.A.F. Kittyhawks. There was no sea or air resistance. Next day the beach-head was extended for ten miles; Cape Sansapor itself and the village of Sansapor were captured. Only small parties of Japanese were encountered, and they fled before the advancing American troops. The occupation of the

     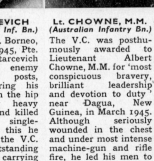

Pte. PARTRIDGE *(8th Australian Inf. Bn.)*	**Cpl. MACKEY** *(2/3 Aust. Pioneer Bn.)*	**Pte. KENNA** *(2/4 Australian Inf. Bn.)*	**Pte. STARCEVICH** *(2/43 Australian Inf. Bn.)*	**Lt. CHOWNE, M.M.** *(Australian Infantry Bn.)*	**Cpl. RATTEY** *(Australian Infantry Bn.)*

Pte. PARTRIDGE *(8th Australian Inf. Bn.)* At Bougainville, Solomons, in July 1945 Private Frank John Partridge, though wounded in arm and thigh, won the V.C. for 'outstanding gallantry and devotion to duty.' His remarkable initiative retrieved a serious situation, inspired his comrades to 'heroic action,' leading to a successful withdrawal which saved two patrols from annihilation by the Japanese.

Cpl. MACKEY *(2/3 Aust. Pioneer Bn.)* East of Tarakan, Borneo, on May 12, 1945, Corporal John Bernard Mackey won the V.C. for 'most conspicuous bravery' in a daring action during which he was killed. In a single-handed charge up a steep hill feature he wiped out two Japanese machine-gun posts. His 'fearless action and outstanding courage' were an inspiration to the whole Battalion.

Pte. KENNA *(2/4 Australian Inf. Bn.)* For his 'magnificent courage and complete disregard for his own safety' during a brief whirlwind action at Wewak, New Guinea, on May 15, 1945, Private Edward Kenna was awarded the V.C. In face of concentrated and highly accurate machine-gun fire and without orders, he single-handed captured a menacing Japanese bunker, killing several of the enemy.

Pte. STARCEVICH *(2/43 Australian Inf. Bn.)* At Beaufort, N. Borneo, on June 28, 1945, Pte. Leslie Starcevich rushed four enemy machine-gun posts, 'fearlessly firing his bren gun from the hip and ignoring heavy hostile fire,' and killed 12 Japanese single-handed. For this he was awarded the V.C. His 'outstanding gallantry' in carrying out these attacks resulted in the capture of a vital objective.

Lt. CHOWNE, M.M. *(Australian Infantry Bn.)* The V.C. was posthumously awarded to Lieutenant Albert Chowne, M.M. for 'most conspicuous bravery, brilliant leadership and devotion to duty' near Dagua, New Guinea, in March 1945. Although seriously wounded in the chest and under most intense machine-gun and rifle fire, he led his men to capture a strongly held enemy position. He was killed in the action.

Cpl. RATTEY *(Australian Infantry Bn.)* Entirely by the 'courage, cool planning and stern determination' of Corporal Reginald Roy Rattey a serious situation in S. Bougainville, Solomons, on March 22, 1945, was turned into a 'brilliant success.' Making a bold rush by himself, he single-handed silenced a Japanese outpost. His brave action enabled his company to gain an important objective.

Photos, Australian Official ; Sport & General

U.S. INVASION AT SANSAPOR

Covered by Australian and U.S. cruisers and R.A.A.F. Kittyhawks, U.S. forces invaded the Vogelkop Peninsula at Cape Sansapor, near the western tip of New Guinea, on July 30, 1944. The capture of the nearby islands of Middelburg and Amsterdam on the same day completed the Allied reoccupation of strategic points along the whole north coast of Netherlands New Guinea. Here crowded U.S. L.C.I.s close in on Cape Sansapor. *Photo, New York Times Photo*

islands of Middelburg (*see* illus. in page 3091) and Amsterdam on July 30, achieved with no fighting, completed the security of the position, and no counter-attacks developed.

The surrender of the 15,000 Japanese at Manokwari, left to their fate by the Japanese Command, and of the diminished garrison at Sorong took place only after the occupation by the Allies of Morotai and Halmahera.

Before the Japanese invasion of the south-west Pacific, Morotai Island's only inhabitants were a small number of Indonesians. Early in the campaign the Japanese made of it an important air and communication base between the Philippines and their new south-west Pacific empire.

The Allied landing on Morotai took place on September 14 on the west coast under the personal command of General MacArthur.

Allies Land in the Moluccas The Japanese were prepared for an attack from the south where they had fortified the beaches. Pitoe airfield, captured on the first day, was unfinished but was speedily made serviceable by the R.A.A.F. engineers. Within a few days all the south-west area of the island was in Allied hands and the air strips were being reconditioned.

During the first landing, the second and third waves of landing craft grounded on a reef a hundred yards from the shore, and it was proof of the absence of enemy air reconnaissance that no advantage was taken of

the accident. All troops got ashore in safety, although 24 hours later the beach was still littered with stranded vehicles. The nearest Japanese bombers were based on the Philippines, and the aircraft on Morotai destroyed by the Allies in earlier raids had never been replaced. By September 17 the Allies were in control of the island. The remaining Japanese had fled to the hills and the Americans were holding a strong line in advance of proposed sites for an airfield and a naval base, on which U.S. engineers were already at work.

Patrolling was active, but as the Japanese did not attack they were ignored, although their numbers were occasionally augmented by small parties crossing from New Guinea.

The capture of Morotai interrupted the Japanese supply line from the Philippines to Halmahera, dominated the approach to their air and naval base **Morotai** Kaoe Bay, and com- **Captured** pleted the isolation of the enemy garrison at Manokwari. At a later date, in January 1945, the Japanese reported that the majority of air attacks on Manila were carried out by heavy bombers based on Morotai, and it was announced in Melbourne on February 14 that over 200 R.A.A.F. Kittyhawks and Beaufighters from Morotai had, in attacks over five days, destroyed Tohohon base (Celebes) where 6,000 Japanese were established.

Incessant and severe bombing weakened the defences of Halmahera, which had been the most important enemy position in the Moluccas. Pilots of planes reported very extensive and elaborate defences on that island, but no air protection, and with communication lines cut it was merely a matter of time before the remaining forces surrendered. On November 21 General MacArthur's H.Q. reported that U.S. troops had landed in the Mapia Islands (145 miles north-west of Biak Island) and the Asia Group (130 miles north of Sorong) to destroy enemy spotting and radio stations which were giving trouble. The preliminary bombardment was carried out by a squadron of which the flagship was British—this was the first

LAST BATTLEFIELDS IN NEW GUINEA

This relief map shows the scene of the last landings in New Guinea preceding the U.S. invasion of the Halmahera Group on September 14, 1944. Announcing the landing at Sansapor on July 30, General MacArthur pointed out that the Allies had established air bases along the entire northern coast of New Guinea from Milne Bay westwards, making enemy operations east of the Halmaheras virtually impossible.

report of operations by the Royal Navy in the south-west Pacific.

Finsch Coast Operations : New Guinea

By July 11, 1944, a force of the Australian 6th Division, continuing their advance from Hansa Bay, controlled a coastal area west of Sepik River (*see* page 3125). From this position a further advance was begun in order to link with U.S. forces established since April on Driniumor River, twenty miles east of Aitape. Papuan infantry under Australian officers worked along the Australian left flank clearing the ground of enemy outposts over a wide zone. The land here consists of low flats with much swamp among reef limestone hills between the spurs of mountain chains lying to the south. The coastal road is no more than a trail in parts, winding around bluffs and following every small inlet.

In the hinterland the Japanese 18th Army, commanded by Lieutenant-General Adachi, occupied extensive areas each with a widespread system of defence. Wewak harbour, although that area was still occupied by the enemy, had ceased to be a potential naval base after the Allied occupation of Humboldt Bay and the Cyclops Mountains airfields (*see* page 3123). Enemy

surface craft could rarely make the Wewak coast owing to the efficient air and naval patrol. Any attempt of the enemy to concentrate aircraft on the coastal airfields was detected at once and drew attacks from R.A.A.F.

The 18th Army's position was already precarious and the Japanese showed their uneasiness by frantic attempts to break through the U.S. lines to the coast, which became more frequent as the pincers of the Allies' attack began to close.

The first serious attack on the U.S. cordon occurred on July 13, but the forward enemy units sent to force a gap were severely battered by U.S. artillery and U.S. and Australian aircraft, which also sank eight Japanese supply barges offshore. The Allied air force kept vigilant coastal patrol and scoured inland trails as well. For some time subsequently small parties of Japanese cut off from the rest were followed through swamp and bush and annihilated before they could rejoin the main army. Ten days later Japanese troops made a second effort to cross

Driniumor River ; this was equally unsuccessful, many of the enemy falling into pits prepared by the Americans. Enemy casualties were estimated at 1,500 killed ; units flung themselves madly against the U.S. lines and were mown down by the guns. During the first week of August the Japanese also failed in an attempt to turn the flank of the U.S. forces on the banks of Driniumor River ; in a counter-attack a successful advance was made along the coast which sealed off more trails to the mountains.

In November, the Australian 6th Infantry Division (veterans of Greece, Crete and Tobruk) commanded by Major-General H. C. H. Robertson, C.B.E., D.S.O., relieved American troops in the Aitape area and took over the Allied defence lines on the river. Heavy rains of the next three months slowed up activities, but in spite of this dogged progress was made.

In a broadcast on January 31, Mr. F. M. Forde, the Australian Army Minister said : " There is a tendency in some uninformed quarters to refer to

GENERAL MacARTHUR LANDS IN THE MOLUCCAS

After an intensive air attack and naval bombardment lasting several days, U.S. forces under the personal command of General MacArthur landed in strength on Morotai Island in the Halmaheras (part of the Moluccas group) on September 14, 1945. They took the enemy completely by surprise and achieved their initial objectives with light losses. Here landing craft unload Marines and supplies at Red Beach, Morotai. *Photo, U.S. Official*

fended position, fell on April 26. On May 13, troops of the 6th Division, under Major-General J. E. Stevens, supported by warships (among them the cruisers H.M.S. " Newfoundland " and H.M.A.S. " Hobart ") made an amphibious landing a few miles east of Wewak, also threatened closely by other forces of the Division advancing from the west. After fierce fighting in which the Japanese had to be blasted out of pillboxes and dugouts in the natural caves of the limestone hills, the Australians captured Wewak peninsula and airfield on the 13th, Wewak village next day. The harbour was not taken until June 5, and even then the Japanese, in an absolutely hopeless position, fought desperately

JAPANESE SURRENDER IN NEW GUINEA

The Australian 6th Division landed east of Wewak on May 13, 1945, and after fierce fighting captured the peninsula and airport. All Japanese forces in New Guinea surrendered at Wewak on September 13 to Major-General H. C. H. Robertson, commanding the 6th Division. Above, Australian troops in the undergrowth after the initial landing. Right, Japanese officers arrive by dinghy for the surrender.

Photos, Australian Official

the role of the Australian Army in New Britain, New Guinea and the Solomons as ' mopping-up.' This is completely misleading. ' Mopping-up ' in the military sense implies the wiping out of unorganized remnants left in the wake of battle. The Japanese in these areas are not unorganized, nor are they remnants. They are aggressive fanatics organized in divisions and brigades, and will sell their lives dearly."

By the first week of February 1945 the enemy had found the plains in the Aitape area untenable. Some had

moved into the Torricelli mountain slopes. Others had been driven east along the coast.

The Australians captured the airfields of But and Dagua, both fiercely defended, by the end of March. On Dagua 32 damaged fighters and 19 medium bombers were found abandoned. All organized resistance in the area had ceased by April 17.

Maprik goldfield area, a hotly de-

for the ridges and tracks overlooking the port. They were cleared by attacks with flame-throwers and bayonets, the enemy retreating to other ridges behind as fast as they were dislodged until their retreat was cut off.

To the south, the Japanese 18th Army, now estimated at 10,000, out of a force originally 30,000 strong, was pinned against the Torricelli Mountains. Another enemy force was firmly entrenched in the tumbled crests of Prince Alexander Range, where each system of defence was repeated on higher ground, the pivots being Mount Tazaki, whose capture was announced on July 3, and Mount Shiburangu. The range was cleared by July 15, only after eight weeks' bitter fighting.

Solomon Islands

In the late autumn of 1944, preparations began for operations to recover the two islands of the Solomons group remaining in enemy hands, Buka and Bougainville. There was already a strong Allied base on Bougainville, at Torokina north of Empress Augusta Bay, which had been held by U.S marines and infantry since their landing in November 1943 (*see* page 2887).

WEWAK DEFENCE AREA IN AUSTRALIAN NEW GUINEA

In the earlier phases of the Allied advance in New Guinea (see Chapter 309), the strongly defended harbour of Wewak was by-passed. A landing in the vicinity was made by the Australians on May 13, control of the harbour, however, not being secured until June 5. It was another six weeks before the mountains sheltering the site were cleared of the enemy.

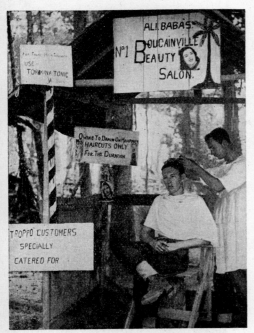

JUNGLE HAIR-CUT

Even while fighting in the jungle swamps of the Solomons, Australian troops managed to secure a brush-up and hair-cut. Here an Australian N.C.O. has 'a little bit off the top' at the self-styled 'Beauty Salon' on Bougainville. An Australian private acts as hairdresser. *Photo, Daily Mirror*

The New Zealand 3rd Division had seized Green Islands to the north-west on February 14, 1944 (*see* page 3089 and illus. in page 3091). The capture of this group assisted in completing the Allied ring round New Britain and New Ireland and disrupted all traffic between Rabaul and Kavieng and between Bougainville and Buka. Three months later the New Zealand division had handed over the group to U.S. forces and returned to their base at Bourail on New Caledonia. They were there joined by other forces from their forward base on Guadalcanal to await repatriation because New Zealand needed men for essential industries (*see* page 3453).

Importance of Green Islands

Green Islands, with a forward air base on Nissan, were valuable to the U.S. air force from which to bomb Japanese bases: Truk was being attacked by Fortresses a month after their occupation, and so was Rabaul.

When in November 1944 Australia assumed responsibility for activities in New Guinea and the Solomon Islands (*see* page 3453), their forces in the Solomons consisted of the 3rd Division under Major-General Bridgeford, C.B., O.B.E., M.C. and the 11th under Major-General K. W. Eather, C.B.E., D.S.O., E.D., forming the Australian II Corps commanded by Lieutenant-General S. G. Savige, C.B., C.B.E., D.S.O., M.C., E.D. The R.A.A.F. and

R.N.Z.A.F. made constant attacks on Japanese bases and supply lines and gave close support to the ground troops.

The U.S. force had made no advance from Torokina, but had fought continuously against fierce enemy attacks. The first Australian advance was to the south-west, to clear Japanese defences from an area of swamps and hills. By the end of January 1945, that district was rid of its last sniper and the main offensive opened. Three thrusts developed: (1) south-west across a low plain to occupy a fertile, cultivated area, which was the enemy's main source of supply of fresh food; (2) north from Torokina, first towards Buka Passage and then across to the north-east coast to isolate enemy bases on Soraken Point and Bonis Peninsula; (3) a direct thrust towards Numa Numa.

Bougainville : South-west Sector

It was announced in Melbourne on January 25, 1945 that the low-lying country south of Empress Augusta Bay had been cleared, and Australian troops had taken the central stronghold of Mawareka, advanced ten miles to the west of Puriata River and controlled 80 miles of waterfront and heights overlooking Numa Numa. By February 18 they were following a tributary, Hupai River, towards Mosigetta, an important junction of the main tracks. By this strategic move the enemy was contained in a triangular area between Gazelle Harbour and the headwaters of Puriata River. This area guarded the approach to the food producing area, and was held by numerous enemy posts each of which had to be destroyed in a separate engagement, usually with hand-to-hand fighting. The country provided natural defences—deep swamps and pathless mud flats. After four weeks of slow advance, the Australians captured Mosigetta, and the western side of the cultivated area had been gained. The nearer that this valuable food area was approached the more dense were the defences, including minefields. Fighting was of savage intensity. The enemy had no option but to retreat south-east when their route to the mouth of Puriata River was closed to them.

TOROKINA SAW THE JAPANESE SURRENDER

The runways of the airfield at Torokina, on Bougainville Island in the Solomons, stretched along the shore. It was from Torokina that the Australians, taking over from the Americans in November 1944, and overcoming fierce enemy opposition, first began to secure control of the island. On September 8, 1945, all Japanese forces in Bougainville and the adjacent islands surrendered at Torokina to Lt.-General S. G. Savige, commanding the Australian II Corps.

One such convoy was ambushed, and promptly "went bush" while its escort wiped out the enemy.

One Australian thrust was made across Puriata River on a 360-ft. bridge, similar to a Bailey Bridge. It was assembled on the bank, rolled into position by tractors, and it carried 32-ton loads. By May 19 all Hongorai River crossing defences were neutralized, and the infantry was attacking strong defences obstructing the road to Buin. Infiltrations still occurred, however, even at the end of July. At the time of the official Japanese surrender, one base only remained in this sector.

Bougainville : Northern Sector

Operations in the north against the Buka area were under the personal direction of the Corps Commander, Lieutenant-General Savige.

ON THE PURIATA RIVER
Australian-manned Matilda tanks being dragged by engineers using bulldozers across the Puriata River, on Bougainville Island in the Solomons, during the fighting in April–May 1945. Right, Australian sappers building a panel bridge over the Puriata which lay on the main supply route to troops in the Hongorai River district.
Photos, Australian Official

Abnormal rains towards the end of the monsoon period in March, which put whole districts under water, and high seas,

Japanese Infiltrations which caused creeks to overflow so that only the heaviest landing craft could make the south-west coast, slowed down the Australian advance. Early in April a considerable number of Japanese troops managed to infiltrate the Australian lines, but although they cut off some units for a time, they did not succeed in forcing a general withdrawal, and were estimated to have lost 500–600 killed, the greatest number of casualties in any single engagement in this theatre of war. Fighting died down by April 8 and the Australian position was then consolidated before the Allied offensive began in great strength against the Hongorai River defences. Observer planes directed concentrated artillery attacks, and enemy transport and troops were bombed without intermission. The weather continued unfavourable and violent thunderstorms interfered with communications; nevertheless, signallers and engineers, working on repairs in heavy rain and gales, maintained the services. Where trails were unfit for trucks, Papuan carriers waded to the forward lines with stores and ammunition.

On February 2, 1945, it was announced that a thrust of 40 miles had been made up the west coast from Torokina without any serious opposition. The advance continued until Downs Ridge was reached whose lower spurs dominated the right flank of the Australian force. These heights were strongly held by the enemy and the ridge was not cleared until March 4. Advance then became more rapid, and by the end of the month the enemy base and airfields of Soraken peninsula were under attack by two forces moving up the east and west coasts of the peninsula. The Australian positions were shelled, but a devastating fire from 25-pounders in close operation with the air force silenced the enemy, whose A.A. fire was accurate but who lacked aircraft.

Penned in the northern half of the peninsula the enemy found his base

ON BOUGAINVILLE

On February 2, 1945, an Australian force was 12 miles north-east of Torokina, advancing in the direction of the Japanese base at Numa Numa on the east coast through a series of fortified ridges defended with mounting violence. Here, Australian-manned Matilda tanks land at Toko Beach, Bougainville. Left, mortar crew outside a dug-out near Numa Numa.

Photos, Australian Official

neutralized, and by the middle of May the Australian advance eastward had overrun Pora Pora and occupied Ratsua, the terminus of an important road to Ruri Bay on the east coast. From Ratsua the Japanese used punts to carry stores up a river to their inland forces. A number of punts at Ratsua jetty were captured, together with much valuable equipment, vehicles, tanks, weapons, ammunition and stores.

A second important Japanese base was cut off on Bonis Peninsula and a cordon drawn right across the northern point of Bougainville, out of which the enemy tried in vain to break. The arrival of the Australians at Ruri Bay was announced on May 20.

Bougainville : Central Sector

About the same time as the advance north began, another force struck across the centre north-eastward from Torokina towards the Numa Numa, Japanese base on the opposite coast. This involved the storming of a series of fortified ranges, spurs of the central mountain complexes. Each slope had to be cleared, each ridge pounded by artillery and aircraft until it could be carried by assault. By the end of March, Smith's Hill and Hunt Hill, commanding the Numa Numa trail, were occupied.

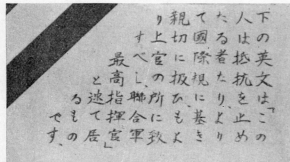

The Japanese with this message has ceased resistance. He should be treated well in accordance with international law. Take him to the nearest Commanding Officer.

C.-in-C. ALLIED FORCES

SOLOMONS SURRENDER

1. Leaflet dropped among enemy lines on Bougainville on August 15, 1945, telling isolated Japanese troops of their Government's capitulation. 2. First contact between Japanese peace envoys and Australians on the Mivo River, Bougainville. 3. At Torokina, Lieutenant-General S. G. Savige signs the surrender document. Before him sit Lieutenant-General Kanda and Vice-Admiral Samijima, whose swords lie on the table.

Photos, Australian Official ; Associated Press

The Australians were then two-thirds of the distance across the island, but the nearer they approached the base the more violent became the fighting. One patrol on April 21 made a deep penetration of the enemy defences, reaching the Numa Numa plantations and returning with valuable information.

Berry Hill, a very strongly fortified peak, after being blasted from the air, was captured on May 19. In a series of arduous engagements, **Japanese Headquarters Overrun** the Australians regained dominating features of the country surrounding the Numa Numa trail, and the Japanese were driven from their headquarters near Wearns Hill by the end of July.

Though the full number of Japanese casualties on Bougainville after the Australians relieved the Americans is not known, 14,460 dead were counted; only 434 prisoners were taken. A high percentage of deaths was probably due to sickness. When the Japanese commander in the Solomons, Lieutenant-General Kanda, began formal surrender negotiations on August 19, he disclosed that there were still 20,000 Japanese on Bougainville, and another

1,000 in nearby islands. In a message to the 3rd Infantry Division, Lieutenant-General Sturdee, Commander of the Australian 1st Army, said : " Your campaign in the last ten months has been strenuous, dogged and continuous. It has been an honour to command such magnificent troops."

New Britain

By mid-April, 1944, the Australian 5th Division with U.S. forces had regained control of all except the northern end of New Britain (*see* page 3117 and map in page 3124). The same Australian division, commanded by Major-General Ramsay, C.B.E., D.S.O., relieved the U.S. troops there, as Australians had done elsewhere, in November 1944, and from that date until the final surrender offensive operations were directed towards regaining all enemy held areas south of Gazelle Peninsula. A broad, fully fortified defence zone extending from Wide Bay to Open Bay prevented the Japanese from escaping by land, and escape by sea or air was also out of the question ; but it was known that they were very well equipped and armed, and had sufficient stores to last for a long period ; they were moreover

self-supporting as they had a very large fertile area under cultivation.

The Australian objective involved a series of minor actions to clear large plantations, to destroy enemy positions on river banks, in native villages, and in small inlets of the two large bays ; and after the shores of these had been secured, there were still fortified areas inland to be broken up.

By the end of March, Tol and Waitavalo plantations. keys to the southern entrance to Gazelle Peninsula. had been captured. In April Wide Bay was occupied after the destruction of a very strong enemy force. In the following two months, the Japanese withdrew slowly north.

All these actions, though they received small attention, entailed unrelenting fighting, and vigorous patrol work never ceased. The Australians were numerically at a disadvantage : as elsewhere **One Australian** in this island campaign **Against Five** they fought at a ratio **Japanese** of one Australian against every five of the enemy. But the absence of Japanese air observation and the refusal of the natives to collaborate with the enemy unless forced into slavery were factors favourable to the Australians. The enemy garrison in New Britain at

AUSTRALIANS INVADE THE OIL ISLAND OF TARAKAN

Troops of the Australian 9th Division landed in force on the island of Tarakan, off the N.E. coast of Dutch Borneo, and one of the world's richest oil-fields, on May 1, 1945. The landings were preceded by a shattering bombardment of enemy installations by U.S. and Australian warships and heavy attacks by Australian and U.S. Liberators. For three days and nights the invasion fleet sailed through enemy waters and reached Tarakan without interference. Here Australians move inshore towards burning oil tanks fired by the enemy.   *Photo, Associated Press*

NEW ZEALANDERS LAND ON GREEN ISLANDS

Under strong naval and air protection, New Zealand forces landed on February 14, 1944, on the Green Islands, off Buka, at the north end of the Solomons, and occupied them against almost negligible enemy opposition and weak air interference. These landings completed the series of flank movements begun in the New Georgia group. 'For all strategic military purposes,' declared General MacArthur, 'this concludes the campaign for the Solomons.' Here, human chains, formed by New Zealand troops, unload supplies.

Photo, U.S. Navy

AUSTRALIANS SECURE ENEMY FUEL-SOURCE IN BORNEO

Photo, Australian Official

Before the Balikpapan landings on July 1, 1945, 'heavies' of the U.S.A.A.F and the R.A.A.F. pounded Japanese defences for 15 days. Balikpapan, with an annual production of 15,000,000 barrels, had been restored by the Japanese to become their main source of oil and aviation spirit. General MacArthur, who accompanied the landing force, declared, 'Our shipping can now, with land-based cover, go to any point in the S.-W. Pacific.' Here a mortar crew of the 7th Division is in action near Vasey Highway, named in memory of Major-General Vasey (see pages 3113 and 3123).

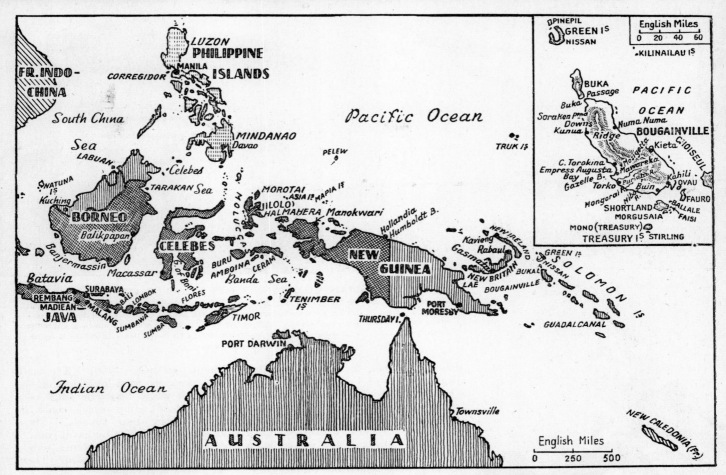

SOUTH-WEST PACIFIC COMBAT AREA

In November 1944, Australian ground forces took over from the Americans all operations in the Solomon Islands and in New Guinea. During 1945, Australian troops made landings in Borneo and reconquered a large part of that important island. This map gives an idea of the immense area covered in these operations. The map inset illustrates the Australian campaign (described in this chapter) which led to the clearing of Bougainville.

the time of the surrender was estimated at 55,000, and the 100,000 Japanese who surrendered on Gazelle Peninsula included civilians brought to settle on the land and 200 Japanese women.

Borneo

At the end of April 1945, Australian forces, after a prolonged period of special training, sailed from their base on Morotai to begin operations for the recovery of Borneo. The very large convoy under cover of an Allied air force passed for three days through enemy waters unhindered.

On May 1 an almost unopposed landing was made on the oil-bearing island of Tarakan off north-east Dutch Borneo, after an extremely severe bombardment by Allied naval and air forces which destroyed the enemy shore defences. The land force belonged to the famous Australian 9th Division, some members of which were veterans of the Middle East campaign and had also fought in New Guinea.

Major-General George Wootten, commander of the 9th Division, had the general direction of the attack, in collaboration with Admiral Royal of the U.S. Navy and Air Vice-Marshal Bostock of the R.A.A.F. The assault forces were under Brigadier D. A. Whitehead. Lieutenant-General Si

AUSTRALIAN PATROL IN NEW BRITAIN

This patrol on the island of New Britain (see map in page 3124) consisted of eight Australian infantrymen, accompanied by three native police boys and a dozen native carriers. It is shown moving along the forest-fringed beach in the Jacquinot Bay area on the south side of the island. First Allied landing on New Britain was made by U.S. troops in December 1943. Australian forces took over in November 1944.

Photo, Australian Official

AUSTRALIAN COMMANDO FORCE LANDS ON SADOE

In preparation for the Australian 9th Division's full-scale invasion of Tarakan, Borneo, on May 1, 1945, an Australian Commando force landed on the nearby small island of Sadoe the previous day, and set up a gun-battery. Left, an Allied aircraft lays a smoke-screen to cover the landing. Right, U.S. landing-craft, with Australian troops on board, nears the shore at Sadoe.

Photos, Keystone

Leslie Morshead, the senior Australian commander, was Corps commander in the field, and the forces engaged included Dutch troops. An Australian Commando had landed the previous day on the islet of Sadoe, between Tarakan and the Borneo mainland, and set up a gun-battery to cover the assault troops as they went ashore on Tarakan. At the same time Royal Australian Engineers cleared the Tarakan beaches of explosive, steel and barbed wire defences.

During the landing itself, a Naval Commando, engaged for the first time after intensive training, marked out beach areas, marshalled the landing craft, gathered information about tidal movements, and controlled much of the beach activity (compare with Beach Groups, *see* page 3150). The only resistance came from low ridges on the left flank where limestone crags concealed 20-mm. guns which could be wheeled back into tunnels. These positions were shelled by naval guns.

The port and oilfields were strongly fortified and fiercely defended. There was a week of strenuous fighting before Tarakan Hill, enemy strongpoint **Tarakan Hill Falls** in the centre of the town, was captured on May 7. The airfield had been taken the day before. The R.A.A.F. was operating from it by the 8th.

Near the town of Tarakan good roads aided rapid advance, but beyond this the swamp and jungle country was heavily mined, and with series of

THE INVASION OF BORNEO BEGINS

1. General Sir Thomas Blamey, Australian C.-in-C. (right), and Lieutenant-General Sir Leslie Morshead, commanding the Australian 2nd Army, inspect troops and assault craft all set for the invasion of Borneo on May 1, 1945. 2. U.S. rocket-firing, troop-carrying craft cover the Australian landings at Tarakan as smoke billows from burning oil installations ashore. 3. Matilda tank moves along the beach.

Photos, Australian and U.S. Official

'MIXED-GRILL' BARRAGE AT TARAKAN

This gun-site on the Borneo island of Tarakan, only 600 yards from the enemy lines, was known to Australian troops, who landed there on May 1, 1945, as 'H.M.A.S. Margy.' Nearest the camera is a 25-pounder; next a 3·7 A.A. gun used as a field artillery piece, while beyond them a Matilda tank joins in. Right, wreckage left by the retreating enemy in a Tarakan oil-field.

Photos, Australian Official: Fox

fortified razorbacks each of which had to be taken by assault. Full control of Tarakan was secured by June 24.

The Japanese garrison was found to be well fed and fully equipped, but the Chinese and half-caste population who met the forward troops even while fighting was in progress were emaciated and in dire need of medical attention. More than 6,000 were tended at a Dutch administrative centre behind the lines. Thousands of native houses had been deliberately fired by the Japanese because their owners showed pleasure at the approach of the liberating forces.

Civilian Conditions on Tarakan

A combined operation in still greater strength was carried out on June 10 by the Australian 9th Division in the important oilfield area of British North Borneo. Landings were made on Labuan Island, on Maura (in Brunei Bay), and at Brooketon. Lieutenant-General Morshead went ashore with the assault force. The U.S.A. 13th A.F. and the R.A.A.F. gave air cover. Again no air opposition was encountered.

By June 13, Brunei town and air-strip were under Allied control. Labuan Island was virtually cleared by the 16th. Three days later, the Australians reached Tutong, an oil centre 35 miles south-west of Brunei, meeting little opposition on the way. On June 20 new unopposed landings were made on the coast of Sarawak at Lutong, refinery centre for the Seria and Miri oilfields, and some 85 miles north-east of Brunei. By the 24th the Seria oilfields had been

ALLIED LANDINGS ON LABUAN ISLAND

Troops of the Australian 9th Division went ashore in great strength on June 10, 1945, at Labuan Island, off British North Borneo, without loss. The landings, supported by units of the U.S. and Royal Australian Navy, were led by General MacArthur and Lieutenant-General Sir Leslie Morshead. Below, left, evacuating wounded to the hospital ships; right, Australian troops in action at Labuan airstrip.

Photos, Australian Official; Acme Pictures

CAPTURE OF BORNEO'S GREATEST OIL-CENTRE

Supported by over 300 warships of the U.S. 7th Fleet, the Royal Australian Navy and the Royal Netherlands Navy, troops of the Australian 7th Division landed near Balikpapan, Borneo's richest oil-source, on July 1, 1945. Three days later the town itself fell. Above, troops sort out supplies. Below, Australian artillery signallers use a captured enemy tricycle to lay lines.

Photos, Australian Official; Paul Popper

captured : the Japanese had fired the fifty wells, some of which were still burning, and destroyed the township before evacuating them. Miri was taken next day : the oilfield, like that at Seria, had been fired.

On July 1 a surprise landing was made at Balikpapan, one of the richest oil producing centres in the Dutch East Indies. Following a heavy naval and air bombardment, the **Surprise Landing at Balikpapan** Australian 7th Division (which turned the tide at Kokoda, New Guinea, in 1942—*see* page 2470), commanded by Major-General E. H. Milford, D.S.O., went ashore. General MacArthur landed with them. After securing a beach-head, the Australians advanced inland in spite of fierce resistance. U.S. heavy, medium and fighter aircraft gave strong support, blasting the ground ahead of the troops. Sepinggan airfield was captured on the 3rd. Balikpapan itself, reduced to ruins by Allied bombing and shelling and oil fires, fell on the 4th. Australian troops then crossed the bay and occupied the anti-aircraft site at Penadjam on the headland of the west entrance.

Resistance stiffened and the Japanese attempted to infiltrate the advance lines and reoccupy their gun positions but were beaten back. Manggar airfield, ten miles to the east, was captured, and the Allied fleet shelled enemy inland positions and escaping units on the coastal road. Advancing from Manggar, one Australian force pressed inland and took the enemy coastal defences on Macassar Strait from the rear, completely annihilating them. North and west of Balikpapan, Dutch

East Indian troops pushed inland. Another landing, unopposed, on the west arm of Balikpapan Bay brought that valuable anchorage under complete Allied control by the 11th. The fighting continued severe, until the carefully built-up defence centre of Mount Batochampar was won on July 15. Sambodja, an oil centre, was occupied without resistance on the 18th.

Operations in all sectors at Borneo were continuing when the unconditional surrender of Japan came on August 14. Although large Japanese forces remained in the south-west Pacific, they were by then powerless to take the offensive.

Hostilities ceased following the Emperor's rescript of August 16, and the first formal acknowledgment of defeat came from Lieutenant-General Kanda's headquarters on August 19 (*see* page 3594) ; but it **Surrender in the S.-W. Pacific** was not till September 6, 1945, that the surrender in the south-west Pacific was signed in St. George's Channel, 28 miles southeast of Rabaul, on board the aircraft-carrier H.M.S. "Glory," where Lieutenant-General V. A. H. Sturdee, commanding the Australian 1st Army, personally received the surrender of General Imamura, Japanese C.-in-C., South-West Pacific, Admiral Kusaka, and all forces under their command.

Local surrenders followed. Japanese forces in Dutch Borneo were surrendered by Admiral Kimada to Major-General E. H. Milford, commanding the Australian 7th Division, on board the frigate H.M.A.S. "Burdekin" on September 8 ; Japanese forces on Bougainville and the adjacent Solomon Islands by Lieutenant-General Kanda, commanding the Japanese 17th Army, and Vice-Admiral Samemija to Lieutenant-General S. G. Savige, commanding the Australian II Corps, at Torokina on September 8 ; Japanese forces in British North Borneo by Lieutenant-General Baba to Major-General G. F. Wootten, commanding the Australian 9th Division, at Labuan on September 10; Japanese forces in New Guinea by Lieutenant-General Adachi, commanding the Japanese 18th Army, to Major-General H. C. H. Robertson, commanding the Australian 6th Division, at Wewak on September 13.

LANDINGS ON BORNEO

The Pacific island of Borneo, scene, in 1945, of a brilliant Australian campaign. Landings were made at Sadoe, off Tarakan, on April 30 ; at Labuan (June 10); and at Balikpapan (July 1). The area of Borneo is 284,000 square miles. Politically the island is divided into : British North Borneo, Sarawak, Dutch Borneo, and Brunei, a Mahomedan state.

Chapter 352

BRITISH COLONIAL RECORD, 1945

To the end of the war, the contributions of the British Colonies continued to be of both military and economic importance to the Allies. African troops played a striking part in the Burma campaign, smaller contingents from other Colonies fought in Europe and the Far East, and Colonial products remained indispensable. In this concluding chapter on the war effort of the British Colonies, Sir John Shuckburgh indicates the future that lies before them

DURING the final stages of the war, Colonial Military Forces served in the main in the Far Eastern Theatre. The African troops in Burma (*see* Chapters 345 and 371) continued the excellent work they had accomplished in previous years. During the early months of 1945 the Parliamentary Under-Secretary of State for the Colonies (the Duke of Devonshire) paid a visit of inspection to the West and East African units in India and Burma. On his return to England, he recounted his experiences in a speech delivered in the House of Lords on April 15. He had seen a number of African combatant units, including the 11th East African Division, the 22nd East African Brigade and the 81st and 82nd West African Divisions, and everywhere he was impressed by the smartness of the African soldiers, sometimes under very difficult conditions, by their keenness in drill and in turning out a guard. But the Africans were no mere " parade ground soldiers." East and West Africans, many of them drawn from " non-warrior " races, had been campaigning in most difficult country and under most arduous conditions. In the Kabaw Valley (*see* page 3531) the East Africans had to man-handle their motor transport for long distances through deep mud and torrential rain. West Africans had, at one stage, to spend six weeks cutting a track through dense jungle to enable their transport to be used at all. On the only occasion on which the Duke saw West Africans actually in action against the enemy, he was full of admiration for their high spirits and absolute steadiness. The morale of these troops was very high and their health was excellent.

The Duke visited a number of field hospitals, which he found efficient and well supplied with medical requisites ;

Good Work by African Troops he found the African " a wonderfully cheerful and uncomplaining patient and immensely courageous in the endurance of pain."

Before the war, said the Duke, the bulk of the African Forces were infantry soldiers armed with rifles only ; there were only a few other units in West Africa and still fewer in East Africa.

During the war the Africans had expanded into complete divisions of all arms. They had learnt the use of complicated modern weapons from bren guns to howitzers. They had become signallers, armourers, drivers, mechanics, cooks, bakers, military police, nursing orderlies and dispensers. They had proved themselves capable of carrying out, with comparatively little European supervision, the whole process of overhauling the armament of a division after a " very long and difficult campaign in unending mud and rain." Another duty in which Africans had proved especially efficient was that of intercepting Japanese wireless messages.

" It was to me," said the Duke in conclusion, " a most remarkable and moving experience to see this great volunteer army. Many of the men in this army have given up good positions at home ; many of them were civil servants. It was a moving experience to see them serving on the other side of the world, and to know that they had proved the masters of a very highly skilled military race. I was deeply touched by the fact that men who, all through those monsoon campaigns, had been able to keep nothing else dry, had kept their photograph of the King dry, and kept it as a treasured possession."

In the operations that marked the closing stages of the Burma campaign, the fine record of the African troops was fully maintained (*see* Chapter 345). The 81st **Battles in** West African Division **Burma** was engaged in hard fighting at Kyauktaw (Arakan) early in January 1945. Later in the month it captured Nyohaung and was there relieved by the 82nd West African Division which had arrived in India from West Africa in the previous year. The 81st Division's advance of some 150 miles greatly assisted the operations directed against Akyab. The 82nd Division continued the advance,

TRIBESMAN'S TROPHY

Record of the African troops was fully upheld in Burma during 1945. At Norak, Kenya, Masai tribesmen gathered to inspect a Japanese officer's sword captured in single and mortal combat in Burma by a Masai Askari of the King's African Rifles. Brought back by Lieut.-General Sir Kenneth Anderson, G.O.C., East Africa Command, it is shown to the Chief and brothers of the brave Askari by a N.C.O. of the Kenya Police.

MALTA RISES AGAIN

Early in 1945 the task was begun of restoring some of the more notable buildings in Malta which had been badly damaged in the George Cross island's 3,215 alerts. Here restoration is in progress at the Church of St. Augustine, Valetta. The stone is brought in by mule from quarries seven miles away. *Photo, Topical*

constantly harassing the flanks and rear of Japanese troops who were attempting to deal with landings on the coast. The additional East African Brigades sent over in 1944 also saw active service before the end of the campaign. One Brigade was used in amphibious operations for the capture of Ramree island ; the other operated for a time west of the Chindwin. (For 11th East African and

ASKARI AWARD

Colour-Sergeant Walisema Abdul Feraj, a veteran Sudanese Askari who had served with the East African forces for over 25 years, received from Major-General E. B. B. Hawkins, D.S.O., G.O.C., Southern Area, the long-service medal at the settlement for discharged Sudanese soldiers near Nairobi in August 1945. It was the Colour-Sergeant's eighth decoration. *Photo, British Official*

81st and 82nd West African Divisional signs, *see* colour plate following page 3938.)

Every preparation was made, on the termination of hostilities in Burma, for a fresh campaign on a grand scale for the reoccupation of Malaya and Singapore. In the event no such campaign proved necessary. The surrender of Japan on August 14 brought to an end the long ordeal of Hongkong, Malaya and other British territories in the Far East. Reoccupation was effected by peaceful means and with the co-operation of the Japanese Government. In agreement with the Chinese and the United States Governments the first units of the British Pacific Fleet entered the harbour of Hongkong on August 30 and took possession of the naval dockyards after a sharp but brief encounter with Japanese " suicide " detachments. On September 5 British, Indian and Gurkha troops landed at the port of Singapore and effected a peaceful entry without untoward incident. By the end of the day the whole island was under British control.

" The return to Singapore," wrote " The Times " correspondent, " was quite extraordinary. The landing had been planned as a carefully phased military operation, so that if the Japanese offered any resistance we should be able to cope with it. But it was like a civic reception." General Itagaki, commanding the Japanese 7th Army in Malaya, Java, and Sumatra, and other Japanese officers met the British troops as they came ashore at 11.30 a.m. " There were also interpreters and guides with white armbands to lead our troops to their objectives. Many staff cars were waiting, and 500 vehicles had been assembled near the cathedral for our use. The Japanese had allowed few people to enter the dock area, but some Chinese were there, cheering and shouting. Four Roman Catholic missionaries, Christian brothers, two Irish and two French, had been allowed in and were overjoyed at our return."

To the vast majority of the people of Malaya release from the Japanese yoke and a return to their old allegiance were entirely welcome. But there was a widespread demand, not confined to Malaya, for some early pronouncement as to future British policy in the country. The Secretary of State for the Colonies (Mr. George Hall), in a written reply of October 10, made a full statement on the subject to the House of Commons. He laid emphasis on " the need to promote a sense of unity and common citizenship which will develop the country's strength and capacity in due course for self-government within the

British Commonwealth." With this object in view, he said, the Government proposed to create a constitutional Union of Malaya " consisting of the nine states in the Malay Peninsula and the two British settlements of Penang and Malacca." Singapore itself would in the first instance be constituted as a separate Colony. Its ultimate incorporation in the Malayan Union would be a matter for later consideration. The peoples of Penang and Malacca would lose none of their rights as British subjects on entering the Union ; but a Malayan Union citizenship would also be created, for which the qualifications would be birth in Malaya or a suitable period of residence there. It would be necessary to conclude fresh agreements with the various Malayan rulers, for which purpose Sir Harold MacMichael (formerly High Commissioner for Palestine) had been sent to Malaya on a special mission. (The controversy that arose over these proposals belongs to the year 1946.)

In his concluding words, Mr. Hall laid emphasis on the right of the Malayan people to be assured of their full share in the rewards of their industry and to feel their country's wealth reflected in their own standard of life.

Rights of the Malayan People

In the European theatre Colonial Units continued, during the last months of the war, to render useful service. Cypriot Transport Companies remained on active duty in Italy and elsewhere in the Mediterranean area until the termination of hostilities. The Jewish Brigade group from Palestine (*see* page 3060) fought in the Italian campaign from March to May 1945. It spent about six weeks in the front line and incurred some 200 casualties. Its services won the commendation of Field-Marshal Alexander. The Mauritius Pioneers reached a strength of nearly 3,000 by May 1945 ; they served, at different times, in the Middle East, Malta, Sicily and Italy. Seychelles Pioneers also served overseas.

Arrangements were made in the spring of 1945 to employ the 1st Battalion, Caribbean Regiment (which had arrived from the West Indies in July 1944), on active service in Italy ; but German resistance collapsed before the plan could be put into effect. West Indians in the R.A.F. again rendered a good account of themselves. A twenty-year-old Jamaican air-gunner (Flight-Sergeant J. M. Hall) was awarded the Conspicuous Gallantry Medal for an outstanding feat of coolness and courage in taking over control of a badly damaged bomber from his wounded pilot

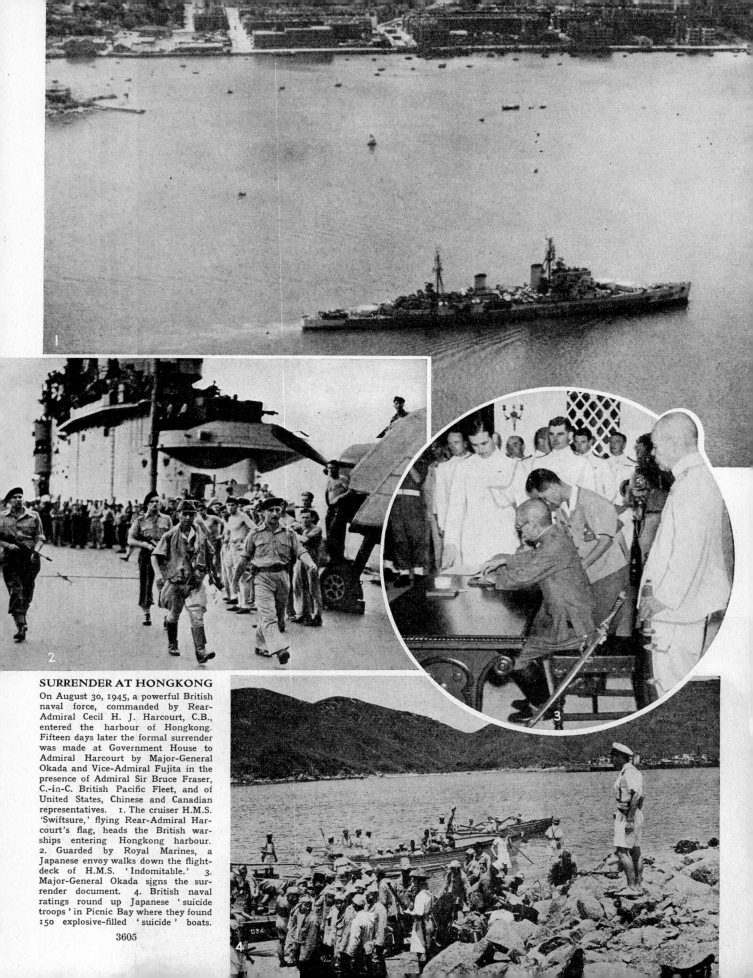

SURRENDER AT HONGKONG

On August 30, 1945, a powerful British naval force, commanded by Rear-Admiral Cecil H. J. Harcourt, C.B., entered the harbour of Hongkong. Fifteen days later the formal surrender was made at Government House to Admiral Harcourt by Major-General Okada and Vice-Admiral Fujita in the presence of Admiral Sir Bruce Fraser, C.-in-C. British Pacific Fleet, and of United States, Chinese and Canadian representatives. 1. The cruiser H.M.S. 'Swiftsure,' flying Rear-Admiral Harcourt's flag, heads the British warships entering Hongkong harbour. 2. Guarded by Royal Marines, a Japanese envoy walks down the flight-deck of H.M.S. 'Indomitable.' 3. Major-General Okada signs the surrender document. 4. British naval ratings round up Japanese 'suicide troops' in Picnic Bay where they found 150 explosive-filled 'suicide' boats.

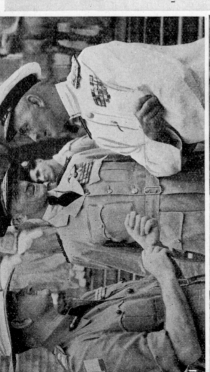

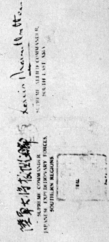
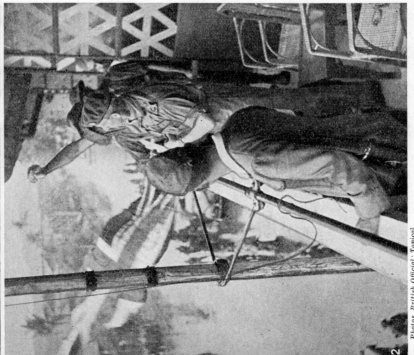

Photos, British Official; Topical

SINGAPORE FREED AFTER THREE YEARS OF OPPRESSION

On the morning of September 5, 1945, surrounded by wildly cheering crowds, British, Indian and Gurkha troops went ashore at Singapore. They were met on the quayside by General Itagaki and other Japanese officers. Apart from damage in the dock area, caused by Allied air raids, the city was undamaged. The official surrender of all Japanese forces in South-East Asia took place on September 12 in the Council Chamber of the Municipal Buildings—the actual document is reproduced above—and was received by Admiral Lord Louis Mountbatten. The Japanese signatory was General Itagaki, deputizing for Field-Marshal Count Terauchi, Supreme Commander, Japanese Expeditionary Forces, Southern Regions, who was indisposed. 1. General Sir William Slim, C.-in-C., 14th Army ; Air-Marshal Sir Keith Park, Allied Air C.-in-C., S.E. Asia ; and Vice-Admiral Sir Arthur Power, C.-in-C., East Indies Station, after the surrender ceremony. 2. Hoisting the Union Jack. 3. Released British prisoners outside the gates of the Changi Prison. 3. An Indian soldier in Singapore mounts guard while Japanese troops fill in trenches dug by British prisoners.

LAYING DOWN OF SWORDS

Under supervision of troops of the 25th Indian Division, Japanese officers laid down their swords at Kuala Lumpur, Malaya, after the surrender of all enemy forces in the area. The official surrender of Malaya took place in Singapore on September 12, 1945.

Photo, Indian Official

and flying over thirty miles to an airstrip behind the Allied lines.

The Colonial war effort in its economic aspect continued to be directed towards the maximum production of raw materials required by the United Nations, and to the reduction of imports (with consequent relief to shipping) by increased local cultivation of foodstuffs and other necessaries of life.

The West African Supply Centre at Accra (Gold Coast) reported at the beginning of the year that West African production was steadily on the increase. Nigeria was producing increasing quantities of tin and columbite (*see* illus. in page 2810), while the Gold Coast was able to meet all demands made upon the Colony for manganese and bauxite. The Nigerian rubber crop of 1944 exceeded that of the previous year by 1,400 tons. The output of palm kernels steadily increased in all four West African territories.

In East Africa, the efforts of Tanganyika to increase its production of pyrethrum met with marked success. In spite of the shortage of manpower, 5,300 acres were brought under this crop. In Kenya there was a widely-expressed desire to assist in alleviating the food situation in Great Britain. In words used by the Governor in the autumn of 1945, "the spontaneous demand to be allowed to help has now assumed the dimensions of a public campaign." Offers were made which were gratefully accepted by the Secretary of State on behalf of the Ministry of Food ; and steps were taken by the Kenya Government to organize the collection of the food.

A notable increase in the production of cereals, mainly maize and wheat, was reported from Northern Rhodesia. The amount of wheat sold in 1944 was more than double the pre-war average. The food-growing campaign in Ceylon Schools (*see* page 3111) proceeded vigorously during the opening months of 1945, and played its part in bringing about the improvement in the local food situation which manifested itself early in 1945. In October figures were published showing that between 1939 and 1945 British Guiana produced 6½ million tons of high grade bauxite (compared with a production in 1933 of only 36,000 tons, in 1936 of 170,000 tons).

Increases in Colonial Production

JEWISH BRIGADE IN ACTION

It was disclosed on March 24, 1945, that the Jewish Brigade, under the command of Brigadier E. F. Benjamin, had been in action on the 8th Army front in Italy. It was the only Jewish Brigade of the war. The unit was mainly Palestinian, but 37 countries of origin were to be traced among its members. It's sign was the Star of David. Here, a patrol of the Brigade rides through an Italian town on a tank.

Photo, British Official

TONGA'S QUEEN IS HONOURED BY BRITAIN

Queen Salote Tubou of Tonga with visitors from Fiji and Samoa during the celebrations in December 1945 to mark the centenary of the foundation of the kingdom of Tonga, British Protectorate in the South Pacific usually styled the Friendly Islands. The Queen was invested by Sir Alexander Grantham, K.C.M.G., Governor of Fiji and High Commissioner for the Western Pacific, with the insignia of a Dame Grand Cross of the British Empire in recognition of her country's war effort. Top picture shows Royal Marines of H.M.S. 'Euryalus' presenting arms during the ceremony.

Photos, Crown Copyright

An event of special interest took place in October 1945, when the Queen of Tonga was appointed a Dame Grand Cross of the Order of the British Empire. She had been an Honorary Dame Commander of the Order since 1932. Few honours conferred by the British Crown can ever have been better deserved. Queen Salote, whose kingdom had been under British protection since 1900, showed herself from the outbreak of the war a staunch and devoted supporter of the Allied cause. She displayed the utmost readiness in rendering assistance, first to the New Zealand military authorities and subsequently to those of the United States, in their plans for the utilization of the island of Tonga as part of the general defence system in the western Pacific (*See* illus. in page 587).

By January the total amount invested in East African War Bonds amounted to over £8,500,000. By the first week in April, Trinidad's total purchases of War Savings Certificates had reached a figure of over $2,700,000 (approximately £675,000), while the same Colony's total contribution to the Red Cross and St. John fund amounted to $780,000 (£195,000).

Financial Aid to Britain

Fiji, by the beginning of the year 1945, had contributed £439,000 to war funds, while Red Cross contributions from the small Colony of Bermuda totalled £12,000 in 1944. The Gold Coast made a gift in money to the Gold Coast Squadron of the R.A.F. In July 1945 the people of Tonga decided to commemorate the victory over Germany by presenting the United Kingdom Government with a fighter aircraft (their third) at a cost of £5,000. During July 1945 the Colonies made further loans to the British Treasury amounting to nearly £520,000. Of this sum £473,000 was free of interest. In addition, loans were made locally in Ceylon and in Fiji to the amounts of Rs.23,586,000 (£1,769,000) and £12,400, respectively.

In a broadcast to the Colonies which he made immediately after the surrender of Japan, the Secretary of State said : " To you all I send congratulations on the occasion of victory and the warmest thanks of His Majesty's Government and of the people of Great Britain for the loyal and generous part that all the varied communities of the British Colonial Empire have played in achieving it. Your contribution has been a noble and valuable one, and has shown itself in many varied forms : in service in the armed forces and the merchant navy ; and in civil defence ;

BRITISH GUIANA CELEBRATES VE DAY

Britain's only possession in South America, British Guiana, with a population of over 330,000, celebrated VE Day with enthusiasm. Georgetown, the capital, was brightly hung with Allied flags, and a day of rejoicing culminated in a broadcast by the Governor, Sir Gordon James Lethem, K.C.M.G., here seen announcing the end of hostilities from the balcony of Government House. *Photo, Associated Press*

in helping to produce vital materials of war ; in the maintenance of essential services in your own lands ; in the gifts and loans of money you have made for the furtherance of the war ; and in voluntary welfare work and hospitality for His Majesty's Forces. The Chiefs of Staff of the three Fighting Services have asked me specially to associate them with this message of thanks."

On the military side, by far the largest contribution came from tropical Africa. African troops served in Abyssinia (*see* Chapter 164) and East Africa (*see* Chapter 163). Their service in Burma has already been referred to in this chapter. Their successful employment, so far from their homes and under conditions so alien to their past experience, constituted one of the remarkable episodes of the war. When Rangoon was liberated early in May, the total strength of the African forces in India and Burma was estimated at 119,000 (East Africans, 46,000 and West Africans, 73,000). At the same time nearly 50,000 African troops were serving in the Middle East and over 200,000 in their home commands in Africa. The total number of Africans in arms amounted in round figures to 372,000, of whom 227,000 were East Africans and 145,500 West Africans.

Not until November 1945 was it learned that a British N.C.O., serving with the 1st/6th King's African Rifles,

African Military Strength

had won a V.C. posthumously at Colito, Abyssinia, in May 1941. He was Sergeant Nigel Grey Leakey, whose " courage and magnificent fighting spirit " were the means of driving off an enemy counter-attack mounted with tanks. With complete disregard for his own safety, and in face of withering machine-gun and rifle fire from the enemy's ground troops and from more tanks in front, Sergeant Leakey leaped on top of a tank coming in from behind, wrenched open the turret, shot the Commander and the crew, with the exception of the driver whom he forced to drive in to cover. Having failed to get the cannon of this tank to fire, he dismounted, calling out " I'll get them on foot," and charged across ground which was being swept by machine gun and shell fire from other enemy tanks. He leapt on to a second tank, opened the turret and killed one of the crew, but was himself shot dead as he did so.

In the Western Pacific, locally raised troops did excellent work in the Solomon Islands campaign and elsewhere. Maltese troops shared in the all-important task of the defence of Malta. Units from Cyprus, Palestine, Mauritius and the West Indies saw service in various fields. Colonial personnel made

a valuable contribution both to the R.A.F. and to the Mercantile Marine.

On the economic side, the most important function discharged by the Colonial Empire was the supply of raw materials urgently needed for war purposes, the normal sources of which had been cut off by the enemy. Bauxite (from British Guiana), tin (from Nigeria), copper (from Northern Rhodesia), sisal (from East Africa) and sea island cotton (from the West Indies) were only a few of the commodities for which reliance had, for the most part, to be placed upon Colonial sources of supply. Immense efforts were made to increase the output of rubber in Ceylon and Nigeria, and of sisal in East Africa. Production of food had to be increased in almost every Colonial territory, it being essential that all overseas territories should, so far as possible, render themselves self-supporting in respect of the main necessaries of life.

To all these tasks the Colonial Empire applied itself with determination and with a large measure of success. The tribute paid to its peoples by Mr. Churchill in June 1943 (*see* page 2814) and by Mr. Hall in August 1945 did no more than justice to their wholehearted and patriotic co-operation.

Chapter 353

THE MERCHANT NAVY'S HEROIC SERVICE

Facts and figures in this chapter sum up the war service rendered to the Allies by their Merchant Navies, and in particular by that of Great Britain, whose merchantmen bore the brunt of Axis attack in the Atlantic, the Arctic and the Mediterranean and did magnificent service in the Far East as well. The history of the Merchant Service in 1944 is told in Chapter 304

I N the last months of the war in the west, large convoys continued to bridge the Atlantic, unloading in the harbours of Britain soldiers, machines of war, and food. London and Southampton were the principal supply bases of the British and American armies of liberation respectively; Antwerp was the main allied intake on the Continent. Across the North Sea ran an immense system of maritime routes over which poured men, weapons and supplies for the build-up for the spring offensive.

Many of these troops and much of this material were transported in Allied warships, but a large proportion was carried by passenger ships, cargo vessels and particularly coasters under the Red Ensign. The convoy routes to the Continent were protected with marked success during this period from the special dangers in the Channel and the North Sea of mine, torpedo and bomb. The most concentrated attacks occurred in the Scheldt Estuary where the enemy employed midget submarines and human torpedoes (*see* page 3497). Thanks to the watchfulness of the Navy he had little success. In the docks of London and Antwerp, ships were hit by flying-

'QUEEN MARY' IN COLLISION

Over 150 British ocean-going passenger ships were converted for troop-carrying in wartime, among them the liner ' Queen Mary ' which, with her sister ship, the ' Queen Elizabeth,' transported four million U.S. troops. Below, the ' Queen Mary's ' damaged bows after she had rammed the cruiser H.M.S. ' Curaçao ' in the Atlantic in 1942. *Photo, Keystone*

bombs and rockets. One ship lying in the Surrey Commercial Docks was unfortunate enough to be hit twice by flying-bombs within a few days.

The opening of the year witnessed the last and heaviest German attempt to cut Britain's sea-lines. Equipped with the " Schnorkel " and other defensive devices (*see* Chapter 342), the U-boats swarmed on all the main convoy routes. During January and February there was a slight increase in the number of Allied vessels sunk by submarines, but Allied methods of attack led to a rise in the number of enemy submarines destroyed, and by March, when the onward drive of the Allied Armies had robbed the U-boats of many of their bases, the last submarine offensive petered out. The convoy system continued in the Atlantic for some weeks after the end of hostilities in Europe, but on May 28 the Admiralty announced that, as from midnight on that date, no further convoys would sail in non-combat areas, and that vessels sailing in such areas would henceforth be released from the necessity of darkening ship at sea.

An analysis issued by the Admiralty on June 13 of Empire, Allied, and neutral merchant ships lost by enemy action from September 3, 1939 to VE Day is given to the right, figures in parentheses representing gross tonnage in thousands. In addition, normal marine risks caused the following losses : British Empire, 610 ships of 1,120,000 gross tons ; Allies other than the U.S.A., 261 ships of 710,000 gross tons ; neutrals, 490 ships of 680,000 gross tons. These figures include Finnish, Hungarian, Italian and Japanese losses up to the time those countries became enemies ; losses of Italian ships after Italy became a co-belligerent are also included. French ships are included up to the date of the defeat of France, after which Free French, but not Vichy-controlled, vessels are included. Five U.S. ships lost by enemy action before December 7, 1941 are included among neutral losses.

Germany's surrendered merchant fleet totalled 1,189,600 tons. One-third was handed to the Soviet Union, to be shared with Poland. The other two-thirds was allotted to (in percentages) : Great Britain and Colonies, 46.04 ; U.S.A., 17.82 ; Australia, 0.19 ; Belgium, 1.33 ; Canada, 1.42 ; Denmark, 2.19 ; Egypt, 0.23 ; France, 7.68 ; Greece, 4.99 ; India, 0.24 ; New Zealand, 0.14 ; Norway, 10.14 ; Holland, 6.59 ; Yugoslavia, 0.86 ; South Africa, 0.14 ; Britain's share was about 365,000 tons, worth over £6,000,000.

After VE Day, the war service of the Merchant Marine continued in and to the Far East, while the supply of the Armies of Occupation on the Continent, the feeding and supply of the devastated areas of Europe, and the continued carriage of the food and material required by Britain engaged many other merchant ships. On May 24 the United Maritime Authority, established by an international agreement of August 1944, came into operation : it continued the arrangements already existing among the United Nations for pooling their ships

Pooling of Allied Ships Continues

	British Empire	United States	All other Allies	Neutral	Total
U-boat	1,360 (7,620)	440 (2,740)	670 (3,260)	300 (930)	2,770 (14,550)
Mine	340 (830)	15 (90)	75 (210)	90 (270)	520 (1,400)
Surface craft	210 (970)	13 (90)	87 (460)	20 (50)	330 (1,570)
Aircraft	440 (1,590)	58 (360)	202 (770)	50 (110)	750 (2,830)
Other or Unknown Causes	220 (370)	12 (30)	138 (330)	30 (60)	400 (790)
Totals	2,570 (11,380)	538 (3,310)	1,172 (5,030)	490 (1,420)	4,770 (21,140)

for " all military and other tasks " and " for the supplying of all liberated areas as well as of the United Nations generally and territories under their control." The arrangement was to extend for six months after the suspension of hostilities in the Far East.

Merchant convoys carried men and supplies to the main Allied bases in the Far East ; and ships under the Red Ensign largely made up the " Fleet Train," a mobile floating supply base, composed of more than a hundred vessels, which supplied food, water, ammunition and fuel at sea to the many types of men-of-war in the British Pacific Fleet. Most of the ships were water-

EX-PRISONERS HOME FROM THE FAR EAST

The first ship to reach England bringing home ex-prisoners of war from the Far East docked at Southampton on October 7, 1945. She was the P. & O. liner 'Corfu,' carrying 1,134 ex-P.O.W., most of them British Army troops who had been in captivity for three-and-a-half years. They were officially received by Lord Nathan, Under Secretary of State for War, and by General Sir Ronald Adam, the Adjutant-General, who read them a message of 'Welcome Home' from the King and Queen.   *Photo, G.P.U.*

borne supply dumps; some were floating repair shops; others were ferries detailed as required to run services to the base ports. In the vast distances of the Pacific Ocean the Fleet could not afford the time to make periodical returns to its bases for supplies and overhaul; instead the base, in the form of the Fleet Train, went to the warships.

All ships in Pacific waters continued to be subjected to the dangers of mine, torpedo and bomb. "Suicide" pilots, who crashed their aircraft loaded with high explosive on to Allied ships, usually selected the broad decks of aircraft carriers on which to immolate themselves, but transports and supply ships also suffered this form of attack.

With the end of the Japanese war, the vast homeward movement of troops which began soon after VE Day was intensified. Large numbers of released prisoners of war, casualties and troops due for demobilization awaited repatriation to Britain and the Empire from the Continent, North Africa, India and elsewhere. Even larger numbers of American forces were scheduled to return as soon as possible to the United States. In addition to all these commitments, a substantial number of men had to be transported outward for occupation and clearing up duties, in place of homeward bound troops. The

bulk of this two-way traffic was carried in merchantmen.

During the war one hundred and fifty-one British ocean-going passenger ships were converted for troop carrying. Stripped of their fittings and given the ubiquitous wartime cloak of grey worn by naval and Allied merchant vessels alike, British controlled ships carried over two million troops on long sea voyages. A further four million were carried between the United Kingdom and the Continent. About forty of this British troop-carrying fleet, including the "Empress of Britain," "Viceroy of India," "Orcades," "Strathallan," and "Windsor Castle" among many famous vessels, were sunk. Twenty-four British liners were converted to hospital ships; of these, the "Newfoundland" and the "Talamba" were sunk. The others now began their last work of mercy in bringing home the wounded, the sick, and the ill-nourished, often ill-used prisoners of war, many of them free only after long years of captivity.

In the course of the year 1945, the following groups were moved in British civilian ships:

30,832 American casualties lifted from north-west Europe to the United Kingdom in hospital ships.

36,500 ex-prisoners of war repatriated from the Far East to the United Kingdom.

32,500 Indian ex-prisoners of war repatriated to India.

40,508 ex-prisoners of war repatriated from Germany to the Dominions. A further 2,670 were sent home via the Middle East.

Over 23,000 more prisoners and internees were repatriated from the Far East during the first quarter of 1946.

For trooping across the Channel and the North Sea, the L.S.I. (Landing Ships, Infantry) were supplemented and later, to a great extent, replaced by the "Royal Daffodil," the "Canterbury," and other pleasure steamers and mail packets well known to peacetime travellers. From Italy, North Africa, India, Burma and the Far East came the big liners packed with homecoming men. An even greater trek westward began to bear the bulk of the American and

Cross-Channel Troopships

THE 'QUEEN ELIZABETH'

On October 12, 1945, it was announced that the liner 'Queen Elizabeth,' allocated under Lease-Lend for ferrying U.S. troops across the Atlantic, would be used for repatriating British troops. She is here being refitted at Southampton before sailing with Canadians to Halifax.

Photos, G.P.U.; Planet

Canadian forces back across the Atlantic. Predominant in this movement were the famous Cunard White Star liners "Queen Mary" and "Queen Elizabeth." During the course of the war, these two gigantic liners between them transported more than four million men; together they brought to the United Kingdom more than one third of the American armed forces serving in the European theatre of war. A trooping operation of a different kind—the transportation of some 40,000 women and 20,000 children in the United Kingdom to join their American husbands and fathers in the States—

was also carried out by big liners.

The Japanese collapse came a little sooner than had been expected, but plans for the transitional period between war and the resumption of international commerce had already been prepared; plans in which the British shipbuilding industry bulked large. During the late summer and autumn, company after company announced its shipbuilding programme, and the total number of ships laid down was something of a barometer of the prospects of overseas trade.

As a result of this programme, most British shipbuilding yards had work on hand that would last at least two years. Some of it was for Britain's hard-hit allies, but the majority of the passenger and cargo liners, tankers, refrigerated ships, coasters, etc., laid down were for British lines. The tramp shipowners alone waited to make replacements until the policy of the United States in the matter of her vast armada of Liberty and other wartime ships was declared. The following statistics, published by the U.S.

Merchant Shipping, 1939–1945

Maritime Commission on January 26, 1946, show the immense preponderance of United States shipping after, as compared with before, the war. At the end of 1945 the United States merchant navy was 5,521 seagoing ships of 1,600 tons gross and over; it had been 1,401 in 1939. The deadweight tonnage of the world's leading merchant fleets in 1945 and 1939 were as follows:

	1945	1939
U.S.A.	56,800,000	12,100,000
British Empire	19,600,000	23,300,000
Norway	3,950,000	6,400,000
Netherlands	2,090,000	3,300,000
Greece	1,700,000	2,700,000
France	1,300,000	2,900,000
Soviet Union	1,200,000	1,500,000

The British shipbuilding industry, stimulated after years of stagnation by the forced pace of war production, was in good shape to meet this demand for new tonnage. (During the war, the Clyde alone built 304 merchantmen in addition to naval construction and repair work.) New means of propulsion, new navigational aids developed during the war were available for adaptation in civilian shipping, and changes had

PRICE OF VICTORY AT SEA

Showing at low tide in the Thames Estuary, east of Southend, these hulks of seven ships lost from a single convoy symbolized the British Empire's shipping losses—11,380,000 tons in all—during the war. Right, the 10,000-ton Liberty ship 'Horace Binney,' mined off Belgium on VE Day, brought to London by P.L.A. wreck-lighters and made seaworthy again—a triumph of salvage.

Photos, Planet; Fox

BRITAIN BUILDS NEW MERCHANT SHIPS

Replacement of the heavy losses of merchant shipping was an urgent task of British shipyards during and after the war. Above, assembling the keel of a 13,500-tons Cunard White Star liner—provisionally labelled '629'—at John Brown's, Clydebank, in November 1945. Right, launching the 'Norhval,' one of two 21,000-tons whaling factory ships built at Haverton-on-Tees.

Photos, L.N.A.; Topical

also been made in methods of welding, an increased use made of prefabrication.

In the last two months of the year, repair and maintenance work began to be put in hand in the repair yards.

Renovation Begins Ship after ship shed her sombre grey, and the guns and other defensive devices with which the Merchant Service had been equipped during the war. By the end of the year a substantial number of vessels had emerged from the repair berths once more in their normal house colours.

During the last few days of the year, natural causes rendered the routine of shipping chaotic. First came a ninety-mile-an-hour gale which disorganized the leave and repatriation services in the Channel and the North Sea, and also held up the departure of Canadian and American forces returning across the Atlantic. Hard on its heels came one of the worst and most persistent fogs of the year—and a large number of floating mines, set adrift by the gale, were an added menace in the sea lanes.

Looking back over the war, it can

G.I. BRIDE SHIP

After serving as a troop transport and, after the war, carrying U.S. soldiers home, the liner 'Queen Mary' took to the United States many British-born wives and children of American service men, two of whom are seen in one of the specially fitted nursery cabins.

be clearly seen that the mainspring of victory was sea power. Without sea power Britain could not have received food, supplies and reinforcements. The Dunkirk and Crete evacuations, the North African and Italian landings, the invasion of France and the subjection of the Japanese island garrisons—in fact, all the main operations of the war —were made possible only by the Allies' wealth of shipping and their

centuries of experience in its efficient use.

Merchantmen went out to trade armed in self-defence. Royal Naval gunners and soldiers of the Maritime Regiment manned the guns in some merchant vessels, but 10,000 merchant seamen also qualified as gunners during the war (*see* illus. in page 2751). Engagements were fought daily between ocean traders and enemy war vessels and aircraft. Men from the bench, the factory, the shop, the desk, and the plough

GERMAN SHIPS DIVIDED AMONG THE ALLIES

The International Reparations Agency, sitting in Brussels, announced on April 23, 1946, that Britain and her Colonies were to receive the largest portion allotted to the Western Allies of Germany's merchant fleet. The allocation was on the basis of the tonnage—in Britain's case 10,870,000 tons—lost by each Allied country during the war. Here are German merchantmen which were sailed under Royal Marine guard from Kiel to the Firth of Forth in June 1945.

Photo British Official

INTERNEES GREET LIBERATION AT HONGKONG

British Marines and naval ratings, going ashore at Hongkong on August 30, 1945, had a sharp but brief clash with Japanese 'suicide' troops in the dockyard area. Four days later a proclamation announced the establishment of a British Military Administration. Here some of the 2,400 internees freed at Camp Stanley sing 'God Save the King' as the Union Jack is hoisted there for the first time for three-and-a-half years. The internees were released in person by Rear-Admiral C. H. J. Harcourt, commander of the British Task Force, appointed C.-in-C., Hongkong, on Sept. 9.

WEWAK FELL TO AN AUSTRALIAN PINCER MOVEMENT

In February 1945, Australian forces in the coastal area of northern New Guinea were closing in on the Japanese base at Wewak from both east and west. Units of the 6th Infantry Division, advancing from the Driniumor River, took But and Dagua airfields (about 25 miles west of Wewak) late in March. At Dagua (above) 32 fighters and 19 medium bombers were found disabled by the R.A.A.F. By mid-May the two forces met ; in the final assault on Wewak that ensued, Matilda tanks covered by infantry screens (below) were used.

Photos, Australian Official

THE 'QUEEN MARY' TAKES HOME U.S. TROOPS FROM EUROPE

In the House of Commons on October 12, 1945, it was announced that, as a result of discussions with the U.S. Government, it had been agreed that, though the 'Queen Elizabeth' and the 'Aquitania' should in future be used for repatriating British troops, the 'Queen Mary' would remain for the time being at U.S. disposal. In return for the use of the 'Queen Mary' an equivalent number of smaller U.S. ships were to be handed over to move British forces from areas where the use of so large a vessel would be wasteful or impracticable. Here the 'Queen Mary' approaches New York in June with over 14,000 U.S. troops returning from Europe. *Photo, Sport & General*

WHEN THE PORT OF LONDON WAS 'TRANSFERRED' TO THE CLYDE

One of Britain's most astonishing moves to counter Luftwaffe attacks was made in late 1940 when the activities of the Port of London were partially transferred to the Clyde Estuary. Under the direction of the Clyde Anchorages Emergency Port, a vast port at sea was devised in safely-enclosed waters where Allied ships could anchor and, without touching land, load and discharge their cargoes overside. Over 600 London dockers journeyed to the Clyde, with some 300 Thames barges and portable grain bucket-elevators. From September 1940–August 1945, the 'Port in the Sea,' discharged and loaded 1,885 ships, cargo totalling 2,056,833 tons. Among the ships here lying off the Gourock anchorages is the 'Queen Mary' (left centre).

served in the wartime ranks of the Merchant Service. Forty British liners were taken over by the Royal Navy and converted into auxiliary cruisers: "Rawalpindi" (see pages 395, 399. 1753) and "Jervis Bay" (see Chapter 125) head the list.

New groups made their appearance in the British Merchant Service. Vessels designated "Empire," including all

'Empire' and 'Sam' Ships shapes, sizes and types of craft, from tugs and motor coasters to large ocean-going cargo ships, were operated for the Ministry of War Transport. "Sams," so called in compliment to their country of origin, were American wartime freighters on charter to the Ministry of War Transport. A large fleet of "Forts" were wartime Canadian-built cargo carriers.

A number of wartime inventions helped navigation at sea. Radar, the all-seeing "eye" which played so important a part in gunnery and in the air, was also of great value at sea—a value not confined to war conditions.

New methods of construction, dual-purpose ships, navigational aids, life-saving appliances, were adopted, many adaptable to general use at sea.

One of the greatest stories of the war is undoubtedly that of the men of the Merchant Service. Though civilians, they fought in every theatre of war. Merchant Service casualties from September 3, 1939 to August 14, 1945 were given by the Prime Minister to the

DEMOBILIZATION OF MERCHANT SHIPPING
The Minister of War Transport announced on December 18, 1945, that cargo ships and tankers, except those employed on trooping or service duties, would be released from requisition on the termination of voyages after March 2, 1946, when the wartime charters expired. Here the S.S. 'Langibby Castle' is in dry dock at Southampton having her first overhaul since the outbreak of war. As a troopship she was damaged by torpedo off the Azores.

House of Commons on November 29, 1945 as:

Deaths	.. .. ..	30,189
Missing	.. .. ..	5,264
Wounded	.. .. ..	4,402
Internees	.. .. ..	5,556

The figure for deaths included those who were known at the time of the statement to have died in internment and those presumed dead in missing ships, but excluded deaths from natural causes; the figures for deaths, missing, and internees included men of all nationalities who served in British registered ships and fishing boats, and British subjects who served on foreign ships requisitioned or chartered by H.M. Government during the war; the figure for internees included those who had been repatriated or had escaped.

The longest strain was in the Atlantic, where the fight began nine hours after the outbreak of hostilities with the sinking of the "Athenia," and lasted to V.E. Day, and a little beyond. During **Long Strain of the Convoys** the war in Europe 75,000 ships were escorted across the Atlantic in 2,200 convoys, the largest totalling 167 ships. (See also colour inset in Chapter 368.) The fiercest test was on the Malta run (see Chapter 240 and Historic Document 264, page 2600). But Malta was saved and remembers with gratitude the "Orari," the "Cornwall" and many another ship.

The worst test, combining continual strain and fierce attack, was the Northern Convoy Route (see pages 2396, 2850, 3035), where nature added blizzards, ice and snow to the air and underwater menace; 829 British and Allied merchant seamen lost their lives on this route. In the 41 convoys that went, 792 ships sailed outward and 62 were lost; 739 ships sailed for home and 28 were lost—a percentage of 7·8 and 3·8 respectively, compared with under one per cent in the Atlantic convoys. The Royal Navy lost two cruisers, six destroyers, three corvettes, three minesweepers and 1,840 men. At this price, over 3,500,000 tons of war material were delivered to the Soviet Union (see also page 3562).

TRANSPORT OF U.N.R.R.A. SUPPLIES
The British Merchant Navy played an important part in transporting food and other essential commodities supplied to stricken Europe by U.N.R.R.A. This herd of cattle, seen on the quayside at Danzig, Poland, was given to U.N.R.R.A. by individual American farmers. Shipped direct from Baltimore, the cattle were intended to increase dairy herds to provide more milk for Polish children. (See Chapter 376.)
Photo, Associated Press

4A¹

BUDAPEST FALLS AFTER SEVEN WEEKS' SIEGE

The 2nd and 3rd Ukrainian Armies, under Marshals Malinovsky and Tolbukhin, completely occupied Budapest, capital of Hungary, on February 13, 1945, after a siege lasting seven weeks. Moscow announced that in the battle for the city the enemy lost over 49,000 in dead and 110,000 in prisoners. Most of the city's finest buildings were destroyed and the Germans blew up the Danube bridges. 1. Soviet self-propelled guns in the streets. 2. Russian gun-crew fire through a hole in a wall. 3. Water from a well in the street : the mains were blown up by the retreating Germans. 4. Soviet artillery observer corrects battery fire from the clock tower of a tall building.

Chapter 354

RED ARMY CONQUERS THREE MORE CAPITALS

In this chapter, the Military Editor, Major-General Sir Charles Gwynn, concludes the history of Soviet military operations in the Balkans and Central Europe, culminating with the liberation of Prague, which he began in Chapter 340 with the entry of the Red Army into Bessarabia. Simultaneous Red Army victories in Germany are recorded in Chapter 362

IN the last week of 1944 Tolbukhin completed the encirclement of Budapest and, extending his drive northwards on the west bank of the Danube, made contact with Malinovsky's troops about Esztergom on the stretch of the river that runs eastwards from Bratislava and Vienna (*see* page 3483). The Germans had therefore lost the defence line of the Danube and were threatened with an additional major disaster if the garrison of over 200,000 men in Budapest could not be relieved. But the initial success of Von Rundstedt's Ardennes offensive (*see* Chapter 336) had been a powerful stimulant to German morale, and even when it became apparent that it had failed to achieve its main object, it seemed probable that it had effectively caused a postponement of a major Allied offensive in the west.

In the first weeks of January the Vistula line was still unbroken and the defence in East Prussia (*see* Chapter 347)

Situation on Other Fronts and in Italy (*see* Chapter 361) still held ; and it is conceivable that, apart from their confidence in the strength of the Vistula position, the Germans may have thought that the Russians in Poland would not resume the offensive until the Western Allies had recovered from the dislocation of their plans caused by Von Rundstedt.

The Germans, therefore, may have felt their general situation to be far from hopeless, and that it might still be possible to retrieve the collapse of the Danube front, or at least to rescue their troops in Budapest from disaster—the most immediate danger.

At any rate, whatever their reasons, the Germans early in January began a series of counter-attacks against Marshal Tolbukhin's Army, which was undoubtedly in a vulnerable situation and could not expect much assistance from Marshal Malinovsky, whose troops were fighting hard on a very wide front.

The somewhat complicated Russian front in Slovakia and Hungary at the end of 1944 was as follows : in the north the southern wing of General Petrov's 4th Ukrainian Army, having cleared the Dukla Pass over the Carpathians, was operating through difficult mountain country towards Presov

and Kosice. On his left Malinovsky's right group was working northwards by the tributaries of the upper Tisza from the Tokaj and Miskolc regions. Farther west Malinovsky was pressing northwards across the upper Ipel and the Slovakian frontier in the Lucenec region, the axis of the thrust being apparently the railway leading to Zvolen. All these operations were evidently designed to clear Slovakia, but German resistance here was strong, and though communiqués reported the capture of numerous small places progress was slow.

Farther west again the Russians had cleared the whole of the lower Ipel and had established bridge-heads across the Hron near its confluence with the Danube. This was an initial step towards Bratislava ; but the immediate objective was evidently Komarno where the main Vienna–Budapest railway skirts the right bank of the Danube. As this railway was the main supply

line for the Germans covering the approaches to Bratislava on both banks of the Danube, their resistance at Komarno was propor-

Russians Draw Nearer to Bratislava tionately stubborn. A considerable part of Malinovsky's force was, moreover, still engaged in the fierce street fighting in Pest which, although it yielded a heavy daily toll of German and Hungarian prisoners, made slow house by house progress.

Malinovsky's army, wholly deployed on the left side of the Danube, was therefore protected from major counter-attacks. Tolbukhin, on the other hand, having crossed the river, had no such protection, and might even be pinned against it by a successful counter-attack. Moreover, he had to face in two directions—eastward towards Buda in order to tighten his hold on the city and to prevent a break-out, and westward to meet any attempt to rescue the

LAKE BALATON BARRED SOVIET APPROACH TO VIENNA

A rapid advance by the 3rd Ukrainian Army on December 5, 1944, brought it to Lake Balaton, the great shallow lake guarding the south-eastern approaches to Vienna. At each end of the lake the Russians encountered stiff resistance, and it was not until March 24, 1945, that they broke through the enemy positions at the north end of the lake to make substantial progress towards the Austrian frontier. Here a German motor-boat patrol is seen on the lake.

LAST BATTLES IN HUNGARY'S CAPITAL

In Budapest on February 13, 1945, all organized resistance ceased after the Royal Palace and its park had been cleared. In the final stages the enemy clung tenaciously to the Government buildings from which they had to be ejected floor by floor. Above, the Pest end of the demolished Elizabeth bridge, which once spanned the Danube. Left, Marshal Malinovsky greets officers in Budapest on the Red Army's 27th anniversary, February 23, 1945. *Photos, Pictorial Press*

encircled city. In addition a substantial part of Tolbukhin's army was far away, holding the passage between the south end of Lake Balaton and the Drava and maintaining contact with Marshal Tito's forces.

During the first days of January Tolbukhin was chiefly engaged in operations against Buda and in some heavy fighting to the south-west of the city, where in the hilly country of the Bakony Forest there were strong German groups whose presence weakened the connexion he had established with Malinovsky at Esztergom. It was this connexion that the first German counter-attacks aimed at breaking, and about January 3 a drive from Komarno towards Esztergom and along the rail-

ways to Buda developed, led by the S.S. Viking and S.S. Totenkopf Divisions, who made attack after attack in an effort to find a weak spot in the Soviet defences.

By January 7 Tolbukhin was forced to evacuate Esztergom, and for the remainder of the month Russian communiqués spoke of counter-attacks repelled on this front and farther south towards Szekesfehervar. The weight of the counter-attacks increased, and on January 23 it was admitted that Szekesfehervar, which the Russians had captured after desperate fighting a month earlier, had also been evacuated.

In these counter-attacks, which developed into what amounted to a counter-offensive on a considerable scale, the Germans employed powerful armoured forces, having drawn strong reinforcements from the west. It is now known that, as soon as it was realized that Rundstedt's coup had failed in its main object, the greater part of his armour, which had lost heavily, was withdrawn, and one of his two panzer armies was dispatched to the Hungarian front. It is difficult to understand why a reserve which would have proved so valuable for defence of the Rhineland or in Poland should thus have been diverted to a theatre of less importance. Possibly the German High Command considered that the immense air superiority of the Allies

in the west had deprived armoured reserves of their offensive potentialities, or that the situation there had been sufficiently stabilized to eliminate danger for a period long enough to admit of an effective counter-stroke on the Danube front. It is possible, too, that by the time the implications of the Russian Vistula offensive in January (*see* Chapter 347) were realized, it was too late to change the direction of the transfer movement.

A third possibility is that, with the collapse of the Vistula front, the proposal to make a final stand in south Germany was seriously considered at Hitler's headquarters. For that course, it was imperative to close effectively the avenue leading to the " Southern Redoubt " by the Danube valley. The reason for the decision to make such a wasteful use of reserves, especially the continuance of the counter-offensive after it had failed to achieve any outstanding initial success and even after the fall of Budapest, is still a matter of intriguing speculation, but it must certainly rank as one of the major mistaken decisions taken by the German High Command. Tolbukhin was for a time hard pressed and had to give ground ; but the ring round Budapest remained unbroken and the Germans,

Protection for ' Southern Redoubt '

right group launched an offensive (announced on January 24) on a considerable scale with success north of Miskolc, but from about February 18 his force west of the Hron facing towards Bratislava had to repel strong German infantry and tank counter-attacks in the Komarno neighbourhood, and fierce fighting continued in this area well on into March, though apparently without much change of positions. On March 1, however, Malinovsky made some gains in the forested hills west of Lucenec, and by March 14 reached and captured Zvolen. Petrov also continued to make progress, but on the whole during March fighting was of a local character with the Germans constantly counter-attacking, probably in hopes of disturbing Russian preparations for a resumption of a general offensive. The counter-attacks extended to the south of Lake Balaton, and on March 24 one of them succeeded in establishing a small footing across the Drava, only to be driven back by a prompt counter-stroke.

Slow Progress in Slovakia

On that date, however, the situation began to change rapidly, for in an Order of the Day Moscow announced that Tolbukhin, having repulsed the attacks of eleven German tank divisions south-west of Budapest and worn the enemy out in defensive fighting, had resumed the offensive and advanced 44 miles on a 60-mile front, recapturing Szekesfehervar and a number of other places. On the following day, it was announced that Malinovsky had also passed to the

exhausted by their efforts, were left without adequate reserves when forced to adopt a defensive attitude.

The recapture of Szekesfehervar proved to be the high-water mark of the enemy counter-offensive, and though hard fighting continued it did not relieve the heavy pressure maintained by both Tolbukhin and Malinovsky on the beleaguered garrison of Budapest. As early as January 18 Malinovsky had gained full possession of Pest, and on February 13 all resistance in Buda ceased with the surrender of Colonel-General Pfeffer-Wildenbruch. During the siege, which had lasted seven weeks, some 50,000 German and Hungarian troops had been killed and 110,000

made prisoner. A few parties that had escaped into the woods to the north-west remained to be mopped up, but the fall of the city left Tolbukhin free to prepare for new operations and removed a block on his most direct line of communications.

Meanwhile, operations in Slovakia had been proceeding steadily if slowly. On January 20 Petrov (see pages 3555 and 3558) captured Presov and Kosice, and about the same time Malinovsky's

THE DANUBE FLOTILLA

On March 25, 1945, the Soviet Danube Flotilla helped in the recapture of Esztergom, north-west of Budapest. In the same area Soviet sailors, near Baitz, captured German shipping with valuable war material. Manoeuvring in the ice, a Russian monitor here hauls some of the enemy ships from their haven to a Russian base.

Photo, Pictorial Press

TOLBUKHIN'S TROOPS FREE AUSTRIA

The liberation of Austria by the 3rd Ukrainian Army, under Marshal Tolbukhin, began on April 1, 1945, when the Russians captured Mattersburg, south-east of Wiener-Neustadt. Twelve days later Vienna, the capital, fell. 1. Soviet troops enter Kirchschlag, set ablaze by the retreating enemy. 2. German six-barrel mortars captured on the Austro-Hungarian frontier. 3. Freed Russian girls in Austria greet their liberators.   *Photos, Pictorial Press*

offensive, and, utilizing units of the Danube naval flotilla, had retaken Esztergom and advanced 30 miles.

By March 26 Tolbukhin had captured Papa and other towns where the Germans were attempting to hold the roads leading to the Austrian frontier, and Malinovsky had captured Banska Bystrica (*see* page 3209) north of Zvolen in the heart of Slovakia. By then Tolbukhin had also taken the offensive south of Lake Balaton and was making rapid progress. On all these fronts German resistance was breaking down and losses in tanks were heavy.

Tolbukhin crossed the Raba River on March 28 and Malinovsky, now operating in strength on the south bank of the Danube, on the same day captured Komarom (opposite Komarno) and the important centre of Györ on the Lower Raba. Tolbukhin, on March 29, reached the Austrian border, capturing Köszeg and other frontier towns. Malinovsky's offensive now began to develop on the north as well as the south bank of the river, and by March 30 it had overcome all resistance in the Hron area and crossed the Nyitra, which joins the Danube at Komarno. This thrust was clearly aimed at Bratislava ; while that south of the Danube was directed towards the approaches to Vienna between Lake Neusiedl and the river.

Tolbukhin's main force at this time was also making progress round the south of Lake Neusiedl, and on April 1 captured the important town of Sopron. Farther south, his left wing, composed partly of Bulgarian troops, achieved a notable success by overcoming determined German resistance in the oil district to the south-west of Lake Balaton, the town of Nagy Kanisza, centre of the field, being captured on April 2. This oilfield had been greatly developed during the war and was virtually the last source of natural oil the Germans possessed. Tolbukhin was also pressing forward towards Graz, and on March 31 captured Szent-Gotthard near the Austrian frontier on the Graz railway.

Also on March 31, north of the Danube, Malinovsky forced a crossing over the river Vag and entered Trnava, on the railway leading to Bratislava from the north-east. South of the Danube his left continued to make progress, capturing the road centre of Magyar Ovar on April 3, and on that day his right group entered Kremnica.

The Germans were still fighting stubbornly, but it was evident that nowhere were they able to halt the Soviet advance, which was now closely threatening both Bratislava and Vienna. On

IN THE CARPATHIANS

On the southern slopes of the Carpathians General Petrov's 4th Ukrainian Army, advancing south from the Dukla Pass, captured Presov and Kosice on January 20, 1945. Large-scale progress was hampered throughout the month of March as the result of determined enemy counter-attacks. Above, Red Army troops march through a Carpathian town. Right, Soviet observers on the look-out from a tree-top.

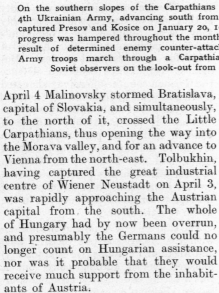

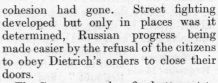

April 4 Malinovsky stormed Bratislava, capital of Slovakia, and simultaneously, to the north of it, crossed the Little Carpathians, thus opening the way into the Morava valley, and for an advance to Vienna from the north-east. Tolbukhin, having captured the great industrial centre of Wiener Neustadt on April 3, was rapidly approaching the Austrian capital from the south. The whole of Hungary had by now been overrun, and presumably the Germans could no longer count on Hungarian assistance, nor was it probable that they would receive much support from the inhabitants of Austria.

By April 5 Malinovsky, south of the Danube, had cleared the country between the river and Lake Neusiedl, capturing Bruck, while Tolbukhin had not only reached the suburbs of Vienna, but, working round to the west, had cut the Vienna–Linz road leading to the upper Danube valley.

On April 8, following the Red Army invasion of Austria, the Soviet Government issued a declaration disclaiming any hostility to the Austrians and confirming their previously announced intention of liberating the country. Two days earlier Tolbukhin appealed to the people of Vienna not to evacuate the city, but to hinder German sabotage and prevent the Germans from using the city's buildings as centres of resistance.

Although Baldur von Shirach recruited some Austrian Volkssturm battalions and the German troops fought desperately in Vienna, there is no doubt that the inhabitants of the city did greet the Russians as liberators, and the murder of Colonel-General Sepp Dietrich, the German commander, by revolver shots fired at him point blank on April 5, was significant of popular sentiments. Dietrich, ordered by Hitler to hold the city to the last, had attempted to organize defences, forcing the inhabitants to dig trenches and construct concrete pill boxes. But defensive works are of little avail if troops with a will to fight are not available in adequate numbers to hold them; and by this time the German losses had been crushing and cohesion had gone. Street fighting developed but only in places was it determined, Russian progress being made easier by the refusal of the citizens to obey Dietrich's orders to close their doors.

The Germans made a final attempt to rally in the northern part of the city, but Malinovsky's advance across the Morava, threatening their line of retreat, dislodged them, and the liberation of the city by **Vienna Freed from the Germans** Tolbukhin's 3rd Ukrainian Army, in co-operation with troops of the 2nd Ukrainian Army, was announced on April 13. Much booty was abandoned by the enemy, who had run out of petrol, and many aircraft were found abandoned on the airfields.

While fighting in Vienna was still in progress, Tolbukhin was also pressing west on both banks of the Danube. By April 15 he had reached St. Pölten on the south side, 28 miles west of Vienna, and on the north side he captured Wagram and many other places on the

BATTLEGROUND OF CENTRAL EUROPE

This map illustrates the last stages of the Red Army's campaign in the Carpathians, Czecho-slovakia, Hungary and Austria, which ended with the relief of the patriots in Prague on May 10, two days after the signing by the Germans of the final act of surrender in Berlin (see Historic Document CCXCVI, page 3640). Other capitals taken on this front during the fighting in 1945 included Budapest, occupied on February 13 after a seven weeks' siege ; and Vienna, taken after stubborn fighting on April 13.

following day. His left wing meanwhile was making progress towards Graz, although the advance here does not appear to have been violently pressed. Malinovsky similarly was making good progress both in Austria north of Vienna, and in the centre of Czecho-slovakia, where the great industrial town of Brno, capital of Moravia, was captured on April 26.

Thus, before the Oder front collapsed about April 19 under Zhukov's final offensive (see Chapter 362), the project

'Southern Redoubt' Made Impracticable

of prolonging resist-ance in the "Southern Redoubt" had been m a d e impracticable. Malinovsky in Czechoslovakia and upper Austria and Tolbukhin in the Danube valley formed an anvil on which the hammer blows of the American 3rd and 7th Armies were due to fall, crushing all communications between northern and southern Germany.

The situation of the Germans in Italy and Yugoslavia had been made equally hopeless, even had they succeeded in resisting Field-Marshal Alexander's and Marshal Tito's offensives. Only in Bohemia did Field-Marshal Schörner make a short-lived attempt to continue the fight when the Nazi edifice finally collapsed in the first week of May, but he was unable to prevent the liberation of Prague by the Red Army on May 10, after a fierce five-day street battle costing 5,000 civilian lives between

Czechoslovak patriots and the German occupying forces.

Malinovsky and Tolbukhin, even though their offensive had not ended with the sensational surrender en masse of the enemy opposing them, had well earned the Order of Victory awarded to them by the President of the Supreme Soviet on April 26. No other group of armies of the Allies could claim such a number of capital cities captured or liberated—Bucharest, Sofia, Belgrade, Budapest, Vienna and Prague.

But reviewing the campaign as a whole, even more remarkable is the way their operations, almost completely separated from the main theatre by the barrier of the Carpathians, fitted into and synchronized with the develop-ment of the Allied plans. Yet it was a long slogging offensive, much of it through very difficult country and under unfavourable weather conditions. The brilliant victory over Von Kleist in Bessarabia (see page 3475) and its rapid exploitation gave the offensive a won-derful start and achieved results of immense importance, political and econ-omic. Malinovsky's dash to Bucharest (see pages 3475–76) deprived Germany of her chief source of natural oil, gave the necessary support to King Michael's coup d'état and secured the by no means negligible co-operation of the Rumanian Army. Tolbukhin's rapid advance into Bulgaria (see page 3476) brought her to heel at a time when she was still offering

obstinate resistance to demands for her withdrawal from Greek territory. Forced to change sides, she not only ceased to be a menace to Marshal Tito, but her troops substantially contributed to the liberation of Belgrade (see page 3481).

Malinovsky's manoeuvre to by-pass the defile at the Iron Gate (see page 3479) and his rapid advance into Hungary as far as the Danube were further notable examples of how success can be ex-ploited, but there followed a long-drawn-out struggle in northern Transylvania and north-west Hungary. This involved hard and continuous fighting before Malinovsky's well-conceived wheel to the north between the Danube and the Tisza separated the Axis forces in the north-east from the army committed to the defence of Budapest and the Danube line.

Yet even then it appeared that the Danube would prove an insuperable obstacle barring the way into western Hungary and Austria. Tolbuk-hin's crossing of the river (see page 3482) was therefore not only a feat of great tactical merit, but a strategical manoeuvre of decisive importance. Exploited rapidly and boldly, it resulted in the complete encirclement of Budapest.

Decisive Danube Crossing

In attempts to retrieve the situation the Germans committed some of their most effective remaining reserves, badly as they were needed elsewhere—possibly they were tempted by Tolbukhin's exposed position and had hopes of achieving a sensational success. But against Tolbukhin's stubborn defence the German counter-offensive exhausted itself, and when he resumed the offensive only a shattered army barred his way to Vienna. It was a notable example of Russian ability to pass rapidly from attack to defence and then to attack again, and the defeat of the German counter-offensive was probably of even greater importance than the capture of Budapest, for its effects were felt in the whole theatre of war.

The capture of Vienna and the link-up with the Americans (see Chapter 369) and Alexander's troops (see Chapter 361) followed almost automatically, but it was a fitting end to a remarkable cam-paign. Seldom can operations in what was in some respects a subsidiary theatre have produced such great results, or have induced the enemy to make such curious mistakes. A remarkable feature of the campaign was the admirable co-ordination of Malinovsky's and Tol-bukhin's operations ; at times their immediate objectives were widely separ-ated, but at the decisive moment and place their main efforts coalesced perfectly.

AUSTRIA'S CAPITAL FREED FROM THE GERMANS

After stubborn fighting, Vienna fell to units drawn from the 2nd and 3rd Ukrainian Armies, under Marshal Tolbukhin, on April 13, 1945. The Red Army captured 130,000 prisoners in the battle for the city and its approaches which began on March 16. Soviet claims included the rout of eleven German tank divisions, including the 6th S.S. Tank Army, the destruction or capture of 1,345 tanks and self-propelled guns, and 2,250 field-guns. In Vienna the Russians applied new tactics, moving through courtyards and breaking down walls instead of advancing along the streets. 1. German barricades in the Mariahilferstrasse. 2. Soviet tank crew in the outskirts. 3. Red Army troops outside the Parliament buildings in the Ringstrasse.

4A²

March 1. Capture of München-Gladbach and Rheydt by U.S. 9th Army disclosed ; U.S. 3rd Army took Oberzerf (Saar River). Over 1,200 U.S.A. 8th A.F. "heavies" attacked Baden and Württemberg ; by night, R.A.F. bombed Berlin. U.S. troops landed on Palawan (Philippines). Iran declared war on Japan ; Saudi Arabia on Germany and Japan.

March 2. German 15th Army in retreat across the Rhine ; announced that U.S. 9th Army had captured Krefeld, Venlo and Roermond and was on the Rhine opposite Düsseldorf ; U.S. 3rd Army took Trier ; British troops with 1st Canadian Army took Weeze on the Niers. R.A.F. struck heavily at Cologne, gave Berlin its eleventh successive nightly raid. U.S. forces seized Lubang Island (Philippines).

March 3. R.A.F. breached Dortmund–Ems canal at Ladbergen (night). Red Army captured Pollnow (Pomerania). Marianas-based Super-Fortresses bombed Tokyo. Japanese forces on Iwo Jima cut in two. For the first time since June 1944, piloted aircraft bombed Britain.

March 4. 1st and 2nd White Russian Armies reached Baltic, isolating vast German forces from the Kolberg area to the E. Prussian border. Announced that Australians on Bougainville had cleared Downs Ridge.

March 5. R.A.F. heavily bombed oil plants near Leipzig. First White Russian Army captured Stargard, Naugard and Polzin ; Red Air Force attacked Königsberg and Stettin. Four-fifths of Iwo Jima in U.S. hands.

March 6. U.S. 1st Army captured Cologne. Second White Russian Army took Polish city of Grudziadz (Graudenz).

March 7. U.S. 3rd Army reached Rhine N.W. of Coblenz. R.A.F. heavily bombed Dessau (night). Russians took Starogard (in former Polish Corridor). Fourteenth Army captured Madaya and Pakokku (Upper Burma) ; Chinese 1st Army occupied Old Lashio.

March 8. U.S. 1st Army captured Rhine bridge at Remagen. "Heavies" of the U.S.A. 8th A.F. attacked Dortmund and Gelsenkirchen in strength ; R.A.F. bombed Hamburg and Berlin. Nineteenth Division entered outskirts of Mandalay ; Chinese captured New Lashio.

March 9. U.S. troops took Bonn ; British forces captured Xanten. Second White Russian Army seized Stolp (N. Pomerania) to complete encirclement of Danzig. Marianas-based Super-Fortresses heavily bombed Tokyo. U.S. troops landed on Mindanao (Philippines).

March 10. Germans withdrew from Wesel bridge-head, blowing up Wesel bridges. Russians captured Lauenburg and Kartuzy, near Danzig.

March 11. West bank of Rhine, from Nijmegen to the Moselle in Alsace, under Allied control. R.A.F. heavily bombed Essen by day ; Berlin received its 20th consecutive night raid. Marianas-based Super-Fortresses attacked Nagoya. Dr. Benes and his Government left London for Slovakia.

March 12. R.A.F. Lancasters and Halifaxes made heaviest attack of the war to date at Dortmund. Russians captured Kistrzin on the Oder.

March 13. U.S.A. 15th A.F. bombed Regensburg area (Bavaria). Heavy attack by Marianas-based Super-Fortresses on Osaka. Maymyo (Burma) captured ; British 36th Division took Mong Mit (Shan States).

March 14. U.S.A. 8th A.F. heavily bombed Hanover and the Ruhr ; R.A.F. demolished Bielefeld viaducts, using 10-ton " Grand Slam " bomb for the first time. Russians captured Zvolen in Czechoslovakia. U.S.A. 15th A.F. and Soviet bombers, fighting together for the first time, simultaneously attacked Novy Zamky (Slovakia). U.S. troops land on Bomblon and Simara (Philippines).

March 14-15. Norwegian Commando force, trained in Britain, seriously disrupted enemy communications in Norway.

March 15. U.S.A. 8th A.F. bombed German General Staff H.Q. at Zossen, 20 miles S. of Berlin ; R.A.F. attacked Gestapo H.Q. at Copenhagen. Russians took Griefenhagen, S. of Stettin. Kobe (Japan) heavily bombed by U.S. Super-Fortresses. All Iwo Jima in U.S. hands.

March 17. U.S.A. 8th A.F. heavily bombed Leipzig, Dresden and Hanover areas ; by night R.A.F. attacked Berlin. Two German destroyers sunk off Corsica by H.M. destroyers " Lookout " and " Meteor." Rangoon bombed.

March 18. U.S. 3rd Army captured Coblenz. Over 1,300 U.S.A. 8th A.F. Liberators and Fortresses bombed Berlin by daylight. First White Russian Army took Kolberg, Baltic seaport. U.S.A. 15th A.F. attacked communications in Yugoslavia, Austria and Hungary. U.S. carrier-based aircraft struck heavily at Japanese Fleet in the Inland Sea. Queen Wilhelmina visited Netherlands.

March 19. U.S.A. 8th A.F. bombed jet-plane plant at Baumenheim (N. of Augsburg) ; R.A.F. destroyed Arnsberg viaduct, near Hamm, with 22,000-lb. bombs. British 2nd Division captured Ava (Burma) ; other 14th Army troops took Amarapura. U.S. forces landed on Panay (Philippines).

March 20. German resistance collapsed W. of the Rhine ; Saarbrücken, Zweibrücken, Kaiserslautern and Worms captured ; Mainz overrun. Red Army took Braunsberg (E. Prussia) and Altdamm on the Oder. British recaptured Mandalay ; British 36th Division took Mogok. Capture of But airfield, New Guinea, by Australians announced.

March 21. U.S. 3rd Army captured Ludwigshaven. R.A.F. Mosquitoes scored direct hits on Gestapo H.Q. in Copenhagen. U.S. forces captured Iloilo (Panay) and San Fernando (Luzon).

March 22. Heavy Allied air attacks on enemy communications leading to the Lower Rhine ; announced that Field-Marshal von Rundstedt had been replaced by Field-Marshal Kesselring as German C.-in-C. in the West. First Ukrainian Army opened offensive in Upper Silesia, S.W. of Oppeln, capturing Neustadt on Czechoslovak border. Rangoon bombed.

March 22-23 (night). U.S. 3rd Army established solid bridge-head across the Rhine, S. of Mainz.

March 23. U.S. 3rd Army captured Speyer ; heavy Allied air attacks on enemy front on the Lower Rhine. R.A.F. Lancasters dropped 22,000-lb. bombs on rail bridge across the Weser at Bremen. Russians took Zoppot, between Danzig and Gdynia. U.S. " heavies " bombed Formosa.

March 23-24. U.S. carrier-based aircraft heavily attacked Ryukyu Islands.

March 24. Twenty-First Army crossings of the Rhine, north of the Ruhr, in great strength ; British 6th and U.S. 17th Airborne Divisions dropped behind E. bank of the river. U.S.A. 15th A.F., based in Italy, bombed Berlin for the first time. Third Ukrainian Army went over to the offensive S.W. of Budapest, recapturing Szekesfehervar,Vesprzem, and Zirc. Firewatching duties abolished in the United Kingdom.

March 25. Mr. Churchill and Field-Marshal Montgomery crossed the Rhine and visited British troops in newly won areas. U.S. 3rd Army captured Darmstadt ; Ludwigshaven cleared. Russians retook Esztergom ; seized Heiligenbeil, last enemy defence point on the Frisches Haff ; Red Air Force heavily bombed Danzig. In Burma 14th Army captured Kume and Langwa.

March 26. U.S. 3rd Army, entering Bavaria, penetrated Aschaffenburg and seized bridge across the Main. Russians captured Banska-Bystrica (Slovakia) and Papa (Hungary) ; Red Air Force bombed Danzig in strength. Fourteenth Army took Myittha on the Mandalay–Rangoon railway. U.S. troops made new landing on Cebu (Philippines).

March 27. All organized resistance on 21st Army Group front ceased ; U.S. 7th Army crossed Rhine N. of Mannheim. R.A.F. attacked U-boat pens at Vegesack (Bremen) with 10-ton bombs. Russians captured 14 suburbs of Danzig. Super-Fortresses attacked Kyushu ; U.S. aircraft and warships pounded Ryukyus. Last V-2 fell in England, at Orpington, Kent.

March 28. Tanks of the U.S. 1st Army entered Giessen, N. of Frankfort-on-Main ; U.S. 3rd Army took Wiesbaden and Aschaffenburg. 2nd White Russian Army captured Gdynia ; other Soviet forces took Györ on the Raba River and Komarom on the Danube. Cebu City (Philippines) occupied. Australian capture of Dagua (New Guinea) announced.

March 29. Mannheim surrendered to U.S. 7th Army ; 21st Army Group offensive from the Lower Rhine bridgehead began at dawn. Third Ukrainian Army reached the Austrian border, captured Köszeg.

March 30. Americans captured Heidelberg and Frankfort-on-Main. U.S.A. 8th A.F. heavily bombed Hamburg, Bremen, and Wilhelmshaven. Second White Russian Army captured Danzig. Super-Fortresses bombed Nagoya.

March 31. U.S. 7th Army crossed Tauber River, E. of Darmstadt ; French 1st Army crossed Rhine in the Speyer area. General Eisenhower called on the Wehrmacht to surrender. R.A.F. bombed U-boat yards at Hamburg. Russians captured Ratibor (Silesia) amd Szent-Gotthard (Hungary) ; crossed Vag River (S. Slovakia). British Fleet attacked the Saki Islands (Ryukyus).

Chapter 355

NAZI GERMANY'S DEATH STRUGGLES

Dr. Frederik Heymann, formerly of the editorial staff of the ' Frankfürter Zeitung ' and foreign editor of ' Bohemia ' (Prague), here describes the last four months of the Nazis' ' Thousand-Year Empire.' Despite the certainty of defeat felt by the majority of the German people, Nazi propaganda carried on to the end its efforts to flog them into continued resistance. The internal history of Germany during 1944 is given in Chapter 313 ; that of the months following the surrender in Chapter 380

IN the two years following Stalingrad, the Germans had become accustomed to gloom. New Year's Day 1945, however, surpassed in its dark forebodings all its predecessors. An overwhelming majority of Germans had, by this time, become conscious of the fact that the war was lost, and their only hope was that it would not drag on too long. But staunch Nazis still pretended to believe in victory, and Germany's military propaganda tried to make the most of the temporary successes of Rundstedt's Ardennes offensive. Hitler in his New Year message went so far as to claim that " the climax of the war has been passed," and that further German counter-strokes would break the will of the enemy. At the same time, he deplored the desertion of Germany's " treacherous Allies." He reminded his followers again that the failure of the attempt on his life on July 20, 1944 (*see* page 3168), had shown the hand of Providence, and ended up by telling the German people that they could not possibly be defeated—either by military weapons or by the time factor.

In reality, Germany's " counterstroke " had already spent its force. By the middle of January it became clear even to the most hopeful Nazis **Defeat on** that Rundstedt's offen- **Both Fronts** sive had been abortive and that, at the very best, it had achieved a slight delay of the Western Allies' push into Germany. The last great Russian offensive had already begun, and by its terrible power and swiftness succeeded in shifting the front in one single, uninterrupted move from the Vistula to the Oder.

After the destruction she had suffered from the air, Germany now became— for the first time since the Napoleonic wars—a vast battlefield, and the names of unquestionably German towns and cities such as Königsberg, Breslau, Glogau and Liegnitz appeared in the reports of the German High Command and of war correspondents, every one of them allegedly a fortress, heroically defended not only by the army but by the entire population. At the same time

the Germans were told that strong counter-measures were in preparation, that the Russians, by pushing their centre forward in the direction of Berlin with their flanks still far back to the east, had put themselves in a most dangerous position which the German High Command would certainly use to its best advantage, though details of these plans had, of course, to remain secret. Hints of this sort continued to be dropped for weeks, even at a time when the German armies to the north of the huge Russian wedge had been wiped out or confined within small pockets of resistance along the Baltic Sea (*see* Chapter 347).

Actually there was never a chance that these counter-measures would be taken. Most of the German effectives still available as fighting reserves in the winter of 1944-45 had already been in action in the course of the Rundstedt offensive. Those remnants of mobile

Panzer formations that had escaped destruction in Belgium and could theoretically be transferred to the east were much too weak to stave off disaster, and Allied air-raids, to which the weakened Luftwaffe had no strength to reply, made this transfer itself a slow, costly, inefficient undertaking.

In striking contrast to what had still been achieved in 1944, the measures now being taken to mobilize new forces showed all the symptoms **More Women** of a desperate makeshift. **Called to** An attempt was made to **Factories** free still more German workers from the war factories by putting women in their places, and a certain amount of propaganda was put out to persuade women who could not undertake a full day's work in a factory to accept at least half-day jobs. Men who had contagious diseases like tuberculosis were put to work, as were war invalids, including the blind. When

COLLAPSE OF THE GERMAN SOLDIER'S MORALE

So low had morale fallen that on November 21, 1944, all German soldiers were required to take a new vow, of faith in Nazism. Left, a declaration issued by Hitler to all troops, printed on ersatz vellum : ' After the end of this war I shall return as a still more fanatical National Socialist than before.' Right, Wehrmacht troops take the new oath ' to die for Hitler and Nazism.'
Photo, Pictorial Press

DESPERATION GRIPS THE GERMAN HOME FRONT

The winter of 1944-45 brought the bitter realities of war home to the German people. 1. Outside Berlin, reserves drawn from youth organizations are trained in musketry. 2. As the Allies drew nearer to the Reich capital, Army field bakeries in the fighting areas had to serve civilians as well as soldiers. 3. Girls train for Luftwaffe duties—part of the drive to press into war service all available German women. *Photos, Pictorial Press ; Associated Press ; Keystone*

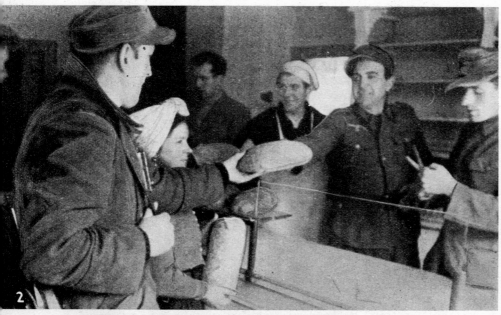

more and more factories were put out of production by air-raids and it became impossible to shift the workers from one place to another, an attempt was made to "loosen up" the whole system of manpower direction by concentrating all the manpower available in one town or city on work in those factories that had escaped damage or could be put into a state of repair within a short time.

The damage inflicted on the German communications system by Allied air-raids was clearly reflected in a number of measures. Travelling by train, already severely curtailed, was now limited to the minimum. On January 23 all public travel by express trains was disallowed, and all existing travel permits were cancelled. Express trains were run, in very limited numbers only, for military and government personnel. This measure was followed by an order forbidding the sending of letters and parcels except locally. From one town to another, only open postcards might be sent, to save weight and time taken in censorship. From January 30 onwards, newspapers, except for special occasions and Sunday issues, appeared as single sheets with two printed pages only.

Two other fields in which transport difficulties became particularly obvious were the distribution of fuel and food. Coal and wood were rationed more strictly and people were advised to help each other by joining in "warmth co-opera-tives," that is, to heat only a small number of rooms in each block of flats and use these as living-rooms for all the inhabitants. On February 3 the Government announced that the rations for periods 72 and 73 would have to suffice for nine instead of eight weeks. A month later even this decision was revoked, and the whole system of food distribution was made "more elastic"; hitherto centrally directed, it was now to be carried out according to stores and reserves available in each district. This "decentralization" was one more symptom of the fact that the whole machine of administration in unoccupied Germany was quickly falling to pieces.

Administration Begins to Break Down

This process had only started when, in the night of January 30, Hitler publicly addressed the German people for the last time. It was the occasion of the twelfth anniversary of the "Third Reich." It was obvious enough that this empire, which had been hailed as "das Tausendjaehrige Reich" (the thousand years' empire) by its ardent followers, had not another year to live, and some anti-Nazis had started to call

IT WAS 1940—IN REVERSE

On January 28, 1945, the German News Agency admitted that millions of German men, women and children were crowding the Eastern roads—'a mass migration without precedent in conditions of deepest winter and biting frost.' It was 1940—in reverse, and in bad instead of good weather (see illus. in pages 1396, 1535, 1551). Top, British troops issue military rations left by the retreating Germans in a newly won Rhineland town to 'displaced persons' (Russians, Poles, French and Dutch). In circle, German refugees watch a heavy U.S. trailer rumble through the streets of Saarbrücken. Right, road-jam of refugees fleeing before the advancing Russians.
Photos, British & U.S. Official.

STAMPS AS PROPAGANDA

These newly designed postage stamps were included in German propaganda for the Home Front in late 1944. Left, a stamp to commemorate the founding of the Volkssturm in October 1944: it depicts three generations springing to arms. Right, issue intended to convince the German people of the effectiveness of rocket-warfare.

1944—its will to let him win. The alleged murderous intentions of the Allies against the whole German people were painted in the darkest colours, and Jews as well as Bolsheviks received the usual attention, this time adorned with references to the horrible atrocities allegedly committed by Russia's "Asiatic hordes" against Germans in the east. He made a final appeal to German youth to fight on fanatically; if this was done, the crisis was sure to be mastered.

If Hitler appealed only to the faithful, the German propaganda machine itself, still led by Goebbels, did not give up the attempt to persuade the people that all was not lost even militarily. Though the daily war reports could, on land, report nothing

Goebbels's Propaganda Continues

it "das Dutzendjaehrige Reich" (the dozen years' empire). Hitler himself had not been heard of for quite a time, and again and again rumours were spread that he was no longer alive or had left Germany. So he decided to prove the contrary and to restore the steadily sinking morale of his party followers by giving a speech over the radio. (Two days before, he received the last "statesman" whom the Germans called an ally — Vidkun Quisling, "Prime Minister" of the so-called Norwegian Government.)

As there was no single fact Hitler could have mentioned as being in any way a basis for hope, he avoided the realm of facts altogether. He claimed, without bothering about logic, that the victory achieved by the Nazi movement in Germany in 1933 was in itself a guarantee for final victory in the war against Germany's enemies. Again, as so often before, Providence was invoked as having shown—by saving Hitler's life on July 20,

Hitler's last Broadcast

COLLECTIONS FOR THE VOLKSSTÜRM

In an attempt to overcome the shortage of clothing for the Volkssturm (see page 3173) in the winter of 1944-45, street-to-street collections were organized. Known as the 'Volksopfer' ('People's Offering'), the campaign was responsible for collecting old uniforms of almost any kind, boots, and anything resembling military equipment. Slogan on the van reads: 'The Führer expects your Offering for the Army and the Volkssturm.' *Photos, Associated Press*

WAR ON GERMANY'S RAILWAYS

With the mounting Allied air attacks on communications in the Reich in the early months of 1945, rebuilding of bombed railway stations became an almost insuperable task. Here, in what remained of a bombed station, a solitary hut serves as booking-office, goods depôt, superintendent's office, telephone-exchange and station workshop. *Photo, Planet News*

but catastrophic losses of territory in the east and, from February onwards, also in the west, there were still air and sea where German successes could be claimed. The Luftwaffe had almost ceased to be a factor with which the Allied air forces had to reckon. Yet there were still the V-weapons. V1 was finished by this time, as the Germans now possessed no bases near enough to Britain to launch them successfully. V2, however, could still be employed to a limited extent, and it was still a weapon on the alleged successes of which German propaganda tried to dwell.

Another such weapon was the U-boats, now equipped with Schnorkel air-masts (*see* page 3494) enabling them to travel long distances under water. A spectacular success of German naval engineering, had it been achieved three years earlier, it might have altered the course of the Battle of the Atlantic. Now, however, with all German naval

GERMANS PUT OUT FLAGS OF SURRENDER

Two days after the fall of Coblenz on March 18, 1945, all German resistance west of the Rhine collapsed. As the Allied armies swept towards the heart of the Reich, they were greeted in many districts by white flags hung out by civilians, who despite orders to evacuate had remained in their homes after the Wehrmacht (and Nazi Party officials) had retreated. Here U.S. 1st Army troops occupy a white-flagged street at Engers, near Coblenz. *Photo, U.S. Army Signal Corps*

bases on the open Atlantic save those in Norway gone and Allied shipping tonnage multiplied, it had no more than a limited nuisance value. It served, however, to provide German newspapers with many a big headline during the last months of the war.

For the rest, German official propaganda was mainly on the defensive. A special effort was made to counteract the effects it was feared the conference of the Big Three in the Crimea (*see* page 3563) might have on the German population. Newspapers, on Goebbels's orders, prophesied an appeal by the Allies to the German people which, it was said, would be only a treacherous attempt to lure them—like Wilson's Fourteen Points—into laying down their arms, in order to enslave them the more easily. When the conference ended without such an appeal being made, Goebbels told the Germans that this made it quite clear that the Allies, on Moscow's order, were determined to annihilate the whole German people, who would answer by a still more determined resistance.

With more and more of the soil of

Germany lost to the conquering armies of the Allies there arose, on top of all the other problems, a new one for the German Government: the problem of refugees. Actually they had created it themselves. To some extent the Nazi authorities attempted a sort of " scorched earth policy ": where possible the population was told to evacuate places threatened by the enemy, to drive away all the cattle and to burn and destroy everything that could be of any use to the Allies.

In the west this order was followed only to a very limited extent. Hard as the Nazi party tried to make the struggle against Britons and Americans " a people's war," they did not succeed. The majority of the German population in the west wanted the war to be over as quickly as possible. They were not much afraid of the conquering armies of the western Allies, whom a

good many Germans regarded as liberators, though this view was never encouraged by Allied propaganda. In some places the Allied armies came near all party officials left hurriedly, and this almost invariably led the population to hang out white flags. Most of these places were occupied without having to suffer from actual fighting and gunfire. Men of the so-called Volkssturm did not resist unless they were forced to do so.

Here and there, however, party and army together prevented any move to surrender, shot at people who were showing the white flag and executed officers who were more intent on saving German lives and property than on fighting on in an utterly hopeless situation. Wherever such resistance was met, it was easily crushed by the

GERMANS GO UNDERGROUND

As the Allied Armies overran the Reich early in 1945, large numbers of civilians were driven underground to live in cellars and shelters. Here German families huddle in sandhill cave shelters at Haltern, between Wesel and Münster, to protect themselves from the shellfire of the advancing Allies. Right, unfinished street shelters at Coblenz after its fall on March 18.

Allied armies, though with grave losses to the desperate defenders and the places they tried to defend.

It was quite different in the east. There the atrocity propaganda of the Nazis had had a very marked effect.

Effects of Anti-Russian Propaganda
One of the reasons for this was that very many Germans—those serving with the Army as well as civilians—knew of the crimes which the Germans themselves had committed in Russia, and thought it not unlikely that the Russians, now they had changed roles with the Germans by invading German soil, would be determined to pay them back ;

and official propaganda—in order to strengthen the will to resist—had done its best to increase these fears.

On March 6 the chief of staff of the German Army, Colonel-General Guderian, appeared before a press conference in Berlin in order to lend the highest possible authority to this sort of talk. He quoted an order of the day by Marshal Zhukov which allegedly showed the Russian intention of destroying the German people. (Actually, Zhukov had said that the Russian Armies were now pursuing the *Fascist beast* into its lair and would destroy it there. It was Guderian himself who identified "Fascist beast" with the German people.) Then the general introduced two German officers who claimed to have got through the Russian lines after having spent several days in the zone just occupied by the Red Army, and who painted in the most lurid colours the awful things which —as they claimed to have heard or seen—the "Asiatic Hordes" had done to German civilians, in particular to German women. These and similar stories were given the strongest possible publicity, and they were not only believed, but even added to by circulating rumours.

Zhukov Misinterpreted

The effect was terrifying even to the German authorities. Huge streams of refugees, literally millions of them, covered the roads leading from the east to the centre of the Reich, crowded the few trains still running, invaded the cities and towns which lay in their way, and all the measures taken to provide food and shelter for them proved utterly inadequate. One of these waves of refugees, amounting to a few hundred thousands, had just swamped Dresden when one of the fiercest air-raids— coming from the west, but intended to help the Red Army tactically by dislocating traffic and communications—hit the town and killed a great many of those who, for lack of room, had not been able to take shelter.

NEW ALLIED CURRENCY FOR THE REICH

The British Chancellor of the Exchequer, Sir John Anderson, announced on October 3, 1944, that Allied forces in Germany were using Allied military marks circulating at par with the Reichsmark, and that the rate of exchange had been provisionally fixed in agreement with the U.S. authorities at 40 Reichsmark to the pound and 10 Reichsmark to the dollar. Below, obverse and reverse of an Allied 10-mark note.

RUBY LOFTUS SCREWING A BREECH RING
Dame Laura Knight, R.A.

IN October 1945 a representative exhibition was held at Burlington House, London, consisting of approximately one-fifth of the 5,000 works of art commissioned or purchased by the War Artists' Advisory Committee set up in the autumn of 1939 to make 'an artistic record of the war in all its aspects.' The collection had been circulating since the early days of the war in Britain, the Empire, and the United States. Here we give a selection of these paintings. Among the well-known artists commissioned was Eric Ravilious (his ÇOASTAL DEFENCES is reproduced on the next page), who was killed while flying over Iceland.

Most of the pictures were painted on the spot, but some were reconstructed from eyewitness accounts, for instance, Raymond Coxon's SHIPWRECKED and Richard Eurich's DUNKIRK BEACHES 1940. (The latter is owned by the Rt. Hon. Vincent Massey, High Commissioner for Canada, and is reproduced here by his permission.) Central seated figure in A. Olivier's OPERATIONS ROOM CONFERENCE, painted at Bomber Command in October 1943, is Air Chief Marshal Sir Arthur Harris. Seated on his left is Brigadier-General F. L. Anderson, U.S.A.A.F., while standing on his right is Air Vice-Marshal R. H. M. S. Saundby. In Dame Laura Knight's 'TAKE OFF', the R.A.F. men depicted are Flight-Lieutenant Stuart White, Flying-Officer Escreet, Flying-Officer Bettles, D.F.C., and Flight-Sergeant Quadling. Miss Ruby Loftus (above) is screwing the breech ring of a Bofors gun —the most highly-skilled operation in the Royal Ordnance Factory where she worked.

SHIPWRECKED
Raymond Coxon

R.A.F. MORSE SCHOOL   Charles Cundall, R.A.

STRETCHER PARTY AT W

COASTAL DEFENCES   Eric Ravilious

'TAKE OFF'

AS CLOTHING   W. L. Clause

OPERATIONS ROOM CONFERENCE   A. Olivier

Dame Laura Knight, R.A.

DUNKIRK BEACHES, 1940   Richard Eurich, A.R.A.

'MULBERRY B' PORT AT ARROMANCHES AS SEEN BY A WAR ARTIST

Pictorial records of the war commissioned by the War Artists' Advisory Committee included these of the 'Mulberry B' port in Normandy. (See also pages 3028 and 3030.) They were painted by Lieutenant Stephen Bone, son of Sir Muirhead Bone, from sketches done on the spot shortly after the port was constructed in the summer of 1944. Supplies are seen coming ashore along the floating pierways. Top, general view of the harbour. *Crown Copyright*

One of the means by which the Nazi party tried to stiffen resistance against the Allies was the so-called "Werewolf" Movement. German broadcasting stations which pretended to be in the occupied territory (actually they were sending from the centre of Germany) read proclamations asking the whole people, including women and youngsters, to do every possible harm to the Allied armies, in particular to their lines of communication. These broadcasts were given a strong publicity within the remaining territory of Nazi Germany but never found many followers in the occupied districts of the west. A few misguided Super-Nazis among the young generation made some such attempts and were quickly disposed of. As a whole the German people, who had been educated to obey any authority and never to act as individuals, were neither willing nor even able to conduct a guerilla campaign. After the middle of April nothing was heard of the "Werewolf" Movement even in the remaining Nazi papers.

'Werewolf' Movement

All through April, the space within which the Nazis still ruled was shrinking rapidly. By the beginning of the month 21 German divisions were trapped in the Ruhr ; they were destroyed in less than three weeks (*see* Chapter 369). On April 13, Vienna was taken by the Russians (*see* page 3625), who were also rapidly approaching the Reich

JEWISH WOMEN SLAVE-WORKERS RELEASED

Many thousands of slave-workers were released by the Allies as they swept into the Reich in the early months of 1945. These Jewish women, among many taken from homes in France, Holland, Belgium, Italy, and Poland, were freed by the U.S. 9th Army from Kaunitz where they had been forced to make munitions. Each was tattooed with a number on the left arm and had a yellow cross daubed on the back of her clothes.   *Photo, Keystone*

capital (*see* Chapter 362). A week later the Americans took Nuremberg and were nearing the frontier of Czechoslovakia. On April 16 Hitler, in an order of the day, which, remarkably enough, was directed only to the German armies in the east, still dared

to predict victory for Germany. "Asia," so he said, thereby meaning the Russian armies, "will bleed to death before the defences of the Reich capital . . . Berlin remains German, Vienna will become German again, and Europe will never become Russian."

It was characteristic of this, as of other last attempts to prolong the death struggle of the Nazi Empire, that the western Allies were hardly mentioned. The Germans must be made to believe that only the fight against the Russians counted, and that all could be saved once the attack from the east could be stopped. There was still behind it the fallacious idea that the western powers would come to an accord with Germany in order to prevent the Russians from going too far west. Hints of this sort appeared also in the long article which Dr. Goebbels wrote for the "Völkischer Beobachter" on the occasion of Hitler's birthday (April 20). "The war," he said there, "is nearing its end. The folly has passed its climax. The perverse coalition between plutocracy and bolshevism is falling to pieces. . . . The head of the coalition [meaning Roosevelt, who died on April 12] is crushed, but the Fuehrer carries on as usual."

Last Attempts to Rally Resistance

It was one of the very last issues of the infamous Nazi paper that carried this article, together with a huge portrait of Hitler. In reality, the Fuehrer

ALLIED ARMIES RECOVER LOOTED METAL

Advancing across Europe in the winter of 1944-45, the Allied armies found ample evidence of the looting of metal from countries formerly occupied by the Germans. In Hamburg alone, some 50,000 church bells stolen from Belgium and Holland, many with historic associations, were discovered ready for smelting. In this dump, also in Hamburg, were piled, irrespective of their artistic merits, metal statues and works of art of many periods.   *Photo, British Newspaper Pool*

GERMANY'S REACTION TO INVASION

As the British and U.S. armies overran western Germany in 1945 they encountered many German civilians who, defying Nazi orders to evacuate, had concealed themselves to await the arrival of the Allied forces. 1. Germans emerge from their homes to surrender to troops of the U.S. 36th Infantry Division. 2. The population of Kyllburg, in the Rhineland, gathers in the streets to hear orders from occupying forces of the U.S. 3rd Army. 3. These townspeople at Brühl, near Cologne, were put to work by a U.S. Military Government unit to clean up bomb damage and search for dead among the debris. 4. In Frankfort-on-Main, after its occupation by the U.S. 3rd Army on March 30, civilians loot a tobacconist's.

R.A.F. UNMASKED HANOVER'S ELABORATE CAMOUFLAGE

was very far from carrying on as usual. He lived in the Berlin Chancellery, trying to direct the resistance of Berlin, whose eastern suburbs were already in Russian hands, and could not make up his mind whether to stay there in his capital or to flee to his "Berghof" at Berchtesgaden where a certain amount of preparation for a last armed resistance (greatly overrated by some observers in Allied countries) had been made. Hitler was, by this time, a nervous wreck, a man whose every hope had been smashed but who could not—did not dare to—give up. On April 22, however, he had a complete breakdown, from which he did not recover. By now he was resolved not to attempt the flight to Berchtesgaden, but to remain in Berlin and there to commit suicide if his last hope—relief by the 12th German army under General Wenck—should fail. This was the plan he revealed to Professor Speer, Minister of Armament and War Production, who visited him on April 23.

Hitler a Nervous Wreck

About this time Hitler became aware that two of his chief lieutenants, Goering and Himmler, had tried to open negotiations with the Allies. Himmler met Count Bernadotte, a relative of the King of Sweden and President of the Swedish Red Cross, on April 24, and offered surrender to the Western Allies only, in the vain hope that he might thus save his life. The Allied answer was that surrender would be accepted only if it was offered to all the Allies, including Russia. Next day the Russian and American armies linked up on the Elbe near Torgau, thereby cutting the remaining body of Nazi Germany in two, and on the 26th Hitler received in his shelter in the Reich Chancellery Field-Marshal Ritter von Greim, whom he appointed Chief of the Luftwaffe in succession to Goering.

Reports by people who saw him during those last few days of his life (in particular a detailed report by a German woman pilot, Hanna Reitsch, who left Hitler and his followers in the last aircraft to get out of the beleaguered city —*see* page 3552) say that he no longer behaved like a human being. He sat for hours, staring and not talking at all, then he got into a frenzy of activity, trying to direct, and give orders to, the "relieving" army of General Wenck which, however, at this time had already been wiped out. Then he heaped reproaches for the fate besetting Nazi Germany on the head of almost everybody save himself, cursing in particular the "traitors" Goering and Himmler.

Hitler's last days—from April 28 to April 30—were filled with preparations for his death. He made two rather loquacious testaments—a "private" and a "political" one—which he managed to send out of Berlin. In his political testament he nominated a new Reich Government. Whereas he himself had been head of state and head of the government at the same time, he now divided these two offices again as they had been up to the death of President Hindenburg. As Reich President, he named none of those who had previously (like Goering and Hess) been designated to this office, but Grand-Admiral Doenitz who was, at the same time, supposed to keep the office of chief of the German Navy and to take over, in addition, the War Ministry. Dr. Goebbels was to become Reich Chancellor, and Bormann, former Deputy Fuehrer, was to become Chief of the Nazi Party. Both Goering and Himmler were solemnly deprived of all their offices and expelled from the

HITLER FACES DEFEAT ON THE RIVER ODER

In January 1945 began the Red Army's sustained advance from the Vistula to the Oder. The enemy's plans to hold up the Russians' advance west of the Oder were completely upset by the speed and vigour of the Red Army's drive. Here Hitler—in one of the last photographs taken of him—discusses strategy with a group of his staff officers at his H.Q. near the Oder as the Russian armies pushed forward.

Photo, Sport & General

Nazi Party. The testament ended with another fierce attack on the Jews on the old familiar lines.

In the evening of April 29—when the Reich Chancellery was already under the steady fire of the Russian guns—Hitler had himself married to Eva Braun, a young woman who for some years had been one of his few intimate friends. There was a wedding meal in which only a few people participated. In the early morning of the next day (around 2.30 a.m.) Hitler received the servants and other staff of the Reich Chancellery to bid them good-bye. Later that morning 180 litres (about 40 gallons) of benzine were brought to the Reich Chancellery. In the afternoon, between 2 and 3 o'clock on April 30, the last act seems to have taken place. There are reasons for believing that Hitler shot his newly wed wife and then himself. It is almost certain that, immediately after they had died, their corpses were carried out into the court of the Chancellery and burned, after great quantities of benzine had been poured over them. Shortly afterwards Dr. Goebbels, together with his family, also committed suicide.

On May 1 Bormann succeeded in informing Grand-Admiral Doenitz who,

Hitler's Marriage and Death

together with other members of the Reich Government, had fled to Flensburg near the Danish border. From Flensburg radio station, Doenitz told the German people on the same day that the Fuehrer had " fallen " in the Battle for Berlin and that he (Doenitz) was taking over (*see* Historic Document 297, page 3640).

From the beginning the " Doenitz Government " was no more than a liquidating commission. Yet it was not this " Government " which finally signed Germany's unconditional surrender. After the Germans had, at the end of the war of 1914–18, invented the legend of the stab in the back of the army, and had coined the slogan " undefeated on the battlefield," the Allies had good reason this time to make the German military leaders sign the surrender, thus unmistakably acknowledging Germany's military defeat.

The German armies in Italy surrendered unconditionally to Field-Marshal Alexander's armies at Caserta on April 29 (*see* Chapter 361). On May 2, at 3 p.m., exactly 48 hours after Hitler's death, the Reich capital surrendered to the Russians. On May 4 all German forces in Holland, North-West Germany and Denmark surrendered to the British (*see* Chapter 357). On the same day the remnants

of the German 9th and 12th armies surrendered to the U.S. 102nd Infantry Division (U.S. 9th Army). On the 6th, Army Group " G," comprising all German forces in Austria, surrendered to the Allied 6th Army Group. Finally, on May 7, Colonel-General Gustav Jodl, in the name of the High Command of the Wehrmacht, signed the unconditional surrender of all German fighting forces at Rheims, and this surrender was confirmed in Berlin next day, when Field-Marshal Keitel (Chief of the Army High Command), General-Admiral Hans Georg von Friedeburg (C.-in-C. Navy) and Colonel-General Stumpf of the Luftwaffe signed on behalf of the German High Command, Marshal Zhukov and Air Chief Marshal Tedder signing for the Allies. Lieutenant-General Carl Spaatz and General de Lattre de Tassigny signed as witnesses. (For text of the instrument of surrender, and broadcasts by German leaders immediately before and after it, *see* Historic Documents 296–300, pages 3,640–41.)

The great slaughter was over, as far as Europe was concerned.

THE CHANGING MAP

German children study a map put up outside an American billet in an occupied area of western Germany, and showing from day to day the increasing encroachment of the Allied forces on the Reich from both west and east.

Photo, U.S. Official

SURRENDER CEREMONY IN THE REICH CAPITAL

Germany's surrender was ratified at 00.16 hours on May 8, 1945, in the Berlin suburb of Karlshorst in a building which had formerly housed the Engineering College of the Wehrmacht. Because of the heavy damage suffered by the German capital, no more suitable building could be found. The German signatories were Field-Marshal Keitel, General-Admiral von Friedeburg, and Colonel-General Stumpf (see illus. in page 3651). For the Allies, Marshal Zhukov signed for the Soviet High Command, Air-Marshal Sir Arthur Tedder for the Allied Expeditionary Force. 1. Marshal Zhukov reads the surrender terms. On his right is Air-Marshal Tedder and on his left General Spaatz. 2. Marshal Zhukov addresses the gathering after the Germans had withdrawn. 3. Allied leaders outside the Engineering College.

THE LAST ACT OF SURRENDER IN THE WEST

Historic Document CCXCVI is the most important of all the documents relating to the war published in this history : it is the terms of the final act of unconditional surrender in Berlin of all Germany's armed forces to representatives of the Allied Expeditionary Force and the Soviet High Command.   Documents CCXCVII to CCC1 are the texts of announcements made by the German leaders who succeeded Hitler to their people immediately before and after this act

Terms of the Final Act of Unconditional Surrender of Germany's Armed Forces signed in Berlin at 00.16 hours on May 8, 1945 :

1. We the undersigned, acting by authority of the German High Command, hereby surrender unconditionally to the Supreme Commander, Allied Expeditionary Force, and simultaneously to the Supreme High Command of the Red Army, all forces on land, at sea, and in the air who are at this date under German control.

2. The German High Command will at once issue orders to all German military, naval, and air authorities and to all forces under German control to cease active operations at 23.01 hours, Central European Time, on May 8, 1945, to remain in the positions occupied at that time and to disarm completely, handing over their weapons and equipment to the local allied commanders or officers designated by representatives of the Allied Supreme Commands. No ship, vessel, or aircraft is to be scuttled, or any damage done to their hulls, machinery, or equipment, nor to machines of all kinds, armament, apparatus, and all the technical means of prosecution of war in general.

3. The German High Command will at once issue to the appropriate commanders, and ensure the carrying out of, any further orders issued by the Supreme Commander, Allied Expeditionary Force, and by the Supreme High Command of the Red Army.

4. This act of military surrender is without prejudice to, and will be superseded by, any general instrument of surrender imposed by or on behalf of the United Nations and applicable to Germany and the German armed forces as a whole.

5. In the event of the German High Command or any of the forces under their control failing to act in accordance with this act of surrender, the Supreme Commander, Allied Expeditionary Force, and the Supreme High Command of the Red Army will take such punitive or other action as they deem appropriate.

6. This act is drawn up in the English, Russian, and German languages. The English and Russian are the authentic texts.

Grand-Admiral Karl Doenitz, C.-in-C. of the German Navy, announced his succession to Hitler on May 1, 1945, in the following broadcast :

GERMAN men and women soldiers of the German Wehrmacht. Our Fuehrer, Adolf Hitler, has fallen. The German people bow in deepest mourning and veneration.

He recognized beforehand the terrible danger of Bolshevism and devoted his life to fighting it. At the end of this, his battle, and his unswerving straight path of life, stands his death as a hero in the capital of the Reich. All his life meant service to the German people. His battle against the Bolshevist flood benefited not only Europe but the whole world.

The Fuehrer has appointed me as his successor. Fully conscious of the responsibility, I take over the leadership of the German people at this fateful hour. It is my first task to save the German people from destruction by the Bolshevists and it is only to achieve this that the fight continues.

As long as the British and Americans hamper us from reaching this end we shall fight and defend ourselves against them as well. The British and Americans do not fight for the interests of their own people, but for the spreading of Bolshevism.

What the German people have achieved and suffered is unique in history. In the coming times of distress of our people I shall do my utmost to make life bearable for our brave women, men, and children.

To achieve all this I need your help. Trust me ; keep order and discipline in towns and the countryside. Everybody do his duty. Only thus shall we be able to alleviate the sufferings which the future will bring to each of us and avoid collapse. If we do all that is in our power to do, the Lord will not abandon us.

The following order of the day was issued on May 1 to the Wehrmacht by Admiral Doenitz as its new Supreme Commander :

THE FUEHRER has fallen. He fell faithful to his great ideal to save the peoples of Europe from Bolshevism. He staked his life, and died the death of a hero. With his passing one of the greatest heroes of German history has passed away. In proud reverence and sorrow we lower our flag before him.

The Fuehrer has appointed me his successor as Head of the State and Supreme Commander of the Wehrmacht. I assume supreme command of the Wehrmacht with the determination to continue the struggle against Bolshevism until the fighting troops and the hundreds of thousands of families of the German eastern territories are rescued from enslavement or extermination. Against the British and Americans I shall continue the struggle so far and so long as they hinder me in carrying out the fight against Bolshevism. The situation demands from you, who have already accomplished such great historical feats and who are now longing for the end of the war, further struggle without question. I demand discipline and obedience. Chaos and downfall can be prevented only by obedience without reserve to my orders. He who at this moment shirks his duty is a coward and traitor, for he brings death or slavery to German women and children.

The oath of allegiance you swore to the Fuehrer now applies to each one of you without further formality to myself. German soldiers : Do your duty. The life of our people is at stake.

Professor Albert Speer, Minister of Armaments and War Production, on May 3 ordered the German people to work for reconstruction in a broadcast as follows :

NEVER before has a cultured people been smitten as grievously as the German people now. Never before has any land been so laid waste by the fury of the war as has Germany. You are all disheartened now and incensed. Instead of faith, desperation has entered your hearts ; you have become tired and cynical. This must not be. The bearing of the German nation in this war has been such that, in times to come, future generations will look upon it with admiration. Let us not stop to cry out our eyes about the past. To work !

The havoc wrought by this war has only one parallel in history—the Thirty Years' War. Yet the decimation of the people by starvation and plagues must not be allowed to reach the proportions of that period. That, and that alone, is the reason why Admiral Doenitz has resolved not to lay down arms. This is the only meaning of the continuance of the struggle to prevent the death of fleeing German men. It is our last duty, and the German people have to shoulder it.

It rests with our enemies to decide whether they wish to grant to the German people the possibilities that lie open to a nation which is defeated but which has shown its heroic spirit in battle, and imprinted its reputation on the pages of history as a generous and decent opponent. Yet each one of us must contribute his share, and in the months to come devote our strength to the work of reconstruction. You must overcome your lethargy, your paralysing despair. I therefore issue this order to you for the immediate future :

1. The most urgent work is the repair of the damage done to the German railway system. As far as the enemy allows it, or where he orders it, the reconstruction work has to be speeded up with every means, to make possible the transportation of food stuffs to areas where starvation stares the people in the face. Remember that the only possibility of rejoining your families lies in the rehabilitation of the German railways.

2. Both industrial factories and workshops of artisans are under an obligation to carry out as quickly as possible any order concerning the repairs of the railway system.

3. The German farmers who in six years of war have obeyed their instructions, fully realizing their responsibility towards the entire German nation, have now to raise their deliveries to the peak.

4. Foodstuffs must have priority in transportation over all other goods. Food, electric current, and gas, as well as coal and wood-producing enterprises, must be supplied before any others. If we work with the same tenacity as we have done during the past years, the German nation can be kept alive without further serious losses. Whether our enemies will allow this we cannot yet foretell. It is, however, my duty to use all my strength to keep the German nation alive.

The direction of our fate no longer lies in our hands. Only divine providence can alter our future. We ourselves can, however, contribute to it by doing our work with determination and industry, by meeting our enemies with dignity and self-confidence, by becoming more modest at heart, and by keeping an unwavering belief in the future of our people which, for ever, will remain our most important concern. May God protect Germany !

Count Lutz Schwerin von Krosigk, Foreign Minister in Doenitz's short-lived government, broadcast to the German people on May 7 news of Germany's unconditional surrender as follows :

GERMAN men and women, the High Command of the Wehrmacht has today, at the order of Grand Admiral Doenitz, declared the unconditional surrender of all fighting German troops. As the leading minister of the Reich Government which the Grand Admiral has appointed for dealing with the war tasks, I turn at this tragic moment of our history to the German nation. After a heroic fight of almost six years of incomparable hardness, Germany has succumbed to the overwhelming power of her enemies. . . .

A government which has a feeling of responsibility for the future of its nation was compelled to act on the collapse of all physical and material forces and to demand of the enemy the cessation of hostilities. It was the noblest task of the Grand Admiral and of the government supporting him, after the terrible sacrifices which the war demanded, to save in the last phase of the war the lives of a maximum number of fellow-countrymen. That the war was not ended immediately, simultaneously in the west and in the east, is to be explained by this reason alone. In this gravest hour of the German nation and its empire, we bow in deep reverence before the dead of this war. Their sacrifices place the highest obligations on us. Our sympathy goes out above all to the wounded, the bereaved, and to all on whom this struggle has inflicted blows.

No one must be under any illusions about the severity of the terms to be imposed on the German people by our enemies. We must now face our fate squarely and unquestioningly. Nobody can be in any doubt that the future will be difficult for each one of us, and will exact sacrifices from us in every sphere of life. We must accept this burden, and stand loyally by the obligations we have undertaken. But we must not despair and fall into mute resignation. Once again we must set ourselves to stride along a path through the dark future. From the collapse of the past,

let us preserve and save one thing, the unity of ideas of a national community which in the years of war has found its highest expression. in the spirit of comradeship at the front and readiness to help one another in all the distress which has afflicted the homeland.

In our nation justice shall be the supreme law and the guiding principle. We must also recognize law as the basis of all relations between the nations. We must recognize it and respect it from inner conviction. Respect for treaties will be as sacred as the aim of our nation to belong to the European family of nations, as a member of which we want to mobilize all human, moral and material forces in order to heal the dreadful wounds which the war has caused.

Then we may hope that the atmosphere of hatred which today surrounds Germany all over the world will give place to a spirit of reconciliation among the nations without which the world cannot recover. Then we may hope that our freedom will be restored to us, without which no nation can lead a bearable and dignified existence.

We wish to devote the future of our nation to the return of the innermost and best forces of German nature, which have given to the world imperishable works and values. We view with pride the heroic struggle of our people and we shall combine with our pride in that struggle the will to contribute as a member of western culture, honest, peaceful labour—a contribution which expresses the best traditions of our nation.

May God not forsake us in our distress, and bless us in our heavy task.

Grand Admiral Doenitz told the German people on May 8 of the cessation of hostilities in the following broadcast :—

GERMAN men and women, when I addressed you on May 1 to announce the death of the Fuehrer and my appointment as his successor, I told you that my first task would be to spare the lives of German men and women. In conformity therewith I ordered the High Command of the Wehrmacht on the night of May 6 to arrange for the unconditional surrender of all German fighting troops in all theatres of war. From 23 hours Central European Time on May 8 the guns will be silent. German soldiers, veterans of countless battles, are now treading the bitter path to captivity and are thereby making the last sacrifice for the life of our women and children and the future of our nation. We bow in respect to their gallantry, which they have proved a thousand times. We remember the fallen and the prisoners.

I have promised our brave men, women, and children to provide them with endurable living conditions so far as it is in my power to do so in the coming difficult time. I do not know yet what I shall be able to do to help you in these hard times. We have to face facts. The foundation on which the German Reich was built is a thing of the past. The unity of state and party no longer exists. The party has disappeared from the scene of its former activity. With the occupation of Germany power has passed into the hands of the occupation forces. It depends on them whether I and the Reich government formed by me will be able to continue in office or not. If I can be of assistance to the Fatherland by continuing in office, I shall do so until the German people have a chance to express their will by appointing a head of State or until the occupation powers make it impossible for me to continue in office. . . .

There is a difficult role ahead for every one of us. We must tread it with the dignity, gallantry, and discipline which the memory of our dead demands of us. We must be inspired by the will to do our best in work and achievement, without which there can be no basis for a future life. We want to march along this road in unity and justice, without which we cannot survive the hardships of the times to come. We may tread the road in the hope that the time will come when our children will live a free and secure life in a Europe at peace. I do not want to lag behind you on this thorny path. If my duty calls me to remain in office, I shall try to help you all I can. If, however, duty requires me to depart, this step will be taken in service to the people and the Reich.

Chapter 356

ATLANTIC AND MEDITERRANEAN AIR FEATS

The use of radar in combating U-boats, the work of aircraft carriers in defence of Atlantic and Northern convoys, and of the Mediterranean Allied Air Forces in Italy and Central Europe, the record of the Royal Air Force in minelaying—these are among the subjects covered in this chapter, written by Captain Norman Macmillan, M.C., A.F.C.

B Y 1945 radar, which was in its infancy when the war began, affected all air operations. During its rapid development from 1939 onwards, probably the greatest technical achievements were the design and production of the magnetron valve, which enabled radar emissions to be reduced from a wavelength measuring several metres to one measured in centimetres. The extremely short wavelength of centimetric radar required much smaller aerials and antennae, two important features in airborne sets. And centimetric emissions could be projected as beams, giving greater accuracy and range.

The U-boat threat to Britain was so serious that Coastal Command was given priority in radar at the beginning of the war, and in September 1939 a Coastal Command aircraft was the first to carry airborne radar. By the end of 1939 Air to Surface Vessel (A.S.V.—pronounced Asvic) Mark I became operational. But it was a broadcast diffusion, and its range was short— about 40 miles ; it was not really efficient, and technical difficulties were numerous.

The Navy's main base was then at Scapa Flow, and a Hudson reconnaissance squadron of the R.A.F., operating off the north-east coast, was the first squadron to be fitted with radar. Sunderland flying boats engaged on anti-submarine work were next, and the Fleet Air Arm attack on the Italian fleet in Taranto harbour (*see page 1315*) followed a triangular A.S.V. search in darkness by a Sunderland of No. 228 Squadron, R.A.F. During the evacuations of Greece and Crete in 1941 A.S.V. radar gave good landfalls against the mountains of the islands and mainland, aiding the night flying of the Sunderlands engaged in evacuation work.

Mark II A.S.V. was fitted to two Whitley squadrons and one Wellington squadron of Coastal Command, and by mid-1941 it was proved that it could be used to find and attack U-boats. A Wellington on a transit flight from Northern Ireland to Iceland in September 1941 claimed to have made the first radar aided attack against a U-boat ; it carried a radar officer, who picked up a U-boat when testing the apparatus. By mid-1942 Catalinas,

Liberators, Fortresses, and Beauforts were also fitted with radar, and the Leigh light (*see illus.* in page 3032) came into use. U-boat commanders could not then use darkness to cover their surfacing to recharge their batteries, for detection by radar and illumination by the Leigh light (and sometimes moonlight only) caused them losses which alarmed the German Admiralty.

In May 1942 an experimental Liberator was fitted with centimetric radar. Piloted by Wing-Commander P. J. Cundy, D.S.O., D.F.C., A.F.C., and flying from Langley Field, Virginia, it picked up a U-boat " blip " on its radar screen many miles away, homed on to the submarine and sank it. The listening receiver which had enabled the U-boat commander to detect the approach of Mark II radar and so allow the submarine to submerge before the aircraft arrived was unable to detect centimetric radar emissions, and the U-boat crews, unaware that British scientists had beaten those of Germany, were bewildered and their morale undermined.

Radar and the U-boats

The 230-lb. depth charges filled with Torpex explosive had to fall within a very limited " hemisphere " about the U-boat to " kill " it. So, if the submarine received any appreciable opportunity to crash dive, the attack was probably innocuous ; hence the importance of this new undetectable radar.

No. 210 Squadron, R.A.F., based at Sollum Voe in the Shetland Islands, was among the first units to be fitted with centimetric radar, primarily to protect Russia-bound convoys. Flying-Officer J. A. Cruikshank, of this squadron, won the V.C. on July 17, 1944, when making the squadron's first successful attack on a U-boat by this means (*see illus.* in page 3188).

To meet these new conditions, U-boats mounted more A.A. guns, and their commanders were ordered to stay on the surface and fight the attacking aircraft. This suited Coastal Command admirably. Sometimes the aircraft pilots closed in and sank the U-boats from a low height despite their vicious anti-aircraft gunfire. At other times

UNDETECTABLE RADAR DEFEATED THE U-BOAT

During his trial for war crimes at Nuremberg in May 1946, Admiral Karl Doenitz, who commanded the U-boat service until he became C.-in-C. of the German Navy in 1943, described the Allied use of radar as ' decisive ' in the battle against the U-boat. ' It forced us into giving up war on the surface,' he declared. Here, early in the war, is a Wellington bomber of R.A.F. Coastal Command with radar devices on the fuselage and beneath the port wing. *Photo, British Official*

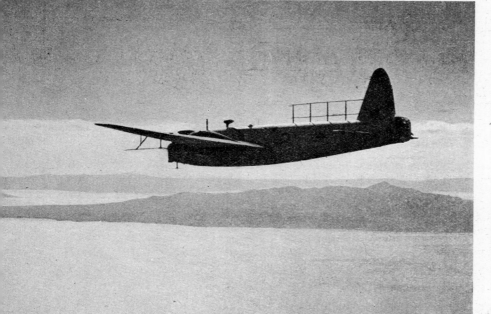

RADAR'S PART IN AIR SUPREMACY

1. Massive aerial system of a 'ground-controlled interception' radar station in England. The transmitter and receiver were underground. These G.C.I. stations directed R.A.F. fighters until they were sufficiently close to the enemy aircraft for their own airborne radar interception equipment to become effective. 2. An airwoman plots aircraft on the cathode-ray tube (see also page 3546). 3. Interior of a 'Chain Home' receiver room, with console (right) and receiver (left). Among the first types of station used in the defence of Britain, they detected low-flying aircraft. 4. Aerial equipment of a 'Chain Home' coastal station. The arrays were mounted on a steel tower 185 ft. high.

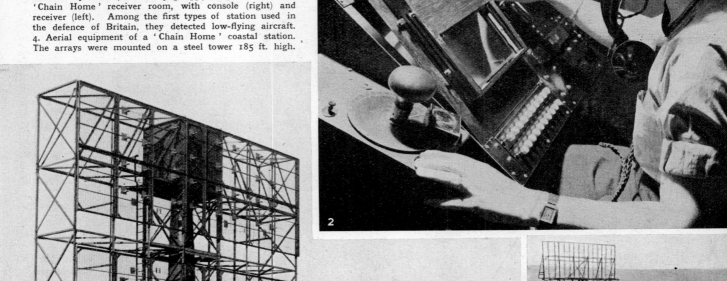

COASTAL COMMAND 'LIT UP' THE NORTH SEA

Shipfinder Force of R.A.F. Coastal Command in 1944-45 made night hazardous for German convoys in the North Sea. Dropping flares of immense candle-power, radar-equipped Shipfinder Wellingtons silhouetted targets for attacking forces flying in their wake. Here a ground crew loads up a Wellington with drop-flares. A Coastal Command Mosquito touches down in Scotland after attacking enemy shipping in Norwegian waters (top). *Photos, Planet News*

A Lancaster carrying centimetric radar crashed at Rotterdam early in 1943. The German Army salvaged the set, but took a year to pass their information—and the secret of the undetectable attack—to the German Navy. Thus it was not until nearly the end of the war that the German Navy, to counteract centimetric radar, introduced the Schnorkel. (*See* page 3035.) It has been facetiously said that Germany loses her wars because her red tape methods are worse than the British. Here (and fortunately for the Allies), owing to German red tape, this invention came too late in the war seriously to menace Allied seaborne supplies. (For fuller details of the last phases of the U-boat war, *see* Chapters 342 and 353.)

In addition to the air patrols of the R.A.F. Coastal Command, the Royal Canadian Air Force, and the United States Air Forces engaged on anti-submarine duties above the Atlantic, No. 836 Squadron of the Fleet Air Arm performed unique **No. 836 Squadron** work. It had 60 aircraft and was entitled to 80 aircrews, and was the biggest squadron in the Naval Air Branch. It provided the aircraft that manned the Merchant Aircraft Carriers (*see* illus. in page 3043), and flew on and off the ships from its base at May Down, near Londonderry. The aircraft were all Swordfish, and they carried depth charges and/or rocket projectiles for action against submarines. These were the aircraft that closed the Atlantic gap; but they did more: they maintained patrol over the convoys they sailed with throughout the ocean crossing, and when the U-boat situation again became serious near the end of the war, right up to the Liverpool Bar Light.

The first M.A.C. ships were grain carrying vessels; later oil tankers and other vessels were used. The first M.A.C. began operating in June 1943, and they continued to be used until the convoy system ended, although their use declined after the Allied acquisition of bases in the Azores (*see* page 2656). The number of M.A.C. ships to a convoy varied from one to four. Grain ships carried four aircraft, the tankers three and some types could carry six. Grain ships had a hangar and a lift to the flight deck, the tankers carried their aircraft on the flying deck, screened by manually removable wind brakes. M.A.C. ships also ferried aircraft across the Atlantic.

M.A.C. ships were manned by Merchant Navy officers and crews, and wore the Red Ensign. The first aircraft to arrive on a M.A.C. ship had the words

the aircraft circled just out of the U-boat's gunnery range and kept watch. The instant the U-boat began to submerge, the aircraft closed in and depth-charged it. If, by submerging, or in the night, a submarine got away, its known maximum speed could be plotted, so that it was certain that it must be somewhere within a prescribed circular area during the succeeding twenty-four hours; aircraft could then be detailed to patrol this whole area so that the U-boat could be picked up again when it surfaced. Thus a U-boat, once sighted, seldom escaped, and U-boats began to get the worst of the terror war at sea. Sometimes if surface warships were near enough to the place of action the circling aircraft called them by wireless to aid in the destruction of the submarine by means of their superior gunfire.

Royal Navy painted out and the words Merchant Navy painted in. But this practice was soon given up, for the use of aircraft in these ships was in principle no different from the mounting of guns in the defensively armed merchant ships which carried naval ratings as gun crews. The Mark III Swordfish carried A.S.V. radar, like that of the Coastal Command aircraft, for anti-submarine search, and were flown by Fleet Air Arm personnel, mostly of the R.N.V.R. branch. These were happy ships, and they played an important part in the safety of the convoys crossing the Atlantic.

British and American heavy bombers continued in 1945 to counter at source the German submarine campaign (*see* Chapters 342 and 346). The laying of sea mines against surface ships and U-boats by aircraft continued to the end of the war in Europe. Bomber

Command laid 47,250 mines, aggregating 33,263 tons, in enemy waters extending from Bordeaux to the Baltic; these sunk over 550 ships and damaged over 480 others, and kept forty per cent of German naval personnel on minesweeping duties. In the Mediterranean and Middle East theatres of war, the Coastal Air Force (*see* page 3650) laid 1,734 tons of mines.

The escort-carriers H.M.S. " Nairana " and H.M.S. " Campania " accompanying the convoys that sailed to Russia had successful air engagements in 1945. On January 30, escorted by ships of the Home Fleet, they attacked shipping a n d installations on the Norwegian coast north of Stadtlandet, d a m a g i n g three supply ships. On February 16, t h e A d m i r a l t y

announced that the escort of a Russia-bound convoy, which included these two carriers, had sunk at least two U-boats and shot down three German aircraft. Next month another convoy for Archangel, similarly escorted, was persistently attacked despite vile weather. At least one U-boat was sunk; ten enemy torpedo-bombers were shot down and many others damaged. No merchant ships were lost on this outward passage, but six per cent were sunk on the return. On the night of May 4 ships of the Home Fleet with the escort-carriers "Searcher," "Queen" and "Trumpeter"

'LILY', THE FLOATING AIRSTRIP

Among revolutionary British inventions during the war were the floating airstrip and the floating pier, disclosed in September 1945. Both were invented by Mr. R. M. Hamilton, who had served as a Petty Officer in the Royal Naval Patrol Service. Known as ' Lily,' because like the leaves of the water-lily it rested on the surface, the floating airstrip consisted of buoyancy cans with hexagonal surfaces, so linked that they ' gave ' to the motion of the sea, yet remained sufficiently rigid to take the weight of an aircraft. The ' Swiss Roll ' flexible canvas-and-wood jetty, which could support a heavily laden lorry, was successfully used at Arromanches (see Chapter 311). 1. Section of ' Swiss Roll ' being laid. 2. A Swordfish touches down on ' Lily.' 3. Experimenting with ' Lily ' at Lamlash, Scotland.

attacked enemy shipping near Narvik. One U-boat depot ship and a tanker were sunk, and a U-boat probably sunk; two A.A. vessels were damaged for the loss of two aeroplanes.

Radar was used by Coastal Command aircraft to attack surface as well as submarine ships. From Stornoway,

Attacks on Enemy Coastal Shipping Lewis, the aircrews of Nos. 58 and 502 squadrons flew their Halifax bombers to the Skager Rak and Kattegat, where, after locating the German convoys by radar, they lighted up the ships with powerful flares. They released their bombs from between 3,500 and 4,000 feet, and when the war ended thousands of tons of enemy shipping had been either sunk or seriously damaged. During January 1945 enemy shipping was attacked six times—in Lyse Fjord on January 8, off the Norwegian coast on January 9, in Leirvik harbour on January 15, and Edj Fjord on January 26; on the 17th and

HOOKING A WALRUS

Important feature of training in the Fleet Air Arm was that of catapulting aircraft from warships and recovering them from the water. In the ' Towed Net ' method of recovery the aircraft taxied on to a towed net, hooked on to it and was hoisted inboard when under the ship's hook. Here, a Walrus aircraft is being hoisted on board after casting off the net.

Photo, British Official

24th targets were found off the Dutch and German North Sea coasts. In February there were three attacks, on the 9th in Forde Fjord, and on the 4th and 24th in the Baltic.

In March eight attacks were made, three off the Norwegian coast (20th, 24th and 30th); two in the Kattegat

(7th and 27th); two in the Skager Rak (25th and 27th) and one at Aalesund (17th). In April the volume of enemy traffic between Norway and Germany increased (some ships carrying reinforcements from Norway to Germany, others taking refugees from north German ports), and Coastal Command made thirteen shipping attacks that month—five in the Skager Rak (4th, 9th, 10th, 19th and 25th); four in the Kattegat (2nd, 4th, 10th and 19th); and one each on the 2nd, 11th, and 14th respectively in Sande Fjord, Norwegian coastal waters, Josing Fjord, and on the 25th a sweep between the Hook of Holland and the Heligoland Bight. The planning of these attacks, which

SWORDFISH'S LAST FLIGHT

The Fairey Swordfish was the only British aircraft to remain fully operational in its original form throughout the war. Carrier-borne, it crippled over a million tons of enemy shipping. Last official flight of a Swordfish was made on October 15, 1945, from H.M.S. ' Ocean.' Below, the final take-off. Left, Vice-Admiral Sir Denis Boyd, Admiral (Air), and Rear-Admiral M. S. Slattery, Vice-Controller (Air), Chief of Naval Air Equipment, who made the last flight.

Photos, British Official

LAST OPERATION AGAINST THE GERMAN NAVY

To the end of the war, the Germans persisted, from bases in Norway, in their violent attacks on Allied northern convoys to Russia. Last offensive operation undertaken by the Royal Navy against the German Navy was a heavy attack on May 4, 1945, on enemy shipping, including a tanker and a 5,000-ton U-boat depot-ship, near Narvik. During the attack Fleet Air Arm bombs blew up both vessels. Below, ratings sweep snow from the deck of the carrier H.M.S. 'Fencer,' bound on Northern convoy, to keep it serviceable for the operation of aircraft.

were successful in sinking or disabling a large number of enemy vessels, required the constant vigilance of reconnaissance aircraft over the narrowing coastal belt still in enemy hands. The ships attacked included destroyers, escort vessels, U-boats, minesweepers, and merchant ships.

In the last days of the fighting there was a great exodus from north German ports to Norway. From April 29 to May 3 inclusive, aircraft of the R.A.F. 2nd T.A.F. put out of action 150 ships, including many U-boats trying to escape, and in the 48 hours before the German unconditional surrender to Field-Marshal Montgomery, Coastal Command aircraft, engaged almost non-stop against them, put out of action nearly 50 vessels, including two destroyers and a number of armed auxiliaries. During attacks just before fighting ended, a new success was scored by the sinking of two U-boats by rocket and cannon fire.

After the surrender the work of Coastal Command continued without pause, shepherding enemy vessels to port, on the watch for submarines that might not have heard their orders, and escorting Allied convoys, with everything at the ready, but without the explosion of depth charges or the rattle of gunfire. Anti-submarine

LAST DAYS IN ITALY

In April 1945, as the German front in north Italy crumbled, Allied air attacks on enemy communications—especially on the vital railway system—were stepped up. Here is the marshalling-yard at the Italian railway keypoint of Parma after it had been heavily bombed by P-47 Thunderbolts of the U.S.A. 12th A.F.   *Photo, U.S. Official*

GERMANS QUIT GREECE

Fearing the cutting of their escape routes into Central Europe, the Germans still occupying Greece began a mass evacuation in September 1944. In this their movements were accelerated by the M.A.A.F. and by big guns of the Royal Navy. Below, enemy A.A. gunners on the Greek coast run to their positions as Allied aircraft approach—a photograph seized among Dr. Goebbels's private collection.

COMMANDING M.A.A.F.

Lieutenant-General John K. Cannon was appointed in the spring of 1945 to succeed Lieutenant-General Ira C. Eaker as C.-in-C. of the Mediterranean Allied Air Forces. This comprised the Mediterranean Strategic Air Force, Tactical Air Force, Coastal Air Force and the Balkan Air Force. As Major-General, he had been appointed Commanding General of the U.S.A. 12th A.F., Mediterranean, in January 1944.

Photo, British Official

patrols and protection to convoys continued until June 4, when the Command completed its last patrol of the European war with the arrival in North Ireland of the last homeward bound convoy.

During the war, Coastal Command dropped 4,778 tons of bombs and depth charges and laid 602 tons of mines.

EX-PRISONERS RETURN BY AIR

In the House of Commons on May 29, 1945, Mr. Churchill stated that to date 156,000 British Commonwealth prisoners of war had been repatriated (over 140,000 by air), with another 10,000 awaiting repatriation in the British and U.S. zones, 8,500 in that part of Austria held by the Red Army, and 400 at Odessa. Here a group of returned P.O.W. leave the Lancaster of R.A.F. Transport Command that ferried them to England from Germany. Besides Lancasters, Dakotas and Fortresses were regularly used for this service.

Photo, Barratt's

Its unceasing vigilance had cost 1,479 aircraft; it had destroyed 175 enemy aircraft. The value of its work, however, was not to be measured by these figures, but by the millions of tons of supplies and millions of men transported safely across the seas through the vigilance of the air force and the navy despite the attacks of a powerful and unscrupulous enemy.

In the summer of 1944, after the ground forces in Italy had been depleted in preparation for the landings on the Riviera (*see* page 3456), Field-Marshal Alexander gave permission for the bridges across the river Po to be cut in order to increase the enemy's difficulties of communication. Previously he had not allowed the air force to destroy these bridges, for he had hoped to capture them intact by the use of airborne troops. There were 23 rail and road bridges (including a few pontoon bridges) over the Po and its tributary the Trebbia. Tactical aircraft began the attack on July 12, 1944, and seventy-two hours later every bridge was out of action. One or more spans were knocked out of all permanent bridges, and pontoons from all floating bridges lay stranded on the river banks for miles downstream. The enemy was forced to rely on small emergency bridges, which he used mostly at night, dismounting them and hiding them by day to conserve them from fighter-bombers for further nocturnal use. During the winter of 1944–45 Allied tactical aircraft in Italy were often weather bound, but as frequently as possible they pounded the enemy communications and supply dumps.

Allied air forces in Italy continued to attack the enemy in the Balkans, concentrating on shipping, motor transport, bridges, airfields, and radar stations in continuation of the general policy to assist Marshal Tito's forces, contain German divisions there which the enemy badly needed elsewhere, and prevent the Luftwaffe from operating with any success from Balkan territory against the Allies in Italy, the Yugoslav partisans, or the Red Army. These duties were undertaken by the Balkan Air Force—a component of the Mediterranean Allied Air Forces—established in June 1944, with British, Yugoslav, Italian, Greek, and Polish personnel.

The spring offensive in Italy began on April 9, 1945, across the Senio river west of Ravenna, after heavy bomber and artillery preparation. The German armies south of the Po were unable to retreat **Air Aid for Last Italian Offensive** owing to the murderous air assault upon their communications, and were virtually destroyed there. The complete collapse of resistance in Italy quickly followed, creating a military triumph, never before achieved, of conquest of the peninsula from the south.

The air force which contributed to the defeat of the German armies in Italy was called the Mediterranean Allied Air Forces. It was created in December 1943 soon after the airfields

GERMAN WARSHIPS ESCORTED BY THE R.A.F.

After Germany's unconditional surrender in May 1945, the famous German cruiser 'Nürnberg' (seen above) sailed with the 'Prinz Eugen' from Copenhagen, where they had been berthed, to Wilhelmshaven. They were under a British escort, which included Liberators of R.A.F. Coastal Command. The two ships were among units of the German Navy, including four destroyers and some 130 warships of various types, taken over by the Royal Navy at Copenhagen.

at Foggia came into Allied use. M.A.A.F. contained more than 250,000 officers and other ranks, who wore the uniforms of many nations. Australia, Brazil, Britain, Canada, France, Greece, Poland, South Africa, the United States, and Yugoslavia were all represented in this force, which at its peak, reached between August and September 1944, contained 173,845 U.S.A.A.F. and 68,896 R.A.F. personnel.

It was divided into four operational entities: the Strategic Air Force, the Tactical Air Force, the Coastal Air Force, and the Balkan Air Force. The complete force was commanded by Lieutenant-General Ira C. Eaker until the spring of 1945 when Lieutenant-General John K. Cannon succeeded him. The first deputy commander was Air Marshal Sir John Slessor, from whom Air Marshal Sir Guy Garrod took over in March 1945.

The strategic air force could dispatch 850 escorted heavy bombers against German war production, and attacked

Air Targets in Twelve Countries targets in twelve different countries. It averaged a weekly bomb load of almost 4,000 tons. It cut one-third of Germany's oil supplies by destroying the Rumanian oilfield production. It brought back a thousand missing airmen from Bucharest after that city's liberation by the Red Army.

The tactical air force made a major contribution to the success of the Allied army's advance up the peninsula from Naples into Tuscany by cutting the German supply system through continual attacks on the three vulnerable railway tracks in a plan called "Operation Strangle."

The complete force dropped over 650,000 tons of bombs on enemy

targets, and destroyed more than 8,700 enemy aircraft. More than 9,000 Allied aircraft were lost, and the killed, wounded, missing and prisoners of war totalled about 40,000. Field-Marshal Alexander announced on July 31, 1945, that M.A.A.F. would end that night. Thereafter the American and British air forces in Italy separated from their unified command, into distinctive organizations for the armies of occupation.

The main preoccupation of home defence in Britain during 1945 centred in the organization to meet the V-weapon attack. (See Chapter 337.) Radar watch was maintained along all the coasts of Britain, for there was always the possibility that a last desperate attempt to bomb Britain might be made by the Luftwaffe in a final act of spite.

But only four comparatively small piloted attacks were made against Britain in 1945. All came in March. On the night of the 2nd–3rd scattered attacks were made, in which bombs were dropped and machine-guns and cannon-guns were used indiscriminately against towns, villages and railways in the midlands and north; six of the attacking aircraft were shot down. Next night a number of enemy-piloted aircraft again attacked England. On the 16th–17th piloted aircraft came in across the coast of north England and dropped fragmentation bombs which caused casualties and damage; and three nights later, when a small number of aircraft raided southern England, one was shot down. The Luftwaffe had shot its last missile against Britain. And to do so it had to use a wide variety of aircraft to make up its small forces, including Junkers 188, Messerschmitt 410, Dornier 217, and Focke Wulf 190, a sure sign of the decline and fall of the German air force.

MAJOR TARGETS IN 1945 OF THE STRATEGIC AIR FORCE BASED IN ITALY	
January	**March—***continued*
8 Targets at Linz (Austria).	22 Oil plants at Ruhland (near Dresden), near Prague, near Vienna, and railways in Austria.
15 Objectives in the Vienna area.	
20 Railyards at Linz and Salzburg; oil storage at Regensburg.	24 Berlin (first attack by M.A.A.F.) and airfields near Munich.
31 Oil plants at Moosbierbaum (N.W. of Vienna) and railyards at Graz and Maribor.	31 Railways in Austria leading to Italy; Graz, in support of Marshal Tolbukhin.
February	**April**
13 Rail centres and communications at Vienna, Graz, and Maribor.	1 Targets in Austria and Yugoslavia, in support of the Red Army.
16 Obertraubling aerodrome at Regensburg (jet-propelled Me. 262 base).	2 Targets in Austria in direct co-operation with the Red Army.
20 Berchtesgaden (attacked for the first time in the War) and neighbouring railways.	9 Forward positions of the German Army opposite the 8th Army: to prevent bombs falling on Allied troops, huge white arrows were dotted all over the 8th Army area pointing northwards, lines of white, amber, and red smoke covered an area up to five miles behind the Allied front, and low altitude A.A. fire was maintained along the front line.
27 Augsburg railways.	
March	
1 Moosbierbaum oil refinery.	
4 Rail targets in Hungary, Austria, and Yugoslavia.	
9 Graz (Austria).	
12 Oil installations in the Vienna area.	
13 Objectives at Regensburg.	
14 Oil and railway objectives in Hungary (jointly with the Red Air Force).	21 Rosenheim and Puchheim on the Munich-Salzburg-Linz railway.
21 Jet plane base at Neuberg and oil refineries in Vienna area.	25 Concentration of rolling stock at Linz.

GERMAN SERVICES CHIEFS SIGN THE SURRENDER

On the outskirts of Berlin on May 8, 1945 (see also page 3639), the heads of the German fighting forces ratified the unconditional surrender terms. Above, left to right, Colonel-General P. F. Stumpf, appointed C.-in-C., the Luftwaffe Reich, after the attempt on Hitler's life in July 1944 ; Field-Marshal Wilhelm Keitel, Chief of the Supreme Command of the Wehrmacht ; and Admiral Hans Georg von Friedeburg, C.-in-C. of the German Navy, who committed suicide on May 23. Below, Air Marshal Sir Arthur Tedder and Marshal Zhukov sign on behalf of the Allied Expeditionary Force and the Russian High Command respectively. On Sir Arthur's right is Mr. A. Vyshinsky, Soviet Vice-Commissar for Foreign Affairs.

Photos, U.S. Official ; Pictorial Press

BALKAN AIR FORCE STRIKES IN YUGOSLAVIA

The formation was announced on August 4, 1944, of the Balkan Air Force—a new composite group of the Mediterranean Allied Air Forces 'for the centralization of the conduct of air operations in the Balkans, except strategic bombing, and for the intensification of air operations in the Adriatic.' Air Vice-Marshal William Elliott, formerly A.O.C., Gibraltar, was appointed its A.O.C. Here a South African Air Force Squadron serving with the Balkan Air Force attacks with rocket-firing Beaufighters targets in the German-occupied town of Zuzemberk, Yugoslavia, early in 1945.

MONTGOMERY BLASTS HIS WAY ACROSS THE RHINE

Under cover of a devastating four-hour air and artillery bombardment—typical of Montgomery's major-assault tactics —21st Army Group stormed the Rhine in bright moonlight on the night of March 23-24, 1945 (see page 3658). Feature of the great assault was the use of a new type of shell, specially designed to deal with German A.A. gun positions. In this greatest barrage of the war, over 1,500 guns—from the lighter Bofors to the 8-inch 'heavies'—took part. Here a 5·5-in. British gun on the west bank of the Rhine blasts targets across the river as a prelude to the crossings.

BRITISH AIRBORNE TROOPS CROSS DORTMUND–EMS CANAL

It was announced on April 2, 1945, that the British 6th Airborne Division had crossed the famous 150-mile Dortmund–Ems Canal ten miles south of Osnabrück, and, in a 15-mile advance beyond Münster, had reached Lengerich in the province of Hanover.   Although the retreating Germans had destroyed the remaining bridges, thanks to the R.A.F.'s persistent smashing of the waterway's banks the water in some sections was only knee-deep and the crossings were made on foot.   Here a stretcher-party carries a wounded man back across the canal beside a partially demolished bridge.

Chapter 357

21st ARMY GROUP CROSSES THE RHINE

The last stages of the campaign of the Army Group under Field-Marshal Montgomery's command are here described by the Military Editor, Major-General Sir Charles Gwynn, who tells the history of the simultaneous campaigns of the Army Groups under American command in Chapter 369. This chapter culminates in the surrender on Lüneburg Heath on May 4—second German surrender in the field, second also to a British commander

By the elimination of the German pocket at Wesel, Field-Marshal Montgomery's 21st Army Group (composed at that time of the 1st Canadian, British 2nd and U.S. 9th Armies) reached the Rhine on March 10 along the whole of its front (*see* page 3572). The U.S. 1st and 3rd Armies had by the same date also lined up on the west bank of the river as far south as the mouth of the Moselle, the former having unexpectedly secured a footing on the east bank at Remagen on March 8 (*see* pages 3572–73).

The stage was therefore set for the final phase of the plan which, back on the Seine in the preceding August, General Eisenhower and Field-Marshal (then General) Montgomery had formed. Under that plan, the main objects were to be the occupation of the Ruhr and the defeat of the German armies in mobile operations in the plains of north-western Germany.

To attain these objects, the Rhine would have to be crossed in force somewhere in the reaches between **Gateway to North-West Germany** Düsseldorf and Emmerich. That was the chief pre-arranged operation to be carried out at the gateway to the decisive area, although no doubt it was also intended to develop a threat along the whole length of the river, and to take advantage of such opportunities as arose of thrusting into southern Germany, bringing the enemy to battle and causing him to disperse his forces.

Upstream of Cologne, however, the nature of the country, especially to the east of the river, made it difficult to decide in advance where attempts to force a crossing might be made. Moreover there was no other objective of the same immediate and decisive importance as the Ruhr to influence a decision.

The Rhine notoriously is everywhere a highly defensible obstacle, wide, swift-flowing and, in its upper reaches, dominated by rugged high ground; but in the reaches north of Düsseldorf selected for the main attack its width, some 600 to 700 yards, its depth of 20 to 25 feet, and its current of three to five miles an hour present an exceptional

problem, both in relation to securing initial footings across the river and to establishing bridges for the passage and maintenance of the main force.

In the face of the weapons of the day, it was clear that landing craft of much the same type would be needed as in an amphibious seaborne enterprise; while for the construction of bridges an immense quantity of engineering equipment would be necessary. After careful experiments on British, French and Belgian rivers most resembling the Rhine in banks and currents, it was decided to use in the main two types of craft for the operation, the L.C.M. (Landing Craft Mechanized) and the L.C.V.P. (Landing Craft Vehicle Personnel) as being best suited to maintain a fast cross-river service of tanks, mobile guns and bulldozers. Both these craft have bows which can be lowered to form ramps for loading and unloading and possess an extremely fast " turn round." The L.C.M., 50 feet long, had a speed of 12 knots and could

carry a crew of five and the equivalent of a Sherman tank; the L.C.V.P., 36 feet long, with a 10-knot speed and a crew of four, could carry 40 fully equipped troops, a bulldozer, or 1,000 gallons of petrol.

The situation was complicated by the fact that the Maas had also to be bridged, which involved some delay in the build-up of material resources between the two rivers. Nevertheless it was essential to **Need for Rapid Build-up** undertake the crossing as soon as possible in order to give the enemy no time to recover from his losses in the Ardennes offensive (*see* Chapter 336) and the subsequent battle of the Rhineland (*see* Chapter 349).

The failure in September 1944 of the airborne attempt to secure a bridge-head at Arnhem (*see* Chapter 325) left no alternative but to seek a solution to the problem of the crossing of the Rhine by deliberate methods. Even before Rundstedt's Ardennes offensive, a start had

PLANNING THE RHINE CROSSINGS
All three Armies of 21st Army Group took part in the Rhine crossing on the night of March 23–24, 1945. British 2nd, under General Dempsey; 1st Canadian, under General Crerar; and U.S. 9th, under General Simpson. The operation was under the overall command of Field-Marshal Montgomery, here seen just before the crossings with General Eisenhower, Supreme Commander, A.E.F., and Lieutenant-General Omar Bradley, commanding 12th Army Group.
Photo, British Official

4B¹

MONTGOMERY'S MEN HEAD FOR THE RHINE

The Rhine crossings of March 23-24, 1945, on a 25-mile front north of the Ruhr, were made by assault troops of 21st Army Group in a great flotilla of 'Buffaloes' and other amphibious craft under a shattering bombardment and dense smoke-screens. 1. Amphibious lorries ('Dukws') in a Rhineland wood where equipment was concentrated before the crossings. 2. Mounted on 'Buffaloes,' these jeep ambulances approach the banks of the great German river. 3. Mobile crane-party of the Royal Navy lift a loaded landing-craft from a transporter on the Rhine. 4. Laying the dense smoke-screens to cover the crossings which took place, for the most part, in bright moonlight. *Photos, British Official ; Keystone*

REICH'S LAST WESTERN BARRIER STORMED

1. In the early dawn of March 24 British troops board assault craft for the Rhine crossing. Banks of the smoke-screens tower in the background. 2. A 'Buffalo' (extreme right), with a R.A.F. party on board, crosses the Rhine under the shadow of a bridge at Wesel which had been blown up by the retreating enemy. 3. Units of the 15th (Scottish) Division scramble ashore, heading for an assembly-point. 4. First Bailey pontoon-bridge to be constructed across the Rhine. Built opposite Xanten and 1,500-feet long, it was the work of VIII Corps Engineers who completed it in exactly 13 hours.

Photos, British Official

Guardsman CHARLTON
(Irish Guards)

At Wistedt, Germany, on April 21, 1945, Guardsman Edward Colquhoun Charlton, co-driver of a tank which had been knocked out, alone, on his own initiative and armed only with a Browning, counter-attacked the enemy. He inflicted heavy casualties, halting them, and though twice wounded continued to fight till he fell. He was awarded the V.C. posthumously.

Cpl. CHAPMAN
(Monmouthshire Regt.)

The V.C. was awarded to Corporal Edward Thomas Chapman for his 'magnificent bravery' on the Dortmund-Ems Canal on April 2, 1945. Single-handed, he repulsed fanatical enemy attacks, gave his battalion time to reorganize a vital position overlooking the only bridge across the canal and greatly aided the success of later operations.

Cpl. TOPHAM
(1st Canadian Parachute Bn.)

Parachuting on to a strongly-defended area of the Rhine on March 24, 1945, Corporal Frederick George Topham, a medical orderly, was awarded the V.C. for 'sustained gallantry of the highest order.' For six hours, most of the time in great pain, he acted with outstanding bravery. 'His magnificent and selfless courage inspired all who witnessed it.'

Photos, Canadian Official ; News Chronicle

been made in accumulating the material required for the undertaking, and by the time the successful issue of the battle of the Rhineland had enabled final selection of the exact point of crossing, resulting from reconnaissance, to be made, everything was on the move towards advanced points of assembly

It had been no easy task, for masses of heavy equipment had to be moved across country in which all avenues of communication had been damaged or, as in the case of canals, put completely out of action. Under these conditions landing craft and other equiment for amphibious operations had to be carried 200 miles overland. As the Rhine crossing would require expert navigation, it fell to British and U.S. naval detachments to surmount the difficulties of these movements. To maintain secrecy, the naval personnel so engaged lived, worked and were dressed like soldiers. This operation was under the overall command of Admiral Sir Harold Burrough, Naval C.-in-C., Allied Naval Expeditionary Force, the senior British and American officers being Captain P. G. H. James, R.N., and Commander William J. Whiteside, U.S.N. Forethought and meticulous planning coupled with an immense display of energy had, however, their reward, and ten days after the elimination of the Wesel pocket the final stages of preparation for the Rhine crossing had been reached.

Here is Montgomery's own brief description of the work of preparation,

Landing Craft Carried Overland

given in his post-war lecture to the Royal United Services Institution already quoted : "The quicker we could engage the enemy in mobile warfare in the north German plains the sooner the end would come. While the battle of the Rhineland was proceeding the details for the crossing of the Rhine were being worked out. Many engineering and administrative preparations

had been initiated back in December before the Ardennes counter-offensive. In particular, work had started on roads and railways necessary to establish our lines of communication across the Meuse [Maas] and Rhine. We had furthermore stocked the 2nd Army depots with some 130,000 tons of stores for the coming operations. And so 21st Army Group launched the operation for crossing the Rhine a fortnight after completion of the battle of the Rhineland. Future history must give the armies great credit for this. It was a most remarkable achievement. The fortnight between the end of the battle of the Rhineland and the crossing of the Rhine was one of intense activity. Formations were regrouped and lined up in their correct positions, covered by a screen of troops holding the river bank. Dense and continuous clouds of smoke were employed to hide our intentions and final preparations."

Montgomery on Preparations for Crossing

It was this smoke screen that especially impressed observers, and its long continuance may well have affected the enemy's morale, keeping him on tenterhooks. An immense intensification of the attack by the Allied air forces on his roads, railways and sources of petrol supply at the same time interfered with the movement of his reserves to meet the coming blow.

At last, on the night of March 23-24 the assault across the Rhine was

BRITISH COMMANDO TROOPS FORCED THE RHINE
Spearheading the Rhine crossings under a barrage of 1,500 guns, British forces of the 1st Commando Brigade made a surprise crossing of the river in the evening of March 23, 1945, four hours ahead of any other troops. Before dawn next day they had captured the town of Wesel, their first objective. Here a detachment is on the look-out for enemy rearguards.

launched on the front Rees–Xanten–Wesel–Dinslaken. The first crossing was made at 9 p.m. in bright moonlight by assault troops in a great flotilla of Buffaloes and other amphibious craft. Four main bridge-heads were established : by the 51st (Highland) Division at Rees, by the 15th (Scottish) opposite Xanten, by the British 1st Commando Brigade at Wesel, and by the U.S. 9th Army (whose spearheads were the 30th and 79th Infantry Divisions) in the area of Dinslaken, some miles north of Duisburg. Wesel, as an important communication centre the key to the crossing, was captured by the Commando Brigade : it had been devastated by earlier air and artillery bombardments.

By the morning footings on the heavily mined east bank had been secured and reinforcements were

Units which Made the Crossing

being ferried across on the whole front of attack. These included, as well as men of the units already mentioned, the 79th Armoured Division, The Black Watch, Argyll and Sutherland Highlanders, Royal Berkshire Regiment, The Royals, Cheshire Regiment, 81st Field Artillery Regiment, Highland Light Infantry, Canadian H.L.I., Manchester Regiment, Royal Scots Fusiliers, Royal Scots, King's Own Scottish Borderers, Royal Tank Regiment (men of the 5th Royal Tank Regiment manning the Buffaloes carrying the troops

in the first assault), Gordon Highlanders, Middlesex Regiment, the Cameronians, 102nd Anti-Tank Regiment, East Riding Yeomanry, Westminster Dragoons, Duke of Cornwall's Light Infantry, Hampshire Regiment, Worcestershire Regiment, Dorset Regiment, Somerset Light Infantry and Wiltshire Regiment.

In the early hours of the 24th, the biggest airborne operation of the war was carried out by the XVIII Airborne Corps (commander, Major-General Matthew B. Ridgeway) of the Allied 1st Airborne Army, and comprising the British 6th (Major-General E. Bols) and U.S. 17th Airborne Divisions. Over three thousand transport planes, operating from twenty-six British and Continental bases and with strong air cover, dropped parachutists north and north-east of Wesel within range of covering artillery. This time, it will be noted, the airborne landings took place after (not, as in the Normandy invasion—see Chapter 311—before) the first assaulting troops had secured a footing. A link between the two forces was rapidly established, the

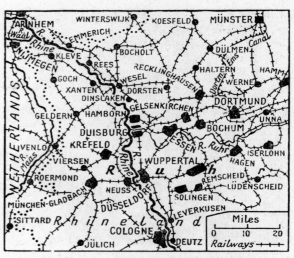

SCENE OF THE RHINE CROSSINGS

This map shows the area of the Rhine crossings by 21st Army Group on the night of March 23-24, 1945 (see text in this page). Also shown is the ground covered by the operations of the British 6th and U.S. 17th Airborne Divisions, the most successful of their kind during the war.

6th Division having meantime seized intact six bridges over the Yssel. The morning saw the river filled with ferrying craft of all types, and bridging operations had started. It must have been a wonderful sight for spectators, among whom Mr. Churchill (see page 3514) and General Eisenhower characteristically were present, often in positions that alarmed their subordinates.

The first British bridge to span the Rhine was that constructed by the VIII Corps Engineers at Xanten. At zero hour (2 a.m.) the commanding officer had gone forward through Xanten, by

British Bridge Across the Rhine

then ablaze under enemy fire, to establish contact with the crossing control, and to fix the exact site for the start of the bridge and the places where the 167 vehicles carrying equipment should assemble. An hour before light, advanced parties had arrived and started work. The enemy was, however, still in possession of the opposite bank at this place, and the main columns of vehicles as they reached the parking places came under fire. It was not till 10.30 a.m., by which time the enemy parties on the east bank had been pinched out by assaulting troops, that work could proceed. The main difficulty to be overcome was the laying of adequate anchors in the strong current. Previous rehearsals on the Maas had shown that extra heavy anchors would be necessary, and that they would have to be laid from a ferry raft working on a cable. Getting the cable across was no easy task, and in the course of the day it was broken several times by derelict

GLIDERBORNE ARMY IN ACTION

Within 30 minutes of their landings east of the Rhine on March 24, 1945, the British 6th Airborne Division had captured its main objectives, taken many prisoners, and seized intact six bridges across the Yssel river. Before nightfall they had linked up with ground forces at points five miles east of the Rhine. Here an airborne anti-tank gun crew—men and weapons landed by glider—take up position at Hamminkeln, north-west of Wesel. *Photo. British Official*

MEETING ON THE LIPPE

Striking east along the northern bank of the River Lippe in the Ruhr—on whose southern bank the U.S. 9th Army was operating—the British 6th Guards Armoured Brigade on March 28, 1945, captured the important communications centre of Dorsten, and linked with the Americans next day. Above, a British tank man gives a light to an American at the meeting.

assault craft, out of control through enemy fire, drifting down stream. Nevertheless the work went on steadily, and by 11.30 p.m. the bridge 1,500 feet

long and its approach roads were open to traffic. By the end of the second day seven bridges in all were in operation to the bridge-head, which by then had been expanded to a width of 25 miles with a maximum depth of six miles.

The enemy's resistance had initially been strongest on the northern flank, where he had concentrated three parachute divisions which, as always, fought stubbornly. The U.S. 9th Army met comparatively light opposition, the two assault divisions **Light Losses of the Crossing** losing only 31 men killed. The comparative ease and speed with which the initial crossing was effected was no doubt due to the perfection of the preparations and to the tremendous weight of the covering fire provided. Naval detachments with the craft they had dragged by road right across Holland

IN RUINED MÜNSTER

Münster, capital of Westphalia, was captured on April 3, 1945, by the British 6th Guards Armoured Brigade in conjunction with elements of the U.S. 17th Airborne Division. Here, a British and U.S. patrol passes the ruined cathedral. Left, U.S. reconnaissance party confers with a British tank-crew over a map. The city had been heavily shelled after the German commandant's refusal to surrender.

Photos, British Official ; British Newspaper Pool

played an important part in the crossing. That the enemy was unable to launch counter-attacks on a considerable scale was due largely to the heavy air interdiction programme which had been carried out, and, no doubt, to the effects of the defeat that the enemy had suffered in the Rhineland.

The American bridge-head at Remagen, by now considerably extended, had also tended to cause dispersion of German reserves, particularly those in

BRITISH DRIVE TOWARDS BREMEN

Troops of the British 1st Commando Brigade on April 5, 1945, cleared the German industrial and railroad centre of Osnabrück in their drive towards Bremen, taking many prisoners. Left, an armoured car of the British 11th Armoured Division, bearing a Nazi street name-plate on its bonnet, pushes towards Osnabrück. Right, British Commando troops search for snipers in the town's ruined streets.   *Photos, British Official*

the Ruhr which might have been used against the U.S. 9th Army. The Germans apparently expected the attack on the Ruhr to develop directly from the Remagen bridge-head and had concentrated for defence north of the Sieg river, only to be caught on the wrong foot when General Hodges broke out of his bridge-head to the south-east on a wider manoeuvre, which is described in Chapter 369.

The bridge-heads on Montgomery's front were quickly joined up, and within four days the deployment of his armies on the east bank of the Rhine was suffi-

Advance to the Elbe Begins

ciently complete for the advance to the Elbe to begin. On March 29 it started at dawn, after some preliminary fighting to secure more elbow room. Each of the three armies had its separate mission. The U.S. 9th Army on the right was directed towards the front Magdeburg–Wittenberge, pressing into the north-west section of the Ruhr as it advanced. In the centre the British 2nd Army was to advance with its left flank directed on Hamburg, while on the left General Crerar's Canadian II Corps, passing through the 2nd Army bridge-head, was to swing north along the Rhine to outflank Arnhem. There later his Canadian I Corps was to cross and establish a protective flank between the Rhine and the Zuider Zee, while the II Corps opened up routes leading northwards towards the coast.

The enemy tried desperately to assemble forces to oppose the advance, especially on the Ems–Dortmund Canal which faced the centre and left of the 2nd Army. On this part of the front there was bitter fighting, but the right

of the 2nd Army, and the U.S. 9th Army, were able to advance rapidly.

On March 28 armour of the 21st Army Group reached the line Borken–Dorsten–Hamborn and, advancing across the Westphalian plain, by March 31 was approaching Münster, by which time the U.S. 1st Army by a very rapid swing northwards was in the area west of Cassel and Paderborn east f the Ruhr.

By April 3 the U.S. 9th Army had reached the Weser near Minden and, having linked up with the U.S. 1st Army near Paderborn, completed the encirclement of the Ruhr. From that date the 9th Army reverted to General Bradley's command. Its subsequent operations therefore form part of the American advance east of the Rhine, which is described in Chapter 369. The rest of this chapter follows exclusively the operations of the 21st Army Group up to the enemy's final surrender. The purpose of these operations, as Montgomery himself stated, was to cut progressively the German east-west lines

AS GERMANY'S SURRENDER APPROACHED

This map shows the area of operations of the Northern Group of armies in north-west Germany as the war in the west collapsed with the unconditional surrender to Field-Marshal Montgomery at Lüneburg on May 4, 1945. The shaded portion, covering the operations of the Anglo-U.S. Airborne Divisions following the Rhine crossings, is reproduced on a larger scale in page 3659.

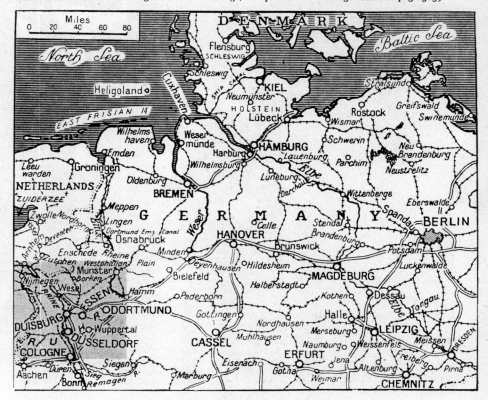

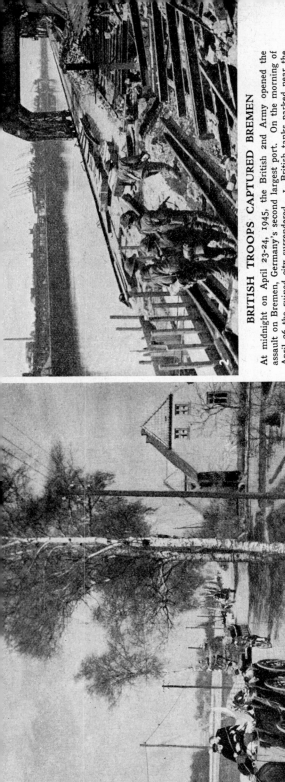

BRITISH TROOPS CAPTURED BREMEN

At midnight on April 23-24, 1945, the British 2nd Army opened the assault on Bremen, Germany's second largest port. On the morning of April 26 the ruined city surrendered. 1. British tanks parked near the city as refugees pass by. 2. British patrol mops up in the fanatically defended dock area where the Nazis held out till the last. 3. Clearing the devastated centre of the city during the last stages of fierce street-fighting.

'TULIPS' FOR BREMEN

During the advance from the Rhine in April 1945 a new British secret weapon was introduced. This was a Sherman tank which fired R.A.F. Typhoon rockets. It was conceived, evolved and tested in a single day as a result of co-operation between the Coldstream Guards and the R.A.F. Known as 'Tulip,' the new weapon, after a few modifications, was capable of demolishing a house at 600 yards. 'Tulips,' played an important part in the storming of the Altenlingen Bridge over the River Ems. Here, outside Zeven (a mile S.W. of Bremen), a tank-man adjusts a 'Tulip' to the range required.

Photos, British Official; Associated Press

SECOND BATTLE OF ARNHEM

The British 49th (West Riding) Division, fighting with the 1st Canadian Army, on the night of April 12-13, 1945, made a surprise crossing of the Yssel river east of Arnhem, which they entered the following day and finally cleared on April 14. Here 'Buffaloes' of the 79th Armoured Division wait at dawn to ferry men and equipment across the river. German prisoners huddle in the background.   *Photo, British Official*

of communications to the coast and to deliver a series of right hooks to round up the enemy, while the left flank formations drove up towards the coast to finish him off.

On April 6 the VIII Corps (commanded by Lieutenant-General H. Barker) of the 2nd Army, having cleared Osnabrück, reached and crossed the Weser near Minden, while a few days later the XII Corps (commanded by Lt.-Gen. Neil M. Ritchie) crossed the river farther north and then turned north for Hamburg.

Meanwhile on April 2 the 1st Canadian Army launched an attack to clear the enemy from the ten-mile-long "island"

Advance in the Netherlands

between Arnhem and Nijmegen. They met stubborn resistance. Extending northwards, by April 7 they were fighting with German troops holding the line of the Yssel round Zutphen (captured that day) and Deventer. That night two battalions of French parachute troops, consisting partly of regular soldiers and partly of members of the *Maquis*, were dropped east of the Zuider Zee, and on the 8th, ground troops, advancing from Zutphen, established contact with them. Heavy fighting continued on this front, resulting in the capture of Deventer on April 11, and the opening of a fresh attack north of Arnhem, finally cleared on April 14.

While this fighting was in progress, the Canadians had also been pressing

northwards on both sides of the Dutch-German frontier, and on April 15 reconnaissance elements reached the North Sea. The capture of Groningen the following day virtually completed the liberation of the northern Netherlands east of the Zuider Zee, and isolated the German Army in the western Netherlands.

At the same time the left and centre of the 2nd Army were closing in on Bremen and Hanover. On April 10 Hanover was captured and the XXX Corps (commanded by General Bryan Horrocks) began the investment of Bremen. On the 12th the Americans crossed the Elbe not far from Magdeburg. The 2nd Army continued to press on between Hanover and Bremen towards Hamburg, and to the west of Bremen were

approaching Oldenburg. Stiff resistance was encountered both at Bremen and Oldenburg, and north-east of Brunswick a German group even made a vigorous counter-attack on the American flank.

The opening of the Russian offensive on April 16 (*see* Chapter 362) of course made the German situation increasingly hopeless; but by that time the death agony of Germany was already far

CANADIANS CAPTURE ZUTPHEN

On April 7, 1945, infantry of the 1st Canadian Army, pushing north to the V-bomb launching sites, captured the ancient Netherlands town of Zutphen on the Yssel river—where Sir Philip Sidney died in 1586—after fierce fighting. Below, Canadian mechanized units cross a partly demolished bridge spanning the moat which surrounds Zutphen.   *Photo, Associated Press*

WITH THE U.S. NINTH ARMY

On March 28, 1945, the U.S. 9th Army, under General Simpson, captured the important river port of Duisburg, on the Rhine. Right, troops cross a Duisburg bridge seized intact. Above, U.S. 9th Army engineers build a pontoon bridge over the Weser in April, while infantry haul themselves across.

advanced in the west. The army isolated in the western Netherlands had lost all strategic meaning; even its defensive line on the Yssel had been penetrated, and the Canadians were advancing south of the Zuider Zee towards Amsterdam. Characteristically the German commander chose this moment for one of the most senseless acts of vindictive vandalism of which the German Army was guilty, when he ordered the flooding of the country (see Chapter 358). The force still holding out at Bremen was in no better position, and by April 18 the 2nd Army had reached Lüneburg and

SCOTTISH TROOPS NEAR THE ELBE

Swinging north from Celle towards the Elbe, the 15th (Scottish) Division on April 14, 1945, advanced 21 miles to reach Uelzen, an important rail junction on the Berlin–Bremen and Hamburg–Hanover lines. Here—only 25 miles from the Elbe and 45 miles from Hamburg—they met fanatical opposition from S.S. formations which held out for five days. Below, a Scottish patrol passes a Red Cross party in the burning town.   *Photo, British Official*

had begun to line up on the left bank of the Elbe, masking Hamburg. The Allies continued to establish themselves on the Elbe between Dessau and Hamburg, but did not cross in force.

The advance of the Allies into Germany had forced the enemy by this time to create new commands: Field-Marshal Busch (earlier commanding an Army Group on the Eastern Front) was appointed C.-in-C. in the north-west, covering Denmark, the Netherlands and the Hamburg–Emden area; Field-Marshal Albert Kesselring (transferred from Italy to replace Rundstedt after the failure of the Ardennes offensive) was put in charge of the "Southern Redoubt" (Bavaria, Austria, and Bohemia).

By April 24 British troops were pressing into the suburbs of Bremen, and on the following day Russian and U.S. troops linked up on the Elbe near Torgau. April 26 saw Bremen completely in British hands, **Bremen Falls to the British** except for the dock area, where fighting continued for a couple of days longer. The Canadians continued to close in on

GERMANS SURRENDER THEIR GREATEST PORT

Hamburg, Germany's second city, was surrendered on May 3, 1945, to the British 2nd Army by the garrison commander, General Wolz, who met the British commander near Harburg and rode into the city at the head of the British troops. Guided by a British naval officer prisoner-of-war, a German colonel and his staff had entered the British lines the previous day with a letter from Field-Marshal Busch, commanding the Hamburg area, requesting surrender negotiations. 1. Inside the British lines the German colonel (second from the right) makes final arrangements for the surrender talks. 2. British officers enter Hamburg Town Hall on May 3 to take over the city from General Wolz. 3. A Hamburg policeman watches a British corporal erect a street sign after the occupation. 4. A corner of Hamburg's badly blitzed dockyard areas.

Photos, British Official; Associated Press

Oldenburg and the British on Hamburg, but not till April 29 was any sensational enterprise undertaken. On that day, having forced a crossing of the Elbe at Lauenburg, south-east of Hamburg, in driving rain, mobile formations of the 2nd Army, reinforced by the U.S. 82nd Airborne Division, were launched in a drive towards Lübeck, in order to frustrate any attempt the Germans retreating before Rokossovsky (*see* Chapter 362) might make to withdraw into Schleswig-Holstein. Lübeck and Wismar were entered on May 2 and contact was made with the Russians.

By the same date a U.S. airborne corps of two divisions, together with the British 6th Airborne Division, had taken up a position facing east on the line Darchau–Schwerin–Wismar, to hold up the retreating Germans. This was a notable and rapidly carried out manoeuvre which, although it met with almost no resistance, was needed to convince the Germans of the impossibility of continuing the struggle in Denmark and Norway—if, indeed, they had had any thought of doing so after hearing of Hitler's death on May 1. While plans for outflanking Hamburg on the Bremen model were actually under way, the commander of the garrison started negotiations on May 2 for the surrender of the city, carried out next day.

On May 3 also, Admiral Doenitz, as Hitler's successor, sent envoys to Field-Marshal Montgomery's headquarters at Lüneburg Heath in a vain attempt to obtain separate armistice terms from **Doenitz** him. By this time the **Seeks** country east of the Elbe **Armistice** was packed with German troops and refugees fleeing before the Russians—the former anxious to come into our lines to surrender and sadly disappointed when told that if they wanted to surrender they must apply to the Russians. The Emden and Cuxhaven promontories were now virtually the only areas where fighting still continued, but May 3 saw the surrender of Oldenburg to the Canadians, and Kiel and Flensburg were declared open towns; the R.A.F. in the five preceding days having put out of action 150 ships, including a number of U-boats attempting to escape to Norway.

On May 4 a fresh delegation from Admiral Doenitz arrived at Field-Marshal Montgomery's headquarters, and this time they were without difficulty convinced that nothing short of unconditional surrender would be accepted. Doenitz having heard their report bowed to the inevitable, and on the same evening General-Admiral Hans Georg von Friedeburg as his representative signed the instrument of unconditional surrender for all German armed forces in north-west Germany, Holland and Denmark, including the garrisons of Heligoland and the Frisian Islands—two days after the cessation of hostilities in Italy (*see* Chapter 361). The armies of the British Commonwealth of Nations had completed their share of the Allied task.

Field-Marshal Montgomery's own account of the surrender was given in characteristic style to war correspondents an hour before the signing of the capitulation. " There **Montgomery's** is a German general **Story of the** called Blumentritt who, **Surrender** as far as I know, commands all forces between the Baltic and the Weser river," he began. " On Wednesday he sent in and said he wanted to come in on Thursday and surrender what they call the army group Blumentritt. . . . He was told, ' You can come in. That's O.K. We are delighted.' . . .

" Now the next thing that happened was yesterday morning (Thursday). Blumentritt said, ' As far as I know there is something going on just above my level and therefore I am not coming

BRITISH TROOPS FORCE THE ELBE

In the early morning of April 29, 1945, the British 1st Commando Brigade and the 15th (Scottish) Division crossed the 300-yards wide lower Elbe in assault-boats and Buffaloes manned by the 79th Armoured Division at Lauenburg, to the south-east of Hamburg, which later in the day they captured. Above, Sherman D.D. swimming tanks after the crossing. Below, Scottish troops land from assault-craft at the double   *Photos, British Official*

ARNHEM MEN RELEASED BY THE 'DESERT RATS'

Breaking out from the Rethem bridge-head across the Aller on April 16, 1945, the British 7th Armoured Division captured Stalag XI B near Fallingbostel. Here they released 6,500 British and U.S. prisoners, including 700 men from Arnhem. Several hundred were found in hospital suffering from malnutrition as a result of forced marches from East Prussian camps. Here, prisoners greet their liberators. *Photo, British Newspaper Pool*

in.' He did not come in. But instead there arrived here to see me four German people — General-Admiral Friedeburg, who is commander-in-chief of the German navy; General Kinzel, chief of staff to Field-Marshal Busch; Rear-Admiral Wagner, staff officer to Friedeburg, and Major Friede, who is staff officer to Kinzel. So the party really was just two chaps—Friedeburg and Kinzel.

" Now this is extremely interesting. They lined up above my caravan and I said, 'What do you want?' They said, 'We've come here from Field-Marshal Busch to ask you to accept the surrender of the three German armies that are now withdrawing in front of the Russians in Mecklenburg between Rostock and Berlin. . . . We are very anxious about the condition of the civilians who are driven along as these armies flee from the advancing Russians, and we want you to accept their surrender.'

Offer to Surrender Three Armies

" I said, 'No, certainly not. These armies are fighting the Russians and therefore if they surrender to anybody it must be to the Russians. It has

nothing to do with me . . .' I then said to them, ' Are you prepared to surrender to me the German forces on my western and northern flanks . . . ? '

" They said, ' No.' So far it had been a very good discussion. Then they said, ' We are most anxious about the condition of civilians in the areas of Lübeck and on the northern flank. . . . We thought perhaps you would make some plan with us whereby you would advance slowly and we would withdraw slowly and all the civilians would be all right.' So far we had not got very far.

" I said, ' No. There is nothing doing. . . . I wonder whether you officers know what is the battle situation on the Western Front? In case you don't, I will show it to you.' I produced a map which showed the battle situation. . . . I said to them, ' You must clearly understand three points : One, you must surrender to me unconditionally all the German forces in Holland, in Friesland, including the Frisian Islands, Heligoland, and all other islands, in Schleswig-

Holstein and in Denmark. Two, once you have done that I am then prepared to discuss with you the implications of the surrender. . . . Three, if you don't agree to Point Number One, I shall go on with the war and will be delighted to do so and am ready. . . .'

" They then said to me, ' We came here entirely for the purpose of asking you to accept surrender of these German armies on your eastern flank. . . . We have no power to agree to what you now want. . . . But two of us will now go back to where we came from, get agreement and come back again. Two will stay here with you.' So yesterday afternoon between 3.30 and 4 o'clock the General-Admiral, accompanied by Major Friede, went back. . . . He was to come back here with the doings. . . . Now they have arrived—they are up top somewhere and my present intention is that they will sign what I have prepared. This piece of paper is really the

Germans Seek Fresh Authority

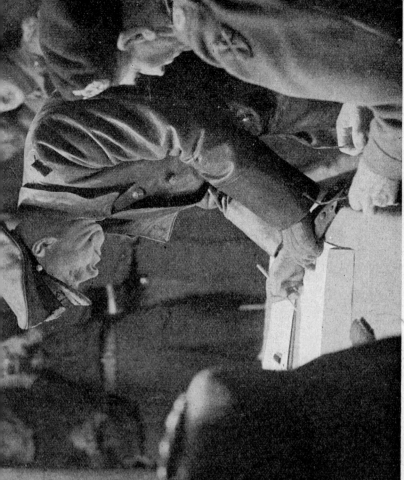

UNCONDITIONAL SURRENDER SIGNED AT LÜNEBURG

General-Admiral von Friedeburg, C.-in-C., the German Navy, signs the instrument of unconditional surrender on May 4, 1945, at 21st Army Group H.Q. at Lüneburg Heath (see also page 367). Friedeburg heads the enemy signatures on the document, reproduced on the left, about which Field-Marshal Montgomery, seated on the German's left, had second thoughts : to Clause I he added in his own hand the words, 'This to include all naval ships in these areas.' He also altered the time of the 'Cease Fire,' corrected the date and initialled it. Seven months later, British troops were putting the finishing touches to a memorial marking the site of the historic ceremony (below). The wording runs : 'Here on 4th May, 1945, a Delegation from the German High Command surrendered unconditionally to Field-Marshal Montgomery all Land, Sea and Air Forces in North-West Germany, Denmark and Holland.'

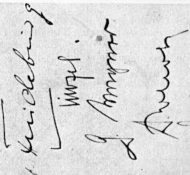

Instrument of Surrender of the forces in accordance with my demands. I am dealing with the commander of the forces facing me and that is why I am doing it alone like this. . . . I have absolutely excluded anything which would be an Allied thing and would require the presence of our Allied Russians and Americans and so on. The forces which surrender will total over 1,000,000—that is their own statement. It will involve some very tricky problems getting them from these places—from West Holland and Denmark. . . . The next scene will be up top in the tent."

It may seem that in all the operations following the opening of the western front the forces of the British Empire played a secondary part, and it is of course true that the Empire was unable to equal the weight of the American

GERMANS IN HOLLAND LAY DOWN THEIR ARMS
In a small hotel at Wageningen, near Arnhem, on May 6, 1945, General Blaskowitz, commanding the German 21st Army of about 120,000 men, surrendered all the German forces in the Netherlands to Lieutenant-General Charles Foulkes, G.O.C., Canadian I Corps. Here General Foulkes reads the surrender orders to General Blaskowitz (right, centre) on whose left is Lieutenant-General Reichelt, his Chief of Staff. Prince Bernhard of the Netherlands was present.

effort. None the less the success of the whole campaign depended largely on the achievement of the Imperial forces. Apart from the heavy losses they had inflicted on the enemy, without the liberation by them of the Channel and North Sea ports, notably Antwerp, the whole western

WEST MEETS EAST
On May 7, 1945, Field-Marshal Montgomery met Marshal Rokossovsky, of the 2nd White Russian Army, at Wismar, scene of the link-up between British and Soviet forces four days earlier. Troops of the British 6th Airborne Division formed a guard of honour for the two great military leaders. Here Field-Marshal Montgomery extends a hand of greeting as he and the Red Army marshal meet.
Photo, British Official

offensive would certainly have been greatly delayed and might possibly have been brought to a complete standstill. Further developments of secret weapons might also have had serious effects on the Allied bases on both sides of the Channel. The strategic role of the 21st Army Group was therefore of exceptional importance.

In the final phase of the campaign this group carried out the only deliberately planned crossing of the Rhine, and that in the area where it must certainly have been expected by the enemy. That it met

Triumph of Meticulous Planning

with such complete success was due to meticulous preparation and admirable execution. The crossing was planned and carried out on so great a scale that it was possible to deploy the full strength of the army on the farther bank with remarkable speed. The enemy was given no time to recover, and although in places he fought stubbornly for a short time, he was never able to offer organized resistance. The end consequently came in a general widespread collapse of morale and physical inability to continue the struggle, and not in decisive battle. If one single operation can be said to have delivered the death-blow to Nazi Germany, it was the 21st Army Group's forcing of the Rhine. That it was accomplished with such apparent ease and with so little loss of life should not obscure the importance of the achievement.

April 1. U.S. 1st and 9th Armies linked up at Lippstadt, cutting off the Ruhr. 1st Ukrainian Army captured Glogau (Silesia); other Red Army forces took Sopron (Hungary). U.S. 10th Army landed in great strength on Okinawa (Ryukyu Islands).

April 2. Announced that Guards Armoured Division had entered Münster, British 6th Airborne Division had crossed the Ems Canal and that British 2nd Army was over 100 miles beyond the Rhine; R.A.F. bombed Berlin again. 3rd Ukrainian Army captured Nagy Kanisza, Hungarian oil-centre. 8th Army made amphibious landing N. of Ravenna. U.S.A. 15th A.F. heavily attacked communications in Austria and N. Italy. Saipan-based Super-Fortresses bombed Tokyo.

April 3. Canadians established bridge-head on Zutphen–Hengelo Canal. 3rd Ukrainian Army captured Wiener Neustadt, Eisenstadt, Neukirchen, and Gloggnitz, on approaches to Vienna.

April 4. British 11th Airborne Division by-passed Osnabrück, crossed the Weser; Kassel surrendered to Americans; U.S. 3rd Army occupied Fulda and Gotha. French 1st Army captured Karlsruhe. By night R.A.F. heavily bombed Harburg oil plants. 2nd Ukrainian Army stormed Bratislava; other Red Army forces took Baden. M.A.A.F. intensively attacked communications in N. Italy.

April 5. British 1st Commando Brigade cleared Osnabrück; Canadians took Almelo, occupied Zutphen; U.S. 3rd Army captured Mulhausen. Heavy U.S.A.A.F. attacks on Bavaria. Russia denounced Russo-Japanese neutrality pact of 1941.

April 6. Canadian and British troops linked up near Zutphen; British troops crossed the Weser near Minden; U.S. 9th Army finally cleared Hamm; U.S. 3rd Army captured Eisenach and Meiningen; U.S. 7th Army cleared Wurzburg; French reached Neckar River S. of Heilbronn. Berlin raided for first time by Continent-based R.A.F. Mosquitoes.

April 6–7. U.S. aircraft struck Japanese naval force off Okinawa, sinking the "Yamato," Japan's largest battleship, two cruisers, three destroyers, and shooting down 417 aircraft. British carrier force attacked the Sakishima group.

April 7. Canadians captured Zutphen; 1,300 Fortresses and Liberators attacked German airfields, depots and rail targets, shooting down 104 enemy fighters. Heavy fighting inside Vienna. Defeat announced of Japanese 15th Army in Burma. Tokyo and Nagoya heavily bombed by Super-Fortresses.

April 7–8 (night). French parachute troops dropped over wide area E. of Zuider Zee to link up with Canadians.

April 8. U.S. 1st Army cleared Gottingen; French Army captured Pforzheim, N.W. of Stuttgart. Russians forced Danube N.W. and W. of Bratislava. New Greek Government formed with Admiral Voulgaris as Premier.

April 9. Heavy R.A.F. raids on Hamburg, Kiel. 3rd White Russian Army captured Königsberg. In Italy 8th Army launched powerful attack across Senio.

April 10. U.S. 9th Army captured Essen and Hanover; in over 5,600 sorties by R.A.F. and U.S.A.A.F., 406 enemy planes shot down; Berlin airfields destroyed. In Italy U.S. troops took Massa. 14th Army captured Thazi, E. of Meiktila (Burma).

April 11. U.S. 9th Army captured Gelsenkirchen in Ruhr pocket; by night R.A.F. raided Berlin three times. Russians established Danube bridge-head in Vienna. 8th Army reached Santerno River (Italy). Russo-Yugoslav treaty signed.

April 12. U.S. 9th Army crossed Elbe; U.S. 80th Division captured Weimar and Erfurt; Buchenwald overrun; British 2nd Army took rail junction of Celle on Aller River; French 1st Army took Rastatt and Baden-Baden. Franklin Delano Roosevelt died; Mr. Harry S. Truman sworn in as President.

April 13. British troops of 1st Canadian Army crossed the Yssel near Arnhem; U.S. 9th Army occupied Dortmund; U.S. 3rd Army captured Jena. Red Armies completed capture of Vienna. Kyaupadaung (Burma) taken. U.S. forces landed on Bohol (Philippines).

April 13–14. Heavy attack by Super-Fortresses on Tokyo.

April 14. British finally cleared Arnhem; U.S. 3rd Army cleared Zeitz; U.S.A. 8th A.F. attacked Gironde estuary positions. Marshal Tolbukhin's troops forced River Traisen, captured Herzogenburg. 14th Army entered Hlaingdet, E. of Thazi. Announced that Australians had almost completed clearing up areas inland from New Guinea coast. Eastern Air Command bombers destroyed Thai power station (Siam).

April 15. All German land exits from W. Holland sealed; U.S. 9th Army cleared Stendal, on the Elbe; U.S. 1st and 9th Armies linked up on Ruhr River N. of Hagen. Russians took St. Pölten (Austria).

April 16. Germans at Groningen surrendered to Canadians; U.S. 1st and 9th Armies linked up to form new pocket in Harz Mountains; in Ruhr pocket enemy resistance ceased almost completely. R.A.F. bombed Swinemünde, sank the "Lutzow." Record total of 1,016 enemy planes destroyed by Allied air forces. Poles crossed Oder and Neisse Rivers. Taungup, last enemy coastal base in Arakan, taken.

April 17. U.S. 9th Army broke into Magdeburg; other U.S. forces took Plauen (Saxony). 2nd Ukrainian Army captured Zistersdorf, oil centre near Vienna. R.A.F. bombed Gestapo H.Q. at Odense (Denmark). Resistance to Australians ceased in But-Dagua area of New Guinea.

April 18. Germans opened sluice-gates and blew up dykes on Zuider Zee; Magdeburg fell to U.S. 9th Army; 3rd U.S. Army cleared Zwickau (Saxony); U.S. 1st Army entered Dusseldorf; R.A.F. in strength attacked Heligoland and island of Düne. 8th Army captured Argenta (Italy).

April 19. U.S. 1st Army captured Leipzig; Heligoland again bombed by R.A.F. 14th Army forces captured Chauk, Burmese oil-centre.

April 20. Battle of Ruhr ended; German Army Group "B" eliminated; capture of Nuremberg by U.S. 7th Army. Red Army took Bad Freienwalde, N.E. of Berlin. Tito's troops seized Bakar, port near Fiume. In Burma 14th Army captured Pyawbwe, Yamethin, and Seikpyu.

April 21. U.S. 9th Army captured Salzgitter (Brunswick). U.S. 7th Army established bridge-head on S. bank of Danube. French took Freiburg; Berlin under fire from Soviet artillery. In Italy 15th Army Group liberated Bologna. Australians' capture of Karawop (New Guinea) announced. Russia signed treaty with Lublin Provisional Government.

April 22. U.S. 1st Army cleared Bitterfeld, captured Dessau; German pocket in Harz Mountains eliminated; French 1st Army took Stuttgart. Russians occupied Opava (Czechoslovakia). 8th Army troops captured Comacchio (Italy). Japanese resistance on Cebu Island (Philippines) wiped out.

April 23. French took Mulheim (Baden). Red Army captured Frankfort-on-Oder, Oranienburg, Kottbus. 5th and 8th Armies reached River Po at several points. In Burma, Pyinmana fell to 14th Army forces.

April 24. U.S. 1st Army reached Elbe, N.E. of Dessau; other U.S. forces (with French) captured Ulm, on the Danube; 1st White Russian and 1st Ukrainian Armies linked up 11 miles S.E. of Berlin. 5th Army seized Spezia naval base; 8th Army took Ferrara.

April 25. Allied forces from E. and W. met at Torgau on the Elbe; Hitler's Berchtesgaden home bombed by R.A.F. U.S.A. 8th A.F. attacked Skoda works at Pilsen; by night Coastal Command bombed enemy shipping from Hook of Holland to Heligoland Bight. Announced that whole of Burma oilfields region had been cleared. San Francisco Conference opened.

April 26. Bremen surrendered to British; French 1st Army captured Constance. 2nd White Russian Army took Stettin; 2nd Ukrainian Army seized Brno (Czechoslovakia). Verona fell to U.S. troops of 5th Army. Toungoo (Burma) captured. Australians captured Maprik, New Guinea.

April 27. U.S. 3rd Army took Regensburg. 1st White Russian Army captured Potsdam, Rathenow and Spandau, all suburbs of Berlin; other Red Army forces seized Wittenberg. Last Germans expelled from Finland. Allied armies entered Genoa, freed Piacenza.

April 28. Augsburg fell to U.S. 7th Army; heavy fighting in centre of Berlin. Enemy forces in N. Italy in complete disintegration; Mussolini executed by partisans at Dongo (Lake Como).

April 29. Allied food-relief by air for Holland began; British crossed Elbe-Trave Canal; U.S. 9th Army linked up with Russians near Dessau. Germans in Italy surrendered unconditionally; British entered Venice.

April 30. U.S. 7th Army occupied Munich, overran Dachau. Tito's troops in Trieste. 14th Army took Pegu (Burma). Australians landed on Sadoe Island, off Borneo. Hitler appointed Admiral Doenitz his successor.

FOUR GERMANS CAME TO SEE FIELD-MARSHAL MONTGOMERY

'There arrived to see me four German people,' was Field-Marshal Montgomery's simple description (see page 3666) of how the enemy emissaries, including General-Admiral von Friedeburg, C.-in-C., the German Navy (with his back to the flagstaff), came to try to arrange an armistice at Lüneburg Heath on May 3, 1945 (see also illus. in page 3674). When Montgomery showed Von Friedeburg his operational map, 'and he realized, apparently for the first time,' said the Field-Marshal later, 'the plight of the German armies on the various operational fronts, he broke down and wept.'

BRITISH AND RUSSIANS MEET ON THE BALTIC

It was near the Baltic port of Wismar, which the British 6th Airborne Division entered on May 2, 1945, after a 50-miles advance from the Lauenburg bridge-head, that troops of the British 2nd Army and the 2nd White Russian Army (under Marshal Rokossovsky) first made contact. On the day of the link-up—May 3—the whole enemy defence system in north-west Germany collapsed, with wholesale surrenders of the panic-stricken Wehrmacht. Everywhere the roads were choked with German troops and civilians fleeing from the 2nd White Russian Army. Here Soviet tank-crews are being greeted by British troops.

Photo, British Official

GERMANS SEEK SURRENDER TERMS ON LÜNEBURG HEATH

At 21st Army Group H.Q. on Lüneburg Heath, near Hamburg, on May 4, 1945, were surrendered to Field-Marshal Sir Bernard Montgomery all German forces in northern Germany, totalling 1,000,000 men. The German emissaries arrived seeking terms on May 3. They were General-Admiral Hans Georg von Friedeburg, who two days before succeeded Admiral Doenitz as C.-in-C., German Navy ; General Kinzel, chief of staff to Field-Marshal Busch ; Rear-Admiral Wagner, Friedeburg's chief of staff ; and Major Friede, of Kinzel's staff, who are here conferring near the British H.Q.

Chapter 358

THE NETHERLANDS ON HER FEET AGAIN

This chapter, telling of the final terrible months of occupation in the northern Netherlands, and of the coming of complete liberation at last with the surrender of Germany, is by Professor Pieter Sjoerds Gerbrandy, Premier of the exiled Dutch Government from September 1940 until the return to Holland, and is in itself a historic document. In spite of their sufferings, the Netherlands people were making good headway against their difficulties by the end of 1945

THE way in which the liberation of the Netherlands from the German yoke was brought about differed very much from what every Dutchman had anticipated. The fact that the country was liberated in two time-separated campaigns had the most terrible consequences for Dutchmen and their country. It was responsible for the misery and starvation in the north-western part during the first half of 1945, the only parallel of which, in the history of the Netherlands, was in the years 1573 until 1575 of the Spanish war.

By the end of 1944 the greater part of the southern Netherlands had been freed (*see* Chapter 332). But conditions in the still occupied northern part had become exceedingly bad. In the big cities of Amsterdam, Rotterdam, Utrecht and The Hague, and the smaller towns like Haarlem, Leyden, Delft and many others, there was no fuel, hardly any electricity and no gas; food had become very scarce, the calories per day falling as low as 450.

The railway strike, involving approximately 30,000 employees, which started on September 17, 1944 (*see* page 3207),

Railway Strike Continues continued until the German surrender, notwithstanding the terrible punishment inflicted by the Germans upon the families of these railway men, and the fact that the Germans made this yet another excuse for cutting off supplies from the population.

By the end of April 1945 all stores of food had been exhausted; but worse than all was the reign of terror exercised by the Germans. When I came back to my country and talked with my family and other people about the first four months of 1945, they mentioned the horrors of famine and cold; but when they talked of the situation as a whole, without exception they always laid emphasis on the terror exercised by the Germans, especially against the male population between the ages of 16 and 45. In nearly every house there was the feeling of constant apprehension because at any moment the Gestapo might knock at the door in order to deport some member of the family.

The Germans used the appalling conditions of the civilians to lure them to the east where they might work for the German war machine. Mobile kitchens moved through the streets of Amsterdam, Rotterdam and The Hague giving out the smell of well-cooked dishes, promised to everybody who would give himself up for slave work in the east. When this method failed, the occupying enemy suddenly, successively, in Rotterdam, The Hague and other cities, ordered families to stand before the doors of their houses; the young members of the population were picked up and sent far away to working and concentration camps. When these " press-gang " methods started they succeeded, for example in Rotterdam, because people were not immediately aware of the danger. Once, however, they had learned what was at stake, they refused to obey the order, and kept away from all the danger spots, or went into hiding in the country. From London the Government, through Radio Orange, gave all the moral support it could to the gallant people who, notwithstanding famine and deadly threats refused to bow down under the German yoke.

In talking to the Dutch people about that time of terror and privation, I found that they assured me that, in the depths of their hearts, there remained always the firm hope of speedy deliverance. This hope was strengthened by the fact that the **Food Relief Arrives** Dutch and British Governments, together with the American, were able to arrange some measure of relief, through the mediation of the Swiss and especially the Swedish Governments. The attempt to send this relief started in October 1944, but it was months before an arrangement, with the agreement of the Germans, took effect, and only relatively small quantities of food came into the country. The mere appearance, however, of Swedish bread was for the starving people a new token of final victory. One cannot, of course, speak of relief without mentioning the unforgettable achievement of the British and American planes in

R.A.F. FLIES FOOD TO STARVING HOLLAND

The cutting-off of the Netherlands by the Allies forced the Germans at last to allow food to be flown in to relieve starvation. On April 29, 1945, R.A.F. Lancasters dropped over 600 tons, including meat, vegetables, flour, tea and salt. For about a fortnight, these ' food drops ' by the R.A.F. and the U.S.A.A.F. continued. Here, food enough to feed 3,280 people for one day is being loaded into the bomb-bay of a Lancaster. *Photo, Keystone*

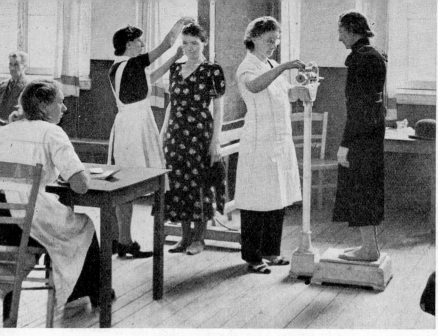
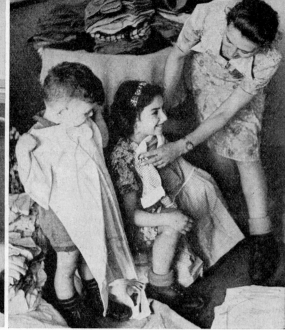

IN HOLLAND AFTER THE LIBERATION

In a Red Cross clinic in Amsterdam, victims of German starvation able to walk are classified for medical treatment to restore them to health. Right, a Dutch mother and her children rescued from the Belsen horror-camp try on new clothes supplied by the British Red Cross. Below, Netherlanders greet Canadian troops who had brought food-supplies by road to the ruined city of Rotterdam.
Photos British Official ; Planet News

dropping great quantities of food a few days before the surrender of the Germans (*see* page 3552), when food supplies in Holland were completely exhausted. Everyone who witnessed the appearance of the planes and the descent of the supplies was overwhelmed with emotion. One of the reasons which made it possible for the people of the Netherlands to hold out under conditions no longer human was the fact that there was a strong and, during the last three years, well organized resistance movement, which had good communications with the Netherlands Government in London. The existence of this resistance movement made itself known in every part of the occupied country through acts of sabotage, and the burning down of the central registries. In some places the resisters guarded ports and installations which had to be kept in order for the day of liberation ; elsewhere they did just the contrary, blowing up dumps and installations used by the enemy. The loss of life amongst this resistance movement was very great, because it was difficult in so densely populated a country to keep the secret communications really secret. One of the surviving leaders estimated the loss of life to have been at least 17,000.

Apart from the resistance movement proper, there were other agencies which kept the spirit of the people alive, amongst them the action taken by the medical profession, which was remarkable. With **Stand Made by Doctors** few exceptions all the medical men took the same line and never gave in to any German threat, even during the most dangerous months. For example, in the second half of January 1945 they sent a flaming protest to the German authorities against the cruelty of the deportations. After having drawn attention to the steady increase in disease, they went on as follows : " More cruel than all this is the ever growing and increasingly gruesome practice of deportation, and forcing of the Dutch male population to work in the German war machine. This compulsion is, in itself, a crime against the first rules of humanity and international law, but the cruelty with which these measures are being carried out represents nothing less than a picture of sadistic vengeance against defenceless men. The men, including cases of obvious disease and ill-health, are hunted out and thrown into camps. Hounded along the roads until exhausted, herded together nearly dead in barracks, trucks, and holds of ships ; completely without food, medical attention or the barest necessities of life, these unhappy people are the prey of disease and misery. We can confirm these accusations with the evidence of eye-witnesses." Then follow some examples of the death-transports from Rotterdam, witnessed during the short halt in Zwolle and Haarlem, where attempts by onlookers to succour the victims were deliberately prevented by the Germans. The description affords a picture that defies all imagination.

Another phenomenon during the first months of 1945, never to be forgotten by the Dutch people, was the endless stream of half-starved men, women and children leaving their families in the cities of Amsterdam, Rotterdam and The Hague in order to try to find food, first in the surrounding country, and later tramping anything up to a hundred miles to the east and to the north. Many of these died on the way, some succeeded in bringing relief to their loved ones, and others, even at the last moment, were robbed by the Germans of their booty collected under the greatest dangers and hardships by long marches in the bitter winter cold, with little or no footgear.

Search for Food

It is the more surprising that the Dutch population held firm because, at

NAZIS' LOOT IN HOLLAND RECOVERED

Among the personal baggage of the Wehrmacht trapped in the Netherlands was much portable booty with which they had hoped to escape to the Reich. After the surrender in May 1945, British and Canadian troops disarming them at Den Helder found among their baggage, as shown above, typewriters, clocks, cameras, beer-mugs and bottles of wine. These goods were returned to their owners when these could be traced.   *Photo, Planet News*

the same time, the Germans had begun the destruction of the country. The greater part of the port of Amsterdam had been demolished. The port of Rotterdam had been severely damaged, and

another part of the town had been mined. Immense areas of the soil had been deliberately inundated, half by sea water. At the same time, large areas became flooded owing to the stoppage of pumps through lack of electricity. Intentional inundation covered over ten per cent of the arable land, including the island of Walcheren where the Allied forces had to break the dyke (*see*

VICTORY PARADE EPISODE AT UTRECHT

Armoured cars of the British 49th (West Riding) Division entered Utrecht on May 7, 1945. Below, as the troops passed by in a victory parade through the streets of the virtually undamaged city, shots were fired by concealed Nazi sympathizers. After a sharp skirmish, Dutch patriots captured the Nazis and the celebrations were resumed.   *Photo, Planet News*

Chap. 332). The flooded areas were among the most fertile in the Netherlands.

Although, once the Germans had been ejected, the soil thus lost could be reclaimed far more quickly than twenty years earlier, nevertheless in the most

Gigantic Task of Restoration

seriously affected part it was bound to take many years to get the land back into good condition. Even as late as the last days of April 1945, the Germans intentionally flooded the Wieringermeer, a polder reclaimed from the Zuider Zee twelve years before the outbreak of the war, and already covered with beautiful farms and villages. In some parts the soil is twenty feet below sea-level, so that even the farmhouses were completely covered with water. Fortunately the percentage of salt in the water of the former Zuider Zee was low; nevertheless all the houses had to be rebuilt. By August 1945 the dyke of this polder had been restored, and the rebuilding of the farmhouses and villages started before the end of 1945, but only years of effort would restore conditions to what they were before the inundations.

Destruction of the soil went hand in hand with plunder of the factories. I saw many factories where nothing was left except bare walls; not only the machinery had been taken away, but in many places the entire equipment, complete with foundations. In consequence of this, one of the difficulties the new

Dutch Government had to face was the fact that those industrialists who had refused to collaborate with the Germans could not start production because they had no tools and no machines. On the other hand, the factories (fortunately the smaller proportion) whose owners had collaborated, could offer new production which the country and the Government so urgently needed. In general the solution was found by removing the collaborators; but this solution had the disadvantage that other experts were not always available.

When I reflect upon my poor country and see the results of the four horrible months of 1945 before the liberation, a depressing picture confronts me. More than 200,000 of the deported population never returned, amongst them 105,000 Jewish Dutchmen; 25,000 died from hunger, apart from the innumerable men and women who would have recovered from their illnesses if they had had sufficient food.

The casualties of the regular armed forces during the five days of the struggle in 1940 were relatively small, amounting to about 4,000; but more than 17,000 civilians, apart from Resistance losses, were killed by the enemy during the time of the occupation. The losses of merchant seamen were between 3,000 and 4,000. We do not yet (in the spring of 1946) know our losses in the Pacific war, but, including civilians, they are certainly more than 100,000.

NETHERLANDS PREMIER

Dr. P. S. Gerbrandy, Premier of the exiled Netherlands Government from September 1940 until its return after the liberation, visited Zeeland Flanders in November 1944 while heavy fighting was still going on. Author of the accompanying chapter, he is here (centre) inspecting damage at Breskens, accompanied by officials and townspeople.

Photo, Pictorial Press

IN RUINED ARNHEM AFTER ITS LIBERATION

On April 14, 1945, troops of the British 49th (West Riding) Division, fighting under Canadian command, finally cleared the town of Arnhem, scene, seven months previously, of the famous stand of the British 6th Airborne Division (see Chapter 325). Below, a corner of the town after its liberation. There was little left intact, and the tasks of reconstruction were formidable. *Photo, Pictorial Press*

Nearly all the bridges, among them the mile-long railway and foot bridges at Moerdijk (the vital link between the north and south of the country—*see* map in page 3298)

Destruction of Homes and Bridges

were destroyed. The destruction of houses surpassed that in any other country in Europe, and about three million people, nearly a third of the population, lost their homes. In the southern part, many little towns of south-western Zeeland were completely wiped out as a result of the fighting there in the autumn of 1944. In the south-east, towns like Venlo and Roermond were partly destroyed. The city of Nijmegen lost its beautiful centre. In the city of Arnhem, which had more than 100,000 inhabitants, every house was either completely demolished, or so severely damaged that little but the walls remained standing. For months in 1945 Arnhem was completely uninhabited. (For military activities in southern Holland, *see* Chapters 325, 332 and 349.) In The Hague, the Germans broke down different parts of the town in the preparation of their so-called defences, whilst another section of the town was sacrificed through the attacks of the R.A.F. against the V1 and V2 launching sites. A drive from Arnhem to the west would take the traveller through one long line of demolished towns and villages.

Shortly after May 5, 1945, the day of liberation, I was able to visit the north-western part of the Netherlands. First of all, my own beloved Amsterdam.

Rejoicing in Amsterdam Certainly the peopl had had consolation during the last days prior to the liberation from the splendid organization which sent relief by air, and trucks laden with food and medicine were already coming in. Those who arranged these relief measures, wherein the greatest difficulties of organization and transport had to be overcome, and the preparation of which I still remember with the greatest admiration, thought only of the fact that every day 5,000 tons of food and coal had to be brought in over severely damaged roads to a starving population.

The condition of the people was so heartrendingly bad that I expected very little enthusiasm. But their mood was high-spirited : "We are free from German terror" was the predominant feeling verywhere.

When I entered Amsterdam and talked to the people surrounding my

IN FLOODED HOLLAND

Worst destruction wrought by the Germans in the Netherlands was the deliberate flooding of vast areas, including the most fertile acres in the country. As much as ten per cent of the arable land was inundated. Here is what remained of the centre of Middenmeer after the floods had subsided, leaving no house habitable Below, Wieringerwerf, where the waters rose twenty feet. Both villages had been built on land reclaimed from the Zuider Zee twelve years before the Second Great War

car, there remained in my mind this impression—"I have never seen a people of such vitality." Tens of thousands gathered on the famous Dam of Amsterdam where they were to be addressed by the Burgomaster and the Allied Generals, and where I had to speak a few words. There you saw the crowds, physically in the most desperate condition, but nevertheless rejoicing, not in the fact that they had got help and food, but that they were free again, that the detestable foe was going for ever, and that they could start the rebuilding of their country.

Immediately after the liberation, in accordance with the promise previously given (*see* page 3214), the Cabinet, on its return to the Netherlands, offered its resignation to Queen Wilhelmina who was at the time residing in a village near Breda in the south of the country. Some time elapsed before the Queen could get in touch with people who could advise her among those who had undergone the occupation, and who had gained the full confidence of the whole nation. It was among them that the Queen (in accordance with the constant pledge given by the resigning Cabinet)

QUEEN WILHELMINA REOPENS THE STATES-GENERAL

For the first time since the German occupation, Queen Wilhelmina of the Netherlands on November 20, 1945, opened the States-General. The ceremony was held, according to custom, in the magnificent Hall of the Knights in the Binnenhof at The Hague. Here Her Majesty, accompanied by Princess Juliana and Prince Bernhard, reads the speech from the throne : one of her principal topics was the future of the Netherlands Indies. *Photo, Pictorial Press*

was to find the person to form the new Cabinet. It was not easy to find a suitable person at once, for political life showed the marks of the occupation. Except for two parties, the former political parties were inactive, at least during the early days of the liberation. There was a movement towards greater unity, and it seemed appropriate to make use of that phenomenon. New forces had come to the front. It was not even certain that the old political parties would reappear in their former structure. For example, there had come into life a movement called " The Netherlands People's Movement " which included members of most former political parties.

One of its leaders, Professor Schermerhorn, a very able man, respected by everybody, and Mr. Drees, one of the prominent men of the Social Democratic Party, were finally charged with the formation of a new government. On June 23, Mr. Schermerhorn and Mr. Drees named their proposed Cabinet to the Queen. It comprised fourteen Ministers, of whom six belonged to the Netherlands People's Movement, others to the different old political parties. Three members of the London Cabinet received portfolios in the new Govern-

New Cabinet Formed

ment, amongst them Mr. van Kleffens, who was reappointed Foreign Minister.

This new Cabinet had to face the most difficult tasks, politically as well as economically. There was no Parliament. Elections were quite impossible because patriots had destroyed the central registries in many towns (to make the Germans' task of government more difficult), and because the population had been scattered all over the country. When it is realized that many hundreds of people belonging to a little town like Dokkum in the north of Friesland, had been in hiding, and that elsewhere small villages were crowded with refugees from all parts of the Netherlands, that evacuation of the inundated areas had spread the population not only over the Netherlands, but also into Belgium and France, it will be understood that General Elections had to wait.

The Government formed an emergency Parliament consisting, for the greater part, of members of the old Parliament (after a purge of collaborators), with a few new members nominated by an organization formed from the political and resistance movements. Until the meeting of this new Parliament, the Government had to continue the London system of ruling by Royal Decree. This system had the disadvantage that the Government could not easily gauge the

spirit of the people, but had the practical advantage that the first measures of reconstruction were not slowed down by debates in Parliament.

The task of reconstruction was a double one. The Government had to put into practice the measures already prepared by the Cabinet in London. It also had to pay immediate attention to economic reconstruction. Of course, in a country where the people had suffered so immeasurably from German terror and plunder, the tasks for the

POST-WAR PREMIER

Successor to Dr. Gerbrandy (see illus. in page 3678) as Premier was Professor Willem Schermerhorn whose Cabinet was announced on June 23, 1945. Aged 51, he was a scientist and leader of the ' Volksbeweging ' (People's Movement) resistance organization during the occupation. The Germans held him as a hostage for some time.

HOLLAND RISES AGAIN

1. The Moerdijk bridge, nearly a mile long, across the Hollandsche Diep, cut by the Germans in 1944, was re-opened late in 1945. A 133-ft. long span from London's former temporary Waterloo bridge was used in the reconstruction. 2. A span of the new bridge at Oosterbeek, near Arnhem (see map in page 3304), also taken from Waterloo bridge. The longest of the Waterloo spans (280 feet) was used for the road-and-rail bridge over the Oude Maas at Dordrecht. 3. Dutch workmen plan a time-table for the use of their only hammer. 4. 'Home' of a family in the Betuwe near Arnhem. 5. The main square of Middelburg, capital of Walcheren,

Government were innumerable, but these two were pre-eminent.

Five special courts to try traitors and collaborators, in accordance with the rules made in London, were set up, in Amsterdam, The Hague, Utrecht, **Dutch Nazis Sentenced** s'Hertogenbosch and Leeuwarden, and each Chamber of the Court consisted of one President, two military members, and two civilian jurists. Many traitors, during the last months of 1945, were sentenced to death, amongst them Mussert and Van Genechten, two of the most detested leaders of the Dutch Nazi Movement. The condemned had only one form of appeal, *i.e.* to the Special Court of Cassation, and when sentenced, they could be deprived of the right to this form of appeal if the Court so decreed.

Tribunals to deal with minor trespassings, infringements of rights, and especially to advise about confiscation, internment, or deprivation of rights, were also set up all over the country; but they worked slowly.

Another application of the measures prepared in London was the restoration of legal rights to those dispossessed by the occupying authorities. Thousands had been robbed of their houses, their factories, their shares and their positions in the limited companies through the insidious German economic system of transferring the wealth of Dutchmen to Germany. But some restoration was possible, by returning to its former owners property found in German hands. Special legislation to this end, formulated by the London Government, amended and improved by the new Government, was put into practice, as well as a form of indemnification of those whose properties were completely lost.

Two of the most important economic measures were (1) the creation of a new stable currency, with complete replacement of the old paper notes by new bank notes, under the immediate control of the Minister of Finance, and with the collaboration of the banks all over the country; (2) the tackling of the problem of rebuilding the houses, bridges, roads, railways and factories, a process that under State control went on steadily into 1946. It is quite impossible to describe all the tasks which the new Government had to fulfil, but some others were the reorganization of the police, the building up of a new army (started already by the exiled Cabinet, but pressed forward by the development of happenings in the Pacific, after the breakdown of Japan and the emergence of nationalist movements in Java and elsewhere), and the repatriation of the enslaved Dutch workers, which at first met with great obstacles, but was, by the end of December 1945, already nearly achieved.

Generally speaking, economic reconstruction went on satisfactorily. As one example of quick reconstruction, I mention that by the end of the year the bridge over the Moerdijk had been rebuilt and put into use. Others could be given from other parts of the country. Able Ministers were trying to effect the recovery of the Netherlands, the first period of indolence of the population was over, and everywhere there was hope that the process would continue satisfactorily. There were, of course, complaints to be heard in some critical

DEFEATED NAZIS LEAVE THE NETHERLANDS

When the final collapse came German troops in Holland numbered 110,000. Disbandment under British and Canadian supervision began on May 9, 1945, when many Nazis were obliged to walk all the way to the Fatherland, so heavy were priority demands on transport, so badly disrupted were communications. Below, disbanded Germans embark in British L.C.T.s at Helden, near Amsterdam, for transport to Harlingen, in Friesland, and so home to the Reich.

circles—one was that the new Cabinet did not sufficiently exercise its authority when preparing and putting into practice its measures. Here lay one of the most vulnerable spots in the political and spiritual condition of the Netherlands.

What the people expected was a quick revival of all the old institutions, so cruelly trampled down by the Germans. They assumed that traitors and collaborators would be summarily dealt with, the press would be brought to life again, the voice of local representatives and of Parliament would be heard clearly, and so on. But to achieve all these things, men and means were needed. In a country so unscrupulously robbed of its élite and so thoroughly plundered, men and means proved inadequate to produce a quick solution of the problems confronting the country. People and Government toiled long to overcome obstacles.

There was insufficient paper to print anything like pre-war newspapers ; the conditions of transport and communications very often did not allow even important officials to fulfil their duties. The administration of public affairs was in many departments in such a state that much-needed information could not be made available to Parliament ; even as late as August 1945

it was barely possible to telephone from The Hague to Middelburg. The Resistance Movement asked for a rigid purge, but the fact that some tens of thousands had to be detained pending trial and after created the problem of providing prisons and camps.

At the end of 1945 there was a feeling that conditions were not as gratifying as the day of liberation had promised. Over the budgetary position of the public finances, notwithstanding the excellent measures taken by the Minister of Finance, hung the threatening shadow of expenditure three or four times as great as had been allowed for.

Recovering loot from Germany, where in one farm could be found thousands of sheets and blankets, many pianos, hundreds of radio sets, accumulations of food and other valuable commodities all stolen from the Dutch, seemed a good idea. But theory and practice differed somewhat. And to all the difficulties at home was suddenly added the emergence of a situation in the

Far East which was also complicated by lack of men and means.

Nevertheless, the reconstruction achieved by the end of 1945 could be regarded with satisfaction, and political life anticipated a considerable strengthening from the general elections held, as the Government had promised, in May 1946. That the people had not lost their old desire to share in the political and spiritual interests of the country and the world was shown by the fact that papers started underground during the occupation, and published openly after liberation, were very widely read. The anti-revolutionary paper " Trouw " (Faith) had nearly half a million subscribers ; " Het Parool" (Watchword) about 400,000, figures never attained by any paper before the war. Among the people was an insistent desire for literature of every kind.

It was, of course, inevitable that much time should elapse before the

Rebirth of Political Life

HOLLAND'S QUEEN PAYS TRIBUTE TO THE DEAD

Queen Wilhelmina of the Netherlands returned to her country on May 3, 1945—three days before the Germans there surrendered. Early in March she had paid her first visit since the occupation when she made a nine-days' tour of liberated areas. She is seen watching Princess Juliana and Prince Bernhard lay a wreath at the reburial ceremony (in November), near Haarlem, of the bodies, found in the nearby sand-dunes, of 400 murdered Dutch patriots.

Photo, Planet News

threads of normal life in the Netherlands could be picked up once more. At the turn of the year life in Holland still wore a strange complexion. The Queen was still living, not in her palace at The Hague, but in an ordinary house. During the winter of 1945-46 people received only ten per cent of the fuel they needed. The public crowded into the open cars of the few available trams on the coldest winter days even in The Hague, which is the very fountain head of the administration and the Government.

Mountainous difficulties had still to be overcome in the field of foreign

HOLLAND'S QUISLING SENTENCED TO DEATH

Anton Mussert, leader of the Dutch National Socialist Party, was arrested by Canadian troops in Utrecht on May 7, 1945 and executed exactly a year later. He is seen (above) during his trial, which began in November before the Supreme Court in The Hague. Queen Wilhelmina refused his request for pardon, and the death-penalty—reintroduced in Holland for the punishment of traitors—was inflicted. *Photo, Keystone*

COAL FAMINE

In the winter preceding the liberation of Holland, one of the scarcest necessities was coal. Official ration for the whole winter was less than half-a-ton per family. These Netherlanders are salvaging water-logged coal from sunken colliers brought up in the course of dredging operations in the North Sea-Amsterdam canal.

trade, and of the acquisition of much-needed raw materials.

A gigantic task lay before the Dutch. But they had regained the freedom they love so much; in the months between June and November 1945 their apparent inertia disappeared. The Queen, descendant of the House of Orange, was the symbol of national unity, as her reception by the population of Amsterdam in July 1945 showed. The way might be long, but the Netherlands was on her feet again.

A HERO'S GRAVE IN THE NETHERLANDS

On the battlefields of the Netherlands—scene of some of the bitterest fighting of the war—lie buried where they fell thousands of British and Canadian soldiers. In many places the inhabitants undertook to tend the graves in perpetuity in memory of the men who gave their lives to free Holland. Here a Netherlands woman lays flowers on a British soldier's grave near Arnhem.

Chapter 359

TRANSITION TO PEACE IN FRANCE

General de Gaulle's Provisional Government, re-established in Paris in August 1944 (see Chapter 335), sought to lead France to political and economic recovery. The elections of October 1945, however, gave three parties an almost equal number of seats in the Constituent Assembly, and the difficulties arising from tripartite government led to General de Gaulle's resignation early in 1946. Mr. Georges Gombault here tells the history of this unsettled period

DURING the first part of 1945, the Provisional Government exercised both legislative and executive powers. The Consultative Assembly (*see* pages 2915 and 3412) discussed the general lines of the Budget, debated foreign policy, called Ministers to account and voted against them. But no notice was taken of its remonstrances; the Government did not regard itself as bound to follow the Assembly's advice.

An opposition began to form in the Consultative Assembly. The purge was regarded as insufficient. The food shortage, a main cause of popular discontent, led to the fall of one Minister of Food after another.

The criticism extended to the whole direction of economic affairs. Economic and financial policy was naturally among the main preoccupations of the Government. Since the return from Algeria to France, two opposing views had been advocated. Mr. Mendès-France, Minister of National Economy, advocated a policy of great firmness, of which stabilization of prices and wages formed an essential part; Mr. Pleven, Minister of Finance, favoured a less drastic cure. General de Gaulle decided in favour of the second method, and the Government supported him. Mr. Mendès-France resigned. But he was justified in the event, for his plan was revived in 1946 by the Gouin Ministry.

Opposition in the Assembly

The municipal elections in towns and communes ended the existence of the local Liberation committees (*see* page 3409). These elections took place on April 23: the French had not gone to the polls since 1937. The elections had not a marked political character. In many communes the lists had been made up of resisters belonging to all parties. One conclusion did, however, emerge from these elections, that the country was strongly attached to the democratic Republic.

The cantonal elections for the Conseils Généraux (virtually county councils) took place on September 23, and were more markedly political. The parties faced each other in each canton. The results foreshadowed those of the elections for the Constituent Assembly: the parties of the extreme Left had great success; the Popular Republican Movement (M.R.P.) won some seats, the Radicals lost some; the Right was overwhelmed.

As a result of these two elections, the parties began to pull themselves together. The Socialist and Communist parties, which had come to life again in the underground movement, sought to re-establish their pre-war organizations. The Radical party, which had never had a very solid structure, tried to strengthen its ranks. The moderates remained dispersed as before. The M.R.P. (*see* page 3410) endeavoured, with the support of the Church, to form the Catholics into a group and to steer them towards social democracy. The unrepentant Right, which had been Pétain's main support, did not dare to make any move as yet.

A purge of the leaders followed in all parties. It was particularly rigorous among the Socialists, who excluded from their ranks the deputies and senators (unfortunately numerous) who had voted for Pétain in the National Assembly of July 10, 1940, at Vichy: the former general secretary of the party, Mr. Paul Faure, was the first to be expelled. The procedure among the Radicals was less strict, but men like Mr. Camille Chautemps, vice-president (i.e. deputy speaker) in the Pétain Ministry, and Mr. Georges Bonnet were struck off the membership of the party. The task of the Communists was simpler, because those of their leaders and their most active members who had not fled abroad were in prison in July 1940: Mr. Daladier had had them arrested after the conclusion of the Russo-German pact of August 1939. The moderate parties confined themselves to bringing to the fore those of their members who had taken part in the Resistance.

Purge of Political Leaders

In the course of 1945, the members of the Resistance rejoined their respective political families, bringing to

THE END OF HITLER'S 'ATLANTIC WALL'

Demolishing the 'Atlantic Wall' (see illus. in page 2905)—which Hitler had boasted was impregnable—occupied French workmen in the early months of 1945. It had been constructed by the Todt Organization largely with forced labour, and covered long stretches of the French and Belgian seaboard. Below, workmen break up a section of the defences in a French coastal town. *Photo, Planet News*

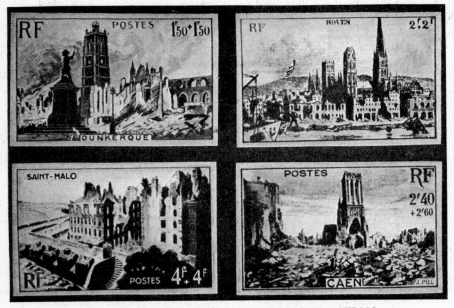

STAMPS RAISE FUNDS FOR RECONSTRUCTION

To assist in the raising of funds for the rebuilding of Breton and Norman towns badly damaged in the war, special postage stamps were issued early in 1945. They depicted the towns as the Germans had left them. Those reproduced above show Dunkirk, Rouen, St. Malo, and Caen. A fifth was of Oradour-sur-Glane (see page 3403) which is to remain in ruins as a memorial to German ruthlessness.   *Photo, French Official*

them, however, a new spirit. An assembly calling itself the States-General of the French Renaissance met in Paris on July 10–11 to reaffirm this programme. That assembly was the last political demonstration by the Resistance.

After the municipal elections in the spring, public opinion expected a change in the composition of the Government.

Ministerial Changes There was a rumour that Mr. Edouard Herriot and Mr. Léon Blum, who had just returned from captivity, would be appointed Ministers of State, together with one of the moderates, Mr. Louis Marin, who had gone to London in 1944. The offer was in fact made to Herriot and Blum, but both declined to take office. General de Gaulle then considered a thorough ministerial reshuffle, but in the end very little change was effected—the Minister of Food resigned and two others were moved to different offices.

Public opinion was disappointed. In its political fanaticism, Vichy had deprived the administration of its best servants, and the new administration was unequal to its task, some of the elements that had replaced the collaborators proving insufficiently experienced. Finally, the nation was ill-satisfied with the methods of the Government: there were complaints that the Government was exercising uncontrolled power and at the same

time that it was not showing enough firmness in the management of public affairs. This state of opinion found expression in the elections for the Conseils-Généraux of September 23, in which Socialists and Communists repeated their success at the municipal elections. The September elections marked the appearance of popular

democratic candidates of the M.R.P. which strengthened its position in the subsequent legislative elections.

There was much in common between these democrats of the M.R.P. and the Socialist Party; but they were divided on a question of supreme importance in France, that of secular education. The M.R.P., reviving the old demands of the Catholics in education, claimed government grants for Catholic schools. The Socialists held to Republican doctrine and practice: all children, whatever their parents' creed, if any, can attend the government schools, which are neutral: it is for the groups that open "free" schools to support them. The issue came before the Consultative Assembly. The question was whether the grants made to Catholic schools by Vichy should be continued. It was decided by 128 votes to 48 to suppress them. The majority was formed by the Radicals, Socialists, and Communists; the minority by the Right wing and the M.R.P.

Catholic School Grants Suppressed

The question of the future institutions of France, widely discussed both in the press and in the Consultative Assembly, had to be decided. Should there be a restoration of the Constitution of 1875, which had in fact been suppressed only by Vichy; or should an entirely new Constitution be worked out? The Radicals favoured the first solution; the Resistance, the Socialists, and the

NEW BANKNOTES FOR OLD IN PARIS

In an attempt to check the widespread activities of the black market, the French Provisional Government in June 1945 ordered the compulsory changing of old banknotes for new. Here in the French capital a crowd of Parisians line up outside the branch of a famous bank to exchange their old notes for those of the new issue.   *Photo, Keystone*

RECONSTRUCTION IN FRANCE

The Minister of Reconstruction in the French Provisional Government estimated in August 1945 that the rebuilding of France would take fifteen years. Rebuilding was then going forward all over the country. 1. Temporary bridge at Nantes. Spanning the Loire, it is some 650 yards long. The old bridge, the 'Pont de la Vendée,' blown up after the Normandy landings, was one of France's 2,300 railway bridges and viaducts destroyed in the war. 2. French labourers, still wearing uniform, settle down to farm what a few months previously had been a Norman battlefield. 3. Workmen on reconstruction in St. Malo. Stones of the older buildings were numbered in an effort to reconstruct the town as it was before the war. 4. Devastated Le Havre: German prisoners are clearing away the rubble.

Photos, New York Times Photos ; Keystone ; Associated Press

DANGER MINES

Communists the second. The Consultative Assembly pronounced in favour of a fully sovereign Constituent Assembly, to be elected by proportional representation; it opposed the submission of the question to a referendum.

The Provisional Government, however, was against a single Assembly with full sovereignty—it felt that the **Decision to Hold Referendum** Assembly's powers should be limited; and it decided on a referendum, to be held on the same day as the general elections, on the two questions (1) Do you wish the Assembly to be a Constituent one? (2) Do you agree that the powers exercised by this Assembly—until the coming into force of the new Constitution—should be those laid down in the proposed law [the text of which was given on the back of the referendum form]?

The Socialists, the M.R.P., the Right wing, and in general all followers of General de Gaulle, recommended the answer "Yes" in both cases; the Communists, who wanted a single sovereign Assembly, recommended "Yes" and "No"; the Radicals advocated the answer "No" to both questions (which would have meant that the body elected would have become a new Chamber of Deputies, the election of a Senate would have followed, and the two bodies sitting together as a National Assembly would have drafted a Constitution).

THEY WERE FORCED TO FIGHT FOR HITLER
When the provinces of Alsace-Lorraine were reincorporated into the Reich on December 1, 1940, after the defeat of France, men eligible for military service were henceforth compulsorily drafted into the Wehrmacht. Among them were these troops who were taken prisoner by the Russians and later sent back to France. They are at the Gare du Nord, Paris, in October 1945, on their homeward journey, still wearing German uniforms. *Photo, Keystone*

The election campaign was lively but not disorderly. The country voted on October 21. It replied to the two questions of the referendum in the way General de Gaulle had advocated: there were more than 15,656,283 votes for a Constituent Assembly, 596,743 against; 10,847,925 votes for relative limitation of the powers of the single Assembly, 5,381,106 against.

On the same day the Deputies were elected—522 in France and 64 in the Colonies. The Socialists obtained 139 seats, the Communists 150, and the M.R.P. 149. The remainder of **New Assembly Meets** the seats went to the Radicals (who suffered a crushing defeat, securing only 25 seats), and smaller groups. The new Assembly met on November 3. Its first task was to designate the head of the Government, General de Gaulle having placed his resignation before it. He was elected unanimously. But he met with difficulties in forming his Cabinet and resigned.

The Constituent Assembly had to choose a new head of the Government. It nominated General de Gaulle again, but this time not unanimously. A long debate followed, at the end of which the Assembly pronounced for a Ministry in which the three big parties should be equally represented.

General de Gaulle then formed his Ministry as follows: five Socialists, five Communists, five members of the M.R.P., and six "experts": this term referred to persons chosen by General de Gaulle and particularly attached to him. A novelty was the appointment of

FRENCH FREE THE PORT OF BORDEAUX
Although the town of Bordeaux was liberated by the F.F.I. on August 31, 1944, it remained useless as a port, since the Germans still held the Gironde estuary. Not till April 1945 did General Leclerc attack the enemy garrison there, overcoming the last German resistance, and reopening the port to shipping on April 19. These wrecked enemy supply ships (below) cluttered the harbour. *Photo, Evening Standard*

Mr. Maurice Thorez, leader of the Communist party, as Minister of State, and the appointment of another Communist to the Ministry of Armaments. During the first phase of the crisis, General de Gaulle had excluded the members of that party, but he accepted them under pressure from the Assembly; he also agreed to confide to them a share in the Ministry of National Defence, which at first he had refused to do. Mr. Thorez, who had been condemned in his absence in 1939 by a military tribunal, was pardoned.

General de Gaulle attended the Constituent Assembly, and obtained a unanimous vote of confidence. The first measure he submitted for adoption was the nationalization of credit: four big deposit banks were nationalized. The commercial banks were, however, simply made subject to control, to the disappointment of both the Socialists and Communists.

Public discontent led to acrimonious debates, notably on the claims of civil servants, who demanded a cost-of-living increase; the Minister of Finance pointed to the situation of the country and agreed only to a partial satisfaction of their demand. A threatened strike of civil servants was averted; their demands continued.

The situation grew more uneasy as the discussion of the Budget proceeded.

DAMAGE IN ROUEN

When the 1st Canadian Army took Rouen on August 30, 1944, they found it extensively damaged both by enemy demolitions and previous Allied bombings (see illus. in page 3199). As the Germans escaped across the Seine, they blew up the Palais de Justice, the telephone exchange and the railway station. Here is a shattered corner of the famous cathedral, heavily bombed in air raids and found to be partly gutted.
Photo, French Official

The German occupation, involving a charge of 400 million francs a day for the maintenance of the army of occupation, and the Vichy regime had ruined French finances. The Budget totalled 400 milliards of francs, and the deficit was estimated at more than 200 milliards. The Constituent Assembly was urged by the Government to act swiftly and the Budget was pushed through with such rapidity that neither the Finance Committee nor the Assembly was able to exercise the rigorous control which is incumbent on a Parliament, and which the situation demanded.

Budget Discussions

Military expenditure was a heavy burden—it approached 200 milliards. On January 1, 1946, the Socialists demanded that it should be cut by 20 per cent. General de Gaulle would agree only to a five per cent cut, apart from possible economies resulting from the bill for the reorganization of the army. The Socialists held to their point of view all the more strongly since there was public indignation at certain abuses due to the lack of parliamentary control. In the end a compromise was effected: the 20 per cent cut was to come into force automatically on February 15 if the bill for

FRANCE HONOURS VICTIMS OF NAZIDOM

It was estimated that the victims of German reprisals in France alone left almost 140,000 orphans. Here is an open-air service held in Paris in July 1945 to the memory of victims of Nazi brutality. The huge wooden cross—to be erected as a memorial—was carried by patriots freed from concentration camps, some of them wearing the striped prison uniform. *Photo, Planet News*

INVASION DAY REMEMBERED ON NORMANDY BEACHES

To mark the first anniversary of the invasion of western Europe, religious ceremonies and military parades were held on June 6, 1945, on the Normandy beaches where the first assault waves came in. At Arromanches (above) a religious service was attended by the British and United States ambassadors to France and by French Cabinet Ministers. Remains of 'Mulberry B' harbour can be seen on the horizon.

Photo, British Newspaper Pool

military reorganization effecting this saving was not introduced by that date. The Left was unwilling either to give way or to provoke a crisis.

This debate led to a hot political controversy between the representatives of the Socialist Party, particularly Mr. André Philip, and General de Gaulle. Mr. Philip claimed that government should be through the Assembly: the Prime Minister, once he had been appointed, must carry out the decisions of Parliament. General de Gaulle contended that the head of the Government should not be a mere instrument of the Assembly but should enjoy real authority. He hinted at resignation: "This, no doubt," he said, "is the last time I shall speak in this place."

This sitting of January 1 was perhaps the most important of the session. The latent disagreement between the parties of the Left **Party** and General de **Disagreements** Gaulle came plainly into view. The head of the Government was left with only one faithful supporter, the Popular Republican Movement; and this group of 150 members was insufficient to assure the existence of the Ministry.

After this Parliamentary encounter,

General de Gaulle went to the south of France, to Cap d'Antibes, for a few days' rest. The Assembly met again on January 15. It held a discussion on foreign policy, in the course of which there was in particular a demand for the breaking off of relations with Franco. General de Gaulle appeared in the Assembly only once during this two-day debate: he intervened simply to reply to Mr. Herriot, who attacked him with some severity; he seemed indifferent to the outcome of the debate.

This quasi-abstention was the more striking since, as was well known, General de Gaulle was interested above all in foreign policy. It was explained when on January 21 he sent to the President of the Consultative Assembly his letter of resignation as head of the Provisional Government of the Republic: "In agreeing," he wrote, "to remain at the head of the Government after November 13, 1945, my purpose was to respond to the unanimous appeal which the National Constituent Assembly had addressed to me and to see through the necessary transition. This transition has today been accomplished."

Public opinion accepted General de Gaulle's retirement calmly, but his

optimism seemed a contradiction of the real situation of the country, which was still suffering cruel privations. The "Monde" wrote of a "premature departure," but considered that it was impossible for General de Gaulle to "remain at a post in which his role of arbiter was vain."

Both people in general and political circles wondered as to the reasons that had determined General de Gaulle to retire and whether he had departed without any intention of returning.

General de Gaulle Retires

The general opinion was that he had abandoned power because, with his authoritarian nature, he despaired of carrying into effect his conception of government. Was he ready to return? If, declared certain newspapers, circumstances should one day require it, he would respond to the country's appeal, but outside the parties. The General himself, in his retreat at Marly-le-Roi, refrained from any declaration. He spent his time writing his memoirs, reading, taking walks, and talking with a few friends.

By 497 votes out of 552, the Assembly appointed Mr. Félix Gouin, its President (a position approximating to that of Speaker in the House of Commons), as General de Gaulle's successor. Mr. Gouin, aged 61, a Marseilles lawyer, Socialist deputy for Aix-en-Provence in the pre-war Chamber, voted against Pétain in 1940, and afterwards

SWIMMING TANKS ON THE RHINE

One of the most important British war inventions was the 'D.D.' (Duplex-Drive) amphibious tank (see also page 3666), which took the Germans by surprise during the Normandy landings, and was subsequently used in the Scheldt estuary, during the crossings of the Rhine and Elbe, and in northern Italy. Buoyancy was achieved by a collapsible screen of treated canvas fitted to the hull of the tank which could be raised and inflated (with compressed air stored in bottles —see photograph above), or lowered at will. Erected, the screen completely surrounded the tank above the tracks (as seen on right), enabling it to float. At the touch of a lever the screen collapsed to lie like a skirt about the hull When water-borne, the tank was propelled by screws at the rear driven by the main driving-shaft. A modified form of the Davis Escape Apparatus, as used by submarine crews, was carried in case of accident.

*Photos, British Official;
Associated Press*

REPAIRING WALCHEREN'S BREACHED DYKES

With the aid of British equipment, including spare Mulberry harbour sections (see Chapter 307) towed from England, Dutch engineers in September 1945 began the colossal task of repairing the dykes at Walcheren blasted by the R.A.F. (see page 3374). Gales considerably hampered progress, breaking open again one repaired dyke, at Nolle, west of Flushing. But by October 3, exactly a year from the R.A.F.'s first attack, the first of the gaps had been sealed. One of the most formidable repair tasks was at Rammekens, where the dykes had been breached by 12,000-lb. bombs. Here, Dutch workmen are at work, carrying sandbags and faggots for the foundations of a new dyke.

Photo, G.P.U.

FRANCE HAILS HER NEW ARMY

On June 18, 1945, France celebrated the rebirth of the French Army. On that same date in the dark hours of 1940, General de Gaulle had broadcast from London (see page 990). Inviting all Frenchmen on British soil to rally to the colours, he had declared 'France is not lost. The same methods which have brought about our defeat can quite well one day bring victory.' Five years later, with Europe freed from Nazidom, fifty thousand troops of the new French Army marched in Paris from the Arc de Triomphe to a saluting base in the Place de la Concorde. Here General de Gaulle, accompanied by Generals Catroux, de Larminat and Leyer, the Army Chiefs of Staff, presented decorations An armoured and motorized procession was led by General Leclerc, the liberator of Paris (see page 3244). Above, the march-past outside the Hôtel de Ville. Right, General de Gaulle decorates the colours of the Marines.

Photos, French Official; New York Times Photos

ALLIED ARMIES CROSS RIVER PO

With the fall of Bologna on April 21, 1945 (see illus. in page 3717), the German defence system in the Po Valley was shattered. Three days later both the 5th and 8th Armies crossed the river in pursuit of a demoralized enemy. First British troops across were the Grenadier Guards and New Zealand infantry, both with the 8th Army.

Engineers of V Corps (top), including men of the 8th Indian Division, build a Bailey pontoon bridge over the Po north of Ferrara. This structure—1,370 feet long—was the longest floating military bridge in Europe and was opened three days after the initial crossings. In the background is the wrecked railway bridge. Left, vehicles of the South African 6th Armoured Division cross the river on a pontoon bridge constructed by U.S. Army engineers.

Photos, British and South African Official

organized Socialist resistance in the "unoccupied" zone of France. He was one of Mr. Léon Blum's defenders at the Riom trials (*see* page 2182 and illus. in page 2181). Selected by the Socialist Party as its representative on General de Gaulle's Committee of National Liberation in London, he crossed into Spain, where he was interned for three months, but succeeded in reaching Britain in August 1942. He went to Algiers when the Provisional Government was set up there, was elected president of the Consultative Assembly in May 1944, and confirmed in that post after the Assembly's return to Paris (*see* illus. in page 3412).

Mr. Gouin decided that drastic steps were necessary if the critical financial situation was to be met, and before forming his Cabinet he asked the three strongest parties whether they would accept the rigorous steps he proposed to take. All three parties agreed: the M.R.P. and the Communists made some reservations, but the Socialist party gave its entire adhesion to his plans. Agreement having thus been secured, Mr. Gouin formed a tripartite Government, with Mr. Francisque Gay, of the M.R.P., and Mr. Maurice Thorez, Communist, as vice-premiers.

The Constituent Assembly gave the Government its confidence by 403 votes to 44. It passed a resolution stating that it counted on the Prime Minister "to assure the economic, financial, and moral recovery of the country while respecting Republican institutions and social laws."

France thus entered a new era. After the euphoria of the liberation, after the phase in which it had seemed as if everything was going to be easy, the country renounced illusions and entered the domain of realities.

To turn from political to social and economic life in France in 1945, four of her chief ports were still in enemy hands at the time of the general German surrender. The garrisons of Lorient, St. Nazaire and La Rochelle surrendered on May 9 to U.S. and French forces; Dunkirk on May 11 to the Czechoslovak troops investing it (*see* illus. in page 3214). Dunkirk was found completely, St. Nazaire nearly completely, destroyed. Destruction elsewhere was immense.

Boulogne, which suffered 417 bombings, had half its houses destroyed; only one-tenth of the remainder were fit for habitation. Cherbourg, badly damaged, had had its port facilities restored, for military use, by American engineers; however, the first Liberty ship bringing goods for civilians (out of a flotilla of 50 released by the U.S. Government for French use) docked there on May 17.

Many Breton and Norman towns were heaps of rubble: St. Malo, which ceased to exist during the eight days' bombardment of the German garrison in August 1944 (*see* illus. in page 3183), had been **War Damage to French Towns** cleared a year later, and preparations for rebuilding had begun. The centre of Dinard was destroyed; one-quarter of the buildings in Le Touquet were wrecked; two-thirds of Wimereux were destroyed. At Rouen, 15,000 houses were destroyed. Blois and Tarascon were very seriously damaged. Complete new plans for Rouen

CELEBRATION OF V.E. DAY IN PARIS

The French capital celebrated V.E. Day (May 8, 1945) with enthusiasm. Great crowds marched arm-in-arm down the Champs Elysées singing the 'Marseillaise,' loud-speakers in the Place de l'Opéra broadcast patriotic music. At a thanksgiving service in Nôtre Dame the Lesson was read by Mr. Duff Cooper, the British Ambassador. Below, crowds outside the Opera House listen to General de Gaulle's broadcast announcing the end of the war. *Photo, U.S. Official*

4 c ¹

FRENCH FOOD SHORTAGE

A bad harvest, caused by the exceptional drought, contributed to the grave food shortage in France during the winter of 1945-46. The wheat harvest was only 43,000,000 quintals compared with 65,000,000 for the previous year. The re-introduction of bread rationing (discontinued on November 1, 1945, and imposed again on December 28) led to strikes in Paris and Lille. 1. Canadian Army lorries help food distribution. 2. French Military Transport Service driver sticks transfer of new insignia on a lorry. 3. Queueing for vegetables in Paris. 4. Parisian baker's assistant puts up a 'Don't Waste Bread!' notice. 5. Angry women in Paris demand more food.

TRIAL OF A TRAITOR

Philippe Pétain, 89-year-old ex-Marshal of France and former head of the Vichy collaborationist 'Government,' was brought to trial in Paris on July 23, 1945, on charges of treason. On August 15 he was sentenced to death, the sentence being commuted by General de Gaulle to life imprisonment. Above, Pétain on trial in the Palais de Justice. *Photos, Keystone*

and Abbeville were drawn up during 1945, and reconstruction went forward steadily, if slowly, everywhere. Excessive overcrowding was common in all the badly damaged towns, and in parts of the Norman countryside where every farm had been at least partially wrecked in the fighting. Special stamps at special prices were issued to commemorate some of these losses and to raise funds for rebuilding.

Food and fuel shortage in many parts of the country, but particularly in the towns, and responsible for most

Lack of Food and Fuel

of the popular discontent, was to a considerable extent due to the breakdown of communications, itself the result of Allied bombing, sabotage by the Resistance, demolition by the retreating Germans, and, in certain areas, actual fighting. Some 2,000 miles of railway track, 71 out of 130 major depots, 19 out of 31 repair yards, 115 out of 332 major junctions, 24 out of 40 important marshalling yards, and 2,300 railway bridges and viaducts had been destroyed. France's locomotives had been reduced to 3,000

(from 17,800), passenger coaches to 4,300 (from 29,100), trucks to 26,500 (from 457,000). Paris was for some time cut off from the outside world, and of the 24 bridges round Lyons, 22 were down. Canals and lock-gates had also been damaged, and more than 2,000 road bridges were destroyed.

There were stocks of coal at the pithead, there was ample surplus food in some country districts; but neither food nor coal could be transported. But not all country districts, even, were well supplied with food: the retreating enemy and the fighting destroyed part of the 1944 harvest, and a drought in the summer of 1945 killed all vegetables in south-central France. Moreover, during the occupation, the Germans had deliberately reduced

France's agricultural productive capacity—food grains to 45 per cent of pre-war, milk to 60 per cent, meat 55 per cent, sugar-beet 50 per cent. While food did not flow evenly or adequately to the towns, the country could not procure sufficient fertilizers, fuel, insecticides, manufactured goods.

During the occupation, rations allocated, but not always obtainable, had never exceeded 1,000 to 1,200 calories a day, and for many months after the liberation they were scarcely, if any, better. The death-rate among newborn babies continued to be very high— the mothers were too weak to feed them, and there was little milk available in most areas. Soap, which was so bad that it rotted materials and led to skin diseases, was allotted at the rate of an

DE GAULLE'S SUCCESSOR AS HEAD OF GOVERNMENT

Mr. Félix Gouin, 61-year-old Marseilles lawyer and Socialist deputy, was chosen as head of the French Government by the French Constituent Assembly in January 1946 to succeed General de Gaulle who had resigned. Gouin had been elected President of the Assembly in May 1944 in Algiers. Above, Mr. Gouin, as President, addresses the Assembly in Paris

COUTANCES, important road junction on the western sector of the Normandy front (see page 3180), was captured by U.S. tanks and infantry with powerful artillery support on July 28, 1944. The town was found to be heavily damaged, among the ruins being that of the railway viaduct.

MARIGNY, some six miles west of St. Lô (see page 3180), was taken on July 26, 1944, by U.S. tanks smashing through the German defences to the south of the Périers–St. Lô road. Although captured with little opposition, it suffered extensively in preliminary Allied bombings.

COUTANCES, administrative centre of the Manche 'département,' which fell to the Americans after two armoured spearheads, moving from Périers and Marigny, had joined about a mile from the town, dates from Romano-Celtic times. Though mauled outside, the Gothic cathedral was intact inside.

MONTEBOURG, in the Cherbourg peninsula and some dozen miles from Cherbourg itself (see page 3175), was seized by American forces on June 13, 1944 : and was lost and not recaptured until June 19 after bitter enemy resistance.   Ruins included the 600-year-old church of St. Jacques.

PÉRIERS, important junction between the Sèves and Ay rivers, was taken by U.S. troops on July 27, 1944 (see page 3180), in an action which jeopardized the position of at least seven German divisions in the Cherbourg peninsula.   Its ancient church was among its many ruined buildings.

ST. LÔ was captured by the Americans on July 18, 1944 (see page 3179), after eight days' fierce fighting.   An important road centre, it was completely in ruins, fire-blackened and shell-shattered.   After its capture the Germans continued to shell it from the nearby hills. *Photos, New York Times Photos*

ALLIED NATIONS CONSIDER REPARATIONS

A conference of eighteen of the nations which had been at war with Germany met in Paris on November 9, 1945, to determine the proportionate allocation of German reparations out of the quota not allotted to Russia and Poland at the Potsdam Conference (see Chapter 380) The Conference, which met in the Luxembourg Palace (above), announced on December 21 its decision to establish an Inter-Allied Reparation Agency   *Photo, Keystone*

ounce or two a month. In these circumstances, the black market (i.e. the clandestine sale of rationed goods) continued to flourish : profiteers on a large scale were involved in it, but many little men who cycled into the country to collect food, some for their own use, some to sell, also kept it going.

Direct war damage was estimated at £23,480,000,000 in value—42½ per cent of France's total pre-war assets.

War Damage in France This figure did not include the cost of occupation (£4,279,000,000), the value of forced deliveries and services (£2,020,000,000), damage to communications other than direct war damage (£2,245,000,000), or destruction of industrial and commercial establishments apart from direct war damage (£210,000,000). France's human losses, military and civilian, were 650,000 killed, with the loss of another 600,000 through excessive mortality and deficiency from normal in births. Men killed in the armed forces left 70,000 orphans ; victims of Nazi reprisals left at least twice as many more. Forty per cent of the conscripts called up in 1945 were rejected, three-quarters of them because they were under weight. French industry had been reduced to 30 per cent of its pre-war capacity. The Minister

of Reconstruction on August 4 estimated that reconstruction would take fifteen years.

Repatriation of prisoners and forced workers from Germany was rapid : 1,365,394 had returned by June 8. Edouard Herriot, released by the Russians in the battle for Berlin, reached Paris on May 21. During the first week of May, Léon Jouhaux (Secretary-General of the C.G.T.), Edouard Daladier (Premier at the outbreak of war) and Paul Reynaud (his successor), Léon Blum (the Socialist leader and former Premier), and Generals Gamelin and Weygand were among the prisoners released. Paul Colette, who fired at and gravely wounded Laval in August 1941 (*see* page 2016 and illus. in page 2014), was freed from Mauthausen concentration camp in Austria.

Warrants were already out for the arrest of all former Vichy Ministers and other alleged traitors and collaborators. Weygand was arrested on his return to France. The French 1st Army arrested Fernand de Brinon (*see* page 3405) on May 11. Marshal Pétain gave himself up on April 26. Pierre Laval, already condemned to death in his absence (*see* illus. in page 3411), flew to Spain, where he was interned, and then to Austria, where he arrived on July 31 in the American zone, to

be immediately arrested and handed over to the French. Joseph Darnand, Secretary of the Interior at Vichy (*see* page 3405) was arrested on June 28 by Allied troops on the Italo-Swiss frontier.

By July 31, the special courts—one in each department of France—set up to deal exclusively with treason trials had passed 1,629 death sentences ; 757 **Treason** sentences of hard **Trials** labour for life ; 5,328 of hard labour for various terms ; 1,136 of solitary confinement ; 11,073 of imprisonment ; 22,137 of national disgrace (*see* page 3410). Acquittals numbered 3,564 ; 25,000 were still awaiting judgement.

These trials were held under the law as it existed before Vichy. The only change was in procedure, made to speed up the hearings. Admiral Esteva (64), former Resident General in Tunisia, was sentenced on March 15 to life imprisonment, loss of civic rights, and the confiscation of his property. General Dentz (64), former C.-in-C. in Syria (*see* Chapter 175), was sentenced on April 20 to death and deprived of his military rank : a sentence later commuted by General de Gaulle to life imprisonment without hard labour. Darnand, sentenced to death on October 3, was shot a week later. Sentence of death passed on Pétain on August 15 was commuted two days later to life imprisonment. Laval, sentenced to death on October 9, was executed six days later, after a vain attempt to poison himself.

Chapter 360

BEHIND THE ENEMY LINES IN ITALY

Chapters 319 and 374 tell the history, from the armistice to the end of the war in Europe, of the increasing part of Italy occupied by the advancing Allies. This chapter describes events in northern Italy, which experienced the full tyranny of occupation by Germany after Italy's change of side in October 1943. Its author is Friedl Orlando, who was on the staff of the Allied Command in Italy working in connexion with partisan activity

THE announcement on September 8, 1943, of the armistice of September 3 between Italy and the Allies (*see* pages 2865 and 2866 and illus. in page 2865) produced an immediate aggressive reaction among the Germans, which meant that the men of the Italian army could either fight their late ally, or let themselves be disarmed and deported as prisoners of war and slave labour into Germany.

The royal family and the Italian High Command had fled into the safety of some unknown Allied camp ; orders came in from nowhere and from everywhere ; surrounded by well-prepared German troops in the homeland as well as in the Balkans, left without air support, means of transport or petrol, few commanders had the stamina to confront the situation and fight the German aggressors. There were exceptions ; but, on the whole, army and air force leaders were puzzled and uncertain.

Not so their men. Some army groups disbanded immediately, every man trying for himself to escape the Germans ; others fought to keep their arms and, when the Germans had suffered a temporary setback, disbanded and fled. In the Balkans thousands joined the Yugoslav and also the Greek partisans ; one group of 40,000 (later the famous " Garibaldi Division ") put themselves en bloc under Tito's orders. The troops in central Italy made towards the Allied lines. But in general the men took the route towards " home " : each man trekked towards the valley of which he knew the hideouts ; each man towards the township where he would be able to tell friend from spy ; each man towards the house where his family would bar the door, if the Germans should come and look for him. Some may even have thought of reorganizing armed resistance ; but the foremost thought in every soldier's mind at that moment was safety for his person and for his weapons, so that, whatever might come, neither he nor the nation should be delivered helpless to the fury of German revenge.

But in central and northern Italy, the soldier soon found that even at home there was no safety. North of the

Italian Soldiers Disband

Allied lines, a Republican Fascist administration had been set up by Mussolini after his rescue from his Apennine prison (*see* page 3233). The Fascist authorities, holding power through Hitler's grace, were only too eager to supply Germany with slave labour and auxiliary fighting forces. In their hands were the communal

DUCE'S LAST 'GOVERNMENT'
On his release by S.S. troops, Mussolini on September 15, 1943, broadcast a 'proclamation' reconstituting the Fascist Party and government on a republican basis with himself as Premier and Minister for Foreign Affairs and Marshal Graziani—C.-in-C., Libya, till his defeat by General Wavell in 1941 (see Chapter 131)—as Minister of Defence. Here Mussolini, grown much thinner, talks with Graziani.

registers, the army records, the ration cards ; they could control the country far better than the foreigners could ever have done, and they were able to keep a watch on every individual. The disbanded soldiers had only one refuge : the mountains. Here they were joined by Allied prisoners, whose camps had been opened on September 8 in accordance with the armistice terms, and who were now hunted by the German-Fascist authorities.

After the Nazi-Fascists regained control of the greater part of the country, the local Committees of National Liberation went underground again. These political organizations, representing the six anti-Fascist parties (*see* page 3234) in all provinces, towns, and often villages and factories, developed clandestinely during the time of the Italo-German alliance. When, largely thanks to their activities, Mussolini fell, they came into the open and brought pressure to bear on Badoglio for the speedy conclusion of an armistice with the Allies. When the Germans occupied the country the Nazi-Fascists immediately seized the C.N.L. leaders. Many were shot ; the luckier ones escaped to join the irregulars in the mountains. Through them, the guerilla bands received their first political colouring and education.

Local Liberation Committees

Meanwhile in the provinces, towns and villages the Committees of Liberation carried on secretly under new leadership, unknown to Germans and Fascists. As the fighting units grew larger, the question came up : how could the political C.N.L. collaborate with the irregular fighting units to the best advantage of the nation ? Parties proved to be divided ; but eventually the point of view of the Communists and Actionists won, and it was established that partisan bands should come under the authority of their local C.N.L., and that, in fact, the partisan movement should be developed so as to become the fighting corollary of the political resistance movement. Adoption of the political programme of the C.N.L.—a programme of national unity, embracing all anti-Fascist opinion from liberal to communist—was demanded from the partisans. All the more important Committees formed a military sub-committee to which the partisan commanders, operating in the particular zone, were responsible. These military sub-committees also co-ordinated the work of the partisans with that of the Groups and Squads of Patriotic Action. These groups were composed of citizens of inhabited places, in great part women, who kept liaison with the partisans, carrying messages to and from

ENEMY WAR INDUSTRY GOES UNDERGROUND

Increasing Allied air attacks on war-production centres in Italy drove the country's German masters to shelter them underground. Here is a section of the well-known Alfa-Romeo plant removed from Milan to the caves at Costozza, near Vicenza. The caves, covering some ten acres, were equipped with air-conditioning apparatus and power, and over a thousand people were employed there making aero-engines.
Photo, British Official

the mountain hideouts, taking up food, clothing and ammunition, reporting German movements and, in the proximity of the Allied lines, doing intelligence work for the Allies. The squads were small, armed detachments of town and village dwellers who attacked Nazi-Fascist administrative offices, executed collaborators and high-ranking Fascists, destroyed records and files— in short, had the task of hampering the Fascist administrative machinery.

With the help of the C.N.L., enrolment of partisans became better organized. As far as possible their number was restricted to the amount of weapons

Enrolment of Partisans

available in an area, i.e. two men were admitted for every one firearm. But while at the outset the partisans could supplement their stocks of arms and ammunition only through attacks on German and Fascist stores, the C.N.L. had further means of supply: they organized secret weapon collections and later arranged for Allied supplies to be dropped from the air. They also vetted new recruits for the partisan forces as to their political loyalty.

But it was never possible to regulate completely the intake of partisans. For one thing, there were the many deserters from the Fascist and German armies. Such desertions, especially of foreign soldiers of the German army, were daily occurrences. Some partisan divisions included Russian, French or Polish

units. There were also cases of desertion by German nationals. Though these deserters mostly brought over their arms, they nevertheless presented a special problem: it was difficult to distinguish them from enemy *agents-provocateurs*, and many a unit suffered a heavy surprise attack after some false sympathizer had found his way into it.

Many of those who worked underground in towns and villages, members of the Squads or Groups of Patriotic Action, came gradually under suspicion and had to flee to the mountains. At the beginning of March 1944 the C.N.L. of northern Italy organized a general strike, lasting several days; its aim was to paralyse Nazi-Fascist war production, and to test the political unity of the country and of the resistance movement. The whole of northern Italy was paralysed by the strike, the biggest ever organized in Europe under Nazi domination. But as a result new people were compromised and had to take to armed resistance. In the end the actual partisan forces numbered 170,000, including women. In areas where sufficient arms were available women participated in the fighting, but in most sections they acted as nurses, cooks, dispatch riders. Only two women commanders are on record: one was a Communist countess, known as "Angela," who commanded a formation in the Turin area; the other, Norma Barbolini, while her brother, commander of the "Modena" division, was recovering from wounds, took over his command of approximately 4,000 men.

Total Strength of Resisters

As the organization of the patriot forces proceeded, as their numbers grew and supplies were somewhat regularized, they were forced to move ever farther from inhabited centres. For reasons of supply they had, at first, kept

GERMANS FEEL MANPOWER SHORTAGE IN ITALY

After the Italian surrender in September 1943, the Germans in Italy were faced with a crisis in their manpower resources. Their demands for Italian labour became so great that Marshal Graziani, Defence Minister in Mussolini's Republican Fascist 'Government,' in April 1944 had to implore the Nazis to cut down these demands. Here Italian workmen help to erect coastal defences for the Nazis on the Adriatic.
Photo New York Times Photos

PARTISANS HELPED TO FREE FLORENCE
Important part in the liberation of northern Italy was played by the Italian partisans whose forces eventually numbered 170,000 In May 1944 all Italian partisans were unified in the Corps of the Volunteers for Liberty (Corpo Volontari della Libertà). When the 8th Army entered Florence on August 12, 1944, it was to find the partisans—some of whom are seen above—in control.   *Photo, British Official*

as near as possible to towns and villages, at great risk to themselves and to the local population. But reprisals grew fiercer—there are tens of Lidices in

Lidices of North Italy

northern Italy. Enough to mention such names as Vado, on the Prato–Bologna road, where 1,400 people were massacred, or S. Pancrazio di Bucine near Arezzo, which was razed to the ground, or Vinca, where, after the male population had fled, a mixed force of German and Fascist S.S. hanged 172 women and children.

The assistance and sympathy of the population was essential to the partisans —their supplies depended on it. The patriots had some funds, raised partly by collections organized by the C.N.L. and partly by attacks made on Fascist offices. Some industrialists also found it worth while to make donations.

Nazi-Fascist propaganda did its best to estrange the population from the partisans. Having failed to set them against each other on political grounds, they described the partisans as bandits and highwaymen. But the patriots enforced a Spartan discipline in their ranks, as the following document shows:

"April 5, 1945.
"The Zone Command (of Liguria) has tried Partisan Dino, vice-commander of the Cichero Division, and has found him guilty of serious crimes, amounting to theft and undue appropriation. He has been sentenced to death. The sentence has been carried out."

When military operations grew more ambitious, entire regions fell to the partisans. In these areas, Fascists were immediately deprived of their

office and free elections for local council, from candidates representing parties and trades, were held. During the elections the partisans acted as a kind of technical instructors. They also provided the police force and, in collaboration with the newly elected local authority, usually organized the collection of wheat and of taxes. A good deal became known about partisan administration when, in summer 1944, the Val d'Ossola (west of Lake Maggiore) was occupied after heavy fighting by the partisans.

Political divisions played a very small part in the patriot movement. All formations accepted simply the programme of national unity of the Committee of Liberation. The particular political colour of a unit derived, in most cases, from loyalty to its leader, but the adherence of a partisan to one or another force was conditioned far more by geographical than by political considerations; a man joining the force operating in his area did not have to swallow the political creed of his commander. Discussion was free and was encouraged. The Communist brigades had political commissars (as well as priests) who had the task of instilling the sense of the purpose of his fight into

HITLER'S JACKAL
Heavily protected by a guard of his German masters, Benito Mussolini, ex-Duce and head of the fast-crumbling Italian 'Fascist Republic' (right), addresses Italian Fascist troops in Milan in January on their way to fight for the Nazis. Behind him stands Pavelini, secretary of the Republican Fascist Party.
Photo, Planet News

every man. For most of these young men, the discussions in their mountain hideouts were their first contact with free political thought, and it was only natural, therefore, that many of them fell under the influence of their commander or political commissar and developed strong sympathies for his way of thought.

In May 1944 all partisan forces were unified in one body called Corpo Volontari della Libertà (Corps of the Volunteers for Liberty) and were put under the orders of a clandestine

Volunteers for Liberty

General Staff for northern Italy, which, in its turn, worked hand in hand with the central Committee of National Liberation. An able army officer, General Raffaele Cadorna, son of the Italian C.-in-C. during the early part of the First Great War, was dispatched north to act as Commander-in-Chief. The vice-commanders were two political figures, chosen from the two parties who were most active in the resistance movement: the Communist Luigi Longo, who, as Gallo, had been political commissar of the Italian Garibaldi Brigade, and had been one of the outstanding figures in the Spanish civil war; and Ferruccio Parri, of the Action Party, who when the north was liberated, became Prime Minister from June to November 1945 of a new all-party government (*see* Chapter 374)— an indication of the solidarity of all Italy with the partisan movement.

ITALY'S PATRIOTS CLEARED MILAN

On May 1, 1945, General Mark Clark, C.-in-C., Allied Armies in Italy, sent special congratulations to the Italian partisans who had liberated the important cities of Milan and Turin before the arrival of the Allied forces. Milan had been entered by U.S. troops of the 5th Army two days previously. Above, partisan light machine-gunners mopping up in Milan as the Germans withdraw
Photo, Evening Standard

What had been scattered bands, bent first and foremost on their own defence, became an active, disciplined fighting body with special strategic functions. These functions were strictly conditioned by the limitations of a partisan force—lack of heavy arms, air support and mechanized transport—and by their particular assets—profound knowledge of the country and superior morale.

In the long peninsula of Italy, with its few lines of communication, sabotage of transport had the most serious consequences for the enemy. The patriots

Patriots Obstruct Alpine Passes blew up trains and tunnels and more than once obstructed the Brenner Pass, a supply line more than ever vital to the Germans after the liberation of the south of France. Earlier the Simplon Pass was repeatedly obstructed, and on one occasion was damaged so severely that for at least two weeks no German supplies could come through it.

Owing to the hit-and-run tactics of partisan warfare, no overall strategic plan can be described on geographical lines. The various tasks depend entirely on the position of the front line and on the situation in the enemy's rear. The first communiqué on Italian partisan activity behind the lines in northern Italy was issued from General Alexander's headquarters on May 22, 1944 (*see* illus. in page 3241). Thereafter communiqués and instructions were issued daily. Here are two taken at random:

June 11, 1944 [the Allied armies were approaching Perugia and Siena] "... The Germans are retreating. They are using main roads like the Orvieto–Siena–Poggibonsi–Florence road and the Terni–Spoleto–Foligno – Perugia –

GRAZIANI IS CAPTURED

Marshal Graziani, Fascist Italy's last commander-in-chief, was detained by Italian patriots at Lecco, Lake Como, on April 27, 1945, as he tried to escape into Switzerland. His trial as a war criminal was later fixed to begin on June 16, 1946. As Italian Governor of Libya, he earned from the Arabs the nickname of 'Butcher.' Here he greets a German S.S general, also a prisoner, before being handed over to U.S military authorities.
Photo, Pictorial Press

Arezzo–Florence road. The time has come for you to strike and strike hard. Do everything possible to impede the enemy's retreat."

July 3, 1944 [directed to the forces in the Spezia zone]. " It is the duty of all patriots in this zone to do everything in their power to hinder the completion of the German defences **Partisan Orders** and to destroy as much as they can of the defences already completed.... Destroy all you can, carry their tools away and make them useless. . . . The leaders of patriot groups in this zone must detail at least two men to note down exact information on the German defences in their area and to make them on as large scale maps as possible. . . The patriot leaders must make sure that the men who gather all this information cross the lines and reach us."

More detailed instructions were sent in code by wireless. There was scepticism on the Allied side for some months, but, when the partisans had proved their worth special Allied liaison officers were dispatched to all the more important partisan commands. Supplies were dropped and, whenever possible, air support was given. Many captured documents testify to the great embarrassment caused to the enemy by the partisans and to the drain their numerous activities constituted on Nazi-Fascist man power. Thus a letter, dated

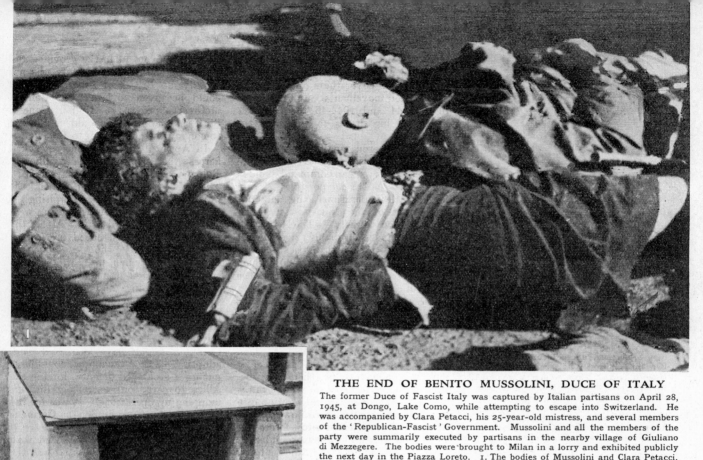

THE END OF BENITO MUSSOLINI, DUCE OF ITALY

The former Duce of Fascist Italy was captured by Italian partisans on April 28, 1945, at Dongo, Lake Como, while attempting to escape into Switzerland. He was accompanied by Clara Petacci, his 25-year-old mistress, and several members of the 'Republican-Fascist' Government. Mussolini and all the members of the party were summarily executed by partisans in the nearby village of Giuliano di Mezzegere. The bodies were brought to Milan in a lorry and exhibited publicly the next day in the Piazza Loreto. 1. The bodies of Mussolini and Clara Petacci. 2. One of many busts of the ex-Fascist leader torn from their niches in Milan. 3. The ex-Duce and his mistress hang head downwards in the Piazza Loreto. 4. Poster pasted up in Milan by a partisan announces Italy's liberation.

CONFUSION IN TRIESTE

New Zealanders, under Lieut.-General Sir Bernard Freyberg, V.C., occupied Trieste on May 3, 1945. They found a confused situation, for Marshal Tito's forces had entered the city four days previously, while 'Chetnik' bands, formerly under Mihailovich, and Italian guerillas were also active. Above, at Monfalcone, near Trieste, youthful patriots greet their liberators.
Photo, British Official

April 2, 1944, from Marshal Graziani, commander of the Republican Fascist army, to Marshal Kesselring, implored him to cut down German requests for Fascist labour and for Fascist soldiers. The following lines are significant : " One of my most urgent problems is to increase as much as possible the number of formations engaged in fighting the rebels; this fight is a necessary and quite indispensable preliminary to the re-establishment of the authority and prestige of the state."

From figures relating to the actions of the Pinero Cichero partisan division. for instance, it appears that in the period

Partisan Gains and Losses

between June 1944 and April 27, 1945, every partisan killed or put out of action three of the enemy. In the same period this division, operating in Liguria and 1,178 strong, fought 359 actions, carried out 157 acts of sabotage and took 2,893 prisoners. Their own losses were 82 dead, 11 missing, 234 wounded.

Large scale attacks by German and Fascist forces were frequent. Often they succeeded in disbanding entire divisions, but always at very great cost to themselves. Winter was particularly unfavourable to the partisans; the Germans needed fewer men to hold the front line, while cold and hunger often compelled partisan units to descend nearer to the valleys. Moreover, they

3706

could no longer rely on one of their main assets for attack, surprise, for there was no foliage to cover them and snow betrayed their movements. In the winters of 1943-44 and 1944-45 the Germans organized big drives to wipe out the resisters.

While numerous small fighting actions were continuously and everywhere in progress, the partisan command avoided big battles as far as possible ; for in large scale operations the superior equipment of the Nazi-Fascist forces counted too heavily. The battle of Montefiorino is probably the biggest (apart from the final battles for the liberation of northern towns), which Italian partisans ever fought. After the corps of " Armando," numbering about 6,000 men had occupied the Radice Pass, important for the German retreat from central Italy, the Germans, in an attempt to dislocate them, attacked with 25,000 men. " Armando's " men fought for several days until their ammunition gave out ; then they dispersed, only to re-form their ranks later on. Through the indiscretion of a Fascist colonel, it became known that in the battle the German-Fascist forces lost 2,080 men killed and 1,200 wounded.

On August 4, 1944, the Allies entered the southern outskirts of Florence (*see* page 3472). But the Germans had blown up all bridges across the Arno, except the Ponte Vecchio, and had firmly installed themselves in the northern part of the city. Patriot forces fought against them for a week, until, on the 11th, the Germans drew out and the Allies crossed the river on the 12th.

After the Canadians took Ravenna on December 4, Lieutenant - General McCreery, commander of the 8th Army, conferred the gold medal. Italy's highest military award, on the local partisan leader, Boldrini, for organizing the

RAVENNA IS FREED

British troops of the 8th Army on December 4, 1944, captured the ancient town of Ravenna, once capital of the Western Roman Empire. Isolated units of the Wehrmacht left behind were skilfully mopped up by Italian partisans as the British troops pushed forward to cut the Ravenna-Ferrara highway. Right, partisans being thanked by their leaders after the city's liberation.
Photo. British Official

partisan movement in the province and liberating the town. As Italy was not an ally, no British or American award could be given to him ; but General McCreery asked the Italian General Staff that he himself should be allowed to convey the gold medal to Boldrini.

In April 1945, the Allies attacked across the Senio river, to liberate Bologna on the 21st (*see* Chapter 361). This was the signal for which the Corpo Volontari had been waiting.

Pushed from the south, fighting with their backs towards the Alps, the German position was, indeed, precarious. Yet there was the Brenner Pass, which, in spite of repeated damage by bombing and

Germans' Escape Hindered

sabotage, still offered some hope of a partial retreat. There was the sea. And there were the Apennines and the southern slopes of the Alps, where the Germans might have dispersed and, adopting partisan technique, could have put up a prolonged defence, forcing the Allies to carry out extremely difficult mopping-up operations. It was for the Italian partisans to hinder the Germans from escape or dispersal.

They also knew that the speed with which the north was liberated was the all-important thing for Italy's future. A slow and piecemeal retreat on the part of the Germans would have meant Italy's ruin for very many years to come. The Germans were known to have planned scorched-earth measures in all details : for weeks, demolition experts had been visiting industrial establishments, mines had been laid, stores of dynamite had been piled up.

On April 24 the Allies entered Ferrara, Modena and Spezia. That day Genoa rose.

MILAN HONOURS ITS DEAD LIBERATORS

On April 25, 1946, Milan celebrated the first anniversary of its liberation by the partisans. Above, left, General Raffaele Cadorna, former leader of the partisans in northern Italy and later appointed Chief of Staff of the Italian Army, decorates the mother of a partisan hero killed in action. Right, Ferruccio Parri, partisan leader and Italian Premier from June–November 1945, addresses a celebration meeting. *Photos, New York Times Photos*

The partisans marched on the town, blocking the three roads of retreat from Liguria, leading to Parma, Piacenza and Milan. Counting roughly a thousand armed men, the partisans were met in Genoa's outskirts by 3,000 German and Fascist troops. Fighting developed. Inside the town, the population, led by the Groups and Squads of Patriotic Action, rose. The Nazi-Fascists found themselves between two fires. On the evening of the 25th, General Reinhold, commander of the German forces in Liguria, signed his surrender. All he asked for was that his troops should be disarmed during the dark hours.

Genoa had given the signal. By April 25 the whole north had risen. While the Allies advanced towards Verona and Piacenza, there was hard fighting in Milan and Turin. By the 27th these two important towns were in the hands of the Corps of Volunteers.

Mussolini was caught while trying to escape to Switzerland and executed immediately. The Republican Fascists refused to believe in **Mussolini** his death, and with the **Executed** fanaticism of despair carried on the fight in the streets of Milan. To convince them that their cause was lost, the Committee of Liberation had his body hung up in a Milan square.

Of all German troops, those stationed in Venezia Giulia and Trieste had probably the best chance of escape. Synchronizing their action with that of the Central Committee of Liberation,

Trieste resistance leaders ordered a rising. After a day or so of fighting, the Germans offered to cease fire, under the condition that they should be handed over to General Freyberg's troops. To avoid unnecessary bloodshed, the Committee of Liberation accepted this condition; they rounded up the Germans, but allowed them to keep their arms until they were able to surrender to the 8th Army. On the morning of the 30th, when the 8th Army was still in the process of occupying Venice, Yugoslav vanguards entered Trieste. They were met by German fire. From this fact derived a whole series of suspicions, accusations and counter-accusations between Italian resistance leaders and followers of Marshal Tito.

Suspicion also cast a shadow on subsequent relations between the Allies and the Italian partisans. Wherever the Allies entered, they declared the Committees of Liberation, which had taken over administration in the towns freed by the Corps of Volunteers, to be merely consultative bodies and established military government instead. The partisan forces were immediately dissolved, individual patriots were disarmed in the street, paid off with the miserable sum the Italian Government could afford, and sent back to their homes that often no longer

existed. True enough, the problem confronting the Allies—the number of these men, the general economic condition of the country and the sudden end of the war—was unprecedented; but the suspicious manner and, above all, the hurry with which the Allies acted, could not fail to cause resentment in these somewhat overstrained men.

On May 2, the German surrender, signed at Caserta on April 29, was published and came into force. Thus the **German** whole of northern Italy **Surrender** had been liberated in **in Italy** one week through the collaboration between regular and partisan armies.

The casualties in the ranks of the Corps of Volunteers had been heavy: out of 170,000 men 26,000 were dead and 20,000 missing. As the Nazi-Fascists never recognized the military status of the Corps, a man classed as "missing" could be assumed to be dead. On this assumption the patriots lost one quarter of their men. 23,000 were seriously wounded.

But their fight was not in vain. Not only did the resistance movement speed up and help to achieve victory, not only did the partisans limit the destruction of the country's economic assets for the future, but they also laid the moral foundation on which alone a new Italy could rise.

GERMAN SURRENDER IN ITALY

The first large-scale surrender made by the Germans was of the land, sea, and air forces
in northern Italy, the Austrian provinces of Vorarlberg, Tirol, and Salzburg, and
parts of Carinthia and Styria to Field-Marshal Alexander on April 29, 1945. Here are
the terms imposed, and Mr. Churchill's announcement of them three days later

**The terms of surrender imposed on April 29, 1945, at
Caserta on the German land, sea, and air forces in Italy :**

First, unconditional surrender by the German commander-
in-chief, south-west, of all forces under his command or
control on land, sea, or air to the Supreme Allied Commander, Mediterranean theatre of operations.

Secondly, the cessation of all hostilities on land, on sea,
or in the air by enemy forces at 12.00 hours G.M.T., May 2
1945.

Thirdly, the immediate immobilization and disarmament
of enemy ground, sea, and air forces.

Fourthly, an obligation on the part of the German
commander-in-chief, south-west, to carry out any further
orders issued by the supreme allied command, Mediterranean
theatre.

Fifthly, disobedience of orders or failure to comply
with them will be dealt with in accordance with the accepted
laws and usages of war.

The instrument of surrender stipulates that it is independent of, without prejudice to, and will be superseded
by any general instrument of surrender imposed by or
on behalf of the United Nations and applicable to Germany
and the German armed forces as a whole.

The instrument of surrender and appendices is written
in English and German. The English version is the
authentic text.

The decision of the Supreme Allied Command, Mediterranean theatre, will be final if any doubt or dispute arises
as to the meaning or interpretation of the surrender terms.

The signing took place in the office of General Morgan
in the presence of British, United States, and U.S.S.R. officers,
including Lieutenant-General Robertson, Chief Administrative
Officer, Allied Force Headquarters ; Major-General Lemnitzer,
Deputy Chief of Staff ; Rear-Admiral H. A. Packer, Chief
of Staff to the Commander-in-Chief, Mediterranean ; Rear-
Admiral S. S. Lewis, Chief of Staff to the Commander United
States Naval Forces in North African Waters ; Major-General
Chauncey, Chief of Staff to Mediterranean Allied Air Forces ;
Air Vice-Marshal G. B. A. Baker, Chief of Staff to the Deputy
Air Commander-in-Chief ; and many other senior allied
staff officers.

**Mr. Churchill informs the House of Commons on
Wednesday, May 2, 1945, of the German surrender in Italy :**

I PROMISED that I would come to the House if anything of
major importance occurred, and I would ask your leave,
Mr. Speaker, and the indulgence of the House, to make a
short statement. There has been a certain amount of matter
issued continuously from tape machines, and I thought
perhaps the House would like to hear a short account which
I have received from Field-Marshal Sir Harold Alexander.

Field-Marshal Alexander, the Supreme Allied Commander
in the Mediterranean theatre of operations, has just announced
that the land, sea, and air forces commanded by Colonel-
General Heinrich von Vietinghoff-Scheel, German Commander-
in-Chief, South-West Command, and Commander-in-Chief
of the army group " C," have surrendered unconditionally.
The instrument of surrender was signed on Sunday afternoon,
April 29, at the Allied Forces Headquarters at Caserta, by
two German plenipotentiaries and by Lieutenant-General
W. D. Morgan, Chief of Staff at Allied Forces Headquarters.
The terms of surrender provided for the cessation of hostilities
at 12 o'clock noon, G.M.T., on Wednesday, May 2, that is
to say 2 o'clock today by our time.

But as all these matters are accompanied by many elements
of uncertainty, it was not until effective confirmation was
obtained by the actual orders issued to the troops from the
German High Command that Field-Marshal Alexander
issued the statement which has now come over the wireless.

The territory under General von Vietinghoff-Scheel,
South-West Command, includes northern Italy to the Isonzo
river in the north-east, and the Austrian provinces of Vorarlberg, Tirol, and Salzburg, and portions of Carinthia and
Styria. It is therefore, geographically, a surrender which
puts us into very close touch with the position of the United
States armies of the north.

The fighting troops of the enemy include the remnants
of 22 German divisions and six Italian Fascist divisions,
but with the combat and echelon troops upon the lines of
communication and throughout this territory, which they
have held for so long, the total numbers who have surrendered
to the allies are estimated to amount to nearly 1,000,000 men.

Not only has a vast area of territory, vital in its character,
fallen into the hands of the Supreme Commander, Sir Harold
Alexander, but the actual surrender which has taken place
so far, comprising the numbers it does, constitutes, I believe,
a record for the whole of this war—and cannot fail but
to be helpful to the further events for which we are looking.

This army in Italy, American and British composed,
commanded by our trusted General and having under him
General Mark Clark, a most efficient and daring American
soldier, has had a marvellous record since they first landed
in the peninsula . . .

What has made it particularly difficult and depressing
for this army is the tremendous inroads which have been
made upon it in order to help forward other great operations.
In June and July of last year what very nearly amounted
to an army was taken from this Command in Italy, while
only a very small corresponding reduction took place on
the enemy's side. Now quite recently, a few months ago,
feeling that it would probably be beyond the strength of
this army, so weakened, to make a decisive attack, we moved
another large addition of divisions to the western front, and
some others went to Greece.

Thus this army was an army stripped of its strength and
facing an enemy force which for all the purposes of war
must have been considered far stronger because it had the
duty of defending mountain ranges and, afterwards, plains
flooded by autumn and winter rains, and which certainly
in the number of divisions, exceeded those which were
left to attack. Moreover those forces left to attack, as I
pointed out in my message of congratulation to Field-Marshal
Alexander, were of so many different nations that only some
personality of commanding qualities could have held them
all and woven them all together.

If you look over the whole list of those men who have
fought, you will find, taking as we may our own contribution
first—it was the largest—the British and British Indian
divisions of the highest quality. In addition to the British
divisions we had the Poles—who have always fought with
the greatest loyalty ; the New Zealanders—who have
marched all the way from the beginning right up to the very
spearpoint of the advance ; the South African Armoured
Division—who were very forward in the fray ; the great
forces of the United States—second in numbers only to our
own. Then there have been the Brazilian forces, which
have made their steady advances ; a negro division of
United States troops, which has also distinguished itself ;
the Jewish Brigade, which we formed a year or so ago,
and which has fought in the front line with courage ; and
finally the Japanese of American birth, who entered Turin.
Finally, there were the free Italians—who have played their
part in clearing their country from the German Fascist
yoke. All these forces, weakened as they had been, were
not discouraged. Divided as they were by racial differences,
they were united and resolved upon their purpose.

Now their reward has come. I am very glad it has come
at a time when it can be singled out. It stands out. It
brings to a conclusion the work of as gallant an army as ever
marched—and brings to a pitch of fame the military reputation
of a commander who has always, I may say, enjoyed the
fullest confidence of the House of Commons.

Chapter 361

THE GERMANS SURRENDER IN ITALY

*This chapter continues the history of the campaign in Italy from the fall of
Rimini in September 1944 (described in Chapter 339) to the unconditional
surrender of all German and Italian-Fascist forces in north Italy and west
Austria, and the junction of Allied forces from north and south in the Brenner
Pass in May 1945. It is written by Mr. Ruggero Orlando, an Italian writer
employed during the period covered by Allied Forces H.Q., Italy*

THE simultaneous advance of the
Allied armies into Germany from
west and east overshadowed the
end of the war in Italy. That long,
difficult and gigantic campaign was a
highly controversial topic for those
politically or technically interested in
the history of the Second Great War.
Already in 1944, Lord Strabolgi published "Conquest of Italy," a book
severely criticizing both political and
military warfare in the Mediterranean.
The unceasing interference of political
leaders with military necessity for
political reasons was stressed in the
diaries of Captain Butcher, General
Eisenhower's naval aide, and in "Top
Secret," a tendentious book by Mr.
Ralph Ingersoll, an American journalist
on the staff of General Jacob Loucks
Devers, U.S. Army, Deputy Supreme
Commander, Mediterranean, 1944.

Official information available at the
time of going to press (June 1946)
makes it impossible to judge these comments accurately; but after 1943 the entire Mediterranean war,
and in particular the
Italian campaign, seems
undoubtedly to have
suffered from continuous delays and
setbacks due to diplomatic reasons and
negotiations. The invasion of Italy
from the south, at first described by
Mr. Churchill as a major war operation,
a direct attack on the "soft under-belly"
of Hitler's fortress of Europe (*see* page
2829), later came to be described as a
"diversionary operation," aimed above
all at pinning down the greatest possible
number of German forces south of
the Alps. This change of attitude at
supreme level was reflected in uncertainty and difficulties on the local
strategic and even tactical planes.

**Changes
in Official
Attitude**

In February 1944, General Devers
said : "Replacements allocated to this
theatre are not adequate to sustain
operations in Italy on the present scale.
At the present time, the United States
part of the 5th Army has an effective
net shortage of 13,072 officers and men."
The American Selective Service System
could not deliver the men considered
necessary by the commanders on the
spot ; and the subsequent withdrawal
of very considerable trained forces for

3709

Operation "Anvil" (the landings in
the south of France—*see* page 3456)
made the situation in Italy worse.
Again, during the winter of 1944–45,
8th Army units were diverted to meet
the political crisis in Greece.

These heavy drains on trained personnel were in part compensated for by
the retraining of anti-aircraft units as
infantry (to form the 473rd Infantry),
and by the arrival between July 1944 and
January 1945 of the U.S. 91st Division,
the Brazilian Expeditionary Force (*see*
page 3473), a Negro division (the U.S.
92nd), the U.S. 10th Mountain Division,
and three Italian combat groups, totalling six divisions and equipped with
British weapons. The gains, however,
says General Marshall, Chief of Staff to
the United States Armies, in his report
to the Secretary of War, "were more
than offset by a February directive from
the Combined Chiefs of Staff which
ordered the transfer of five British and
Canadian divisions to the European
Theatre." The uncertain and changing
nature of the central planning is confirmed in the next sentence : "The
directive was later amended to send
three to France, one to the eastern
Mediterranean, and retain one division

in Italy for possible use in the impending
final battle."

The torrential rains (*see* page 3473) at
the end of the summer campaign of 1944
undoubtedly helped the German defenders. Instead of being the beginning
of deployment in the
Po valley, the conquest
of Rimini by the 8th
Army (September 21)
and of the Apennine Futa Pass,
between Florence and Bologna, by
the 5th Army (September 23) (*see*
page 3473) were but the closing touch
of the liberation of central Italy.
Mr. Churchill revealed that the forcing
of the mountain line strongly fortified
and "held by a hostile German Army
practically as large as our own," cost
the Allies nearly 50,000 casualties. On
September 28 the Prime Minister explained why operations had slowed down:
"General Alexander has now definitely
broken into the basin of the Po, and here
we exchange the barriers of mountain
ridges for the perpetual interruption of
the ground by streams and canals."

**Winter
Campaign
Impossible**

Autumn began with the Allied Armies
deployed along a line between Viareggio,
on the Ligurian Sea, and the marshes
of Comacchio on the Adriatic. On the

THROUGH MUD AND FLOOD ON THE ITALIAN FRONT

The German defence of Italy was helped by the heavy rains which set in at the end of the summer
campaign of 1944. In spite of foul weather, however, Canadian troops of the 8th Army on
October 24 overcame all resistance on the west bank of the Savio between Cesena and the
Adriatic, where these transport vehicles (below) make their way through flood and mud, to
reach the mouth of the river.   *Photo. British Official*

Cpl. HUNTER
(43rd Marine Commando)
The V.C. was awarded post-humously to Corporal Thomas Peck Hunter for his 'magnificent courage and leadership' on the night of April 1-2, 1945, in northern Italy. Twice offering himself as a target in order to save his Commando troop, he was the means of securing a vital objective at the cost of his own life. His skilful use of his bren gun demoralized the enemy

Pte. BURTON
(Duke of Wellington's Regiment)
In Italy on October 8, 1944, Private Richard Henry Burton displayed 'magnificent gallantry and total disregard of his own safety' for which he was awarded the V.C. During the attack on an important hill position, with most of his comrades either dead or wounded, he twice dashed forward on his own initiative, directing such accurate fire with his bren gun that the enemy retired.

Capt. BRUNT, M.C.
(Sherwood Foresters)
For a 'magnificent action' in Italy on December 9, 1944, Captain John Henry Cound Brunt, M.C., was posthumously awarded the V.C. During violent counter-attacks by the 90th Panzer Grenadier Division, by personal example he rallied his men—outnumbered by at least three to one—to drive off the enemy. He personally killed at least a score of Germans. Next day he was killed

Major LASSEN, M.C. (Two Bars)
(Special Boat Service)
The only non-British or Empire recipient of the V.C. in the war of 1939-1945, Major Anders Lassen, M.C., reached Britain from Denmark in 1940 and joined the British Army. On the night of April 8-9, 1945, he displayed 'magnificent leadership' in face of overwhelming odds in a reconnaissance raid on the shores of Lake Comacchio, Italy, during which he was mortally wounded

western half of the front stood the 5th Army (part American, part British, with the Brazilian Expeditionary Force), under the command of Lieutenant-General Mark Clark, U.S. Army. Its centre was the city of Lucca. On the right, the Adriatic sector along the Romagna plateau and the southern approaches of the Po delta, was deployed the 8th Army, commanded by Lieutenant-General Sir Oliver Leese. Its centre was Cesena, on the river Savio.

On November 4, Field-Marshal Sir John Dill, head of the British Joint Staff Mission in Washington, died. Sir Henry Maitland Wilson was appointed his successor, Sir Harold Alexander, C.-in-C. Allied Armies in Italy, becoming Supreme Allied Commander, Mediterranean, with promotion to the rank of Field-Marshal (to have effect from June 4, date of the capture of Rome). Field-Marshal Alexander's successor as C.-in-C. of the Allied Armies in Italy (15th Army Group) was Lieutenant-General Mark Clark, who was succeeded as commander of the 5th Army by Lieutenant-General Lucian K. Truscott (commanding the U.S. VI Corps at Anzio). Lieutenant-General Sir Richard L. McCreery (who commanded the X Corps at Salerno and Cassino and planned and executed the crossing of the Garigliano) succeeded Sir Oliver Leese (promoted to command Allied Land Forces, South-East Asia—*see* page 3530) as commander of the 8th Army.

A sudden thrust by the British V Corps, forming the spearhead of the 8th Army, led to the capture on November 9 of Forli with its airfield. But no hopes of a forthcoming winter campaign were raised.

Partisans Told : "Lie Low"

Two days later, indeed, Field-Marshal Alexander broadcast to the Italian partisans in the north his order for the winter : "Lie low." The next five months of Italian warfare saw the Allies mainly on the defensive. Patrols were active and, above all, intense liaison work proceeded between the Allied armies and the partisan forces of northern Italy's Committee of Liberation (*see* page 3701). A joint strategy was evolved, half military and half insurrectional—a subject of profitable study for historians. Field-Marshal Alexander became a very popular name

KESSELRING, C.-IN-C. WEHRMACHT IN ITALY
Field-Marshal Albert Kesselring was placed in command of the Central Italian Front in September 1943, and in the following spring succeeded Rommel as C.-in-C. of the Wehrmacht in Italy on the latter's departure for the Western Front. On March 22, 1945, it was announced that he had replaced Rundstedt as German C.-in-C. in the west. Above Kesselring during an inspection tour in Italy
Photo. Associated Press

CLEARING THE MINES FROM BRITAIN'S BEACHES

With the threat of invasion finally past, restrictions governing access to many of Britain's beaches were removed early in 1945. Clearance of anti-invasion obstructions was carried out by the Royal Engineers who were also employed in the dangerous task of locating mines laid along the shore. It was stated on May 31, 1945, that 98 officers and men had been killed in the course of this work. Here mines are being exploded on a beach, under the supervision of Sappers. Bringing in recovered mines through barbed-wire defences (below).

Direct colour photographs by Fox Photos

ADMIRAL RAYMOND A. SPRUANCE

ADMIRAL WILLIAM F. HALSEY

GENERAL OMAR N. BRADLEY

GENERAL MARK W. CLARK

Between June 1944 and August 1945, Admiral Spruance and Admiral Halsey alternated in command of the U.S. 5th Fleet. Admiral Spruance, awarded the U.S. Navy Cross in June 1945 for 'extraordinary heroism,' commanded the U.S. 5th Fleet at Iwo Jima and Okinawa. General Bradley, commanding U.S. Ground Invasion Forces in June 1944, later took control of the 12th (Central) Army Group. In December 1944, Lieut.-General Mark Clark, previously commanding the 5th Army, became Allied C.-in-C. in Italy.

Direct colour photographs by the U.S. O.W.I. and Pictorial Press

HARRY S. TRUMAN—THIRTY-THIRD PRESIDENT OF THE UNITED STATES

On April 12, 1945, Franklin Delano Roosevelt died suddenly after serving less than three months of his fourth term in office. Senator Harry Shippe Truman, the Vice-President, succeeded him as thirty-third President of the United States. Mr. Truman, born in 1884 on a farm in Missouri, where he spent the first thirty-three years of his life, did not enter national politics till 1934, when he was elected Senator. He was appointed Chairman of the Senate War Investigating Committee shortly after America came into the war, and was chosen as Democratic candidate for the Vice-Presidency in July 1944. (See page 3254.)

THE ROYAL NAVY'S PART IN OPERATION 'TORCH'

Operation 'Torch' was the code-name for the Allied landings in North Africa on November 8, 1942. Important political details of ' this majestic enterprise,' as it was described by Mr. Churchill, given by the Prime Minister at a secret session of the House of Commons a month after it occurred, were not made public till after the war. Of the forces involved, Mr. Churchill declared that, though the U.S. land and air forces were predominant, ' on the sea, the proportion was overwhelmingly in our favour.' Here are British battleships and an aircraft-carrier of the covering force of more than 350 British, American, Canadian, Polish, Netherlands and Norwegian men-of-war (see page 2392). The landings are described in Chapter 256.

British Official.

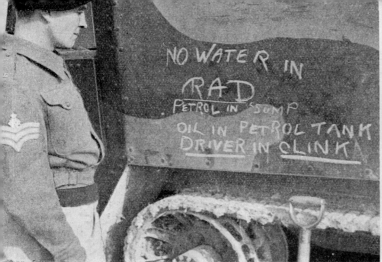

ON THE ROAD TO RAVENNA

British and Canadian forces of the 8th Army captured the famous medieval city of Ravenna on December 5, 1944, and pushed on towards Ferrara. Right, 75-mm. S.P. guns on half-tracks, acting as tank-busters, manned by men of the King's Dragoon Guards, formed the spearhead of the advancing Allies. Left, typical Army humour on one of these S.P. guns outside Ravenna.

among tens of thousands of irregulars, whose operations were officially recorded and when no longer under security veil, were broadcast daily by Allied Headquarters from autumn 1943 to the end of the Italian campaign. The co-ordination between Armies and patriots in Italy was considered the best achieved in any theatre of operations, and accounted for the perfect timing of the popular revolt which broke out in northern Italy at the beginning of the Allied spring offensive (*see* page 3706).

The liaison between troops and partisans was put successfully to the test in two offensive operations during the

Partisan Army Liaison winter: when British and Canadian forces of the 8th Army captured Ravenna (December 5) and when the New Zealand 2nd Division occupied Faenza after the hardest battle of the season (December 14–16). The famous Byzantine mosaics of Ravenna and Dante's tomb escaped unscathed. The conquest of Faenza

was followed by battles of the 8th Army's infantry through difficult and heavily mined country, in appalling weather conditions as the Allies closed in on the Senio river, next German defence line, guarding the Po valley from the south-east.

On December 26 the Germans attacked the left flank of the 5th Army in Tuscany. Their offensive, doubtless intended to coincide with Rundstedt's attack in Belgium, was in fact launched at the moment when that breakthrough had spent itself (*see* Chapter 336). Negro troops of the 92nd Division withdrew down the Serchio valley, north of Lucca, and abandoned the town of Barga (27th). Two brigades (the 19th and 21st) of the 8th Indian Division (which was commanded by Major-General Dudley Russell) were rushed from the ·8th Army front to stem the

onslaught, and helped the Americans to stop the enemy offensive. By December 29, most of the lost ground was regained, though, owing to subsequent wintry conditions, the reconquest of the last of it was not completed until February 6, 1945. German **Engagement in Tuscany** propaganda tried to boost this thrust into a major offensive. It was rather a local engagement, in a sector where the situation had long been, and remained, confused. Barga is sited in a lovely mountain landscape, famous in Italian literature, a plateau between the Apennines and the pre-Apennines of Garfagnana. The Germans had plenty of artillery in the former, and the Americans in the latter, and Barga was for some time a sort of no-man's-land.

During the first weeks of 1945, heavy snow closed most mountain passes to military traffic, and communications were extremely difficult. Operations for some weeks were confined in the main to activity by the Mediterranean Allied Air Forces (*see* Chapter 356)

SCOTS AND IRISH ENTER FORLI

Stiff opposition was encountered by the 8th Army as it advanced to capture Forli on November 9, 1944. The Ronco, last river before the town, was crossed on November 1 and a firm bridge-head established by the British V Corps. Left, Gurkhas wade the swiftly flowing Ronco with a life-line. Right, townspeople at Forli greet Highland infantry and tanks of the North Irish Horse, first troops to enter the town   *Photos. British Official*

ITALIANS IN THE ALLIED ARMIES

Fighting alongside the Allied armies in Italy towards the end of 1944 were three all-Italian groups, each two divisions strong. Here an Italian unit, equipped with British guns, ammunition and clothing, waits to go into action on a sector of the 8th Army front. The men shelter behind a Churchill tank while the tank's guns answer the enemy's fire. *Photo, British Official*

enemy from the whole coastal sector south of the Po di Primaro.

There were at this time, twenty-six German divisions in Italy, including some of their best troops such as the 26th Panzer, the 19th Light, the 232nd, the 4th and 1st Parachute Divisions, and in order **Relative Strength of Forces** to prevent their transfer to Germany or retreat to the " Southern Redoubt," which it seemed possible Hitler might try to organize, a plan known as Operation " Grapeshot " was drafted whose aim was to trap and destroy the German armies of northern Italy in Italy. The Allied 15th Army Group (5th and 8th Armies) then consisted of the following divisions : seven American,

against targets in Austria, South Germany, the Balkans, and north Italy, and in the supply of Italian and Yugoslav partisans. The reconstituted Italian Air Force was used not for contacts with the patriots in north Italy, but to supply Marshal Tito's forces, and to protect them against German shipping covering the Dalmatian shores.

Canadian troops of the 8th Army reached Lake Comacchio on January 6, 1945, cutting off a number of enemy detachments in the swampy ground north of Ravenna. American and Brazilian units of the 5th Army opened a local offensive on the night of February 18–19, and occupied several heights in the upper Reno valley, west of the road between Pistoia and Bologna. On March 3, a local offensive on the 8th Army front enabled Italian regular and partisan forces to clear the

NEW ZEALANDERS CAPTURE FAENZA

The important Italian town of Faenza fell to troops of the New Zealand 2nd Division fighting with the 8th Army on December 16, 1944, after a fierce two-days' battle in which Italian patriots took part. Below, New Zealand infantry make a difficult passage as they enter Faenza over the ruins of a bridge which had once spanned the River Lamone. *Photo, British Official*

C.-IN-C., FIFTH ARMY

Lieutenant-General Lucian K. Truscott, Jr., who commanded the U.S. VI Corps at Anzio, was appointed commander of the 5th Army in Italy (announced December 6, 1944) in succession to Lieutenant-General Mark Clark, who succeeded Field-Marshal Alexander as C.-in-C., Allied Armies in Italy. Truscott founded the U.S. Rangers in England and took part in the Dieppe raid (see Chap. 243).

one South African, twelve British, six Italian, one Indian, two Polish, one New Zealand, and one Brazilian, plus a Jewish brigade. The average strength of a German division was some 10,000 ; that of an Allied division was much less. The Allies were superior in aircraft and, on the whole, in equipment ; but they were outnumbered.

" Grapeshot " was based on strong concentration of effort around Bologna. Two spearheads, one from the 5th, the other from the 8th Army, were to push forward respectively from the rugged mountains south-west of the city, and

CROSSING OF THE SENIO RIVER

The final Allied offensive in Italy began on April 9, 1945, when nearly 1,000 Allied Fortresses and Liberators struck a powerful blow at German positions directly opposite the 8th Army between the Senio and Santerno rivers. Over 3,000 100-lb. H.E. and 180,000 fragmentation bombs were dropped, the whole area being afterwards covered with an impenetrable wall of smoke and dust 4,000 feet high. That night the 2nd New Zealand Division, under Lt.-Gen. Sir Bernard Freyberg, V.C., stormed the Senio and spanned it with Bailey bridges. 1. New Zealand infantrymen scaling the high dyke of the Senio. Those in the foreground are carrying sections of a footbridge. 2. British-manned Vickers heavy machine-guns support the New Zealanders' attack. 3. Churchill tank plunges through the smoke and dust raised by the T.A.F. dive-bombers. 4. Maori medical orderlies lead the way for a casualty who is being helped by two German prisoners.

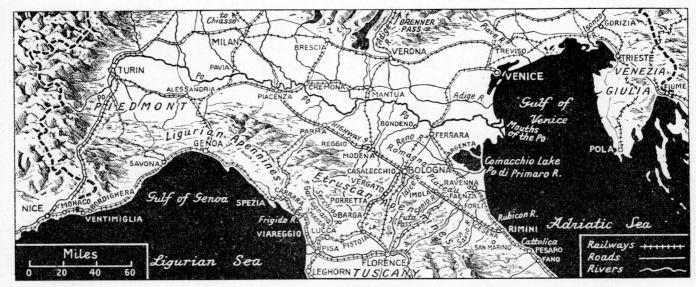

CLOSING STAGES OF THE CAMPAIGN IN ITALY

This map shows where the last battles in Italy were fought, from the fall of Rimini in September 1944 to the final surrender by General von Vietinghoff-Scheel of all German and Italian-Fascist forces in northern Italy and western Austria on April 29, 1945. It also includes the area where the Partisan troops were most active.

from the eastern plain—the Senio river front. The right wing of the 8th Army was to march towards Ferrara, to clear the southern bank of the Po. Then both Armies, from the line Bologna–Ferrara, were to cross the Po and the Adige, and, pursuing the enemy, close the Alpine passes.

On March 27, General Mark Clark broadcast to the patriots. He said: "Overhaul your equipment. Prepare to hamper the eventual enemy retreat and prevent enemy sabotage and destruction." On April 2, the 8th Army in a daring amphibious operation gained a very useful foothold between Lake Comacchio and the Adriatic, a precau-

tion against possible German counter-attack on the extreme right of the Allied flank. On the extreme left of the front, the Americans with similar purpose began an advance on April 5 which, with support from the British destroyers "Marne" and "Lookout," carried them to the city of Massa and across the Frigido river on the 10th. Their ad-

vance was the signal for local partisans to rise and seize Carrara.

In the evening of April 9, after a heavy air bombardment (*see* table in page 3650) and an artillery barrage said

BRITISH COMMANDO FORCE AT LAKE COMACCHIO

By a daring amphibious operation, a British Commando force with the 8th Army landed at dawn on April 2, 1945, north of Ravenna on the narrow sandspit between Lake Comacchio and the Adriatic, overrunning German defences and taking over 200 prisoners. It was here that Major Lassen, M.C. (see page 3710) won the V.C. Right, 'Kangaroo' tank after the operation. It was in radio contact with all positions. Below, Commando signalmen occupy slit trenches recently used by the Nazis. *Photos, British Official*

to have been greater than that at El Alamein, the 8th Army crossed the Senio river in strength between a point about nine miles north of Faenza and the southern shore of Lake Comacchio. On that date, the formations under 8th Army command were: British 6th Armoured Division; British 56th and 78th Infantry Divisons; 8th and 10th Indian Infantry Divisions; New Zealand 2nd Division; 5th Kresowa and 3rd Carpathian Divisions and Polish 2nd Armoured Brigade; Cremona, Fruili and Folgore Groups (each two divisions strong) of Italian infantry;

TWO ALLIED ARMIES REACH THE RIVER PO

On April 23, 1945, it was announced that both the 5th and 8th Armies had reached the banks of the River Po. The following day the 8th Army captured the industrial city of Ferrara and the ancient town of Modena. Above, Italian partisan troops, who had assisted in the liberation of Modena, round-up a group of cheerful-looking German stragglers in the outskirts of the town.

Photo. British Official

plus a considerable contingent of smaller units, including the 1st Jewish Brigade.

Flame-throwers went into action along the whole front ahead of the 8th Indian Division, the New Zealanders, and the Polish Corps. The British 78th Infantry and 6th Armoured Divisions swept through to join the 56th Division and the New Zealanders in the battle for Argenta Imola fell to the Poles on April 15, on which day the 5th Army joined in the offensive by an assault in the rugged central sector south of Vergato. On April 16, Field-Marshal Alexander issued an order of the day : "Final victory is near. The German forces are now very groggy and only need one mighty punch to knock them out for good. The moment has now come for us to take the field for the last battle which will end the war in Europe. You know what our comrades in the west and east are doing on the battle-fields. It is now our turn to play our decisive part. It will not be a walk-over ; a mortally wounded beast can still be very dangerous You must be prepared for a hard and bitter fight, but the end

Battle for Argenta

is quite certain—there is not the slightest shadow of doubt about that."

Although the Germans concentrated their defence against the 8th Army, they were defeated in the terrific battle for the "Argenta gap," half-way between Ravenna and Ferrara. Argenta itself was taken on April 18 against, according to General Mark Clark, "some of the best troops of the German army in formidable natural positions, strengthened throughout the winter months with all the ingenuity and thorough ness of the German High Command." On April 20 U.S. forces of the 5th Army cut the Via Emilia between Bologna and Modena, and South African troops entered Casalecchio, three miles south-west of Bologna.

ONE MORE RIVER!

But it isn't only "one more river" – this time it is THE river !

It is the mighty Po!

Do you remember the hell of the rivers Sangro, Rapido, Liri, Volturno and Garigliano ? Do you remember the lives that were sacrificed in crossing these rivers ?

Put these rivers all together and the result will be smaller than the

Po!

Also when you crossed these rivers, the Germans were in retreat and had no time to prepare defenses.

But covering the Po you will find a blanket of death. Artillery, Nebelwerfers, Mortars and Spandaus.

The whole Po area is a network of canals and is impassable for tanks.

Rush
In!
Various
Exiting
Revelations
Prepared
Oh Boy!

And here are a few facts about the Po:

At its shallowest part (between Adda and Mincio) it is 7 ft. deep.
At the deepest part (near Pavia) it is 20 ft. deep.
The width varies from 208 to 1,040 yds.
The banks are mostly sheer and between 18 and 30 ft. high.
The speed of the Po exceeds 20 m. p. h.

"PO" means death and suffering.
P.O W means security and comfort!

Think it over, only

<u>Fools rush in ...!</u>

AND 'ONE MORE RIVER' IT WAS

In an ingenuous attempt to undermine the morale of troops of the 8th Indian Division advancing towards the banks of the River Po in April 1945, the Germans dropped leaflets behind the lines. The grisly picture painted by the Nazis had no effect on the Indians who read the sheets with derision—and proceeded to cross yet 'one more river.'

see plate following page 3102

ALLIED FORCES DRIVE TOWARDS BOLOGNA

Fighting with the 8th Army, the 8th Indian Division, with New Zealanders and Poles, spearheaded the crossing of the flooded River Senio on April 10, 1945. Farther south, troops of the Gurkha Brigade captured Medicina in their drive towards Bologna. Here Indian troops advance up a ridge ; the man nearest the camera carries a ' Lifebuoy ' flame-thrower (see plate following page 3102). *Photo, British Official*

INDIAN TROOPS STORMED THE SANTERNO

Against fanatical resistance, troops of the 8th Indian Division helped to breach the powerful defences of the Senio river, twelve miles west of Ravenna, on April 10, 1945, when two young Sepoys, Namdeo Jadhao and Ali Haidar, won the V.C. (see page 3525). Next day they stormed the Santerno river with flame-throwers in close support. Here, Indian troops cross an improvised bridge spanning the Santerno
Photo, British Official

On April 21, a date celebrated in Italy as the anniversary of the foundation of Rome by Romulus, the ancient city of Bologna was liberated by the simultaneous entry of 8th Army troops from the east, 5th Army troops from south and **Bologna Liberated** west. Seat of one of the oldest and most famous universities in Europe, Bologna is also an important industrial centre and controls the most important Apennine passes and all the big roads on the southern bank of the Po. Two days later, spearheads of both Armies reached that greatest of Italian rivers. On the 24th, Ferrara and Modena fell to the 8th Army, and both armies crossed the Po at several points : first troops of the 5th Army across were the U.S. 10th Mountain Division, first of the 8th, the Grenadier Guards and New Zealand infantry. On the same day, the 5th Army entered the naval base of Spezia.

Since the offensive began, more than 40,000 prisoners (including Lieutenant-

BOLOGNA FALLS TO THE FIFTH AND EIGHTH ARMIES

Climax of eight months' hard and difficult fighting across the fifty miles of mountainous country between Florence and Bologna was reached on April 21, 1945, when U.S. troops of the 5th Army and Polish forces of the 8th Army simultaneously entered the ancient city of Bologna which had been abandoned by the enemy. Here U.S. troops relax in one of the city squares.

Photo, U.S. Official

General Count von Schwerin, commanding the 76th Panzer Division, and Major-General Schellwitz, commanding the 305th Infantry Division) had been captured. Enemy resistance remained nevertheless strong and organized.

Insurrection in the north broke out on April 24 (*see* page 3706), the patriots rapidly securing control of Genoa, Milan and other cities.

5th Army Meets the French On the 27th, the 5th Army liberated Piacenza and entered Genoa. It then drove on beyond Savona, to make contact with the French who had crossed the frontier and captured Ventimiglia and Bordighera on the 27th.

On April 29, Colonel-General Heinrich von Vietinghoff-Scheel, Kesselring's successor in Italy, unconditionally surrendered all German and Italian-Fascist forces in northern Italy and western Austria, aggregating over 1,000,000 men. The surrender (see Historic Document CCCII, page 3708) was signed at Allied Force Headquarters, Caserta, by two German plenipoten-

MOPPING-UP IN RUINED ARGENTA

The vital 'Argenta Gap,' sole practicable route for enemy mobile forces west of Lake Comacchio, was brought almost completely under Allied control by the capture on April 18, 1945, of Argenta town by troops of the 8th Army who afterwards pushed on along the road to Ferrara. Here a British patrol mops up among the devastation in ruined Argenta

Photo, British Official

ALLIES FROM SOUTH AND WEST LINK AT BRENNER

On May 4, 1945, troops of the U.S. 7th Army (part of General Eisenhower's command), after a night drive in snow and ice through the Brenner Pass, made contact at Vipitino, ten miles south-west of the Pass, with forces of the 5th Army driving north, thus completely overrunning the Nazis' 'Southern Redoubt.' Above, after the link-up at Brenner, with Nazi prisoners from Italy (left) tramping to captivity. *Photo, U.S. Official*

7th Army (*see* Chapter 369) near the Brenner Pass on May 4. The Allied forces in Italy had joined hands with those who had landed in the west.

"The Italian triumph," said General Marshall, "is a striking demonstration of the solidarity of the United Nations. Fighting under the 15th Army Group, at some time during the Italian campaign, were **Alexander's Polyglot Armies** Americans, British, Canadians, French, New Zealanders, South Africans, Poles, Indians, Brazilians, Italians, Greeks, Moroccans, Algerians, Arabs, Goums, Senegalese, and a brigade of Jewish soldiers.

"The entire campaign was slow and bitter. The Allied troops did not have the superiority they enjoyed in western Europe, where geography had compelled us to make the great effort. None the less, the Italian campaign was a heavy contribution to the successes on the western front, pinning down German forces which Hitler needed badly to reinforce his weakened armies, both in the east and the west."

tiaries, one on behalf of General von Vietinghoff-Scheel and the other on behalf of Obergruppenführer Karl Wolff, supreme commander of the S.S. and police, and German general plenipotentiary of the Wehrmacht in Italy. Lieutenant-General W. D. Morgan, Chief of Staff of Allied Force Headquarters, signed for the Allies. The surrender was not made public until May 2, the day it came into effect, by which date the Allies had entered Venice, Padua, Milan and Turin, all of which they found controlled by the patriots.

Spearheads of the 5th Army entered Como and reached the Swiss Frontier at Chiassa, thus splitting all enemy forces in northern Italy, **Brazilian Success** on April 29. On that day also the entire German 148th Infantry Division surrendered to the Brazilian Expeditionary Force headed by General Mascarenhas da Moreas, the Brazilians taking over 6,000 prisoners and over 1,000 enemy vehicles; and the New Zealand 2nd Division reached the Piave. The South African 6th Armoured Division with U.S. Infantry took Treviso on the 30th.

The New Zealand 2nd Division, under Lieutenant-General Sir Bernard Freyberg, V.C., crossed the Isonzo and linked with Yugoslav troops on May 1, received the surrender of the German commander in Trieste (*see* page 3707) and entered Gorizia on May 2. Troops of the U.S. 85th and 88th Divisions of the 5th Army made contact with troops of the U.S.

NEW ZEALANDERS ENTER TRIESTE

The famous Adriatic port of Trieste was surrendered by the German commander to General Freyberg on May 2, 1945, and the following day was entered by New Zealand troops of the 8th Army whose armour here pushes through a crowded street. Trieste belonged to the Austro-Hungarian Empire up till 1918 and, despite Yugoslav claims, was awarded to Italy by the Treaty of St. Germain because of its predominantly Italian population. *Photo, British Official*

May 1. British and U.S. bridge-heads across Lower Elbe linked up ; U.S. 3rd Army reached Czech border N.E. of Passau ; French 1st Army crossed Austrian frontier in Bregenz area. Charlottenburg and Schöneberg districts of Berlin cleared. 2nd New Zealand Division linked with Tito's forces in Italy. Australian 9th Division landed on Tarakan, N.E. Borneo.

May 2. British 2nd Army reached Baltic at Wismar ; U.S. 9th Army made second link with Russians at Ballow, N. of Arneburg ; 2nd T.A.F. heavily attacked Kiel (night). Berlin fell to 1st White Russian and 1st Ukrainian Armies. German surrender in Italy came into effect. Anglo-Indian amphibious force landed near Rangoon. Stand-down of British Civil Defence Services and Royal Observer Corps ; air-raid warning system discontinued.

May 3. Collapse of whole German defence system in N.W. Germany ; Hamburg surrendered to British 2nd Army ; Oldenburg surrendered to Canadians ; Americans captured Braunau, Hitler's Austrian birthplace. British link-up with Russians on Wismar-Wittenberge line ; Red Army freed Teschen on Polish–Czech frontier. New Zealand troops entered Trieste and Gorizia. Rangoon liberated.

May 4. All German forces in N.W. Germany, Holland and Denmark surrendered unconditionally to 21st Army Group at Lüneberg ; on U.S. 9th Army front remnants of German 9th and 12th Armies surrendered ; U.S. 7th Army captured Berchtesgaden, Salzburg, and Innsbrück and drove through Brenner Pass to Italy. Russians took Zlin (Bohemia), linked with Americans on the Elbe, near Dessau.

May 5. 2nd White Russian Army took Swinemünde and Peenemünde, site of Baltic V-bomb research station : British 7th Armoured Division crossed Danish frontier and entered Jutland. Patriot rising broke out in Prague. U.S. 3rd Army captured Linz, capital of Upper Austria. Davao (Mindanao, Philippines) fell to U.S. troops.

May 6. 2nd White Russian Army forced the Stralsunder Fahrwasser, on the Baltic, captured island of Rügen. U.S. 3rd Army entered Pilsen. 5th Army crossed Austrian frontier from Italy. Australian 9th Division captured Tarakan airfield (Borneo). Super-Fortresses bombed Honshu and Kyushu (Japan).

May 7. Germany's unconditional surrender to Western Allies and the U.S.S.R. signed at Rheims ; 3rd Canadian Division occupied Emden ; 1st Ukrainian Army captured Breslau ; British troops of 1st Canadian Army entered Utrecht. Australian and Dutch troops stormed Tarakan Hill.

May 8. V.E. Day. Germany's unconditional surrender signed in Berlin. 1st Ukrainian Army captured Dresden. Capitulation at Oslo of all German forces in Norway. Tito's troops freed Zagreb (Yugoslavia). Admiralty issued wireless surrender orders for German Fleet.

May 9. Goering and Kesselring captured by U.S. troops in Austria. Channel Islands liberated after 5 years of enemy occupation. German garrisons at Lorient, St. Nazaire, and La Rochelle surrendered. Surrender of Germans in the Dodecanese. Marianas-based Super-Fortresses heavily bombed Japan. Fresh U.S. landing on Mindanao (Philippines).

May 10. Prague entered by Russian tanks. Kiel occupied. First U-boat to surrender to Royal Navy (U 249) put in at Portland, Dorset. U.S. troops crossed Asa River estuary in S. Okinawa. All lighting restrictions lifted in Great Britain.

May 11. German garrison at Dunkirk surrendered. U.S. 3rd Army linked with Russians E. of Pilsen. 14th Army forces entered Sandoway (Burma). Australians across the Hongorai River (Bougainville). Chinese entered Foochow.

May 12. British troops went ashore at Jersey (Channel Islands). S.S. General "Sepp" Dietrich captured by U.S. troops in Austria. Germans in Crete surrendered. Aircraft of British Pacific Fleet heavily bombed Miyako and Ishigaki (Saki group, Ryukyu Islands).

May 13. Rear-Admiral Brüning, commanding German naval forces operating from Holland, arrived at Felixstowe. In New Guinea, Australian 6th Division made amphibious landing E. of Wewak.

May 14. Scots Guards took possession of Heligoland ; Ernst Kaltenbrünner, Gestapo chief, captured by U.S. 3rd Army troops. Marianas-based Super-Fortresses heavily attacked Nagoya (Japan). Australians in New Guinea cleared Wewak village.

May 15. British and Norwegian Naval Mission arrived in Bergen. On Okinawa U.S. forces penetrated defences of Naha, the capital. Australians made further crossing of Hongorai River (Bougainville). Japan abrogated treaty with Germany.

May 16. British troops went ashore on Alderney (Channel Islands), taking 3,200 German prisoners. U.S. 7th Army captured Robert Ley, German "Labour Front" leader. U.S. 77th Infantry Division seized "Chocolate Drop Hill," Okinawa, after 5-day battle. Aircraft of British E. Indies Fleet attacked Japanese cruiser in N. Malacca Straits.

May 17. British carrier-based aircraft heavily bombed Saki group (Ryukyus). White Paper on Burma issued in London.

May 18. Chinese announced capture of Foochow. "Sugar Loaf Hill," N.E. of Naha, Okinawa, captured. U.S. Navy aircraft heavily damaged industrial targets in Central Kyushu, shot down 62 enemy planes. U.S. troops on Mindanao captured Valencia. Admiralty announced that central area of North Sea was open for fishing.

May 19. Marianas-based Super-Fortresses in strength attacked Tokyo. On Okinawa, "Carbuncle Hill" stormed.

U.S. and Filipino forces captured the Ipo Dam, N.E. of Manila. Marshal Tito claimed right to occupy Trieste.

May 20. British aircraft bombed the Saki group. Announced in Melbourne that Australian 9th Division held two-thirds of Tarakan and that on Bougainville the 3rd and 11th Divisions had reached Ruri Bay, cutting off enemy communications along the E. seaboard. Tito withdrew troops from Carinthia.

May 21. Australians captured "Hill 105" on Tarakan (Borneo). Off Formosa, a single U.S. aircraft destroyed a convoy of 5 enemy ships, totalling 17,000 tons. Acting premier of Syria asked Allies to evacuate all foreign troops from Syria.

May 22. U.S. troops took Yonabaru, second town of Okinawa. On Tarakan, Australians seized "Helen's Hill." Announced from Washington that Japanese were attacking the U.S. with explosives dropped from small long-range balloons. Field-Marshal Montgomery appointed C.-in-C. of British Forces of Occupation in Germany.

May 23. Over 550 Super-Fortresses dropped 4,500 tons of incendiaries on Tokyo in heaviest raid on Japan to date. Resignation of Mr. Churchill and the Coalition Government.

May 24. German cruisers "Prinz Eugen" and "Nürnberg" sailed from Copenhagen to Wilhelmshaven under British naval escort. Australians in New Guinea encircled Wewak. Aircraft of British Pacific Fleet raided the Saki group. U.S. Ryukyus-based Thunderbolts bombed Kyushu.

May 25. Super-Fortresses mass-raided Tokyo at night, dropping 4,000 tons of incendiaries. 14th Army forces seized Bassein, centre of Burmese rice trade. General de Gaulle invested Field-Marshal Montgomery with Grand Cross of the Legion of Honour.

May 26. Tokyo again raided heavily by Super-Fortresses ; buildings damaged included the Imperial Palace. Mr. Churchill announced new Cabinet.

May 27. S.H.A.E.F. announced the change of its H.Q. from Rheims to Frankfort-on-Main. Chinese troops recaptured Nanning, capital of Kwangsi.

May 28. 450 Super-Fortresses attacked Yokohama, dropping over 3,200 tons of fire bombs. Japanese "suicide" attacks on U.S. shipping off Okinawa.

May 29. Australians in Tarakan, capturing "Freda's Hill," reached the N.W. coast at Cape Djoeta. Belgian Socialists demanded abdication of King Leopold. French shelled Damascus.

May 30. U.S. troops captured Shuri Castle on Okinawa. On Luzon, Montalban Dam seized, completing U.S. control of Manila's water supply. British and U.S. citizens evacuated from Damascus.

May 31. Osaka, Japan's second city, heavily bombed by 450 Super-Fortresses. General Chiang Kai-shek resigned Chinese Premiership, succeeded by Dr. T. V. Soong. Norwegian Government returned to Oslo.

Chapter 362

BERLIN FALLS TO THE RED ARMY

This chapter, the last in the account of the campaigns in eastern Europe by Major-General Sir Charles Gwynn, the Military Editor, carries the Armies of Marshals Zhukov and Koniev from the Oder to Berlin, with the surrender of which on May 2, 1945, the war against Germany virtually ended. Simultaneous operations by the Soviet armies in the south are recorded in Chapter 354

B Y the end of March 1945, Zhukov had cleared the east bank of the Oder, eliminating the last bridgeheads the Germans held across the river (*see* page 3559). He had also liquidated all blocks on his lines of communications, and in conjunction with Rokossovsky had annihilated the Germans in Pomerania on his right flank. On his right Rokossovsky was in process of completing the mopping up of Danzig, and on his left Koniev had reached the Neisse on a broad front. Farther south Malinovsky and Tolbukhin were ap-

in Hungary and Slovakia continued to advance, Marshal Zhukov (1st White Russian Army) and Marshal Koniev (1st Ukrainian Army) were apparently not quite ready. Not until April 19 was it announced that their final offensive had started on the 16th with a crossing of both the Oder and the Neisse by Polish tanks and infantry. By that time Vienna had fallen, and in the west the Allies had reached the Elbe. It is not yet clear why Koniev and Zhukov remained comparatively inactive for so long. Presumably the

main reason was the necessity of completing a build up of material and troops which would ensure success. Breslau and Glogau, which still held out, may have delayed Koniev, for they blocked his best lines of communication. Moreover, it had become evident that though, on their western front the morale of the Germans was breaking and resistance becoming patchy, yet they were determined to hold the Oder–Neisse line at all costs, possibly hoping that if that could be achieved the western Allies might concede more favourable terms.

It was therefore essential that the success of the Russian offensive when delivered should be assured. An unsuccessful attack launched before the Allies had closed up to the Elbe might have

Soviet Offensive Develops

enabled the Germans to carry out the scheme for making their final stand in the south. So long, however, as Zhukov and Koniev remained poised, the Germans could not disengage with safety nor transfer troops to reinforce their western front. Whatever were the reasons for the somewhat intriguing delay in launching it, the Soviet offensive quickly developed in devastating fashion in spite of desperate German resistance. It took three days of hard

LAST NAZI CALL-UP

The Red Army launched its final offensive on April 16, 1945, with a crossing of the rivers Oder and Neisse. By this time the Germans were helpless to stem the Russian tide. These German photographs—among the last to be taken of their own troops —show members of the Volkssturm (above) and a youthful Nazi (right) in action on the Oder front.   *Photos, Associated Press*

proaching Vienna (*see* Chapter 354); while in the west General Eisenhower's armies were well across the Rhine and had encircled a large German force in the Ruhr (*see* page 3661 and Chapter 369).

All therefore seemed well set for the final effort to crush the last remnants of German resistance. But although the Allies in the west and the Russians

ON THE FRISCHES HAFF

The 3rd White Russian Army on March 15, 1945, fought its way along the water-logged shore of the Frisches Haff in East Prussia to cut in two the enemy formations defending Königsberg, which fell on April 9 (see page 3560). Above, remains of Nazi transport column at Frauenburg, on the Frisches Haff, after attack by Soviet Stormoviks. Right, some of the seven thousand Germans taken at Heiligenbeil, last German defence point on the Frisches Haff, on March 25.

fighting to enlarge bridge-heads over the two rivers and to get the main forces in motion, but after that the issue was never in doubt.

Koniev appeared at first to be making for Dresden and Zhukov for Berlin, the suburbs of which were reached on April 22. The following day Orders of the Day announced that Zhukov had taken Frankfort - o n - Oder, Oranienburg (site of a notorious concentration camp), and other towns and had broken into Berlin from the east, north-east, and north; and that Koniev, having penetrated the deep defences of the Neisse, and captured Kottbus and other towns in a wheel northwards, had entered Berlin from the south. By April 25 Zhukov, having at an early stage initiated an outflanking movement north of the city, had linked up with Koniev north-west of Potsdam, thus completing Berlin's encirc ement.

Frankfort-on-Oder Captured

Koniev meanwhile with his left continued to advance towards Dresden, crossed the Elbe, and near Torgau joined hands with the Americans on April 25 (see Chapter 369), U.S. and Soviet patrols having had some difficulty in recognizing each other. This great event elicited an exchange of messages to the Allied troops from Marshal Stalin, Mr. Churchill and President Truman, in which the link-up was taken as an assurance of the determination of the Allies to prosecute the war together till the last remnants of German resistance were crushed. Although these messages were an acknowledgment of a great comradeship in arms and a call for a final effort, their main purpose probably was to dispel any lingering hopes the Germans might entertain of driving a wedge between the Allies or of obtaining divergent terms from them.

There was to be no race to Berlin, however, and evidently each of the Allies had its assigned task. The Russian attack on Berlin, where it was known that Hitler had decided to make a last ditch stand, was therefore vigorously maintained and made steady progress in street to street fighting.

On April 27 the satellite towns of Rathenow, Spandau and Potsdam (spiritual home of German militarism) were taken, making the ring of encirclement all the closer. Hitler, who appears at first to have expected his armies in the north to come to his assistance, about this time gave up all hope, and

Himmler, deserting his master, offered to surrender to the western Allies, only to be turned down since he appeared still to hope to maintain resistance to the Russian advance. (See also announcements by German leaders in pages 3640–41.) The Germans in the north were in fact in no position to come to Hitler's rescue, for in addition to the pressure exercised on them from the west Rokossovsky had on April 26 crossed the lower Oder, taken Stettin and was thrusting rapidly into western Pomerania. It is not clear how much opposition Rokossovsky was meeting, but probably it was feeble for from British sources came reports that German units retreating before him were reaching the British lines and entreating officers in vain to accept their surrender to save them from falling into the hands of the Russians.

The Germans obviously were by now in a hopeless position. Koniev's link with the Americans in Saxony was consolidated and barred all communication between north and south. In the south the U.S. 3rd and 7th Armies were pressing on towards Bohemia and Austria, overrunning Bavaria. In Italy the Allies were in full pursuit of the Germans attempting to retreat across the Po (see page 3716). In the north, British and Americans were across the Elbe (see page 3666), and, with Rokossovsky pressing on through

East–West Link Consolidated

RUSSIANS HEAD FOR THE REICH CAPITAL

Final Russian onslaught against Berlin began from the east on April 16, 1945, with the Oder and Neisse crossings. Nine days later, with the link-up between the 1st White Russian and 1st Ukrainian Armies, north-west of Potsdam, the capital's encirclement was complete. 1. Red Army tank heads for the city. 2 Soviet troops man a gun-post along a Berlin motor-road Below, German river-craft abandoned on the Oder *Photos, Pictorial Press*

Pomerania and into Mecklenburg, retreat into Denmark offered the only hope of temporary escape.

On May 1 Hitler's death in Berlin and his succession by Grand Admiral Carl Doenitz was announced. On the following day the fall of Berlin after seventeen **Berlin** days' fierce fighting was **Surrenders** proclaimed in Order of the Day No. 359 issued by Marshal Stalin : "Troops of the 1st White Russian Front commanded by Marshal Zhukov, with the support of troops of the 1st Ukrainian Front commanded by Marshal Koniev, after stiff street fighting, have today, May 2, completely captured Berlin, capital of Germany, centre of German imperialism, and hotbed of German aggression. The Berlin garrison, with General of Artillery Weidling and his staff at their head, ceased resistance at 3 p.m., laid down their arms, and surrendered. By 9 p.m. our troops had taken over 70,000 prisoners in Berlin " (in addition to more than 100,000 taken earlier in the fighting for the city).

This for the Russians meant a final triumph, exclusively their own and therefore probably even greater than the enemy's unconditional surrender to all the Allies which was to follow. It was saluted by 24 salvos from 324 guns in Moscow, where great victory celebrations were held. Never can revenge for unprovoked attack have been so complete, though the cost was terrific. To Marshal Stalin and to Zhukov it was a personal triumph ; but to the Russian people who had seen their lands devastated and their families slaughtered or led into captivity it probably meant even more. To the world in general, which such a short time before had thought the fall of Leningrad, Moscow and Stalingrad inevitable, the Russian recovery was a sheer miracle. Even when the tide turned at Stalingrad and Germany's ultimate defeat could be predicted, few could have imagined that the Red Army would traverse those hundreds of miles to take the aggressor's capital by storm.

The speed with which Zhukov's offensive developed may produce the impression that it encountered feeble resistance, but it was undoubtedly one of the most remarkable feats accomplished by the Red Army. When he started Zhukov had secured only a tiny bridge-head, little over a mile deep, across the Oder. Most of the forty miles between the river and Berlin was intersected by trenches, houses were strongly fortified, and there were many water channels to be crossed. Nevertheless, after a three-day infantry and artillery battle had broken the crust of the defence and extended the bridge-head, the main role was assigned to armoured formations. There was no question of making a gap, and the tanks, looking for weak spots, had to work their way through defences in depth. Their orders were to " by-pass cities and inhabited points and move forward in forced marches." Sappers accompanying the armour gave invaluable assistance by bridging canals, often under heavy fire. Manoeuvring ever more widely, in four days of incessant fighting the tanks reached the outskirts of Berlin only to find resistance stiffening. But a way had been opened for the infantry, and motorized divisions swung to the right, outflanking the city on the north. Then followed street fighting in which the Germans were either driven underground or attempted to hold the main public buildings in the heart of the city.

Tempelhof and its airfield were over-run on April 27. The outer districts of the city were captured in succession, Charlottenburg in the west, Moabit **Russian Gains in Berlin** in the north-west and Schöneberg in the south, by April 29. Mopping up had to be done thoroughly, for Germans concealed in cellars seized chances of emerging to attack forward Russian parties from the rear. The streets were often under cross-fire and progress could be made only by blasting a way through the walls of adjoining houses, as had been done in Vienna (*see* page 3627). As resistance in the suburban districts was broken, the Russians in ever stronger force and in a closer ring pressed on into the heart of the city where fanatical groups were holding the main government buildings.

The fight for the Reichstag alongside the Spree at the corner of the Tiergarten was particularly fierce, and marked the culmination of the struggle. For hours the Reichstag, neighbouring structures, and the Tiergarten were pounded from the air and by heavy guns and mortars. At first German anti-aircraft guns gave some protection, and transport aircraft attempted to maintain communications. But soon, as the guns were silenced, the aircraft that came in could not get out.

The final assault was delivered across the Spree under intensified supporting bombardment of the whole area. The Russian infantry made an astonishing charge over narrow footbridges and closed with the enemy in desperate hand-to-hand combat. In the peak of the struggle, an unknown man

SOVIET DRIVE THROUGH UPPER SILESIA

The 1st Ukrainian Army under Marshal Koniev, in its drive through Upper Silesia, captured the powerful German defence point of Neisse on March 24, 1945. (1) Marshals Rotmistrov (see page 3223 and illus. in page 3077) and Koniev in a forward observation post during the offensive. (2) Soviet transport passes Nazi barricades and abandoned guns in the town of Neisse. (3) Wrecked German baggage train clutters the streets. *Photos, Pictorial Press*

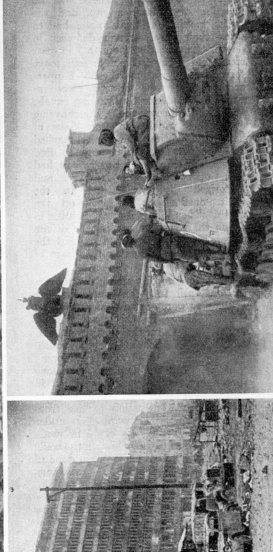

BATTLE FOR BERLIN

After stiff street fighting, during which the entire Government quarter of the city including all the Ministries, was laid in ruins, Berlin was captured on May 2, 1945, by the 1st White Russian Army, commanded by Marshal Zhukov, with the support of the 1st Ukrainian Army under Marshal Koniev. The end came when Soviet forces met in the Tiergarten (see map) after a hard-fought advance from north and south. I. Soviet mortar-crews in a residential quarter. 2. German 'King Tiger' tank disabled outside the ruined Potsdam Station (see map). 3. Soviet artillery enters the capital from the N.E

RED ARMY ARTILLERY SHELLS BERLIN

British and American military observers permitted to study the Red Army at the front paid high tribute to the precision of both Russian guns and Russian marksmanship. Soviet artillery played an important part in the capture of Berlin which fell on May 2, 1945, after 17 days of fierce fighting. Here Red Army gunners go into action on the outskirts of the Reich capital.

Photo, Pictorial Press

penetrated into the main building and from an upper window thrust out a Red banner evoking tumultous cheers. A few minutes after that, the Red banner was hoisted on the roof as a symbol of victory.

The Russian troops were in a state of exaltation which allowed nothing to stop them, and it is not surprising that the Germans, assailed by tanks, close range artillery and frenzied infantry, lost their will to continue a hopeless struggle. Nevertheless, it was a cool, skilful and determined encircling manoeuvre that defeated the German defence so quickly.

The capture of Berlin virtually brought the war to an end. With Hitler's death it is clear that, with

German Commanders Give Up Hope the exception of Shörner in Bohemia, all the high German commanders had given up hope of continuing resistance either in the southern redoubt or by retreat into Denmark and Norway. The South-West Command, which included Italy and the southern provinces of Austria, surrendered to Field-Marshal Alexander on April 29 (*see* page 3717), and the whole of the troops in north-west Germany, Denmark and Holland to Field-Marshal Montgomery on May 4 (*see* page 3666). Desperate attempts were continued to escape surrender to

the Russians and at the last minute to drive a wedge into Allied unity. But, faced by the firm resolve of the Allies to accept nothing short of unconditional surrender and the continued advance of the Russians, the attempt was soon abandoned.

On May 3 Rokossovsky's forces joined hands at several points with those of Montgomery on the Wismar–Wittenberge line, and in the following days completed the capture of all German ports on the Baltic coast. Koniev was also advancing on Dresden and, despite stubborn resistance, stormed that city on May 8, shortly after the final act of Germany's unconditional surrender was ratified and confirmed in Berlin at 00·16 hours on May 8.

Thus the greatest war in history was brought to a formal end, and this time the signatures of the heads of all the German fighting Services gave indisputable proof that the reputedly invincible Wehrmacht acknowledged complete defeat.

The isolated outlying German groups quickly accepted the situation and followed the lead of the main army.

The largest group was that penned into the Courland promontory. The troops were in any case in a desperate situation, for Rokossovsky's drive along the Baltic coast had deprived them of the **Surrender in** bases from which they **Courland** had received supplies by sea. When their surrender was completed, May 13, they had eaten all their horses and were on the edge of starvation. In attempts to excuse the strategic blunder that had for so long left the remnants of two armies powerless to affect the situation, it was claimed that the force had retreated to Courland in order to stage a counter-offensive. In the end about 200,000 men laid down their arms there.

In East Prussia, Marshal Vassilievsky (3rd White Russian Army) captured Pillau on April 25, and though a die-hard remnant continued resistance in the sand dunes enclosing the Frisches Haff till Doenitz surrendered, virtually the whole Province had been cleared before May 8.

Only in Bohemia was there a deliberate attempt to carry on the struggle, but

ALLIED PENETRATION OF THE REICH ON APRIL 6, 1945 (Allied-held areas are shaded)

by May 10 Field-Marshal Schörner's troops (*see page 3626*), threatened with encirclement, began to surrender in disorderly scattered parties.

The completeness of the victory was, of course, mainly due to the spirit of unity that had been established between the Allies, and to the skill and loyalty with which their efforts had been co-ordinated. To the Western Allies may be assigned the chief credit for frustrating German attempts to interrupt sea communications, for establishing a mastery over the Luftwaffe, and for disrupting from the air Germany's industrial capacity and internal mobility.

Their armies also intervened with decisive effect in the last years of the war.

Yet the part played by the Soviet Union by engaging and defeating the greater part of Germany's Army, the instrument on which she primarily relied, cannot be overestimated. It was undoubtedly the decisive factor in

WAR IN ITALY ENDS WITH GERMAN UNCONDITIONAL SURRENDER

The Italian campaign ended on April 29, 1945, with the unconditional surrender by General Heinrich Gottfried von Vietinghoff-Scheel of all German and Italian-Fascist forces in northern Italy and western Austria, numbering nearly 1,000,000 men. The instrument of surrender was signed at Allied Force H.Q., Caserta, by two German agents in civilian clothes and by Lieutenant-General W. D. Morgan, Chief of Staff of Allied Force H.Q. One German signed on behalf of General von Vietinghoff-Scheel and the other on behalf of Obergruppenführer Karl Wolff, supreme commander of the S.S. and German police in Italy. 1. One of the German representatives signs the surrender. 2. Lieutenant-General Morgan signs on behalf of the Allies. 3. Scene of the ceremony, with the Germans on the extreme left and Lieutenant-General Morgan, with head bowed, on the right. 4. General von Vietinghoff-Scheel.

Photos, British Official ; Associated Press.

RUSSIANS TAKE BRESLAU AFTER EIGHTY-TWO DAYS' SIEGE

Photo, Pictorial Press

Troops of the 1st Ukrainian Army, under Marshal Koniev, on May 7, 1945, completely captured the city and fortress of Breslau, capital of Silesia, on the River Oder. The Germans had earlier announced the garrison's surrender because of lack of supplies after a siege which had begun on February 14 and lasted 82 days. The Germans, headed by the fortress commander, General von Niklos, and his staff, laid down their arms and surrendered to the Russians. Since its investment, the city had been crumbling to pieces, block by block, in bitter street fighting of the kind shown here.

RED ARMY HAILS CAPTURE OF THE REICH CAPITAL

'A city of death and destruction,' surpassing in its horror even Warsaw and Leningrad, was how Russian observers described Berlin after its fall to the Red Army on May 2, 1945. The city was taken block by block in 17 days' bitter street fighting with remnants of the German 9th Army, S.S. troops and other fanatical Nazis holding out till the end. Above, men of a Red Army tank unit hail their triumph in the Königs-Platz. The 1870 Victory column is in the background. Below, Russian patrols approach the ruined Reichstag, over which the Red Flag was hoisted on April 30.

Photos, Pictorial Press 4 D

HITLER'S 'LAST STAND' TROOPS IN BERLIN MARCH TO CAPTIVITY

After Berlin had finally surrendered to the Red Army at 3 p.m. on May 2, 1945, straggling columns of German prisoners, many halt-crazed by the ordeal through which they had come, began to be marched to prison camps on the city's outskirts. Many laughed hysterically and could not stop laughing as they trailed through the shattered city. Here, some of the 120,000 prisoners taken in eight days' fighting for the capital emerge from a ruined building on their way to captivity. Hundreds of German military engineers were at once ordered to restore Berlin's public services put out of commission in the fighting

Photo Pictorial Press

making victory complete and in saving the Western Allies, if not from defeat, at least from being unable to develop decisive offensive power. No one has more frankly and fully admitted the debt the Western Allies owe to the Soviet Union than Mr. Churchill, and he of all men should be best qualified to judge.

Russia received material assistance from the industrial resources of Britain and America, and she benefited increasingly by the destructive effects of the western air offensive. But it must always be remembered that from the moment Russia was attacked the Luftwaffe's offensive against Britain virtually ceased. Its engagement on the Russian front, and possibly even more the diversion of Germany's industrial capacity to meet wastage on that front, prevented a renewal of full scale air attack. If Russia had collapsed or been rendered impotent as a result of her early defeats, it is questionable whether under renewed air attack by the Luftwaffe and a possible earlier appearance of Hitler's secret weapons in consequence of reduced demands on his industrial resources, Britain could have remained the secure base from which the Allied western offensive

Assistance from Britain and America

developed. During Russia's period of greatest danger, Great Britain was sending her all the assistance she could, but Pearl Harbor had not yet forced the U.S.A. into the war, and by the time it did the first crisis at Moscow had passed ; and although Germany, in view of Britain's amphibious potentialities, maintained substantial forces to guard the western sea board, that did not materially affect the strength of the forces initially used against the U.S.S.R. Almost certainly, the greatest benefit Russia derived from British action at that critical time was the postponement of the date of the German onslaught, owing to the diversion of the Luftwaffe to the capture of Crete and to the losses it suffered then. That postponement in all probability had far-reaching results, for it may have saved Moscow by involving the Germans in a disastrous winter campaign. If that was the result, seldom can an apparently disastrous episode have produced such favourable strategical consequences.

Nevertheless, it was mainly due to her own efforts that Russia survived the initial German onslaught ; and the postponement of Hitler's attack would not have mattered if his confident belief in decisive victory within three months had been well based.

Failure to capture Moscow, and enforced withdrawal under the pressure of the astonishingly prompt and fierce counter-offensive which Zhukov had prepared, brought the Germans, as they themselves admit, to the brink of complete disaster. They may have been saved by their executive skill, but the exceptional severity of the winter, which affected even the suitably clothed Russians, contributed to their escape. This was nevertheless perhaps the real turning point of the war. Coinciding as it did with the addition of America with all its resources to the Allied ranks, Germany's ultimate defeat could thereafter confidently be predicted. She had lost many of her best war experienced troops, the reputation of her army for invincibility, especially under winter conditions, had been shattered. Even in her southern drive, where her success had been greatest, she suffered a set-back when the Russians recaptured Rostov on November 28, six days after the Germans took it, and Sevastopol held out.

But Germany still retained great offensive power, and in the summer of 1942 she displayed her remarkable power of recovery. She was able to mount a formidable offensive although she had increasingly to rely on satellite troops and formations of second-class quality to hold comparatively quiet sectors. It has been argued that the Russians had never to meet German troops of as uniform high quality as those the western Allies encountered in Africa and Italy. Considering the vast area covered by operations in Russia, that may be partly true, and certainly after 1941 elements of weakness were revealed of which the Russians were quick to take advantage. But for offensive purposes high quality German troops were always available, and it was in defence that weaknesses were chiefly discovered.

Summer Campaign, 1942

Successful as the 1942 German offensive was in overrunning valuable territory, it failed to destroy the Russian southern armies and left those of the centre and north and in reserve comparatively free to prepare for the counter-stroke. Timoshenko, though defeated, by rapid retreat saved his armies, and, rallying at Stalingrad and in the Caucasus, brought the German drive to a standstill. Moreover, the determined stand made at Voronezh forced the Germans to modify their plans, and kept open railway communications from Moscow towards Stalingrad. The Soviet counter-offensive at Stalingrad, which trapped

CAMPAIGN ON THE EASTERN FRONT

As a conclusion to his detailed account of events on the eastern front, begun in Chapter 181 and continued at intervals in other chapters through this HISTORY OF THE SECOND GREAT WAR, *General Gwynn summarizes the great movements of this stupendous campaign from 1941 to 1945*

A T the end of the first month of the invasion, the Germans claimed that the Russians were on the brink of collapse, having lost all control and become capable of only local resistance. Yet stubborn fighting in the Smolensk region and in the approaches to Leningrad had already begun to check the impetus of the offensive. The evacuation of Smolensk, announced on August 13, 1941, had taken place only a few days earlier and the threat to Leningrad did not reach its maximum till September 8. Timoshenko's counter-offensive east of Smolensk during September forced the Germans on to the defensive, and it was not till October 3 that they were able to resume their drive towards Moscow which was to end in the disastrous winter campaign.

The time gained by Timoshenko was therefore to prove of the utmost importance ; but the resistance of Leningrad had more immediate and permanent results. Although cut off completely by land, it stood siege under conditions of appalling suffering from starvation,

cold and constant air and artillery bombardment for over two years, and eventually became the base for a highly important counter-offensive. During that period it not only brought the German northern offensive to a halt, thus protecting the communications from Murmansk and Archangel to Moscow, but contained very considerable German forces. The siege, partly no doubt owing to its great length, has attracted attention mainly as an example of amazing endurance, but the strategic results it achieved with the assistance of Voroshilov's field armies should not be under-estimated.

Events on the Leningrad front were, of course, overshadowed by the desperate fighting to save Moscow after Hitler, on October 3, launched the offensive he believed would prove decisive. There, as at Leningrad, much of the credit for the stubbornness of the defence directed by Zhukov should go to the civil population, but undoubtedly it was winter and German unpreparedness to meet its rigour that saved the city.

RED ARMY ADVANCES INTO POMERANIA

On March 5, 1945, Marshal Zhukov's 1st White Russian Army captured Stargard, Naugard and Polzin, powerful strongpoints in the German defences in the Stettin area, forestalling an enemy counter-plan aimed at the right flank of the Soviet salient. Above, German refugees' 'covered wagons' trek westwards in Pomerania. Below, Russian cavalry enter Naugard, 30 miles north-east of Stettin.
Photos, Pictorial Press

Paulus's army and started the second Russian winter offensive, was undoubtedly the decisive turning point of the war, synchronizing as it did with the defeat of Rommel at El Alamein and the opening of the Tunisian front.

From that time onwards the North African and Italian operations constituted an effective second front, all the more because the German forces engaged there perforce had to be of high quality owing to their comparatively small size and the high standard of armament of the Western Powers.

The Russian winter campaign of 1942–3 was amazingly successful, though it ended with a serious reverse; but not before the Germans, desperately battered, had been driven back to and beyond their starting point of the previous summer, and had been compelled to draw on their main strategic reserves.

The results of the winter campaign of 1942–43 made it clear that Germany could no longer hope to bring about a complete Russian collapse; but it was still open to question whether by exploiting her apparent superiority under summer conditions Germany might be able to establish a firm defensive front in Russia, leaving her in possession of vast territories of great economic value and with opportunities for employing her strategic reserves against the Western Allies should they attempt to land in France. There was every sign that Russia intended to exploit during the summer the offensive power she had developed, but equally there were signs that the Germans, still trusting to superiority under summer conditions, would not stand passively on the

Russian Collapse Averted

defensive but would attack, if only to break up Russian offensive preparations and to secure a more favourable stabilization line.

In the event the Germans struck first, the Russians apparently having deliberately awaited attack in defensive positions against which they hoped the Germans would shatter their armour. The great battle of the Kursk salient (July 1943) which resulted, proved conclusively that the Germans had met their masters under all conditions. Their offensive, in spite of some initial success, broke down, and the great Russian counter-offensive which had begun at Stalingrad was resumed and was maintained virtually without intermission to the end. Even when a pause on certain sectors of the front

became necessary, another flared into activity.

Defeated in the Kursk salient, the Germans were left with no alternative but to withdraw as speedily as possible to the Dnieper and Melitopol line while retaining their positions in the Crimea

Germans Withdraw to the Dnieper

and in the north round Leningrad. It must be admitted that their withdrawal was skilful, but Russian pursuit was fierce, and before a rallying position on the Dnieper could be effectively occupied Soviet forces secured bridgeheads across the river.

When Tolbukhin broke the Melitopol line, Koniev thrust from Kremenchug towards Krivoi Rog, and Vatutin took Kiev, it was clear that the Dnieper line was crumbling. But Vatutin's bold thrust westwards from Kiev implied a greater danger, for it threatened the main line of communication of all the Germans in the Ukraine. Von Manstein was compelled to concentrate his reserves to meet it; and he was able to draw on the Reichswehr's central reserves, for till after the winter the Allies could not open their expected attack in the west.

Without time for full preparation, the counter-stroke with which Von Manstein attempted to crush Vatutin and restore the situation was perforce delivered piecemeal as his reserves arrived, and though it recovered some ground it did little more than delay Vatutin's offensive. Its partial success may have encouraged Hitler to cling to dangerously exposed positions in the Dnieper bend.

The Russian offensive continued to develop and before the spring thaw

(1944) brought it to a pause the whole of the Ukraine was recaptured and all the German forces in it, having suffered heavy disasters, withdrew in divergent directions, part to cover Rumania, part into Poland. As a final blow Tolbukhin recaptured the Crimea.

The annihilation of Von Arnim's army in Tunisia and the subsequent invasion of Sicily and Italy may well have contributed to the German failure to rally on the Dnieper, and intensification of the Allied air offensive had also begun materially to affect the issue; in particular it made it increasingly important for the Germans to protect the oilfields of Rumania and the war industries of Italy. It was an astonishing feat for the Red Army to have maintained a virtually uninterrupted offensive for ten months during which it advanced over 500 miles, through country twice devastated by the tide of war, and fought many hard engagements. No clearer proof could have been given of the completeness of Russian recovery and of the offensive power developed under all conditions coupled, evidently, with remarkable administrative capacity. The subsidiary offensive which in January 1944 raised the siege of Leningrad, and left the Germans in a dangerous salient in Latvia and Estonia, proved how uniform the recovery had been.

German Failure to Rally

The Soviet offensive was resumed in the summer of 1944 after a surprisingly short pause. The attack by the three White Russian Armies was admirably conceived and carried through with devastating results. It was delivered almost immediately the success of the Normandy landing was assured. The offensive was soon taken up all along the front and did not pause till in the centre the frontiers of East Prussia and the line of the Vistula had been reached. In the north the Germans in Latvia and Estonia were completely isolated by the three Baltic Armies, while in the south, after Rumania and Bulgaria had been forced to change sides, the offensive was maintained to the end without a pause.

After the reopening of the western front the successive waves of the Allied offensive were synchronized as far as practicable, although pre-arranged dates may have been upset by particular events. Thus Zhukov's great drive from the Vistula to the Oder in January 1945 had probably been intended to coincide with the battle of the Rhineland, which was delayed by Rundstedt's Ardennes offensive. Thereafter the crossing of the Rhine and collapse of German resistance in the west may have come earlier than the date Zhukov was working to for his Oder offensive. On the whole, however, the final

blows of the Allies were admirably co-ordinated, and Mr. Churchill has testified to the punctuality with which the Russians fulfilled their promises. Both he and General Marshall agree that even after the western front was fully developed, the Russians had still to deal with two-thirds of the German Army.

To what should we ascribe Russia's amazing recovery apart from the fact that she had immense man-power resources to draw on ? Primarily it was the courage, patient endurance and amazing physical strength of the Russian soldier, all the more astonishing in view of the many different races and surroundings from which he came.

Secondly, Russia was fortunate in producing leaders who refused to accept defeat and developed into commanders of exceptional brilliance. It was probably advisable to replace the older commanders by men who had acquired in the first year of the war intimate experience of modern conditions, but once the latter had been placed in high command it is evident that they commanded confidence to a remarkable degree. Compared with the constant dismissals of German commanders, the security of tenure enjoyed by Russian generals is all the more notable.

The Russian system of training must have been astonishingly efficient to ensure replacement of the desperately heavy casualties by an unending stream of well-trained men. But perhaps the most surprising achievement was that of the administrative Services which kept the huge machine in motion.

RUSSO-AMERICAN LINK-UP AT TORGAU

Allied troops from the east and west joined forces for the first time at Torgau, thirty miles north-east of Leipzig, on April 26, 1945. Here, Russians and Americans chat across the bonnet of a jeep. Above, Major-General E. F. Reinhardt, commanding the U.S. 69th Division, with Major-General Rusakov, commander of the Soviet 58th Guards Division. *Photos, Pictorial Press*

Chapter 363

EMPIRE CHANGE-OVER FROM WAR TO PEACE

In this chapter, covering events in the Dominions during the year 1945, internal politics, the aid given to Britain both in the last months of war and the first of peace, and the sacrifices made in the cause of the United Nations are the chief topics. The history of the Dominions in 1944 is given in Chapter 338

THE failure on February 5 of the attempt to find General McNaughton (*see* page 3450) a seat in Parliament for Greynorth (where he was beaten by a Progressive Conservative) led the Premier, Mr. Mackenzie King, to state that his defeat would force the Government to consider holding a general election very shortly, notwithstanding his own frequently expressed reluctance to do so while the soldiers were still fighting in Europe. The 19th Parliament of the Dominion of Canada was dissolved on April 16, a few hours before its term automatically expired on the 17th; but the fighting was in fact over before election day, June 11. The results, declared on June 19, gave the Liberal Party still the largest number of seats in the House, but with much reduced strength, the figures of the principal groups being: Liberals 119 (155 at the dissolution); Progressive Conservatives 65 (40); Co-operative Commonwealth Federation 28 (10); Social Credit 13 (10). Seven Independent Liberals and three of eight Independents could generally be counted on to support the Government, which thus had a precarious majority of seven.

CANADA

Mr. Mackenzie King himself was defeated at Prince Albert, Saskatchewan, a seat he had held for nineteen years: he polled a 263 majority of civilian votes, but the service vote put him out by 129. In Saskatchewan, where a year earlier the C.C.F. had gained a sweeping victory in the provincial elections (*see* page 3449), that party won 18 out of 21 seats in the Federal House. The C.C.F.'s other ten seats were five (out of 17, with 10 Liberal) in Manitoba; four out of 15 in British Columbia; and one in Nova Scotia. The Social Credit Party was successful only in Alberta, where it won 13 out of 17 seats. The Progressive Conservatives won a victory in Ontario, securing 48 seats to the Liberals' 34. A record number of candidates (965), including a record number of women (19), presented themselves to the electors; 430 lost their deposits. General McNaughton was again defeated; but the other members of Mr. King's Cabinet, with the exception of the newly appointed

Mackenzie King Defeated

Mr. D. L. McLaren, Minister of National Revenue, held their seats.

Mr. King (who was returned at a by-election at Glengarry on August 6) declared that the result showed that not only were most Canadians justly proud of their contribution to victory, but also recognized that the country's war effort had been wisely organized and directed, and had repudiated the

CANADIAN CROSS

Mothers or widows of all Canadian soldiers who gave their lives in the Second Great War received this silver cross from the Canadian Government. Each cross was accompanied by a personal note from the Canadian Minister of Defence, General A. G. L. McNaughton, saying 'This memorial cross is forwarded to you on behalf of the Government of Canada in memory of one who died in the service of his country.'

Photo, P.N.A.

efforts of those who had "ignored Parliament and Parliamentary methods" and sought by "high pressure" publicity to gain control of the Government. The Government interpreted the service vote (118,537 Liberal, 109,679 C.C.F., 86,530 Progressive Conservative) as showing lack of support for total conscription, favoured only by the Progressive Conservatives.

General McNaughton continued to be Minister of Defence until August 21, when he resigned to assume the chairmanship of the Canadian section of the Joint Permanent American-Canadian Defence Board: he had been a minister

for eight months—several of them the most critical in the history of the Canadian services—without a seat in the Federal Parliament. The only precedent was the case of Sir Wilfred Laurier who was Minister of Inland Revenue from October 1877 to February 1878 without a seat in the House of Commons.

Before Parliament was dissolved, however, the crisis caused by the difficulty of maintaining Canada's fighting forces at strength had been resolved: a reduction in the incidence of casualties among the Canadians in Europe during January and February, when the brunt of the fighting fell on the U.S. 1st and 3rd Armies and the British 2nd Army in the Ardennes, enabled the Minister of National Defence to issue a statement on March 7 that the reinforcement crisis was over. Six days later he told the press that the position overseas was so satisfactory that men with long service abroad could be relieved in greater numbers without affecting the army's fighting strength.

The 1st Canadian Army, formed to take part in the invasion of Normandy, and containing throughout its existence large numbers of British (*see* page 3567) and other Allied units, ceased to exist on June 30. It had liberated much of France, Belgium and the Netherlands. Its commander, General H. D. G. Crerar, C.H., C.B., D.S.O. (*see* plate facing page 3331), returned to Canada, the remaining Canadian forces in Europe, under the command of Lieutenant-General Guy Simonds, becoming known as Canadian Forces in the Netherlands. The total casualties among all Canadian forces on all fronts from September 3, 1939, to August 14, 1945, were 37,476 killed; 1,843 missing, 53,174 wounded, 9,045 prisoners of war—a total of 101,538.

End of First Canadian Army

The part Canada was to play in the Pacific was the subject of a statement by the Prime Minister in April. The forces employed would be volunteers, and "Canada's effort to maintain her just part in the further prosecution of the war against Japan will, as measured in numbers, necessarily be very much less than has been the case in the war in Europe." Speaking at Edmonton in May, he gave the forces for the

BALLOON BOMBS FALL ON CANADA

Japanese long-distance balloon bombs were first reported over British Columbia and the prairie provinces of Canada on May 22, 1945. Carrying high explosive and incendiaries, they were able to stay aloft for about a week at a height of some five miles and to descend automatically. Above, one of over 350 balloons rendered harmless in Canada. The balloon was of tough paper : also shown is the 'chandelier,' carrying mechanism and bombs. *Photo, Paul Popper*

Pacific war as some 50,000 soldiers, 13,000 sailors, and an undetermined number of airmen. The Navy Minister, presenting the naval estimates in April, said that the naval unit which would take part in the Pacific war would include two cruisers, a number of destroyers and frigates, and, if the necessary arrangements for their acquisition could be made, two aircraft carriers Canadian-manned, but with airmen of the British Fleet Air Arm.

The arrival in Guam of Canadian troops and aircraft was announced in Washington on August 6, among the famous regiments mentioned being Princess Patricia's Light Infantry, the Seaforth Highlanders of Canada, the 48th Highland Regiment of Canada, and the Royal 22nd (French Canadian) Regiment.

An announcement in January by the Minister of Defence that the North Atlantic was "alive with U-boats," and that ships were being sunk daily caused serious alarm, not only in Canada; it was somewhat modified by the Navy Minister's statement of February 13 that although U-boat activity had been slightly greater during January, shipping losses both then and in December

had been less than in earlier times. There had been losses off the Canadian coast, but not "day by day."

Agreements signed in Ottawa on April 3 by Colonel Llewellin, British

Minister of Food, and Mr. J. G. Gardiner, Minister of Agriculture, provided for the purchase in 1946 by Britain of not less than 450,000,000 lb. of Canadian bacon and ham, 60,000,000 lb. of beef, and all eggs available subject only to shipping space ; three months later, Britain made an agreement to take all surplus eggs until the end of 1947. To help the United Nations' deficiency of sugar, Canada saved 184,000,000 lb. by cutting the civilian ration from June to October from 2 lb. to 1 lb. per month. To make supplies of meat available to liberated Europe, meat rationing, suspended on March 1, 1944, owing to a shipping "bottleneck," was reintroduced from September 10, the ration being 2 lb. of carcass meat a week—just under 1½ lb. of actual meat ; Tuesdays and Fridays became meatless days in all Canadian restaurants from July 13. Canada's 1945 production of wheat suffered from severe drought—one of the factors in the world food crisis of 1946.

The Empire Air Training Scheme (*see* Chapter 132, and pages 588-9, 687, 776, 1184, 1187, 2202, and illus. in page 1962), established in 1940, was formally closed in Canada at a ceremony near Ottawa attended by the Governor-General, the Earl of Athlone, on March 29 ; some 125,000 airmen had passed through the 250 schools created and administered by Canadians in Canada. The Air Minister announced on April 5 that the Royal Canadian Air Force would be represented by a squadron in the air police force that would be required for the occupation of Germany.

ALLIES PLANNED ICEBERG AIRFIELDS

How Britain, Canada and the U.S. planned to build mobile iceberg airfields weighing 2,000,000 tons each was not disclosed till February 1946. Under Operation 'Habakkuk,' it was intended to use them as advanced bases for anti-U-boat warfare. Main structural material was to be pykrete, which was about 86 per cent ice and 14 per cent wood pulp. Here, a workman at Lake Louise, Alberta, Canada, chips ice blocks for 'Habakkuk' beams during experimental work.

CANADA IN THE HEART OF EMPIRE

For over five years an office building in Lincoln's Inn Fields, London, housed the H.Q. in Britain of the Royal Canadian Air Force. At a civic ceremony on October 30, 1945, the northern side of the square, known for 300 years as Newman's Row, was renamed 'Canada Walk.' Here a name-plate is unveiled by a member of the Canadian W.A.A.F.

Photo, Central Press

With the closing of the 8th Victory Loan on May 12, 1945, Canada had raised in two War Loans and eight Victory Loans a total of 10,774,784,900 Canadian dollars (£2,410,466,910), exceeding the aggregate target figure of 8,600,000,000 dollars by 2,174,784,900 dollars. Her total wartime financial aid to Britain to September 2, 1945, was 4,600,000,000 dollars—ninety per cent of her total aid to the Allies. In addition 200,000,000 dollars' worth of war plants in Canada had been bought from Britain, and 800,000,000 dollars' worth of securities had been repatriated to supply Britain with Canadian dollars.

It was announced on October 24 that responsibility for maintaining the Alaska Highway (*see* page 2319), built by the United States Army with Canadian assistance, would pass from the United States Army to the Canadian Army on April 1, 1946. It was to be maintained for peacetime use. The total cost of building the road, from Fort St. John in British Columbia to Fairbanks in Alaska, had been 115,000,000 dollars.

The Charter of the United Nations Food and Agricultural Organization was signed in Quebec on October 16 by thirty nations, the Soviet delegation signing three days later. On October 28, Sir John Boyd Orr, the British nutrition expert, was appointed Director-General, and Syria and the Lebanon were admitted to membership. Canada ratified the United Nations Charter on October 25, and on December 12 the House of Commons approved, by 169 votes to nine, of participation in the Bretton Woods agreements.

When the Family Allowances Act (*see* page 3468) came into force on July 1, 1,273,755 families out of the estimated 1,467,000 had registered ; in 3,644 families there were ten or more children under 16, in two fifteen or more. During the first month, the mothers in 1,237,754

Lt. GRAY, D.S.C. (R.C.N.V.R.)	C.S.M. OSBORN (Winnipeg Grenadiers)
The V.C. was awarded posthumously to Lieutenant Robert Hampton Gray, D.S.C., a Canadian fighter pilot who, when serving in the British aircraft-carrier H.M.S. 'Formidable' on August 9, 1945, led an attack on enemy shipping in the bay of Onagawn Wan, Honshu (Japan). Though his aircraft was in flames, he pressed home the attack to destroy an enemy cruiser, sacrificing his life.	For displaying 'heroism and self-sacrifice' while serving with the Canadian forces in the defence of Hongkong in December 1941, Company Sergeant-Major John Robert Osborn was awarded the V.C. posthumously. After leading a desperate bayonet attack to capture Mount Bulter, Osborn threw himself on a hand grenade about to explode killing himself, but saving the lives of his comrades.

Photos, British and Canadian Official

families, on behalf of 2,956,844 children under 16, actually received allowances, totalling 17,560,934 dollars (about £3,900,000).

The appointment of Field-Marshal Sir Harold Alexander, Supreme Allied Commander in the Mediterranean, to succeed the Earl of Athlone as Governor-General of Canada was announced on July 31.

The status of Newfoundland (*see* page 2801) came up for discussion in the House of Lords (London) in January 1945, when Lord Cranborne, Secretary of State for the Dominions, said

NEWFOUND-LAND

ALEXANDER, CANADA'S NEW GOVERNOR-GENERAL

On July 31, 1945, the King approved the appointment of Field-Marshal Sir Harold Alexander, Supreme Allied Commander in the Mediterranean, as Governor-General of Canada. Raised to the peerage in the New Year Honours of 1946, as Viscount Alexander of Tunis, of Errigal in the County of Donegal, he sailed to take up his appointment on April 5, 1946. He here inspects the R.C.A.F. guard of honour as he entered Parliament Buildings, Ottawa, for his installation.

Photo, Keystone

NEWFOUNDLAND GOVERNOR
On January 16, 1946, Mr. Gordon Macdonald, Regional Controller of the Lancashire, Cheshire and North Wales coal-producing areas since 1942, was appointed Governor of Newfoundland and knighted by the King. Sir Gordon succeeded Vice-Admiral Sir Humphrey Walwyn who had held the post since 1936. *Photo, Keystone*

that the prolongation of the war must postpone the setting up of machinery to examine the constitutional future of the island, and made impossible any attempt to forecast its future economic circumstances. Parliament had expressed the view, shared by the Newfoundland people, that any pronouncement on the constitutional future depended for its validity on the chances of normal economic security.

In December the Prime Minister, Mr. Attlee, stated in the House of Commons that it had been decided to **Newfoundland** set up as early as **Convention** possible in 1946 an **to be Called** elected National Convention of Newfoundlanders. Elections, held on June 21, were broadly on the basis of the former parliamentary constituencies, all adults being entitled to vote. The resulting convention had the following terms of reference : " To consider and discuss the changes that have taken place in the financial and economic situation of the island since 1934 and, bearing in mind the extent to which the high revenues of recent years have been due to wartime conditions, to examine the position of the country and to make recommendations to His Majesty's Government as to the possible future forms of government to be put before the people at a national referendum."

The Dominions Under-Secretary announced on February 13, 1945, that Newfoundland had lent Great Britain

to that date 12,300,000 dollars free of interest during the war.

The death on July 5 of Mr. John Curtin, Prime Minister of Australia since October 1941, and Minister of Defence since February 1942, brought Mr. Joseph Benedict **AUSTRALIA** Chifley to the Premiership. Aged 60—the age at which Mr. Curtin had died after a long illness—Mr. Chifley had been an engine driver in early life. He was a close friend of Mr. Curtin, and the only change from Curtin's Cabinet in the new Government he announced on July 13 was the replacement of Senator Collings (then in his 80th year) by Mr. Johnston at the Ministry of the Interior.

On August 2, Mr. Arthur Calwell, Minister of Immigration, announced in the House of Representatives two draft agreements with the United Kingdom, one covering free passages for British ex-servicemen and women and their dependents, the second covering assisted passages for United Kingdom civilians not eligible for free passages. The Australian Government had also approved in principle a plan to bring out 50,000 orphans from Britain and other war-devastated countries in

the first three years after the war. Australia, he said, was always open to healthy immigrants from the Dominions, the U.S.A., and Europe who would not become a charge on the community ; but he emphasized that the maximum additional population Australia could absorb was about 140,000 per annum. As the average excess of births over deaths was about 70,000 per annum, this meant that annual immigration could not satisfactorily exceed 70,000. He also estimated that the re-settlement of Australian ex-servicemen and women and the provision of additional housing for them might take up to two years.

The Empire Air Training Scheme ended in Australia, as in Canada, (*see* page 3735) on March 29 ; it had turned out in Australia 35,000 fully trained airmen.

Egg rationing was introduced in Australia on February 26. The adult meat ration (averaging **Meat Ration** 2 lb. a week, excluding **Cut in** unrationed bacon, ham, **Australia** offals, etc.), cut by 9 per cent on January 26, was cut by a further 12 per cent on May 7, when supplies to restaurants were also cut by 25 per cent. In announcing this second cut Mr. Chifley

NEWFOUNDLANDERS BID FAREWELL TO THEIR GUNS
The only Empire formation in the British 2nd Army, the 59th Newfoundland Heavy Regiment, R.A., formed in 1940, bade farewell on June 2, 1945, to the guns they had fought from the Normandy beaches to Hamburg. The ceremony took place at Bergedorf, near Hamburg, the inspection and salute being taken by Brigadier Francis Cleeve, D.S.O., M.C., commanding No. 3 Army Group, Royal Artillery (above). (See also illus. page 1182.) *Photo, Newfoundland Official*

said "the choice facing Australia is either to cut the present rate of consumption or cut down on export to Britain. But to reduce supplies to Britain at present would be unthinkable, and every Australian will share that opinion." Later in the same month, Mr. Scully, Minister of Agriculture, said that Australia viewed the position in Britain "with grave concern" and that she would do "all humanly possible to maintain our commitments to Britain," but food production was being gravely hampered by the worst drought in the history of Australia. All restrictions on clothing were removed on September 27.

A conference of the United Nations Relief and Rehabilitation Administration opened at Lapstone on February 15. It urged the participating governments to establish immediately depots for medical supplies to be sent quickly wherever they were needed, and to set up more forward bases close behind the military lines. It also decided that the principle of medical officers entering relief areas with adequate supplies should be adopted by all governments. A resolution moved by Dr. Evatt, Australian Minister for External Affairs, that relief should go to areas immediately they were liberated was passed unanimously.

Australia, to which the Japanese menace had come so close, celebrated V.J. Day (August 15) with wild rejoicing. Ships in harbour were illuminated, crowds danced in the streets of the leading cities, great victory parades were staged in Sydney and Melbourne. Mr. Chifley made a nation-wide broadcast in which he declared that the unstinted thanks of all free people were due to Mr. Churchill, President Roosevelt, Marshal Stalin and Generalissimo Chiang. "Especially do we honour Mr. Churchill," he said, "with whom we had the honour to stand alone against aggression." In a message to General MacArthur, he said, "Australia is deeply indebted to you for your wonderful courage and devotion." A loyal Address of Congratulation, moved by Mr. Chifley and seconded by Mr. Menzies, leader of the Opposition, was adopted by Parliament on August 29.

On August 17 the Prime Minister announced that the War Cabinet had told the British Government that Australia, as a principal Pacific Power, wished to furnish a force to participate in the occupation of Japan, and to share with the United Kingdom the responsibility for command in the South-West Pacific. General MacArthur and the United States Minister in Canberra, to whom the Australian claim for representation at the Japanese surrender was referred, acceded to the claim, said Dr. Evatt on August 24, "in recognition of the outstanding part Australia had played in the war against Japan."

United States Appreciation of Australia

Australian ships took part in most of the major, as well as many minor, engagements of the Pacific war, and they assisted U.S. landings at Arawe and Cape Gloucester (New Britain), Aitape and Hollandia (New Guinea), Wake Island, Biak Island, Morotai (Halmaheras) and Leyte (Philippines).

MELBOURNE'S V.J. THANKSGIVING SERVICE

Australia celebrated V.J. Day (August 15, 1945) and her final freedom from the Japanese menace with wild rejoicings. Ships in harbour were illuminated, crowds danced in the streets, great victory parades were staged in Sydney and Melbourne. The Prime Minister, Mr. Chifley, delivered a nation-wide broadcast. Below, the vast crowds gather outside Melbourne's Shrine of Remembrance for the public thanksgiving service.　　　*Photo, Associated Press*

AUSTRALIA'S PREMIER

Mr. Joseph Benedict Chifley's selection as Prime Minister of Australia in succession to Mr. John Curtin, who died on July 5, 1945, was announced a week later. Born in 1885, Mr. Chifley was leader of the Australian Labour Party. An engine-driver in early life, he became Commonwealth Treasurer in 1941.
Photo, Central Press

Australian soldiers, many of them veterans from the fighting in Egypt, Libya and Greece, were mainly responsible for the land operations which brought about the reconquest of New Guinea ; they served in the Philippines, and landed in Borneo, Celebes and Timor. When in November 1944 they took over from the Americans complete responsibility for New Guinea and the Solomons, the Japanese still held all Bougainville except the Torokina sector on the west coast (then slightly smaller than the area the Australians held for eight months at Tobruk) and a few other areas. By July 25, 1945, the Australians had reconquered 3,000 square miles (*see* Chapter 351).

Civil Government Again in Papua
An act to restore civil government in Papua and mandated New Guinea south of the Markham River (temporarily amalgamated under one administration until six months after the war) was passed by the House of Representatives on July 20. Most of the settlemen's in New Guinea and many in Papua, an area with a native population of about a million, had been destroyed.

General Sir Thomas Blamey, C.-in-C. Australian Military Forces, represented Australia at the formal surrender of Japan in Tokyo Bay. An announcement of October 26 said that a detachment of 1,500 volunteers was to take part in the occupation of Japan. General V. A. H. Sturdee, who, as commander

of the Australian 1st Army received the Japanese surrender in the South-West Pacific (*see* page 3602), in December succeeded General Blamey as C.-in-C. Australian Military Forces pending their subsequent control, as before the war, by a Military Board.

Out of a population of 7,200,000, Australia provided close on a million men for full time service in the fighting forces, and 60,000 women in the auxiliary forces. Two out of three men between 18 and 40 served full time in one of the fighting services. Casualties from September 3, 1939 to August 8, 1945—78,086 in the army, 14,629 in the Air Force, 2,816 in the Navy—were 23,365 killed, 6,030 missing, 39,803 wounded, 26,363 prisoners of war. Australians won over 11,000 war decorations.

In August the War Cabinet decided that demobilization should begin not later than October 1, and on September 20 it was announced that 200,000 men would be released before the end of January 1946. The Advisory War Council was dissolved on August 30. The cost of the war to Australia to the middle of 1945 was £A2,110,000,000 or approximately £A287 10s. per head of the population. By January 26, 1945, twelve public loans totalling £A772,000,000 had been raised, and a further loan was opened in March.

A new graving dock, the " Captain Cook " dock, big enough to accommodate the largest battleships or liners such as the " Queen Elizabeth " —one of the largest docks in the world, and the only one of its size in the south Pacific—was opened by the Governor-General at Sydney on March 24 (*see* illus. in page 3451). First conceived in

1938, it was under construction when Singapore fell, after which it was rushed to completion five years ahead of schedule. Constructed of local stone, it was completed by machinery and equipment made in Britain and shipped to Australia without loss at the height of the U-boat campaign.

Australia ratified the United Nations Charter on September 19.

The announcement was made on September 4 that H.M. the King had approved the appointment of the popular Lieutenant-General Sir Bernard Freyberg, V.C. (*see* page 3443) to be Governor-General of New Zealand in succession to Marshal of the R.A.F. Sir Cyril Newall. Born in London, brought up and educated in New Zealand, General Freyberg fought in Gallipoli and in France during the First Great War, winning his V.C. at Beaumont Hamel. He retired on account of ill-health in 1937, but returned to active service in 1939 to command the New Zealand Expeditionary Force which he led in Greece. He superintended the evacuation of Allied forces to Crete, where he was Allied C.-in-C. in 1941. He and his

NEW ZEALAND

FOOD FOR BRITAIN

Towards the end of 1945, gifts of foodstuffs were shipped from Australia under a 'Food for Britain' campaign. On November 25, the aircraft-carrier 'Unicorn' sailed from Sydney with over 400 tons of food, including 15,000 lb. of sweets and chocolates for British children. Here British naval ratings at Sydney load more gift-food on H.M.S. 'Nepal.'
Photo, Planet News

division (New Zealand 2nd) served with the 8th Army throughout the campaigns in North Africa and in Italy, where they particularly distinguished themselves at Cassino. Crossing the Isonzo on May 1, New Zealanders reached Monfalcone, making there the first link with Marshal Tito's Yugoslav forces in Venezia Giulia, and on May 2 they received the surrender of the Germans in Trieste (see page 3718).

To increase exports to Britain, by an estimated 1,500 tons of meat and 5,000 tons of butter annually, the weekly meat ration was cut in June from 1s. 9d. worth to 1s. 6d. worth, butter ration from 8 ozs. to 6 ozs.

The House of Representatives ratified the United Nations Charter and the constitution of the Court of International Justice on August 7.

Total New Zealand casualties of the war were 10,033 killed, 2,129 missing, 19,314 wounded, 8,453 prisoners of war.

After the cessation of hostilities in Europe, Sir Pierre van Ryneveld, Chief of the South African General Staff, broadcast on May 9 an account of the part played by South Africa in the war. In September 1939 the Union possessed

the disasters of Sidi Resegh and Tobruk, South Africa had over two divisions in the field, and her field strength remained at the equivalent of two divisions —the 6th Armoured Division of some 22,000 Europeans (including 1,500 Rhodesians) and 3,000 non-Europeans, and another division made up of about 140 Specialist Units (Engineers, Signals, etc.) totalling 21,000 Europeans and 16,000 non-Europeans. The S.A.A.F. grew to a maximum of 34 squadrons (considerably larger than the R.A.F. a few years before the war), and the South African Naval Forces, including 3,000 personnel seconded from the Royal Navy, manned 64 vessels. In May 1945 the Union's Defence Forces totalled 175,000 Europeans, 75,000 non-Europeans plus 35,000 well trained and well equipped

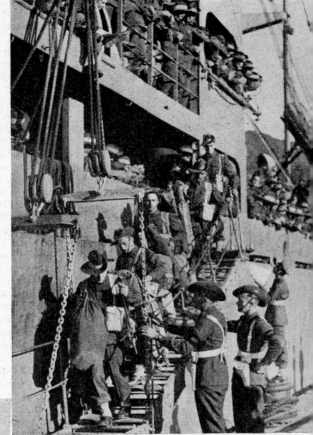

AUSTRALIA'S VICTORY

Among the nine Allied signatories to the Japanese surrender instrument on board the U.S.S. 'Missouri' in Tokyo Bay on September 2, 1945, was General Sir Thomas Blamey, C.-in-C. Australian Land Forces (left), to whom all enemy troops in Borneo, British New Guinea and the Bismarck-Solomons area had been ordered to surrender. Above, Australia's contingent in the British Commonwealth Occupation Force lands at Kure, Japan.

Photos, British Official; Keystone

one Fairey aeroplane, one Bristol Blenheim, six Hurricanes, four anti-aircraft guns, and a few hundred bren guns. Within a few weeks, Field-Marshal Smuts, the Premier, approved of plans for raising a field army of two divisions, an air force of 35 squadrons, and a fleet of 51 vessels of the minesweeping and anti-submarine types—a programme requiring the recruiting of 120,000 European personnel. Before

SOUTH AFRICA

officers and men serving part time.

At the beginning of the war £14,000,000 worth of vehicles were ordered, mostly from Canada, and safely delivered. When in the middle of 1940 Union troops went to East Africa, there was not sufficient shipping to take them, and they therefore went the whole way by road, 11,000 vehicles and 30,000 men being moved 4,000 miles along the Great North Road through Central Africa to the Abyssinian frontier, where under the

outstanding leadership of Major-General Dan Pienaar they formed the spearhead of the successful British campaign which freed Abyssinia (see Chapter 164). The same South African forces were largely responsible for stopping Rommel at El Alamein in June 1942 (see Chapter 224). The South African 6th Armoured Division served throughout North Africa and formed an important part of the highly cosmopolitan army with which Field-Marshal Alexander finished the campaign in Italy.

All those who joined the armed forces of South Africa were volunteers. The total number who served was 354,049, made up of 197,820 European men, 24,975 European women, and 122,254 non-European men. They won 4,537 awards, including four V.C.s. Total casualties were 6,840 killed, 1,841 missing, 14,363 wounded, 14,589 prisoners.

The 6th Armoured Division returned to South Africa after the surrender of the Germans in Italy, but 12 S.A.A.F. squadrons, with engineer, signal, transport, workshop and security units, remained in the Mediterranean area to maintain and safeguard lines of communication to the Far East.

On September 10, Mr. Strauss, Minister of Agriculture, announced that the Union Government had offered cheese, dried fruit, citrus fruits, jam **Fruit and other Foods for Britain** and other foods, to the value of about £6,000,000 to Britain during 1945, and that 43,000 cases of meat and sugar had been earmarked for U.N.R.R.A., but that the amount of food that the Union could make available to Britain, the Netherlands and other countries would be affected by the prevailing drought over a large part of South Africa.

The appointment of Major Gideon Brand van Zyl to be Governor-General from January 1, 1946, was announced on October 28. Major van Zyl, a lawyer, aged 72, was the first Union-born man to be appointed Governor-General. He sat in the House of Assembly from 1918–1942, and was appointed Administrator of Cape Province in 1942. On his taking up office, Mr. N. J. de Wet, appointed Officer Administering the Government in 1943 (*see* page 2806), would relinquish that appointment.

Field-Marshal Smuts attended the San Francisco conference (*see* Chapter 381) as South Africa's representative, and was mainly responsible for the drafting of the preamble to the Charter. On his return to South Africa, in a speech at Pretoria on July 21, he described the Charter as " a declaration of war against war " in which the higher law of humanity was laid down in unmistakable terms. The Union Government ratified the Charter by executive action on October 9.

The wartime Coalition Government broke up when Mr. B. Madeley, Minister of Labour and leader of the South African Labour Party, tendered his resignation in October ; at the same time the nine other Labour members of the Assembly went into opposition. The Dominion Party decided also to withdraw at its congress in Durban on November 20, a decision involving the resignation of Colonel Stallard, Minister of Mines. On November 28, Smuts paid tribute for invaluable service to the Union rendered by Mr. Madeley and Colonel Stallard, and added, " The Coalition was a great success. Our opponents prophesied it was a house built on sand, but it stood for six years

through the storm and we have parted good friends."

In his broadcast on V.J. Day, Field-Marshal Smuts said, " It is the greatest occasion for thanksgiving that at the very moment in history when man has produced a weapon with which he can destroy himself this greatest of wars has come to an end, and an opportunity is thus granted to humanity so to order the affairs of the world in future that no human agency shall ever again bring war upon mankind." A proclamation of October 5 vested in the State the sole right to search or prospect for uranium or thorium, or to mine, dispose of or isolate from any substance or export these substances, and laid it down that every person who had discovered or might discover uranium or thorium must immediately notify the authorities.

" Southern Rhodesia's war effort, and the presence on the world's battle-fronts and in all arms of Rhodesians who have **SOUTHERN** been worthy ambassa- **RHODESIA** dors of their country, have aroused an interest in this country in thousands of people to whom, hitherto,

NEW ZEALAND CELEBRATES VICTORY IN EUROPE

While in Australia celebration of victory in Europe (May 8, 1945) was subdued—it being emphasized that for Australian fighting forces there remained elimination of the Japanese—in New Zealand V.E. Day meant the return of the victorious New Zealand 2nd Division from the battlefields of Italy. Below, a section of the great crowd which surged through the grounds of Government Buildings in Wellington, New Zealand, on V.E. Day. *Photo, Sport & General*

Southern Rhodesia has been but a name," said Sir Godfrey Huggins, Prime Minister of Southern Rhodesia. Some idea of that war effort is given in the following facts:

Out of a total European population in 1940 of just under 69,000, of whom some 19,000 were men of military age **Contribution in Manpower** (18–45), over 10,000 (including 1,400 women) served full-time with the military forces of the British Commonwealth—8,000 in the Army, nearly 2,000 (including two Rhodesia squadrons) in the Royal Air Force, and 350 with the Royal Navy. Fatal casualties were rather more than six per cent of the enlisted personnel.

The Rhodesia Fighter Squadron of the R.A.F. went into action at Dunkirk on June 2, 1940, and served continuously during the Battle of Britain, fighting both day and night battles. It carried out, in 1942, the first Typhoon attack on enemy territory. A Rhodesia Bomber Squadron served with Bomber Command.

The first station of the Empire Air Training Scheme to be ready anywhere in the Commonwealth was opened in May 1940 in Southern Rhodesia, which eventually had ten stations.

Both prices and consumption were controlled by the Government, and a Government Food Production Committee helped to increase agricultural production, particularly of maize, wheat, potatoes and ground-nuts. Butter was rationed (at amounts varying according to supply of from a quarter of a pound to half a pound per head per week), and it was made an offence to eat an egg between 4 p.m. and 5 a.m., but thanks to the efforts of her farmers, Southern Rhodesia was able to maintain a good diet standard throughout the war. The Government set up two factories to turn out essential war material, women entering industry in considerable numbers. Southern Rhodesian industry provided the Eastern Group Supply Council with a wide variety of goods, including military boots (55,000 pairs in 1943, 440,000 pairs in 1944–45), ingot tin and 28,000 tons of timber. Southern Rhodesian mines produced chrome, asbestos, mica, tungsten, tantalite and coal to meet the Allied needs.

Southern Rhodesia's war effort was

SMUTS AT SAN FRANCISCO
Field-Marshal Jan Smuts, South Africa's Prime Minister, was responsible for drafting the preamble to the Charter adopted by the United Nations Conference on International Organization which opened in San Francisco on April 25, 1945. Over a quarter of a century before he had helped to draft the League of Nations Covenant. He is seen here on arrival at San Francisco
Photo Keystone

financed entirely from home resources by a population of some 69,000 Europeans and 1,350,000 Africans of low productive capacity, to whom a "tickey" (3d.) meant approximately as much as 5s. to a European. Her last pre-war budget amounted **S. Rhodesia's Wartime Finance** to £5,300,000: the figure for 1944–45 was more than £10,000,000. From the outbreak of war up to the end of March 1945 she spent a total of £25,988,000 on war purposes alone, besides maintaining and in some cases developing her administrative and civilian services.

An announcement of importance for Southern Rhodesia's future was that made on April 4, 1945, by the Colonial Office of the constitution of the recently created Standing Central African Council (*see* page 3454). Its members were the Governor of Southern Rhodesia, Vice-Admiral Sir Campbell Tait (chairman); the Governors of Northern Rhodesia, Sir John Waddington, and of Nyasaland, Sir Edmund Richards; and the Prime Minister of Southern Rhodesia, Sir Godfrey Huggins; with nine others, three each appointed by Waddington, Richards, and Huggins. It held its first meeting in Salisbury, capital of Southern Rhodesia, on April 24.

SOUTH AFRICAN ARMOURED FORCES · 'MARCH PAST'
At the famous Monza motor-racing track, north-east of Milan, a 'march past' was held in May 1945 of the entire South African 6th Armoured Division which had played such a vital part throughout the Mediterranean campaign. The salute was taken by Commodore F. C. Sturrock, Minister of Railways and Harbours and Acting Minister of Defence for the Union of South Africa.
Photo British Official

Chapter 364

STEPPING-STONES TO JAPAN'S MAINLAND

This chapter continues the history of the war in the Pacific from Chapter 322, and covers the American conquest of Luzon in the Philippines, Iwo Jima in the Volcano Islands, and Okinawa in the Ryukyus—the last bringing the Allies to a distance of only 750 miles from Tokyo. Its author, the distinguished war correspondent Mr. A. D. Divine, O.B.E., D.S.M., served with the forces which carried out these successive invasions

ON February 4, 1945, twenty-six days after the landing under General MacArthur's personal command of Lieutenant-General Krueger's 6th Army in Lingayen Gulf, MacArthur's forces entered Manila. In those twenty-six days they had advanced 115 miles. Inevitably the interest of this campaign before Manila lies primarily in the reasons for its almost staggering speed. Between the landing at Lingayen and the crossing of the Pasig River there was no battle, no major clash of armed forces. There was, in point of fact, to be no major battle commensurate with the size of the forces potentially engaged throughout the whole campaign of Luzon.

To arrive at the reason for this it is necessary to go farther back than the landings on Lingayen Gulf. The whole campaign of the Philippines must be looked upon as an exercise in sea power, an exercise in which the American command grasped to the full the potentialities of the combination of weapons, and in which the Japanese showed themselves, to a degree almost incomprehensible, without grasp of the realities and without knowledge of their advantages. The Philippines were lost to the Japanese long before General MacArthur ever landed in Lingayen Gulf. They were lost when the Japanese Fleet, with its ancillary air and with the potential advantage of its shore-based air, failed to prevent the American Fleet, under the direction of Fleet-Admiral Nimitz and the command of Admiral Halsey, from raiding at will from Cape Engano to Mindanao.

To make that defeat doubly sure, the Japanese command fought a campaign thereafter of complete inco-ordination of arms, exemplified by the successive stupidities of the Battle for Leyte Gulf (*see* page 3402) and the attempts to reinforce Leyte (*see* page 3401). By the time Mindoro came into American hands (*see* page 3275) the Japanese on Luzon were already in parlous plight. Their hope of seaborne reinforcement had disappeared with the destructive defeat of the Japanese Fleet on October 24 and 25. They were faced with an enemy overwhelmingly superior at sea, in the

LUZON

air and on the land. Their force, weakened by the useless sending of reinforcements to Leyte, was hopelessly small to defend an island 500 miles in length from north to south and poorly provided with internal communications.

The Americans extracted the last possible benefit from their command of the sea. By elaborate feinting in the Verde Islands Passage, south of Manila Bay, they created in the mind of General Tomoyuki Yamashita the impression that they intended to land in the Batangas area. Then, moving north with the speed that can be achieved only by ship-borne arms, they descended early on January 9 upon Lingayen.

Yamashita's defensive plan was never to become clear. It seemed almost that he had no plan. Colonel Harishi Hashimoto, Chief of Staff of the Japanese forces in Manila, stated in evidence before the U.S. Military Commission that the landing was made two months ahead of Japanese expectations. There was a concentration to the south of Manila in some hope, apparently, of staving off the expected invasion there. There was no defence of the Lingayen Gulf. The invasion fleet of 850 ships came in to the beaches without the loss of a single transport, and the 14th Army Corps was disembarked with the loss of very few men on the southern shore, while the 1st Army Corps landed unopposed at Damortis.

What interference there was in the landings came from airmen of the Kamikaze Corps (suicide pilots) who, during the preliminary bombardment and the necessary mine-sweeping operations, caused heavy damage and some loss to the Luzon Attack Force under Admiral Kinkaid. What Japanese forces there were in the vicinity of Lingayen and in the great central plain withdrew to the surrounding mountains. With two divisions, General MacArthur and General Krueger blocked any hopes Yamashita had of fighting a campaign from the Caraballo Mountains. Another division covered the enemy forces which hovered on the right flank. The U.S. 37th Infantry moved down the central plain upon Manila (*see* map in page 3744).

From the Caraballo Mountains Yamashita sent in his exiguous armour. It is necessary here to remember that Japanese armour in the East was throughout the reconquest quantatively inferior and qualitatively almost negligible. It is improbable that General Yamashita had more than 300 tanks in the whole of the Luzon area. Two hundred of those were wasted in attack ill-devised against an enemy prepared and wholly superior in anti-tank weapons.

Exiguous Enemy Armour

By January 11, the 37th was only 88 miles from Manila. On the 25th it was

FILIPINOS GREET U.S. LIBERATORS

When Lieutenant-General Krueger's U.S. 6th Army went ashore in Lingayen Gulf, north-west Luzon, 129 miles north of Manila, on January 9, 1945, and seized four important beaches, they encountered negligible enemy resistance. Below, Filipinos race across the sands to greet their American liberators. Lingayen Gulf was the scene of Japanese landings on December 22, 1941 (see page 1976).
Photo, Keystone

announced that U.S. troops had captured Clark airfield and the nearby Fort Stotsenberg. Not until they reached the subdivided river beds of the Pampanga area was there even serious demolition to impede their progress. The only holding action of the slightest importance was the Japanese attempt half-way between Lingayen and the capital to establish positions on a spur of the Zambales range where the plain narrows to a waist at Bamban.

Meanwhile, with that fluidity of base line which absolute amphibious power gives to a commander, General MacArthur had prepared fresh landings near Subic Bay on the far side of the momentous battleground of Bataan, and at Nasugbu in the area of the original feint—from which any forces originally concentrated there had long been withdrawn—new U.S. troops went into action.

The denial of Manila Bay to General MacArthur was the sole military advantage left within Yamashita's purview. If he could have kept the Americans out of that harbour he could have at least hoped to postpone for a little the "build-up" of the forces for the invasion of Japan. But he could not keep them out. There was left for the Japanese nothing save guerilla warfare.

By February 6 Manila was under American control, and by the 8th American infantry of the 37th Division were across the Pasig River co-operating with the 11th Airborne Division, which had reached the city from the southward, in a final clearance. The Japanese, compressed into the intricate area of the Intramuros, the ancient Spanish walled city, were making a last stand.

By February 21 the Japanese holdings had been compressed to an area less than half a mile long and only 500 yards wide, and General MacArthur announced that 16,000 Japanese dead had been counted in Manila since the battle began on February 4. At the same time he stated that 92,000 Japanese had been killed in the six weeks that had followed the landings at Lingayen, while American casualties were 2,676 killed and some 10,000 wounded. The figures of Japanese dead must be accepted with some reserve, but the almost incredible disparity between the totals of dead— 2,000 as against almost 100,000—can indicate one thing only—the overwhelming strength of the American forces, a strength in aircraft, guns, tanks, armoured vehicles and ammunition infinitely beyond anything the Japanese could hope to summon.

Japanese Last Stand at Intramuros

The Intramuros fighting was a traditional "last stand." It was, however, the last stand of a section only— Yamashita's main army was scattered north-west and east of the capital. The west in these days was cleaned up: Bataan, of terrible memory, was overrun in a remorseless return (February 16); Corregidor was battered into silence and captured a few hours later. As the Intramuros fell (February 24),

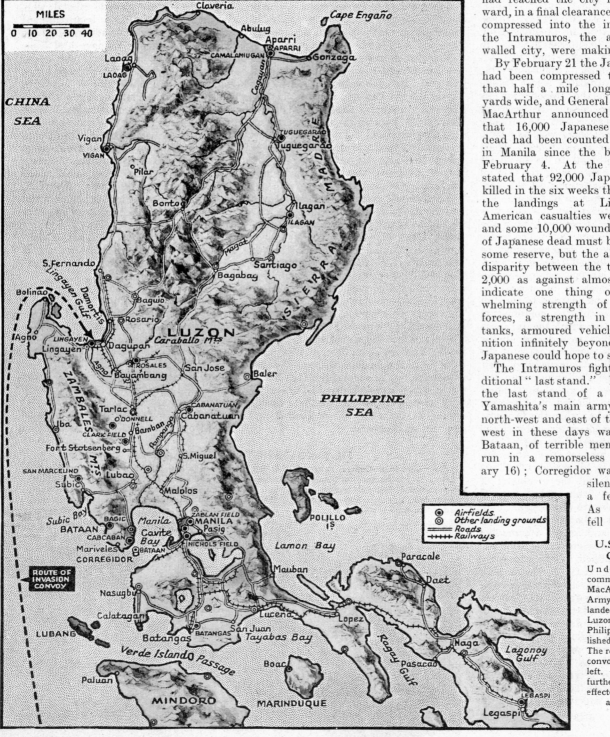

U.S. LANDINGS ON LUZON

Under the personal command of General MacArthur, the U.S. 6th Army on January 9, 1945 landed at Lingayen on Luzon, largest of the Philippines, and established four beach-heads. The route of the invasion convoy is shown on the left. Three weeks later further landings were effected near Subic Bay and at Nasugbu.

RECAPTURE OF THE PHILIPPINE CAPITAL

Manila, capital of the Philippines, was entered by U.S. forces from three sides on February 4, 1945, when opposition was met from enemy snipers. After blowing up the Quezon and Ayala bridges across the Pasig River (1), fanatical Japanese continued to hold out in Intramuros, the old walled city on the south bank. It was not till February 24, after bloody fighting, that Intramuros finally fell—four days after its 40-feet walls had been breached by artillery (4). U.S. infantry patrolled the streets on the look-out for snipers (2) ; while homeless Filipinos sought safety behind the U.S. lines (3). *Photos, U.S. Official and Signal Corps ; Paul Popper*

Yamashita played his last card in Manila, standing astride the city's water supplies in the hills towards the east. Swiftly these small holding forces were dislodged. The campaign degenerated into a series of mopping-up operations north and north-east in the high mountains of the Sierra Madre. It was still incomplete when Japan surrendered.

The campaign of the Philippines was a story of overwhelming force brought against an enemy incompetent by reason of numerical inferiority, deficiency of supplies and equipment,

IWO JIMA

and uninspired leadership to defend his chosen terrain. On Iwo Jima the enemy had an ample sufficiency of men for adequate defence. He had, for the special nature of his defence, sound material, his leadership and his planning were good, and he had all the advantage of what was probably the strongest defensive terrain utilized in the Second Great War.

Iwo Jima is the centre island of the three tiny specks of the Volcano group. It is shaped like a leg of mutton, five miles long, with the crater of Suribachi poised upon the exposed end of the bone. The cone itself is not more than 500 feet high. The main island rises in the centre not more than 300 feet, but that 300 feet is seamed, scored, honeycombed with excoriated volcanic vents. Hundreds of natural caves communicate

with deep sulphur-exuding tunnels. Steep and broken gulleys cut across the surface; ragged sea cliffs surround it. Only in the triangle to the south is there level sand, and even the sand is utterly treacherous : fine, shifting, black pumice dust in which a man cannot dig a fox-hole, in which the beaches are a quicksand. Only on these beaches could a landing be effected.

The importance of Iwo Jima lay in one thing only—the possibility of its use as a base from which long-range fighters could cover the Super Fortresses on their missions to Japan. To the Japanese it had already ceased, under a succession of air attacks from Saipan, to be an effective base either for offence or defence. It was 750 miles south of Tokyo.

The plan for the attack, which was under the overall command of Vice-Admiral Spruance, provided for a three-day bombardment of the tiny island combined with heavy bombing attacks and sustained raiding by ship-borne aircraft. The main weight of the bombardment was, however, to come from a force of seven of the older battleships—subsequently increased—supplemented by a strong force of cruisers, destroyers and gunboats. The known defences of the island included 6-inch and

probably 8-inch batteries, well set in concrete emplacements at the base of Suribachi and in the volcanic embrasures of the north. Besides these, photographic reconnaissance showed innumerable pill-boxes, gun-pits, trenches and mortar sites behind the beaches and over the whole surface of the island.

At 8 o'clock on February 16, while Corregidor, 1,500 miles away off Luzon, was being recaptured, the battleships stood in to the attack. No more sustained bombardment has ever been carried out on so small and concentrated a target in the history of war. The weight of metal that was brought against Iwo Jima must stand in relation to the size of the target as an all time high in sea bombardment. In the course of the three days, nine battleships fired incessantly at well-spotted targets. One of them alone, the "Tennessee," fired 1,377 rounds of 14-inch and 6,380 rounds of 5-inch against selected targets. Under the battering of the heavy guns, under the rain of shells from the cruisers, the destroyers, the gunboats that thrust right in against the rocks, under the incessant barrage of bombs, rockets and cannon fire from

MANILA'S 'BATTLESHIP ISLAND'

Guarding Manila Bay was Fort Drum, 335-foot long battleship island,' built by the U.S. Navy in 1905, mounting 6-inch and 14-inch naval guns and heavily protected by reinforced concrete ' plates ' 36 feet thick. (See map in page 2092.) Recapturing it from the Japanese in February 1945, U.S. troops pumped 5,000 gallons of petrol and oil mixture into vents in the walls, set a 30-minute fuse and blew it, with its enemy garrison, right out of Manila Bay, opening the way for the Allied fleet. Right, direct hit on the fort by the U.S.A. 5th A.F. Below, U.S. infantry land on the island by a 'Trojan Horse' catwalk from an invasion craft moored alongside.

Photos, Keystone ; Fox Photos

'OLD GLORY' HOISTED AGAIN AT CORREGIDOR IN THE PHILIPPINES

In Luzon on February 16, 1945, the recapture of Bataan was followed within a few hours by the landing on Corregidor of U.S. parachute troops and infantry. Twelve days later, General MacArthur announced from Manila that the last remnants of the enemy garrison on Corregidor had been eliminated. To mark the return of U.S. troops, the Allied commander here salutes the Stars and Stripes run up on the same flagstaff from which it was hauled down by the Japanese on May 6, 1942 (inset). In the background are troops of the U.S. 503rd Parachute Regiment.

RED ARMY STORMS THE AGGRESSOR'S CAPITAL

Final struggle for the Reich capital was waged in a chaos of blazing buildings, dive-bombing by Soviet Stormoviks and hopelessly commingled German civilians and troops clamouring for shelter. Many officers and men tried to escape capture by donning civilian clothes and mixing with the terror-stricken homeless. Main resistance to the Russians centred in the Government quarter where fanatical S.S. troops resorted to shooting members of the Wehrmacht attempting to desert. 1. To the cheers of his comrades in the street, this Soviet soldier flew the Red Flag from the roof of the burnt-out Reichstag on April 30, 1945. 2. A Russian mobile unit fires a multiple gun against the background of a blazing building. 3. Russian officer addresses his troops at the badly-shattered Brandenburg Tor.

MACARTHUR'S MEN GO ASHORE AT LINGAYEN GULF IN THE PHILIPPINE ISLAND OF LUZON

Against surprisingly little resistance, very large forces of Lieutenant-General Krueger's U.S. 6th Army, under the personal direction of General MacArthur, who went ashore with his men, landed on Luzon Island on January 9, 1945. Heavy bombing and an intensive bombardment of shore installations by a powerful Allied fleet, including an Australian naval squadron, preceded the invasion. Here, U.S. troops come ashore at Lingayen from Coast Guard landing barges. A Coast Guard (left) directs traffic beside the striped signal flag, while in the background lies a mass of landing craft.

the sea, the surface of the island changed before the eyes of the invaders. The trees of the northern section turned from green to bare grey skeleton trunks, the scrub of the south disappeared, the very slopes of Suribachi changed from a weathered grey to the brown of fresh-broken rock.

To the bombardment there was virtually no reply. One cruiser was moderately damaged by fire from a 6-inch battery. Not until the L.C.I.s covering the underwater demolition teams went in did the grim, well-disciplined defence open fire. This was the " invasion repulse " claimed by the Japanese. In actual fact the little force though heavily damaged, withdrew only on completion of a detailed examination of the beach approaches.

At dawn on February 19 a vast fleet lay off Iwo Jima, and to the north the fast carrier force of the 5th Fleet, under the command of Vice-Admiral Mitscher, stood between the invasion forces and any attempt by Japan to interfere by surface craft or by air.

The scene was one of the most remarkable among the many landings of the Second Great War. The United States battleship " Tennessee " occupied the **Amphibious Attack on Iwo Jima** central position 2,500 yards off the main landing beach on the south-western side of the island, selected in accordance with the weather forecast which promised winds from the westward. From her on either side extended a line of battleships, cruisers and destroyers, which ringed and commanded the entire circumference of the island. With a slowness that was as impressive as it was methodic, the assault landing craft gathered at the line of departure, and at 9 a.m. the first wave of the U.S. V Marine Corps swept in under the thunder of a rolling barrage. As the craft touched down the barrage lifted from the beaches to the ridges beyond. It held the Japanese defence penned in the depths of its caves and its deep gun-pits through the first critical moments of the landing. Not until approximately noon was the Japanese reaction to become serious, and not until 2 p.m did it reach its full height.

But what there was even in the first stages was sufficient to pin the right flank, where the 5th Marine Division landed, to the desperate, shelterless slope of the open sand. The centre, below No. 1 airfield (*see* map in page 3754), was more successful. The extreme left flank was held by withering fire from the slopes of Suribachi. None the less the position was established, and Vice-Admiral Richmond K. Turner,

in overall command of the operation, and General Holland M. Smith, commanding the Marines, had good reason to be proud of their achievement.

At dusk, however, the position was precarious. Intolerable mortar fire—on Iwo Jima the Japanese produced their most modern weapons, including rocket guns and gigantic mortars—had broken all attempts to advance on the left. In the centre the advance had taken the Marines across the narrow portion of the island and, as darkness fell, the position was in the shape of a ragged L, the 4th Division astride the island, the 5th pinned on the open sand. Had General Yamashita attacked during the night with all available force, he might have engineered a great disaster. The only attack that came, however, was weak and easily broken up. By dawn fresh waves of men, new material, the organization that was beginning to come out of the appalling chaos of the sandy beach with its tanks and jeeps sucked into the quicksand, its rim of wrecked and battered landing craft, redressed the position.

This day the first airfield was overrun in the face of intense opposition from heavy defences to the north. It was becoming apparent rapidly that this was not a case of shore-line defence. With every yard of the advance fresh Japanese fortifications were opening up. By the end of the second day the pattern of Iwo Jima was sealed. There was no room here for the battle of manoeuvre, no room for generalship in the full sense. This was a " soldier's battle "—only the soldier could win it

and only the soldier could pay the price.

Optimistically, it had been hoped by many before the landing craft went in that Iwo Jima would fall within three days ; but on the third day it was necessary to land the 3rd Marine Division, which had been held in reserve. For twenty-six days the men of the V **Strength of Japanese Defences** Marine Corps advanced against an enemy who had with brilliant tactical eye turned Nature to his purpose. There was not a rock from south to north in that island that was not defended. There was not a defensive point that was not directed to cover the movement of an attacker from those two treacherous beaches where alone he could land. There was not a spot in the island from

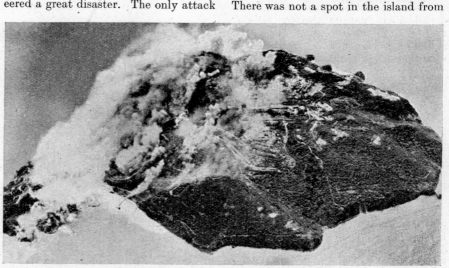

AMERICANS RETURN TO CORREGIDOR
Important island-fortress guarding Manila Bay and scene of an heroic stand by the Americans in 1942 (see page 2094), U.S. parachute troops and infantry landed on Corregidor on February 16, 1945, after a three-days' heavy naval and air attack during which it was plastered with over 2,000 tons of bombs and shells. Here, bombs from B-24's of the U.S.A. 13th A.F. rain on the island, blowing up a large ammunition dump. (See also page 3747.) *Photo, Keystone*

the first day until the last that was not potentially within range of Japanese guns and heavy mortars.

There was endless gallantry in this desperate fighting. Not the least of its episodes was the capture on February 23 of the broken volcano of Suribachi, heavily defended, desperately held, by men of the 28th Regiment—an exploit standing high even in the great record of the U.S. Marines. Its loss deprived the Japanese of an observation post from which the movements of every man of the invasion force could be watched with the naked eye, and from which concealed mortars and light guns had caused intolerable harassment of the southern flank. By the time Suribachi was taken the Americans had suffered 5,372 casualties (644 killed) on land, apart from considerable casualties upon the ships.

Through all this period the battleship force maintained its bombardment, spotting being carried out either from the ships' own aircraft or by shore parties. But the advances were measured in yards—sometimes in feet.

To evaluate properly the courage of the Marines, it is essential to emphasize the courage and tenacity of the Japanese **Japanese Courage and Tenacity** defenders. Where they stood they died, and they died under a concentration of fire that was equalled perhaps not more than twice in the course of the war. On the irregular circle of the main portion of the island, a circle only 2½ miles in diameter, there was poured every type of projectile then in use. The seamed and tortuous surface was drenched with napalm, the terrible jelly fire that falls from the air. The caves and the pillboxes were smoked out with long-range flame-throwers. From

the air everything from 2,000-lb. bombs to cannon shell was poured into the defences. With the capture of Suribachi, the full artillery of the three divisions was in effective operation, the guns so thickly on the ground that the difficulties of storage and dumping were at times almost insuperable.

Behind the creeping forward lines, the Seabees began their immense war of construction : roads were built of netting and steel plates from the shifting sand of the tide-marks ; shelters were made with sandbags in the uncertain sand ; fuel, food, ammunition dumps were dug in ; work went forward on No. 1 airfield. On March 1 the western beaches were brought into the full picture, and slowly, painfully slowly, the advance crept on, pushing forward

with its tremendous concentration of force. Later, Motoyama airfield was secured in a long series of yard by yard advances. Motoyama "town," that miserable sulphur village of the centre, was overrun. The hideous area of the sulphur mines beyond, where volcanic crater interlocked with volcanic crater and the ground of the island looked like the surface of the moon, was taken, and by March 5 the enemy had been driven into the coastal strip at the extreme north of the island. By March 10 the remnants of the Japanese garrison were split into three small pockets of resistance. All organized resistance ended on March 16 when elements of the U.S. 3rd and 5th Divisions broke through the enemy lines at Kitano Point.

IWO JIMA INVADED
The securing of five-miles-long Iwo Jima ('Sulphur Island'), midmost of the Volcano Islands and only 750 miles from Japan, was vital for American attack on the enemy mainland. Though U.S. landings began on February 19, 1945, after a powerful three-days' naval shelling, it was not until March 16 that the island finally fell. Right, Iwo Jima from the air ; the volcanic Mt. Suribachi is seen at the tip on the right and also (extreme left), in the bottom photograph, of the invasion force going in.

The cost was heavy. The V Marine Corps casualties were 4,189 dead, 441 missing, 15,308 wounded. To these it was necessary to add considerable naval casualties (*see* Chapter 365). The Japanese were estimated to have lost approximately 21,000 men plus some 700 prisoners.

Ten days after Iwo Jima had been secured, on Monday, March 26, elements of the United States 10th Army, with Marines, landed on the little islets of Kerama Retto. With this **OKINAWA** step the subjection of Japan itself came within measurable distance. The little group of islets which makes up the Kerama group is almost precisely in the centre of the long chain of the Ryukyu or Nansei Shoto Islands which, like a series of giant's stepping stones, link Formosa with Japan and form the outpost barrier between the Pacific Ocean and the East China Sea.

Once again the operation was essentially an exercise of sea power. Once again it proceeded without interference from the Japanese Navy. To ensure that immunity, to provide for the proper use of that power, Fleet-Admiral Nimitz, under whose command the operation proceeded, assembled the most powerful fleet that the world had ever known.

It was necessary as a first step to take the Kerama group in order to obtain an anchorage and to secure positions commanding the Okinawa beaches. The objective of the operation was Okinawa itself. This, the main island of the chain, is approximately 65 miles from north to south with a maximum width of about ten miles, a long, narrow, irregular island, subdivided by constricted waists of land with irregular peninsulas projecting east and west to the sea (*see* map in page 3755). It was believed to be garrisoned by a force of 60,000 men under General Mitsuru Ushijima, together with a certain number of impressed Okinawan troops.

Though hilly, Okinawa had none of the natural defences of Iwo Jima. The landing beaches were good and there was

Landing on Okinawa a considerable number of possible alternative landing places. The tactics of the landing followed in broad essentials the tactics at Luzon. A feint was made at the southern portion of the island where the capital, Naha, and the old capital, Shuri, are situated, and which contains the bulk of the population. Then, with the exquisite flexibility of amphibious tactics, the force, under Vice-Admiral Turner, was swung in on the beaches below

U.S. MARINES GO ASHORE ON IWO JIMA

Preceded by one of the greatest naval bombardments of the war, lasting three days and directed by Vice-Admiral Spruance, a landing was effected by the U.S. V Marine Corps on the Japanese island of Iwo Jima, in the Volcano group, on February 19, 1945. 1. Marines advance under fire up the beach ; Mt. Suribachi is seen in the background. 2. Light ammunition trucks are man-handled ashore from landing craft. 3. Unloading supplies on the volcanic sands a few hours later. *Photos, Associated Press ; Paul Popper*

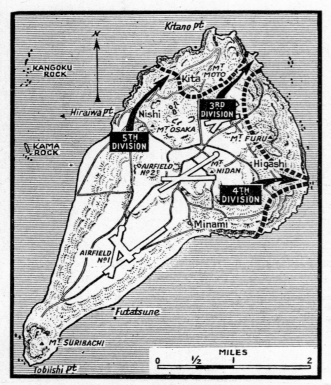

JAPANESE FORCES ARE SPLIT

The battle for Iwo Jima, as it appeared on March 10, 1945, six days before the end. The remnants of the Japanese garrison had been split into three groups, the largest being a half-mile-square pocket round Kitano Point, at the north end of the island. The U.S. 4th Marine Division, killing 564 of an enemy force of 750, pushed through to the east coast at Tachiwawa Point.

CONQUERORS MEET

On March 14, 1945, the U.S. flag was formally raised over Iwo Jima, a proclamation issued suspending Japanese rule, and Fleet Admiral Chester Nimitz was appointed Military Governor. Here Lt.-Gen. Holland M. Smith (right), commanding the U.S. Marines, and Maj.-Gen. Clifton B. Cates, commander of the U.S. 4th Marine Division, meet within sight of the northern tip of the island.
Photo, Central Press

day they held a depth of more than three miles. As mechanized equipment poured in over the landing beaches, the beach-head rapidly expanded. By Monday, April 2, American Marines had crossed the island, reaching the eastern coast at Nakagusuku Wan. The Japanese defence was cut in two and from that moment the result of the campaign was never in doubt.

It is the more curious, therefore, that almost from this moment a deadlock began which was to last far beyond the estimated duration of the campaign, and was to involve heavy and lamentable casualties.

The 10th Army, under General Buckner, consisted of the XXIV Army Corps and the III Marine Corps. General Buckner had at his command a force very considerably in excess numerically of the Japanese defence, infinitely better equipped with artillery and quick-firing weapons, having at its disposal the strength of almost two armoured divisions, supported by tremendous air-power from the escort-carriers attached to the landing force, with the almost unlimited support of the Fleet carriers behind it, and the immeasurable advantage of the mobile batteries of the Fleet guns which could—as at Iwo Jima—virtually surround the enemy's positions.

It appears to have been assumed largely that the Japanese command would withdraw towards the northern portion of the island to take advantage of the succession of narrow isthmuses and of the increasing ruggedness of the hills. But from the first General Ushi-

the Yontan airfield. The landing on April 1 was preceded by a tremendous bombardment from the sea. The Japanese command, hampered by a force too small to defend the enormous indented coastline of the island, was caught " on the wrong foot " by the feints, and the beaches below Yontan were virtually undefended. Under Lieut.-General Simon Bolivar Buckner the U.S. 10th Army swarmed ashore without opposition and almost without loss. By 11 o'clock in the morning they had secured Yontan airfield and the Katena strip. By the end of the first

ON THE QUICKSANDS OF IWO JIMA

Only possible landing places on Iwo Jima were the quicksands to the south of the island (see map above). Left, U.S. Marines construct sandbagged gun emplacements on what had once been the enemy's No. 1 airfield ; Mt. Suribachi is seen in the distance. Right, urgent U.S. casualties are treated on the beach. Poles in the sand supported plasma bottles for blood-transfusion before casualties were taken off by sea
Photos, Associated Press

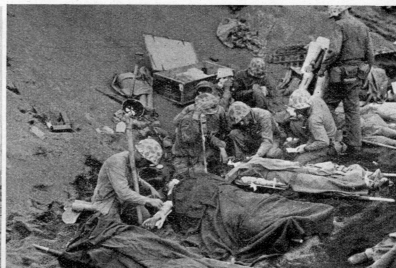

jima concentrated his defence in the south. General Buckner, however, committed the III Marine Corps to a mopping-up operation to the north, and wheeled the XXIV Army Corps against the main enemy force. The wheel was executed slowly and without apparent decision, and General Ushijima had time to improvise defences on a front of some 11,000 yards in width.

The campaign has been compared to that of Iwo Jima. The comparison is incorrect and unfair to the heroic men of the V Marine Corps. The Okinawa terrain had none of the natural defensive qualities of Iwo Jima; the enemy had no previously prepared fixed defences between Yontan and Shuri. Only the incredible fanaticism of the Japanese soldier held the line, and that fanaticism for almost two months was sufficient against an invader who held absolute command of the air, who had the equivalent of two armoured divisions, who to an overwhelming strength in artillery had added the stupendous power of the guns of the Fleet, and who had almost unlimited superiority in men, equipment and supply.

Fanaticism Against Strength

It is easy to over-simplify, but to any serious student of it must appear that there was faulty leadership. In the end General Buckner brought back the III Marine Corps. Instead of attempting to break the deadlock by landing it in rear of the enemy, he committed these troops—the finest amphibious body in the Pacific—on his right flank, crowding two army corps on a front of little more than eight miles, and eventually with

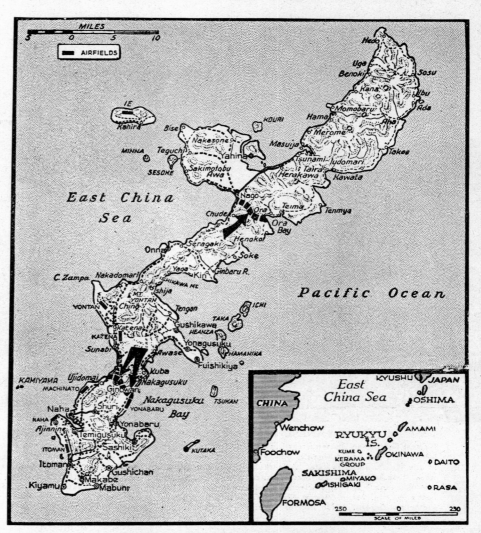

AMERICAN HEADWAY ON OKINAWA

Six days after landing near the Yontan airfield in the west of Okinawa, U.S. marines, driving north, on April 7, 1945, reached the vicinity of Nago on the west coast and Ora Bay on the east. Troops of the U.S. 10th Army, pushing south, were meeting stiff opposition as they neared Naha, the capital. Okinawa is one of the most densely populated islands in the world.

U.S. TROOPS MAKE FOR OKINAWA'S BEACHES

Not a single craft was lost during the landing on Okinawa on April 1, 1945, by troops of the U.S. 10th Army, under Lieutenant-General Simon Bolivar Buckner, in which over 1,400 ships were involved. The left flank of the operation was protected by units of the British Pacific Fleet, under Vice-Admiral Sir Bernard Rawlings. Here, amphibious craft head for the beach as a U.S. battleship fires a broadside. *Photo, L.N.A.*

drawing one of his army divisions because of overcrowding. The expedient worked, but at a heavy price in men. The élan of the Marines on the right flank and the fear they inspired in the Japanese command caused a thinning of the Japanese right. Even as the Marines flooded into the waste where Naha had stood, the 7th Division (Army) broke through the gap beyond Yonabaru town and the campaign became a mopping-up operation. On June 21 the American flag was hoisted over Okinawa, four days after the death of General Buckner in action.

Estimated to last approximately forty days, the campaign had taken eighty-two. The casualty figures were equally enlarged. The Americans lost, killed and missing, approximately 12,000 men, with 35,000 wounded. The final figures with regard to the Japanese casualties were given as 101,853 dead, with 7,902 prisoners. It is difficult to accept these figures in view of the fact

JAPANESE RESIST FANATICALLY ON OKINAWA

Fiercest fighting on Okinawa raged in the southern section where some 60,000 of the enemy, fighting fanatic-ally, in mid-April 1945 began to oppose the U.S. advance with a heavier artillery concentration than that used in any Pacific island to date. As a result, the campaign, which had been planned to last approximately six weeks, took 82 days. 1. U.S. Marines enter ruined Naha, the capital, on May 27. On the extreme left is a General Sherman tank. 2. Smoke-screened hillside overlooking Naha as U.S. troops advance towards the city under heavy fire. 3. Major-General Lemuel C. Shepherd (left), commanding the U.S. 6th Marine Division, and Lieutenant-General Simon Bolivar Buckner, commanding the U.S. 10th Army, who was killed in action on June 17.

Photos, Paul Popper ; Fox Photos ; Keystone

innumerable sinkings of minor vessels in connexion with the landings and covering operations, the Japanese Navy as a fighting force ceased to exist.

As with the Navy, so with the Japanese Air Force. The toll taken of the Japanese air in the Philippines, in the covering operations for Iwo Jima and in Okinawa, crippled the striking power and, in the upshot, the defensive power of the **Japanese Air Force Crippled** Japanese Metropolitan Air Force. Only the suicide tactics of the Kamikaze organization kept Japanese airmen in the picture, and even that, by the end of Okinawa, was becoming a diminishing asset. Though the Japanese military forces involved were not, in relation to the actual size of the Japanese armies, large, the loss in military prestige and in material was not to be despised.

Meanwhile the stupendous achievement of American production was beginning to play its full part. The material losses of these three campaigns with the sea losses that accompanied them were far more than made up. The losses of personnel, grievous as they were, were never strategically important. Japan finished up each campaign weaker than before. The Americans finished immeasurably stronger. By the end of Okinawa the Philippines were already a vast base for the forthcoming invasion. Even while the fighting was continuing, the work of preparing Okinawa for its

that in mid-May an estimate of 51,000 Japanese dead had been made. If the Japanese had lost the same proportion of men by wounds as had the Americans, this would have meant 200,000 men out of action by mid-May. In point of fact resistance continued strongly for another month, and the only assumption possible is that in the early days of the campaign at any rate, over-optimistic estimates of Japanese dead were made. There seems little evidence to indicate that the size of the Japanese garrison was much in excess of the original Intelligence estimates of 60,000.

These three campaigns were all undertaken with a single objective—to provide bases for the eventual invasion of Japan. They succeeded, however, in doing vastly more than this, for with the crippling of the Japanese Fleet in the Battle for Leyte Gulf, with the sinking of the "Yamato," the second and last of Japan's modern battleships, in her abortive sortie against the Okinawa invasion force, and with the almost

BURNING OUT THE ENEMY AT KUSHITAKE
Driven from their hillside hiding-place, Japanese troops, one carrying a white flag, here surrender to U.S. Marines on Okinawa. Above, U.S. fire-bomb explodes on an enemy stronghold at Kushitake, on southern Okinawa. When the flames subside every Japanese above ground in the area will be burned to death and those underground suffocated, the fierce flames drawing off all oxygen in their path. *Photos, Keystone; New York Times Photos*

PRISONERS ON OKINAWA

Fiercest fighting in the Pacific was on Okinawa, in the Ryukyus, where American casualties totalled over 12,000 in dead and missing during 82 days' fighting. Although the initial landing, by the U.S. 10th Army, was on March 26, 1945, the island did not pass into American hands until June 21. The enemy lost almost 8,000 in prisoners alone, some of whom here trek to the beaches for transportation. *Photo, L.N.A*

Japanese Expansion up to 1930...........
Areas of Expansion after 1930.........
Allied Advance up to August 15, 1945

eventual role as a staging area for the invasion of Japan was well under way.

The military operations that followed the hoisting of the flag on Okinawa were small and unimportant. They consisted of the seizure and consolidation of other small islands in the chain. But the vital factor in this period was the " build-up," and that proceeded unhampered by the enemy—swiftly, inexorably.

These three campaigns—one vastly easier than had been anticipated, one vastly more difficult, and one made more difficult than it need have been— were, in combination, the greatest successes of the Pacific war. With the earlier capture of the Marianas they made possible, first, the wiping out by incendiary bombing of the great cities of Japan and, secondly, the provision of everything that was necessary for the staging of the eventual descent on the mainland. They, and not the atomic bomb, were the decisive factor in the subsequent Japanese surrender.

WAR ENDS IN THE FAR EAST

Position in the Far Eastern Theatre of War on the date of Japan's surrender, when very large areas of the territory conquered by the enemy were still in Japanese hands, as can be seen from the key. The Russians continued their Manchurian offensive for some days (see Chapter 367). This map does not show Allied advances in China.

Courtesy of The Times

June 1. Chungking announced that Chinese troops had captured Pinyang (Kwangsi) and Suilo. On Okinawa U.S. forces linked up south of Shuri. S.E.A.C. announced formation of 12th Army in Burma. U.S. Army Persian Gulf Command ceased transporting U.S. war supplies to Russia via Persian Gulf.

June 2. S.E.A.C. announced heavy defeats of enemy in the Kama bridge-head E. of the Irrawaddy and in the Shan Hills ; " staircase " N.W. of Kalaw captured.

June 3. Carrier-based aircraft of U.S. 3rd Fleet attacked Kyushu airfields. On Okinawa U.S. troops cut off Chinen peninsula to control Nakagasuku Bay, former enemy naval base. Land Forces Adriatic disbanded. Last convoy reached the Clyde, Scotland.

June 4. By day 450–500 unescorted Super-Fortresses bombed Kobe (Japan), dropping 3,000 tons of fire bombs. U.S. Marines landed near Naha (Okinawa). U.S. " Mars " Tank Force transferred from Burma to China theatre. On Tarakan, Australians captured " Margy Hill " and " Hill 102."

June 5. Announced that Australians had captured Wewak harbour, last Japanese base in New Guinea. Field-Marshal Montgomery and General Eisenhower awarded Order of Victory, highest Soviet military decoration. Allied Control Commission met in Berlin.

June 6. 400 Super-Fortresses inflicted heavy attack on Osaka (Japan). U.S. Marines cleared Oroku peninsula on Okinawa, reached the coast near Itoman. Brazil declared war on Japan.

June 7. First Allied cargo-ship to use Wewak (New Guinea) for three years entered the port. King Haakon of Norway landed at Oslo. Last joint statement on the war against U-boats issued by Mr. Churchill and President Truman. King and Queen visited the Channel Islands.

June 8. Super-Fortresses heavily bombed Tokyo, Osaka, Nagoya, Kobe and Kyusha areas. Japanese announced formation of People's Volunteer Corps, including every able-bodied man, woman and child, to resist invasion. Field-Marshal Montgomery presented with the freedom of Antwerp by the Burgomaster.

June 9. Australians on Tarakan penetrated strong enemy defences in the hills near Djoeta. 14th Army troops in Burma captured Kalaw, pursuing Japanese forces trying to escape into Siam.

June 10. Australian 9th Division landed in great strength on Labuan Island, on Mauru, and at Brooketown in British North Borneo, capturing Labuan town. Super-Fortresses heavily attacked industrial targets on the Japanese mainland, including Yokohama. Australians landed at Matchin Bay, North Bougainville. Guards Armoured Division became an infantry division again.

June 11. In N. Borneo Australians, with air support, advanced several miles inland towards Brunei against only light opposition. S.E.A.C. announced that an estimated 108,240 Japanese troops had been killed in Burma since Fabruary 1, 1944. General Election in Canada : Mr. Mackenzie King's Government returned again.

June 12. Australian columns in N. Borneo reported less than ten miles from Brunei. On Okinawa U.S. artillery, in support of ground forces, put down one of the heaviest barrages of the Pacific war.

June 13. Brunei fell, with little opposition, to troops of the Australian 9th Division ; airstrip also captured ; reported that the Dyaks (head-hunters) were attacking Japanese patrols with blow pipes and poisoned darts.

June 14. British officials went ashore in N. Borneo to restore civil administration. Tokyo described Japanese situation on Okinawa as " desperate." Ribbentrop captured in Hamburg. White Paper on India issued.

June 14 and 15. Truk, Japanese stronghold in the Carolines, heavily bombarded by British Pacific Fleet and bombed by British carrier-borne aircraft.

June 15. Australian 9th Division, well beyond Brunei, drove along the coast towards the Miri oilfields in Sarawak. 520 Super-Fortresses heavily bombed Osaka. Chungking announced that Chinese had recaptured the Ishan airbase in Kwangsi. Victory parade in Rangoon to mark liberation of Burma.

June 16. Australians in N. Borneo took Timbalai airstrip. U.S. 10th Army captured three dominating positions on the Yaeju Dake plateau, last enemy defence line before the S. tip of Okinawa.

June 17. 450 Marianas-based Super-Fortresses bombed Japanese industrial towns of Omura, Kagoshima, Hamamatsu and Yokkaichi. In S.W. Kiangsi Japanese captured Lungnan and Tingnan. Polish leaders met in Moscow.

June 18. Chinese recaptured treaty port of Wenchow on the Chekiang coast. In Burma, British, Indian and Gurkha troops seized hill positions on Toungoo-Mawchi escape road to the Shan Hills. On Okinawa U.S. troops cleared Oroku pocket

June 19. Over 450 Marianas-based Super-Fortresses bombed Fukuoska, Toyohashi, and Shizuoka. Australians in N. Borneo reached Tutongi : other Australians, landing on Brunei Bay, took Weston.

June 20. Australian 9th Division troops landed at Lutongon, on Sarawak, others S. of Brunei Bay ; R.A.A.F. and U.S. bombers raided Balikpapan (S. Borneo). Carrier-based aircraft of British E. Indies Fleet bombed Sumatra and shipping in Malacca Straits. Liner Queen Mary arrived at New York with 14,000 U.S. troops from Europe.

June 21 and 22. Japanese " suicide " aircraft attacked U.S. warships off Okinawa, 59 being shot down.

June 21. All organized resistance on Okinawa ceased after 82 days' fighting. Marianas-based Super-Fortresses heavily attacked Japanese industrial targets. Australian 9th Division gained full control of entrance to Brunei Bay.

June 22. Australians in Sarawak liberated 150 Sikh and Punjabi troops captured by Japanese troops earlier in the war.

June 23. Announced that Australians in Borneo controlled 80 miles of coastline. U.S. forces landed near Aparri, last port left to enemy on Luzon. Rangoon port open to shipping. Prof. Willem Schermerhorn formed new Dutch cabinet.

June 24. Announced that Australian 9th Division had captured Seria oilfields (N. Borneo), overcome all resistance on Labuan island and gained full control of Tarakan. Balikpapan (Dutch Borneo) heavily raided by R.A.A.F. and U.S.A.A.F.

June 25. Australians captured Miri in Sarawak. Announced that Chinese controlled nearly 200 miles of Chekiang coast. San Francisco Conference ended.

June 26. 500 Marianas-based Super-Fortresses bombed Japanese towns, including Nagoya and Osaka ; other Super-Fortresses attacked oil refinery at Yokkaichi.

June 27. 2,700-ton aircraft-carrier U.S.S. " Bunker Hill " steamed into New York harbour under her own power for repair after having been wrecked, but not sunk, off Okinawa on May 11.

June 28. All resistance on Luzon ceased. 450–500 Super-Fortresses from Marianas heavily bombed Nobeoka and Okayama (Japan).

June 29. U.S. and Australian bombers heavily attacked Balikpapan oilfields for ninth consecutive day. Tarakan oilfields reported back in production. Tokyo announced evacuation of war industries to Manchuria.

June 30. Chinese recaptured Linchow air-base. U.S. troops made unopposed landing on Kume Island, 50 miles W. of Okinawa.

NAVAL SUPPORT FOR ISLAND INVASIONS

U.S. landings on Iwo Jima (February 19, 1945) and Okinawa (April 1) were covered by forces of the Allied fleets massed on a scale hitherto unknown in the Pacific. 1. Flame-tipped rockets streak towards Okinawa from U.S. Navy L.S.M. (R)s—Landing Ships Medium, Rockets. 2. Fire-fighting parties on the flight-deck of the 33,000-ton U.S. aircraft-carrier 'Saratoga', hit off Iwo Jima on February 21 by 7 bombs which killed 123 of the crew. 3. U.S.S. 'Tennessee', 32,000-ton battleship, taking part in the naval bombardment of Iwo Jima.

Chapter 365

FAR EASTERN NAVAL EXPLOITS, 1945

*The advance of the American and British navies to the coasts of Japan, an
operation closely linked with the air activity described in Chapter 368, and
the driving of the enemy from the Indian Ocean are the subjects of this chapter,
which concludes the history of Allied naval exploits in the Far East*

AMERICAN naval losses in the three years following Pearl Harbor were revealed on December 7, 1944 ; they amounted to about 230 combat ships, totalling 3,750,000 tons, and included two battleships, nine aircraft-carriers, nine cruisers, 51 destroyers, and 33 submarines ; but the United States had replaced these losses many times over : in the same period she had built 42,000,000 tons, and at the beginning of 1945 probably possessed a fleet larger than all the other navies of the world combined.

The year 1945 opened in the Pacific with great naval activity off the Philippines, where the invasion of Luzon (*see* page 3743) was preceded by bombardment from a powerful Allied fleet, including battleships, cruisers, destroyers and rocket-firing craft—an operation in which, on January 6, Sir Bruce Fraser, commander of the British Pacific Fleet, narrowly escaped death : he was on the bridge of the U.S.S. "New Mexico" as an observer when he was knocked down by blast from a bomb which killed Lieutenant-General Sir Herbert Lumsden, Mr. Churchill's special military representative with General MacArthur, and Mr. W. Chickering, correspondent of "The Times."

The fleet escorting the invasion armada included an Australian squadron under Commodore J. N. B. Farncomb. Japanese aircraft and light naval forces **Heavy Attack on Allied Shipping** heavily attacked Allied shipping, both before and during the landings, sinking the escort carrier U.S.S. "Ommaney Bay" for the loss of 79 planes, two destroyers, one midget submarine, and other vessels. The cruiser H.M.A.S. "Australia" was holed five times, and the destroyer H.M.A.S. "Arunta" was damaged, but neither withdrew from action until the operations were concluded.

The landings on Iwo Jima (*see* page 3746) were preceded by a similar violent naval bombardment, beginning on February 16 and covering the invasion, which was under the overall command of Vice-Admiral Richmond K. Turner, and was supported by a fleet of over 800 warships including the battleships "Tennessee," "Idaho," "Nevada," "New York," "Texas," and

"Arkansas," most of them commanded by Vice-Admiral R. A. Spruance. The U.S. escort-carrier "Bismarck Sea" was sunk, and the 33,000-ton aircraft-carrier "Saratoga" was hit by seven bombs, but not sunk, off Iwo Jima on February 21.

Just over a month later, naval attacks on the Saki group (southernmost of the Ryukyu chain) began on March 26. This was the occasion of the first major Pacific action of the British Pacific Fleet (*see* page 3402) which, in conjunction with Admiral Spruance's U.S. 5th Fleet and under overall American operational command, was led by Vice-Admiral Sir Bernard Rawlings, with aircraft-carriers under Rear-Admiral Sir Philip Vian. The battleship H.M.S. "King George V" and the aircraft-carrier H.M.S. "Illustrious" were among the vessels taking part. Heavy sea and air attacks on the Ryukyus continued until the landings on Okinawa on April 1 (*see* page 3754), the British Pacific Fleet continuing to concentrate on the Saki group. Over 1,400 ships, under the overall command of Admiral Spruance, were involved in the Okinawa landings, the left flank of which was protected by the British Pacific Fleet. The enemy developed a strong counter-attack.

During the evening of April 6, Japanese aircraft attacked U.S. ships and shore installations in force, sinking three destroyers and the U.S. minesweeper "Emmaus," hit by five Japanese Kamikaze (suicide) pilots (*see* Chapter 368), and damaging several other destroyers and smaller craft, for the loss of 106 machines. Early next day, a considerable enemy surface force, described by Tokyo radio as a suicide force, left the Inland Sea : it was led by the 45,000-ton 16-inch gun battleship "Yamato," the most powerful ship remaining to Japan, and included an Agano class light cruiser. It came under heavy Allied air attack in the middle of the day. No air opposition developed, though the Allied planes encountered heavy A.A. fire. The "Yamato," the Agano class cruiser, and three destroyers were sunk some fifty miles off Kyushu, three other vessels were left burning, and only three escaped. One heavy U.S. unit suffered damage.

Allied Losses off Okinawa

Japan's desperate and suicidal attempts to halt the conquest of Okinawa continued. On April 21, Admiral Nimitz's H.Q. announced Allied and enemy losses between March 18 and

AUSTRALIAN WARSHIPS WERE AT LUZON LANDINGS

Among the Allied fleet covering the invasion of Luzon, in the Philippines, on January 9, 1945, was an Australian squadron. This force was heavily attacked by Japanese aircraft and naval units while en route for Luzon on January 5, 6 and 7, when the 10,000-ton cruiser H.M.A.S. 'Australia' was holed five times and the destroyer 'Arunta' damaged, though both remained in action Below, the 'Australia' after the attack: 3 officers and 41 ratings were killed.

April 18 in the Okinawa operations and associated attacks on Japan. They were as follows: American, five destroyers, one destroyer-transport, two minelayers, one gunboat, four landing-craft, and two ammunition ships; Japanese, one battleship, two light cruisers, five destroyers, five destroyer-escorts, 28 small cargo ships, many torpedo boats and small craft, and 2,569 aircraft.

The Kamikaze pilots did score successes, however. The destroyers "Long-shaw" and "Drexler," the auxiliary transport "Bates," and a landing ship were sunk on June 11, the 2,100-ton destroyers "Twiggs" on June 16 (136 killed or missing including all her officers) and "William D. Porter" on June 10 (61 wounded). The 27,000-ton aircraft-carrier U.S.S. "Bunker Hill," flagship of Vice-Admiral Marc Mitscher, was wrecked but not sunk on May 11 when three Kamikaze pilots crashed into her, killing 392 men, wounding 264 and destroying 70 aircraft. Mitscher himself had a narrow escape from death. The fires aboard her were got under control, and her commander, Captain George Seitz, with outstanding seamanship took her across the Pacific to Puget Sound for preliminary repairs. She reached New York under her own steam on June 27.

In the twelve weeks from the end of March, three of the newest and most powerful aircraft-carriers in the

American Losses

END OF JAPAN'S LAST BIG BATTLESHIP

The 45,000-ton 'Yamato', Japan's last remaining modern battleship, was sunk off Kyushu on April 7, 1945, as she led a 'suicide' force heading for Okinawa in support of an enemy counter-attack which had begun the previous day. She here attempts to escape bombs and torpedoes of attacking U.S. carrier aircraft. Fires flame up amidships, while near-misses explode off the port bow. Two enemy cruisers and three destroyers were sunk in the same engagement.

Royal Navy, the "Indefatigable," the "Victorious" and the "Formidable," which were serving with the British Pacific Fleet in the Ryukyus, were hit by five Kamikaze aircraft. Seventy men were killed, 34 seriously wounded, but all the carriers remained in action. The destroyer "Ulster" was put out of action, however. British naval aircraft accounted for 140 enemy planes destroyed or damaged during these Japanese attacks, which were as fierce as any by the Luftwaffe on the Mediterranean and North Russia convoys.

On July 11, Mr. Artemus Gates, Under-Secretary of the Navy, reported that the U.S. Navy possessed two 45,000-ton aircraft-carriers (the "Midway" and the "Franklin D. Roosevelt"), 27 other first-line carriers of 27,000-tons and 10,000 tons, and 69 escort carriers; and declared that the United States Fleet had gained control of Pacific waters "right up to the Japanese coast." Three days later the truth of his words was demonstrated: the Japanese homeland was bombarded for the first time by Allied warships— a development following on frequent bombings by land- and carrier-based aircraft (described in Chapter 368). The target, the port and industrial centre of Kamaishi (which lies 275 miles north-east of Tokyo) received 1,000 tons of shells in a two-hour bombardment by a force of the U.S. 3rd Fleet under the command of

JAPANESE FAIL TO SINK THE 'FRANKLIN'

One of the worst naval disasters of the war occurred on March 19, 1945, when Japanese aircraft struck at but failed to sink the 27,000-ton U.S. aircraft-carrier 'Franklin' some sixty miles off the south coast of Japan. In the explosions following the attack over 200,000 lb. of the carrier's ammunition and a large quantity of octane spirit blew up, killing over 800 of the crew. Below, the 'Franklin' lists badly as the cruiser 'Santa Fé' comes alongside. *Photos, U.S. Navy*

HEROIC STRUGGLE BY BRITISH SUBMARINE

Early in 1945 H.M.S. 'Shakespeare,' while attached to the East Indies Fleet, survived one of the stiffest battles of the submarine war during which she sank a medium-sized Japanese merchant ship and fought off 25 air attacks. A shell from an enemy merchantman tore a hole in her pressure hull, flooding the engine-room; and though four more shells ripped into her, the crew continued to fight the enemy air attacks. Here 'Shakespeare's' gun-crew is standing by during a pause in the action. *Photo, British Official*

during this attack. Among British warships taking part were the 35,000-ton battleship "King George V," the 23,000-ton aircraft-carrier "Formidable," the cruisers "Newfoundland" and "Black Prince," the destroyers "Barfleur," "Grenville," "Quickmatch," "Troubridge," and "Undine." American ships participating included the "Iowa," which made naval history by broadcasting a running commentary of the action during the bombardment. No opposition of any kind was encountered.

An American cruiser squadron bombarded installations round Cape Nojima, 80 miles south of Tokyo, on the night of July 18–19. Nine U.S. destroyers entered Tokyo Bay and attacked an enemy con- **Japanese** voy on the night of July **Coast** 22–23, and on the 23rd **Bombarded** destroyers of the 3rd Fleet swept close inshore in Sagami Bay (south-west of Tokyo Bay). On the 25th a U.S. cruiser and destroyer force under Rear-Admiral J. C. Jones bombarded the Kushimoto seaplane base and other targets at the southern tip of Honshu.

During the night of July 29–30, a powerful Allied squadron, including the battleships H.M.S. "King George V" and U.S.S. "Massachusetts," fired over 1,000 tons of shells from a range of about six miles into the port and industrial centre of Hamamatsu. An Allied destroyer force steamed before dawn on July 31 into Suruga Gulf, on the south coast of Honshu, and carried

Rear-Admiral J. F. Shafroth and comprising the 35,000-ton battleships "Indiana," "Massachusetts" and "South Dakota," the 13,000-ton cruisers "Chicago" and "Quincy," and four destroyers. No opposition was met from shore batteries, aircraft or warships. Both before and during the bombardment, some thousand carrier-borne aircraft ranged over a wide area of north Honshu and Hokkaido, meeting no opposition. Next day, Muroran, whose population was swollen with refugees from the devastated cities of Honshu (see Chapter 368), was blasted from 1,000 yards range by another task force of the 3rd Fleet, including three of the biggest battleships in the world, the new 45,000-ton "Iowa," "Missouri," and "Wisconsin." Again there was no opposition.

Under cover of darkness, during the night of July 16–17 the U.S. 3rd Fleet and British Pacific Fleet, which had met at a secret rendezvous 500 miles from Japan, carried out one of the heaviest naval bombardments of the war, their target being a 60–80 mile stretch of the Honshu coast

north of Tokyo. Battleships approached to within six miles of the shore, cruisers and destroyers frequently steamed close inshore at high speeds to bombard the targets at very short range. More than 2,000 tons of shells were poured into Japanese industrial centres in that area

BRITISH EAST INDIES FLEET ATTACKS SUMATRA

'Softening-up' attacks were delivered against Sabang, off the north tip of Sumatra, Japanese-occupied naval base guarding the northern end of the Malacca Straits, beginning on April 12, 1945. Forces employed were units of the British East Indies Fleet, under the command of Vice-Admiral Harold Walker, including the 30,000-ton battleship 'Queen Elizabeth' (left), and the French battleship 'Richelieu' (right), here seen with an escort carrier (centre) during the operations. *Photo British Official*

BRITISH PACIFIC FLEET HASTENS DEFEAT OF JAPAN

On May 28, 1945, Vice-Admiral Sir Bernard Henry Rawlings, K.C.B., K.B.E., commanding a British task force, arrived at Guam on board his flagship H.M.S. 'King George V' for talks with Admiral Chester L. Nimitz, C.-in-C., Pacific Ocean Areas. The 'King George V' and the aircraft-carrier H.M.S. 'Illustrious' had been among units of the British Pacific Fleet which, in conjunction with Admiral Spruance's U.S. 5th Fleet and under overall American operational command, had taken part in their first major Pacific action when they attacked the Saki Islands, in the Ryukyus, on March 26 and 27. 1. H.M. destroyers 'Whelp' and 'Wager' refuel with oil from H.M.S. 'Duke of York' en route for the Japanese mainland in August 1945. 2. Admiral Rawlings and Admiral Nimitz on board the 'King George V' at Guam. 3. H.M.S. 'King George V' steams into Guam harbour, her company dressing ship.

Photos, British Official

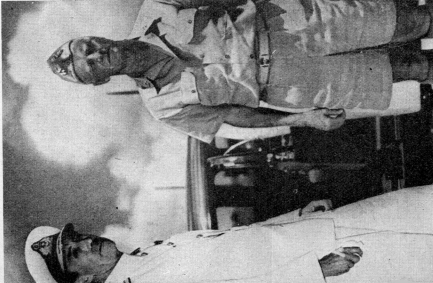

SECRET NAVAL BASE IN THE INDIAN OCEAN

Details of Port 'T,' a secret British naval base dug out of the jungle by Royal Marines on Addu Atoll, a group of waterless coral islets in the Indian Ocean (see map left), was not disclosed till July 1945. Port 'T' became a vital link on the convoy route to Australia and a base for naval operations in the Indian Ocean. Left, the barrel of a heavy gun is being lowered into position at the port. Above, a well camouflaged gun position.   *Photo, British Official*

out a five-minutes bombardment of Shimizu, port and aluminium centre. British cruisers and destroyers forming part of the 3rd Fleet steamed inshore on August 10 to bombard Kamaishi, target of the first naval bombardment of Japan. Paramushiro and other targets in the Kuriles were bombarded from close inshore by the U.S. cruisers "Concord" and "Richmond" on August 13. The next day saw the surrender of Japan.

While powerful United States and British fleets had moved steadily nearer the Japanese homeland, ships of the British East Indies Station were busy in the Indian Ocean and round the East Indies. Operating with the British Pacific and East Indies Fleets were, in addition to warships already mentioned, the battleships "Howe," "Queen Elizabeth," and "Valiant," the French battleship "Richelieu," the battle-cruiser "Renown," the aircraft-carrier "Indomitable," the cruisers "Argonaut" and "Euryalus," and the Dutch light cruiser "Tromp." Destroyers of the East Indies Fleet bombarded Sigli (Sumatra) on March 17; Port Blair in

East Indies Operations

the Andamans on March 19; and on the 26th, in co-operation with Liberators, sank an enemy convoy of ships escorted by two submarine chasers in the Andaman Sea. During the third week of April, Sumatra suffered naval attack: battleships and cruisers bombarded Sabang, destroyers bombarded Kota Raja, and naval aircraft bombed Padang and Emmahaven. Japanese aircraft rising in defence were repulsed. Battleships, cruisers and destroyers bombarded

Leading Seaman JAMES MAGENNIS (R.N.)   **Lieutenant IAN FRASER, D.S.C. (R.N.R.)**

For bravery in the attack by H.M. Midget Submarine XE-3 on the Japanese cruiser 'Takao' in the Johore Straits, Singapore, on July 31, 1945 (see page 3771), Lieutenant Ian Edward Fraser, the commander, and Leading Seaman James Magennis were both awarded the V.C. As there was sufficient depth of water for the XE-3 to place herself for the attack only under the midship portion of the 'Takao,' Lieutenant Fraser forced his craft right under the centre of the cruiser, where her hatch would not open fully; but Leading Seaman Magennis, the diver, managed to squeeze his way out and fix limpet mines to the cruiser's hull, scraping off several years' growth of barnacles. Later, though exhausted and armed only with a spanner, he daringly released one of the mine-carriers which had become jammed against the XE-3's hull.   *Photo, Planet News*

airfields on Car-Nicobar in the Nicobar Islands on April 30. Avenger aircraft operating from the escort-carrier "Shah" attacked the 10,000-ton Japanese cruiser "Haguro" in the northern Malacca Straits; a destroyer force consisting of the "Saumarez" and the "Virago" (both of which played a part in the sinking of the "Scharnhorst"—*see* page 2851), the "Venus," the "Verulam," and the "Vigilant," led by Captain M. L. Power ("Saumarez"), intercepted and sank her with torpedoes.

Aircraft from carriers of the British East Indies Fleet bombed enemy airfields in Sumatra, and shipping in the Malacca Straits, without loss on June 20. From July 5–10, undisturbed by the enemy, a naval force commanded by Rear-Admiral W. R. Patterson on board the cruiser H.M.S. "Nigeria," and including the escort-carriers "Ameer" and "Emperor," the destroyer "Roebuck" and the 6th Minesweeping Flotilla,

HYDROGRAPHIC SURVEY

Sergeant of the Royal Marines photographing drawn charts with a huge camera taking plates 48½ ins. by 40½ ins. The negative was transferred to a sensitized zinc plate from which copies were printed. This was a task carried out in H.M.S. 'White Bear,' a hydrographic survey vessel serving with the East Indies Fleet and acting as headquarters for smaller vessels able to penetrate narrow creeks and rivers.

was engaged in sustained mine-sweeping operations in the approaches to the Malacca Straits. Simultaneously, a combined air attack and bombardment was carried out against enemy installations in the Nicobar Islands; while carrier-borne planes bombed airfields in north-west Sumatra. No casualties or damage was suffered by

H.M. ships in these operations; one pilot was lost.

From July 24–26, another force, under the command of Vice-Admiral H. T. C. Walker, and including the destroyers " Paladin " and " Rotherham," the 7th Minesweeping Flotilla, and minelayers of the Royal Indian Navy, among them H.M.I.S. " Punjab," gave support to minesweeping operations off the west coast of Malaya and the north of the Malacca Straits, and attacked enemy installations. Kamikaze planes unsuccessfully attacked this force on July 26.

Great assistance in isolating Japan from her sources of supply in Burma, Malaya and the enemy-held islands was given by the American and British submarine services : 189 ships were reported sunk by the former, 158 by the latter

WARSHIP IN DRY-DOCK AT SEA

After an attack by enemy aircraft, the 33,000-ton U.S.S. battleship ' Mississippi ' was towed for repairs to a giant floating dry-dock (see illus. in page 3397) in June 1945 at an anchorage off the port of Guiuan at Samar Island (see map in page 3268) in the Philippines. She was the first battleship in the Philippines area to be serviced in a floating dry-dock.

in the course of the last seven months of the war. Japanese submarine casualties in 1945, all sunk by American ships or aircraft, were 28 ; Japan's total loss of submarines throughout the war was 130, 9½ by British attack.

A new American naval command, the Philippine Sea Frontier (under Rear-Admiral James L. Kauffman) was set up at the beginning of 1945 to include all South-West Pacific waters except actual battle areas of the U.S. 7th Fleet : its main task was to facilitate the flow of supplies to the 7th Fleet and to General MacArthur's troops in the Philippines.

In July the existence of a secret British naval base in the Indian Ocean

PACIFIC FLEET PRINTED ITS OWN NEWSPAPER

Typical example of the Royal Navy's capacity for ' carrying on ' was the production and distribution of ' Pacific Post,' the British Pacific Fleet's own newspaper, written and printed by the Navy for the Navy. Its offices were in Sydney, New South Wales, and it had a circulation of almost 40,000. Here, ratings in a Pacific Fleet destroyer read their paper during a lull.
Photos, British Official ; New York Times Photos

AMERICAN FLAG FLIES OVER JAPANESE TERRITORY

After fighting against fanatical enemy resistance every foot of the ascent of 300-ft. high Mt. Suribachi, the volcano commanding the whole of Iwo Jima, U.S. Marines on February 23, 1945, captured it and while still under fire hoisted the Stars and Stripes—with a length of Japanese piping as flag-pole. This was only four days after the initial landings on the island. The enemy had laid down a heavy rain of fire on the beaches from caves in the sides of Mt Suribachi. Iwo Jima was the first territory of the pre-war Japanese empire to fall to the Allies.

3767

JAPANESE 'SUICIDE' PLANES HIT BRITISH CARRIERS

As the Allied navies drew nearer the Japanese homeland, the defeated enemy formed a corps of Kamikaze or 'suicide' pilots for their aircraft. On July 8, 1945, it was reported that during twelve weeks' operations by the British Pacific Fleet in the Saki Islands, three of Britain's newest aircraft-carriers, the 'Indefatigable,' the 'Victorious' and the 'Formidable,' had been hit by five Kamikaze planes. Though damage was caused, 70 men being killed, the ships remained in action. Here, firefighters go into action after the suicide hit on H.M.S. 'Formidable.'

ENEMY'S BITTER LAST STAND AS OKINAWA FALLS

Some of the fiercest fighting in the Pacific campaign occurred during the 82-days' struggle, begun on April 1, 1945, for the island of Okinawa, in the Ryukyu group and some 750 miles from the Japanese capital. Typical of Okinawa was this desolate battlefield near Shuri (see map in page 3755), peppered with rain-filled shell-craters and dotted with blasted tree stumps, after the U.S. 10th Army artillery had blown the enemy from their positions. The demolished radio tower in the left foreground was one of eleven in this vital nerve-centre of resistance manned by some 80,000 fanatical Japanese. Until they were blown from them, the enemy concealed themselves in caves in the small hill to the left. Below, U.S. Marines crouch at the entrance to a cave after hurling an explosive charge to force out Japanese troops making a desperate last stand.

Photos, U.S. Army Air Forces and Marine Corps

ADMIRAL NIMITZ WELCOMES BRITISH AID IN THE PACIFIC

Photo, Associated Press

Full-scale co-operation between the British Pacific Fleet and U.S. naval forces, begun off the Saki Islands, in the Ryukyus, on March 26 and 27, 1945, contributed materially towards hastening the end of the war against Japan. Addressing the ship's company, under the shadow of the 14-inch guns of the British battleship 'King George V' in Guam Harbour in May (see illus. in page 3764), Admiral Chester L. Nimitz, U.S.N., C.-in-C., Pacific Ocean Areas, declared, 'From the very beginning we have welcomed your coming and we will continue to welcome your help.'

was revealed. Work began on "Port T" in September 1941 when the 1st Royal Marine Coast Regiment, under Lieutenant-Colonel (later Major-General) W. B. F. Lukis, went ashore on Addu Atoll, a group of waterless coral islets 500 miles from Colombo and 3,000 from Australia, to establish coastal batteries, searchlights, signal towers, roads, camps and jetties. The hot and humid climate, the difficulty of keeping food fresh, the lack of fresh water, and the resultant fevers and malaria made it necessary to evacuate in the first three months nearly one quarter of the force originally landed.

Four miles of roadway were laid across a swamp infested by giant crabs, the men working thigh-deep in foul

'Port T' Ready for Use

mud to lay its foundations. The batteries were in position within six weeks, and "Port T" was ready for use before Japan entered the war. The first convoy of troops, escorted by the cruiser H.M.S. "Emerald," arrived at the base on January 3, 1942. "Port T" remained a vital link on the convoy route to Australia, and for operations in the Indian Ocean, throughout the war. It could accommodate the largest ships— the "Queen Mary" put in there.

Ships serving in the Pacific had to face bad weather conditions as well as the enemy : an announcement of the loss in a typhoon of three American destroyers, the "Spence," the "Hull," and the "Monaghan," was made on

AMERICAN HOSPITAL SHIP OFF LEYTE

Evacuating wounded by hospital ship from the battlefields of Leyte in the Philippines after the landings on October 20, 1944. Even hospital ships were not immune from attack by Japanese 'suicide' pilots : on April 28, Washington announced that the U.S. hospital vessel 'Comfort' had been hit by a 'baka' suicide glider-bomb (see Chapter 368) as she evacuated wounded from Okinawa, badly damaging her and killing 29. *Photo, New York Times Photos*

January 10. On June 5 another typhoon damaged 21 units of the U.S. 3rd Fleet, none being sunk on this occasion, however, and most of them back in service some six weeks later.

Great gallantry was displayed on July 31, 1945, in a successful attack by a midget submarine on the Japanese heavy cruiser "Takao." Lieutenant Ian E. Fraser, D.S.C., R.N.R., brought his

craft, XE-3, up an eighty-mile passage, through mined waters, past hydrophone posts, and through an anti-submarine boom to the "Takao," at her moorings in very shallow water in Johore Strait, Singapore. Despite severe exhaustion through lack of oxygen, Leading-Seaman James Magennis, diver on the XE-3, placed "limpet" charges under the "Takao's" keel, damaging the vessel seriously. Lieutenant Fraser then piloted his submarine back to safety. For this exploit both he and Leading-Seaman Magennis were awarded the V.C. on November 13, 1945.

THE 'INDOMITABLE' IN HONGKONG BAY

After almost four years, a powerful force of British warships on August 30, 1945, entered Hongkong harbour (see also illus. in page 3605). Under the command of Rear-Admiral Cecil H. J. Harcourt, it included the battleship 'Anson' and the aircraft-carriers 'Indomitable' and 'Venerable.' Below, the 30,000-ton 'Indomitable' rides at anchor in Victoria Bay, Hongkong, as a Chinese junk passes nearby. *Photo, British Official*

'CHINA INCIDENT' ENDS : SINO-SOVIET TREATY, 1945

Here are the surrender terms signed by the Japanese which ended the undeclared war
they had waged against China for more than eight years. Extracts from President
Chiang Kai-shek's V.J. Day broadcast and the articles of the treaty of friendship
and alliance of 1945 between China and the Soviet Union complete the page

Japanese Surrender to China, September 9, 1945.

THE formal surrender of a million Japanese troops in
China, signed at Nanking at 1.04 a.m. (British Summer
Time) on September 9, 1945, brought to an end the
"China Incident," as Japan called the war which was
precipitated by her unprovoked attack on July 7, 1937. The
instrument of surrender acknowledged that "the Emperor of
Japan, the Japanese Government, and the Japanese Imperial
General Headquarters" recognized the "complete military
defeat of the Japanese military forces by the Allied forces,"
and stipulated :

1. All Japanese land, sea, air and auxiliary forces in
China (south of the Great Wall, and excluding Manchuria),
as well as in Formosa and French Indo-China north of
latitude 16 degrees, will cease hostilities and will remain
at the stations they now occupy. They are now non-
combatant troops, and in due course will be demobilized.
They will assemble, preserve from damage, and turn over
to forces specified by Generalissimo Chiang Kai-shek all
arms, ammunition, equipment, supplies, records, information, and other assets of any kind belonging to the Japanese
forces.

2. All Allied prisoners of war and civilian internees
formerly under Japanese control in the areas named above
will be liberated at once, and the Japanese forces will
provide protection, maintenance, and transportation to
places as directed.

3. Henceforth, all Japanese forces hereby surrendered
will be subject to the control of Generalissimo Chiang
Kai-shek. Their movement and activity will be dictated
by him, and they will obey only the orders and proclamations issued or authorized by him or orders of their Japanese
commanders based upon his instructions.

4. Local Japanese commanders will be required to
implement these orders, subject to drastic punishment
for violation of them.

Broadcast by Chiang Kai-shek, President of the Chinese Republic, on China's V.J. Day (September 3, 1945).

NOW that the war is over we shall brook no further delay
in the inauguration of constitutional democracy. The
highest ideal of the national revolution is the participation
of all the people in national politics. The most important
measure for the realization of this ideal is to return the
power of government to the people. The convocation of the
National Assembly is indispensable to the return of such
power to the people. I earnestly hope that the people as a
whole and leaders of all walks of life will give sincere support
to the Government for the early convocation of the National
Assembly and the attainment of democracy.

The successful conclusion of the prolonged war is the
time to begin the task of national reconstruction. The
Government's administrative policy will be guided by
impartiality and sincerity. . . . The Government is prepared
to consult all leaders before the convocation of the National
Assembly. It is also ready to consider a reasonable increase
in the number of delegates to the Assembly and to seek a
rational settlement of other related problems.

As a safeguard to the freedoms of the people, the National
Government has, besides the enforcement of the law for the
protection of personal freedom, decided to abolish the wartime press censorship so that the people may have freedom
of speech. It will promulgate a law to facilitate political
assembly and organization. . . . Only thus can we tread the
path of democracy traversed by the United States and
Great Britain and establish a model democratic state in the
Far East.

If we want to attain democracy, we must have the rule
of law as the foundation of constitutional government, and
the Constitution as the safeguard of the people. Disreputable

practices like the employment of armed force in political
controversy and the seizure of territory in defiance of Government orders are relics of the days of the war lords. They
should not be found in a modern democratic state and could
not be tolerated in national rebuilding. Only when domestic
problems are peacefully solved by political means, and all
shades of opinion observe the law of the country, can we
avoid the mistakes made in the early days of the Republic . . .

The most important condition for national unity is the
nationalization of all armed forces in the country. There
should be no private army within the country's boundaries,
nor should armed forces be kept by any political party. . . .
On behalf of the Government I solemnly state that all armed
forces, if they submit to recognition by the Government,
shall receive the same treatment without discrimination.

Treaty of Friendship and Alliance between the U.S.S.R. and the Republic of China, signed on August 14, 1945.

1. The high contracting parties undertake jointly with
the other United Nations to wage war against Japan until
final victory. The high contracting parties pledge themselves to render each other all necessary military and other
help and assistance in this war.

2. The high contracting parties undertake not to enter
into separate negotiations with Japan and not to conclude
an armistice without mutual consent with either the present
Japanese Government or with any other Government or
authority established in Japan which will not clearly renounce
all aggressive intentions.

3. The high contracting parties undertake after the end
of the war against Japan to take jointly all the measures in
their power to prevent a repetition of aggression and violation
of the peace on the part of Japan. If one of the high contracting parties becomes the victim of aggression, the other
contracting party will immediately render to the party
involved in military operations all military and other aid and
support at her disposal. This article remains in force until
such time as, at the request of both high contracting parties,
responsibility for the prevention of further aggression by
Japan is placed in the hands of the United Nations organization.

4. Each of the high contracting parties undertakes not
to conclude an alliance of any kind and not to take part
in any coalition directed against the other contracting party.

5. The high contracting parties, taking into account the
protection and economic development of each country,
agree to work together in friendly co-operation after the
advent of peace and to act on the principle of mutual respect
of each other's sovereign and territorial rights and not to
interfere in the internal affairs of the other contracting
party.

6. The high contracting parties agree to give each other
all possible economic help in the post-war period to speed
up the reconstruction of both countries and in order to bring
about the well-being of the world.

7. This agreement is drawn up in a way which respects
the rights and obligations of the high contracting Powers
and all member Powers of the United Nations.

8. This agreement is subject to ratification which is to
take place as soon as possible. The exchange of the instruments of ratification will be made in Chungking. The agreement comes into force immediately after its ratification, and
will remain valid for 30 years. If neither of the high contracting parties gives notice during this period of its desire
to terminate the agreement, it will remain in force for an
indefinite period thereafter, subject to each of the high
contracting parties being able to terminate the agreement
by giving one year's notice to the other contracting party.

[The principal terms of important agreements signed at
the same time are published in page 3566.]

Chapter 366

CONTINUING CIVIL WAR IN CHINA

The year 1945 saw the end of China's eight-year-old struggle against Japan, but not the dawn of peace for her : civil war between the Kuomintang Government under Chiang Kai-shek and the Communist forces of the north under Mao Tse-tung continued throughout that year and on into 1946, despite pertinacious efforts by both Chinese and Allied leaders to compose their differences. The history of China during 1944 is recorded in Chapter 323

MILITARY operations in China during the last months before Japan's surrender were little more than a pendant to the vastly greater enterprises going forward against the Japanese from the Kuriles to Burma (*see* Chapters 351, 364, 365, 367, 371). It was in fact in Burma, where they helped to open the Ledo Road, that Chinese troops made probably their most significant contribution to these culminating campaigns (*see* pages 3277 and 3538).

Within China, the beginning of 1945 found Japan's final great offensive checked (*see* page 3280), but the enemy was still in possession of most of the important gains he had secured (*see* map in page 3280).

The vulnerability of these gains, in view of the Allied advance west and north in the Pacific, was already evident when on January 13 carrier-borne planes of Admiral Nimitz's fleet swept over Hongkong, Swatow and Amoy. For years the east China ports had been useless to the Chinese in **Military Position Against Japan** face of unchallengeable Japanese sea dominance ; now Japan's gains on land in the same area were made valueless by loss of that dominance. Moreover, General MacArthur's campaign in the Pacific was steadily gaining for the Allies a position in which land-based bombers could harass the narrow Japanese communications corridor connecting Manchuria with Indo-China ; and although the Chinese were still too weak in heavy arms—and above all too short of mechanized transport—to be likely to mount a large-scale offensive, their continuous small-scale harassing activity over a vast area was a steady drain on Japan's military budget.

After an uneasy winter of seeming stalemate, there came signs that the enemy was being forced to pull out, to leave his southern China conquests to their detached garrisons with the doubtful aid of sedulously sponsored independence movements, and to move his main defence line back to the original limited object of the 1937 attack on China—the line of the Yellow River protecting Manchuria's industries. The

Chinese began to move forward. Their first notable success came in March with the recapture of the airbase at Suichwan in Kiangsi province, East China, abandoned by the U.S.A. 14th A.F. in February. A month later, away to the west, they recovered from their last local setback (loss of the airbase of Lahokow in Hupeh) to launch a general counter-attack in Honan and Hupeh provinces against Japan's north-south corridor. By May full Japanese retreat was evident in the east, the Chinese on the 18th regaining the key port of Foochow on the Fukien coast and sweeping on to capture exactly a month later the port of Wenchow, 150 miles to the north, and only 250 miles south

of Shanghai. On June 25 the Chinese High Command announced that Chinese forces were in control of nearly 200 miles of the Chekiang coast.

From the west, too, pressure was intensified. In Hunan, a drive began in May against the Japanese supply base and communications centre at Paoching. The seriousness of the threat in this quarter **Chinese Sixth Army Flown In** was made clear by the disclosure in Chungking on May 28 that the entire Chinese 6th Army with guns, horses and equipment had been flown by the American Air Transport Command over a thousand miles from Burma into Hunan over the Himalayan "hump." This vast

CHINESE TROOPS RECAPTURE KWEILIN
The Chinese High Command announced on July 29, 1945, that their forces, trained and equipped by the U.S. Army, had driven the Japanese from the city and important air base of Kweilin, capital of Kwangsi province in south-west China. Formerly main forward base of the U.S.A. 14th A.F., it had been lost during the Japanese offensive late in 1944 (see page 3279). Here, Chinese troops re-enter the ruined city. *Photo, Keystone*

air trooping operation—the first in which an entire army had been flown from one operational theatre to another —brought into the central China picture a formidable body of troops, American-trained and equipped, which had proved its merit in the gruelling Burma campaign. For the first time, China was able to bring against the inferior Japanese divisions left in China an army equipped and trained to up-to-date standards.

In the south, where Japan's biggest gains of late 1944 had been scored, the enemy had been deprived of Nanning by May 27, and a few days later the Chinese took Pinyang, sixty miles to the north. By the end of the month, pressing from west and south, the Chinese had reached and recaptured the air-base town of Liuchow, junction of the railways leading north-west to Kweiyang, north-east to Hankow.

Continuing their drive against the retreating Japanese, Chinese troops on July 29 re-entered Kweilin, capital of Kwangsi and until 1944 main forward base in south China of the United States Army 14th Air Force. Despite the limitations imposed on it by the loss of its forward bases, this Air Force carried out during 1945 attacks of a scale and range which reflected the improved supply position both by air and by road from India. (The Ledo Road, pushed through Japanese-occupied Burma with such audacity—*see* Chapters 299 and 345—was abandoned on November 1: it was worthless as a peacetime commercial highway.) In one long-range sweep against Tsingtao on the Shantung coast of north China on February 10, Mustangs of the U.S.A. 14th A.F. destroyed 46 Japanese aircraft on the ground. Fighters of the same force destroyed 92 parked planes in attacks on an aerodrome near Shanghai on April 1 and 2.

By the end of July, the Japanese were concentrating their forces—then estimated by Chunking at about 1,000,000, with another 1,000,000 "puppet" troops in reserve—at vital centres such as Canton, Hankow, Shanghai, and the Shantung peninsula. Then, on August 9, came the Soviet attack in Manchuria (*see* page 3780) and, five days later, Japan's capitulation. China was free from the Japanese threat after eight years and a month of unremitting if sometimes feeble struggle. But the freedom which followed Japan's collapse called for further vast endeavours before it could become the basis of a unified and peaceful sovereign state. China ended the war with a million enemy troops under arms and undefeated in the field sprawled over wide areas of her territory; with the armies of her new Russian ally in occupation of three great provinces which her own troops could not immediately reach; with an autonomous army answerable to a dissident regime intermingled with enemy and Allied troops all over the north.

The major problem, which in the succeeding months prolonged misery and strife in large areas of China, was the quarrel between the one-party regime of **Kuomintang-Communist Quarrel** the Kuomintang, recognized by the world as the legal Government of China under the Presidency of Chiang Kai-shek, and the Communist-dominated coalition which by stout guerilla fighting throughout the war had extended its authority from a small sparse area of central Shensi province in the north-west to innumerable pockets of resistance and free administration throughout the Japanese-occupied areas of north China. For ten years before Japan

JAPANESE C.-IN-C. SURRENDERS IN CHINA

Acknowledging 'complete military defeat,' the Japanese in China formally surrendered to the Chinese at an impressive ceremony in the Central Military Academy at Nanking, the pre-war capital, on September 9, 1945. The surrender, which involved about 1,000,000 troops, was made to General Ho Ying-chin, Chinese C.-in-C. (centre at table on left), acting for Generalissimo Chiang Kai-shek, by General Okamura, commanding the Japanese Army in China (centre at table on right).

SOVIET-CHINESE TREATY OF FRIENDSHIP

A treaty of friendship and alliance between the Chinese Republic and the Soviet Union was signed at the Kremlin, in Moscow, on August 14, 1945 (see Historic Document 306, page 3772). Here, Mr. Wang Shih-chieh, the Chinese Foreign Minister, signs the instrument, while Generalissimo Stalin and Mr. Molotov, Soviet Commissar for Foreign Affairs, look on. The agreement was to come into force immediately and remain valid for thirty years. *Photo, Pictorial Press*

and eliminate their potential influence from the promised constitution-making body. The Kuomintang believed the Communists were ever seeking to extend their territorial control by armed force; indeed, it was indisputable that the great areas of the north claimed as Communist had become so by virtue of Communist military occupation after the withdrawal of the main Chinese forces and the break-up under Japanese pressure of Kuomintang administration. Certainly genuine efforts had been made in Chungking to broaden the central Government: Generalissimo Chiang Kai-shek resigned the office of President of the Executive Yuan (Prime Minister) on May 31 (remaining President of the Republic and Generalissimo), and was succeeded by the liberal Dr. T. V. Soong, the Foreign Minister—at that time in San Francisco for the United Nations Conference. Dr. H. H. Kung, brother-in-law of the Generalissimo, resigned the Vice-Premiership, and was replaced by Dr. Wang Wen-hao, Minister of Economics and chairman of the Chinese War Production Board. Dr. Wang Shih-chieh, Minister of Information (*see* page 3281) and formerly a member of the Permanent Court of Arbitration at The Hague, took over the post of Foreign Minister.

Government Changes

After the defeat of the Japanese it soon became clear that the Communists had every intention of extending their influence by force of arms, claiming, possibly rightly, that they had at least

attacked there had been open civil war between Kuomintang and Communists, and the uneasy truce of 1937 had been as much a reaction to the threat of Japan as it was an immediate cause of that threat's being translated into action.

Thrown together in apparent collaboration at the outbreak of war, Kuomintang and Communists did not maintain amity long after the stalemate which in 1939 followed the bitter campaigns of the first 18 months' resistance to Japan. Armed clashes became increasingly frequent, while the long heritage of bitterness earned compound interest in innumerable accusations by each side against the other of dictatorship, defeatism, corruption, maladministration. It is to the credit of the leaders, both Kuomintang and Communist, that (partly under pressure from the Allies) attempts were made to achieve harmony by discussion; but by the end of the war little progress had been made (*see* page 3281). Latterly the Communists concentrated their efforts on a demand for a coalition government, refusing to hand over control of their armies to any other regime, while the Kuomintang maintained that it was its duty to retain the substance of power until a new national constitution could be fully put into effect by a unified nation from which such things as local armies not answerable to the High Command had already disappeared.

Armed Clashes

Either argument can be written reasonably enough; the gap was due less to declared aims than to mutual distrust. The Communists believed the Kuomintang insincere in its plans for transition to democracy and feared the defeat of Japan would be the signal for a renewed attempt to wipe them out

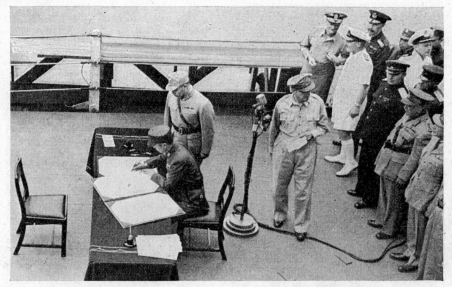

CHINA AT JAPANESE SURRENDER TO THE ALLIES

At the Japanese surrender ceremony on board the U.S.S. 'Missouri' in Tokyo Bay on September 2, 1945 (see Chapter 372), General Hsu Yung-chang is here signing on behalf of the Chinese Republic. At the microphone stands General MacArthur, and behind him (left to right) are Admiral Chester L. Nimitz, who signed for the U.S.A.; Admiral Sir Bruce Fraser (for Great Britain); Lieutenant-General K. N. Derevyanko (for the U.S.S.R.); General Sir Thomas Blamey (for Australia); and Colonel Nicholas Cosgrave (for Canada). *Photo, Pictorial Press*

as good a mandate to rule and that they ruled better than their opponents.

During the war, the nature and armament of the Communist forces had prevented them from occupying sizable cities or lines of communication (though six weeks before Japan's surrender they made the remarkable claim that they had captured Tsinan, capital of Shantung province). But at the first hint of total Japanese collapse on August 12 General Chu Teh, Commander-in-Chief of the Communist forces, ordered "all forces in liberated areas to issue an ultimatum to the Japanese and their puppets, giving a time limit for surrender, and to take charge of all administrative affairs in any Japanese and puppet-occupied cities." Had there been previous agreement between Kuomintang and Communists, this order would have been the best way of quickly clearing the enemy from the whole country and restoring free Chinese administration. But there was no agreement : although throughout the year there had been comings and goings between Chungking and Yenan, proposals and counter-proposals, the atmosphere had deteriorated rather than improved. Chiang Kai-shek telegraphed to the Communist leaders in Yenan telling them that the Big Four were conferring jointly on the Japanese surrender and ordering Communist forces not to take independent action, but to remain in their actual positions. The Central Government, he said, had made full provision for disarming the enemy, reoccupying enemy-held territory, and ensuring order.

Communists Issue Orders to Japanese

These instructions were much resented in Yenan, and Chiang was bitterly attacked over the Yenan radio, Chu Teh at the same time appealing to Britain, the U.S.A. and the U.S.S.R. for representation at the surrender, "reserving the right to dispute any arrangements or treaties made without my consent." He asked the United States to halt lease-lend shipments to the Central Government " to lessen the danger of civil war," and sent his troops forward against the Japanese, whose chief anxiety here as elsewhere seems to have been to make an orderly surrender as quickly as possible to any formation which demanded it.

From Chungking, however, Chiang Kai-shek showed his desire to reach agreement by telegraphing to the Communist leader Mao Tse-tung on August 16 inviting him to Chungking. Mao twice refused the invitation, suggesting, however, on the second occasion (August 20) the sending of a representative (past years had seen more than one such representative later repudiated). On the 26th Chiang made a new and generous appeal to Mao " to discuss and formulate our national policies," and two days later Mao arrived in Chungking, accompanied by the U.S. Ambassador, Major-General Patrick J. Hurley (*see* illus. in page 3282), who had flown to Yenan with Chiang's third invitation.

The signature in Moscow on August 14 of the Sino-Soviet treaty of friendship

MUSIC FOR RELEASED INTERNEES IN CHINA

Soon after the cessation of the war against Japan, Allied internees in occupied China began to reach the ports for repatriation. Above, at Tsingtao, on the Yellow Sea (see map in page 3280), these ex-internees, among 1,800 British, Americans, Russians and Italians to be freed in that area, were entertained by the Royal Marines band from the cruiser H.M.S. 'Bermuda.' Below, U.S. armoured forces welcomed by Chinese as they stream into Tsingtao.

and alliance (*see* Historic Document CCCVI, page 3772)—the outcome of negotiations begun on July 1—by which the U.S.S.R. recognized the Chungking Government as the legal Government of China, had a modifying effect on the Yenan Communists, whose press ceased its vituperative attacks on Chiang Kai-shek and his Government.

U.S.S.R. Recognizes Chiang Kai-shek

Japanese forces in south China surrendered to the Chinese 1st Army in Canton on August 19. Chinese National troops crossed the Yangtse and entered Nanking, capital of the Chinese Republic, on August 25. V.J. Day was celebrated in China on September 3, when Generalissimo Chiang broadcast on the National Government's aims, and appealed for unity :" If we want to attain democracy

CHINA AND THE CHARTER

The United Nations Charter, signed on June 26, 1945, at the San Francisco Conference (see Chapter 381), was ratified by China on August 24. Generalissimo Chiang Kai-shek, President of the Chinese Republic, using a brush, here signs his name to the document signifying his country's ratification of the Charter. *Photo, U.S. Official*

we must have the rule of law as the foundation of constitutional government, and the Constitution as the safeguard of the people. . . . Only when domestic problems are peacefully solved by political means, and all shades of opinion observe the law of the country, can we avoid the mistakes made in the early days of the Republic and establish a great charter worthy of the heroic efforts of our revolutionary martyrs and the freedom-loving people during the last fifty years." The most important condition for national unity, he said, was the nationalization of all armed forces in the country. There should be no private army within the country's boundaries, nor should armed forces be kept by any political party (*see* Historic Document CCCV, page 3772).

The formal surrender in China, in which the Japanese acknowledged "complete military defeat," was signed

Japan Surrenders to China

at a ceremony in Nanking at 1.04 a.m. B.S.T. on September 9 (*see* Historic Document CCCIV, page 3772). It was made by General Yasutsuga Okamura, Japanese C.-in-C., China, to General Ho Ying-chin, Chinese C.-in-C., acting on behalf of Generalissimo Chiang Kai-shek. Chinese sovereignty over Formosa, in Japanese possession since 1895, was proclaimed in Chungking on August 30.

Negotiations between Chiang Kai-shek and Mao Tse-tung continued in Chungking until October 11, when a joint communiqué was issued announcing general agreement on broad principles, and Mao left Chunking. Both sides had pledged themselves to avoid civil war by all possible means, and to

co-operate for peacetime reconstruction. It was also agreed that differences should be submitted to a projected "People's Political Commission," whose decisions were to be binding, which was to meet under the chairmanship of Generalissimo Chiang and consist of representatives to be appointed by the National Government, the Communists and other party and non-party groups. (But no method of selecting the persons to sit on this committee, or of registering their decisions, was suggested.) The Kuomintang promised to recognize the equality of all political parties and to guarantee freedom of conscience, of assembly, and of the press. Political prisoners were to be released, and the right of arrest, trial and punishment was to be restricted to the regular police and judiciary. The Communists agreed to allow Government troops to garrison the big cities of north China, though they asked that these should not be allowed into the countryside, where there was danger of clashes with Communist troops already in possession.

The agreement seemed a triumph; but distrust remained, nor had fighting ceased. Two days before the agreement was announced, Yenan accused Government forces of using Japanese and "puppet" troops against the Communists in central China, Shansi and Kwangtung. The allegations were denied in Chungking. On October 13 it was disclosed that the National Government 92nd Army was being flown from Nanking to Peiping in U.S. Army transport planes to establish Government control in north China. A week later Yenan announced that it was withdrawing its new 4th Army, up to then stationed in strength in the Shanghai, Nanking, Hangchow, and Ningpo areas, from all areas south of the Yangtse.

But dispatches from both Chungking and Yenan reported increasingly heavy fighting in north China, involving, it was estimated, about a million men. By the end of October, fighting centred in four zones : (1) a triangle formed by south Shansi, north Honan, and south Hopei ; (2) along the Tatung-Puchow railway in Shansi ; (3) in east Suiyuan (Inner Mongolia) ; and (4) in Shantung, along the Tsinan-Tsingtao railway. General Yen Hei-shan, National Government Commander of Shansi on October 29 reported very heavy fighting in that province, with National Government casualties of 15,000 and Communist losses also severe. The National Government Commander of Suiyuan reported that Communist forces, supported by tanks and field guns, were strongly attacking Tatung and had captured several other towns.

On November 1 it was announced in Chungking that an agreement had been reached at Changchun (Hsinking), capital of Manchuria, between the National Government and the Soviet High Command

Red Army Leaves Manchurian Ports

whereby Government forces were to land troops in Manchuria by sea and air, the Red Army withdrawing, in implementation of the Russo-Chinese treaty, to Vladivostok, Korea and Port Arthur. On October 30 and succeeding days, Government troops arrived at Hulatao, Yingkow and other Manchurian ports on board U.S. transports. They found that the Russian garrisons had withdrawn, but that strongly armed Chinese Communist forces of the 8th Route Army were in the areas round these ports in such strength as to make landings difficult or impossible. Landings were effected at Chinwangtao (Hopei Province), however, and a drive inland began against strong opposition.

Heavy fighting continued in other areas : in Shansi the Communists took Tatung and gained control of most of the province. In south Hopei they gained a considerable victory in the Tzehsien area, claiming the capture of

FREE AGAIN

Left to right: Sir Percy McElwaine, Chief Justice, Straits Settlements; Sir Charles Shenton Thomas, Governor and C.-in-C., Straits Settlements ; Sir H. Trusted, Chief Justice, F.M.S. ; Sir Horace Seymour, British Ambassador to China, who met the prisoners ; Sir Mark Young, Governor and C.-in-C., Hongkong (see Chapter 199); and Mr. C. R. Smith, Governor of British North Borneo, released at Mukden, arrive at Chungking on August 28, 1945.

tions Committee, of pro-Communist activities on the part of various State Department officials. General George C. Marshall, formerly Chief of Army Staff, appointed the President's special envoy to the National Government, reached Chungking on December 23. On January 5, 1946, the National Government and the Communists agreed to appoint delegates to confer with General Marshall for an immediate end of the civil war. Five days later a communiqué was issued announcing a definite agreement which the delegates undertook to recommend to Chiang Kai-shek and Mao Tse-tung. Its principal points were : (1) immediate cessation of hostilities on both sides ; (2) cessation of

70,000 Government troops. Extensive rail sabotage by them was reported.

On November 10 Government troops began an all-out assault on a 35-mile front to break through into Manchuria. After a battle lasting over a week, Government troops stormed the walled town of Shanhaikwan, drove through the Great Wall, and fanned out into Manchuria.

Advance by Government Forces

Widespread guerilla activities and destruction of communications by the Communists continued. The fall of Hulutao was reported on November 25 in Chungking, and Government forces reached Jehol and made advances in other areas. Advancing along the Manchurian railway from Shanhaikwan, Government troops entered Mukden without incident (reported December 13); and on December 27 at a joint Russo-Chinese ceremony Changchun (Hsinking), the capital, was formally taken over by Chinese airborne troops. *See* map in page 3781.

Meanwhile, Yenan radio alleged that American troops in Manchuria were collaborating with the Kuomintang in attacks on the 8th Route Army—allegations which Lieutenant-General Wedemeyer, C.-in-C. of the American forces in the China theatre, declared to be unfounded. U.S. Army Air Force planes were accused of machine-gunning Communist troops, and U.S. ground forces were involved in several local skirmishes along the north China railways, which they were guarding, and on the Yangtse.

By December 1 there were 53,000 U.S. Marines in north China, 35,000 U.S. Army personnel elsewhere in the country. Those in Communist areas

CHINESE GOVERNMENT IN CONTROL OF MUKDEN

When Chinese Government troops in October 1945 reached ports in Manchuria to take over areas evacuated by the Russians, they found strongly-armed Chinese Communist forces in control. But on December 13 they were reported, after an overland advance through the Great Wall, to have entered Mukden without incident. Here, Government troops stand on guard at H.Q., Mukden. Above, train with refugees crowding into Mukden for safety. *Photos, L. N. A.*

were regarded by Yenan as advance agents of the Kuomintang. General Wedemeyer declared that he was ignoring Communist protests about their presence and employment " because I am instructed to deal only with the Central Government," and stated that " in a few isolated clashes the Americans had in no case taken the initiative."

General Hurley's resignation as U.S. Ambassador was announced on November 27 : he made charges, investigated and dropped by the U.S. Foreign Rela-

destruction of lines of communication ; (3) the setting up of an Executive Headquarters in Peiping to carry out the agreement for the cessation of hostilities ; (4) necessary instructions and orders to be issued by the Executive H.Q. in the name of the President of the Republic. A truce was signed, to come into effect on January 14 ; and Chungking announced the end of the civil war. But the announcement was premature : spasmodic fighting, with brief truces, was continuing many months later.

July 1. Australian 7th Division landed in strength near Balikpapan (Borneo) after 15-days' bombing and bombardment by Allied aircraft and warships. Announced in Chungking that Chinese commando forces had crossed Indo-Chinese frontier.

July 2. Nearly 600 Super-Fortresses from the Marianas heavily attacked targets at Shimonoseki, Kure, Ube, Kumamoto and Shimotsu (Japan). Australian 7th Division held 3-mile stretch along shore of Macassar Strait (Borneo). Announced that British submarine "Trenchant," operating in the S.-W. Pacific under U.S. command, had sunk the Japanese cruiser "Asigara."

July 3. 500 Super-Fortresses dropped 3,000 tons of incendiaries on Japanese industrial towns of Himeji, Tokushima, Takamatsu and Kochi. In S.-E. Borneo Australians captured Sepinggan airfield. Australian 6th Division in New Guinea took Mt. Tazaki, overlooking Wewak. On Bougainville Australian 3rd Division secured the line of the Mibo River.

July 4. Australian 7th Division captured Balikpapan; other Australian forces took Manggar airfield on Macassar Strait (Borneo). In Burma Japanese forced the Sittang River east of Pegu.

July 5. General MacArthur announced the liberation of the whole of the Philippines. Allied 15th Army Group in Italy disbanded. Provisional (Lublin) Government of Poland recognized by Britain and U.S.A. General Election in Great Britain. Death of Mr. Curtin, Australian Premier.

July 6. Over 400 Super-Fortresses bombed Shimotsu, Kofu, Akashi, Chiba and Shimizu (Honshu, Japan). U.S. Navy bombers heavily attacked Korea and sank enemy shipping in Yellow Sea and round Japan.

July 7. Australian 7th Division landed at Penagam, in control of Balikpapan Bay (Borneo). U.S. Navy Privateer planes attacked enemy shipping in Korean and Japanese waters.

July 8. North of Balikpapan, Australians cut all enemy escape routes in area of Pandarasi oilfield (Borneo). U.S. aircraft attacked airfields in Osaka and Nagoya regions (Japan). Announced that over 5,000,000 tons of war supplies had been sent to Russia since 1941 by Persian Gulf route.

July 9. Heavy damage inflicted by 550 Super-Fortresses from the Marianas on Japanese towns of Gifu, Sakai, Wakayama, Sendai and Yokkaichi. Commonwealth Air Conference opened in London.

July 10. 2,000 carrier-based aircraft from U.S. 3rd Fleet heavily attacked Tokyo without opposition except from A.A. fire; Okinawa- and Iwo Jima-based U.S. aircraft struck at wide area of Honshu (Japan). Liberators of Eastern Air Command bombed Bangkok, capital of Siam, wrecking vital bridge. German submarine U530 surrendered at Mar del Plata, near Buenos Aires.

July 11. Australians made unopposed landing at Jinabora, Balikpapan, captured Pandarasi oilfield (Borneo). In

New Guinea, Australians, with bayonets and flame-throwers, captured important ridges inland from Wewak.

July 12. Australian 7th Division launched powerful offensive on Mt. Batochampar (S.-E. Borneo). 550 Marianas-based Super-Fortresses by night bombed targets at Nagoya and Tokyo Bay (Japan). Admiral Lord Louis Mountbatten and General MacArthur met at Manila for two-days' conference.

July 13. All resistance ceased in Brunei Bay (N. Borneo). At midnight S.H.A.E.F. was disbanded, General Eisenhower becoming Commander of American forces in Europe and Military Governor of the U.S. zone in Germany.

July 14. For the first time in the war Japanese mainland bombarded by Allied warships when units of the U.S. 3rd Fleet and carrier-borne aircraft attacked industrial centre of Kamaishi (Honshu). At Regensburg, Germany, U.S. troops unearthed Reichsbank's gold reserve.

July 15. 1,000 U.S. carrier-based aircraft again heavily attacked Japan, concentrating on Muroran on south coast of Hokkaido, where U.S. warships devastated the port; U.S. bombers from Iwo Jima and Marianas bombed Kyushu and Honshu airfields. Australians captured Mt. Batochampar (Borneo). Liberators of Eastern Air Command bombed Siamese port of Singora. Announced that Australian 6th Division captured Prince Alexander Range, overlooking Wewak (New Guinea). Italy declared war on Japan.

July 16. Some 500 Marianas-based Super-Fortresses made heavy attack with fire bombs on Oita and other targets in Japan, this being the first raid under the strategic command of General Spaatz.

July 16-17 (night). U.S. 3rd Fleet and British Pacific Fleet poured over 2,000 tons of shells into enemy industrial centres on the Honshu coast, north of Tokyo, in one of the heaviest naval bombardments of the war.

July 17. Some 1,500 British and U.S. naval aircraft took up the previous night's attack on the Japanese coast, concentrating on air bases round Ishinomaki Bay, against only A.A. opposition. Singora (Siam) bombed again. Berlin (Potsdam) Conference opened.

July 18. Carrier planes of U.S. 3rd Fleet attacked Japanese warships at entrance to Tokyo Bay. In S.E. Borneo, Australian 7th Division captured oil centre of Sambodja, N.E. of Balikpapan.

July 19. Over 600 Super-Fortresses, biggest force to date sent against Japan, struck at Choshi, Hitachi, Okazaki, and Fukui. Over 200 U.S. bombers and fighters attacked Shanghai. In Burma Gurkhas recaptured Laya station. Australians in N. Borneo occupied Marudi. U.S. Senate ratified Bretton Woods agreement.

July 20. U.S. Mustangs attacked Nagoya, Okazaki, and Toyohashi areas of Japan. Announced from Chungking that Japanese forces in China were withdrawing from less important positions.

July 21. U.S. naval aircraft attacked enemy shipping in the Tsushima Straits,

between Japan and Korea; Thunderbolts raided Truk (Carolines), Yap, and other enemy-held positions in the Pacific.

July 22. Super-Fortresses bombed Ube (Honshu); at night U.S. destroyers, entering Tokyo Bay, attacked an enemy convoy. U.S. Okinawa-based bombers raided Shanghai airfields. Australians landed at Tempadeong (S.E. Borneo).

July 23. Heavy air and naval attacks on enemy convoy in Sagami Bay, S.W. of Tokyo Bay. Reported that Australians had gained control of virtually all navigable waters in Balikpapan Bay (Borneo).

July 24. Between 1,000–1,500 U.S. and British carrier-borne aircraft of the U.S. 3rd Fleet struck heavily at remnants of the Japanese fleet at Kure in the Inland Sea; Super-Fortresses bombed Osaka and Nagoya. Far East Air Force bombers raided Shanghai.

July 24-26. British East Indies Fleet attacked installations and airfields off the W. coast of Malaya.

July 25. British and U.S. carrier planes renewed attacks on Japanese warships near Kure and Kobe. French 1st Army dissolved.

July 26. Over 350 Super-Fortresses bombed industrial targets on Kyushu and Honshu, including Omuta, Matsuyama and Tokuyama. Ultimatum to Japan issued by Great Britain, China, and the U.S.A. from Potsdam. Labour Government formed in Britain.

July 27. Super-Fortresses dropped 60,000 leaflets over 11 Japanese war-production centres, warning them that they would be destroyed from the air, and urging the inhabitants to evacuate. Disclosed that the newly-formed British 12th Army in Burma in its first action had defeated enemy forces trying to cross the Sittang River into Siam from the Pegu Yomas.

July 28. Six of the 11 Japanese towns marked out for destruction were heavily bombed by some 600 Super-Fortresses from the Marianas; British and U.S. carrier aircraft made concentrated raid on remnants of Japanese fleet in Inland Sea; U.S. aircraft from Okinawa attacked Kagoshima (Kyushu). U.S.A. ratified United Nations Charter. Mr. Attlee, new British Premier, and Mr. Bevin, new British Foreign Secretary, in Potsdam.

July 29. Chinese recaptured Kweilin, capital of Kwangsi province, lost in the 1944 Japanese offensive. British 8th Army disbanded. Secret list of German war casualties discovered at Flensburg.

July 29-30 (night). U.S. and British warships intensively bombarded Hammamatsu (Japan) for 70 minutes.

July 30. Over 1,000 British and U.S. carrier-aircraft heavily attacked Tokyo and Nagoya regions. Mediterranean Allied Air Force, created in 1943, dissolved. Allied Control Council met in Berlin.

July 31. Allied destroyer force bombarded Shimizu, 80 miles S.W. of Tokyo; Far Eastern Air Force from Okinawa bombed Nagasaki; leaflets dropped on 12 more Japanese cities. 12th Army Group disbanded. Field-Marshal Alexander appointed Governor-General of Canada.

Chapter 367

SOVIET CAMPAIGN IN MANCHURIA

*In fourteen days from the Soviet declaration of war against Japan, on August 8,
1945, forces of the Red Army and the Red Navy conquered and occupied the
greater part of the Chinese province of Manchuria, held by the Japanese since
1931. In this chapter, the Military Editor, Major-General Sir Charles Gwynn,
records that lightning campaign. The return of the province to Chinese rule is
described in Chapter 366*

ON August 6, 1945, President
Truman announced that the
first atomic bomb had been
dropped on Hiroshima. The Soviet
Government's declaration of war on
Japan two days later was, however, not
connected with that epoch-making
event. Although General MacArthur,
presumably aware of the imminence of
the declaration, may have decided to
use his new weapon in anticipation of
Russia's action, it is improbable, on the
other hand, that the Russians were fully
informed as to what was
about to happen; and we
have it on Mr. Churchill's
authority that their action
was in punctual fulfilment
of an undertaking made at
Yalta, to declare war on
Japan three months after
V.E. Day. Furthermore, it
is evident that at the time
the undertaking was given,
no one was in a position
to estimate definitely when
the atomic bomb would be
ready, what its effects would
be, or what progress the
American operations might
make in the three-month
period. The undertaking
must have been based on
Soviet the time
Position interval cal-
in Far East culated to
be required
for the reinforcement of the
Soviet forces in the Far East
by transfers of troops and
material from the European
front, and for the completion
of preparations for the
invasion of Manchuria.
Although the Russian forces
in the Far East were at all
times of substantial strength,
their role had been defensive,
and much reorganization
was necessary before they
could undertake a major
offensive campaign.

When, on August 9, Soviet
troops crossed the frontiers
it soon became clear that
the offensive was on a massive
scale, and that the plan of

campaign had been carefully worked out.
How far the Japanese had adequate
forces to meet the attack is more doubtful. They undoubtedly over a long period
had expended much energy on perfecting their defensive precautions. Their
strategic road and railway system had
been greatly developed, strongly fortified
zones had been prepared on the lines of
probable invasion, war industries on a
large scale had been established in
Manchuria, and their Kwantung army
(*see* illus. in page 3288) was reputedly

RUSSIA'S FAR EAST WAR CHIEFS
On August 8, 1945, the Soviet Union declared war on Japan. Here,
at Darien, are, left to right, Marshal Malinovsky, commanding the
Transbaikal Army; Marshal Meretskov, commanding the First Far
Eastern Army; and Marshal Vasilievsky, Commander-in-Chief.
Russia's 2nd Far Eastern Army was under Army-General Purkayev.

substantial numerically and composed
of their best troops. On the other hand,
it was known that some divisions had
been withdrawn to meet the American
offensive in the Pacific. At least one
division of the Kwantung army had
been identified on Leyte Island. Others
were believed to have been withdrawn
to the home islands, in view of the threat
of an American landing. Japan was in
fact paying the penalty for the gross
over-dispersion of her resources resulting
from her original aggressive campaign;
and with almost complete
destruction of her navy and
her loss of air power even
the short lines of sea communication with Manchuria
were no longer secure.

The form the Russian
offensive took was well designed to exploit fully, by
convergent drives from
exterior lines, both superior
Soviet numbers and the
shape of the Manchurian
frontiers. Three main attacks
were launched simultaneously, all initially in the
direction of Harbin: (*a*) by
the 1st Far Eastern Army
under Marshal Meretskov
westwards from the southern
end of the
Maritime **Lines**
Province **of Russian**
north of **Attack**
Vladivostok (*b*) by the 2nd
Far Eastern Army under
Army-General Purkayev
across the Amur south-
westwards up the Sungari
valley, and (*c*) by the Transbaikal Army under Marshal
Malinovsky eastward from
Manchuli along the Chinese
Eastern Railway. In addi-
tion, subsidiary operations
were undertaken from the
Blagoveshchensk region
across the Amur, and across
the Ussari at Hulin, both
clearly of a defensive character to protect the Trans-
Siberian Railway from
Japanese counter-strokes
based on railways which

led to these points. General Purkayev, who appears to have been the peacetime commander in the Far East, was also responsible for operations undertaken for the conquest of the southern half of the Island of Sakhalin. Admiral Ivan Yumashev, Commander of the Soviet Pacific Fleet, was in charge of amphibious operations to capture ports on the east coast of Korea, and Japanese bases in the Kurile Islands. His river flotillas also co-operated with Purkayev in the latter's Amur and Ussari operations.

All these far-reaching operations were under the supreme command of Marshal Vassilievsky, who had **Russian** become commander of **Commanders** the 3rd White Russian Army following Army-General Chernyakhovsky's death in February 1945 (*see* page 3560). Before that, Vassilievsky was Chief of Red Army Staff and for long Stalin's principal strategic adviser. Malinovsky and Meretskov had made great reputations on the European front, the former in the Ukraine and in Rumania, the latter on the Leningrad front and in Finland.

Although the three main attacks were all delivered against well fortified areas and encountered strong opposition, they met with immediate success, achieving an average advance of ten to

MALINOVSKY'S MEN IN HAILAR

By August 10, 1945, second day of Russia's campaign in the Far East, the Red Army had made important gains on all sections of the Manchurian front. The most dramatic advance was by Marshal Malinovsky's armoured troops which swept forward a hundred miles to capture the important road and rail centre of Hailar (see map below). A Soviet patrol here probes a deserted street in Hailar. *Photo, Pictorial Press*

fifteen miles on August 9. On the Transbaikal front Manchuli and Dalainor in the strongly fortified zone covering the railway were captured; and farther south, in the Lake Buirnor area, where the Japanese had not expected attack, an important advance was made through difficult country. On the main front not only had the fortified zone to be pierced but beyond it lay the Khingan mountains. The thrust from Lake Buirnor had, however, the effect of turning the fortified zone, and opened a line of advance which led through mountain tracks, outflanking Hailar. This town was a strong centre of communications in the western foothills of the Khingan range, blocking the main pass through it.

On the Khabarovsk front the Russians crossed the Amur and Ussari and captured Fuyan, on the right bank of the Amur. In the Maritime **Bombing** Province, Meretskov **of Com-** advanced ten miles in **munications** heavily fortified, difficult country. Intense bombing attacks were also started on August 9 against the chief centres of the Japanese lines of railway communication, and millions of leaflets were dropped urging the Japanese to petition the Emperor to end the war. The second atomic bomb fell that day on Nagasaki.

Progress on August 10 was unchecked. The main Transbaikal force advanced some twelve miles, capturing Argun and other important points; while mobile troops, apparently those from the Buirnor area, made an astonishing bound of a hundred miles, striking

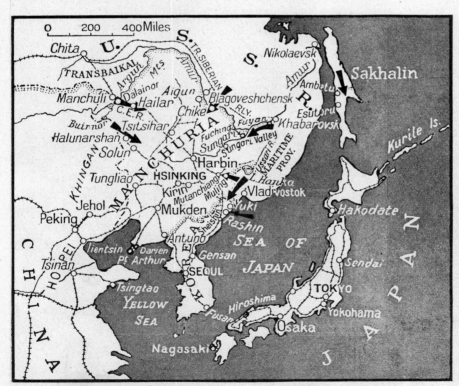

SOVIET ADVANCE IN MANCHURIA

The Soviet Armies' chief lines of penetration into Manchuria during the short Russian war with Japan are indicated here. While some troops of the 2nd Far Eastern Army forced the Amur and Ussari rivers, others advanced into the southern (Japanese) half of Sakhalin. Marshal Malinovsky's forces seized Hailar and Tsitsihar. Pushing west and south from the Maritime Province, Marshal Meretskov's troops reached Mutanchiang and Yuki. *By courtesy of The Times*

SOVIET NAVAL FLOTILLA REACHES HARBIN

Troops of the 2nd Far Eastern Army, under General Purkayev, on August 20, 1945, occupied Harbin, large city and vital communications junction in central Manchuria: Japanese at Harbin here lay down their arms at the feet of a Soviet soldier. Below, citizens welcome forces of the Russian Amur Naval Flotilla which had approached Harbin by river and entered the city with the first infantry detachments. *Photos, Pictorial Press*

into the foothills south of Hailar and capturing that town, which lies 60 miles inside Manchuria. The 2nd F.E.A. extended its hold on the south bank of the Amur and on the west bank of the Ussari, where Hulin was captured. The Amur was also forced in Blago-veshchensk region and Aigun taken. The 1st F.E.A. advanced a further 18 miles, taking a number of towns on the Chinese Eastern Railway at its eastern end. On August 10, too, Russian naval units joined in the attack on Japanese shipping in the Korean ports of Sheishin and Rashin started by Soviet bombers the previous day.

Soviet Naval and Air Assault

On August 11 the advance was still more marked. On the Transbaikal front mobile troops, crossing the Khingan mountains, advanced another fifty miles, while the main force captured a number of towns west of the range. The 2nd F.E.A., attacking vigorously, advanced 20 miles, took Fuching on the Sungari and Hsiaokiaho west of the Ussari. The 1st F.E.A., still operating in mountainous and wooded country, covered from ten to fifteen miles and

AT PORT ARTHUR

Airborne troops of the Transbaikal Army landed at Port Arthur on August 22, 1945, and disarmed the Japanese garrison. Later, Marines of the Red Navy hoisted the Soviet naval flag (above). By an agreement, signed on August 14, 1945 (see page 3566), Port Arthur, captured by the Japanese in their war with the Russians in 1905, was to be used jointly by China and the U.S.S.R. for thirty years. The monument on Haku-gyoku-zam hill commemorates the Japanese dead of 1904-5.   *Photo, Pictorial Press*

captured many towns including Muling.

The Tokyo broadcast on August 10 announcing that the Japanese Government was ready to accept the Allied ultimatum of July 26 with the proviso that the sovereignty of the Emperor was maintained (*see* Chapter 372), although it did not bring the cessation of hostilities, probably affected the determination of Japanese resistance.

On August 12, the fourth day of the Soviet offensive, steady progress was made on all fronts and many important towns were occupied. The powerful Japanese naval base of Rashin in Korea, 15 miles from the Soviet frontier and fifty sea miles from Vladivostok, was stormed by Russian troops, landed and supported by the Soviet Pacific Fleet.

Soviet Advance

On August 14 Japan surrendered unconditionally, but, the Emperor having

MARSHAL MALINOVSKY'S TROOPS ENTER MUKDEN

Scene of Japan's final victory over the Tsarist forces in 1905 and the capital of Manchuria until 1932, the important city of Mukden, with a peacetime population of over half-a-million, was occupied by troops of Marshal Malinovsky's Transbaikal Army on August 20, 1945. Here a group of Chinese watch from the kerbstone the Russian troops as they swing into the town.

Photo, Pictorial Press

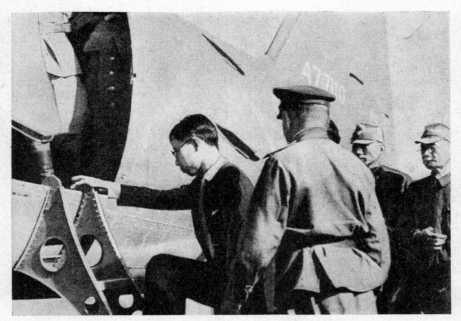

PUPPET 'EMPEROR' ARRESTED

As troops of Marshal Malinovsky's Transbaikal Army entered Mukden on August 20, 1945, they found at the airport P'u Yi, the Chinese-born 'Emperor' of the Japanese puppet-state of 'Manchukuo' (Manchuria). He and his suite were arrested and interned. Here, the puppet 'Emperor' is escorted on board the aircraft which took him to Soviet General Staff H.Q.

Photo, Keystone

Korean coast after heavy fighting. On Sakhalin Japanese frontier defences had been penetrated. Between August 9 and 13 some 8,000 prisoners had been taken—an unusually large number for Japanese armies to lose, but not enough to indicate a general willingness to surrender.

On August 15 further progress was made on all fronts, but on the following day on all three main fronts and at Sheishin in Korea the Japanese attempted a counter-offensive. It was, however, an abortive effort which failed even to bring the Russians to a temporary halt.

On August 16 the Japanese Emperor issued a rescript to all his troops to surrender, and on the 17th Marshal Vassilievsky, in reply to a proposal to cease hostilities made by the commander of the **End of the Kwantung Army** Kwantung army, suggested mid-day of August 20 as the time-limit by which Japanese H.Q. should order its forces to lay down their arms. As the Japanese surrendered their arms, he said, the Soviet troops would discontinue war operations.

The Emperor's order on August 17 brought the war to an end; but owing to the difficulty of communicating the order in a confused situation, fighting continued for some days, and the Russian armies pressed on towards their original objectives. On August 18

as yet given no order to the armed forces to cease resistance, fighting continued. By that day Malinovsky's force was operating in strength east of the Khingan mountains, and was advancing rapidly. Purkayev, having cleared the salient south of the Amur between the Ussari and Sungari, had made considerable progress up both banks of the latter river. Meretskov, who was probably meeting the stiffest resistance since his advance constituted the most immediate threat to Harbin and Hsin-king (Changchun), had reached and crossed the Mutan river, capturing the important railway junction of Mutan-chiang from suicide detachments fighting to the end. The Soviet Pacific Fleet had also captured Sheishin on the

RUSSIAN ACTIVITY IN MANCHURIA

The Soviet armies, after occupying industrial areas created by the Japanese in Manchuria, removed large quantities of factory equipment. Left, gutted interior of the Ten-ho weaving and dyeing factory in Mukden, after the Russians had blasted a wall and removed the machinery. Right, Memorial to Soviet tank-troops erected in Mukden and surmounted by a real tank.

SURRENDER OF JAPANESE IN MANCHURIA

On August 23, 1945, after fourteen days' fighting, Generalissimo Stalin announced that the Red Army had occupied the whole of Manchuria and Southern Sakhalin and that the Japanese Kwantung army had surrendered. Here, Marshal Vassilievsky, C.-in-C., Soviet troops in the Far East (centre), and Marshal Meretskov, commanding the 1st Far Eastern Army (left), meet Lieutenant-General Hata, Chief of Staff of the Kwantung forces.

Photo, Pictorial Press

in some sectors resistance was still met, but in others troops had begun to surrender in thousands, among them the encircled garrison in a fortified zone in the area of Hailar, which laid down its arms, yielding 5,000 prisoners headed by Major-General Nomura : it was symptomatic of the Japanese acceptance of defeat that General Nomura did not feel compelled to commit suicide.

During the following days the number of Japanese surrendering increased —on August 19, 100,000 prisoners were counted—but the **Airborne Troops Occupy Towns** Russians were taking no chances and continued to a d v a n c e, refusing to accept the risk of giving fanatical elements an opportunity to organize die-hard opposition. On the 19th Malinovsky's army occupied Tsitsihar, while airborne troops landed at Harbin, Kirin, Hsinking (Changchun) and Mukden, at all of which places they found the garrisons ready to surrender. Next day Malinovsky's troops, presumably mobile spearheads, occupied Mukden and Changchun ; Purkayev occupied Harbin, Meretskov Kirin. Resistance ceased in the southern (Japanese) half of Sakhalin. The prisoners this day included four generals commanding Japanese armies in the combat areas.

On August 22 Soviet airborne troops landed at Darien and Port Arthur and proceeded to disarm the garrisons there. Facilities at these two ports, the lease of which by China to Tsarist Russia was perhaps the main cause of the Russo-Japanese war of 1904, were granted to the U.S.S.R. by an **Sino-Soviet Treaty** agreement (*see* p a g e 3566) with China signed simultaneously with the Soviet-Chinese treaty (*see* Historic Document 306, page 3772). Their recapture by Soviet arms obliterated the memory of disastrous defeat. The ambitions of the Russian Navy were further satisfied by the occupation of the northernmost of the Kurile islands, leading to permanent possession of the group.

Marshal Stalin's Order of the Day addressed to Marshal Vassilievsky and his army and naval commanders on August 23 announced that they had completed their task. By that date virtually the whole of Manchuria had

been occupied and P'u Yi, the unfortunate puppet emperor of Manchukuo, had been captured at Mukden and interned.

The task as originally set had been by no means an easy one, for the Kwantung army was a formidable force and for years had been engaged in perfecting defensive arrangements. To reach the decisive objectives long distances had to be covered, and much of the country to be traversed was highly defensible. In the event, determined resistance was encountered only in the fortified zones on the frontier, and by the time they had been forced it must have become clear to all Japanese commanders that their government had accepted defeat, and in the final phases, while the Emperor's order to cease resistance was awaited, it is not surprising that disorganization and loss of morale set in.

Nevertheless the conduct of the campaign afforded another striking demonstration of Russian military efficiency. The transfer of troops from west to east and the completion of preparations for an offensive on a great scale in the time available after the collapse of Germany were in themselves remarkable feats. The strategic plan of campaign was admirably suited to the circumstances, and its tactical execution showed how thoroughly the lessons of the German war had been absorbed. The frontier defences were crushed by the weight of artillery fire, centres of resistance were bypassed, and mobile armoured forces broke through, thrusting boldly and at great speed into the comparative vacuum behind the defensive zones.

The use of air power to disrupt the enemy's rearward communications and finally the employment of airborne troops to secure points which might become centres of resistance, all followed the pattern of the most striking features of the final phases of the war in Europe.

Malinovsky's handling of the situation on the Transbaikal front was outstand-ingly skilful. He was confronted with a highly fortified zone behind which lay the densely wooded and formidable Khingan mountains, offering a second defensive position. His attack from the Buirnor area, which evidently took the Japanese by surprise, was a bold and well executed solution of his problem, reminiscent of his manoeuvre to outflank the Iron Gate defile in Rumania and his passage of the Little Carpathians to enter the Morava valley in Austria (*see* pp. 3479, 3625). He took risks in committing his mobile armour to an advance by difficult mountain tracks, but the bypassing of the strong garrison near Hailar cut the supply line of the Japanese in the fortified frontier zone.

The latter part of the campaign developed into little more than the advance of armies of occupation, and it is doubtful how far the **Eighty-one Generals Captured** Japanese fought with real determination even in the initial encounters. The weight and vigour of the Russian attack did not give them much chance ; but there is no definite indication of low morale. Once the Emperor's order to cease resistance was given there was, however, little show of unwillingness to obey it, and neither mass nor individual suicides were reported. The Russians undoubtedly expected displays of fanaticism, and the rapidity of their final advance was presumably dictated by determination to crush any signs of such developments. The rate at which prisoners were collected—before the end of the month the figure of 513,000 including 81 generals was reached— gives proof of the completeness with which the surrender was carried out. It is rather curious, however, that the amount of material captured was comparatively small : between August 9 and 28 only 587 planes, 347 tanks, 955 guns of all calibres, 711 mortars, 3,355 machine-guns and 1,789 lorries was the record of booty collected ; more may have been secured later.

Chapter 368

ALLIED AIR SUPREMACY IN THE EAST

Air strength was the chief factor in the Allied reconquest of Burma, and, with naval power, gave the Allies victory in the Pacific. This Chapter, by Capt. Norman Macmillan, M.C., A.F.C., which covers air activities in the East during 1945, continues the record from Chapter 306. Air operations in the west during 1945 are described in Chapter 346

THE complicated plan of operations that led to the advance through central Burma and victory at Rangoon (*see* Chapters 345 and 371) could not have been developed without air transport. The size of General Slim's force for the move south to Rangoon had to be **Air Transport** fixed by the air delivery **in Burma** rate over the roadless divide between the sea and the lower Irrawaddy valley—and what air transport could achieve can be gauged by Eastern Air Command's announcement on April 20 that in the year ending March 31, 1945, over 550,000 tons of arms and supplies (a cargo that would have filled 55 Liberty ships, and ranged from ammunition and rations to bulldozers and pneumatic hammers) had been flown into Burma. Eighty per cent was landed at forward airfields, the rest parachuted or dropped to troops at the front. Of this total, 250,000 tons was flown in between January and March, during which time, in addition, Eastern Air Command flew in 236,000 men and evacuated over 70,000.

On January 3, 1945, the Allies occupied Akyab, and on January 21 landed on Ramree Island (*see* page 3536). Sea transport built up the supplies on Ramree, air transport lifted them over the divide to the selected zone in the Irrawaddy valley, and road transport fed the army's needs from the air landing bases.

Although it was British policy to spare Mandalay as much as possible, heavy bombers attacked it on January 12 and 13. Fort Dufferin held out for twelve days after tanks entered the city on March 8, and fighter-bombers breached the fort walls with bombs before its capture (*see* illus. in page 3539). The 14th Army secured the main airfield at Meiktila on March 31, and supplies poured in by air from Ramree. While military columns moved on Rangoon from the north, Indian parachute troops were dropped at Elephant Point, on the west bank of the Rangoon river, on May 1 (*see* Chapter 371). The city fell on May 3. From the battle of Imphal (*see* page 3004) to the fall of Rangoon, the R.A.F. alone flew nearly a quarter of a million sorties in Burma.

On May 31, S.E.A.C. announced that all U.S.A.A.F. units had been withdrawn from Eastern Air Command, which then again became solely a Royal and Royal Indian Air Forces formation. Major-General George E. Stratemeyer, appointed in July overall commander of U.S. Air Forces in China, was succeeded as head of E.A.C. by Air-Marshal W. A. Coryton.

Air attacks on the Japanese escape routes to Siam continued. Bridges over the Mekong river were bombed and broken. The Andaman and Nicobar island groups and Sumatra came under increasing air attack from naval aircraft with the British East Indies Fleet (*see* page 3765) and the R.A.F.

India-based Super-Fortresses sank the 50,000-ton King George V graving dock at Singapore on February 1— scuttled in 1942, it had been raised by the enemy. They bombed Singapore again on March 11, and the railway yards at Kuala Lumpur on March 10. Royal Australian Air Force Liberators

AIR 'WAR' AGAINST MALARIA IN BURMA

An important factor making for Allied victory in Burma was the marked improvement in methods of combating tropical disease. In 1943, three Allied soldiers in every thousand fell sick of malaria every day. By 1945, the incidence was reduced to one in every four thousand. R.A.F. Hurricanes, spraying the potent insecticide D.D.T. in the form of white vapour (below), destroyed the malaria-spreading mosquitoes in their swampy breeding-grounds.

SQUADRON-LEADER SCARF

For 'supreme heroism' against 'tremendous odds,' Squadron-Leader Arthur Stewart King Scarf, R.A.F., was awarded the V.C. posthumously, it was announced on June 22, 1946. After a Japanese attack on the R.A.F. station at Butterworth, Malaya, on December 9, 1941, his was the only aircraft to survive, yet he pressed on to bomb the enemy air base at Singora, Thailand, as sole remaining member of a sortie already arranged. Over the target he was mortally wounded.

AMERICA'S SHIPBUILDERS HELPED TO WIN THE WAR AT SEA

A vital contribution to the ultimate victory of the Allies at sea was the prodigious output of the American shipbuilding yards. Early in 1940 some 100,000 workers were employed ; by the peak year of 1943 the number had risen to well over 700,000, fourteen per cent being women. Output increased from 1,100,000 deadweight tons of merchant shipping in 1941 to 8,000,000 tons a year later and then to 16,500,000 in 1943. Workers, many of whom are wearing protective headgear, are here leaving one of the shipyards of the South, where several new shipbuilding works were established. *Direct colour photograph by Pictorial Press*

BRITAIN'S CONVOYS SIGNIFIED ATLANTIC VICTORY

IN the House of Commons on October 4, 1944, Mr. A. V. Alexander, First Lord of the Admiralty, declared : ' We have now reached a stage at which most of our shipping problems appear to be over.' Eight months later, on June 6, 1945, President Truman and Mr. Churchill issued their last joint statement on the war against the U-boats. They described it as ' a long and perilous struggle, demanding not only the utmost courage, daring and endurance, but also the highest scientific and technical skill.' 781 German submarines had been sunk, though at the peak of the battle in 1941 and 1942 ' the issue hung in the balance.'

The Convoy System played an important part in the struggle, notably in the Atlantic and on the Murmansk route to Russia. In five years and eight months 75,000 merchant ships were escorted in or across the Atlantic in 2,000 ocean convoys, the largest of which totalled 167 ships —all covered by escorts of the Royal Navy. The total number of ships lost was 574, equivalent to one in every 131 that sailed. Nearly 1,500 merchant ships were escorted by the Royal Navy in 75 convoys to and from North Russia, and 173,000 in some 7,700 British coastal convoys. The photographs in this and the facing page were taken during a two-day attack by enemy bombers on a British convoy in the Bay of Biscay in September 1943. Though U-boats joined in, both they and the bombers were driven off, without loss to shipping. Left, crew man A.A. guns during the air attack. Above part of the convoy.

LAST OF THE WAR-TIME POSTERS
In early summer 1945 British Railways (top left), and London Transport (centre) issued striking Victory posters. Earlier in the year British citizens were still being exhorted—by means of other posters shown here—to continue their war-time duties. This selection completes the series of representative war posters of the Second Great War begun on page 551.

made a thousand-mile daylight flight on January 27 to bomb the Mandalin-Simon hydro-electric plant in Java, a visit repeated on February 11; R.A.A.F. Kittyhawks and Beaufighters from Morotai attacked Tohohon in Celebes on February 14. The preliminary strategic air assault for the reconquest of Malaya and the Netherlands East was just beginning when Japan surrendered.

The invasion of Luzon (January 9, 1945—*see* page 3743) was preceded by air attacks on bridges, tunnels and roads, and dummy parachutists were dropped to create a false impression as to the actual points of Allied attack. Subsequent operations were supported by strategic bombing here, as in other campaigns.

Air operations over a wide area supported the attack on Luzon : carrier-aircraft of the U.S. 3rd Fleet attacked Formosa and Okinawa, largest of the

Air Support for Luzon Attack

Ryukyu Islands, on January 2 and 3 (this was the first attack on the Ryukyus), and reconnoitred without interference 540 miles of the Chinese coast from Formosa to Hongkong, destroying 111 Japanese aircraft, damaging 220, sinking 27 enemy ships and damaging 68. The rail system and 24 airfields on Formosa were heavily bombed again by carrier-aircraft on the 7th. On the 11th, carrier-aircraft sank 25 enemy ships and damaged 13 in four convoys off Indo-China, and destroyed 39 flying-boats and seaplanes in Indo-China harbours. The area was attacked again next day, when 16 more ships were sunk, and 15 more damaged. In the two days 112 aircraft were shot down, all the operations being carried out at a cost of 16 U.S. planes.

On January 13 carrier-aircraft attacked Hongkong, Swatow, and Amoy. China-based Super-Fortresses hit targets in Formosa, including Okoyama and the Toko seaplane base, on January 16 and 17. Carrier-aircraft attacking the same island on the 20th and 21st shot down 47 Japanese planes, destroyed 102 and damaged 162 on the ground. From the reoccupation of the Philippines to June 17, Allied aircraft based in the Pacific dropped 10,000 tons of bombs on Formosa, and heavy attacks continued. Off Formosa on May 21 a single U.S. plane destroyed a convoy of three transports and two freighters aggregating 17,000 tons.

After bombardment since January 23, during which 3,128 tons of bombs were rained on the two-and-three-quarter-square-mile island of Corregidor (which commands the entrance to Manila Bay),

3787

R.A.F. GROUND CREWS IN ACTION IN BURMA

Since the reconquest of Burma in 1945 depended largely on air power and supply, R.A.F. ground staff were keymen. 1. Unloading a L-5 Sentinel liaison aircraft from an invasion barge on the Arakan coast. These light machines were much used to transport wounded, etc. In Central Burma: R.A.F. fitters recondition Merlin engines for Spitfires at a forward airfield (2); and (3) an improvised 'control tower,' made from strips of white cloth stretched on bamboo frames, in action.
Photos, British Official

men of the 503rd Parachute Regiment dropped on to the island on February 16 from two long trains of Army C-47 transport planes and, with infantry landed on the beaches, began its re-conquest. Puerta

Air Patrols Over South China Sea

Princessa on Palawan Island (west Philippines) was captured with its two airstrips on March 1 : these airfields controlled the Sulu Sea, and also the sea-lanes of the South China Sea between Japan and her conquests in south-east Asia and the East Indies. Thereafter U.S. Navy Liberators based on the Philippines and Morotai maintained daily patrols over the South China Sea.

On April 1 the U.S. 10th Army landed on Okinawa (*see* page 3754) under an air " umbrella " of 1,500 naval planes. The violent sea-air battle which followed is described in page 3761. (By the end of the first week of the invasion U.S. Marine fighter aircraft were in action from Yontan airfield.) In the struggle for Okinawa, Allied aircraft losses exceeded 1,000, and heavy naval losses were suffered from enemy air attack, particularly by "Kamikaze"

BY AIR TO RANGOON

Indian parachute troops of the 14th Army were dropped on May 1, 1945, at Elephant Point, not far from Rangoon, two days before the Burmese capital's capture by powerful forces of infantry landed from ships of the Royal Navy on May 2 (see Chapter 371). Here, Indian parachute troops are aboard a Dakota air-craft on their way to Rangoon.

pilots. Although these suicide pilots, belonging to the Kamikaze (suicide) Corps, were first encountered during the Battle for Leyte Gulf (*see* page 3402) in October 1944, they were not mentioned in official communiqués until April 1945. Their object was to crash their planes on the decks of Allied ships, immolating themselves in the process, and their sacrifice achieved a certain amount of success : the 27,000-ton air-craft-carrier U.S.S. "Ticon-deroga" was heavily damaged on January 21 (144 killed or missing, 193 wounded) by two suicide planes off Formosa; the

FAMOUS RAILWAY

The advance of the British 36th Division down the Myitkyina-Mandalay 'railway-corridor' (see page 3543) was one of the great exploits of the fighting in Burma in 1944-45. Over a section of the line in an area heavily pitted with shell-holes, air-craft of the U.S.A. 10th Air Force are (left) parachuting food, ammunition and medical supplies to advancing troops.

Photos, British Official

10,000-ton cruiser " Nashville " was seriously damaged by one suicide plane off Negros (Philippines) on December 13 (133 killed, 190 wounded). Other instances are given in page 3762.

Over Okinawa, Kamikaze attacks became more bitter and better organized : 111 were shot down by ships' guns and U.S. fighters during the nights of May 27–28 and 28–29 alone. There also the " baka," first mentioned on April 28 when one crashed into the U.S. hospital ship " Comfort," also made its appearance ; it was a small, wooden-built, piloted, rocket-assisted glider bomb, carried to its launching point slung under a master aircraft. During its dive the pilot accelerated to about 650 m.p.h. by using his rockets, and steered his glider on to the target—usually a ship—perishing in the crash. The warhead contained more than a ton of explosive.

Okinawa, captured on June 21, was soon almost covered by airfields for Allied combat aircraft in preparation for the final all-out assault on Japan proper. From these airfields, interdiction of the

Okinawa as Allied Air Base

enemy sea-lines between Japan and Korea and the north-eastern China ports became practicable : in 49 days Allied aircraft sank 50 supply ships and damaged 64 others in the Tsushima Strait ; Shanghai was attacked by over 200 bombers and fighters from Okinawa on July 18 and 19, by 300 on the 24th.

The Australian 9th Division landed in Brunei Bay, north-west Borneo, on June 10 (*see* page 3601) and seized the naval anchorage and airfields. These new facilities completed a chain of strategic bases from which Allied land-based and seaborne aircraft could cover the coast of the Asiatic mainland from Korea to Singapore. The Japanese were now hemmed in to the west of a

END OF A JAPANESE DESTROYER OFF LEYTE

The fate of an enemy destroyer, part of a convoy attempting to reinforce the Japanese base at Ormoc, Leyte (taken by U.S. troops on December 10, 1944), is vividly shown here. Left, a B-25 of the U.S. Far East Air Force flattens out over the destroyer which is vainly trying to escape. Right, a few seconds later the target is struck with a direct hit amidships which caused her complete destruction. *Photos, U.S. Navy*

line from the northern Kuriles to Victoria Point, and the pockets of their forces (e.g. on Bougainville and at Wewak) to the east and south were completely cut off.

While all these widespread operations were going on, the air attack on the Japanese mainland, shared by land-based and carrier-borne machines, was **Attacks on Japanese Mainland** mounting steadily. Super - Fortresses from the Marianas attacking Tokyo, most frequent objective in Japan, on January 27 met the strongest opposition they had encountered. On February 10 Tokyo suffered an earthquake, and an hour later the Kanto factory area, embracing both Tokyo and Yokohama, was hit by Super-Fortresses. By 7 a.m. on February 16 a very powerful force of the U.S. 5th Fleet under Vice-Admiral Mitscher, and including 15–20 aircraft carriers, had moved up to within 300 miles of the island of Honshu ; during that day Tokyo and Yokohama were subjected to incessant bombing for nine hours by 1,500 carrier-borne aircraft. The attack continued next day, and ended in a decisive victory : 332

Japanese planes were destroyed in combat, 177 on the ground, and at least another 150 probably destroyed on the first day ; an unknown number were brought down on the second. An escort carrier was left down by the bows, ablaze and sinking, at Yokohama, 13 other vessels were sunk, 22 damaged. The cost was 49 U.S. planes, 30–40 pilots.

On February 25 aircraft of the 5th Fleet, which attacked Tokyo and Yokohama throughout the day, were joined by over 200 Super-Fortresses from the Marianas ; together they devastated 667 acres of the industrial centre of the Japanese capital.

Over a thousand tons of a new type of incendiary—a 6-lb. bomb filled with jellied petrol and dropped in 500-lb. clusters—dropped on Tokyo on the night of March 9 razed over 15 square miles of the city. By March 21 Mustang and Black Widow (*see* illus. in page 3394) fighters were reported in operation from Iwo Jima ; on April 7 Mustangs from Iwo Jima escorted Super-Fortresses from the Marianas in an attack on Tokyo and Nagoya. Pathfinders preceded an attack from 3.0 to 4.45 a.m. on May 23 on the congested Shinagawa district of

Tokyo : the target area was brilliantly illuminated, and three square miles were burnt out by 4,500 tons of incendiaries (about 750,000 bombs). In another heavy attack three days later,

UP IN SMOKE

First of many attacks on the Japanese mainland by carrier-based aircraft was made on February 16-17, 1945, when Tokyo and Yokohama were incessantly pounded, resulting in the destruction of enemy shipping and 332 Japanese aircraft. Below, struck by a carrier-based U.S. Navy bomber, an enemy destroyer blows up off Kyushu. The nature of the explosion suggests that her magazine was hit. *Photo, U.S. Navy*

U.S. WARSHIPS IN THE PACIFIC—

4. Hole made by a 500-lb. bomb, dropped by an enemy 'suicide' aircraft, on the flight deck of the U.S.N. carrier 'Bunker Hill' off Okinawa on May 11, 1945 (see page 3762). 5. 'Kamikaze' aircraft flies low over a U.S.N. escort-carrier, its port engine and wing-tips aflame after direct hits by the carrier's guns from which smoke still drifts.

'KAMIKAZE' AIRCRAFT ATTACK—

1. Japanese 'Zeke' ('Zero') 'suicide' aircraft desperately tries to manoeuvre on to the deck of a U.S. Pacific Fleet warship before crashing into the sea. Another—a twin-motored type—is hit by A.A. fire, and with its engines belching flames (2), strikes the sea with a terrific splash (3), after an unsuccessful attempt to dive on a U.S. carrier.

JAPANESE SUICIDE GLIDER-BOMB

The 'baka,' a new Japanese 'suicide' glider-bomb, first reported in action against shipping off Okinawa on April 28, 1945, was later used against Super-Fortresses attacking the Japanese mainland. With wooden wings and fuselage, it was carried to within close range of the target by a master aircraft, whence it was rocket-assisted and directed by a pilot killed when it exploded. This 'baka' was found intact on Yontan airfield, Okinawa. The warhead weighed over a ton.

when the fires were fanned by a 70 m.p.h. gale, the Imperial Palace was damaged.

Nagoya was attacked almost as often as Tokyo : a force of Super-Fortresses which bombed targets there on January 23 met strong opposition and fought running battles up to a hundred miles out at sea, both approaching and leaving. In five incendiary raids during March by forces of 250 and 300 Super-Fortresses, Nagoya was hit three times, Osaka once, when six square miles of it were burnt out, and Kobe once.

Incendiary Raids on Nagoya

Between March 27 and May 11 Super-Fortresses based on Tinian carried out mine-laying operations aimed at sealing off the three entrances to the Inland Sea of Japan ; by August 3 every important harbour in Japan itself and along the coast of Asia from Korea to the Soviet frontier had been mined.

The first attack on Japan by aircraft other than Super-Fortresses or carrier planes was made on April 19 when Mustangs from Iwo Jima hit Utsugi naval air station which lies 25 miles

SENTINEL AT OKINAWA

A U.S. L-5 Sentinel liaison aircraft flies over blazing Okinawa to observe the effects of Allied artillery and mortar fire. Nick-named 'Jungle Angels' in Burma, these light monoplanes, powered with a single 6-cylinder engine developing 185 h.p., and with a wing-span of 34 feet, were used for many purposes, including transport of supplies and wounded, artillery-spotting and the directing of troop movements in the jungle. *Photo, Central Press*

south-west of Tokyo. Between April 21 and May 9 the airfields on Kyushu Island, used by the enemy planes attacking Allied shipping off Okinawa, were the principal object of attack.

Aircraft plant on Honshu was attacked by Super-Fortresses on May 6 ; the main fuelling centre of the Japanese army and navy at Tokuyama and other oil centres on May 9 ; the seaplane plant at Fukae on the 10th. Over 500 Super-Fortresses dropped 3,500 tons of fire bombs on Nagoya from a low level on May 16 ; the port, docks and industrial plant of Yokohama received 3,200 tons of fire bombs on May 28.

On May 30 Major-General Lemay, Commanding General of the 21st (Super-Fortress) Bomber Command, said at Guam (announced as Pacific Ocean Areas Advanced H.Q. on February 14) that raids to date on Tokyo had cost fifty Super-Fortresses, 550 airmen ; in Washington Mr. Forrestal, the Navy Secretary, said that the overall strength of the Japanese air force had been reduced by thirteen per cent as a result of losses inflicted in April alone.

American Losses Over Tokyo

Leaflet raids began during May—from May 5 to June 3, between 500,000 and 1,000,000 emphasizing the futility of continued resistance were dropped on Japanese cities.

In a raid on Kobe on June 4 (3,000 tons of fire bombs) one at least out of eight Super-Fortresses lost was brought down by " baka " bombs launched from

Japanese fighters in the attempt to ram the American bombers. Osaka was bombed by instruments through thick cloud on June 6. A number of industrial towns were hit on June 17 (when one, Kagoshima, was left entirely ablaze), 19, and 21. Seventy of a force of about 450 Super-Fortresses which bombed Nagoya, Osaka and other towns on June 26 were forced by adverse winds and heavy rain to land on Iwo Jima on the return journey. The naval station of Sasebo and two other towns received 3,000 tons of incendiaries on June 28. Next day Tokyo announced the mass evacuation of war factories to Manchuria. On July 9 it was announced in Guam that as a result of the first 41 incendiary raids on Japan, 30 Japanese cities had been virtually reduced to ashes, the total burnt-out

BORNEO BOMBED

Liberator and Beaufighter aircraft of the Royal Australian Air Force gave valuable support to troops of the Australian 9th Division both before and after the landings in Brunei Bay, north-west Borneo, on June 10, 1945. Above, R.A.A.F. crews being briefed by Australian Army liaison officers before taking off from Palawan in the Philippines. Left, Brunei after bombing by the R.A.A.F. It was captured on June 14.
Photos, British Official

area being estimated at 130 square miles. Naval and transport bases, industrial towns, oil installations, airfields continued to be relentlessly attacked.

A U.S. Navy Department announcement of February 27 stated that since December 1, 1944, carrier-based planes of the U.S. 3rd and 5th Fleets had destroyed 1,610 Japanese planes, damaged 1,078, sunk 187 ships and probably sunk or damaged another 402 for the loss of 178 aircraft.

On March 18 and 19 naval planes attacked the Japanese fleet sheltering in the Inland Sea of Japan: six freighters were sunk, 200 aeroplanes shot down, 275 destroyed on the ground, and damage **Damage in Japanese Waters** was done to a battleship of the new 45,000-ton "Yamato" class, as well as to a number of other war vessels. Attacks over and near Japan by naval aircraft were intensified during July: on the 6th, Navy planes made extensive raids in Korea, and in the waters round Japan and in the Yellow Sea damaged or left ablaze ten enemy ships; on the 7th Navy Privateers sank or damaged many small ships in the same areas and round the islands of the northern Ryukyus. On the 10th a powerful task force of Admiral Halsey's 3rd Fleet commanded by Vice-Admiral J. F. McBain approached Honshu to within

3792

carriers "Amagi" and "Katsuragi" damaged; and extensive damage was done to land installations in spite of strong opposition and very heavy A.A. fire. Twenty-one enemy planes were destroyed in combat, 271 on the ground, for the loss of 27 American and British aircraft.

While carrier-planes were concentrating mainly on shipping in their July attacks, Super-Fortresses continued their attacks on land objectives: on the 12th, some 500 dropped more than 3,000 tons of high explosive and incendiary bombs at night on Ichinomiya, a munitions centre nine miles north-

R.A.F. IN COCOS ISLANDS

The Cocos or Keeling Islands, a group of some 20 small coral-islands in the Indian Ocean, 700 miles south-west of Sumatra and annexed to Singapore in 1903, provided bases for R.A.F. aircraft of South East Asia Command. Here, Spitfires of No.136 (Fighter) Squadron are lined up on a Cocos airstrip. This top-scoring squadron was credited with 100 'kills,' besides 150 'probables' and 'damaged.' *Photo, British Official*

fifteen miles' flying distance of Tokyo Bay: some 2,000 carrier-aircraft attacked targets round Tokyo. Not a single Japanese aircraft or warship gave battle.

The first bombardment of the Japanese mainland came on July 14 (*see* page 3763). On the 15th 1,000 carrier-aircraft attacked Japan. Again there was no opposition, though 24 planes were lost through bad weather. In the two days' attacks 129 locomotives were destroyed, 82 planes were destroyed or damaged on the ground, 374 small ships were sunk or damaged, and heavy damage was done to installations. British carrier-aircraft joined in the assault at dawn on the 17th—there was no opposition except A.A. fire. A British-American force of carrier-aircraft attacked Japanese warships at Yokosuka on July 18; at Kure on July 24 U.S. carrier-planes heavily damaged the 30,000-ton battleships "Ise" and "Hyuga," left burning the heavy cruiser "Tone" and the light cruiser "Oyodo," and damaged a large aircraft-carrier and the heavy cruiser "Aoba," while British planes sank an escort carrier of the "Kobe" class and five cargo vessels and destroyed 12 grounded aircraft. Another British-American attack on July 28 left "Hyuga" and "Ise" beached and burning; the cruisers "Tone," "Aoba" and "Oyodo" out of action, 54 enemy ships sunk, 90 others with the escort carrier "Kaiyo" and the aircraft-

British Aircraft Join in Assault

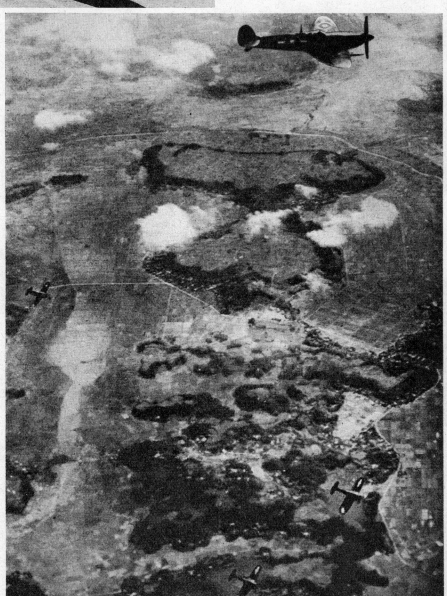

FIRST 'SEAFIRE' OVER JAPAN

As the Allied navies drew nearer the Japanese mainland against diminishing opposition in 1945, carrier-borne fighter aircraft began to make increasingly frequent sorties over enemy territory. Here, a 'Seafire' of the Fleet Air Arm (see page 3391 and illus. in page 3392), carrying out escort duties for the first time over Japan, flies above a heavily-bombed area. These naval equivalents of the 'Spitfire' first went into action over the Normandy beaches in June 1944.

TOKYO IS 'SCORCHED TO THE GROUND'

On May 26, 1945, after a raid by 500 Super-Fortresses dropping 4,000 tons of incendiaries, the Japanese radio admitted that Tokyo was 'literally scorched to the ground,' the Imperial Palace severely damaged and that 'what was once the world's third metropolis ' was ' virtually laid waste.' On June 9, the enemy announced that in raids on the capital 3,100,000 had been rendered homeless. Destruction in the (1) Asukasa, (2) Sumida river industrial districts. 3. U.S. B-29's head for Tokyo.

CONDEMNED AIRCRAFT DUMPED AT SEA

Some 300 Fleet Air Arm aircraft were taken on board Royal Navy escort-carriers in Sydney Harbour, New South Wales, in late 1945, and dumped at sea. Including U.S. 'Corsairs,' 'Hellcats,' 'Avengers,' and British 'Barracudas,' stripped of all useful equipment, they were described, though some were new, as 'surplus, obsolete, and of no value to anybody.' Above, loading condemned planes on board the carrier 'Pioneer.' *Photo, Planet News*

west of Nagoya, and other places; before dawn on the 16th some 450 attacked Oita, a port in the north-east of Kyushu, and other towns with 2,500 tons of fire-bombs; on the 19th more than 600 struck heavily at dawn at Choshi, the biggest fishing port on the east coast of Honshu; on the 24th more than 600 dropped 4,000 tons, including 4,000-lb. bombs, on Osaka, Nagoya and satellite industrial towns. Also on the 24th several hundred Liberators and Mustangs, from Iwo and Okinawa, bombed and strafed wide areas of south Honshu. Smaller forces attacked the coal liquefaction plant at Abel (Honshu), oil refineries at Kawaraki on Tokyo Bay, chemical centres and oil refineries at Omuta and elsewhere.

On July 27 Super-Fortresses dropped 60,000 leaflets on eleven towns —centres of war production or transport **Towns** —warning them that **Warned in** they would be targets **Leaflet Raids** for heavy air attacks, urging their inhabitants to leave them immediately, and appealing to the Japanese to overthrow their militaristic government, make peace, and thus save their country from destruction. (The announcement of this raid at Guam was accompanied by the statement that a million and a half leaflets were being dropped by Super-Fortresses on Japanese cities every day.) On the 28th six of the warned towns were heavily bombed. Twelve more cities received 720,000 leaflets on July 31; four of them were attacked on August 1 by a

record force of 820 Super-Fortresses which dropped 6,632 tons of H.E. and incendiaries—a bomb load exceeding any dropped by the R.A.F. or U.S.A.A.F in a single raid on Germany.

In operations designed to cut off supplies of food, raw materials and fuel, bombers and fighters based on Okinawa destroyed or damaged 250 enemy vessels totalling 250,000 tons between July 3 and August 1.

A statement issued from Guam on August 5 said that 31 towns had been warned, ten of which had been destroyed; in the past 35 days Super-Fortresses had dropped nearly 50,000 tons of bombs on Japan, as well as 3,000,000 copies of the

surrender ultimatum issued at Potsdam on July 26 and signed by Mr. Churchill, Mr. Truman, and Generalissimo Chiang-Kai-shek. In addition, every Monday morning U.S. planes were dropping over Japan a million copies of a miniature newspaper called "Rakusen" (Parachute News), made up like a typical Japanese daily, and containing articles, pictures and cartoons.

On August 6 President Truman announced, "Sixteen hours ago [i.e. at 8.45 a.m. on the 6th] an American aeroplane dropped one bomb on Hiroshima. That bomb had more power than 20,000 tons of TNT and more than 2,000 times the blast-power of the British 'grand slam', which is the largest bomb yet used in the history of warfare." The first bomb charged with the power of atomic fission (*see* Chapter 379) had fallen. On the same day four towns on the "death list" were hit by 580 Super-Fortresses with 3,850 tons of H.E. and incendiaries. A second atomic bomb, even more powerful than the first—described as already obsolete —was dropped on the shipbuilding and arms centre of Nagasaki on August 8: it was 48 hours before the pall of dust and smoke permitted effective aerial reconnaissance. Also on August 8 the Soviet Union declared war on Japan (*see* page 3780).

The ordinary air offensive was maintained in strength: the very day of the surrender (August 14) (*see* Chapter 372) saw a force of 800 Super-Fortresses drop 6,000 tons of high explosive and incendiaries on Honshu targets. Battered from the air, cut off by Allied air and sea power from contact with the riches of the immense empire she had conquered with such apparent ease, Japan could no longer hold out.

R.A.F. TRANSPORT COMMAND FLIES OUT EX-PRISONERS

Repatriation from South-East Asia began on August 18, 1945, organized by R.A.P.W.I. (Recovery of Allied Prisoners of War and Internees), which in two months evacuated 18,500 Allied nationals from Siam alone. Here at Bangkok, the Siamese capital (occupied on September 12), ex-prisoners, some on crutches, wait to embark on a R.A.F. Transport Command aircraft for Rangoon, first stage on the long way home. *Photo, British Official*

Chapter 369

ALL GERMANY IN ALLIED HANDS

In this, the final chapter describing the campaign in western Europe, the Military Editor, Major-General Sir Charles Gwynn, traces the advance of the United States Armies and the French 1st Army from their crossings of the Rhine to the final unconditional surrender of all German land, sea and air forces at Rheims on May 7, 1945.   For 21st Army Group advance, see Chapter 357

WHILE Field-Marshal Montgomery's armies were preparing for their crossing of the Rhine (*see* Chapter 357) and General Patton's U.S. 3rd and General Patch's U.S. 7th Armies were clearing the Saar pocket, General Hodges's U.S. 1st Army was occupied in consolidating and expanding the footing it had, on March 8, so surprisingly gained across the Rhine at Remagen (*see* pages 3572–73). At first it seemed improbable that his bridge-head would provide an opening for a major thrust, on account of the difficult nature of the country to the east ; but it would in any case be a source of anxiety to the Germans and cause dispersion of their reserves.

The footing originally gained was very small and all communication to it depended at first on the captured Ludendorff railway bridge, which had suffered some damage and was exposed to observed artillery fire and air attack (*see* illustrations in page 3572). Nevertheless the success was exploited with great energy, and, before German resistance solidified, high ground overlooking the bridge was captured. Bridging equipment was also rapidly brought forward, and before the railway bridge collapsed on March 17 several temporary bridges were in operation.

Bitter fighting continued with German reinforcements constantly arriving, especially on the north side of the bridge-head, from which it was evidently expected that a thrust towards the Ruhr might develop. By March 25 the bridge-head had, however, been expanded to a width of thirty and a depth of ten miles, and although on its northern flank the enemy had by then consolidated a strong defensive position on the line of the Sieg river, Montgomery's crossing had produced a new and more serious menace to the Ruhr.

The expansion of the Remagen bridge-head in depth had cut the main Frank-fort–Cologne motor road (March 16), increasing the enemy's difficulties of maintaining north–south communication, and now General Hodges brought off a surprise coup which caught the Germans on the wrong foot. Having deceived them by maintaining heavy pressure on the Sieg front, on March 26 he used his main force to break out of the bridge-head to the south-east. His armour drove to Limburg, seizing a bridge over the Lahn river, and raced along the highway towards Frankfort. Other armoured columns were directed eastward, and, covering forty miles a day, reached Marburg and Giessen by March 28. From there they swung northwards through the hill country west of Kassel, one of the most important centres of strategic communication in western Germany.

By this time the U.S. 3rd Army had also come into the picture across the Rhine. On the night of March 22–23, one of its formations (XII Corps commanded by Major-General Manton S. Eddy) effected a brilliant surprise crossing **U.S. 3rd Army Across the Rhine** with improvised material at Oppenheim, south of Mainz. By the 24th this bridge-head was expanded to a width of fifteen miles, and on the 25th the 4th Armoured Division led a breakthrough to a depth of 27 miles, seizing an undamaged bridge over the river Main. In the confused movements entailed by mopping up the Saar, columns of the U.S. 3rd and U.S. 7th Armies had crisscrossed each other ; but admirably quick Staff work sorted out the tangled lines of communication, and there was little delay or loss of momentum in the further exploitation of the unforeseen capture of the Oppenheim bridge-head. Part of the 3rd Army crossed the Rhine at Mainz to deal with the German group between Mainz and Frankfort, which had been by-passed by the first armoured thrust, while the remainder of the Army drove north-eastward towards the line of the Fulda river and Kassel, making contact on their left with the right of General Hodges's 1st Army. During the last week of March, therefore, these two armies had embarked on a massive drive into the heart of Germany.

Farther south the U.S. 7th Army had also crossed the Rhine on a fifteen-mile front between Gernsheim and Mannheim ; and, taking the latter city, had advanced 27 miles eastward. On its right the French II Corps also crossed

BADGES OF ARMY GROUPS UNDER AMERICAN COMMAND

Below are badges of Allied Army Groups and Armies in the central and southern sections of the Western Front at the time of the surrender in May 1945. The 6th Army Group, commanded by General Jacob L. Devers, comprised the U.S. 7th Army (Lieutenant-General Alexander M. Patch) and the French 1st Army (General Jean J. de Lattre de Tassigny). The 12th Army Group, under General Omar N. Bradley, consisted of the U.S. 1st (General Courtney H. Hodges), U.S. 3rd (General George S. Patton, Jr.), U.S. 9th (Lieutenant-General William H. Simpson), and U.S. 15th (Lieutenant-General Leonard T. Gerow) Armies.

6TH. ARMY GROUP
[White on Red]

12TH. ARMY GROUP
[Red, White & Blue; Black Border]

1ST. ARMY
[Black on Khaki]

3RD. ARMY
[White on Blue: Red Ring]

7TH. ARMY
[Red Triangle with Yellow Border on Blue]

9TH. ARMY
[White on Red]

15TH. ARMY
[White & Red; Khaki Border]

FAMOUS BRIDGE COLLAPSES INTO THE RHINE

On March 17, 1945, nine days after its sensational capture by a lieutenant of the U.S. 1st Army (see illus. in page 3572), the Ludendorff bridge spanning the Rhine at Remagen, south of Bonn, collapsed into the river, many U.S. engineers working on it losing their lives. But by this time temporary bridges had been built and were in use. *Photos, Associated Press*

Paderborn, thus, as recorded in page 3661, completing the encirclement of the Ruhr and a large area south of it.

On April 6 General Eisenhower was able to write to General Marshall: "As you can see from the reports, our plans have been developing almost in exact accordance with original conceptions. You must expect, now, a period in which the lines on your map will not advance as rapidly as they did during the past several weeks because we must pause to digest the big mouthful that we have swallowed in the Ruhr area. It should not take too long and, of course, in the meantime maintenance will be pushed to the limits to support our next main thrust. My G2 [Major-General K. W. D. Strong, of the British Army] figures that there may be 150,000 German soldiers left in the Ruhr, but a number of them will change into civilian clothes before we liquidate the whole thing. He is confident, however, that we will capture 100,000. The enemy has been making efforts to break out of the area, but our persistent policy of knocking out his communication to the eastward, and his lack of mobility within the pocket both make it very difficult for him to launch a really concerted attack. I am confident that he can do nothing about it."

Eisenhower on ' Digesting ' the Ruhr

C.-IN-C., U.S. FIFTEENTH ARMY

A new army, the U.S. 15th, under Lieutenant-General Leonard T. Gerow, entered into the line of the 12th Army Group on the Western Front, on March 30, 1945, giving the U.S. 1st and 9th Armies more freedom to increase the weight of their offensive into Germany. The C.-in-C. of the new army was born in 1888.

near Germersheim, made contact with the U.S. 7th Army south of Heidelberg, and on April 1 established a bridge-head for the French Army at Philippsburg.

The Rhine had ceased to be an obstacle, and an offensive on an immense scale had begun to develop east of the river. The enemy's defence had been completely shattered and the speed with which the offensive had been pressed, combined with the disruption of his transport system and shortage of motor fuel, left him quite incapable of co-ordinating a new defensive system on any sector

Rhine Ceases to be an Obstacle

of his front. He continued to offer bitter resistance at isolated points, but these were by-passed by armoured columns and left to be mopped up later. The U.S. 15th Army, commanded by Lieutenant-General Leonard T. Gerow, was at this time brought forward to occupy, organize and govern the parts of Germany already conquered, and so to give the leading armies greater freedom of action in their surge eastwards ; in particular, by holding the line of the Rhine on the Ruhr front, it enabled the U.S. 9th Army to press boldly forward, and on April 1 to make contact with the U.S. 1st Army near Lippstadt, west of

VICTORS AND VANQUISHED IN GERMANY

Infantry of the U.S. 3rd Army crowd on board an assault-boat raft, carrying also a tank-destroyer, about to be ferried across the Rhine. General Patton's forces broke through to the river near Coblenz on March 9, 1945. Below, German prisoners march listlessly to captivity along the grass-covered centre strip on the Frankfort motor-road near Giessen (taken by the U.S. 3rd Army on March 29) as vehicles of the U.S. 6th Armoured Division head for Kassel.

That sums up the situation at this stage admirably, and seldom has so good an opportunity been afforded of looking into the mind of a commander at a given moment and receiving his appreciation of the situation based on the information available at the time. In the event the Ruhr pocket was to yield 300,000 prisoners; elements of eighteen German divisions from the 1st Parachute, 5th Panzer and 15th Armies had been enclosed by skilfully conceived and rapidly executed manoeuvres, in what General Eisenhower describes as the " largest double envelopment in history."

The pause envisaged by General Eisenhower proved to be hardly perceptible. Leaving strong forces to deal with the Ruhr pocket, the 1st and 9th Armies (the latter now having rejoined General Bradley's 12th Army Group)

soon started to press eastward. The 9th Army advancing from the Weser to the Elbe, with its armour covering twenty to thirty miles a day, met little or no resistance. By mid-April it had reached the Elbe near Wittenberge and Magdeburg and had established bridge-heads across that river. The 1st Army similarly drove eastward to the Mulde, south of Dessau, by-passing Leipzig and a somewhat aggressive enemy group in the Harz mountains.

The Elbe–Mulde line represented the limits of the advance in accordance with agreement reached with the Russians. The by-passed pockets at Leipzig and in the Harz mountains were speedily reduced, but the liquidation of the Ruhr was a more serious affair. Not only did the Ruhr lie right across the Allied lines of communication, but a force of the size contained in the pocket might have been difficult to hold if it had made a well co-ordinated and determined attempt to break out ; even to break down stubborn defence might entail heavy sacrifice. Liquidation without delay was therefore essential.

Extensive operations developed during the first week after the encirclement, infantry and armour of the 1st and 9th Armies driving into the area from north, east and south while the 15th Army guarded the west side. With all communications to the east cut, and deprived of mobility within the pocket by persistent air attack and shortage of petrol, the Germans, who were commanded by Field-Marshal Model, were given few opportunities of taking co-ordinated action, and the attack made steady progress. Ninth Army troops entered Essen on April 9, to find that no work had been done in the huge Krupp armament factories since the R.A.F. raid of March 11 (*see* illus. in page 3550). Dortmund fell on the 13th, and with the capture of Düsseldorf (where cheering civilian crowds greeted the entry of troops of the U.S. 1st Army) on April 18, resistance in the Ruhr virtually ended a week before patrols of the 273rd Regiment, 69th Division, under V Corps of the U.S. 1st Army, probing east of the Mulde, made the long awaited junction with the Red Army, meeting elements of the Russian 58th Guards Division near Torgau on the Elbe on April 25 (*see* illus. in page 3733).

With that event, the centre of General Eisenhower's great command reached its final objective. The operations of his left wing under Field-Marshal

Operations Against the Ruhr Pocket

Montgomery are described in Chapter 357 ; it remains only to follow the operations of the armies of his right.

The U.S. 3rd Army, having captured Kassel on April 4, pressed on eastward to the south of it. Mühlhausen was taken the following day and the advance continued into Thuringia, though at a slower rate. Erfurt was reached April 11, and cleared next day after violent fighting.

North Cut Off from 'Southern Redoubt'

Weimar to the east of it, where the Constituent Assembly of the new German Republic met in 1919 and adopted the so-called Weimar Constitution, was occupied without opposition on April 12. The university town of Jena, with the Zeiss optical works, was captured and the Saale river crossed on April 13. At this stage, the left of the U.S. 3rd Army continued its advance eastward to reach the upper Mulde in prolongation of the U.S. 1st Army front ; and beyond that river the advance continued to the Dresden–Munich highway south of Chemnitz (surrounded by April 19). This thrust closed the main avenue by which the German Armies in the north might have joined those in the south for a last stand in the "Southern Redoubt," although probably it had

HEIDELBERG INTACT

The ancient town of Heidelberg, on the Neckar River and famous for its university, the oldest in Germany, fell practically undamaged into the hands of the U.S. 7th Army on March 30, 1945. Only German forces to remain were a few snipers who were soon rounded up by the incoming U.S. troops and marched to the cages on the outskirts of the town. *Photo, Keystone*

WHITE FLAG AT LEIPZIG

At Leipzig, captured by the U.S. 1st Army on the night of April 19–20, 1945, fanatical S.S. troops held out in the huge monument on the outskirts which commemorates the victory over Napoleon in 1813. The Nazis were forced to surrender by heavy artillery fire at point-blank range. Here a white flag flutters from the monument as U.S. troops move in. *Photo, Associated Press*

already become too late for any large force to make the attempt.

The main strength of the U.S. 3rd Army after the crossing of the Saale was directed south-east toward the mountains of Czechoslovakia and the Danube Valley, in order to complete the encirclement of the strong German force in Bohemia, already threatened from the north and east by the Russians (*see* page 3626) and to co-operate with the U.S. 7th Army in its advance into Bavaria. Meantime the 7th Army, after clearing up the pockets by-passed by the 3rd Army, was advancing through Baden and north-western Bavaria

U.S. AND FRENCH ATTACK IN SOUTH

Towards the end of March 1945, Lieutenant-General Alexander M. Patch's U.S. 7th Army and the French 1st Army, under General de Lattre de Tassigny, launching offensives in the south, linked up south of Heidelberg. 1. U.S. shells explode near the ruined bridge across the River Main at Würzburg. This famous Bavarian town was cleared on April 6 after fierce street fighting. 2. In Schweinfürt, centre of Germany's ball-bearing industry and heavily damaged in repeated attacks by Allied bombers, civilians are detained for questioning. The town was entered on April 11 by the Americans. 3. The only building standing at Ulm, taken jointly by the U.S. 7th and French 1st Armies on April 24, was the Gothic cathedral with one of the tallest spires in Germany.

U.S. THIRD ARMY ACROSS THE DANUBE

Troops of General Patton's U.S. 3rd Army crossed into Czechoslovakia on April 21, 1945, to capture the town of Asch, two miles inside the frontier. Five days later other units of the same army reached the Danube, and within 24 hours captured Regensburg (Ratisbon). 1. U.S. patrols comb Asch for snipers. 2. Tank of the U.S. 65th Infantry Division is ferried across the Danube. 3. Particularly troublesome snipers, captured near Regensburg, were forced to lie down, head on hands. *Photos, U.S. Official; Associated Press*

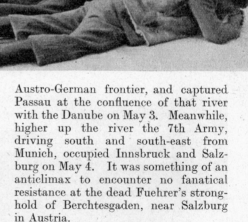

towards Nuremberg. On its right the French were directed on Stuttgart and were responsible for clearing the Black Forest area.

Both armies encountered considerable resistance, and though the U.S. 7th Army had reached Würzburg by April 3

U.S. 7th Army Reaches Nuremberg

and was in touch with the French in Baden, sharp fighting continued for some days round Würzburg, which was by-passed. Farther south, at Heilbronn on the Neckar, General Patch's forces fought a hard nine days' battle before they cleared the town on April 12. By the middle of the month, the right of the U.S. 3rd Army was driving southwards into northern Bavaria, and after capturing Coburg, former capital of the Grand Duchy of Saxe-Coburg-Gotha, on April 11, entered Bayreuth on April 14. Late in the evening of the 16th advanced troops of the U.S. 7th Army broke into Nuremberg. Nuremberg was bitterly defended by a garrison of 4,000 fanatical S.S. men, but the city, much damaged, was finally captured on April 20. The 7th Army then swung south into the Bavarian plain, racing towards Munich.

By this time the 3rd Army had spread along the north-west border of Czechoslovakia, and on April 21 captured the town of Asch, two miles inside the Czech frontier. The following day the French in the south, having completed the occupation of Stuttgart and Freiburg, reached the Swiss frontier north-west of Constance, cutting off all the Germans in the Black Forest area.

The whole of General Eisenhower's right wing was by now sweeping south-eastwards in the Danube valley in a line broken only by a few German

pockets. The armour of the U.S. 3rd Army in a rapid dash approached Regensburg (Ratisbon) on the Danube (April 23) and the following day, higher up the river, the 7th Army's 44th Infantry Division, with troops of the French 1st Army, captured Ulm, scene of one of Napoleon's most remarkable victories, leaving a German pocket at Gemund behind it.

The pace of the sweep continued to increase. On April 22 the U.S. 7th Army crossed the Danube at Dillingen; on the 26th, the U.S. 3rd Army cleared both Ingolstadt and Regensburg, the river port at which, for so long during the war, oil from Rumania had been delivered to Germany. On that day also, farther to the south-east, 3rd Army troops crossed the Austrian frontier. On April 28 the 7th Army captured Augsburg and next day entered Munich where all resistance ceased on April 30; the famous beer cellar where the Nazi movement was born being still recognizable. There was now little more to be done than to gain contact with the Russians in Austria and to close the back door on the German forces in Italy. The western frontier of Czechoslovakia had been sealed off, leaving the Germans there no hope of escape from the advancing Russians.

By May 1, U.S. 3rd Army armour in force had reached the river Inn on the

Austro-German frontier, and captured Passau at the confluence of that river with the Danube on May 3. Meanwhile, higher up the river the 7th Army, driving south and south-east from Munich, occupied Innsbruck and Salzburg on May 4. It was something of an anticlimax to encounter no fanatical resistance at the dead Fuehrer's stronghold of Berchtesgaden, near Salzburg in Austria.

The surrender of the Germans in Italy on April 29 (*see page 3717*) and in north-west Germany on May 4 (*see page 3666*) proved infectious, and everywhere German

German Willingness to Surrender

senior commanders showed willingness to abandon the struggle. Nevertheless, it was necessary to press on in order to prevent fanatical groups forming in the inaccessible mountain regions, and to round up wanted individuals who might be trying to escape into neutral countries. From Innsbruck a column of the U.S. 7th Army drove on into the Brenner Pass till it made contact with the 5th Army coming up

U.S. TROOPS SEIZE HOME OF NAZISM

When U.S. 7th Army units entered Munich, the capital of Bavaria, on April 29, 1945, they found it heavily damaged by Allied bombers. Above, released British prisoners chat with the U.S. guard outside the famous Beer Cellar, birthplace of the Nazi party (see also page 1807). Right, wreckage of the Victory Arch in the Ludwigstrasse.

Photos, Keystone

BERCHTESGADEN IN ALLIED HANDS

Formations of General Patch's U.S. 7th Army which captured Berchtesgaden on May 4, 1945, found Hitler's mountain retreat still smoking from the effects of the R.A.F. raid of April 25. Here, American and French troops inspect the grounds of the badly damaged house in which the Fuehrer, gazing out on the snow-capped Bavarian Alps, had planned world-conquest.

from the south (*see* illus. in page 3718). The 3rd Army also continued its advance down the Danube, entering Linz on May 5. On that day the enemy's Army Group G, commanded by General Schulz and comprising all German forces in Austria and Bavaria, surrendered unconditionally to General Devers, whose 6th Army Group thus brought its immensely long advance from the south coast of France to a triumphant conclusion: since August 15, 1944, it had advanced an average of more than three miles a day.

The surrender on May 4 of the armies facing Field-Marshal Montgomery was followed less than three days later by a general unconditional surrender to the Allies. Very early on May 7 Colonel-General Gustav Jodl (Chief of Staff of the German Army), General-Admiral Hans Georg von Friedeburg (C.-in-C. of the German Navy), and Major Wilhelm Oxenius (A.D.C. to Jodl) reached the school-house at Rheims which for the past three months had been General Eisenhower's G.H.Q. They were offered the surrender terms

Germany Surrenders to the Allies

SAIPAN—WHENCE U.S. HEAVY BOMBERS SET OUT FOR JAPAN

The capture of the Mariana Islands (see page 3264), between June 15 and August 10, 1944, marked an important development in the air war in the Pacific by bringing the Japanese mainland within bombing distance for Pacific-based Super-Fortresses (see maps in pages 3274 and 3490). The round trip to Tokyo and back was under 3,000 miles, and the first bombing mission left Saipan for the enemy capital on November 24, 1944. Here, B-29 Super-Fortresses are parked, each in its own bay, on a vast airfield constructed on Saipan   *Photo, New York Times Photos*

NUREMBERG FALLS TO THE U.S. SEVENTH ARMY

Nuremberg, medieval city of Bavaria and scene of spectacular Nazi Party rallies, fell on April 20, 1945, to American troops after four days' bitter fighting. On April 16, the 3rd and 45th Infantry Divisions of General Patch's U.S. 7th Army broke into the city from four directions. Particularly stiff resistance was put up by some 4,000 S.S. troops. Above, U.S. armour, watched by children, probes the ruins of the old inner city. Below, the desolate Zeppelin Stadium from whose tiered rostrum Hitler had formerly harangued his Party and the world. *Photos Keystone*

GERMAN SURRENDER IN THE WAR ROOM AT RHEIMS

1. The ceremony at Rheims, May 7, 1945 (see page 3802) : left to right, facing the Germans, Lt.-General Sir Frederick Morgan (British Army) ; General François Savez, French Deputy Chief of Staff for National Defence ; Admiral Sir Harold Burrough (Royal Navy) ; Lt. Gen. W. Bedell Smith, Chief of Staff to General Eisenhower ; Major-General Ivan Souslaparov, head of the Russian Military Mission in France ; General Carl Spaatz, Commanding General, U.S. Strategic Air Forces in Europe ; and Air-Marshal Sir J. M. Robb. 2. The German delegates : left to right, Major Wilhelm Oxenius, A.D.C. to Jodl ; Colonel-General Gustav Jodl, Army Chief of Staff ; and General-Admiral Hans Georg von Friedeburg, Navy C.-in-C. 3. General Eisenhower about to address his staff. On his left is Air Chief Marshal Sir Arthur Tedder.

Photos, U.S. Official; British Newspaper Pool; Keystone

U.S. ARMIES TAKE 325,000 PRISONERS IN RUHR 'POCKET'

The Ruhr was encircled on April 1, 1945, when the U.S. 1st and 9th Armies made contact near Lippstadt. Field-Marshal Model tried to strike out from Hamm in the north and from Siegen in the south, but enemy attempts to break through the Americans were everywhere forced back. On April 14 the 'pocket' was split at Hagen, and two days later the eastern half collapsed, 80,000 prisoners being taken in 24 hours. Prisoners taken by American troops during their 18-days' liquidation of the Ruhr 'pocket' totalled 325,000, including 30 generals. Here, near Gummersbach, an industrial centre east of Cologne, are some of 82,000 prisoners captured by the XVIII Airborne Corps of the U.S. 9th Army.

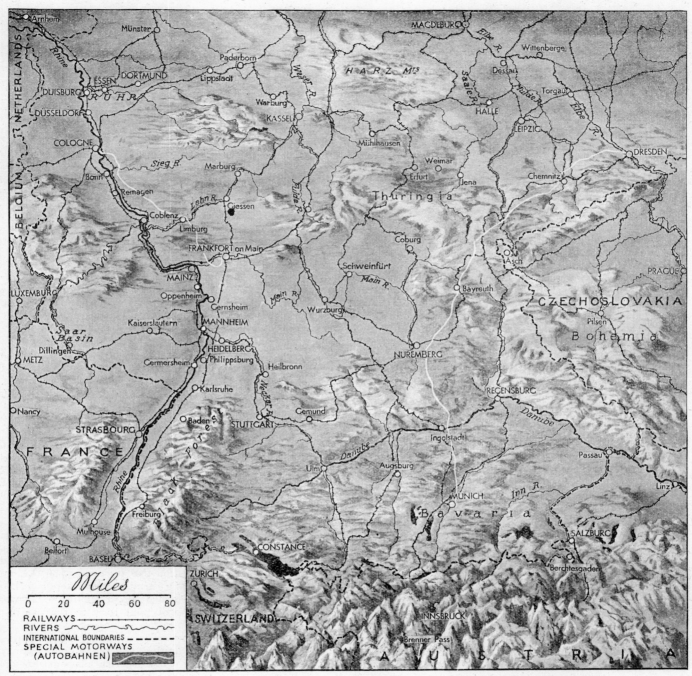

LAST BATTLEGROUNDS IN CENTRAL EUROPE

This map shows the area covered in the final stages of the war in Europe by the Allied Sixth and Twelfth Army Groups, ending with the linking of American and Russian forces at Torgau and at Prague, of Americans of the 7th Army and Americans of the 5th at the Brenner Pass.

in writing : these called for the unconditional surrender of all German land, sea, and air forces to the Allied Expeditionary Force and the Soviet High Command, all such German forces to remain where they were until otherwise ordered. They answered "yes" when asked if they understood the terms ; and at 2·41 a.m. on May 7 Germany's unconditional surrender was signed by Colonel-General Jodl on behalf of Germany, by General Bedell Smith (Chief of Staff to General Eisenhower) on behalf of the Allied Supreme Command, by General Souslaparov for the Soviet Union, and by General Savez for France.

In Czechoslovakia the Germans under Field-Marshal Schörner continued to offer stubborn resistance to the Russians (*see* page 3626). Moreover the Czech liberation forces, which had succeeded in gaining control of Prague, were in considerable danger. The U.S. 3rd Army, therefore, advancing probably farther than had been originally intended, entered Pilsen, second largest city in Bohemia, on May 6, and pushed

on towards Prague, entered by a small number of Americans as well as by Russian tanks on May 10. General Patton's advance and rapid movements, which had sealed off the western side of Czechoslovakia, helped greatly to convince Schörner that it was useless to continue the attempt he at first made to prolong resistance, even after Doenitz had given the order for unconditional surrender. The massive drive of General

SURRENDER IN BAVARIA AND AUSTRIA

On May 5, 1945, the German Army Group G, comprising the 1st and 19th Armies, surrendered near Haar to General Jacob L. Devers, commanding the 6th Army Group, seen (right centre) explaining the terms to the Germans on his left. At Innsbruck that day (left), Major-General Edward H. Brooks (at head of table), commanding the VI Corps, U.S. 7th Army, accepted the surrender of the 19th Army from Lieutenant-General Erich Brandenberger (back to camera).

Eisenhower's right wing through Bavaria into Austria, coupled with the victory of Alexander's armies in Italy, must have convinced all Germans that the idea of holding out in the Southern Redoubt must be abandoned.

As on Eisenhower's northern front the decisive battle had been fought between the Rhine and Maas, so also on his southern and centre fronts the really decisive battle was fought west of the Rhine in the Saar. It is true that the encirclement of the Ruhr and the liquidation of Army Group B within it had decisive effects, for it eliminated the last source from which the enemy could draw warlike supplies. The half-hearted and patchy resistance offered in the Ruhr once it was encircled hardly, however, deserves to rank as a decisive battle. That in no wise diminishes the credit due to the American armies for brilliant and rapid exploitation of unforeseen footholds across the Rhine. The use made of the somewhat unpromising bridge-head at Remagen was masterly: it was the main factor in securing the encirclement of the Ruhr.

Tribute must also be paid to the energy, initiative and speed displayed by subordinate commanders and troops, and by the Service of Supply in dealing with unexpected situations. On no occasion were the armies so surprised by unexpected success as to be unready, as sometimes happens, to seize the opportunity. But perhaps what showed best how highly skilled and efficient the American armies had become was the rapid sorting out of the tangled situation in the Saar and the direction of the armies to their new objectives. Those who can recall the confusion and congestion that occurred when General Pershing's armies in 1918 were launched in their final offensive into the Argonne can hardly fail to note the contrast and to realize how essential it is to give rapidly organized armies opportunities of acquiring experience and training under active service conditions before they are called on for a decisive effort.

Tribute to American Skill

Those who argue that the war might have been won in 1944 seem apt to ignore the dangers of premature attempts. The experience gained in Tunisia, Sicily and Italy and in Normandy, apart from the vast extent of material preparations necessary for reopening and expanding the western front, was needed to turn the American armies into the magnificent war machine they became. Those gallant armies might have failed through lack of experience if their initial test had been too severe, and the cost and loss of time in retrieving early failure cannot be estimated.

DOCUMENT THE GERMANS SIGNED AT RHEIMS

These two pages of typescript formed the main surrender document signed at Rheims on May 7, 1945. The brief instrument was signed by Colonel-General Gustav Jodl (for the Germans), Lieut.-General W. Bedell Smith (on behalf of General Eisenhower), General Ivan Souslaparov (for the Soviet High Command), and Major-General Savez (French Army).

ACT OF MILITARY SURRENDER

1. We the undersigned, acting by authority of the German High Command, hereby surrender unconditionally to the Supreme Commander, Allied Expeditionary Force and simultaneously to the Soviet High Command all forces on land, sea, and in the air who are at this date under German control.

2. The German High Command will at once issue orders to all German military, naval and air authorities and to all forces under German control to cease active operations at 2301 hours Central European time on 8 May and to remain in the positions occupied at that time. No ship, vessel, or aircraft is to be scuttled, or any damage done to their hull, machinery or equipment.

3. The German High Command will at once issue to the appropriate commanders, and ensure the carrying out of any further orders issued by the Supreme Commander, Allied Expeditionary Force and by the Soviet High Command.

4. This act of military surrender is without prejudice to, and will be superseded by any general instrument of surrender imposed by, or on behalf of the United Nations and applicable to GERMANY and the German armed forces as a whole.

5. In the event of the German High Command or any of the forces under their control failing to act in accordance with this Act of Surrender, the Supreme Commander, Allied Expeditionary Force and the Soviet High Command will take such punitive or other action as they deem appropriate.

Signed at Rheims at 0241 on the 7th day of May, 1945.
France

On behalf of the German High Command.

Jodl

IN THE PRESENCE OF

On behalf of the Supreme Commander, Allied Expeditionary Force.

On behalf of the Soviet High Command.

W. B. Smith   *Sousloparov*

Major General, French Army
(Witness)

-1-   -2-

3808

August 1. Record force of 820 Marianas-based Super-Fortresses heavily bombed Hachioji, Mito, Nagaoka, and Toyama (Japan) after warning by leaflet; Kawasaki (Tokyo Bay) also attacked.

August 2. U.S. Liberators and Mustangs from Okinawa bombed Kagoshima and Fukuoka, attacked Kyushu airfields and set nitrogen factories ablaze at Marushima. The King received President Truman on board H.M.S. " Renown " in Plymouth Sound.

August 3. Admiral Nimitz announced that Super-Fortresses had mined every important Japanese harbour as well as all those from Korea to the Soviet frontier, thus achieving a " complete shipping blockade of the Japanese homeland."

August 4. General MacArthur, appointed C.-in-C. of all Allied forces based on the Ryukyus, announced that these islands, with the Philippines, " form a great semi-circular base from which a mighty invasion force is being forged for the final conquest of Japan."

August 5. Over 400 U.S. aircraft from Okinawa heavily attacked Tarmuizu (S. Kyushu). Super-Fortresses dropped warning leaflets on 12 more Japanese towns. S.E.A.C. announced that over 10,000 Japanese had been killed or captured in Burma following the enemy's break-out from the Pegu Yoma. Melbourne announced the seizure of the " Tachibana Maru," Japanese so-called hospital-ship, carrying arms and troops.

August 6. First atomic bomb dropped, by a single Super-Fortress, causing unprecedented devastation at Hiroshima (Honshu); emergency meeting of Japanese cabinet called; four " warned " enemy cities bombed by Marianas-based Super-Fortresses. Australians in S.E. Borneo completely cleared Balikpapan Bay and coastal airstrips.

August 7. Super-Fortresses from the Marianas heavily attacked the Japanese naval arsenal of Toyakawa; Mijakonojo and Kagoshima (Kyushu) also bombed. Chinese captured Yeungkeong, coastal town 150 miles W. of Hongkong, isolating the Japanese forces on the Liuchow peninsula.

August 8. The U.S.S.R. formally declared war on Japan, hostilities to begin at midnight. Heavy Super-Fortress raids on Yawata, Fukuyama and Japanese industrial and military targets. Chinese forces captured Kukiang Island, last enemy foothold near the port of Foochow.

August 9. The Red Army at dawn attacked along a 1,000-mile front in Manchuria, crossed Amur and Ussari rivers. At Nagasaki (W. coast of Kyushu) second atomic bomb dropped, obliterating the great port; Super-Fortresses dropped 3,000,000 leaflets on Japan calling for an end to the war before further atomic bombs were dropped.

August 10. Tokyo radio announced that the Japanese Government was prepared to accept the Allied peace terms as laid down at Potsdam, provided that the Emperor's sovereignty was maintained. Red Army made important gains

on all Manchurian sectors. British cruisers and destroyers with the U.S. 3rd Fleet, steaming inshore, bombarded Kamaishi, 90 miles N. of Sendai. Royal Netherlands Air Force attacked Tjilatjap, on the S. coast of Java.

August 11. Hostilities continued in Manchuria; Soviet bombers attacked railway targets and shipping in Korean ports. British and U.S. carrier aircraft heavily bombed Tokyo area.

August 12. Red Army advance continued in Manchuria; aided by Soviet Pacific Fleet, Russians captured enemy naval base of Rashin (Korea) and port of Yuki. Far Eastern Air Force heavily attacked Kyushu, including military base of Miyazaki.

August 11–13. British and U.S. carrier-aircraft destroyed 1,300 enemy planes in Kanto Plain round Tokyo. Allied naval force attacked Paramushiro and other targets in the Kuriles.

August 13. Rapid Russian advances in Manchuria included the capture of Halun-Arzhan, Sholun and Zamlinao. Moscow reported an advance by Marshal Malinovsky's troops of 200 miles in four days.

August 14. President Truman and Mr. Attlee announced Japan's unconditional surrender. Fighting continued in Manchuria, the Red Army shattering the entire network of Japanese communications in eastern Manchuria, capturing Korean port of Seishin, advancing into the southern (Japanese) section of Sakhalin. U.S.S.R. and China signed at Moscow a treaty of friendship and alliance. Pétain sentenced to death in Paris, the sentence being commuted to life-detention.

August 15. Russians announced continuation of Manchurian offensive, as enemy had given no " cease fire " order. In Burma, Lord Louis Mountbatten ordered the suspension of hostilities " so far as consistent with the safety of Allied forces."

August 16. Japanese in Manchuria launched a counter-offensive on all fronts; overcoming counter-attacks, troops of the 1st Far Eastern Army occupied Wanching; other Red Army forces captured Chiamussu on the Sungari river. In Burma, fighting continued in the Karen hills, where the Japanese were apparently unaware of the end of the war.

August 17. Russians in Manchuria took 20,000 prisoners; Wuli, Ninguta and Tumin occupied. In S.E. China, General Ku Chu-tung issued surrender instructions to the Japanese. U977, with a crew of 32, surrendered at Mar del Plata, in the Argentine.

August 18. Shigemitsu, the new Japanese Foreign Minister, broadcast to the Japanese people, openly admitting defeat and warning them against taking an over-optimistic view of the Potsdam declaration. Japanese in the Shanghai area liberated 6,000 British subjects. R.A.F. dropped over 500,000 leaflets in Burma calling on the enemy to lay down their arms; A.-A. fire met near Moulmein.

August 19. Japanese surrender envoys

arrived at General MacArthur's H.Q. at Manila. Japanese forces in S. China surrendered at Canton. Russians announced that resistance by the Kwantung army in Manchuria had ceased on most sectors.

August 20. Soviet Transbaikal Army occupied Mukden (capital of Manchuria until 1932); 2nd Far Eastern Army took Harbin in central Manchuria; enemy resistance ceased in Karafuto (Japanese Sakhalin). Chinese High Command announced that Chinese troops were advancing virtually unopposed through Japanese-occupied China. Last Japanese at Tarakan surrendered to Australians.

August 21. Red Army, advancing unopposed through Manchuria, took 52,000 prisoners, including 4 generals of the Kwantung army. U.S. Navy statement announced that Japan had lost all but 49 of the 369 warships with which she entered the war.

August 22. Soviet airborne troops landed at Port Arthur and nearby port of Dairen, disarmed garrisons; Red Army units landed in Kurile Islands and received Japanese surrender.

August 23. Stalin announced the occupation of all Manchuria, S. Sakhalin, and the Kurile Islands. Japanese declared that nearly ten million people had suffered—death, wounds or destruction of homes—in Allied air raids.

August 24. Soviet High Command announced that the 1st Far Eastern Army was advancing along the E. coast of Korea, having captured Kanto, and that in Manchuria another 14,000 Japanese had been taken prisoner. The Chinese Government ratified the United Nations Charter.

August 25. Chinese High Command announced that Chinese troops, having crossed the Yangtse, had entered Nanking.

August 26. Japanese envoys arrived at Rangoon from Saigon. Chinese troops entered Shanghai and advanced rapidly through the whole of China; Chinese communist troops captured the Boca Tigris forts controlling Pearl river approaches to Canton.

August 27. British, U.S., Dominions and Dutch warships anchored in Sagami Bay, near Tokyo.

August 28. Preliminary arrangements for enemy's surrender in the S.E.A.C. theatre signed at Rangoon by Lt.-Gen. F. A. M. Browning and Lt.-Gen. Numata. Russians completed occupation of Japanese Sakhalin.

August 29. Troops of the U.S. 11th Airborne Division landed at Atsugi airfield, near Tokyo; Allied warships entered Tokyo Bay. Russians announced the capture of a total of 513,000 prisoners (including 81 generals) in Manchuria.

August 30. U.S. troops entered Yokohama, where General MacArthur set up his H.Q.; Yokosuka naval base formally surrendered to General Clement, U.S. Army. British naval force entered Hongkong harbour.

August 31. U.S. 8th Army troops completed occupation of Yokohama; British Marines went ashore at Yokosuka to take over a section of the naval base.

BRITISH TROOPS IN NORWAY AGAIN

On May 11, 1945, some 300 British and Norwegian troops, including men of the British 1st Airborne Division, which fought at Arnhem (see Chapter 325), arrived by air in Norway, flown in aircraft of R.A.F. Transport Command. They formed the vanguard of the Allied forces of liberation whose task was to take over from the 400,000 Germans still in occupation. 1. Supplies being unloaded from a Halifax at Gardermoen airfield, near Oslo. 2. British airborne men being welcomed on entering the capital by lorry to take part in a triumphal procession. 3. Crowds throng the quayside at Oslo to greet units of the Royal Navy after the liberation. *Photos, British Official ; Keystone*

Chapter 370

ALLIES LIBERATE NORWAY AND DENMARK

Northern Norway was freed by the Russians during 1944 (see Chapter 316), but the rest of the country remained, like Denmark, under German occupation until the capitulation of Germany's armed forces in north-west Germany on May 4. In this chapter, Mr. O. F. Knudsen, of the Royal Norwegian Embassy in London, and Mr. Elias Bredsdorff, of University College, London, tell the history of their respective countries during 1945

THE passive warfare waged throughout the early years of the German occupation of Norway came to an end in the autumn of 1944 when the Red Army entered north Norway, driving before them some eight divisions of German troops defeated in Finland (*see* page 3203). From **NORWAY** that time the Germans attempted to extricate all the troops they could spare from Norway in order to send them to the hard-pressed fronts in Germany. The struggle inside Norway took on increasingly the character of a military conflict. The Norwegian Forces of the Interior, co-operating with the Allied Air Forces and Navies, set themselves to disrupt all communications throughout Norway. Organized sabotage groups, with the help of parachutists and arms and ammunition dropped from the air, conducted a carefully planned offensive against all means of German communication—railways, harbours, shipping, petrol storage dumps, etc.

Norwegian parachutists from Britain cut the three railway lines linking north Norway with south, and in the night of March 14–15 a Norwegian Commando unit trained in Britain, acting in co-operation with the Forces of the Interior, cut every railway line connecting Oslo with the German disembarkation ports in south Norway. On February 8, men of another Norwegian Commando unit seized thirteen tugs at Fredrikstad in daylight and sailed eleven of them to Sweden (two had to be scuttled for lack of fuel), capturing the salvage vessel "Uredd" on the way. Ships were blown up in Oslo and other ports. German shipping trying to evacuate troops by sea was subject to constant attack (*see* page 3498).

The disruption of communications brought about an increasing food shortage throughout the country. In addition, the German forces in Norway—amounting to about a tenth of the total population—were thrown back entirely on the country's internal food supplies. The Norwegian people were approaching starvation. Grain and potato supplies were critically low, and even fish was scarce.

German terrorism increased. On February 9 and 10, 34 hostages were shot following the assassination on February 8 of Major-General Karl Martinsen, head of Quisling's Security Police. They included lawyers, doctors, professors and business men, and were executed for "murder and sabotage," "secret Communist organization," and aiding refugees. On March 16, 14 other patriots were shot. R.A.F. Mosquitoes attacked the Gestapo headquarters in Oslo on December 31, 1944 (previously bombed on September 25, 1942—*see* illus. in page 2176—and since repaired), and early in 1945 the Germans transferred 30 hostages to cells in the Gestapo building, presumably in the hope that their presence might prevent further attacks. Among these hostages was Einar Gerhardsen, chairman of the Labour Party.

Although the Germans were evacuating troops from Norway, they seemed to have no intention of abandoning the country without a struggle. It had a high strategic value and was well suited for a last desperate stand. The German naval bases strung out along the west coast from Alta Fjord to Bergen sheltered some 300 U-boats, used against the Atlantic sea routes and the Murmansk convoys. Norway, together with Denmark, offered a protection for Germany's northern flank and blocked the Baltic.

A large part of the 50,000 German Navy men in Norway were helping to man the 300 coastal batteries which lay between Lyngen Fjord in the north and the Swedish frontier in the south. The Luftwaffe, too, had about 50,000 men in Norway, and was constantly improving the airfields. German aircraft in Norway numbered 300–400, mostly fighters. The German troops in Norway—they numbered a quarter of a million or more—included several élite units, particularly the Alpine Divisions. About 30,000 men were concentrated in the Narvik area, where the Germans seemed intent on establishing their line against the slowly advancing Russians and Norwegians. The S.S. Lieutenant-General Rediess, Chief of the German Gestapo in Norway, had

German Occupation Forces

FOOD FOR DEVASTATED FINNMARK

Distribution of relief among the people of Finnmark, Norway's northernmost province, 70,000 of whom had been left homeless by the Germans in 1944 (see page 3203), provided a serious problem for the Russian and Norwegian liberating forces early in 1945. Here, food is distributed by inhabitants dressed in heavily padded traditional costume dating back to the 17th century.
Photo, Norwegian Official

KING HAAKON AND PRINCE OLAV AT OSLO

On June 7, 1945, after exactly five years in exile, King Haakon returned to Norway, sailing from England in the cruiser H.M.S. 'Norfolk.' Accompanied here by the Crown Princess Martha, who had shared his exile in Britain, the King drives through cheering crowds in Oslo, the capital. Right, Crown Prince Olav, C.-in-C., Norwegian Forces, takes the salute on Oslo quayside on arriving on board the cruiser H.M.S. 'Devonshire' on May 13.

4–5,000 police troops under his command, and there were also about 6,000 men in Norwegian armed quisling units.

Norwegians were alarmed at the prospect of the Germans' making a last stand in Norway : it was feared that the remainder of the country would be ruined as Finnmark had been (*see* page 3203), and that the economic destruction of Norway would be virtually irreparable. The Norwegian Army in Britain was a small body of specialist troops, and the Norwegian Home Front was already doing all it could against extremely heavy odds. It looked as though substantial Allied help would be needed to overcome the German forces which the Norwegians were doing their best to bottle up in Norway, despite the prospect that this might prolong the war there.

The situation changed radically, however, upon the collapse of the German forces in Germany. The German Commander-in-Chief in Norway, General Böhme, broadcast to his troops at 10.15 p.m. on Monday, May 7 : "From the Supreme Command has come the news that all military operations are to cease." Urging his troops to maintain discipline and order, he said : "Of you, my comrades, I expect an exemplary attitude that will compel the respect of our enemies." He went on to say : "We expect the Norwegian people to show the same discipline as the German soldier has shown to the Norwegians in Norway."

The Norwegian people did, in fact, show remarkable self-control. In the critical days just before the German capitulation, the Home Front Leaders issued directions instructing the people to ignore rumours, abstain from demonstrations and do nothing to provoke the enemy. Many directives to the

NAZI TROOPS LEAVE NORWAY

Before being sent home to Germany, enemy troops in Norway were subjected to a rigid 'screening.' Hoping to evade Allied justice, many S.S. men had disguised themselves as ordinary members of the Wehrmacht. First Germans to leave Norway in mid-July 1945 here go on board a transport at Mandal whence they sailed for Lübeck. Left, German soldier comes up for identification before being allowed to embark. He is being closely watched by Norwegians in the foreground.

Photos, Associated Press ; Central Press ; British Official ; Planet News

same effect were issued by the Norwegian Government and High Command in London. These directives the Norwegian people followed, and as a result the process of liberation was effected smoothly and happily.

Home Front forces took charge of the Government buildings, the Gestapo headquarters, and other strategic points

Home Front Leaders Take Control

in the capital. The Norwegian Government in London authorized the Home Front Leaders to maintain law and order on its behalf. Special temporary officials were appointed from the ranks of the Home Front to assist in eight Government Departments. Vidkun Quisling, with several of his "ministers," surrendered voluntarily on May 10. He was imprisoned in the former Gestapo prison in the Möllergatan in Oslo where many patriots had suffered torture and death. The German Reichs Commissioner Terboven and the Gestapo chief Rediess committed suicide.

On May 8 an Allied Military Delegation arrived by air in Oslo and proceeded immediately to the German Military Headquarters at Lillehammer to settle the formalities of surrender. On May 10 transport planes brought advance units of the Allied Liberation Forces, consisting of nearly 3,000 men of the British 1st Airborne Division and 140 Norwegians, to begin the disarming of the German occupation forces. The immensity of this task was made clear in the words of Crown Prince Olav, Norwegian Commander-in-Chief. "Every fourth male adult in the country is an enemy," he said in an

QUISLING ON TRIAL

Most notorious of all collaborators, Vidkun Quisling, leader of the Norwegian Nazi Party, came up for trial at Oslo on August 20, 1945, three months after his surrender to the Home Front. Violently protesting his innocence, he was found guilty on September 10 and executed by a firing squad on October 24. Here he listens to his defence counsel.

Photos, Associated Press

NORWAY'S NEW PARLIAMENT MEETS

At the Norwegian elections on October 8, 1945, the Labour Party secured a victory over all other parties combined. On November 1, Mr. Einar Gerhardsen (below), 48-year old Labour leader, resistance organizer and Prime Minister in the Coalition Government formed in the previous June, became Prime Minister of a new Labour Government. Above, King Haakon reads his speech at the opening of the new Parliament. On his left is Prince Olav.

Order of the Day. Crown Prince Olav arrived in Oslo on May 13 on board the cruiser H.M.S. "Devonshire," together with five members of the Norwegian Government from London. The remaining members of the Government, including the Prime Minister, Johan Nygaardsvold, arrived on May 31. They were received by Paal Berg, head of the Norwegian Resistance organization, who emphasized that no differences divided the Home Front and the Government.

King Haakon himself returned on board the cruiser H.M.S. "Norfolk," re-entering his capital on June 7, 1945, on the fifth anniversary of his departure in 1940 and the fortieth anniversary of Norway's restoration as an independent kingdom in 1905. Immense enthusiasm marked the return of both the King and the Government. In accordance with a pledge given in January 1945, Johan Nygaardsvold tendered the resignation of himself and his Cabinet to King Haakon on June 12. At the King's invitation, Einar Gerhardsen, Labour Party Chairman and Mayor of Oslo, who had spent three years in Oranienburg Concentration Camp, formed a new national coalition Government con-

sisting of six Labour, two Communist, two Conservative, one Liberal, one Agrarian and three non-party members. The Storting met for the first time since 1940 on June 14.

The arrest of traitors proceeded smoothly : by June 12, 15,924—about half the membership of Quisling's Nasjonal Samling (*see* page 2719) were in gaol. The trial of Quisling began on August 20. He pleaded "not guilty"

BRITISH FAREWELL PARADE IN NORWAY

In the grounds of the royal palace, Oslo, on December 18, 1945, King Haakon inspected a farewell parade of some 2,000 British troops whom he thanked for the part they had played in liberating his country. They included a composite Guards battalion, the Royal Artillery, R.A.S.C., East Yorkshires and Green Howards. The King was accompanied during the inspection by General Graham, C.-in-C., British forces in Norway. *Photo, Associated Press*

after the liberation, goods to a value of only 106,000,000 kroner (approximately £5,000,000) were exported. To co-ordinate and promote Norwegian exports, an Export Council was set up in November. A number of commercial and financial agreements were concluded with European countries, most important being the Anglo-Norwegian Financial Agreement signed on November 8, which fixed the rate of exchange at 20 kroner to the £1, and authorized the free use of Norwegian sterling balances, to which no limit was set, within the sterling area, Norway giving reciprocal rights to Britain.

Steps Towards Recovery

The Norwegian forces, together with the British, American and Russian forces in Norway, had by September 19 evacuated some 225,000 Germans and repatriated the 46,000 Russian prisoners-of-war in Norway. All Soviet forces stationed in northern Norway were

to charges ranging from high treason and abetment of murder to embezzlement. After much valuable information had come to light, he was found guilty and sentenced to death on September 10. After an unsuccessful appeal to the Supreme Court, he was executed by a firing squad on October 24. (The death penalty, hitherto unknown in Norway, had been provided for treason and other grave crimes by two decrees issued on October 3, 1941 and January 22, 1942 by the Norwegian Government in London.) Several of Quisling's ministers were subsequently tried and condemned, some to death, others to terms of imprisonment and loss of civil rights.

Supplies of food and other essential commodities arrived in sufficient quantities and at a satisfactory rate. The value of imports rose from 116,000,000 kroner (just under £6,000,000) in June to 149,000,000 kroner (just over £7,000,000) in October. The food position improved rapidly, although the clothing situation remained difficult. Unemployment, which had been feared, did not occur—indeed there was a shortage of labour in particular trades. After the calling in of banknotes on September 8 the German-created inflation was checked and production

and labour-effort began to increase. To co-ordinate industrial effort, an Economic Co-ordinating Council was established in July under the chairmanship of the Prime Minister. Home industry made more rapid recovery than the export trade. In the first six months

NARVIK REMEMBERED

Allied representatives on May 28–29, 1946, commemorated in Norway the 6th anniversary of the Battle of Narvik (see pages 808–816). Here British naval officers pay tribute at the grave of Captain B. A. W. Warburton-Lee, V.C., of the destroyer 'Hardy.' Admiral Sir William Whitworth is in the centre. Left, General M. E. Béthouart, who commanded the French forces at Narvik, salutes the British memorial in graveyard there.

withdrawn by September 28, and the last British forces had left before the end of the year.

Norway went to the polls on October 8 —the first General Election in any liberated country. The Labour Party— already the largest party—increased its representation to 76 out of a total of 150 seats in the new Parliament, thus

GERMAN WAR GEAR LEFT IN NORWAY

Allied forces began to arrive in Norway by air on May 9, 1945. From the 350,000 armed Germans there men of the British 1st Airborne Division collected vast quantities of war material. 1. One-man submarines lined up on trailers on a Norwegian beach. 2. Stacks of German rifles being checked. 3. Germans assist a R.A.F. sergeant to make an inventory of spare parts at Kjeller aerodrome, near Oslo. 4. Snow covers the 700-foot keel of the 45,000-ton German battleship 'Tirpitz' in Tromsö Fjord, her resting-place since R.A.F. Lancasters sank her with 12,000-lb. bombs on November 12, 1944.

4 F²

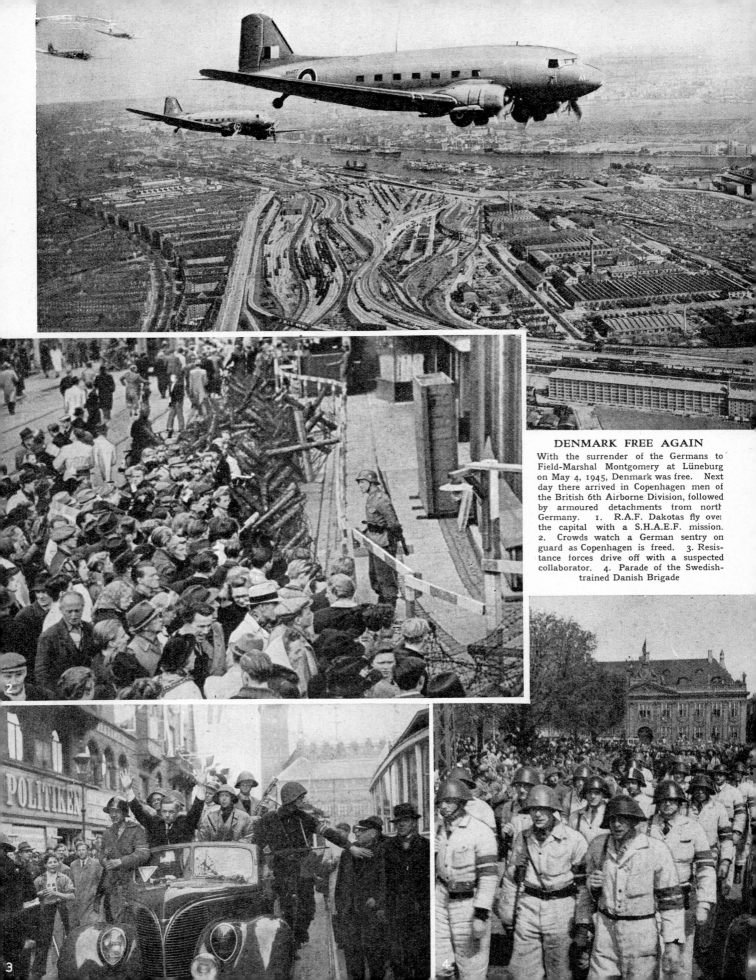

DENMARK FREE AGAIN

With the surrender of the Germans to Field-Marshal Montgomery at Lüneburg on May 4, 1945, Denmark was free. Next day there arrived in Copenhagen men of the British 6th Airborne Division, followed by armoured detachments from north Germany. 1. R.A.F. Dakotas fly over the capital with a S.H.A.E.F. mission. 2. Crowds watch a German sentry on guard as Copenhagen is freed. 3. Resistance forces drive off with a suspected collaborator. 4. Parade of the Swedish-trained Danish Brigade

securing an over-all majority. The Communist and Christian Popular Parties made considerable progress, the first winning eleven (against none previously) and the second eight (against 2). The right-wing parties—Conservative, Liberal and Agrarian—suffered a setback. The Coalition Government resigned on November 1 and Einar Gerhardsen formed a Labour Cabinet in which Trygve Lie was Foreign Minister.

At the opening of Parliament on December 11, King Haakon emphasized the difficult tasks of reconstruction facing the country. The **Norway's Reparations Claim** immensity of these tasks can be gauged from the fact that Norway's reparations claim against Germany amounted to 21,000,000,000 kroner—about £1,000,000,000. Biggest item was the direct cost of the German occupation—12,000,000,000 kroner. In Finnmark Province, where German devastation was total, 12,000 houses and 500 business premises were destroyed in a region of 70,000 inhabitants. It was estimated that the rebuilding of Finnmark would cost 560,000,000 kroner and require 12,000,000 man-days. In the whole of Norway, 100,000 new houses were estimated to be needed.

The Norwegian Parliament ratified the San Francisco Charter on November 14.

This most notable year in Norwegian history also included, on November 27, the celebration of King Haakon's fortieth anniversary as Norway's elected monarch.

As a revenge against the frequent acts of sabotage and the preparations for the formation of a Secret Danish Army, the Germans, **DENMARK** and the Hilfspolizei (*see* page 3201) under their wing, increased their counter-sabotage in 1945. Private houses, newspaper buildings, theatres, and overcrowded passenger-trains were blasted by the Germans, and every week saw new German murders of outstanding Danish personalities, physicians, teachers, clergymen, business men, and others.

On February 19, following the murder by patriots of a notorious local informer at Odense, Hilfspolizei men cordoned off Odense district hospital, murdering four resident doctors, and placed high explosive bombs at fifteen buildings in different parts of the town. The greater part of the main street was reduced to ruins, three of the town's four newspaper offices were wrecked, scores of families were made homeless. An express train from Aalborg to Copenhagen, containing only Danish civilians, was wrecked on February 24, killing ten, injuring 36. Robert Christensen, Chief Engineer of the biggest shipyard in Copenhagen, was murdered in his home by Hilfspolizei men on April 20.

Yet Danish sabotage did not stop, its most important achievement in 1945 being the complete wrecking of the industrial centre "Torotor," which was working for the German war machine. Danish acts of sabotage, it was announced in Copenhagen in February 1946, totalled 2,671—ten in 1940, 19 in 1941, 122 in 1942, 969 in 1943, 867 in 1944, 684 in 1945 (that is to say, up to May 5). The largest number in any one month was 222 in April 1945. Of the total, attacks on railways numbered 1,810.

In 1945, 26 new names were added to the long list of executed prisoners in Denmark. On March 21 the Gestapo headquarters in Copenhagen was bombed by Royal Air Force Mosquitoes. Several members of the Gestapo were killed and also some Danish prisoners, kept as hostages on the top floor of the building, but the majority of these prisoners, including the President of the Danish Freedom Council, Professor Mogens Fog, were liberated by this attack. On April 17 the Gestapo

KING CHRISTIAN RE-OPENS DENMARK'S 'RIGSDAG'

On May 9, 1945, the Danish 'Rigsdag' was re-opened by King Christian (below) who, accompanied by the Queen, drove through cheering crowds in Copenhagen after the ceremony. Four days earlier, Mr. Vilhelm Buhl, ex-Premier, had formed an all-party cabinet with Mr. Christmas Möller (right), leader of the Conservatives, as Foreign Minister, here arriving in the capital after his return from London where he had been chairman of the Danish Council. (See illus. in page 2732.)
Photos, British Newspaper Pool ; Keystone

'MONTY' IN DENMARK

A British naval squadron, headed by the cruiser 'Birmingham' and including the cruiser 'Dido,' on May 9, 1945, arrived in Copenhagen harbour to take over the remnants of the German Navy (see illus. in page 3500) which had surrendered on the 7th. Here, Field-Marshal Montgomery, with H.M.S. 'Birmingham' in the background, shakes hands with naval officers on touring the docks. Left, German naval officers go ashore from the 'Dido.'

headquarters in Funen was also destroyed by the Royal Air Force.

During the last two or three months of the occupation Denmark suffered another German invasion : hundreds of thousands of refugees, especially from East Prussia, came on foot, by ship or by train. To accommodate them, the German authorities took over schools, hotels and public buildings.

On May 4 the news came that the Germans in Holland, North-West Germany and Denmark would capitulate next day. The illegal Resistance Movement—an army of approximately 55,000 men—suddenly appeared in public wearing arm bands in red, white and blue.

For many months before the liberation there had been organized contact between the leaders of the Danish political parties and the leaders of the Resistance movement (the Freedom Council), and they had agreed to form a Danish Government, until a General Election could take place, one half being representatives of the Resistance movement and the other half the leaders of the political parties. The result was that already on May 4 a proclamation announced the formation of a new all-party Government whose Prime Minister was the Social Democrat, Vilhelm Buhl. Christmas Möller (see illus. in page 2732) was Foreign Minister, Professor Mogens Fog Minister for Special Affairs.

The Resistance movement took over control and, assisted by the Danish Brigade, 4,000 strong, trained and armed in Sweden, arrested over 12,000 Danish collaborators by May 27, including Dr. Fritz Clausen, the Danish Nazi leader. Troops of the British 6th Airborne Division, followed by armoured divisions which raced across the country from Germany, entered Copenhagen on May 5. Field-Marshal Montgomery arrived by air on the 13th, and drove for six miles through wildly cheering crowds to Amalienborg, where King Christian conferred on him the seven-hundred-year-old Order of the

Dannebrog, the highest Danish Order of Knighthood.

There was some sharp fighting in Copenhagen on May 5 and for a few days after between Danish patriots and Danish quislings, as well as with groups of Germans who refused to surrender. The cruisers "Prinz Eugen" and "Nürnberg" fired for 25 minutes on May 5 in support of German troops. In the fighting 59 Danes were killed, some 200 injured. The German Commander on the island of Bornholm in the Baltic also refused to surrender, and Soviet troops went ashore there on May 9 after a preliminary bombing. General Korotkov, the Soviet Commander, explained that Russian troops had occupied the island because it lay behind the Soviet zone of occupation in Germany. Soviet forces left the island on April 5, 1946.

LUFTWAFFE SECRETS SHOWN TO R.A.F.

Immediate task confronting the Allies after the unconditional surrender in Europe was the disarming of all enemy forces. Here, a Luftwaffe officer (extreme right) demonstrates to R.A.F. disarmament officers the secrets of the main 'ops' room from which the German Fighter Command in Denmark was controlled. Below, youthful Germans lay down their arms as they cross the frontier from Denmark into Germany on the journey home. *Photo, British Official*

RUSSIANS AT BORNHOLM

Despite the general German capitulation, 15,000 Nazi troops on the Danish Baltic island of Bornholm refused to surrender. The island was invaded by the Russians on May 9, 1945, and the German garrison rounded up. Here, General R. H. Dewing, C.B., D.S.O., head of the Allied Mission to Denmark, inspects a Soviet guard of honour.

The German troops in Denmark were disarmed by the British; the German refugees were left to the care of the Danes, who, more fortunate than other liberated peoples, had ample food, Denmark's productive capacity having been scarcely touched by the occupying power.

Parliament reopened on May 9. It introduced the death penalty, unknown before in Denmark, in a new penal code of May 26. A General Election was held on October 30—the first free election since 1938. **General Election in Denmark** The most marked change was the set-back suffered by the Social Democrats, for sixteen years the Government Party, who lost so many seats that they refrained from forming a new government. The seats gained by the three largest parties, with the figures for the 1943 election in brackets, were: Social Democrats, 48 (66); Conservatives, 26 (31); Farmers' Party, 38 (28). The Communist Party gained 18 seats (3). A new minority Government was formed on November 7 by the Farmers' Party, with Knud Kristensen as Prime Minister, Gustav Rasmussen as Minister of Foreign Affairs.

From San Francisco on June 5 came a unanimous invitation to Denmark to join the United Nations, and a Danish delegation, headed by Henrik Kauffmann, Minister in Washington, took its place at the Conference.

Chapter 371

CAPITULATION IN SOUTH-EAST ASIA

This chapter records the final stages in the Burma campaign which, although minor operations continued right up to the Japanese surrender in August 1945, culminated with the occupation of Rangoon on May 3. It deals also with subsequent local surrenders in the South-East Asia Command and the difficulties they met. Earlier 1944–45 operations in Burma are described in Chapter 345

WITH the fall of Mandalay (*see* page 3535), the bulk of the Japanese forces in Burma were left to the south of that city. They had been reinforced by remnants of Japanese divisions driven south-west from the Ledo Road sector, and though the actual numbers of the enemy were not then known, there were formations from ten enemy divisions and two independent brigades facing General Slim. The 14th Army had the three victorious divisions of XXXIII Corps, and an independent tank brigade. Slim still had the IV Indian Corps " up his sleeve," however, commanded by Lieutenant-General Frank W. Messervy, a Western Desert commander (*see* Chapter 224) of great experience and reputation.

The Japanese grouped below Mandalay were now vulnerable to a " block " on their main lines of communication coming by rail and road from Rangoon through Thazi and Meiktila. Slim had kept IV Corps back for a long-range penetration exploit which was to cut off the main enemy forces and leave the road to Rangoon open ; and after the fall of Mandalay he brought it into operation. The first move in the plan, called by Slim the " Union Jack " plan, was a surprise capture of Meiktila.

The Meiktila dash was the most secret operation of the 1944–1945 Burma offensive. The Japanese had been deceived into believing that in January IV Corps was in the north (where, indeed, 19th division, then part of IV Corps, really was). In actual fact, the main divisions of the Corps (5th, 7th and 17th Indian Divisions, with 255th Independent Tank Brigade) had worked their way south until by February 5 they were near the Irrawaddy, between Pakokku and Chauk. The Corps had removed all its " flashes " and other means of identification and, starting on Christmas Day 1944, had marched south from Kalemyo on the Chindwin, through the Gangaw Valley, with the East Africans, the Lushai Brigade and Chin Levies in front as a cover. Supply throughout had been by air. The obvious objective was Chauk and the Burma oilfields. The Japanese thought so. Slim meant them to.

Two of the divisions, 5th and 17th, together with the tanks, had been geared for speed. These two divisions were on a basis of two motorized brigades and one airborne brigade per division—an arrangement designed to get them from Meiktila to Rangoon in the shortest possible time. At first light on St. Valentine's Day, 7th Division began its crossing of the Irrawaddy, almost opposite the ancient capital of Burma, Pagan. At this point the main river channel is half a mile wide, but at that time of year the waters spread over an area up to two miles broad and are treacherous with sandbanks and currents. On the eastern bank, above the beach there are 70-ft. sandstone cliffs, fissured by streams. The Japanese did not expect a crossing there, but they had machine-gun nests set in the cliffs, and machine-gun fire met the boats as

Advance on Pagan

MEIKTILA FALLS AFTER SURPRISE 'DASH'

Centre of Burma's main rail and road communications, Meiktila, eighty miles south of Mandalay, was captured on February 28, 1945, after a surprise ' dash ' by the 17th Indian Division thrusting eastwards across the Irrawaddy. Here in the shadow of a Burmese temple, crews of three-inch mortars pour their shells into the town from the outskirts. Right, radio telephonists of the 14th Army set up a command post in one of Meiktila's many temples

Photos, British Official

FOURTEENTH ARMY RACES THE BURMA MONSOON

With five weeks to go before the monsoon, the 14th Army in Burma in April 1945 was 340 miles from Rangoon. The Japanese were trying to hold a line from Meiktila stretching westwards towards the Irrawaddy. Here, troops of the 6th/7th Rajput Rifles mop up in Pyawbwe, the railway town 26 miles south-east of Meiktila, occupied on April 20. Left, forward observation post in the jungle east of Toungoo, reported captured on April 26. *Photos, British and Indian Official*

they came within range. But the landing was a success; British and Indian troops got ashore, established bridge-heads, and picked off the machine-gunners. When the sun came up, more troops, including Gurkhas, crossed unopposed. Pagan, "the city of 5,000 pagodas," and one of the wonders of the East, where no Japanese had been quartered and which had, therefore, escaped damage, was captured intact.

On February 19, 17th Division, with Sherman tanks, Priest self-propelled guns, armoured cars, scissors bridges and trucks, made another river crossing east of Pakokku and began the rush on Meiktila, 85 miles away. The surprise still held; but speed was essential and the armour churned over dusty roads and rough tracks trampled across the scrub desert.

The Japanese had not tried to hold Pagan, but they resisted in some of the villages. The tanks made short work of them, clearing Taungtha on February 24, and on the 27th seizing an airstrip 14 miles from Meiktila. Within

a few hours the first Dakotas touched down there carrying technicians, control personnel, and a U.S. airborne anti-aircraft unit. Then came plane after plane loaded with infantry. Before nightfall a concentration of heavy and light A.A. batteries had been set up, and a defensive perimeter established. Meiktila was captured next day, after fanatical resistance by the Japanese garrison had been overcome, and the British forces advanced to cut the Rangoon–Mandalay railway near Thazi. (Thazi itself was not taken till April 10.) The main airfield at Meiktila was not reported taken until March 31.

The capture of Pakokku by Gurkha and Indian troops was announced on March 7. Resistance in the oilfield area centred on Chauk was more stubborn.

With the capture of Meiktila, Slim

had broken the back of Japanese resistance in Burma. He had split the Japanese Army and had cut the main force off from Rangoon. This force was now between the hammer of XXXIII Corps (pushing south from Mandalay) and the anvil of IV Corps at Meiktila, and **Large Enemy Force Liquidated** although pushed for time (the monsoon was now only six weeks away), Slim decided that it must be eliminated before he continued the advance on Rangoon. In the first week of April the two Corps closed in, and on April 7 S.E.A.C. issued an announcement that "in the central Burma plain our troops have reached the end of a definite phase of operations. The large Japanese force cut off between Mandalay and Meiktila has been liquidated and its remnants driven into the hills south-east of Mandalay."

The time had come for the last move of the "Union Jack" plan. Slim moved XXXIII Corps south-westwards, behind IV Corps, to the Irrawaddy and the oilfields round Chauk. At the

ALLIES CUT OFF JAPANESE WEST OF PEGU

On April 30, 1945, S.E.A.C. announced that the 14th Army had captured Pegu, important road and rail junction 50 miles north of Rangoon, thus cutting the enemy's last escape route from Rangoon and lower Burma to Siam usable by motor transport. Here, Sherman tanks go forward through the blazing outskirts of the town. Right, a British patrol on the Pegu canal passes the ruins of a village in a monsoon-flooded area east of Waw. *Photos, British Official*

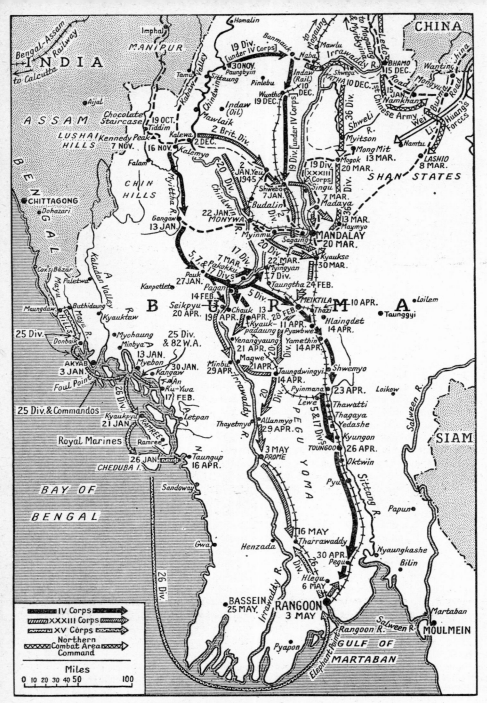

ALLIED RECONQUEST OF BURMA

This map shows the general lines of Allied advance on all sectors after the enemy had been thrown out of Assam and dislodged from Tiddim. For the sake of continuity, it includes that part of Burma covered in the winter operations of 1944-45 (see page 3536) as well as the part covered in the last stages of the campaign up to and after the occupation of Rangoon on May 3, 1945.

the way Pyawbwe, railway town 26 miles south-east of Meiktila and one-time Jap Army H.Q., after a three-day battle in which 1,100 Japanese were killed. The drive continued in oppressive heat and against fanatical resistance. By April 26, Yamethin, Shwemyo, Pyinmana, Lewe, Thawatti, Thagaya, Yedashe, Kyungon, Toungoo, Oktwin and Pyu were all in British hands.

The speed of the advance outpaced the planning capacity of the Japanese; the only opposition came from snipers in roadside culverts and in chaungs, and from mines. Only very occasionally did enemy planes appear in the sky, whereas complete air cover was given to the Allied troops by the R.A.F., the R.I.A.F. and the U.S.A.A.F.

The Allied salient in Burma was probably, as it has been called, " the narrowest ever known in war": it consisted at this time virtually of the road and railway and a couple of hundred yards on either side. There were Japanese **'Narrowest Salient in War'** to the left and Japanese to the right. But this factor mattered little to the men of 17th Division as they bowled along the Rangoon road towards Pegu. They were more concerned about the monsoon, which broke early in the area. For three days it hardly stopped raining. The Japanese decided to make a stand at Pegu in order to keep clear the only escape road from Rangoon and Lower Burma to Siam usable by motor transport. There was a stiff fight before the town fell on April 30, and then the Japanese blew up two important bridges along the remaining 36 road-miles to Rangoon.

Besides the drive by IV Corps, Mountbatten planned also an amphibious assault on Rangoon itself. He wanted to avoid the pinning down of the 14th Army in southern Burma when the monsoon came. The 26th Indian Division (Major - General Chambers), belonging to XV Indian Corps, was pulled out of west coast operations (see page 3536) for the task, and the three-service planning began at Ramree on April 7. It was a rush job—and many army units had to be collected from distant bases. May 2 was set as D day—a date which gave no time for rehearsals. The operation was of a kind new in the Burma theatre —"triphibious" invasion by land, sea and airborne forces.

The problems were many and tough. Rangoon River has treacherous bars and narrow channels. The seaborne troops had to be put into their landing craft over thirty miles from their objective, and that is a long journey

same time he gave IV Corps the order to go ahead with its armoured push south on Rangoon. Fifth and 17th Divisions, and the tanks, were ready. They now virtually constituted the Corps, as 7th Division, after crossing the Irrawaddy, remained with XXXIII Corps in the oilfields.

The final dramatic race with the monsoon started: there were five clear weeks before the monsoon was due, and

there were 340 road-miles to cover. The Japanese attempted to make a stand along a line running roughly from Meiktila west towards the Irrawaddy. Hlaingdet, guarding the path through which they might have escaped to the Shan States, was entered on April 14. On the 20th it was announced that British and Indian tanks and infantry of 17th Division were 70 miles south of Meiktila, having captured on

COPENHAGEN'S V.E. DAY GREETING FOR THE ROYAL DRAGOONS

Copenhagen, the capital of Denmark, celebrated V.E. Day (May 8, 1945) three days after its liberation. The city had been in German hands from April 9, 1940. On May 7 armoured cars of the Royal Dragoons arrived in the capital to join troops of the British 6th Airborne Division who had landed earlier in the day. They were given an overwhelming reception. On V.E. Day British troops paraded the streets to the accompaniment of cheering by the Danes (above).

JAPAN SIGNS INSTRUMENT OF TOTAL SURRENDER—

At 10.30 a.m. (Tokyo time) on September 2, 1945, on board the U.S. battleship 'Missouri' moored in Tokyo Bay, Japan formally signed her unconditional surrender to the Allies. The ship had been chosen for the ceremony in compliment to President Truman who was born in Missouri. Some fifty Allied generals and admirals were present, in addition to the delegates empowered to sign on behalf of their governments, and the Allied armada included the battleships 'H.M.S. King George V' and H.M.S. 'Duke of York.' The 'Missouri' flew the flag which had flown above the Capitol in Washington on the day of the Pearl Harbor attack.

—ON BOARD U.S. BATTLESHIP 'MISSOURI' IN TOKYO BAY

First to sign the instrument of surrender were the two Japanese delegates, Mamoru Shigemitsu, the new Foreign Minister (1) ; and General Yoshijiro Umetsu, Chief of Imperial General Staff (2), both watched by General MacArthur. Allied delegates signing included General MacArthur, as Supreme Allied Commander (3) ; Fleet-Admiral Chester Nimitz, for the U.S.A. (4) ; Admiral Sir Bruce Fraser, for Great Britain (5) ; Lt.-General Kuzma Derevyanko, for the U.S.S.R. (6) ; General Sir Thomas Blamey, for Australia (see illus. in page 3740) ; Air Vice-Marshal Isitt, for New Zealand   (See also Hist. Doc. CCCVII and illus. in page 3842.)

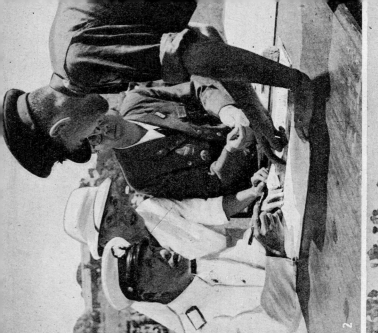

JAPANESE SURRENDERS IN SOUTH-EAST ASIA COMMAND

1. Field-Marshal Count Terauchi, Supreme Commander of the Japanese Expeditionary Forces in the Southern Regions, salutes Admiral Lord Louis Mountbatten, Supreme Allied Commander, S.E.A.C., at Saigon, Indo-China, on November 30, 1945, after handing over his ceremonial swords. 2. Vice-Admiral Tiezo Hara signs the surrender to Brigadier J. A. Salomons, D.S.O., in the Andaman Islands, Bay of Bengal, on October 9 at Port Blair. 3. Lieutenant-General Takazo Numata, representing Field-Marshal Count Terauchi, and Rear-Admiral Kaigye Chudo (right) arrive by air on August 26 at Rangoon to discuss details of surrenders in S.E.A.C.

BRITISH BRIDGE-LAYING TANKS IN BURMA

Existence of the British Army's bridge-laying tank, first used on the Continent, was not disclosed till June 1945. It was known as the ' Scissors ' type, because the bridge was carried folded, scissors-wise, on top of it. Hydraulic mechanism inside the tank unfolded the bridge and lowered it across the gap to be spanned. Here, in Burma, a Churchill tank carrying a ' scissors ' bridge crosses a ' scissors ' bridge already in position. *Photo, British Official*

in such craft if there is the slightest swell in the sea—particularly for Indian troops not used to the sea. The one practicable channel for the landing craft ran almost under the muzzles of Japanese coastal guns at Elephant Point on the west bank. These guns were well sited and well dug in—difficult, therefore, to neutralize by bombing from the air. India's new parachute troops were to deal with them.

Rumours that the Japanese were pulling out of Rangoon subsequently **Parachutists** proved true—they had **Land Near** drained the city to send **Rangoon** men north, to make the stand at Pegu. But no chances could be taken, and the schedule was adhered to. Guided by smoke bombs placed by British " Pathfinders," the American aircrews and the Canadian jumpmasters put down hundreds of stocky little Indian Army parachutists on D day minus one just where they were wanted. The parachutists found only 37 Japanese. They killed 36 of them and wounded the other severely. Elephant Point was theirs.

Off the river mouth lay the ships with men and stores : they had started from their base in Arakan and steamed 400 miles down the Burma coast. To prevent enemy interference, the East Indies Fleet had attacked the Nicobar

Islands (*see* page 3765) and Port Blair in the Andamans on April 30. The sea was getting up, and the weather staff reported that a bad monsoon storm was travelling rapidly towards them. That storm missed the waiting armada by only a few miles. On schedule the landing craft were sent off in the choppy sea on their long journey to their landing points. Progress in the small vessels, not intended for use in rough water, was slow. Hundreds of the men spent five hours in the misery of seasickness before they were landed.

In the van were men of the Lincoln Regiment, spearhead in so many of 26th Indian **Seaborne** Division's victories. **Troops Reach** They, and many other **Rangoon River** units, were put off at points on either side of Rangoon river 25 miles southeast of the city. Through blinding rain they got ashore on to a river bank of knee-deep mud. Despite the appalling conditions, they made rapid progress through the slime of the paddy-fields to break into the city from the landward side in support of the troops who landed on the bomb-battered quays.

The first wave ashore included a battalion of the Jats, the Frontier Force Rifles and the 8th Gurkhas, who landed on the west bank. The east bank force, besides the Lincolns, was made up of Garhwalis and Punjabis. Sherman tanks of the 19th Lancers (an Indian regiment) supported their assault.

The city was an empty shell. On the riverside, warehouses and wharves, fired by the Japanese before their main body left several days earlier, were still smouldering, despite the torrential rain. There was no water in the city mains with which to fight the fires,

RECAPTURE OF BURMA OILFIELDS

On April 19, 1945, S.E.A.C. announced that British and Punjabi troops in an encircling movement had captured Chauk, one of the chief centres of Burma's oilfields, and had seized intact much valuable equipment. In the Mt. Popa–Kyaukpadaung area the Japanese had dug themselves in round the oilfields which they had plainly hoped to hold. Below, Sikh troops in foxholes at the edge of an oilfield just north of Chauk. *Photo, British Official*

S.E.A.C.'S BIGGEST COMBINED OPERATION

At dawn on May 2, 1945, on the Rangoon River, 25 miles south-east of the Burmese capital, British and Indian troops landed in the largest amphibious combined operation in south-east Asia. Rangoon was completely freed within 24 hours of the landings and the Burma campaign virtually at an end. 1. The invasion force sails up the river. 2. R.I.N. assault craft approach the city quays. 3. Disembarking near Elephant Point. 4. R.A.F. Regiment unit manhandles 20-mm. A.A. guns through a sea of mud on the river landing-beaches.

Photos, British and Indian Official

even had there been an effective fire-fighting force. As troops advanced from the waterfront they found smoke and the smell of recently burned buildings—many fired by the Japanese, others by the looters who swept through the city as soon as Japanese control was off.

Occupation of Rangoon was completed on May 3. In the advance from Mandalay to Rangoon, the 14th Army killed 31,364 Japanese, took 683 prisoners and captured 450 guns, 51 tanks.

An Order of the Day issued by Admiral Mountbatten next day said, "The occupation of Rangoon by a successful combined operation was the culmination of a long series of con-

FOURTEENTH ARMY GENERALS IN BURMA
A roadside conference on the outskirts of Prome after its fall on May 2, 1945 : (left to right) : Lieutenant-General Sir Montagu Stopford, K.B.E., C.B., D.S.O., M.C., who commanded XXXIII Corps during the campaign and was later C.-in-C. the 12th Army ; Major-General F. W. Messervy, C.B., D.S.O., commander of IV Corps and leader of the main dash by land to Rangoon ; and Major-General Douglas D. Gracey, C.B., C.B.E., M.C., commanding the 20th Indian Division.

and inflicted 250,000 casualties. The liberation of Burma, in which we have had the active assistance of the Burmese, marks not only the successful accomplishment of the first stage in your advance, it will also be your springboard for further and greater victories."

The first deep-water ships entered Rangoon on May 8 after the river had been swept clear of mines, but not till June 23 was the port announced as again open to shipping.

Contact between IV Corps from the north and XV Corps from Rangoon was made some 25 miles north-east of Rangoon on May 6, when men of the 7th Gurkha Rifles met 26th Indian Division troops near the town of Hlegu.

While the campaign for the capture of Rangoon was going on, other forces were clearing the oilfields. The East

TROOPS OF THE B.N.A.
Burma's own troops helped to free Prome on May 2, 1945, and were in action on the approaches to the city (right). Three days earlier it had been announced that native forces, originally trained and armed by the Japanese to fight the British, were co-operating with the Allies as the 'Burma National Army.' Above, Frontier Force Rifles hoist the flag at Prome.

certed operations carried out by the 14th Army. . . . The fall of the capital ten days before the rains brings to an end the battle of Burma, for although isolated enemy pockets remain their doom is sealed. . . . In the process we have killed 97,000 Japanese

AMERICAN FIELD SERVICE IN ACTION

Throughout the Burma campaign the American Field Service rendered untiring first aid to the Allied fighting forces. All voluntary workers, they drove ambulances and jeeps fitted with stretchers right up to the firing line, tended the wounded and drove them back to safety. On the Sittang Bend (left), an A.F.S. volunteer attends to a Gurkha hit by shrapnel. Right, an A.F.S. driver fits out a village child with an Army shirt. *Photos, British Official*

African troops which preceded IV Corps in the secret advance from Kalemyo (*see* page 3820) emerged near Seikpyu, opposite Chauk, on February 22; and when IV Corps started the advance on Rangoon from Meiktila, XXXIII Corps was sent south-westwards (*see* page 3821), with instructions to clear the oil area and advance on Rangoon along the Irrawaddy river. The Japanese, finding two strong forces —each with a tank brigade—both making south, decided to deploy the major part of their remaining forces before Lieutenant-General Sir Montagu Stopford's XXXIII Corps, composed of 20th Division, 7th Division, and 254th Tank Brigade.

A large force concentrated for the defence of the Yenangyaung oilfields was trapped and broken up by XXXIII Corps in a series of aggressive thrusts. The important railhead town of Kyaukpadaung was captured on April 13. Chauk fell to an encircling movement by British and Punjabi troops on the 19th, Seikpyu was taken on the 20th. Yenangyaung, main centre of Burmese oil production, and Magwe were captured on April 21, and on the 25th S.E.A.C. announced that the whole of the oilfields region had been cleared of the enemy. The oilfields had been thoroughly destroyed in 1942, and the Japanese had succeeded in obtaining only 800 barrels a day, compared with 8,000 before the war. XXXIII Corps pressed on down the Irrawaddy Valley, taking Prome on May 3. It was met on May 17 by troops advancing from Rangoon who had captured Tharrawaddy on the 16th.

Oilfields Cleared of the Enemy

In the west, Taungup, the enemy's last base in Arakan, was captured on April 16 by XV Indian Corps, bringing to a victorious end the Arakan campaign which began in December 1942 (*see* page 2691).

The remnants of the Japanese force in Burma had been split into three groups: (1) some 50,000 east of the Rangoon–Mandalay railway trying to

BURMESE TRIBESMEN HELP ALLIED ARMIES

It was disclosed on December 19, 1944, that a force of tribesmen in the Burma hills, known as the 'Kachin Rangers' and fighting under American command, had been operating inside enemy lines in north Burma (sometimes as deep as 150 miles), had killed some 3,000 Japanese, blown up bridges, wrecked trains and rescued over 200 Allied airmen who had baled out over enemy territory. Here, a patrol with rifle and Bren-gun is on the look-out by a jungle trail.

escape into the Shan Hills and Siam ; (2) some 12,000 stranded in central Burma between the Rangoon–Mandalay and Rangoon–Prome railways ; (3) about 6,000 in the south-west. Operations to round them up or destroy them continued in monsoon conditions. Serious fighting flared up on the Sittang river, north-east of Pegu, during the early part of July, when enemy forces penned in the Pegu Yomas, and seeking to escape across the Sittang, secured a bridge-head over the river and drove Gurkha troops from Nyaungkashe. Stubborn resistance was still being met, despite the infliction of more than 11,500 casualties—including only a few hundred prisoners—when Japan surrendered.

The formation of a new British Army in Burma, the 12th, was announced on June 1. Based on Rangoon, and commanded by Lieutenant-General Stopford, it formed part of the 11th Army

P.O.W. SIGNAL WITH HOME-MADE FLAG

About a thousand Allied prisoners of war were found in the Rangoon area after the occupation of the Burmese capital on May 3, 1945. Prisoners too weak to march were left behind ; others were forced to accompany the retreating enemy towards Pegu. Both groups had to devise means of signalling their presence to Allied bombers. These released prisoners display a Union Jack they had made for this purpose from scraps of Japanese blankets. *Photos, British Official*

group under Lieutenant-General Sir Oliver Leese. When Japan surrendered on August 14, S.E.A.C. was preparing to launch a major expedition into Malaya. This operation, known as "Zipper," had Singapore as its objective, and was to have been an amphibious blow aimed at beaches in the Port Swettenham area. Troops, ships, aircraft and landing craft were all assembled and September 9 had been chosen as D day. As it was, an Allied force was able to sail peacefully into Singapore on September 5 (see page 3604).

BURMA'S GOVERNOR ARRIVES AT RANGOON

The Governor of Burma, Sir Reginald Dorman-Smith, arrived at Rangoon on October 16, 1945 (when the Governor's flag was flown from Government House for the first time since February 22, 1942), to take over the administration of the country from the military. Left, the Governor greets prominent Burmans on arrival. Below, R.A.F. Spitfires fly over the cruiser H.M.S. 'Cleopatra' in the harbour as Sir Reginald comes ashore in a naval motor-launch.

BRITISH TROOPS LAND IN BATAVIA

A serious situation developed in Java after the Japanese surrender owing to the setting up of a 'Provisional Indonesian Republican Government' headed by Dr. Soekarno, an Indonesian nationalist leader, and the inability of S.E.A.C. to land forces rapidly. Allied liberating forces did not disembark until September 28 when British, Dutch and Indian troops went ashore at Batavia, among them these Seaforth Highlanders. *Photo, British Official*

The official surrender of all Japanese forces in South-East Asia took place on September 12, General Itagaki (commanding the Japanese 7th Army in Malaya, Java and Sumatra) signing for Japan, Lord Mountbatten countersigning after the Japanese delegates had withdrawn (*see* illus. in page 3606). General Ichida (Chief of Staff of the Japanese Burma area) signed the surrender of the troops left in Burma at Rangoon on September 13; Lieutenant-General Ishiguro (commanding the Japanese 29th Army) formally surrendered Japanese forces in Malaya at Kuala Lumpur on the same day.

At the time of Japan's capitulation, the area under S.E.A.C. was being **South-East Asia Command Extended** extended, with a view to later operations, to include French Indo-China and Java—the latter coming under the Command actually on August 15. The result was that S.E.A.C. had at its disposal insufficient troops adequately to occupy all the recovered areas under its authority. Not until the end of September did S.E.A.C. take over all its areas, and this lapse of time before Allied forces could secure local surrenders gave the Japanese in Java, Sumatra and Indo-China time to prepare a legacy of trouble.

The great task of releasing Allied prisoners of war and internees and sending them home began at once. From Singapore alone, 40,000 men were repatriated during the first three weeks of September, and through the staging post at Bangkok poured the 50,000 prisoners released in Siam and French Indo-China (*see* illus. in pages 3777 and 3795). The Dakotas of R.A.F. Transport Command which had nourished the 14th Army now flew at full operational pressure on their new errand of mercy. The end of 1945 saw Malaya, Siam, and Burma free of Japanese and all Allied prisoners there repatriated. The French were taking over in Indo-China after some initial trouble, and a S.E.A.C. garrison had reoccupied Hongkong. The Civil Affairs problems of the whole area were, however, still acute; much of the primary distribution and repair work had to be done by the military. The food situation was particularly threatening as much of the rice-growing country had fallen out of production.

The most serious difficulties arising from the limitations of S.E.A.C.'s forces occurred in the Netherlands Indies. When, **Difficulties in Java** by direction of the Supreme Allied Commander, General MacArthur, and by arrangement with the Netherlands authorities (who had not the necessary forces at their disposal), a small British contingent under Lieutenant-General Sir Philip Christison (formerly commanding the XV Indian Corps) landed in Java on September 28 to rescue Allied prisoners, round up the Japanese, and take over administration, they found a so-called "Provisional Indonesian Republican Government" in control of large areas, and in carrying out their mission they found themselves forced at times to act against armed opposition from Indonesians using weapons and ammunition transferred to them, against the surrender terms, by the Japanese. The Nationalist movement in the Netherlands Indies was no new thing, and had been fanned for his own purposes by the enemy. While the British troops went on with their duties, their leaders brought together the Indonesians and the Dutch in order that they could work out their own problems.

JAPANESE SURRENDER IN DUTCH TIMOR

All Japanese forces in Dutch Timor were surrendered by Colonel Kaida Tatsuishi to Brigadier L. G. H. Dyke, of the Australian Army, on September 11, 1945. The ceremony took place on board the minesweeper H.M.A.S. 'Moresby' in Koepang harbour. Here the enemy envoy, facing Brigadier Dyke, signs the instrument. *Photo, Pictorial Press*

Chapter 372

DISASTER OVERWHELMS JAPAN

Battered from the air and from the sea, cut off from her rapidly gained and almost as rapidly lost vast overseas empire, Japan was compelled to surrender unconditionally to the Allies less than four years after her unprovoked attack on Pearl Harbor. The last months of war and the first months of peace in Japan are described in this Chapter. For Japanese home affairs in 1944, see Chapter 324

THE conquest of Okinawa brought the Americans' main forces to within immediate striking distance of the heart of the Japanese Empire. The Pacific war was primarily a naval war. Japan had begun it with a considerable battle fleet. By June 1945 the effective strength of the Japanese Fleet was reduced to the two hermaphrodite battleships of the " Ise " class and the 33,000-ton " Nagato." She had virtually no cruisers effective, her carrier strength was reduced to five ships including escort-carriers, and her destroyer strength was approximately thirty. In actual fact few of these ships were capable of serious action, and none had accompanied the " Yamato " on her suicide dash to Okinawa (*see* page 3761). The Japanese Navy had ceased to exist as a fighting force, and off the Japanese coast stood four Allied Fleets all composed of fast up-to-date ships and each vastly superior to the whole remaining naval strength of Japan.

With the Air Force it is a little more difficult to be precise, but it is improbable that the total remaining air strength of Japan consisted of more than 3,000 of all types of planes and, once again, the fighting efficiency of by far the greater portion of these was doubtful in the extreme. The air sweeps of the Allies were virtually unopposed (*see* page 3793).

Japan's Depleted Air Force

There remained the Army. There was only one major land campaign in the whole course of the Japanese war—that fought in Burma (*see* Chapters 295, 345, 371). Immense movements and manoeuvrings took place up and down the length of China, but owing to the extreme inadequacy of Chinese arms in every branch of current equipment, they bore little or no resemblance to the other campaigns of the Second Great War, and cannot be estimated on the same level.

The island conquests and the campaigns in New Guinea and the Philippines, bitter as they were, were not on the scale of the war in Europe. In the large scale operations of Luzon, for example, the total of American dead was barely 3,000. In Okinawa, the most costly of the island assaults, the total

killed and missing in action in two months was just 12,000. Though Japanese casualties, due in part to the immense American superiority in arms and equipment and in part to the fanaticism with which the Japanese fought, were invariably out of all proportion to Allied losses, it cannot be said that the Japanese army had suffered any serious weakening of its strength.

But a very large part of the Japanese army was outside the Japanese mainland : enemy documents state that on September 1, 3,400,000 army and navy personnel were deployed throughout Japanese-occupied territories. The destruction of Japanese air and sea power made their return to the Empire impossible. The armies of Manchuria, of northern and southern China, of

STERN ORDERS FOR PRISONERS AT SEA

Below is a facsimile of orders issued to Allied prisoners transported on Japanese prison-ships—as promulgated by the ' Commander of the Prisoner Escort, Navy of the Great Japanese Empire.' As may be seen, threat of the death penalty covered such breaches of discipline as ' talking without permission and raising loud voices ' and ' using more than two blankets.' The offer of preferential treatment in Clause 6 must have provoked smiles from the prisoners—not merely on account of its pidgin-English.

Commander of the Prisoner Escort
Navy of the Great Japanese Empire

REGULATIONS FOR PRISONERS

1. The prisoners disobeying the following orders will be punished with immediate death.

   a) Those disobeying orders and instructions.
   b) Those showing a motion of antagonism and raising a sign of opposition.
   c) Those disordoring the regulations by individualism, egoism, thinking only about yourself, rushing for your own goods.
   d) Those talking without permission and raising loud voices.
   e) Those walking and moving without order.
   f) Those carrying unnecessary baggage in embarking.
   g) Those resisting mutually.
   h) Those touching the boat's materials, wires, electric lights, tools, switches, etc.
   i) Those climbing ladder without order.
   j) Those showing action of running away from the room or boat.
   k) Those trying to take more meal than given to them.
   l) Those using more than two blankets.

2. Since the boat is not well equiped and inside being narrow, food being scarce and poor you'll feel uncomfortable during the short time on the boat. Those losing patience and disordering the regulation will be heavily punished for the reason of not being able to escort.

3. Be sure to finish your "Nature's call", evacuate the bowels and urine, before embarking.

4. Meal will be given twice a day. One plate only to one prisoner. The prisoners called by the guard will give out the meal quick as possible and honestly. The remaining prisoners will stay in their places quietly and wait for your plate. Those moving from their places reaching for your plate without order will be heavily punished. Same orders will be applied in handling plates after meal.

5. Toilet will be fixed at the four corners of the room. The buckets and cans will be placed. When filled up a guard will appoint a prisoner. The prisoner called will take the buckets to the center of the room. The buckets will be pulled up by the derrick and be thrown away. Toilet papers will be given. Everyone must cooperate to make the room sanitary. Those being careless will be punished.

6. Navy of the Great Japanese Empire will not try to punish you all with death. Those obeying all the rules and regulations, and believing the action and purpose of the Japanese Navy, cooperating with Japan in constructing the "New order of the Great Asia" which lead to the world's peace will be well treated.

The End

Indo-China and Malaya were lost as far as the defence of Japan was concerned.

But the invasion forces were all the same calculated on a scale sufficient to overcome an army estimated at approximately 3,000,000 in Japan itself—

Allied Invasion Preparations Japanese figures later showed that the combined naval and military strength in Japan totalled 4,000,000. The speed of the "build-up" in the Philippines, the Marianas, the Marshalls, and the Ryukyus achieved an almost incredible acceleration. On August 4 General MacArthur's command was extended to include the Ryukyu Islands, which meant that he became Supreme Commander of the Allied invasion forces.

Behind the incessant air assault (described in pages 3789–3795) the gigantic strength of America was coiled for the final spring.

Then on August 6 came the destruction of the city of Hiroshima with a single atomic bomb (*see* page 3795), followed on August 8 by the declaration of war by the U.S.S.R. (*see* page 3780), and the dropping of a second atomic bomb on the city of Nagasaki.

While representatives of Great Britain, the U.S.A. and the U.S.S.R. (the last not yet at war with Japan) were in conference at Potsdam (*see* Chapter 380), a "peace feeler" from Japan reached the first two through the third. The Allies' response was the Potsdam ultimatum of July 26 (*see* Historic Document 308, page 3842). Domei, the official Japanese news agency, announced on the 27th that the Government would ignore this ultimatum; but on August 10 Tokyo broadcast that the Government was willing to accept the Potsdam declaration provided that "the said declaration does not comprise any demand which prejudices the prerogatives of His Majesty as a sovereign ruler." On the 11th, Mr James Byrnes, U.S. Secretary of State, handed to the Swiss Legation in Washington for transmission to the Japanese Government a reply on behalf of the U.S.A., Great Britain, the Soviet Union and China, stating that "from the moment of surrender, the authority of the

Emperor and the Japanese Government to rule the State shall be subject to the Supreme Commander of the Allied Powers who will take such steps as he deems proper to effectuate the surrender terms. The Emperor will be required to authorize and ensure the signature by the Government of Japan and Japanese Imperial General Headquarters of the surrender terms necessary to carry out the terms of the Potsdam declaration."

Allied sea and air bombardment of Japan continued, and on August 14 the Japanese Cabinet decided to accept the Allied terms. Next day the Emperor Hirohito broadcast for the first time to the Japanese nation. The Second Great War was over.

During its last stages, the war weariness inside Japan already manifest in 1943 grew, and by 1945 the possibility of defeat was admitted even in higher circles. On February 14, a Foreign Office spokesman said, "Shigemitsu's [the Foreign Minister's] principle is not to reject any hand which offers peace." On April 5, the day of the Soviet denunciation of the Russo-Japanese neutrality pact (*see* page 3566), General Koiso resigned, and a new cabinet was formed by Admiral Baron Kantaro Suzuki who in his first state-

Internal Political Moves

SURRENDER ENVOYS FROM JAPAN REACH MANILA
Sixteen surrender envoys from Japan, including General Takashima, vice-Chief of the Japanese Imperial General Staff, arrived at Ie, off Okinawa, and were flown on to Manila on August 19, 1945. Here the U.S. official interpreter refuses to shake hands with Lieutenant-General Takashiro Tanabe on the Manila airstrip. The surrender was announced to enemy troops still in hiding on Luzon by means of streamers each attached to three balloons, in the manner shown above.

ALLIED AIR MIGHT OVER JAPAN

Over a thousand carrier-based aircraft of the U.S. 3rd Fleet staged an exercise off the coast of Japan on August 22, 1945, as a preliminary to the entry into Sagami and Tokyo bays of the Allied landing forces and the signing of the unconditional surrender aboard the U.S.S. 'Missouri' on September 2. Left, members of Admiral Halsey's staff examine charts of Tokyo Bay with Japanese pilots.

Though the Allied idea that Japan's "paper cities" would collapse under sustained bombing was exaggerated, there is no doubt that the powerful attacks of 1945, comparable with those rained on Germany in 1944, did relatively greater damage. The drift of workers from their factories (*see* page 3290) became so serious that in January the Government issued an order aimed at compelling essential workers to stay in the bombed cities.

On March 10 a new mobilization law affecting all Japanese males between 12 and 60, females between 12 and 40 came into force. A week later it was announced that all schools, except those of the first grade, would be closed from April 1 for one year " in order to link pupils and teachers closely with

national defence and mobilize them for war production." Evacuation of civilians from defence areas, the speedy construction of fortifications, arrangements for the instruction of civilians in the handling of arms, the evacuation of children from the larger cities were also announced during March. **Defence Against Invasion** On May 21 came the mobilization of two million students in a Students Defence Corps; and on June 28 the formation of a special Army Command to strengthen the defences of Tokyo "in anticipation of Allied attempts at invasion." The mass evacuation of war factories to Manchuria was announced on June 29; while a Tokyo broadcast of July 2 stated that owing to the scale of the Allied air attack all but 200,000 people had been evacuated from the capital (whose normal population was some six millions).

A Tokyo broadcast of April 23 stated that from March 1 to the middle of April 700,000 houses had been destroyed, the industrial area of Tokyo being " mostly in ruins." The same station later declared that the raid of May 26 had " virtually laid waste what was

ment declared that the war situation " warrants not the least bit of optimism in our nation's survival." On May 22, a domestic broadcast by the Procurator General spoke of " a tendency towards peace agitation." During July, Tokyo radio hopefully prophesied a modification of the unconditional surrender demand, and followed this with a direct appeal to the United States for a " more lenient attitude," declaring that there were no problems between Japan and a " liberal " America.

AFTER THE SURRENDER

Lt.-Gen. A. E. Percival (left), British commander at Singapore in 1942, and Lt.-Gen. Jonathan Wainwright, who held out at Corregidor after General MacArthur's escape, stood behind the latter when he signed the surrender in Tokyo Bay on September 2, 1945 (see illus. in page 3824). Here the three commanders are seen together at Gen. MacArthur's H.Q. in Yokohama. Right, bronze plaque on the deck of the U.S.S. 'Missouri,' marking the site of the surrender ceremony.

once the world's third metropolis." On June 10, Domei said, " The Allies have achieved their first target in the invasion of Japan. Tokyo, Nagoya, Yokohama, Osaka and Kobe have ceased to exist. The nation must prepare for imminent battle on its own soil."

The Domei agency on August 23 gave a summary of casualties and damage resulting from Allied air attacks (including the atomic bomb **Total of** damage) as 260,000 **Air Raid** killed, 412,000 injured, **Damage** 9,200,000 homeless, 2,210,000 houses demolished or burnt out, 44 of Japan's 206 cities almost completely wiped out, 30 per cent of the built-up areas of 37 others (including Tokyo) destroyed. The total of nearly ten million sufferers in one way or another represented nearly a sixth of the Japanese home population.

Allied observers, when they reached Japan, however, found the people in less desperate situation than these figures would suggest. In face of sustained attack, the great majority of city workers had migrated to the untouched country, where close family ties with the peasantry from which they had so recently sprung ensured that they would find shelter. When

the terror subsided the Japanese (as had the Chinese of Shanghai, Canton, Hankow and Nanking) returned to the cities and built themselves makeshift shanties on the sites of their former homes : in Japan, as in Germany, the Allies had to deal with a vast urban population living in squalor and want, pauperized by the destruction of the industries on which it had depended, cut off from its normal food supplies, yet clinging to the sites of its homes.

The breakdown of Japanese industry which preceded the surrender was due to the mass migration of the workers and to the Allied block- **Breakdown** ade, which prevented **of** raw materials from **Industry** reaching the country, rather than to air raid damage to factories. General MacArthur's first report on the state of Japan estimated, for instance, that at the end of the war her production industry was intact as to 73 per cent, her precision machine industry as to 88 per cent of total capacity. The power industry, reduced to 28 per cent of its wartime peak capacity, had suffered most : but even that remained capable of producing enough for normal home needs. Admiral Nimitz stated on October 5 that Japan's fighting forces were stronger on land and in the air at the time of her surrender than at the outbreak of war, but that her defeat was inevitable once she had been stripped of her sea power ;

GENERAL MacARTHUR LANDS IN JAPAN

On August 30, 1945, 42,000 U.S. troops, mostly airborne, entered Yokohama without incident and occupied a large part of the Kanto Plain surrounding Tokyo. In the afternoon General MacArthur arrived by air from Manila and set up his headquarters in the New Grand Hotel in Yokohama. The General, smoking a long-stemmed corncob pipe, is here about to land from his transport aircraft ' Bataan ' at the Atsugi airfield. *Photo, New York Times Photos*

BRITISH AND DOMINIONS FORCES IN JAPAN

Main landings of Allied forces in Japan began on August 30, 1945: five days earlier the Japanese had announced the impending withdrawal of their troops on Honshu from the area left white on the map. 1. Royal Marines take over a fort in Tokyo Bay. 2. An A.B. of the Royal Australian Navy puts up a notice outside British Landing Force H.Q. in Yokosuka. 3. H.M.S. 'Duke of York,' with H.M.S. 'King George V' in Sagami Bay.

HEADQUARTERS BLF

DUKE OF YORK

in importance to the concern over the situation in Luzon."

By the end of March, with Iwo Jima lost, with the remains of the Japanese Fleet crippled by naval air attack on its protected bases in the Inland Sea, and with the Americans approaching Okinawa, the influence of these "newly developed factions" became apparent. On March 30 the I.R.A.A. was dissolved and replaced by an organization known as the *Dai Nippon Seijikai*—the Political Association of Great Japan—with General Jiro Minami (commander of the Japanese Armies in Manchuria at the time of the 1931 "incident") as President. The new organization issued a manifesto declaring that Japan was already "a battlefield" and announcing its aim as the formation of "a strong organization from all circles." Within a week General Koiso had resigned (*see* page 3834). His successor, the 78-year-old courtier Admiral Suzuki (formerly Grand Chamberlain), brought Minami into the Cabinet as Minister without portfolio; while Shigenori Togo, Tojo's Foreign Minister who had conducted the diplomatic smoke-screen for Pearl Harbor, came back to the Foreign Office. Concealed behind the Imperial connexion of the aged Premier, the Japanese diehards were making their last throw.

On May 15 the Japanese Cabinet decided that in view of Germany's

Militarists' Last Throw

General MacArthur reported that "while air raids destroyed important plants in the Tokyo area, shortage of raw materials was a more effective factor in curtailing production."

During the culminating battles of the war the increasing precariousness of Japan's economic and social position was reflected in the political situation. On January 14 Japan's Fascist-model single political party, the Imperial Rule Assistance Association, met with other sectional groups "to discuss changes in the political structure and urge the Government to take decisive steps to reform the administration." The following day the official news agency commented: "Newly developed factions are clamouring for a bold and unprecedented renovation . . . The agitation is becoming one of the matters of greatest concern to the people—equal

Agitation for Reforms

JAPANESE ARMED FORCES ARE DISBANDED

By September 30, 1945, 1,833,600 of the 2,253,000 Japanese troops in the homeland had been demobilized. Here, in a Tokyo street, the pavements strewn with their personal belongings, Japanese await disbandment. Above, small arms, ready for shipment, seized by U.S. forces at the Ustunomiya arsenal. Each piece was packed separately in oiled cloth to prevent rusting.

unconditional surrender (*see* page 3802), all treaties with her, including the Tripartite (Axis) Pact, had ceased to be operative. In June, parallel with the official and unofficial moves towards peace, Japanese propaganda moved to the theme of home defence. The "People's Volunteer Corps" was said to number a hundred million people (approximately the total population of the home islands). The Diet voted Suzuki dictatorial powers on June 10, and four days later he assured the Press that preparations for home defence were "complete and perfect."

In July Japan was under attack from the air and from the sea for 22 consecutive days and nights. Her de-

IN THE CITIES HIT BY ATOMIC BOMBS

Two bombs charged with the energy created by atomic fission were used by the Allies—one on Hiroshima on August 6, 1945, the other on Nagasaki two days later. 1. Nagasaki family returns to live in the ruins. 2. Bomb-victim at Hiroshima erects 'forward address' notice. 3. Hiroshima children wear masks as a protection against the odours rising from the ruins.

his G.H.Q. at Manila accompanied by competent Army, Navy and Air Force officers, the Japanese party to proceed on August 17 under safe-conducts in white-painted Japanese planes of a specified type from Satanomisaki (Kyushu) to the island of Ie, near Okinawa, whence they would be flown in American planes to Manila. The Japanese Government asked for, and was granted, an extension of the time limit for the despatch of envoys, the Emperor issuing on August 16, however, an Imperial rescript to the

MacArthur's First Order to Japanese

fence had been broken before the dropping of the atomic bombs gave her reason for surrender plausible to her own people.

Admiral Suzuki resigned on August 15. His Ministers of War and of the Navy were joined by many lesser apostles of expansion in traditional suicide. The Suzuki Cabinet was replaced by an administration led by Hirohito's cousin, Prince Higashikuni. Shigemitsu, once more Foreign Minister, in a broadcast on August 18, said, "The Japanese people have been beaten and must revise their thinking." The *Dai Nippon Seijikai* was dissolved. The "100 million souls" of the "People's Volunteer Corps" were disbanded on August 22, and the Supreme War Council was reconstituted as "a conference for the termination of the war."

On August 15, General MacArthur sent a radio message from Manila calling on Japan to cease hostilities immediately, and to send a Japanese representative to

EMPEROR ADVISES COLLABORATION WITH THE ALLIES

In a forty-word rescript, the Emperor Hirohito on November 27, 1945, at the opening of the 89th session of the Japanese Diet, advised his people to do their best to carry out General MacArthur's orders. Although special seats had been reserved for them, no women attended the ceremony, which is shown above. Below, the Emperor greets the bows of his subjects in western style by removing his hat during a tour of industrial centres   *Photos, Keystone; Associated Press*

Allied armada including powerful ships of the British Pacific Fleet. "Today the guns are silent. A great tragedy has ended. A great victory has been won," said MacArthur.

For the first time in her history, Japan was under foreign domination. General MacArthur entered Tokyo at the head of his troops on September 8. He at once announced the imposition of a press **Japan Under Foreign Domination** and radio censorship. On September 12 he ordered the dissolution of the Black Dragon society—the secret terrorist organization which for many years had played a predominant part in Japan's imperialistic policy, and had been responsible for many political assassinations—and the arrest of seven of its leaders.

General Hideki Tojo, Prime Minister from October 1941 to July 1944, tried to commit suicide on September 11 when U.S. troops arrived at his house to arrest him as a war criminal. Field-Marshal Sugiyama, C.-in-C. of the

entire armed forces to cease hostilities immediately. Tokyo announced that three relatives of the Emperor, carrying his instructions, had left for Manchuria, China and the southern areas, and that the Japanese envoys for Manila would leave on August 19. They duly arrived at Ie whence they were flown to Manila.

Two days later the Japanese made the following announcement: "Our armed forces in the territory within a line extending from a **Allied Landing Area Cleared** point east of the Kamo river in Chiba Prefecture through the city of Chiba, the estuary of the Tama river, Fuchu, Hachioji, Otsuki to the southern end of Izu Peninsula will be made to evacuate this area as speedily as possible. Government offices and public institutions within the area will function as usual while the general public is required to go about its business calmly as usual." (*See* map in page 3837).

The greatest fleet of transport planes ever assembled had meanwhile been concentrated on Okinawa, some from as far away as Britain, Egypt and Australia. At the same time, powerful forces were converging on Japan by sea. Owing to a series of typhoons, the first Allied landings, timed for August 26, had to be postponed; the advance party landed by air on August 29, the main landings took place on the 30th.

Many thousands of Allied prisoners found in Japan were set free. Commander Harold Stassen, the Relief Commissioner charged with their care,

reported that not a single camp was humanely run. Eighty per cent of the prisoners were suffering from tuberculosis, pellagra, dysentery or beri-beri, due to diet deficiencies, and very many of them bore the marks of brutal ill-treatment.

The war ended formally at 10·30 a.m. Tokyo time (2·30 a.m. B.S.T.) on September 2 when the unconditional surrender of Japan (*see* Historic Document 307, page 3842) was signed on board the battleship U.S.S. "Missouri" in Tokyo Bay, which was filled by a great

Japanese Home Army, committed suicide with his wife on September 12. Warrants were issued for the arrest of a number of other persons as war criminals; by September 17 all the members of the Pearl Harbor Cabinet were under arrest or dead. The names of the International War Crimes Tribunal, to sit in Tokyo, were announced by General MacArthur on February 18, 1946: they included Sir William Webb (Chief Justice of Queensland) as chairman, Justice Stuart McDougall of Canada, and Lord Patrick, a Scottish judge, and Dean of the Faculty of Advocates of Scotland.

MacArthur ordered the elimination of all Japanese Government organizations which "establish or maintain restrictions on freedom of thought, religion, assembly or speech" on October 4. Twenty-one of the largest banks were seized on September 30. Prince Higashi-kuni resigned on October 8, and a new cabinet was formed under Baron Kijuro Shidehara. MacArthur ordered the enfranchisement of women on October 11.

On September 30, the Japanese War Ministry reported to the Allied Commander that 81 per cent (1,833,600) of the 2,253,000 troops under arms in the homeland had been demobilized. Japanese Imperial G.H.Q. was formally closed down, and the Army General Staff disbanded, on October 16. An Imperial rescript of October 17, ordering the freeing of political prisoners, affected some million-and-a-half persons. The cultivation of the opium poppy, coca leaf, and hemp was forbidden on the 18th. A directive of November 6 ordered the immediate dissolution of the four biggest financial and industrial trusts in Japan. Conscription was abolished on November 9. All Imperial assets were "frozen" on November 20. The reform of the feudal system of land tenure was begun on December 9.

Most drastic, perhaps, of all changes was the abolition of Shintoism as the State religion on December 15. This

Demilitariz-ation Begins

ENEMY SURRENDERS IN THE SOUTH-WEST PACIFIC
The surrender of the Japanese forces in the S.W. Pacific area was signed on board the aircraft-carrier H.M.S. 'Glory' in St. George's Channel, 28 miles south-east of Rabaul in New Britain on September 6, 1945. At a preliminary conference in the captain's cabin are (left to right) Admiral Kusaka, commanding the Japanese South-East Navy; General Imamura, Japanese C.-in-C., South-West Pacific; Lieutenant-General V. A. H. Sturdee, commanding the Australian 1st Army, who received the surrender; Brigadier E. L. Sheehan, and Captain W. Buzzard, R.N.

was followed on December 31 by the issue of an Imperial rescript to the Japanese people in which Hirohito repudiated "the false conception that the Emperor is divine and that the Japanese people are superior to other races and are fated to rule the world. The Emperor is not a living god."

An Allied directive of the same date ordered the suspension of all current teaching of Japanese history, geography, and morals in Japanese schools, text books and manuals on these subjects to be handed in at collecting centres.

New textbooks thoroughly purged of all militaristic teaching were to be distributed as soon as ready.

By the end of 1945 several organized political parties were forming, among them a Labour Party, a Liberal Party, the New Japan Party, demanding a curb on police powers, and the Centre Political Party, a right-wing group including many former members of the Diet. On January 13, 1946, MacArthur authorized the Japanese Government to hold general elections at a date not earlier than March 15 of that year.

The Soviet Government was anxious to see established in Japan an Allied Control Council which would act only on decisions reached by unanimous agreement; but this was strenuously opposed by the United States, which, in view of difficulties in the Allied Control Council for Germany, considered that in case of disagreement the final word should be given to General MacArthur. The Foreign Ministers of Great Britain, the United States and the Soviet Union meeting in Moscow in December (*see* page 3564) agreed, with the concurrence of China, to the establishment of an Allied Council for Japan, with its seat in Tokyo, under the chairmanship of the Supreme Commander for the Allied Powers (or his deputy), the other members representing the Soviet Union, China, and, jointly, the United Kingdom, Australia, New Zealand and India. General MacArthur, while expressing his intention to try to make this Council work, did not conceal that he regarded it as impracticable. He continued into 1946 to be effective Allied dictator of Japan.

Allied Council for Japan

DEATH SENTENCE FOR 'TIGER OF MALAYA'
The Japanese general Tomoyuki Yamashita, one-time conqueror of Singapore and Corregidor and known as the 'Tiger of Malaya,' was brought before an American military court at Manila in December 1945, charged with war crimes in the Philippines, sentenced to death and hanged on February 22, 1946. He here listens to the death sentence being pronounced by Major-General Russell B. Reynolds (seated, extreme left). *Photos. Associated Press; British Official*

JAPAN SURRENDERS UNCONDITIONALLY TO THE ALLIES

The official text of the instrument of surrender signed by representatives of Japan on board the United States battleship 'Missouri' in Tokyo Bay on September 2, 1945, and the terms of the 'Potsdam Declaration' issued on July 26 by Mr. Churchill, President Truman, and President Chiang Kai-shek are given below. (*See also pages 3824-5*).

Terms of Japan's Unconditional Surrender to the Allies, September 2, 1945.

1. We, acting by command of and on behalf of the Emperor of Japan, the Japanese Government, and Japanese Imperial General Headquarters, hereby accept the provisions in the declaration issued by the heads of the Governments of the United States, China, and Great Britain on July 26, 1945, at Potsdam and subsequently adhered to by the Union of Soviet Socialist Republics.

2. We hereby proclaim the unconditional surrender to the Allied Powers of the Japanese Imperial General Headquarters and of all Japanese armed forces and all armed forces under Japanese control, wherever situated.

3. We hereby command all Japanese forces, wherever situated, and Japanese people to cease hostilities forthwith, to preserve and save from damage all ships, aircraft, and military and civil property, and to comply with all requirements which may be imposed by the Supreme Commander for the Allied Powers or by agencies of the Japanese Government at his direction.

4. We hereby command the Japanese Imperial General Headquarters to issue at once orders to the commanders of all Japanese forces and all forces under Japanese control, wherever situated, to surrender unconditionally themselves and all forces under their control.

5. We hereby command all civil, military, and naval officials to obey and enforce all proclamations, orders, and directives deemed by the Supreme Commander for the Allied Powers to be proper to effectuate this surrender and issued by him or under his authority, and we direct all such officials to remain at their posts and to continue to perform their non-combatant duties unless specifically relieved by him or under his authority.

6. We hereby undertake for the Emperor, the Japanese Government, and their successors to carry out the provisions of the Potsdam declaration in good faith, and to issue whatever orders and take whatever action may be required by the Supreme Commander for the Allied Powers, or by any other designated representatives of the Allied Powers, for the purpose of giving effect to that declaration.

7. We hereby command the Japanese Imperial Government and the Japanese Imperial General Headquarters at once to liberate all Allied prisoners of war and civilian internees now under Japanese control and to provide for their protection, care, maintenance, and immediate transportation to places as directed.

8. The authority of the Emperor and the Japanese Government to rule the State shall be subject to the Supreme Commander for the Allied Powers, who will take such steps as he deems proper to effectuate these terms of surrender.

The 'Potsdam Declaration' of July 26, 1945.

1. We, the President of the United States, the President of the National Government of the Republic of China, and the Prime Minister of Great Britain, representing the hundreds of millions of our countrymen, have conferred, and agree that Japan shall be given an opportunity to end the war.

2. The prodigious land, sea, and air forces of the United States, the British Empire, and China, many times reinforced by their armies and air fleets from the west, are poised to strike the final blows upon Japan. This military power is sustained and inspired by the determination of all the Allied nations to prosecute the war against Japan until she ceases to resist.

3. The result of the futile and senseless German resistance to the might of the aroused free peoples of the world stands forth in awful clarity as an example to the people of Japan. The might that now converges on Japan is immeasurably greater than that which when applied to the resisting Nazis necessarily laid waste to the lands, the industry, and the method of life of the whole German people. The full application of our military power, backed by our resolve, will mean the inevitable and complete destruction of the Japanese armed forces, and just as inevitably the utter devastation of the Japanese homeland.

4. The time has come for Japan to decide whether she will continue to be controlled by those self-willed militaristic advisers whose unintelligent calculations have brought the Empire of Japan to the threshold of annihilation, or whether she will follow the path of reason.

5. The following are our terms. We will not deviate from them. There are no alternatives. We shall brook no delay :—

6. There must be eliminated for all time the authority and influence of those who have deceived and misled the people of Japan into embarking on world conquest, for we insist that a new order of peace, security, and justice will be impossible until irresponsible militarism is driven from the world.

7. Until such a new order is established and until there is convincing proof that Japan's war-making power is

(*Continued on page 3847.*)

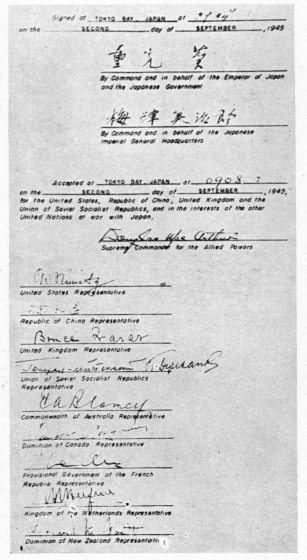

Signed at TOKYO BAY, JAPAN at
on the SECOND day of SEPTEMBER, 1945

By Command and in behalf of the Emperor of Japan and the Japanese Government

By Command and in behalf of the Japanese Imperial General Headquarters

Accepted at TOKYO BAY, JAPAN at 0908 7
on the SECOND day of SEPTEMBER, 1945, for the United States, Republic of China, United Kingdom and the Union of Soviet Socialist Republics, and in the interests of the other United Nations at war with Japan.

Supreme Commander for the Allied Powers

United States Representative

Republic of China Representative

United Kingdom Representative

Union of Soviet Socialist Republics Representative

Commonwealth of Australia Representative

Dominion of Canada Representative

Provisional Government of the French Republic Representative

Kingdom of the Netherlands Representative

Dominion of New Zealand Representative

THE MEN WHO 'SHOT' THE WAR WITH CAMERAS

Some of the most vivid photographs of the war—in Burma as in other theatres—were the work of the Army Film and Photographic Unit (whose badge is reproduced in colour facing page 3483). Although the members of the A.F.P.U. —most of them professional press and film cameramen in civilian life—were non-combatants and were normally unarmed, they were frequently to be found in forward positions, collecting material for invaluable pictorial records of the war. At Tobruk, for instance, four sergeants of the A.F.P.U. were at work for an hour before the 8th Army reoccupied the town in 1942. Here, an A.F.P.U. cameraman records the struggle for an oilfield in Burma in 1945.

ALLIED PRISONERS RELEASED NEAR TOKYO

Accurate figures of Allied prisoners of war and internees in Japanese hands were difficult to obtain even after the war ended. Many prisoners had died in captivity and the enemy did not immediately give the Allies complete information as to the location of camps, especially of those in outlying districts. On August 22, 1945, the War Office announced that about 250,000 Allied nationals were held in some 150 camps in Asia and the Pacific islands. These included 38,000 British servicemen and 112,000 British civilians. Here, Allied nationals, released near Tokyo following the Allied landings in Japan at the end of August, greet their liberators. *Photo, British Official*

Photo, Keystone

THE END OF JAPAN'S ONCE-POWERFUL FLEET

In the waters of Kure Bay, south of Hiroshima, in Japan's Inland Sea, these war vessels, remnants of the once-powerful Nippon fleet, lay at their moorings after the enemy's unconditional surrender on August 14, 1945. The remaining ships consisted of one battleship (the 26-year-old 32,720-tons 'Nagato'), four aircraft-carriers, four cruisers, 51 submarines and 38 destroyers. The battleship was destroyed in the atomic bomb test at Bikini on July 25, 1946; the aircraft carriers, cruisers and submarines were scuttled, and the destroyers distributed among the Allied Powers.

BRITISH OCCUPATION FORCE TAKES OVER IN JAPAN

It was announced on January 31, 1946, that 'B.C.O.F.' (British Commonwealth Occupation Force) would help to occupy Japan. It was to represent Great Britain, Australia, New Zealand, and India, with Lt.-General J. Northcott, former Australian Chief of Staff, as C.-in-C. It also included a R.A.F., R.A.A.F., R.N.Z.A.F. and R.I.A.F. component and a British Pacific Fleet Squadron. Above, band of the Queen's Own Cameron Highlanders at Kure, where troops of the 2/5 Royal Gurkha Rifles (below) also parade. Right, badge of 'Brindjap,' the British and Indian contingent serving with B.C.O.F., which is commanded by Maj.-Gen. D. T. Cowan, C.B., C.B.E., D.S.O.   *Photos, Indian Official*

REPORT ON THE EFFECTS OF THE ATOMIC BOMBS

Below is the end of the Potsdam declaration of July 26, 1945 (concluded from page 3842), and a summary of the report (published by H.M. Stationery Office in 1946, price 1s.) of a British Mission of scientists sent to Japan to study the effects of the atomic bombs dropped one on Hiroshima and the other on Nagasaki. [*See* Chapter 379, colour plate facing page 3862, illustrations on pages 3900 and 3901 and diagram on page 4034].

destroyed, points in Japanese territory designated by the Allies shall be occupied to secure the achievements of the basic objectives we are here setting forth.

8. The terms of the Cairo declaration [*see* page 2636] shall be carried out and Japanese sovereignty shall be limited to the islands of Honshu, Hokkaido, Kyushu, Shikoko and such minor islands as we determine.

9. The Japanese military forces after being completely disarmed shall be permitted to return to their homes with the opportunity of leading peaceful and productive lives.

10. We do not intend that the Japanese shall be enslaved as a race nor destroyed as a nation, but stern justice will be meted out to all war criminals, including those who have visited cruelties upon our prisoners. The Japanese Government shall remove all obstacles to the revival and strengthening of democratic tendencies among the Japanese people. Freedom of speech, of religion and of thought as well as respect for fundamental human rights shall be established.

11. Japan shall be permitted to maintain such industries as will sustain her economy and allow the exaction of just reparations in kind, but not those industries which will enable her to re-arm for war. To this end access to, as distinguished from control of, raw materials shall be permitted. Eventual Japanese participation in world trade relations shall be permitted.

12. The occupying forces of the Allies shall be withdrawn from Japan as soon as these objectives have been accomplished and there has been established, in accordance with the freely expressed will of the Japanese people, a peacefully inclined and responsible government.

13. We call upon the Government of Japan to proclaim now the unconditional surrender of all the Japanese armed forces and to provide proper and adequate assurances of their good faith in such action. The alternative for Japan is complete and utter destruction.

The Effects of the Atomic Bombs at Hiroshima and Nagasaki.

HIROSHIMA stretches over flat ground in all directions for roughly two miles from the centre. The main commercial and residential area of Nagasaki lies on a small plain near the head of a long bay. From here the valley of the river Urakami runs north for three or four miles, and a smaller valley branches north-east for less than two miles; both valleys are narrow and are separated and flanked by abrupt hills rising in places to 1,000 feet. The smaller valley is crowded with dwellings without plan. The Urakami valley contained large steel, engineering and armament works, together with smaller factories and a host of home workshops with an attendant jostle of workers' dwellings.

Hiroshima had been virtually undamaged by air attack before the atomic bomb fell. The bomb exploded near its centre and thence spread its destruction with great uniformity. Directly or indirectly, it initiated innumerable fires among the wooden houses and workshops, which burned unchecked for days and gutted the Old Town and the industrial zone enclosing it. The more modern industrial buildings on the edge of the town, however, at 1½ miles and more from the centre, escaped with only minor damage.

In Nagasaki the centre of damage was in the industrial area in the Urakami Valley. The harbour and the commercial area, nearly two miles distant, escaped with only minor damage; and so did the housing in the smaller valley, screened by the intervening ridge of hills.

Both in Hiroshima and in Nagasaki, the scale of the disaster brought city life and industry virtually to a standstill. Even the most destructive conventional attacks had no comparable effect in paralysing communal organization.

In great areas of destruction, rising here and there like islands, reinforced concrete buildings remained showing few signs of external damage. Reinforced concrete buildings of normal construction were usually safe from partial collapse beyond 600 yards from the centre of damage, and from structural damage beyond ½ mile. Reinforced concrete buildings of very heavy construction in Hiroshima, within 200 yards of the centre of damage, remained structurally undamaged.

Light single-storey concrete buildings, such as are employed for factories and warehouses, failed at about a mile from the centre of damage in both cities. The most striking feature of damage to steel framed single-storey factory sheds was their mass distortion, in the direction away from the explosion.

Of the machines housed in these sheds, only five per cent had suffered serious damage from the atomic bomb. This low figure is to be ascribed to the absence of fire. Nearly two-thirds of all machines in the Urakami valley had been housed in smaller workshops and sheds of timber. These shops were burnt down almost without exception to a distance in excess of 1¼ miles from the centre of damage; fifty per cent of the machines in them was destroyed or irreparably damaged.

Japanese houses are constructed on a frame of 4-in. or 6-in. square timbers. The roofs are a source of weakness, their covering of pantiles bedded in mud on ½-in. boarding being disproportionately heavy. The walls are of bamboo covered with 3 ins. of mud, which is sometimes protected by ¼-in. boarding; much of the wall space is occupied by paper-covered screens. Complete collapse of these buildings from blast extended to 1¼ miles from the centre of damage in Hiroshima, and to an average of 1½ miles in Nagasaki. Fire completed the destruction almost to the same distance.

PEOPLE who were directly under the explosion in the open had their exposed skin burnt so severely that it was immediately charred dark brown or black; these people died within minutes or at most hours. Very severe burns were occasionally reported at nearly 1½ miles from the centre of damage; mild burns at distances of 2½ miles and more.

Fire was not confined to wooden Japanese houses, but raged fiercely in many concrete buildings, in some machine shops, and in other buildings not normally subject to fire. It is certain that firespread did occur in both cities; but more striking is the vast numbers of separate points of fire.

The most important radio-active action at Hiroshima and Nagasaki appears to have been that from penetrating radiation, for convenience called gamma rays. The gamma rays pass through the skin without affecting it. They do not attack the cells in the blood-stream, but the primitive cells in the bone marrow, from which most of the different types of cells in the blood are formed. Therefore serious effects begin to appear only as the fully-formed cells already in the blood die off gradually and naturally, and are not replaced. Deaths probably began in about a week after the explosion, reached a peak in about three weeks, and had for the most part ceased after six or eight weeks.

It is estimated that people in the open have a fifty per cent chance of surviving the effects of gamma rays at ¾ mile from the centre of damage. The gamma rays are capable of penetrating considerable thickness of building and other material.

The effects of gamma rays on human reproduction necessarily form a long-term study, but at distances up to 1¼ miles from the centre of damage, pregnant women who survived had either miscarriages or premature infants who died very soon. Two months after the explosion miscarriages, abortions, and premature births throughout Hiroshima were nearly five times as frequent as in normal times, and formed more than one quarter of all deliveries. Sperm counts made in Hiroshima show that a high proportion of men exposed to gamma rays, up to perhaps ¾ miles from the centre of damage have reduced power of reproduction.

Official casualty figures for Hiroshima are 78,150 dead, as well as 13,983 missing. Those killed by air attack during the whole war throughout Great Britain, including London, numbered 60,000. The standard figure for an atomic bomb in British conditions would be approximately 50,000 dead.

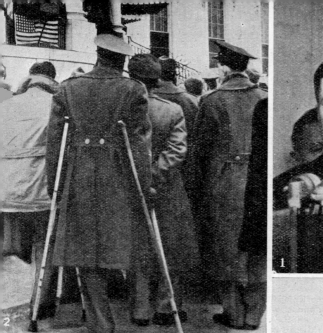

ROOSEVELT'S FOURTH TERM

Franklin Delano Roosevelt, 32nd President of the U.S., only President to be chosen for more than two terms, died on April 12, 1945, at Warm Springs, Georgia, aged 63. On January 20, 1945, when he spoke his fourth inaugural address, it was America's first wartime Presidential inauguration since Lincoln. 1. Delivering his fourth inaugural address from the White House. On his left is his son, Colonel James Roosevelt. 2. Disabled soldiers listen to the speech. 3. The funeral procession passes down Delaware Avenue, Washington, to the Capitol. 4. Tomb at Hyde Park, New York, Roosevelt's birthplace. Below, memorial coin struck in January 1946.

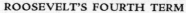

Chapter 373

AMERICA AT THE WAR'S END AND AFTER

The emotional impact on the American people of the atomic bomb and of the death of President Roosevelt ranked with that of the end of the Second Great War. Quick acceptance of President Truman and rapid progress toward reconversion, despite a post-war wave of strikes, eased the transition from war to peace, states Selden Menefee, author of " Assignment : U.S.A.," and of Chapters 251, 294, and 321 in this history of the year 1945.

IN terms of its emotional impact on the American people, the sudden death of Franklin Delano Roosevelt, in his thirteenth year as President, tops the list of events in the United States during 1945. His sudden passing was a profound shock to his friends and enemies alike. Men who had sneeringly referred to him as " that man in the White House " during the 1944 election campaign first were incredulous, then wept when they heard the news.

For three days the nation was in deep mourning. Flags everywhere were at half mast, most shops were closed. Tens of millions of Americans felt the loss as deeply as if a member of their own families had died. **Death of Roosevelt** A woman in Detroit said, "It doesn't seem possible. It seems to me that he will be back on the radio to-morrow, telling us that it was just a mistake." Soldiers on Okinawa cried unashamedly. When the President's body was brought by train from Georgia to Washington, D.C., silent crowds lined the tracks at every town. Half of Washington's population turned out to pay tribute to the flag-draped coffin on its black horse-drawn hearse as it was taken from the railway station to the White House. And when it had passed, an elderly Negro woman remained sitting on the Pennsylvania Avenue kerb, rocking back and forth and crying: "Oh, he's gone. He's gone for ever. I loved him so. He's never coming back. . . ."

For the common people of America, over the years Franklin D. Roosevelt had evolved from a friend into a father-symbol—someone on whom they knew they could depend. Many Americans in uniform could not remember any other president. They knew him as the man who foresaw America's entry into the war and did his best to prepare for it, against Congressional opposition—and the man who started to prepare for peace long before victory was won, by proposing that the United Nations be made a permanent organization for enforcing world peace. When a nation-wide opinion poll asked Americans late in 1945 to name " two or three of the greatest men who have ever lived in

this country," Franklin D. Roosevelt was named by 61 per cent, Abraham Lincoln by 57 per cent, and George Washington by 46 per cent.

After the first shock of Roosevelt's death, all eyes turned on President Truman, who was not well known to the American people. He was something of a political accident—an average Midwesterner from Missouri who failed in business after the last war, who had been a local politician until the notorious Boss Tom Pendergast of Kansas City decided to back him for the Democratic nomination to

the U.S. Senate in 1934. Truman remained loyal to Pendergast even after he was sent to jail; but no breath of scandal had ever touched Truman. In the Senate he had made his mark. As a hard-working, liberal, conscientious Senator he won an enviable reputation as head of a Committee to investigate war expenditures. In 1944 he was a compromise selection for the Vice-Presidency, accepted by the Democratic politicians who feared that Vice-President Henry Wallace was too liberal to be acceptable to the right wing of the Party. Truman campaigned well, but

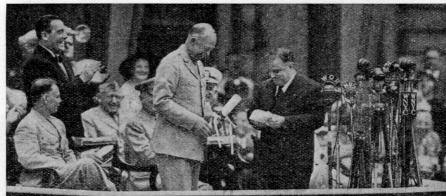

EISENHOWER'S RETURN

General Dwight David Eisenhower, Supreme Allied Commander in Western Europe, arrived in Washington on June 18, 1945, after triumphal receptions in Paris and London. Next day he was given a thunderous welcome in New York. Left, ' V for Victory ' sign at a Washington reception. Above, Mayor La Guardia presents him with the freedom of New York.

after the election he faded out of the public eye except on such occasions as when he appeared at a National Press Club party and played the piano while cinema actress Lauren Bacall sang torch songs. What kind of a President would he make ?

Mr. Truman won the country by his modesty and humility. It was a relief

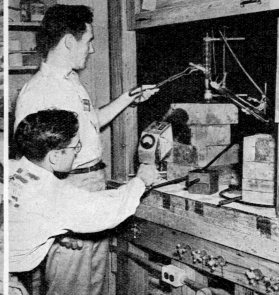

TENNESSEE HOME OF THE ATOMIC BOMB

The atomic bomb (see Chapter 379) was first used operationally at Hiroshima on August 6, 1945 (see page 3795). Here is the vast Clinton plant at Oakridge, near Knoxville, Tennessee, where part of the apparatus for constructing it was located. Right, research-workers, wearing special uniforms with chest-badges containing film to record radiation exposure.

Photos, New York Times Photos ; Associated Press

even to some of Roosevelt's staunchest supporters to have an average American, a man whom they could always understand, in high office. Truman courted Congress, hoping to avoid the bad relations with the Senate and House which had dogged the Roosevelt Administration. He made it clear that he was no crusader, but only a man who was pledged to keep the gains of the preceding twelve years, win the war, and see the country safely into the peace.

By the end of June a poll gave 87 per cent approval of the way he was handling his job, and only 3 per cent dis-

Popular Approval of Truman

approved. This surpassed even Roosevelt's peak of popularity. In September a poll was taken on the President's handling of U.S. foreign relations. Some 24 per cent said " excellent," 48 per cent " good," and only one per cent " poor." (The rest were undecided.)

As the battle for Germany drew to a close, talk of the post-war world reached a new peak. The newspapers devoted columns of space daily to the San Francisco Conference (*see* Chapter 381), and more columns to the controversy over when reconversion should begin. V.E. Day came as a bit of an anti-climax after the gradual breakdown of the German military machine and after at least two false reports of surrender. New York and a few other cities held impromptu celebrations on May 7, but in most places people went about their work in war plants and shops with the remark, " Well, that's two down and one to go." In San Francisco there was no public demonstration whatsoever.

When, however, General of the Army Dwight D. Eisenhower, after a triumphal reception in London and Paris, arrived by air in Washington on June 18, he had an enthusiastic welcome from hundreds of thousands of people as he drove to address Congress. Next day in New York he was given an overwhelming ovation from crowds estimated at four million, in the evening receiving the Freedom of New York from Mayor La Guardia. Eisenhower's appointment as Chief of Staff of the Army was announced on November 20, following the retirement of General Marshall, who, past the statutory retiring age of 64, was subsequently appointed the President's special envoy in China (*see* page 3778).

On V.J. Day, enthusiastic San Franciscans staged a three-day celebration that bordered on mob disorder. Even staid Washington had a night of delirious celebration, as did

nearly every American city. Most Americans identified themselves emotionally with the Pacific war much more than with the European war, and only after Japan's surrender did they feel a sense of release.

American war workers had turned in a good performance on the production lines. In the five years since the fall of France, U.S. industry and labour had turned out 297,000 combat planes, 3,600,000 trucks, 86,000 tanks, 87,000 warships of all sizes, 5,200 merchant ships, 434 million tons of steel, and 41,000 million rounds of ammunition. The war had cost more than £71,000 million, or more than the expenditures of the British Commonwealth and Empire and the Soviet Union combined; and it had cost 252,146 American lives, out of a total of 1,070,000 casualties. The cost was high but few begrudged it. The war had been a heavy drain also on American resources —some experts estimated that United States oil supplies would last only twelve more years at wartime rates of consumption, and her iron ore only eight years.

During the war, living standards reached and remained on a level

TRIBUTE TO U.S. MARINES

A special three-cent stamp commemorating the achievements of the U.S. Marines in the Second Great War was issued on July 11, 1945. Purple in colour, it depicted the raising by U.S. Marines of the American flag on Mount Suribachi, the volcano commanding Iwo Jima, on February 23, 1945 (see illus. in page 3767)

higher than ever before in the nation's history. When hostilities ended, petrol rationing was dropped. Shoe rationing soon followed. In November all food rationing, except of sugar, was ended, with the world sugar shortage making rationing of that commodity probable until 1947. Some shortages still persisted at the end of the year, especially of meats and fats; but farm production was so high that food rationing was felt to be no longer necessary.

The country was, however, faced by a real danger of inflation. Living costs had risen by about a third during the war, and threatened to go higher because of the shortage of consumers' goods as compared with the demand. Price controls were therefore extended to the middle of 1946, despite some business opposition, and manufacturers made strenuous efforts to turn over to peacetime production.

The Army started cancelling contracts in April, when the Allies were sweeping through Germany. More orders were **Army Contracts Cancelled** revised after V.E. Day; and in the week following the dropping of the atomic bomb on Hiroshima, the armed services sent out 30,000 telegrams cancelling the great bulk of remaining contracts. Almost immediately after victory, shipment of the armed forces home began. By the end of the year, over half of the 8,000,000 men in the Army had been demobilized, and nearly half of the 3,750,000 men in the Navy. Supply of civilian clothes to the demobilized caused such a drain on supplies that a civilian could not buy a shirt or suit of standard quality and size.

The housing shortage was an immense problem. During the war, residential construction had been limited to war housing, much of it temporary. Now some 3,000,000 returning men needed homes. There were none available in the larger cities except for purchase at inflated prices. More than a million families were sharing accommodation with others, and many people were living in trailer-caravans. In Atlanta, Georgia, 2,000 people answered an advertisement for a single flat. In Minneapolis, Minnesota, a man, his wife and baby spent seven freezing December nights in their car because they could not find even an hotel room. Home construction went slowly because materials were scarce and costs so high that houses of a type which sold for £1,500 before the war could not be built to sell for less than £2,500.

Reconversion brought the index of industrial production, which had reached a peak of 232 per cent of the pre-war level in February and March, down to 163 per cent in October. Then it started to rise again. New cars, refrigerators and vacuum cleaners began to appear in shop windows, though few were available for purchase as yet.

Before the war's end, government economists had predicted that 8,000,000 people would be unemployed during the reconversion period; but at the end of 1945 the number without work was still under 2,000,000. Many women war workers had left the labour market, and many demobilized men were taking a rest before starting to work again. Low-paid jobs in service industries were still going begging. It was anticipated, however, that the £40,000 million national income of 1945 would decline to £30,000 million in 1946.

The greatest threat to an ordered changeover to peace economy was the wave of strikes. Patriotic pledges had held back both union leaders and members from striking during the war; but four days after V.J. Day the United Auto Workers (C.I.O.) presented the automobile industry with a demand for a thirty per cent wage increase, so that the workers' "take-home pay" would be as large for the peacetime forty-hour week as it had been for 48 hours (with 8 hours at overtime rates) during the war. The U.A.W. selected General Motors, the largest company, for the initial test, and called out 175,000 G.M. workers late in November. This in turn affected other companies depending on G.M. for parts. President Truman appointed a fact-finding board to try to

KING AND PRESIDENT MEET IN PLYMOUTH SOUND

H.M. King George VI and President Harry S. Truman of the United States met on board the 32,000-ton battle-cruiser H.M.S. 'Renown' as she lay off Plymouth Sound on August 2, 1945. The President, who was on his way back to the U.S. from the Potsdam Conference (see Chapter 380), lunched with the King and afterwards received him on board the American cruiser 'Augusta.' The two heads of State are here pacing the quarterdeck of the 'Renown.' *Photo, G.P.U*

bring the sides together, and asked the board to examine the company's books to determine whether the increase could be afforded. But G.M. refused to agree to this procedure, arguing that ability to pay was no criterion for wage increases, and its representatives walked out of the hearing. Industrialists generally seemed disposed to stage a sit-down strike rather than submit to peacetime regulation of profits and higher wage rates. At the end of the year over 400,000 workers were on strike, and if the stoppages spread, increasing lack of consumer goods, with a consequent increased danger of inflation, threatened the country. The danger was heightened by the facts that union membership had soared during the war to a total of 14,500,000 members, while industry had acquired a cushion of some £10,000 million in wartime profits with which to soften the impact of labour troubles.

During his first months in office, President Truman followed a middle-of-the-road course in domestic politics. But with the war's end, he asked the Congress to enact a far-reaching programme providing for legal authority for his fact-finding committees on labour disputes, government planning for full employment, increased unemployment compensation, extension of social security legislation, protection of Negro job rights, a housing programme, and other liberal measures as a precaution against post-war chaos. A combination of Republicans and conservative Democrats operated through the peculiar American system of Congressional committees to bottle up virtually all of this legislation before it could come to a vote.

The American public was disposed to back Truman. The C.I.O. was critical of his proposal to give fact-finding committees power to delay and investigate strikes; but labour supported every other **Public Backing for Truman** portion of his programme. A majority of Americans believed that big businessmen were making more than a fair profit, and that the government should have the right to decide what a fair profit was. Nine out of ten wanted price control continued; two-thirds of all Americans favoured the forty-hour week, and almost as many favoured a legal minimum wage of 65 cents an hour.

NEW YORK CELEBRATES JAPAN'S DEFEAT

Although the defeat of Japan was not officially celebrated in the United States until September 2, 1945, after the signature of the surrender terms in Tokyo Bay (see page 3824), there were wild scenes of enthusiasm as soon as the news of the 'cease fire' came through on August 15. Here a vast crowd gathers in Times Square, New York, round a replica of the famous Statue of Liberty erected as part of the 'drive' for the purchase of Liberty Bonds.   *Photo, Pictorial Press*

Three-fourths of the public thought that social security legislation should be extended to cover all workers, instead of excluding those in homes, on farms and in very small businesses. And by a vote of five to two, Americans told interviewers for the National Opinion Research Centre that they thought President Truman should take a stronger stand in trying to get Congress to carry out his recommendations.

The record of Congress was much better in the international field than in domestic affairs. Congress approved the ratification by the Senate of the United Nations Charter on July 28 by a vote of 89 to 2, after only two weeks of hearings and debate. Every measure presented by the Administration in the field of foreign policy was similarly approved, although sometimes by much narrower margins. After some delay, the full appropriations requested by U.N.R.R.A. were voted. Membership in the Food and Agriculture Organization was approved. The Reciprocal Trade Agreements Act was renewed and extended, and the lending powers of the Export-Import Bank increased. The Bretton Woods agreements for an International Bank and Monetary Fund were approved after a bitter fight. The entire Administration programme for an orderly expansion of world trade was thus approved by the same Congress that blocked the entire Administration domestic programme.

The end of the war was the signal for President Truman, on August 15, to release the findings of the Army and Navy inquiry boards into the circumstances which had enabled the Japanese to make so successful an attack on Pearl Harbor on December 7, 1941. The Navy report criticized Rear-Admiral Husband Kimmel, in command of Pearl Harbor at the time, and Admiral Harold Stark, C.-in-C. Pacific Fleet, though it found no "serious offences committed nor serious blame incurred" by any of its personnel. The Army report extended its censure from Lieutenant-General Walter Short, in command at Hawaii at the time, to include Mr. Cordell Hull, the Secretary of State, and General George C. Marshall, the Chief of Staff. Courts-martial were not recommended, but the reports did tell a shocking tale of unpreparedness, confusion and lack of co-operation between the service branches.

On September 6 the Senate voted unanimously for a Congressional investigation, and eight days later a committee of ten, all lawyers—five members of the Senate, five of the House

Pearl Harbor Inquiries

U.S. INDUSTRY TURNS FROM WAR TO PEACE

By the end of 1945, America's major industries were being reconverted to produce peacetime goods. Above, workers in a California factory finish a wartime order for aircraft wings, while in the foreground others produce food cabinets and soda-fountain equipment. Below, some of the 40,000 U.S.A.A.F. aircraft on an Arkansas dump. Engines and other salable parts have been removed, while the metal is earmarked for salvage. *Photos, Associated Press; Keystone*

of Representatives—was set up. It opened its investigations on November 15; its report, issued after it had listened for weeks to testimony from almost everybody still living who had had any connexion with the disaster, was published on July 21, 1946. Eight members signed the majority report which, placing the blame squarely on the local commanders, Admiral Kimmel and General Short, found them guilty of errors of judgement, but not of dereliction of duty.

They exonerated President Roosevelt (placed first in the list accused by the two Senators who signed a sharp and bitter dissent from the majority report) from all blame; but both the War and

ALLIED FAR EASTERN ADVISORY COMMISSION

On August 22, 1945, Washington proposed the creation of an Allied Far Eastern Advisory Commission to ' formulate policies for the carrying out of the Japanese surrender terms,' a proposal agreed to at the London Council of Foreign Ministers in September. The Commission's first meeting was held on October 29 at the State Department, Washington, under the chairmanship of Major-Gen. Frank R. McCoy. Russia was not represented. Front row, left to right : Mr. T. A. Stone (Canada) ; Mr. C. A. Berendsen (New Zealand) ; Mr. P. E. Naggiar (France) ; Mr. Wei Tao-ming (China) ; Lord Halifax (Great Britain) ; Mr. James F. Byrnes (U.S.A. Secretary of State) ; Dr A. Loudon (Netherlands) ; Dr. H. V. Evatt (Australia) ; Major-Gen. McCoy (U.S.) ; Sir Girja Shahkar Bajpai (India) ; and General Carlos Romulo (Philippines). *Photo, Keystone*

Navy Departments were held to have failed in the full discharge of their duties, officers named in the committee's censure including Lieutenant-General Leonard Gerow (who commanded the U.S. 15th Army in Europe—*see* illus. in page 3797) and Admiral R. K. Turner (director of amphibious operations in the Pacific—*see* illus. in page 2882).

The ending of Lend-Lease shortly after V.J. Day created hardly a ripple in the United States. The British reactions to President Truman's announcement on the subject, which Britons considered unnecessarily abrupt, caused some surprise. Congress had voted Lend-Lease for war purposes only, and would have bitterly opposed its extension after the end of hostilities. The American public was never well-informed on the subject of Lend-Lease ; more than two-thirds of the people thought that the United States should be paid back for the war materials sent to Britain, and almost as many did not know that they were getting " mutual aid " from Britain—the total value of such reciprocal aid up to June 30, 1945, being £1,080,300,000. Sixty-five per cent of college graduates, but only 29 per cent of those who had simply passed through the elementary schools, knew about " reverse lend-lease."

Opinion was similarly uninformed in regard to the British mission headed by Lord Keynes which came to America in September to negotiate a grant or loan to assist in restoring Britain's trade.

PEARL HARBOR INQUIRY

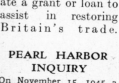

On November 15, 1945 a U.S. Congressional committee of inquiry into the Pearl Harbor attack in 1941 began its sittings in Washington. It consisted of five members of the Senate and five of the House of Representatives. The Committee (right) here examines the first two witnesses. On the walls are relief maps of the Hawaiian islands.
Photo, Keystone

In a Gallup poll held while the negotiations were on, disapproval of " a loan of three to five thousand million dollars to help England get back on her feet" was expressed by sixty per cent, approval by only 27 per cent. Behind this unfavourable opinion was the memory of unpaid loans after the First Great War, kept alive by isolationist propagandists.

Lord Keynes was considered by American officials to be an extremely able negotiator, and the terms finally agreed

Negotiations for Loan to Britain upon undoubtedly were as favourable as Congress could be expected to approve When this agreement was announced early in December, after twelve weeks of negotiation, the concessions made by the British were sufficient to gain widespread editorial approval in the American press. One factor in favour of the loan was the widespread realization that American prosperity as well as military

The agreement was for a total U.S. loan of $4,400,000,000 (£1,100,000,000) to Britain, consisting of a credit agreement for $3,750,000,000 (£937,500,000), to be spent mainly on American goods needed for reconverting British industry, and a final sum in settlement of Lease-Lend of $650,000,000 (£162,500,000). The credit, which could be drawn upon at any time between the date of ratification of the agreement and December 31, 1951, was to be repaid over a fifty-year period starting on December 31, 1951, with interest at two per cent, except during years when Britain's income from home-produced exports and invisible current transactions was less than the average annual amount of U.K. imports during 1936–38. For her part Britain agreed to support the American programme for an international policy of lowering barriers to world trade, including the modification of the sterling bloc policy after one year, and acceptance of the Bretton Woods proposals (*see* page 3256). The loan agreement, approved by the British Parliament before the end of the year, was ratified by Congress, after a stiff fight in both the Senate and the House of Representatives, on July 13, 1946.

The American public was profoundly shaken by the news of the atomic bomb. A great majority approved the use of the bomb as a means of ending the war ; but they viewed it with mixed feelings, nevertheless, because of the danger that

security depended on full participation in world affairs.

it might be used against the United States at some future time. Most people realized that within a very short period —possibly five years—other countries could develop their own atomic bombs ; nevertheless, they felt that such secrets as America possessed should be kept under American control for as long as possible. In the background was a feeling of guilt over having unleashed this new death-dealing device. Most Americans believed that in the end mankind would be better off as a result of atomic fission, and that it will make future wars less likely ; but five people out of six thought that there was a real danger of the world's urban population being annihilated in another war.

Mr. Clement Attlee, British Prime Minister, and Sir John Anderson, who had supervised atomic energy research for the British War Cabinet, arrived by air in Washington on November 10 for talks between the United States, Britain and Canada on atomic energy, the conference lasting from November 11–14. A joint statement, signed by President Truman, Mr. Attlee and Mr. Mackenzie King and issued on November 15, declared their willingness to exchange fundamental scientific information with other of the United Nations that would fully reciprocate as soon as effective, enforceable safeguards against its use for destructive purposes could be devised, and advocated the setting up at

Mr. Attlee Visits the United States

BRITISH PREMIER IN WASHINGTON

Mr. Clement Attlee arrived in Washington on November 10, 1945, for talks between Britain, the U.S. and Canada. On November 13 he addressed a joint session of Congress when he declared : ' Man's material discoveries have outpaced his moral progress. The greatest task that faces us today is to bring home to all people before it is too late that our civilization can only survive by the acceptance and practice in international relations and in our national life of the Christian principle that we are members one of another.' Above, Mr. Attlee and President Truman at the White House. Right, the British Premier addresses Congress.
Photos, Keystone

the earliest practicable date of a commission under the United Nations to prepare recommendations as to safeguards to be submitted to the United Nations Organization. The proposed Atomic Energy Commission was set up on January 24, 1946, during the first meeting of the General Assembly of the United Nations in London (*see* Chapter 387).

A bill to provide for "Government control of the production, ownership and use of fissionable material," and imposing penalties up to twenty years' im-

Bill to Control Atomic Energy prisonment or a fine up to $20,000 (£5,000) or both for disseminating information "on restricted data with intent to injure the U.S.A. or to secure advantage for a foreign nation," proposed in December by Senator Brien McMahon, head of the Special Committee on Atomic Energy set up by the Senate, was approved by the full Senate on June 1, 1946, and sent to the House of Representatives.

During his stay in Washington, Mr. Attlee addressed a joint session of Congress, emphasizing the ties that bound the United States and the United Kingdom, and explaining the point of view and programme of the British Labour Party, with its freedom-loving tradition. "We in the Labour Party," said Mr. Attlee, "declare that we are in line with those who fought for Magna Carta and Habeas Corpus, with the Pilgrim Fathers and with the signatories of the Declaration of Independence."

AGREEMENT ON U.S. LOAN TO BRITAIN

On December 6, 1945, after 12 weeks of negotiation, agreement was reached in Washington between representatives of Great Britain and the United States for a loan to Britain of £1,100,000,000. Here the U.S. Secretary of State, Mr. James F. Byrnes, puts his signature to the agreement. On his left is Mr. Fred M. Vinson, Secretary of the U.S. Treasury, and on his right Lord Halifax, British Ambassador to Washington, and (extreme left) Lord Keynes, who led the British mission. Immediately behind Mr. Byrnes is Mr. Dean Acheson, U.S. Assistant Secretary of State. The agreement was ratified by Congress on July 13, 1946. *Photo, Keystone*

Many points of friction with the Soviet Union developed during 1945, most noticeably over the situation in the Far East. On the initiative of Mr. Byrnes, U.S. Secretary of State, while he was in London in September for the meeting of the Council of Foreign Ministers (*see* Chapter 378), a Far Eastern Advisory Commission was created to formulate policies for the carrying out of the Japanese surrender terms. Russia suggested that the Advisory Commission should be preceded by the appointment of an Allied Control Council for Japan—a proposal that was opposed by the U.S.A. (*see* page 3841); and no Russian representative was present when the Commission held its first meeting in Washington on October 29.

Two working committees were set up to consider (a) basic policies and objectives in Japan, including the study of directives sent to General MacArthur and the implementing of orders issued by him;

Far Eastern Affairs

(b) Japanese war crimes. Representatives of the Commission were appointed to visit Japan and familiarize themselves at first hand with the situation there. At the Moscow meeting of the Foreign Ministers in December (*see* page 3564), agreement was reached on the constitution of an Allied Control Council and a Far Eastern Commission for Japan, the latter to supersede the Far Eastern Advisory Commission; and on January 2, 1946, Lieutenant-General Derevyanko, who signed the Japanese surrender instrument on behalf of his country (*see* page 3825), was appointed Soviet delegate on the Allied Control Council; Mr. Andrei Gromyko, Soviet Ambassador in Washington, Soviet representative on the Far Eastern Commission.

MOTOR FACTORY WORKERS STRIKE

In the United States the return to peace was marked by a wave of strikes, the workers' 'no-strikes-during-wartime' pledges no longer holding good. By the end of 1945, some 400,000 employees of General Motors alone were out. Below, a procession of workers with placards parade outside the G.M. works in Detroit. *Photo, Associated Press*

September 1. Russians withdrew from British, American and French zones of occupation in Vienna. At Monte Cassino, Italy, Polish cemetery dedicated in ceremony attended by Field-Marshal Alexander.

September 2. Japanese signed instrument of unconditional surrender on board U.S. battleship "Missouri" in Tokyo Bay; 13,000 U.S. troops landed in Japan; Japanese forces surrendered in Luzon (Philippines). Annamites in French Indo-China attacked members of French colony in Saigon. Minesweeping of Malacca Straits begun. Censorship ended in Britain. U.S. Lend-Lease agreement with Britain terminated.

September 3. British prisoners of war and internees sailed for home from Tokyo. British troops landed at Hongkong. In Malaya, Royal Marines took over Penang. British military authorities lifted restrictions on fraternization. Allied victory march in Brussels to celebrate first anniversary of city's liberation.

September 4. General MacArthur ordered immediate demobilization and disarmament of Japanese army and prohibited broadcasts in foreign languages. General Sir Bernard Freyberg, V.C., appointed to succeed Sir Cyril Newall as Governor-General of New Zealand. Wake Island surrendered by Japanese commander. General Franco informed of decision of Allied conference on the re-establishment of international zone of Tangier.

September 5. British and Indian forces landed at Singapore. In Germany, Hugo Stinnes and 43 other industrialists arrested by British Control Commission. Rioting continued at Saigon, Indo-China.

September 6. Surrender of all Japanese in S.W. Pacific area signed on board H.M.S. "Glory" off Rabaul. General Eisenhower announced termination of Press censorship in Europe. Greek Regent, Archbishop Damaskinos, arrived in London.

September 7. British naval base at Singapore handed back to British control. British, American, Russian and French troops held victory parade in Berlin. Australian House of Representatives ratified United Nations Charter.

September 8. Troops of 1st U.S. Cavalry Division entered Tokyo; U.S. flag raised in presence of General MacArthur. Surrender of all Japanese on Bougainville and adjacent islands signed at Australian H.Q. Surrender of Japanese forces in Netherlands East Indies and Dutch Borneo signed.

September 9. Formal surrender of 1,000,000 Japanese signed in Nanking by General Okamura; the document specified that the surrender to General Chiang Kai-shek covered all ground, sea, air and auxiliary forces "within China (excluding Manchuria), Formosa, and French Indo-China north of latitude 16 N." U.S. troops landed on Korea, liberating hundreds of British and American prisoners of war; surrender instrument signed.

September 10. General MacArthur ordered dissolution of Japanese Imperial H.Q., established radio and Press censorship in Japan. Commander of Japanese forces in N. Borneo surrendered at Labuan. In Malaya, S.E.A.C. troops landed at Port Swettenham and Port Dickson. Quisling sentenced to death by Norwegian court. Sweden suspended neutrality regulations in force since the outbreak of the war.

September 11. Japanese General Tojo arrested after attempting to commit suicide. Surrender of Dutch Timor signed off Koepang. Chinese forces entered Hanoi, Indo-China. First meeting of Foreign Ministers opened in London. Sir Arthur Tedder promoted Marshal of the R.A.F.

September 12. Surrender of Japanese forces in S.E. Asia received at Singapore by Lord Louis Mountbatten. First S.E.A.C. troops flown to Bangkok, Siam. Field-Marshal Montgomery made "Citizen of Honour" of Brussels. Revealed that Field-Marshal von Busch died on July 17 in prisoner of war hospital in England.

September 13. Japanese 18th Army finally surrendered at Wewak, New Guinea, to Australians. Surrender of Japanese troops in Burma took place in Rangoon to British 12th Army. Japanese Military H.Q. formally abolished. Anglo-U.S. trade and financial discussions began in Washington.

September 14. Surrender of all Japanese forces in Malaya made at Kuala Lumpur. Field-Marshal Montgomery granted Germans in British occupation zone the right to form political parties.

September 15. Togo, former Japanese Foreign Minister, surrendered to the U.S. 8th Army. Aircraft of R.A.F. Fighter Command flew over London to commemorate the Battle of Britain.

September 16. Japanese in Hongkong surrendered to Admiral Harcourt. Lord Wavell arrived in Delhi.

September 17. Trial began at Lüneburg of Josef Kramer, commandant of Belsen concentration camp, and 44 of his staff. Chinese national flag hoisted over Formosa after 50 years of Japanese occupation. Yugoslav Government claimed whole of province of Venezia Guilia on the ground that it is "geographically, economically, and by the will of its population" a constituent part of Yugoslavia.

September 18. President Truman announced the resignation of Mr. Stimson as Secretary of War, succeeded by Mr. Robert Patterson. First shipment of rubber left Singapore. New graving-dock, second largest in the world, opened at Cape Town.

September 19. Mr. Attlee and Lord Wavell broadcast on Government's proposals for self-government for India. International traffic resumed on the Rhine from Duisburg to the sea. William Joyce ("Lord Haw-Haw") sentenced to death for treason in the Central Criminal Court, London.

September 20. British and American warships arrived in Shanghai. New British submarine "Achates" launched at Devonport.

September 21. Field-Marshal Montgomery given a civic reception in Prague.

September 22. In Germany British Military Government announced that local and provincial councils, composed of selected Germans, would be established at once and that when these were functioning satisfactorily the Germans would be allowed to elect their own local councils. The liner "Ile de France" handed back to French authorities at Southampton.

September 23. Announced that a further relaxation of non-fraternization orders would, from October 1, permit British occupation troops to enter German homes. Denmark declared to be the first Continental country free of mines, 2,000,000 having been lifted.

September 24. General MacArthur issued orders to the Japanese calling for the establishment of economic control and for the production of essential commodities; war production prohibited and all heavy industries placed under Allied control. Petroleum agreement signed by Great Britain and the United States.

September 25. American troops landed at Aomori, southern terminus of the rail ferry between Honshu and Hokkaido. World Trade Union Conference met in Paris. Diplomatic relations resumed between U.S.S.R. and Hungary. Announced that British ships would cease to use the Panama Canal to conserve foreign dollar payments.

September 26. U.S. officer killed and other Allied casualties sustained in clashes with Annamite nationalists near Saigon, Indo-China.

September 27. Emperor Hirohito made formal call on General MacArthur at U.S. Embassy in Tokyo. In Germany, larger food rations announced for children between 9-17 and for victims of Nazi persecution approved by Allied Kommandatura in Berlin. In London, international agreement signed for establishment of European Central Inland Transport Organization, signatories including Britain, the U.S.S.R., and France.

September 28. General Patton reported to General Eisenhower on "de-nazification" programme in Bavaria. Malta again became Mediterranean H.Q. of British Fleet. King and Queen visited ships of the Home Fleet in the Firth of Forth.

September 29. British troops began the occupation of Java without interference from Indonesian nationalists. Dutch forces landed at Batavia.

September 30. British officials in Germany announced the inauguration of a clothing levy to be made on the Germans. U.S. Marines landed at port of Tientsin (China). Hungarian Provisional Government recognized by the United States.

Chapter 374

DEMOCRATIC ITALY VOTES FOR A REPUBLIC

Internal affairs in the increasing area of Italy under Italian control are described by Friedl Orlando in this chapter, which follows events up to the declaration of the Republic in June 1946. The last stages in the military campaign in Italy are recorded in Chapter 361 ; the history of German-occupied Italy after the Italian surrender is told in Chapter 360

THE year 1945 opened with a serious revolt of the Sicilian separatists. Ever since the Allied landing in Sicily, the separatist movement had grown in strength, and by illegal means had obtained arms. It was supported by the big Sicilian landowners and local Fascists who feared that, in the new democratic Italy, there would be no room for them. Their propaganda met with some success amongst the population. The armed rising in the beginning of January had to be quelled by force.

The episode brought home once more to the Allies the necessity of conferring greater prestige, power and freedom of action on the central Government in Rome. Several steps were successively taken in that direction : on January 15 the control of news and information was handed back to the Italian Government ; on February 24 the political section of the Allied Control Commission was abolished. Henceforth the Italian Government could enter into direct negotiations with Allied and neutral countries, although it was required to keep the Allies informed of all its more important dealings in the international field. Internally, it could promulgate laws and degrees without prior consultation with the head of the Allied Commission.

Official representatives had already been dispatched to London and Moscow (*see* page 3241). Alberto Tarchiani was now appointed Ambassador in Washington and Giuseppe Saragat Ambassador in Paris. Both were political personalities, chosen because no trained diplomat free from the taint of Fascism was available.

The main preoccupations of the Bonomi Government were the political purge and the improvement of economic conditions. The most spectacular Fascist trial opened in Rome on **Fascist Trials** January 22 against General Mario Roatta (*see* page 3231), retained by Badoglio as Chief of Staff until the Allies asked for his removal, and 14 other prominent Fascists. Startling revelations were made during the hearings concerning Fascist intervention in the Spanish Civil War, and the murder of Mussolini's political opponents in exile. The public conscience was badly shaken when, in the middle of the trial, Roatta suddenly disappeared on the night of March 4 from a military hospital to which he had been removed on February 3 following a heart attack. Complicity in high quarters was suspected. The Bonomi Government announced that in future it would keep a firmer hand on men held in connexion with the purge : "socially dangerous elements of the old regime" were to be interned ; Military Intelligence passed under the direct control of the Minister of War ; the

ANTI-FASCIST RIOTS IN THE ITALIAN CAPITAL

There were violent anti-Fascist demonstrations during March 1945 after the mysterious escape of ex-Lieutenant-General Mario Roatta, then on trial as a war criminal. Roatta, former Italian Chief of Staff, had been dismissed by Marshal Badoglio at the request of the Allies on November 12, 1943. Here, the crowds, under the shadow of the Red Flag, demonstrate outside the Colosseum against the Government's slackness in carrying out the 'purge.' *Photo. Keystone*

Supreme Allied Commander, Mediterranean, also sent his Chief of Staff, Lieutenant-General W. D. Morgan, to Belgrade, for discussions with Marshal Tito, without any immediate useful result. But negotiations between the Allied and Yugoslav authorities continued; while in Washington on May 29 President Truman saw Dr. Subasitch (Yugoslav Foreign Minister, then in the United States for the San Francisco Conference).

Commander-in-Chief of the Carabinieri was replaced by General Brunetti.

On March 12 the High Court found all the accused, except four minor persons, guilty. Among the heaviest sentences were: Filippo Anfuso, at the time of his arraignment "Republican-Fascist" Ambassador in Berlin, condemned in his absence to death; Roatta (in absence) and Santo Emanuele, of the Secret Service, to life imprisonment; General Angioi, head of the Military Intelligence Service, to twenty years' imprisonment.

On June 4 the High Court condemned to death Pietro Koch, head of the Fascist counterpart of the S.S., who, after the Italian surrender, was detailed to suppress the underground resistance movement, and equipped a torture chamber in Rome which vied with the worst set up by the Gestapo. He made no effort to defend himself.

After the surrender of the German forces in Italy (*see* page 3717), northern Italy also came under Allied Military Government, though the retirement of the Germans was followed by certain local difficulties. Yugoslav troops entered Venezia Giulia (*see* page 3707) and, contrary to previous understanding between Marshal Tito and Field-Marshal Alexander, now occupied the whole province. The French occupied the Aosta Valley in Piedmont, an area which had long been Italian, although the inhabitants speak French. After discussions between the French and Italian Governments and the Supreme Allied Command, the French withdrew from the Aosta Valley in June, and were replaced by Americans. The Italian Government subsequently granted a large degree of autonomy to the area.

The position in Venezia Giulia (Istria) was complicated by the rival claims of Yugoslavia (*see* opposite page) and Italy

A.M.G. AIDS FOOD DISTRIBUTION IN ITALY

Among the many duties of Allied Military Government in Italy up till almost the end of 1945—when virtually the entire country was handed back to Italian control—was the co-ordination of supplies and distribution of wheat. Here, at a northern port, sacks of cereal go into the hold of a schooner bound for the south. Above, also under A.M.G. supervision, Indian Pioneers repair a railway track at Ancona to help food distribution. *Photos, U.S. Official*

to the area, which included the port of Trieste—the core of the dispute. All sections of opinion in Italy were opposed to the Yugoslav claim. Even Togliatti, the Communist leader (*see* illus. in page 3239), after at first supporting it as "an act of justice and restitution," on May 16 came out, like the leaders of all other political parties, in support of Italy's claim.

Trieste itself was meanwhile garrisoned by British, Dominion, United States and Yugoslav troops. No incidents occurred, but the situation was confused and feeling was tense. On May 15 the British and United States Ambassadors in Belgrade presented notes in friendly and identical terms, emphasizing that the disposal of the disputed territory must form part of the peace settlement and could not be affected by military occupation following the enemy's withdrawal. Field-Marshal Alexander,

On June 9 an agreement for the temporary military administration of Istria was announced, its principal terms being (1) that part of the area including Trieste, the railways and roads from Trieste to Austria via Gorizia, Caporetto, and Tarvisio, as well as Pola, to be under command and control of the Supreme Allied Command; (2) Yugoslav troops in this area, limited to a detachment of Regular troops not exceeding 2,000, to occupy a district selected by the Supreme Commander and not to have access to other areas; (3) Marshal Tito to withdraw Yugoslav forces in the area to come under Allied Military Government by 8 a.m. on June 12; (4) the agreement not to prejudice the ultimate disposal of Venezia Giulia.

Yugoslav withdrawal proceeded in quiet and orderly fashion and without incident. On June 12 the Yugoslav flag was lowered from the Trieste town hall, and the Stars-and-Stripes and the Union Jack were run up. Great pro-Ally demonstrations occurred in the city, which was bedecked with Italian flags.

General Morgan, for Allied Mediterranean H.Q., and General Jovanovitch, for the Yugoslav High Command, signed an agreement on June 20 defining the demarcation between Allied and Yugoslav zones of occupation (*see* map in column 3, where this line is shown as the Morgan Line): it ran from a point four miles south of Trieste to the Italo-Austro-Yugoslav frontier. This agreement also stipulated that the Allies should hold the town, airfield and port of Pola, from which the Yugoslav troops withdrew on June 21.

The rival claims to Trieste continued, however, to present a major problem to the Allies. The Italian Government made repeated offers to enter into direct negotiations with the Yugoslav Government, but these led to nothing, Tito maintaining his claim to a frontier on the Isonzo. At the London meeting of the Council of Foreign Ministers held

in September (*see* Chapter 378), Signor de Gasperi, Italian Foreign Minister, presented his country's case, declaring that Italy was ready to make sacrifices to compensate for Fascist aggression, but reaffirming the Italian character of Trieste and the coastal towns of Istria. Dr. Kardelj, deputy Prime Minister of Yugoslavia, reiterated Yugoslav claims to the whole of Venezia Giulia.

The Foreign Ministers on September 19 instructed their deputies to conduct investigations and report (a) on a line which would in the main be the ethnic line leaving a minimum under alien rule; (b) on an international régime which would assure that the port and transport facilities of Trieste should be available for use on equal terms by all international trade, and by Yugoslavia, Italy, and the States of central Europe. A commission of experts, appointed by the Foreign Ministers' deputies to study the question on the spot and make recommendations, presented its report to the Foreign Ministers of Great Britain, U.S.A., the Soviet Union and France when they met in Paris on April

VENEZIA GIULIA

Trieste and the surrounding country, in Italian possession since 1918, was claimed by Yugoslavia at the end of the Second Great War. This map shows various frontier lines suggested between Italy and Yugoslavia, and the area which the Foreign Ministers' Conference of June 1946 proposed to place under international administration.
By courtesy of The Daily Telegraph

25, 1946. The commission could not agree on a definite line for the future Italo-Yugoslav frontier, but it was in general agreement on the ethnographic and economic aspects of the region. Once more the Italians and Yugoslavs were invited to present their points of view. Italy advocated a frontier approximating to the proposed Wilson Line of 1919; while Yugoslavia claimed the restoration roughly of the 1914 frontier (*see* map above). All the Foreign Ministers advocated different frontiers, the Soviet Minister supporting the Yugoslav claim in its entirety. No agreement was reached, and the discussion was deferred to a later meeting.

When the Foreign Ministers met again in June they finally agreed to the main provisions of the treaty with Italy, to be put before the Peace Conference on July 29. Trieste and an area round it, indicated in the map, should, they thought, become a free territory guaranteed by the Security Council of the United Nations, in direct contact with both Italy and Yugoslavia, the Italo-Yugoslav common frontier to follow roughly the line advocated by the French in April. Certain readjustments of the Franco-Italian frontier in favour of France were included. Italy was to renounce all rights and titles to her territorial possessions in Africa, which should continue for twelve months

RESTORING HIDDEN WORKS OF ART

The Allied Government in Italy in February 1944 announced the setting up of a Commission for Monuments and Fine Arts whose tasks included compiling inventories of famous works of art and restoring looted masterpieces to their owners. Here, paintings are being returned to Florence in a U.S. lorry in July 1945. They had been stowed away on the Upper Adige river, near Bolzano, as the Allies advanced. Heralds in medieval dress trumpet their arrival.

TRAGEDY FOR TRIESTE

Rival claims of Italy and Yugoslavia to Trieste after the surrender of the Germans there (see page 3718) produced a situation with international complications. 1. Lt-General Sir Bernard Freyberg, V.C., commanding the New Zealand 2nd Division, meets Marshal Tito's representative, General Borstnar, in Monfalcone, 15 miles from Trieste, on May 1. 2. Among the wrecked ships lying in the harbour was the overturned Italian liner 'Rex,' once holder of the Atlantic Blue Riband. 3. Vatican City relief lorry, labelled 'Food for Trieste,' is escorted by a British military policeman. 4. On November 4, crowds demonstrate in support of Yugoslav claims.

under the existing Allied administration; the final disposition of the territories to be made by the four Powers on one or a combination of the bases of (a) independence; (b) incorporation in neighbouring territories; (c) trusteeship under the United Nations as a whole or any one of the United Nations. Italy was to pay reparations to Russia to the value of $100,000,000.

Through the swift and concerted action of Allied Armies and the partisan forces, most of the northern Italian industrial plants had been saved. Yet they received during 1945 little raw material and no coal, nor was transport working. As A.M.G. gradually handed the provinces back to Italian authority, the Government was faced with a huge unemployment problem, intensified by the return of Italian prisoners of war. Moreover, at the end of 1945, Italy was still in complete uncertainty about her future. Until the Government knew how much reparations

BRITISH IN ITALY

During 1945, Allied military control in Italy was steadily relaxed, until by December 31 the Allied Commission had returned to Italian administration the whole country except Venezia Giulia, South Tyrol, and Udine. 1. Allied soldiers early in November outside the H.Q. of the British Military Police in Rome which had been named 'New Scotland Yard.' 2 Major-General I. B. Erskine, head of the British Military Police, holds an inspection in Milan. 3. Battalion cooks prepare an al fresco meal near Trieste in Venezia Giulia.

Italy would have to pay, and the rate at which the Allies were willing to back the A.M.-Lire (money issued to Allied occupation troops), economic reconstruction was extremely difficult. Trade between the industrial north and the agricultural south helped to stabilize prices. During the summer, U.N.R.R.A. abolished the restrictive clauses (see page 3447) concerning supplies to Italy, and in the second half of the year started importing fertilizers, coal and raw materials. On August 1 the Italian Government regained control of foreign trade, and in the same month Italy concluded a commercial agreement with Switzerland. An economic delegation left for Warsaw and Prague to negotiate coal supplies

from Poland and Czechoslovakia. American credit to Italy was further extended, and Britain, too, announced a small sterling credit to back part of the A.M.-Lire spent by British troops in Italy.

After the liberation of northern Italy, negotiations between the Northern and Southern Committees of Liberation followed in Rome for the formation of a new Cabinet that would include all sections of Italian political opinion. These negotiations were long and protracted: the main stumbling block was disagreement amongst the parties concerning the future position of the Committees of National Liberation. These bodies, covering the six anti-Fascist parties which had worked together during the clandestine period, had organized the resistance in the north

under the German occupation and had even administered patches of territory behind the lines (see pages 3701-3703). Now, the Left wing parties were unwilling to restrict the rights and activities of bodies which had proved efficient, had sprung spontaneously from the people and undoubtedly commanded their support. The Liberals, on the other hand, held that the C.N.L. would now but double the functions of the regular organs of Government.

At the beginning of June the six parties agreed that in future the C.N.L. should have merely consultative functions. In territory administered by A.M.G., the Allies adopted the same view. With this controversy settled, the Bonomi Government resigned on June 12 and on the 19th Ferruccio Parri, of the Action

ATOMIC BOMB HELPED TO END THE WAR AGAINST JAPAN

The first atomic bomb to be used in warfare was dropped on Hiroshima, Japan, on August 6, 1945, by a Super-Fortress of the U.S.A. 20th Air Force. It was followed three days later by another on Nagasaki. Both bombs caused unbelievable destruction, which provided the Japanese with an excuse for capitulation. Preliminary experiments were carried out on Alamogordo bombing range, New Mexico on July 16, when this awe-inspiring mushroom of smoke and flame rose to a height of 40,000 feet. *Photo, U.S. Army*

WITH THE BRITISH AND CANADIANS IN NORMANDY

One of the turning-points in the struggle following the Allied invasion of France was reached on July 18, 1944, after the capture of Caen—most important road-junction in Normandy—nine days earlier, when British and Canadian troops of the British 2nd Army broke into the area east of the river Orne. This attack, which took them across the river and into the plains, was preceded by the most devastating tactical bombing operation carried out to that date. (See Chapter 314.) Above, wounded being carried from the battlefield near Colombelles—an industrial district north-east of Caen. Left, British and Canadian troops round up Germans in the same area.

Direct colour photographs by Associated Press

GERMANS SURRENDER UNCONDITIONALLY TO
FIELD-MARSHAL MONTGOMERY AT LUNEBURG

ON May 4, 1945, there was signed at 21st Army Group H.Q., on Lüneburg Heath, near Hamburg, a field surrender of all German forces in north-west Europe. The signing was preceded by 'feelers' from the Germans. On May 2—the day on which hostilities ceased in Italy—General Blumentritt, commanding all German forces between the Baltic and the Weser river, sent an envoy to Field-Marshal Montgomery's H.Q., saying that he wished to surrender his Army Group to the British next day. On May 3, instead of Blumentritt, there arrived a German delegation headed by General-Admiral von Friedeburg, C.-in-C. of the German Navy in succession to Admiral Doenitz, and General Kinzel, chief of staff to Field-Marshal Busch, C.-in-C., North-West Germany, offering surrender of the three German armies facing the Russians in Mecklenburg, between Rostock and Berlin.

Field-Marshal Montgomery refused this offer, pointing out that this was a matter for the Russians and demanding instead the unconditional surrender of all German forces in Holland, Friesland, Schleswig-Holstein and Denmark. The Germans, who had no powers to discuss these points, returned to Hamburg. Next evening (May 4) they arrived back at Lüneburg to sign—without protest—the surrender document which declared that all hostilities would cease at 8 a.m. B.D.S.T., next day, the Germans to lay down their arms and to surrender unconditionally. The German Command further agreed to carry out 'at once and without argument or comment' all orders issued by the Allied Powers 'on any subject.' In the event of any doubt or dispute arising, the decision of the Allied Powers was to be final. The instrument of surrender was written in both English and German, the former being described as the 'authentic text.' Here, Field-Marshal Montgomery reads the terms to the Germans. On his right is Admiral Friedeburg, next to whom is his staff officer, Admiral Wagner. Friedeburg committed suicide at Flensburg on May 23.

WITH VICTORY THE LIGHTS GO UP AGAIN IN BRITAIN

Lifting of the lighting restrictions, which had been in force all over Britain since the outbreak of war, was a symbol that danger in Europe was over. On May 8, 1945, after Mr. Churchill's broadcast had announced the end of hostilities, all public buildings in London were floodlit, among them the Guildhall of the Middlesex County Council in Parliament Square (left) and the Clock Tower of the Houses of Parliament (right). On September 17, 1944, a system of half-lighting, or 'dim out' had been introduced, and on April 23, 1945, normal lighting was allowed—except in a five-mile coastal belt. On May 10, all lighting restrictions were lifted.

Party (*see* illus. in page 3707), became Prime Minister. Parri, a Milan intellectual, had been Vice-Commander of the Partisan Army. He was one of the most popular men in the country, highly respected for his integrity, and his appointment as Prime Minister was a gesture expressing the pride and gratitude with which the whole country regarded the Resistance movement. But the Government had no electoral mandate. In anticipation of elections as soon as the country (or the greater part of it) was returned to Italian control, the preparation of electoral laws and lists was put in hand ; constituencies were defined ; a system of proportional representation was worked out, and universal suffrage was proclaimed. For the first time in Italian history women were given the vote.

The purge was continued by the Parri Government. Many prominent Fascists such as Bottai, Federzoni, Rossoni, were sentenced to death or to life imprisonment, some of them in their absence. It was the Government policy to strike at the leaders while showing leniency towards people in secondary positions. But the scrupulousness with which the Government proceeded led to great

The 'Purge' Continues

DE GASPERI ADDRESSES CONSULTATIVE ASSEMBLY

At the abortive Foreign Secretaries' meeting in London in September 1945 (see Chapter 378) Italy's case was presented by Mr. Alcide de Gasperi, Foreign Minister in the Parri Government, who here reports to the Consultative Assembly on his return. (Count Sforza, President of the Assembly, is seated in the chair, top left.) On December 4 Mr. de Gasperi succeeded Parri as Premier.

delays in the opening of trials and the pronouncement of verdicts ; and this caused dissatisfaction among the people, and the holding for a long time under great suspense of those under suspicion.

These difficulties, the prevailing economic distress, and the popular reaction to Yugoslav claims resulted in the resurgence of right-wing parties. Conservative policies, advocated by elder statesmen like Orlando and Nitti, found followers. Discontented elements formed themselves into a group, the *Uomo Qualunque* (man-in-the-street) movement, which described itself as anti-anti-Fascist, and opposed the purge in any form. This movement gained some support among big industrialists.

On November 23 the Liberal Ministers, belonging to the only right-wing group represented in the Government, resigned, partly through dissatisfaction at their failure to secure increased representation in the Cabinet, and partly in protest against a new purge decree promulgated by the Government. These resignations caused a grave crisis, threatening as they did the end of the coalition of the six parties which had fought the Germans. Parri resigned, and it was ten days before, on December 4, Alcide de Gasperi succeeded in forming a new coalition Government. As leader of the Christian Democrats, he was somewhat more acceptable than Parri to right-wing opinion.

New Government Formed

By the end of the year A.M.G. had handed back to Italian control all Italy except Venezia Giulia, Udine and South Tyrol. The Allied Supreme Command had restored control of the Italian army to the Government.

ITALIAN PRISONERS RETURN FROM RUSSIA

Unemployment in Italy in late 1945 was complicated by the repatriation of prisoners of war who began arriving home in thousands. Those seen above had come from Russia. Dejected and clad in miserable rags, they were once part of the forces sent by Mussolini to Hitler's aid which had suffered heavy defeats during the siege of Stalingrad and along the Voronezh-Volga line (see page 2497 and illus. in page 2498).

Photos, Keystone

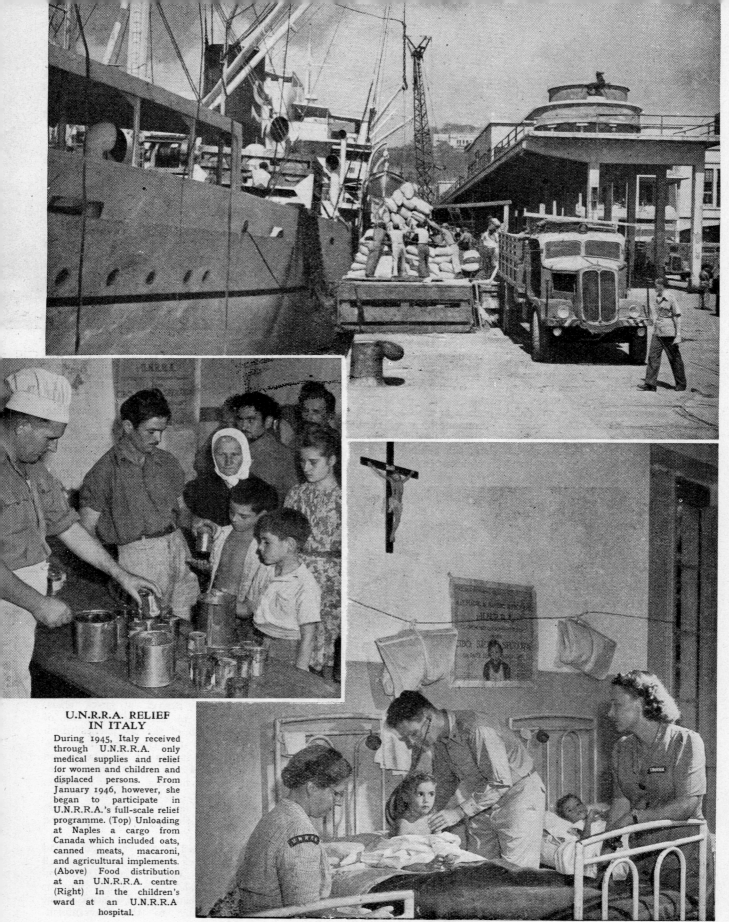

U.N.R.R.A. RELIEF IN ITALY

During 1945, Italy received through U.N.R.R.A. only medical supplies and relief for women and children and displaced persons. From January 1946, however, she began to participate in U.N.R.R.A.'s full-scale relief programme. (Top) Unloading at Naples a cargo from Canada which included oats, canned meats, macaroni, and agricultural implements. (Above) Food distribution at an U.N.R.R.A. centre (Right) In the children's ward at an U.N.R.R.A hospital.

Italy had been promised admission to the United Nations, once the peace treaty had been signed, by the Potsdam decisions published on August 2, in which Great Britain, the United States, and the Soviet Union acknowledged that "Italy was the first of the Axis powers to break with Germany, to whose defeat she had made a material contribution . . . Italy has freed herself from the Fascist régime and is making good progress towards the re-establishment of a democratic government and institutions."

Victor Emmanuel III Abdicates

The *Consulta*, a nominated consultative council set up to serve as a parliament pending the election of a Constituent Assembly, met for the first time on September 25, 1945. On March 9, 1946, it approved bills concerning the elections and the organization of the Constituent Assembly. June 2 was chosen as the date for the general election and also for a referendum to decide whether Italy should remain a monarchy or become a republic—a question which had caused dissension and difficulty in Italian politics ever since the fall of Mussolini (*see*

Chapter 319). The abdication of King Victor Emmanuel III in favour of the Crown Prince was announced on May 9, and next day the Prince was proclaimed King Umberto II.

The final results of both election and referendum were announced by the Court of Cassation on June 18. Of the 556 seats for which votes were cast, the Christian Democrats secured 207, the Socialist Party 115, the Communist Party 104, the National Democratic Union 41, Uomo Qualunque 30, the rest going to splinter parties. Eighty-nine per cent of registered electors voted in the referendum, the result being : for a Republic, 12,717,923 ; for the Monarchy 10,719,284 ; invalid papers, 1,498,136. The King disputed the validity of the provisional result issued on June 10 (Republic, 12,672,767; Monarchy, 10,688,905) ; but wiser counsel prevailed. On June 13 he followed his father and his wife and children into exile, and on June 28 the new Constituent Assembly elected Enrico de Nicola Provisional President of the new Italian Republic.

TWO YEARS AFTER—IN WAR-SHATTERED CASSINO

By the end of 1945 a semblance of life had begun to reappear in Cassino, scene of one of the fiercest battles in the Second Great War (see Chapter 302 ; also page 3879). Here, former shopkeepers display their wares in what was once the town's main thoroughfare. A disabled German tank stands in the foreground. Above, in October this sign-board warned the troops that the town, where rebuilding was in progress, was 'out of bounds' because of malignant malaria. In the background is Monastery Hill.

Photos, Associated Press ; Keystone

Chapter 375

FIGHTING ENDS IN THE BALKANS

In this chapter Miss Edith Trumpler summarizes briefly the trend of events in Greece, Rumania, Bulgaria, Hungary, Yugoslavia, and Albania in the months preceding and following the end of the war in Europe. Fighting was at an end, but political tension was high throughout the period. For the history of these countries in 1944, see Chapters 327 and 331. The rebirth of Austria is also recorded here

THE newly appointed Regent (*see* page 3371) vainly appealed to all parties to cease fighting, while the Republican General Nikolaos Plastiras, head of the Govern- **GREECE** ment formed on January 3, threatened to lead an "army of liquidation" against the insurgent E.A.M. troops. Punitive measures by the British army gradually forced E.A.M. troops northwards and, as E.A.M. loosened its military grip, moderate leaders of the Left ceased to support it.

A Trades Union Congress mission of inquiry, headed by Sir Walter Citrine, was in Greece from January 22–30. It found that "scarcely any person of note in Greek public life, including the trade union movement, seemed to be completely clear from suspicion of undesirable collaboration of some kind." It also found "a very widespread dread

among all kinds of people that the British Government might throw overboard its responsibility by a premature withdrawal of British troops."

Negotiations between E.A.M. and the Government continued, and the Varkiza agreement, signed on February 12, brought the civil war to an end. In the "Peace without Vengeance" the resistance leaders agreed to the handing over of their arms and the return of prisoners and hostages, while the Government promised amnesty for all political acts committed before December 1944, an early free plebiscite to decide the constitutional question and the subsequent election of a constituent assembly.

Increasing discontent led to the fall of the Plastiras Government on April 7. A new Government under Admiral Petros Voulgaris included Republicans and Royalists. But political tension

developed again, and on August 11 Voulgaris, at the Regent's request, formed a "Service" government.

In view of their obligations to Greece, the British and U.S. Governments suggested to the Hellenic Government that the forthcoming elections should be supervised by British, American, Soviet and French official observers—a suggestion accepted by the Greeks and agreed to by the French, but not by the Russians, who declined to participate because they were "opposed in principle to supervision of national elections by foreign states." The Greek Cabinet announced January 20, 1946, as the intended date of the elections. Royalist and right-wing parties supported this proposal, but the Left and Centre parties opposed it, on the ground that all parties had not been consulted. Voulgaris resigned and, unable to solve the Government crisis, the Regent assumed office as Premier until on November 1, Panagotis Kanellopoulos, leader of the National Unionist Party, formed a Government whose main object was to prevent financial disaster : the drachma, fixed at 2,000 to the £ in June, had continued to fall.

Three weeks later the 82-year-old Liberal leader, Sofoulis, replaced Kanellopoulos, including in his Government the "best known figures in all the moderate and republican parties" (Bevin, House of Commons). At the same time, the Regent announced the postponement until 1948 of the plebiscite on the King's return — a decision which provoked a sharp protest by King George of the Hellenes. The Regent resigned, but following urgent appeals from the British and U.S. ambassadors in Athens consented to withdraw his resignation.

Regent Resigns

On January 20, 1946, the Regent by decree fixed the general elections for March 31. Despite E.A.M.'s threat, carried into effect, to boycott the elections, they were held and showed a sweeping victory for the Populist (Royalist) party, which secured 191 seats out of 317. The Allied Electoral Mission, which comprised 240 observer teams, reported that the elections "were

GREECE'S HIGHEST AWARD FOR BRITISH GENERAL

At a ceremony in Athens on March 24, 1945, the Greek Regent, Archbishop Damaskinos, presented Lieutenant-General R. M. Scobie, commanding Allied forces in Greece, with Greece's highest military award—the Grand Cross of George I (with swords). Here are (left to right) Lieutenant-General Scobie, Archbishop Damaskinos, and General Plastiras, then Premier of Greece, after the presentation. *Photo, British Official*

WITH BRITISH AND INDIAN FORCES IN GREECE

Named 'Red Eagle Bridge' in honour of the 4th Indian Division, whose sappers built it, this Bailey bridge (above left) spanning the Aliakhmon River on the main Salonika-Athens road is here being opened to traffic in September 1945. It greatly aided distribution of food supplies. Right, British troops pile up arms surrendered by E.L.A.S. under the Varkiza agreement of February 12.

on the whole free and fair, and the results represented a true and valid verdict of the Greek people. Even had the Leftist parties which boycotted the election taken part . . . [it] would not have altered the general outcome." A right-wing Cabinet was formed by Mr. Konstantinos Tsaldaris.

The Dodecanese islands, where the Germans surrendered on May 9 (*see* page 3493), remained under British military rule pending the signing of the peace treaty with Italy : the Foreign Secretaries, meeting in Paris in June 1946, favoured their cession to Greece.

The Rumanian Coalition Government under General Radescu (*see* page 3322) broke up from within because of the determined struggle of **RUMANIA** the National Democratic Front to gain supremacy. Widespread disturbances in Bucharest and the provinces were followed by Soviet intervention, on the ground that Rumania was a back area of the Red Army where order must be maintained.

Mr. Vyshinsky, Vice-Commissar for Foreign Affairs, flew to Bucharest on February 27 and demanded and secured Radescu's dismissal. Prince Stirbey tried and failed to form a Government, and then King Michael called upon Dr. Petre Grozea, leader of the Ploughman's Front (*see* page 3322), to do so, a change which led Radescu to seek sanctuary with the British Political Representative.

Rumanian administration of Transylvania (*see* page 3326), suspended in October 1944 by Marshal Malinovsky on account of excesses against the Hungarian inhabitants, was restored during March ; and a far-reaching land reform decree was signed by the King on

U.N.R.R.A. RELIEF CENTRE IN GREEK MOUNTAINS

Among relief distribution centres for U.N.R.R.A. in Greece in 1945 was the village of Karpenision in the Aetolian mountains. During the German occupation it had been the H.Q. of the British Military Mission and of the E.L.A.S. 15th Division. The Germans raided it twice—in November 1943 and in 1944—leaving it in ruins. Here Greeks with mules set out for their homes from the village with U.N.R.R.A. supplies. *Photos, British Official*

PARTISANS
ON CRETE
It was announced on April 9, 1945, that the R.A.F. had established a base at the eastern tip of Crete and was flying in supplies to the Greek partisans engaged in harassing the German garrison of some 10,000 men still holding out in the northwest corner of the island. Here partisans lend a hand at servicing R.A.F. Spitfires at the base.
Photo, British Official

March 22. But Britain and the U.S.A. refused to recognize the Grozea Government, which they did not regard as truly representative.

King Michael Breaks with Government

King Michael called upon Dr. Grozea to resign in order that a wider government could be formed, a demand Dr. Grozea ignored. The King thereupon appealed to Russia (which had conferred the Order of Victory on him on July 19), Great Britain and the U.S.A., to assist him in setting up a government that would be recognized by all three of them so that the country would be in a position to conclude peace treaties and join the United Nations, and on August 23 he broke with the Government and left the capital.

Grozea went to Moscow in September and secured substantial relaxations in the armistice terms (*see* page 3328), such as reduction in deliveries to Russia of food and industrial plant, handing back of railways to Rumanian control, and the repatriation of Rumanian prisoners of war.

The opposition leaders Maniu and Bratianu continued to denounce the Government as a dictatorship. On November 8, the King's birthday, large crowds demonstrated in Bucharest in favour of the monarchy. Some fifteen lorries and buses loaded with Communists drove among the crowds, and a struggle ensued in which eleven were killed and 85 injured.

At their meeting in Moscow in December (*see* page 3564), the Foreign Ministers of the U.S.S.R., Great Britain and the U.S.A., in reply to King Michael's appeal of August, advised him to include one member of the National Peasant Party and one member of the National Liberal Party in the Government and appointed a commission consisting of Mr. Vyshinsky, Mr. Averell Harriman and Sir Archibald Clark Kerr to proceed to Bucharest to consult with the King and the Rumanian Government. Two members were added to the Government on January 7, 1946. Great Britain and the United States recognized it on February 5, provided elections were held in the following May.

On January 1, 1945, Moscow announced that persons mainly responsible for Bulgaria's entry into the war, who had been taken into custody by the Red Army (*see* page 3325), had been handed over to the Bulgarian authorities for trial. The three former Regents, Prince Kyril, Professor Filoff and General Michoff (*see* illus. in page 2798) were executed on February 1.

BULGARIA

Ninety-eight other persons, including two former Prime Ministers, Bojiloff and Bagrianoff, 68 deputies and eight of King Boris's personal advisers, were condemned to death at the same time; Muravieff (*see* page 3324) and 26 others to life imprisonment with hard labour. In the first three months of 1945, 11,000 persons were tried by the People's Courts for collaboration, and death sentences were passed in 2,680 cases, among the condemned being many senior army officers.

When in August the U.S.A. and Britain insisted that more liberal election laws were required than those existing if the general elections proposed to be held on August 26 were to be free, the Bulgarian Government decided, after a show of resistance, to postpone the elections. Four opposition parties—the Independent Agrarians, the Independent Socialists, the Democrats and the Radicals—were given legal status on September 9; but they decided to abstain from voting, " not wishing to expose Bulgarian voters to the terror perpetrated by the Government." Bulgaria went to the polls on November 18 with only an unofficial opposition. Eighty-six per cent of votes cast were for the Fatherland Front, twelve per cent for the opposition.

At the Foreign Ministers' Conference in Moscow in December, Russia agreed to give friendly advice to the Bulgarian Government to include within it two representatives of democratic groups not already participating in it. Negotiations between Colonel Gheorghieff, the Prime Minister, and Opposition leaders opened on January 4, 1946, but broke down after a few days. Discussions with Government and Opposition leaders held by Mr. Vyshinsky in Moscow equally failed.

At the beginning of 1945, Hungary was a battlefield (*see* page 3326), but by the early part of April the Red Army had cleared the Germans from the country (*see* Chapter 354).

HUNGARY

On January 21, an armistice was signed in Moscow between the U.S.S.R., Great Britain, and the U.S.A. and the Hungarian Provisional Government: it was on similar lines to the surrenders signed by Bulgaria and Rumania (*see* page 3328), and included the proviso that Hungary was to evacuate Czechoslovak,

DOWNING ARMS AT RHODES
On May 9, 1945, all German forces in the Dodecanese and the Aegean, including the garrison at Rhodes, totalling some 20,000 men, were surrendered on the island of Symi (*see* page 3493) to Brigadier J. Moffatt on behalf of the Allied Supreme Commander, Mediterranean. Here, German troops on the island of Rhodes stack their arms, ammunition and equipment after the surrender of their C.-in-C., Major-General Wagner.

ALLIED CONTROL COMMISSION FOR RUMANIA

The Allied Control Commission began its sittings in Bucharest in October 1945. Left to right : Major Jiglov, Russian liaison officer ; Lt.-Colonel Bolton, British liaison officer ; Air Vice-Marshal Stevenson, British Commissioner ; Major-General Vasilev, Chief of Staff ; Admiral Bogdenko, assistant Vice President ; General Schuyler, head of the U.S. Mission ; Lieutenant Balic, U.S. Navy ; and Mr. Finagenov, head of the Economic Section. *Photo. British Official*

Yugoslav and Rumanian territory occupied since December 31, 1937.

One of the new Hungarian Government's first acts was the promulgation on March 18 of a far-reaching measure of land reform that ended the ancient feudal system of land tenure under which, in 1938, 36 magnates owned more than a million acres, while 1,200,000 peasants owned only 950,000 acres.

A law providing for universal, secret and equal suffrage for all Hungarians (men and women) was passed on September 19, and general elections were announced for November 4, each party to put forward its own list of candidates. On October 6, however, municipal elections in Budapest resulted in an overwhelming victory for the Smallholders' party, which secured 151 seats against 52 for the Communists, 51 for the Socialists, and ten others. On October 17, Marshal Voroshilov, chairman of the Allied Control Commission, informed the party leaders that elections should be held on a single Government list as in Rumania. This method of election was not favoured by either the American Government, which had made recognition of Hungary conditional on free elections there, or that of Britain. The Hungarian Government therefore rejected Voroshilov's demand, but agreed to the formation of a coalition Government, whatever the outcome of the elections. These, held on November 4 "fairly, freely and without disturbance,"

Smallholders' Victory in Hungary

gave the Smallholders 245 seats, the Communists 70, the Socialists 69, National Peasants 23, Democrats 2. The Smallholders' leader, Zoltan Tildy, formed a new coalition Government recognised by all three Allies.

A five-year economic treaty with Russia which would have given the U.S.S.R. virtually a fifty-fifty share in Hungary's entire economic life was initialled in Moscow on August 27. The British and American Governments lodged vigorous protests against the signing of a treaty with a country with which the Allies were still technically at war, and the agreement was never ratified by Hungary. The new Government liquidated the Russo-Hungarian trading company formed to operate it.

King Peter refused to accept the Tito-Subasich agreement (*see* page 3361), and demanded Subasich's resignation. This provoked Mr. Churchill to declare in the House of Commons on January 18 that the agreement would be put into effect " even if we were so unfortunate as not to be able to obtain the consent of King Peter." Subasich did resign, but was asked by the King to form a new Government. On February 15 he left for Belgrade. A fortnight later the King chose as Regents three out of six candidates proposed to him by Subasich and on March 7 a new Government of National Unity was announced headed by Tito and including Dr. Milan Grol, a well-known democrat, and Dr. Subasich.

YUGO-SLAVIA

Field-Marshal Alexander, C.-in-C., Mediterranean, visited Belgrade towards the end of February to co-ordinate future Allied operations with those of the Yugoslav army, to arrange for further material help to Yugoslavia, and to decide on administrative arrangements between the Allied forces in Italy and Tito's forces when they linked up.

On April 11 in Moscow Marshal Tito and Mr. Molotov signed a twenty-year treaty of friendship, mutual alliance, and post-war collaboration. While in Moscow, Tito made an official claim for the cession of Trieste and the Istrian peninsula, in an interview with the

POLITICAL RIOTS IN BUCHAREST

On November 8, 1945, the twenty-fourth birthday of King Michael of Rumania, large crowds in Bucharest, the capital, demonstrated in favour of the monarchy. As a result of clashes between monarchists and Communists, eleven people were killed and 85 injured. Here, the crowds gather in Royal Parade, outside the Palace. The equestrian statue is that of King Carol I. *Photo, Associated Press*

LIFE BEGINS AGAIN IN HUNGARY'S CAPITAL

1. Crowds stream across the Kossuth bridge, first to be patched up, towards the Parliament building, which escaped major damage. 2. Marshal Tolbukhin (right) whose troops helped to capture Budapest on February 13, 1945, with Field-Marshal Alexander and (behind) Major General Lemnitzer, U.S. Army. 3. In December 1945 internal postage on a letter cost 60 pengos. The pengo (pre-war value about a shilling) had slumped to over 60,000 to the pound sterling. 4. First meeting of the newly elected National Assembly on November 29. The Rev. Zoltan Tildy, Premier and leader of the Smallholders' Party, is fourth from the right.

"Red Star" on April 15. (For the developments arising from this claim, *see* page 3859.) Yugoslavia also demanded Carinthia (Austria), where Yugoslav troops overran another area under 8th Army operational control but withdrew on May 20 under protest.

A new Federal State of Yugoslavia was created during the months of April and May, in furtherance of Tito's announcement of December 1944 (*see* page 3362). Regional governments were set up for Serbia, Croatia, Slovenia, Montenegro, Bosnia-Herzegovina, and Macedonia.

Among laws passed during the third session of the National Liberation Council from August 7–26 were one

RESTORING TIRANA, CAPITAL OF ALBANIA
British parachute troops, with Albanian partisans, played an important part in freeing Albania in late 1944. On November 18 the Germans announced their evacuation of Tirana, though its capture by partisans was not officially disclosed until three days later. Here, repair work goes on in Tirana after its liberation. The peacetime population was some 40,000.

TITO-ALEXANDER TALKS
Field-Marshal Alexander had talks in Eelgrade with Marshal Tito which began on February 24, 1945. They discussed co-ordination of Allied-Yugoslav operations and the delivery of Allied help to the partisans. Above, the Field-Marshal and the Marshal discuss tactics with the aid of a map.

concerning the form of the Constituent Assembly, which was to be sovereign and to consist of two Houses, separate and equal—the Federal Assembly chosen by direct vote to represent political trends, and the Assembly of the Nations to express local and regional aims ; two laws governing the elections for the new Constituent Assembly ; and a fourth law providing for agrarian reform based on the principle that " the land shall be owned by him who tills it."

Elections were announced for November 11. But before then the two non-Communist Ministers of any standing had resigned—Dr. Grol on August 18, because he considered the electoral laws " restricted and in many cases suspended political liberties," Dr. Subasich at the beginning of October on the ground that his agreement with Tito was not being carried out. The oppo-

sition, led by these two ex-ministers, decided to boycott the elections, in which, however, an additional ballot box was provided at each polling station so that electors who wished could record their vote against the National Front. Ninety per cent of votes cast went to the National Front.

On November 29 the Constituent Assembly, meeting for the first time, proclaimed Yugoslavia a republic, the Assembly assuming the functions of head of the State pending the drawing up of a new constitution. The British and U.S. Governments recognized the republic on December 22.

During the war, ten per cent of Yugoslavia's population was killed. Italian and German invasion and civil strife shattered her economic life and destroyed her communications. Famine was rife. It was estimated that she had lost sixty per cent of her national wealth, and that her national income had fallen by seventy per cent. Only U.N.R.R.A. assistance saved thousands from starvation, the food available in many of the ruined villages being still well below 1,500 calories a day at the beginning of 1946.

General Draha Mihailovich, leader of the Chetniks and most noted of the alleged quislings and war criminals tried in Yugoslavia, was captured on March 13, 1946, after being hunted " from mountain to mountain, and from wood to wood." Accused of collaboration with the Germans and of having used his forces against Tito's partisans, he was brought before a military tribunal in Belgrade in June, condemned to death on July 15, and was executed two days later.

After the evacuation of Tirana by the Germans (*see* page 3371) a Provisional Government set up at Berat in October 1944 **ALBANIA** under 38-year-old Colonel Enver Hoxha, leader of the Communist-controlled Democratic Front, moved to the capital on November 28.

Elections held in December 1945 and stated by Allied correspondents to be free and orderly, gave the Provisional Government 93 per cent of all votes cast. Early in January 1946, the newly elected Constituent Assembly proclaimed Albania a republic and forbade King Zog to return.

In the declaration published on November 1, 1943, following the Moscow

TITO MONEY IN ISTRIA

Limits of the Yugo-slav occupation zone in Istria were defined on June 20, 1945 (see page 3860). Left, Yugoslav 1-lira note, depicting a partisan, issued in Istria.

AUSTRIA UNDER ALLIED CONTROL

The Allied Control Council for Austria, announced on August 8, 1945, consisted of the four commanders of the occupying armies here seen at the opening of the Parliament of the Austrian Republic in Vienna on December 19. Left to right : Lt.-General Sir Richard McCreery (Great Britain), who commanded the 8th Army in Italy ; General Mark Clark (U.S.), former Allied C.-in-C., Italy ; Marshal Ivan Koniev (U.S.S.R.), former Commander of the 1st Ukrainian Army ; and General Emile Marie Béthouard (France). *Photo, Associated Press*

Conference (*see* page 2940), the United Kingdom, the U.S.A. and the U.S.S.R. stated their wish to see a free and independent Austria re-established. Vienna was freed from the Germans by the Red Army on April 13 (*see* pages 3625 and illus. in page 3627). The formation of a Provisional Government headed by Dr. Renner, the 75-year-old Social Democrat who had headed the Austrian peace delegation in 1919, was announced by Moscow radio on April 29. On May 2, Mr. Law, Minister of State, stated in the House of Commons that the matter of the Austrian Provisional Government was being taken up with Moscow by the British and U.S. Governments ; and that the occupation of Austria was to be carried out by British, American, Russian and French forces, whose zones were under consideration.

On August 8, the setting up of the Allied Control Council was announced. The country was divided into four zones (*see* map facing page 4014), each under a Military Commissioner, who together formed the Control Council. Vienna, like Berlin, was divided into four different sectors, and was the seat of the Control Council. Formal entry of British, U.S. and French troops into the city took place on August 23.

Vienna had been badly damaged in the fighting ; all bridges except one

AUSTRIA across the Danube were down ; there was no gas and only about half an hour's electricity a day ; garbage, not removed for six months and piled high in the streets, led to outbreaks of typhus. The food situation, too, was grave, and was aggravated by the division of the city into sectors.

The Allied Control Council, meeting for the first time on September 11, issued a proclamation that (1) free elections were to be held as soon as the necessary conditions existed ; (2) free activity would be allowed to three parties, Socialists, Communists and the People's Party (Catholics) ; (3) Vienna's food rations would be raised from 800 to a minimum of 1,550 calories a day from September 23. Communications between the zones of occupation were restored, following which, from September 24–26, a conference of provinces was held, with Allied approval and under the chairmanship of Dr. Renner, to discuss the personnel of the more representative government he formed on September 27. Full liberty of the Press, subject only to Allied military security, was restored on October 1.

On condition that elections were held not later than December 31, 1945, Great Britain, the U.S.A., France and the U.S.S.R. formally recognized the Austrian Provisional Government on October 20. On November 25, the first free general elections to be held for

fifteen years drew 90 per cent of registered voters to the polls. Members of the National Assembly and of the diets of the eight provinces were elected. The People's Party secured 85 seats, the Social Democrats 76, the Communists 4 in the National Assembly. The same party secured majorities in all diets except those of Vienna and Carinthia, where the Social Democrats were first. The parties had agreed to continue government by coalition, whatever the election results. Dr. Renner resigned, and on December 4, Dr. Leopold Figl, 43-year-old leader of the People's Party, was appointed Chancellor by the new Assembly. Dr. Renner was unanimously elected first post-war President of Austria.

On December 22, 1945, the Austrian Government lodged a formal claim to

AUSTRIA'S PRESIDENT

Dr. Karl Renner, who, at a joint session of the National Assembly and the Bundesrat (an assembly representing the provinces), was on December 20, 1945, chosen unanimously as first President of Austria's post-war Republic. Born in 1870, he founded the Workers' Bank. He was imprisoned by the Nazis in 1934.
Photo, New York Times Photos

the northern part of South Tyrol, the former Austrian province of Alto Adige (no claim was made to Trento—formerly Trentino—the southern part). The claim was discussed, but not accepted, at the Foreign Ministers' Conference in May 1946.

Notes in identical terms from the British, American, Russian and French Governments were handed to President Renner and Chancellor Figl on January 7, 1946, recognizing Austria as a State " with the same frontiers as 1937 pending a final delimitation," President Renner as duly elected head of it, and the new Government as the *de jure* Government.

LIFE IN LIBERATED AUSTRIA

1. Repair work in progress in the autumn of 1945 on one of the bridges spanning the Danube Canal in Vienna. The canal and its locks had been damaged in the fighting between the Germans and the advancing Russians, rendering it useless. 2. Arrival of an U.N.R.R.A. train at the Ostbahn station in Vienna on March 8, 1946. Carrying wheat supplies, it was met by Chancellor Figl and members of the Austrian Government. 3. A patrol of the 2nd Battalion London Irish Rifles, stationed at Turrach See, searches for S.S. troops who had been living as bandits on the countryside. 4. In the main square at Spittal, a British military policeman and an Austrian police officer share point duty.

Photos, British Official ; Associated Press

Chapter 376

A NEW POLAND WITH NEW FRONTIERS

Poland, first victim of the war of 1939-45, was completely freed from the Germans before the end of February 1945. This chapter records the political difficulties that arose after her liberation, and the changes that were proposed in her frontiers as a result of the Second Great War. For her history in 1944, see Chapters 316 and 317

On the same day that the Lublin Committee proclaimed itself the first Provisional Government of Liberated Democratic Poland (*see* page 3204), the Polish Government in London issued a statement in reply in which it said, "The Polish Gov-

Two Polish Governments ernment protests emphatically against this attempt against the sovereign rights of the Polish nation made by the Lublin Committee which has illegally assumed the title of Provisional Government ... The direction of the struggle rests in the hands of the [London] Polish Government, recognized as the only legal representative of the Polish State by the United Nations and by the neutral countries." The Soviet Government, however, recognized the new Provisional Government on January 5, 1945.

On January 17, Warsaw, in enemy hands since September 1939, was freed (*see* page 3554). Next day the Lublin Government moved to the capital. By the time Mr. Churchill, President Roosevelt, and Marshal Stalin

met at Yalta (*see* page 3563) the Germans had been expelled from pre-war Poland except in the "Polish Corridor" and the city of Poznan (*see* illus. in page 3559). In the statement issued by the heads of government of Great Britain, the United States, and the Soviet Union on February 12, they said: "A new situation has been created in Poland as a result of her complete liberation by the Red Army. This calls for the establishment of a Polish Provisional Government which can be more broadly based than was possible before the recent liberation of western Poland. The Provisional Government now functioning in Poland should, therefore, be reorganized on a broader democratic basis with the inclusion of democratic leaders from Poland itself and from Poles abroad. This new Government should then be called the Polish Provisional Government of National Unity.

"Mr. Molotov, Mr. Harriman, and Sir. A. Clark Kerr are authorized as a Commission to consult in the first instance in Moscow with members of

the present Provisional Government and with other Polish democratic leaders from within Poland and from abroad, with a view to the reorganization of the present Government along the above lines. This Polish Provisional Government of National Unity shall be pledged to the hold-

Commission of Three Appointed ing of free and unfettered elections as soon as possible on the basis of universal suffrage and the secret ballot. In these elections all democratic and anti-Nazi parties shall have the right to take part and put forward candidates.

"When a Polish Provisional Government of National Unity has been properly formed in conformity with the above, the Government of the U.S.S.R., which now maintains diplomatic relations with the present Provisional Government of Poland, and the Governments of the United Kingdom and the United States, will establish diplomatic relations with the new Polish Provisional Government of National Unity ...

"The three heads of Government consider that the eastern frontier of Poland should follow the Curzon line, with digressions from it in some regions of 5–8 kilometres in favour of Poland (*see* map in opposite page). They recognize that Poland must receive substantial accessions of territory in the north and west ... The final delimitations of the western frontier of Poland should await the peace conference."

Immediately the Yalta decisions were made public, the Polish Government in London declared that neither it nor the Polish nation could recognize them, and went on, "The intention of the three Powers to create a Polish Provisional Government

Anders Becomes C.-in-C. of National Unity can only legalize Soviet interference in Polish internal affairs." General Anders, appointed on February 26 Acting C.-in-C. of all Polish Armed Forces in place of General Bor-Komorowski (*see* pages 3205–06), said in an Order of the Day that he was assuming his duties "in Poland's direst hour" and that "with our standards covered with glory we are facing the greatest tragedy of our nation." (General Bor. liberated

SOVIET ARTILLERY IN THE STREETS OF CRACOW

Save for its rubber-tired wheels, this horse-drawn Russian artillery entering Cracow (which fell to troops of the 1st Ukrainian Army on January 19, 1945) might have stepped from the pages of "War and Peace." Cracow, on the Vistula, medieval capital of Poland and a powerful stronghold in the enemy defences covering the Silesian coal basin, was taken by the Red Army during one of its greatest weeks of the war when it liberated vast areas of Polish territory. See also illus. in page 3555.

Photo. Pictorial Press

by the U.S. 7th Army on May 6, resumed the functions of C.-in-C on May 28.)

Not all the London Poles, however, were in agreement with the policy of the Arciszewski Government. A number

Statement by Mikolajczk

resigned from the National Council, and on March 15 Mr. Mikolajczk, the former Premier (*see* page 3212) and leader of the opposition group, made the following statement of policy :

" 1. I consider close and lasting friendship with Russia, within the wider friendship of the United Nations, is the keystone of a future Polish policy.

" 2. To remove all doubt as to my attitude, I wish to declare that I accept the Crimea decision in regard to the future of Poland, its sovereign independent position, and the formation of a Provisional Government representative of national unity.

" 3. I support the decision arrived at in the Crimea that a conference of leading Polish personalities be called, with a view to constituting a Government of national unity as widely and fairly representative of the Polish peoples as possible and one which will command recognition by the three major Powers."

The difficulties between the London Government and the Soviet Union were not helped by the arrest in February of Madame Archiszewska and other workers with the Polish Red Cross by the Russian political police, announced on March 1 ; nor the disappearance, announced on April 6, of the Deputy

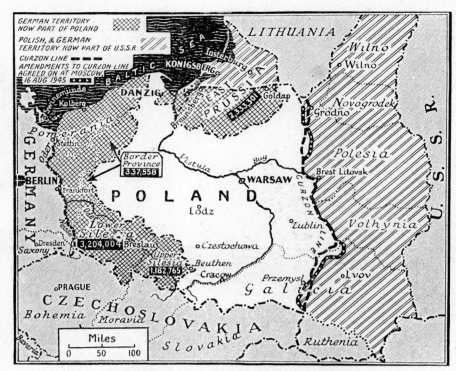

POLAND'S PROPOSED NEW FRONTIERS

A treaty between the U.S.S.R. and the Polish Provisional Government of National Unity, signed in Moscow on August 16, 1945, accepted the Curzon Line, with variations indicated on the map, as the Soviet-Polish frontier. The parts of East Prussia, Silesia and Pomerania (with 1939 population figures), taken over by Poland at the end of the Second Great War, subject to ratification in the peace treaty with Germany, are also shown   *Courtesy of " The Observer."*

POLISH LEADER

Mr. Tomasz Arciszewski, Premier of the London Polish Government, 1944-45. Born in 1877, he began life as a factory worker. In the First Great War he led the armed resistance of Polish workers against the Germans. He was appointed head of the Executive of the Polish Socialist Party in 1931 and from 1939-44 was leader of the Underground Socialist Party in Poland.

Photo. Keystone

Prime Minister, Mr. Jan Jankowski, leader of the Christian Democrats, and fifteen other leaders who, on March 27 and 28, had presented themselves, at an indirect invitation from the Soviet Commander, to General Ivanov, representing the High Command of the 1st White Russian Front. The negotiations of the Commission in Moscow consulting on the reorganization of the Polish Government reached a deadlock a few days after the second announcement, which was followed on April 11 by another, that Mr. Wincenty Witos, three times Premier and for twenty years leader of the Peasant Party, had been taken from his home to an unknown destination.

The Commission of Three having failed to make headway in the formation of a new Government, Mr. Molotov, Mr. Eden and Mr. Stettinius discussed the Polish question in Washington on April 22–24, prior to the meeting of the San Francisco Conference. The discussions were continued in San Francisco parallel with the main Conference, until on May 3 Mr. Molotov informed Mr. Eden and Mr. Stettinius of the arrest of the missing leaders. The talks were suspended, and at a press conference a week later, Mr. Eden said, " I must emphasize that the list of sixteen Poles reported as having disappeared . . . .

included nearly all the leading figures of the Polish underground movement. . . . Most of them were just the type who should, in our view, have been consulted about the new National Government." Three of them, indeed, had been mentioned by the British Government to the Commission of Three as entitled to be consulted.

Marshal Stalin, in a statement published on May 18, denied that the arrested Poles had been invited for negotiations by the Soviet authorities, and said that they had been arrested " in accordance

Stalin on Polish Arrests

with the law protecting the Red Army rear from diversionists," and by agreement between the Polish Provisional Government and the Soviet Military Command.

The Commission of Three later resumed their work in Moscow, and on June 13 announced that they had agreed to invite to Moscow four members of the Provisional Government, including Mr. Edward Osobka-Morawski, the Prime Minister (*see* page 3204) ; three other leaders from inside Poland, and three from abroad, including Mr. Stanislaw Mikolajczk. In a series of talks from June 17–21, conducted exclusively between the Poles, the three groups reached agreement. A week

U.N.R.R.A. SUPPLIES FOR STARVING POLAND

The return to peace in late 1945 found Poland heavily scarred with war-wounds, her population virtually starving and with over 1,100,000 war orphans. Left, the hollow shell that was the railway station in the former free city of Danzig. Right, at Gdynia, Poland's Baltic port, the U.S. ship 'Virginia' unloads U.N.R.R.A. supplies which included 397 horses and 318 cows.
Photos, Associated Press

later the formation of a new Cabinet headed by Mr. Osobka-Morawski (Socialist), and in which Mr. Mikolajczk (Peasant Party) and Mr. Wladyslaw Gomulka (Communist) were Deputy Premiers, was announced in Warsaw.

The trial of the arrested Poles took place in Moscow from June 18–21. All the accused except one admitted the charges wholly or in part. General Leopold Okulicki, commander-in-chief of the Polish Home Army, was condemned to ten years' captivity, Mr. Jankowski to eight years; others received lesser sentences. Three were acquitted (including two who had pleaded guilty). Great freedom was allowed the prisoners in setting forth their political views, and the trials, by bringing into the open fears, hatreds and misunderstandings that had previously been only hinted at, provided a healthier atmosphere in which the new Polish Government, recognized by Great Britain and the United States on July 5, could begin the difficult work of reconstruction.

The setting up of the new Polish Government, and subsequent withdrawal of recognition from the London Government, placed the Polish forces under Allied command in a curious position. On July 2, **Polish Forces with the Allied Armies** Polish Military Headquarters in London issued a statement that " the status of the Polish forces, which total about 250,000 men and women, remains unchanged, despite the apparent changing character of the political situation in Poland. . . . There is no question of troops not getting their pay. There is no fear of mass desertion . . . .

" The II Polish Corps in Italy under General Anders's command remains an integral part of the 8th Army, under the Supreme Command of Field-Marshal Alexander, and continues to take orders from him. The 1st Polish Armoured Division and the Parachute Brigade in Germany continue to accept responsi-

POLISH-SOVIET AGREEMENT SIGNED

A treaty on the Soviet-Polish frontier and an agreement on the payment of reparations or damage done during the German occupation of Poland were signed in Moscow on August 16, 1945, by Mr. Molotov, Soviet Foreign Commissar, and Mr. Osobka-Morawski, the Polish Premier. Here, the Polish premier signs, watched by Generalissimo Stalin, Mr. Molotov, and Mr. A. Y. Vyshinsky, Foreign Vice-Commissar.
Photo, Planet News

bility under the supreme command of Field-Marshal Montgomery. Polish troops quartered in Britain continue to perform their duties under the supreme command of the British military authorities. The Polish Air Force and Navy are still operating under the direct command of the R.A.F. and British Admiralty respectively."

Mr. Churchill, in his speech to the Commons of February 27 on the Yalta conference, had said: "H.M. Government are resolved that as many as possible of the Polish troops shall be enabled to return in due course to Poland of their own free will . . . In any event, H.M. Government will never forget the debt they owe to the Polish troops who have served them so valiantly, and for all those who fought under our command I earnestly hope it may be possible to offer them the citizenship and freedom of the British Empire if they so desire."

The communiqué issued on August 2 following the Potsdam Conference said, "The Three Powers are anxious to assist the Polish Provisional Government in facilitating the return to Poland as soon as practicable of all Poles abroad who wish to go, including members of the Polish armed forces and merchant marine. They expect that those Poles who return home shall be accorded personal and property rights on the same basis as all Polish citizens."

Speaking in the Commons on November 23, Mr. Ernest Bevin, the Foreign Secretary, said that some 23,000 out of the 67,000 Poles in Britain, 14,000 out of the 110,000 in Italy and the Middle East, and a few hundreds of those in north-west Europe had so far expressed a wish to return, and added, "The Polish Provisional Government have agreed to concert with our Ambassador in Warsaw the terms of a statement covering the points on which the Polish soldiers, sailors and airmen under our command particularly want information. I hope this will enable many more to take the decision to go back to Poland and to help in the reconstruction of their country. I want to make it clear, however, that there is no intention of using compulsion." But six months later, only 29,800 had in fact opted to return to Poland, leaving about 100,000 overseas and 60,000 in the United Kingdom to be settled outside Poland.

Poles Reluctant to Go Home

When the new Government took office, hostilities in Poland had been over for four months, but what was little

PEACE RETURNS TO RUINED WARSAW

The clearing of the enemy from Warsaw, capital of Poland, brought almost insuperable problems of reconstruction for its inhabitants. After five years and four months of German occupation, it was liberated on January 17, 1945, by troops of the 1st White Russian Army with units of the 1st Polish Army (see illus. in page 3554), but as a result of both the German bombing in September 1939 and the ill-starred 63-day rising in the summer of 1944 (see pages 3205-3206) it had virtually been obliterated. 1. Mobile repair-unit in October 1945 restores the city's public services. 2. Buyers and vendors in an open-air market in a badly-bombed street. 3. All that remained of the once-famous Ghetto quarter.

less than chaos existed in the country. There was a universal shortage of consumer goods and livestock; the splitting up of the great estates was under way, involving the creation of an entirely new economy; the upper and middle classes had been largely dispossessed of their capital and property. A decree of January 3, 1946, nationalizing the mines, petroleum resources, armament factories, and other enterprises brought some forty per cent of the working population into State employment.

END OF A CAMPAIGN

Poles enlisted by the Polish (London) Government were placed in a curious position with the setting up of the Polish Provisional Government of National Unity. 1. General Wladyslaw Anders, who commanded Polish forces in Russia, Middle East and Italy (see pages 2736 and 3054, also illus. in page 1948). 2. Polish tanks 'laid up' in Italy. 3. Some of 2,000 Polish troops who had elected to return to Poland sail from Tilbury on December 30, 1945.

Photos, G.P.U. and Associated Press

In Warsaw, the seat of the Government, there was scarcely a habitable building. In many places typhus and typhoid raged. Throughout the country people were ill and ill-fed—Mr. Hoover in March 1946 said that the situation in Poland was the worst he had seen in Europe, that 5,000,000 children there were undernourished, and that despite gallant efforts by Polish organizations, U.N.R.R.A. and other bodies, there was no overall organization to care for and rehabilitate Poland's 1,100,000 war orphans.

Armed bands, some of them remnants of the resistance movement antagonistic to the government, some of them just bandits, infested the forests, ravaging the villages and the countryside. Under an amnesty proclaimed on June 1, about 6,000 members of the former Home Army came in up to October 1; but on October 15 the Provisional Government announced an agreement with Marshal Rokossovsky, Russian Commander in Poland, under which a general of the Red Army with special

powers and having at his disposal a military unit was to be attached to every provincial capital in order to combat "all acts of banditry and marauding."

Throughout the country a pathetic stream of returning refugees trickled sadly and anxiously towards what was left of their homes. Another stream poured steadily westwards, many from the **Refugees and Settlers** areas returned to the Soviet Union under the readjustments of Poland's frontiers, to find homes in the four new "voivodships" (administrative districts) of Western Pomerania, Upper and Lower Silesia, and Mazuria (East Prussia), from which those Germans who had not fled before the Red Army were being ruthlessly driven into the Allied-occupied zones of Germany. A treaty, signed on August 16, and ratified on January 3, 1946, between Poland and the Soviet Union settled Poland's eastern frontier (*see* map in page 3875). Under an agreement signed at the same time the Soviet Union relinquished in favour of Poland all claims on German assets in the whole territory of Poland, including the areas newly acquired from Germany, and ceded to Poland fifteen per cent of all reparations due to Russia from Germany, the Polish Government in return undertaking to make coal deliveries to the Soviet Union at a specially agreed price.

Politically the state of the country remained confused. Despite the broadening of the Government, power rested mainly in the hands of the Communists. **Political** Political freedom was **Confusion** restricted, and when a month after the formation of the new Government there was a demonstration in Lublin in favour of the Peasant Party (Mr. Mikolajczk's party), the demonstrators were arrested.

But Mr. Mikolajczk continued to challenge the Communist domination of the administration, and when the Government proposed that in the elections shortly to be held, the electorate should be asked to vote for a single list of candidates, he resolutely refused to agree.

POLES' LAST RESTING-PLACE NEAR MONASTERY HILL, CASSINO

On September 1, 1945, sixth anniverary of the German invasion of Poland, the Polish cemetery at Monte Cassino, Italy, where a thousand Poles who fell in the attack on the Hitler Line (see Chapter 302 and page 3865) lie buried, was dedicated in a ceremony attended by Field-Marshal Sir Harold Alexander and General Wladyslaw Anders, G.O.C., Polish II Corps. The battlefield cemetery is constructed in a series of stone-revetted terraces in a dip between Monastery Hill and the ring of neighbouring heights round which the fiercest of the fighting raged. Above, the ceremony in progress. The entrance is flanked by two large Polish eagles, finely sculptured in stone. Below, the cemetery seen from Monastery Hill.

OCCUPATION FORCES IN AUSTRIA'S CAPITAL

On August 8, 1945, a joint statement issued in London, Washington, Moscow and Paris announced the setting up of Allied control machinery in Austria and delimitation of the zones of occupation. Vienna, the capital, was to be administered by an inter-Allied governing authority under the direction of the Allied Council. Left, outside Vienna's famous Opera House, a group of Soviet soldiers stands beside one of many poster-portraits of Stalin, while a solitary American looks out across the square. Above, in the courtyard of the 18th-century Schönbrunn Palace—British H.Q. for Vienna—which had escaped serious damage in the fighting, the changing of the guard takes place for the first time on August 6. The 2nd Battalion of the Lancashire Fusiliers took over from the R.A.F. Regiment (seen here) ; the band of the 4th Hussars played during the ceremony.

Photos, British Official ; Pictorial Press

THE COMMONS GIVE THANKS FOR DELIVERANCE

The British Premier, Mr. Winston Churchill, on May 8, 1945, announced the end of the war in Europe in a broadcast at 3 p.m. (see page 3506), afterwards repeating the contents of his broadcast to the House of Commons. He then moved ' That this House do now attend at the Church of St. Margaret, Westminster, to give humble and reverent thanks to Almighty God for our deliverance from the threat of German domination,' the identical resolution moved at the time of the 1918 Armistice. Here, the Premier and the Cabinet, preceded by the Speaker and the Serjeant-at-Arms bearing the Mace, cross to St. Margaret's. (Mr. Attlee and Mr. Eden were in San Francisco.)

'WE WANT THE KING!' SHOUTED LONDON'S VICTORY CROWDS

Thousands of people who crowded into London on V.J. Day (August 15, 1945) thronged the Mall and the approaches to Buckingham Palace, many of them scaling the base of the Victoria Memorial. They sang and shouted 'We want the King!'. The King and Queen, accompanied by the Princesses, responded to the calls by appearing on the balcony and were greeted with prolonged cheers. In all, the royal party appeared six times. By night the palace was floodlit—as were many other famous London buildings for the occasion—and the crowds in the Mall continued to celebrate the end of the war until the small hours.

Photo, P.N.A.

Chapter 377

CZECHOSLOVAKIA RESUMES INDEPENDENCE

Of all the countries in Central and Eastern Europe, Czechoslovakia alone enjoyed a tolerably smooth transition from occupation by the Nazis to renewed independence. Dr. Frederik Heymann, formerly foreign editor of the Prague paper 'Bohemia,' describes the transition period here. For the history of Czechoslovakia and her exiled government during 1944, see Chapters 316, 317

THE liberation of Czechoslovakia began in the east (*see* page 3214), and it was in the east, too, that the Czechoslovak authorities started taking over the administration of the areas freed from German and Hungarian forces. As the provisional capital—while Prague was still in the hands of the enemy—they chose Kosice, the main city of eastern Slovakia. It was there that Dr. Frantisec Nemec, as representative of the Czechoslovak Government in London, began the task of unifying the various insurgent movements which had been organized—frequently under Communist leadership—in so-called National Committees. In Bohemia and Moravia these committees had still to work underground, but they had now come into the open in the east. In the first half of February this work of unification made considerable progress, and on the 17th of that month President Benes announced that the government would soon return from London to Czechoslovakia.

The President, accompanied by Mr. Jan Masaryk, left London on March 11, and arrived on the 17th in Moscow, where he had discussions with Marshal Stalin and Mr. Molotov and with other members of the Czechoslovak Government, including the Premier, Monsignor Jan Sramek. On April 3 the President arrived in the provisional Czechoslovak capital, and four days later the names of a new Provisional Government were announced. Mr. Zdenek Fierlinger (54), Czech and a diplomat of long standing who had been ambassador to the Soviet Union since 1943, became Prime Minister. Though he belonged to no party, he was a left-wing Socialist. Leaders of the Catholic, Social National, Communist, and Democratic Parties, five in all (three Czech and two Slovak), became Vice-Premiers, among them Monsignor Sramek (Czech, Catholic). Jan Masaryk, son of the founder of the Czechoslovak Republic, remained Foreign Minister.

Provisional Government Formed

On April 9 the new government announced its political programme with the following main points : a close alliance with the Soviet Union whose army was to be supported by every means ; an alliance with Poland (the

Czechoslovak Government recognized the Lublin Committee as Provisional Government of Poland on January 31) ; friendly relations with Yugoslavia and Bulgaria ; a rapprochement, if possible, with democratic governments of Austria and Hungary ; and the consolidation of the existing friendly relations with Great Britain.

Under an agreement signed in London on February 26, food, medical supplies and other help from U.N.R.R.A. reached the liberated parts of the country by air and through Black Sea ports.

On April 23 a call went out from the government to the Czechs in Bohemia and Moravia to rise in arms against their German oppressors and to start a general strike. Czech resistance, indeed, came much more into the open, answered by fierce reprisals from the Germans, particularly in Prague, where street fighting

began early in the morning of May 5. Throughout the night of May 5–6 and during the following days, desperate appeals for help went out to the Allies from the Prague radio station held by the patriots—the Germans made an unexpected stand in Prague, and the patriots were insufficiently supplied with weapons and ammunition to overcome them. Red Army tanks (*see* page 3626) and American troops (*see* page 3807) entered the city on May 10, to receive an enthusiastic welcome.

The city suffered some damage, notably in the centre where the famous Old Town Hall was burnt down by the Germans. Compared with Warsaw or Budapest, however, Prague, one of the most beautiful cities in Europe, suffered little destruction.

On May 16 President Benes, after six years of exile, arrived in his capital,

CABINET GOES HOME

President Benes left London on March 11, 1945, to return to Czechoslovakia via Moscow, where he had talks with the Russians. Right, accompanied by his wife, he bids farewell to England. On his right are Mr. Gusev, Soviet Minister in London, and Mr. Jan Masaryk, his Foreign Minister (extreme left). Below, crowds at Kosice, the temporary capital, greet the President's return.

Photos, Planet

together with the members of the government. He was greeted by huge crowds, who went wild with joy when the presidential banner rose again over the ancient Hradcany castle in place of the hated swastika.

Once freed and restored, the Czechoslovak Republic was faced with a number of difficult problems. Most of

Rebuilding National Foundations

them arose out of the need to rebuild the state on safer foundations than those on which it had rested during the first two decades of its existence. Though Czechs and Slovaks formed the majority of its people, a large measure of freedom and minority rights, including participation in the government, as well as state-sponsored schools, universities, theatres, etc., had been granted to the national minorities within its borders, in particular to the Sudeten Germans who formed about one-fifth of the population. But Czechoslovakia's constructive solution of the minority problem had been frustrated by the violence with which the Sudeten Germans had embraced the Nazi creed with its German expansionism. Though some Sudeten Germans had remained faithful to Czechoslovakia, the majority had been a most active and efficient fifth column.

The use of the term " Sudeten " was banned by a decree of May 23, which changed the official name of the Sudetenland to " border areas," and there was complete unanimity among the Czechoslovak people that this dangerous and unreliable element must be moved from their country. The Berlin Conference (see page 3923) recognized the need, though it asked the Czechoslovak Government to carry out the expulsion

"in an orderly and humane manner." The Prague Government gave assurance to this effect, but in the beginning little difference was made between Nazi Germans and those who had been anti-Nazis and had themselves suffered under the Nazi rule. Later anti-Nazis, though they too had to leave, were allowed to take along whatever movable property they possessed. Germans who had not been Nazis, but had not fought actively against them either, were allowed a limited amount of money and luggage; whereas Nazis had to leave everything behind. Things were made rather difficult for the reception areas (in the main the American zone of Germany) by the fact that in many cases only women, children and aged people were sent away while ablebodied men were kept to work in mines and factories. Later in the year, when Czech and some Slovak workers had moved in greater numbers into the " border areas," most of the German workers, too, were moved into Germany. Some Czechoslovak industries, however, continued to feel a serious shortage of manpower.

The problem of the Hungarian minority in Slovakia was, said Dr. Benes,

U.N.R.R.A. AID FOR CZECHOSLOVAKIA
An agreement was signed in London on February 26, 1945, between Mr. Jan Masaryk, Czechoslovak Foreign Minister, and Sir Frederick Leith-Ross, Deputy Director-General of U.N.R.R.A., whereby U.N.R.R.A. supplies were made available for the rehabilitation of Czechoslovakia. Medical supplies had been sent by air a month earlier. Here, Mr. Masaryk signs the agreement. On his left is Sir Frederick Leith-Ross. *Photo, Keystone*

capable of solution on an exchange basis. Moreover, the number involved was very much smaller (about 700,000). An agreement signed in Budapest on March 1, 1946, provided for the exchange of equal numbers, with compensation on a basis of equality, the position of the balance of Hungarians left in Slovakia to be considered in the peace treaty.

Those Czech and Slovak Jews who had survived the ordeal of concentration and extermination camps—they were a pitifully small percentage—returned and had their property restored. Those Jews who, in the census of 1930, had given their mother-

Jewish Property Restored

tongue as German or who had studied at German schools and universities in Czechoslovakia, and had, many of them (in particular doctors), found refuge in England during the war, were repatriated by the Czechoslovak Government, but had great difficulty in obtaining permission to practise again. Some emigrated a second time.

There was another group of non-Czechoslovak people, though of Slav origin, in the easternmost and most backward region of Czechoslovakia: in Sub-Carpathian Ruthenia. There, mixed with a great number of other small minority groups (among them Hungarians, Jews, Rumanians and Gipsies), lived about half a million people whose language was almost identical with that spoken in the Ukraine. After a long period of Hungarian misrule, it became, under the Treaty of St. Germain, part of Czechoslovakia, whose government, from 1919 onward, helped this poor and backward region by building roads and hospitals, by giving land

R.A.F. SERVICE BETWEEN LONDON AND PRAGUE
By the month of August 1945 R.A.F. Transport Command was operating a regular air service between the Croydon (London) airport and Prague, capital of Czechoslovakia. Here, R.A.F. Transport Command Dakotas and Stirlings are parked on the tarmac at Prague's airfield. The Stirlings were being used to repatriate Czechoslovak nationals from Britain.
Photo, British Official

PRAGUE, LAST EUROPEAN CAPITAL TO BE FREED

On May 5, 1945, a rising was launched in Prague by the Czech National Committee. Later in the day the patriots urgently appealed by radio for help from the U.S. and Red Armies— though the capital was in Czech hands, 300 German tanks were approaching. Desperate street fighting developed, and German bombers attacked the city. Not until May 8 (three days after the general German surrender), did the enemy agree to withdraw. 1. In the uniform of a general of the Czechoslovak Army, President Benes inspects Soviet troops in the capital at a farewell parade on December 1, when all Russian and U.S. forces were withdrawn from Czechoslovak territory. 2. Entry of the first Soviet tanks into Prague on May 10. U.S. infantry entered the capital at the same time. 3. Citizens of Pilsen line the streets to welcome the U.S. 3rd Army on May 6.

to the peasants and creating new industries. By 1938 the Ruthenians had also achieved, within the framework of the republic, a remarkable measure of self-administration. A majority, however, mainly among the poorer people, had always been pro-Russian, and when the Curzon Line was accepted as the basis of the Polish-Soviet border (*see page 3874*), and the Ukrainians formerly under Polish rule were returned to the Ukrainian Soviet Republic, the Ruthenians (or Carpatho-Ukrainians) also voiced their desire to join that republic.

Ruthenia Ceded to U.S.S.R.

Mr. Fierlinger arrived in Moscow on June 21, and on the 29th concluded an agreement with the Soviet Government (unanimously ratified by the Czechoslovak Provisional National Assembly on November 23) by which Sub-Carpathian Ruthenia was transferred to the Soviet Ukraine.

By this territorial change Czechoslovakia and Rumania—once closely allied in the " Little Entente "—lost their common frontier, while the Soviet Union acquired a " bridge-head " on the southern slopes of the Carpathian mountains and became a direct neighbour to Hungary

Though the loss of this easternmost province caused little resentment, there was disappointment in some circles that it was to Soviet Russia Czechoslovakia was losing part of her territory. Hardly any open criticism was made, as Czechoslovakia could not now oppose Russia on any major issue. Altogether, the popularity of Russia, and of the

Red Army in particular, suffered some setbacks in the course of the year, less so in the western provinces than in Slovakia, where the Russian army had not in all cases treated the population as Slav brothers ; but Russian influence remained nevertheless very strong indeed.

On August 30 Dr. Benes signed a decree setting up machinery for the creation of a Provisional National Assembly of 300 members (200 Czechs, 100 Slovaks) : local National Committees elected District Councils on September 16, and these a fortnight later elected Provincial Councils by choosing names from a single list. These councils met in Prague on October 14 to elect members of the Provisional National Assembly, which held its first meeting on October 28.

Four decrees signed by President Benes on October 24 nationalized (1) the mines, natural resources, and big iron and steel enterprises (including armaments) ; (2) certain large enterprises in the food and drink industries ; (3) the banks ; and (4) the insurance companies. Small industries, communal enterprises and the distributive trades were not affected. Most of the undertakings involved had been under national administration since the surrender of Germany and the collapse of the Protectorate Government. Their value was to be assessed at " current market prices," and compensation was to be paid in Government bonds, cash or other values from a special fund, except in the case of " nationally unreliable " people and " disloyal " Czechoslovaks,

CZECHOSLOVAK PREMIER

On April 7, 1945, the constitution of the new Czechoslovak Provisional Government was announced, with Mr. Zdenek Fierlinger (above) as Premier. Formation of the new body had resulted from discussions in Moscow between Czechoslovak and Russian leaders. Aged 54, Mr. Fierlinger had been Ambassador in Moscow from 1943.

who were to receive no compensation. All foreign trade was brought under State control by a decree of October 29. The film industry was nationalized on August 13, production, distribution, import and export being brought under State control.

An agreement with the Soviet authorities made over to the Soviet Union as war booty factories set up in Czechoslovakia by the Germans during the war, except in the case of machinery earlier looted by the Germans from the country and reinstalled there after the beginning of the air war on Germany.

American and Russian troops withdrew simultaneously from Czechoslovakia on December 1.

Between August 1 and December 1 the Czech People's Courts sentenced a total of 1,370 German and Czech war criminals, 86 to death and 76 to long terms of imprisonment. Dr. Emil Hacha, puppet president of the Protectorate, died on June 27 while awaiting trial.

The first general elections since 1935 were held on May 26, 1946. In Bohemia-Moravia, the Communists secured 93 seats, Social Nationalists 55, Christian Democrats 46, Social Democrats 37 ; in Slovakia, Christian Democrats 43, Communists 21, Freedom Party 2, Labour Party 2. On June 4 President Benes (whose re-election as President of the Republic it was agreed by all parties should take place at the first meeting of the new Assembly on June 14) charged Mr. Klemens Gottwald, the Communist leader, with the formation of a new Cabinet, Mr. Fierlinger having refused a Communist invitation to remain as Prime Minister of a new Government.

REMEMBRANCE AT LIDICE

Czechoslovakia in June 1946 commemorated the fourth anniversary of the massacre of Lidice (see page 2569), the mining village, 20 miles west of Prague, wiped out by the Nazis on June 10, 1942, because, they alleged, it had harboured the killers of Reinhard Heydrich. All that marked the site was this cross erected by the Russians over the mass grave of the village's murdered men.

October 1. Czechoslovakia resumed diplomatic relations with Rumania. King Leopold of the Belgians issued proclamation to the Belgian people before leaving Austria for Switzerland.

October 2. In Indo-China truce declared between French authorities and the Annamites. Announced that General Patton had been relieved of his command of the U.S. 3rd Army and of his post as Military Governor of Bavaria, and had been replaced by Lieutenant-General Truscott. Council of Foreign Ministers in London terminated its first session. First travelling Post Office train for five years left Euston for Aberdeen.

October 3. In China fighting in Kunming between Chungking troops and Chinese Communists. French battleship " Richelieu " covered landings of Allied troops in Indo-China. Darnand, head of Vichy militia, sentenced to death, executed seven days later. Constitution of World Trades Union Federation adopted in Paris. General de Gaulle visited Saarbrücken in French occupation zone. President Truman recommended Congress to establish a commission on control of atomic energy development. First gap in Walcheren dykes sealed.

October 4. In Tokyo Allied H.Q. ordered removal of Japanese Home Minister Yamazaki, release of political prisoners, abolition of secret police and abrogation of all laws restricting freedom of thought. Trial opened in Paris of Pierre Laval on charges of treason.

October 5. Japan's Prime Minister, Higashi-Kuni, and his entire Cabinet resigned. In London troops of the Household Cavalry mounted guard in Whitehall for the first time since the outbreak of war.

October 6. Baron Shidehara, appointed Japanese Prime Minister, pledged that Japan would follow the course of democracy. General MacArthur abolished Shintoism as Japanese state religion. Indictment of leading German war criminals signed in Berlin by the chief prosecutors of U.K., U.S.A., U.S.S.R. and France.

October 7. In Paris Laval and his counsel withdrew from court as a protest against the conduct of the trial. First party of released prisoners of war from the Far East arrived in England, at Southampton.

October 8. Rudolf Hess flown from Britain to Germany to stand trial as a war criminal. Palestine Jews demonstrated in Tel-Aviv, Jerusalem and Haifa against British immigration policy. Indonesian extremists arrested all " moderate " officials, forbade sale of food or goods to Europeans or Eurasians. Norwegian General Election. President Truman declared at Press conference that U.S. would not share secret of atomic bomb production with any other nation.

October 9. Andaman Islands reoccupied by British troops. South Africa ratified United Nations Charter. Military Government in Burma gave place to civilian administration. British and Dutch officials arrested by Indonesian extremists. Laval sentenced to death while absent from court.

October 10. U.S. Secretary of State announced plans for the formation of Far East Advisory Council to sit at Washington. The U.S.A. recognized the Hungarian Government. In Britain, the Chancellor presented a bill to nationalize the Bank of England ; 30,000 dockers out on strike.

October 11. General MacArthur presented Baron Shidehara, the Japanese Prime Minister, with a five-point programme for social and political reform. It was announced that all U.S. forces were to leave Palestine, beginning on October 12.

October 12. Negotiations between French and Annamites at Saigon broke down. Dutch Prime Minister, Mr. Schermerhorn, broadcast on position in Java. General de Gaulle declared : " We never want to see a German Reich again." Return of " Queen Elizabeth " and " Aquitania " to British service announced.

October 13. Indonesian People's Army declared war on Dutch, Eurasians, and Amboinese in Java. Announced that British, Chinese and Russian forces were to join the U.S. in the occupation of Japan. Syria and Lebanon agreed on a joint policy towards Palestine.

October 14. Major-General Hawthorn, British officer commanding Allied forces in Java, issued a proclamation listing offences against the military administration.

October 15. Conference of International Labour Organization opened in Paris. Laval executed. Sir Reginald Dorman-Smith, Governor of Burma, returned to Rangoon for the first time since 1942. General MacArthur declared Japanese disarmament completed. Dr. van Mook expressed willingness to open discussions with Indonesians on basis of Queen Wilhelmina's 1942 declaration.

October 16. At Batavia Indonesians held first " national " conference. Announced that British Government was prepared to recognize Dr. Renner's Austrian Provisional Government. Thirty nations signed Charter of United Nations Food and Agriculture Organization, Argentina and the U.S.S.R. abstaining.

October 17. Archbishop Damaskinos, the Greek Regent, assumed the Premiership. At Hamburg trial opened of U-boat crew accused of murdering British and Allied seamen in the Atlantic in March 1944. German H.Q. in Norway disbanded.

October 18. In Berlin Allied Military Tribunal held its first open session and received indictments against 24 leading Nazis. Indonesians rejected status within the Netherlands Empire offered them by the Dutch.

October 19. Marshal of the R.A.F. Sir Arthur Tedder succeeded Lord Portal as Chief of Air Staff. In Rome Signor de Gasperi, Italian Foreign Minister, disclosed that Italian Government was sounding the Allies about a revision of the international status of Italy.

October 20. Great Britain, the U.S., the U.S.S.R. and France gave official recognition to Dr. Renner's Provisional Government.

October 21. Elections to Constituent Assembly and Referendum on its standing held in France. British and U.S. Governments expressed strong regrets to the U.S.S.R. at the terms of the Soviet-Hungarian economic agreement (initialled in Moscow, August 27).

October 22. In the Shantung province of China, fighting broke out between Chinese Communists and Government forces. Allied Control Council announced " fundamental principles of judicial reform " for Germany. Announced that no more permanent commissions in the Indian Army would be granted to British officers.

October 23. Budapest radio announced the decision of the four major Hungarian political parties to hold elections on November 4, as arranged. Russia proposed to Austria an exchange of diplomatic representatives.

October 24. United Nations organization called into existence at Washington. Execution at Oslo of Norwegian traitor, Vidkun Quisling. Formal surrender at Rangoon of General Kimura, C.-in-C., Japanese forces in Burma. Mr. Stalin received Mr. Harriman, U.S. Ambassador, at Sochi in the Caucasus.

October 25. Robert Ley, former German Labour Front leader and one of the leading Nazis on trial at Nuremberg, committed suicide in his cell. French 2nd Armoured Division arrived at Saigon, went into action.

October 26. Finnish–Russian border agreement announced. Mr. Bevin told House of Commons that there were from twenty to twenty-five million displaced people on the move in Europe. Sir Ben Smith, Minister of Food, said that world food prospects for coming year were " seriously disquieting."

October 27. In Navy Day Address in New York President Truman gave 12 points of U.S. foreign policy. Dr. Benes decreed the nationalization of some 1,000 Czechoslovak industrial and financial concerns. Sir John Boyd-Orr nominated Director-General of United Nations Food and Agriculture Organization.

October 28. Chinese Central Government offered terms to Yenan Communists with view to stabilizing political situation in N. China. Dr. Benes declared that Sudeten Germans must leave Czechoslovakia in interests of European peace.

October 29. Mr. Attlee announced British Government's decision to set up atomic research station near Didcot. Fighting reported in N. China between Government and Communist forces. Trial of General Yamashita, " the Tiger of Malaya," opened at Manila.

October 30. Brigadier Mallaby, British commander in Sourabaya, murdered by Indonesian extremists while conducting " cease fire " parleys. Chinese Government troops began landing from U.S. ships at Chinwangtao. Czechoslovak Provisional National Assembly confirmed Dr. Benes as President.

October 31. General Christison, Allied C.-in-C., announced that unless Brigadier Mallaby's murderers surrendered, the whole weight of Allied forces would be brought against them.

MEMBERS OF BRITAIN'S LABOUR CABINET OF 1945

CLEMENT R. ATTLEE
Prime Minister

HERBERT MORRISON
Lord President of the Council

ERNEST BEVIN
Foreign Secretary

ARTHUR GREENWOOD
Lord Privy Seal

HUGH DALTON
Chancellor of the Exchequer

SIR STAFFORD CRIPPS
President of the Board of Trade

A. V. ALEXANDER
First Lord of the Admiralty

LORD JOWITT
Lord Chancellor

J. CHUTER EDE
Home Secretary

VISCOUNT ADDISON
Dominions Secretary

LORD PETHICK-LAWRENCE
Secretary of State for India

G. H. HALL
Colonial Secretary

J. J. LAWSON
Minister for War

VISCOUNT STANSGATE
Minister for Air

JOSEPH WESTWOOD
Secretary for Scotland

GEORGE A. ISAACS
Minister of Labour

EMANUEL SHINWELL
Minister of Fuel

ELLEN WILKINSON
Minister of Education

ANEURIN BEVAN
Minister of Health

TOM WILLIAMS
Minister of Agriculture

Chapter 378

PEACE COMES TO BRITAIN AFTER SIX YEARS

Describing the three months' interval between the end of the war in Europe and the cessation of fighting in the Far East on August 15, 1945, this concluding chapter on the Home Front tells of the coming to full power of a Labour Government. It then records outstanding events in Great Britain, Northern Ireland and the Channel Islands up to the close of the year. Some idea is given of how the gigantic task of directing the nation's whole way of life into the paths of peace was begun with courage and determination in face of manifold difficulties both at home and abroad

THE rejoicings over the end of hostilities in Europe were brief—Japan had still to be defeated, and though Allied leaders were hopeful that 1945 would see the end of that campaign too, the people had been warned of the possibility of a long-continued struggle in the Far East, and prepared themselves to face it.

On May 18, Mr. Churchill sent letters in identical terms to the leaders of the Labour, Liberal and National Liberal Parties proposing the maintenance of the Coalition Government "until a decisive victory has been gained over Japan." "If you should decide to stay with us," he said, "all united together until the Japanese surrender is compelled, let us discuss means of taking the nation's opinion, for example a referendum, on the issue whether, in these conditions, the life of this Parliament should be further prolonged."

The Labour Party Conference, then meeting at Blackpool, decided with only two dissident votes to reject the Prime Minister's proposals. "The need for bring- **Labour Wants Autumn Election** ing to an end when conditions allow a Parliament the life of which has been prolonged year after year has been recognized by all of us," said Mr. Attlee in his reply, "and by no one more emphatically than yourself. . . . We consider that the fair and just solution of the problem is an election in the autumn. . . . I do not think that it would be right or possible to obtain from Parliament another prolongation of its life. I could not consent to the introduction into our national life of a device so alien to all our traditions as the referendum. . . . Hitler's practices in the field of referenda and plebiscites can hardly have endeared these expedients to the British heart."

But Mr. Churchill, feeling that an election to be fought on a party basis pending in the autumn would interfere with the smooth working of the Coalition Government, decided on immediate resignation, and at noon on May 23, 1945, tendered the resignation of the Cabinet he had formed on May 11, 1940.

The King invited him, as leader of the strongest party in the House, to form a new government to hold office until a new Parliament was elected. Mr. Attlee resumed his position as Leader of the Opposition. With the breakup of the Coalition, the wartime ministries of Home Security and Economic Warfare disappeared, their residuary functions being taken over respectively by the Home Office and the Foreign Office.

P.M. GOES ELECTIONEERING
The General Election campaign in Britain opened on June 4, 1945, when Mr. Churchill, Prime Minister of the 'Caretaker' Government which followed the breakup of the Coalition, outlined his party's policy in a broadcast. Here he begins his election tour, at Uxbridge, where he told his audience, 'It was not by my desire that the election has come about.' *Photo, Sport and General*

On June 15, the 37th Parliament of the United Kingdom—fourth longest in British history—was dissolved after a life of nine years six months and twenty days. The election campaign had already opened, on June 4, with a broadcast by the Prime Minister. Electioneering by broadcasting was on a much larger scale than in 1935, when five broadcasts were made by the Government, four by the Labour Party, and three by the opposition Liberals. In 1945, the Government was allotted ten periods, the Labour Party ten, and the Liberals four following the 9 p.m. news bulletin, the peak hour of listening. The Government relied in its appeals almost exclusively on Mr. Churchill's immense popularity and success as a war leader. His portrait and the phrase " Help him to finish the job " constituted the major part of Conservative propaganda, and during the last days of the campaign the Prime Minister made a rush tour of the Midlands, the North, Scotland, and London. Everywhere he received an enthusiastic personal reception, but encountered lively political opposition.

The principal points in the policy put forward by the Labour Party were the nationalization of the coal mines and the transport system, an effective and com- **Labour Party Policy** prehensive scheme of social security, a clear cut programme for export trade, rapid rehousing to provide good accommodation for all, a foreign policy based on loyal co-operation in the United Nations organization, and the maintenance of controls to the extent required to effect a smooth transition from war to peace conditions. Polling day was July 5, except in 23 constituencies where, owing to local holidays, polling was, by a special act, held in 22 cases on July 22, and in one case on July 19. To allow time for the receipt of Service votes from overseas, to record and collect which elaborate steps had been taken, the results were not declared until July 26, in the middle of the conference of representatives of the United Kingdom, the United States, and Soviet Russia which met at Potsdam on July 17 (*see* page 3923). The Labour Party secured a sweeping majority : 393 seats (compared with 164 in the previous House) against the Conservatives' 189 (formerly 358). Only 12 Liberals were returned (instead of 18) ; Liberal Nationalists, now indistinguishable from Conservatives, numbered 13 (instead of 26). Independents numbered 14, Northern Ireland representatives nine Unionists and two Nationalists. Four "splinter" parties secured only eight seats between them.

Among Cabinet Ministers in Mr. Churchill's interim government who lost their seats were Mr. L. S. Amery, Mr. Brendan Bracken, Sir James Grigg, Mr. Hore-Belisha, Mr. Richard Lloyd, Mr. Harold Macmillan. Mr. Churchill's son-in-law, Mr. Duncan Sandys, and his son, Major Randolph Churchill, were also defeated. Sir Archibald Sinclair and Sir William Beveridge, whose social security report formed the basis for the social security plans of all parties, both lost their seats.

Mr. Churchill, who had flown back from Berlin to London to hear the **Mr. Churchill Resigns** election results, tendered his resignation at once, having held office as Prime Minister for 1,902 days covering the most momentous period in the history of the British Isles. The King at once invited Mr. Attlee to form a Government. Mr. Attlee, First Lord of the Treasury and Minister of Defence as well as Prime Minister (as Mr. Churchill had been) filled the first seven Cabinet posts and on July 28 returned to Potsdam (where he had been with Mr. Churchill in an advisory capacity for the opening of the conference) as leader of the British delegation with his Foreign Secretary Mr. Ernest Bevin. Mr. Attlee chose the rest of the Cabinet (*see illus.* in page 3888) and his other Ministers after his return to London at the end of the Conference, which lasted until August 1.

On August 6 came the dropping of the first atomic bomb on the Japanese

Lieutenant FURNESS
(Welsh Guards)

In late May 1940, during the retreat to the French coast, Lieut. the Hon. Christopher Furness performed a 'magnificent act of self-sacrifice against hopeless odds' for which he was posthumously awarded the V.C. While covering the withdrawal of transport from Arras his carriers were disabled, the crews killed or wounded, whereupon he fought the enemy hand-to-hand, single-handed, till he was killed. The transport got through.

Sergeant DURRANT
(Corps of Royal Engineers)

For 'gallantry, skill, and devotion to duty' when in charge of a Lewis gun in a motor-launch in the St. Nazaire raid on March 28, 1942, Sergeant Thomas Frank Durrant was awarded the V.C. Answering a German destroyer's demand to surrender with a burst of fire, he continued to work his gun though badly wounded, until he was taken prisoner, when he died. For his part in this raid, Lt.-Col. A. C. Newman was also awarded the V.C. (See page 2255.)

Captain LIDDELL
(Coldstream Guards)

While capturing a bridge over the River Ems near Lingen, Germany, on April 3, 1945, Captain Ian Oswald Liddell displayed 'outstanding gallantry' for which he was posthumously awarded the V.C. 'His superb example of courage,' ran the citation, 'will never be forgotten by those who saw it.' It was disclosed after his death that he was one of eight Brigade of Guards officers (Coates Mission) selected to protect the Royal Family in case of invasion.

industrial town of Hiroshima. Following the announcement of this event by President Truman, Mr. Attlee released a statement which had been prepared by Mr. Churchill before the change of government, setting out the history of the research which had gone to the production of this latest logical development of man's continued use of the finest fruits of his scientific intelligence for purposes of destruction. Research into the possibilities of the release of energy by atomic fission, it was explained, had been undertaken by His Majesty's Government in 1941. Interchange of ideas between British and American scientists went on, and in October 1941 (before the United States came into the war) President Roosevelt suggested the merging of British and American efforts, as a result of which a number of British scientists went to the United States. By the summer of 1942 the work done confirmed the report made in the autumn of 1941 by the British Government committee of scientists presided over by Sir George Thomson, that the atomic bomb could be produced by the end of the war.

EISENHOWER GETS CITY'S FREEDOM

General of the Army Dwight D. Eisenhower, Supreme Allied Commander, on June 11, 1945, flew to London from his H.Q. at Frankfort-on-Main to receive the following day a sword of honour and the Freedom of the City of London which the Court of Common Council had unanimously decided to confer on him. Here, in Guildhall, he is receiving from the Lord Mayor, Sir Frank Alexander, as a token pending the completion of his own sword, one once owned by Wellington.
Photo, G.P.U.

VICTORY STAMPS

To mark the victory celebrations on June 8, 1946, special issues of British stamps were printed to the total cash value of £2,800,000, made up of 240,000,000 of the 2½d. denomination and 24,000,000 of the 3d. The former were blue, the latter deep violet, both being twice the normal breadth. After V.E. and V.J. Days postmarks (centre) bore the ' V ' sign and victory bells.

"By God's mercy," said Mr. Churchill's statement, "British and American science outpaced all German efforts. These were on a considerable scale, but far behind. The possession of these powers by the Germans at any time **Mr. Churchill** might have altered the **on the** result of the war, and **Atomic Bomb** profound anxiety was felt by those who were informed. Every effort was made by our Intelligence Service and the R.A.F. to locate in Germany anything resembling the plants that were being created in the U.S. In the winter of 1942–43 most gallant attacks were made in Norway on two occasions by small parties of volunteers from the British Commandos and Norwegian forces at very heavy loss of life, upon stores of ' heavy water,' an element in one of the possible processes ; the second of these attacks was completely successful." (*See* page 3202 and Chapter 379.)

But the first bomb was pronounced already out-dated when a second "better" one was dropped on Nagasaki three days later. Tokyo broadcast acceptance of the Potsdam ultimatum next day : the hideous weapon could be said to

have justified itself. Thousands of Japanese civilian men, women and children had been killed : but probably many more thousands of Allied, and of Japanese, service lives had been saved, since the Allies were spared the need of an armed invasion of the Japanese homeland with all the carnage that would have involved. Formal acceptance of the Allied terms of unconditional surrender was handed by the Japanese Minister to the Swiss Foreign Office at 8.10 p.m. on August 14, and at midnight Mr. Attlee broadcast news

of Japan's surrender, proclaiming August 15 and 16 Victory-over-Japan days (*see* Hist. Doct. 310, p. 3905).

The State opening of the new Parliament by King George VI coincided with the end of hostilities in the Second Great War. The speech from the Throne (*see* Hist. Doct. 311, p. 3905), setting out the Government's programme, was read to an assembly of both Houses and in the presence of the Diplomatic Corps. When the House of Commons reassembled in the afternoon, the Prime Minister read the terms of the

THANKSGIVING DAY AT ST. PAUL'S

Sunday, May 13, 1945, was observed throughout Britain as a day of thanksgiving. In London, Their Majesties, accompanied by the Princesses, drove through cheering crowds to St. Paul's Cathedral where the special service was conducted by the Archbishop of Canterbury. The vast congregation included European crowned heads, Allied Service leaders, the Diplomatic Corps, and Mr. Churchill and the War Cabinet. Here, the royal carriages pass down Ludgate Hill.

Photo, Planet News

Japanese surrender and then moved, "That this House do now attend the Church of St. Margaret, Westminster, to give humble and reverent thanks to Almighty God on the victorious conclusion of the War."

On August 21, Mr. Attlee announced in the House that the Government had decided to appoint an advisory committee, with Sir John Anderson as chairman, to assist them on the technical side on questions raised by the discovery of how to release atomic energy. Its members were Sir Alexander Cadogan, Permanent Under-Secretary of the Foreign Office, Field-Marshal Sir Alan Brooke, C.I.G.S., Sir Alan Barlow, Second Secretary of the Treasury, Sir Edward Appleton, Director of the Department of Scientific and Industrial Research, Sir Henry Dale, President of the Royal Society, Professor P. M. S. Blackett, Sir James Chadwick, and Sir George Thomson. On the recommendation of this committee, it was announced on October 29 that it had been decided to set up at Harwell near Didcot in Berkshire a research and experimental station covering all aspects of the use of atomic energy.

Committee on Atomic Energy

Relaxation of wartime restrictions continued. On May 9, 84 defence regulations (including 18B under which the Home Secretary could, without formal charge, detain persons whose activities he considered to be a possible danger to the State) were revoked in entirety, 25 others in part. Fifty persons still detained under 18B were released. All lighting restrictions everywhere in the United Kingdom were lifted on May 10. Shipping movements

SURRENDERED U-BOAT COMES UP THE THAMES
London had its first view of a surrendered U-boat on May 22, 1945, when the U776 sailed up the Thames to be moored for public inspection below Westminster Bridge. The U-boat, flying the White Ensign, was reputed to have a range of 10,000 miles at a surface speed of 10 knots, but when surrendered had done only one patrol of 54 miles and fired only one torpedo—which missed.
Photo, Daily Press

and casualties were published by Lloyd's on May 29 for the first time since September 1939, and from midnight on May 28–29 convoys ceased to sail in non-combat areas, and the necessity of darkening ships at night was lifted. Lighthouses and lightships round the British coast, blacked out during the war, showed full lights on May 30.

Restrictions on travel between Great Britain and Northern Ireland were relaxed from May 17. All internal censorship in Great Britain, and censorship of mails and of documents carried by passengers to Northern Ireland, ceased at the same time. Censorship of the press ended in Britain on September 2, exactly six years after it began. Submission of news had remained voluntary throughout the war; editors, co-operating willingly with the Chief Press Censor Rear-Admiral G. P. Thomson in preventing any breach of security, had submitted for censorship 665,500 items, totalling 183 million words.

Restrictions Relaxed

The last civilian internment camps in the Isle of Man were closed by the beginning of September. Double summer time (introduced in 1941 as a war measure) ended on July 15, summer time on October 7, the following winter

THE KING BIDS FAREWELL TO THE CIVIL DEFENCE
A farewell parade was held in Hyde Park on Sunday, June 10, 1945, of 2,500 men and women representative of Britain's Civil Defence services in every region of Great Britain and Northern Ireland. They were inspected by the King, accompanied by the Queen and Princess Elizabeth. Here, a section marches past the saluting base. Stand-down of the Civil Defence took place on May 2.
Photo, Planet News

LONDON GETS BACK TO NORMAL

Famous paintings from the national collections, stored for safety during the war eighty feet beneath Piccadilly Circus in the Underground, brought up again, February 1946.

The fine equestrian statue of George III by Wyatt which had been removed 'for the duration' to Berkhamsted, Herts (see illus. in page 1912), returned to Cockspur Street, in mid-April 1946.

On January 30, 1946, 20 tons of priceless manuscripts were brought back to the British Museum from Skipton Castle, Yorkshire, where they had been for six years.

Removal of surface pipes, laid along London streets to provide water for fire-fighting (see page 1720), began in July 1945. Here, dismantling pipes across London Bridge.

By the autumn of 1945 removal of the thousands of public surface shelters erected in the streets had begun. Demolition squads are here at work in Haymarket during March 1946 (see page 831).

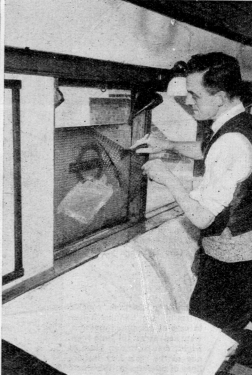

It took sharp-edged stripping-knives—and razor-blades to finish it off—to remove the protective netting (see page 2114) from the windows of London's buses and tube-trains.

From 1942 Britain made use of pneumatic camouflage devices constructed from barrage balloon material. Here is a dummy Sherman tank which weighed only 17 lb. and fitted into a holdall when deflated. Right, heavily armed British 'Neptune' tank, navigable on both land and water.

Most striking of London's wartime buildings was 'The Citadel' in the Mall, overlooking Horse Guards Parade. With walls eight feet thick and heavily guarded by A.A. guns, it was the Admiralty's bomb-proof secret H.Q.

BRITISH WAR SECRETS

After the defeat of France, when Britain's ports in the south and east were virtually closed, two emergency ports for ocean-going traffic were built on the west coast of Scotland— at the Gareloch on the Clyde and at Cairnryan on Loch Ryan. Above, deep-water berth at 'No. 1 Military Port,' Gareloch.

(See also page 3618.)

Britain's 'oil defences,' capable of setting the Channel ablaze in case of attempted invasion, were kept secret till June 1945. Right, demonstration blaze of one of the secondary inshore lines of oil-defence: the whole area is swept with fire and smothered in thick smoke

being the first winter of Greenwich mean time since that of 1939–1940. The basic petrol ration, restored on June 1, was increased in September from a mileage of 120 to one of 150 miles a month, and coupons were made valid for use in the month of issue and the month following (instead of only in the month of issue).

On July 10 the Dover Command which, since December 1939, had been a separate command, reverted to its peacetime status as part of the Nore Command. G.H.Q. Home Forces, formed in the summer of 1940 when invasion seemed imminent, was disbanded on July 15. Under the command of Sir Alan Brooke and later of Sir Bernard Paget, it had grown into a powerful field army and provided many divisions for North Africa, Sicily, Italy, and the whole 21st Army Group for the final campaign in western Europe. At

G.H.Q. Home Forces Disbanded

BOMBERS TO FURNITURE

Change-over from war to peace production in many sections of British industry was well advanced by the late summer of 1945. Below, in a factory at Walthamstow, London, where orders for R.A.F. Mosquito aircraft—the famous wooden bombers—are being completed, other workmen are making much-needed Utility furniture.
Photo, Topical Press

PACKING UP U.S. LORRIES

With the end of the war in Europe, the Americans in Britain were faced with the task of preparing for shipment to the Far East some 35,000 U.S. Army vehicles. Most of them had left by January 1, 1946. Above, at the U.S. base at Ashchurch, Glos., lorries are crated after being reconditioned and sprayed with rust-preventive, so that they will be serviceable within six hours of arrival at the end of their journey.
Photo, U.S. Official

the time of its disbandment the C.-in-C. was Lt.-General Sir Harold Franklyn.

The last of the training areas used by United States troops in Britain in preparation for the invasion of France were returned to the War Office during the summer. Of the 3,036,332 acres in the west, the Midlands, Lancashire, Wales and Northern Ireland placed at their disposal, less than 50,000 remained under United States control at the end of the war in Europe. The great American warrior, General Dwight D. Eisenhower, who had led the Allied armies to victory in the west, on June 12 drove in an open carriage through cheering crowds to the Guildhall to receive the Freedom of the City of London. In a warm and modest speech, Eisenhower said,

"No man could alone have brought about this result. Had I possessed the military skill of a Marlborough, the wisdom of a Solomon, the understanding of Lincoln, I still would have been helpless without the loyalty, vision and generosity of thousands upon thousands of Britons and Americans. My most cherished hope is that after Japan joins the Nazis in utter defeat neither your country nor mine need ever again summon its sons and daughters from their peaceful pursuits to march to the drums of war. But—a fact important for both of us to remember—neither London nor Abilene [Eisenhower's birthplace] will sell her birthright for physical safety or her liberty for mere existence."

Great crowds acclaimed him when he appeared later on the balcony of the Mansion House. In the afternoon he was received in audience by the King at Buckingham Palace, who conferred on him, its first American recipient, the Order of Merit.

Collection of war damage insurance premiums ceased with the one due on July 1. Mr. Aneurin Bevan stated on August 24 that 700,000 bombed houses in the London region needed further repair, though they were considered fit for habitation; about 70,000 in " bomb alley " also needed further attention. In the blitzed city areas outside London repairs had, broadly speaking, been completed. Sir Malcolm Trustram Eve,

K.C., Chairman of the War Damage Commission, stated in September that notification of damage to 3,281,953 separate properties had been received, with hundreds more coming in each week. 3,024,822 were in respect of dwelling houses (the total number of dwelling houses in England and Wales in 1939 was about 11,200,000), 25,989 of agricultural properties ; 1,400,245 were in London, 386,822 in Scotland, 76,556 in Wales, 64,604 in Northern Ireland. In all these cases the cost of repairs or rebuilding had to be met ; 1,018,538 claims did not exceed £25, 394 exceeded £10,000. Properties scheduled as total losses, for which a value payment was to be made, numbered just under 200,000. The Commission had already paid £271,281,171. These figures did not cover damage to public utilities such as railways, docks, electricity, gas and water undertakings, all special objects of attack.

Total Service casualties for the United Kingdom were : killed, 244,723 ; missing, 53,059 ; wounded, 277,090 ; prisoners, 180,405. (During the war of 1914–1918, 812,317 men from the United Kingdom were killed, 1,849,494 wounded.)

Five Acts passed by the old House of Commons received the Royal Assent on June 15 : the Treason Act, which made no change in what constitutes treason, but made all cases of treason and misprision **New Acts of Parliament** of treason triable in the same way as cases of murder, i.e. before a jury with the ordinary laws of evidence applying, and in cases of treason committed abroad abolished the accused's right to apply to the Attorney-General to order a trial at bar with three judges ; the Requisitioned Land and War Works Act, to conserve the use or value of assets created at the public expense on requisitioned or other land ; the Family Allowances Act, which provided for the payment to the mother, from a date to be specified by Order, of a weekly allowance of 5s. for each child after the first up to the age at which school attendance ceased to be compulsory; the Education (Scotland) Act, which applied to Scotland with necessary modifications the Education Act (1944) for England and Wales (see Historic Document 277 page 3017) ; the Distribution of Industry Act, which was intended to abolish distressed areas by offering to industrialists help in establishing new industries in the former " special areas " (to be extended and renamed " development areas ").

One of the first acts of the new House was to ratify, with the approval of all

CROYDON'S UNEXPLODED BOMB

After 200 days sappers of the Royal Engineers on Dec. 17, 1945, succeeded in freeing Croydon, near London, from the threat of a 4,000-lb. unexploded German bomb which had lain buried since January 1941. Nicknamed ' Hermann ' by the local inhabitants, the bomb is here being hauled from the 40-foot shaft at the bottom of which it was found. Its 2,000 lb. of high explosive had been sterilized by steam-heating.   *Photo, Planet News*

HELPING EX-SOLDIERS TO FACE THE FUTURE

In 1944 the War Office began to make plans for the rehabilitation of returned prisoners-of-war, known as the Civil Resettlement Scheme. Left, at No. 1 Civil Resettlement Unit, Hatfield House, Herts, repatriated prisoners are instructed in such subjects as rationing and post-war credits. Right, the Guildford 'demob' depot, one of several where demobilized servicemen were able to choose civilian outfits.   *Photos, P.N.A.; Illustrated*

parties, the United Nations Charter (August 23). The bill for the nationalization of the Bank of England, introduced on October 10, was the first measure of nationalization brought forward by the Government, and it went through before the end of the year with little opposition. In November, Mr. Morrison outlined the programme of nationalization of industry which the Government proposed to undertake during the life of Parliament. First on the list was the coal industry (the Coal Industry Nationalization Bill was published on December 20), to be followed at a later stage by the electricity and gas industries, and by railways, canals and long distance road haulage services—road passenger transport was to be co-ordinated with the national transport scheme, within which dock and harbour undertakings were to be brought.

President Truman's unilateral announcement on August 20 that Lend-Lease ceased forthwith caused by its abruptness a certain amount of consternation in Britain, a considerable part of whose food had been supplied during the war years under the terms of the Lend-Lease agreement. It was true that those terms stipulated that with the end of hostilities would come the end of the supply of goods by America on Lend-Lease terms ; but it was generally felt that President Roosevelt would have found a more tactful way of impressing on the people of Great Britain that though they had stood unaided between the United States and the Nazis for over a year they could not expect continued support, except on commercial terms, from that great country.

Talks between a delegation headed by Lord Halifax, British Ambassador in Washington, and Lord Keynes, a Director of the Bank of England, on the one hand and the United States Treasury on the other opened in Washington on September 11. After twelve weeks of hard bargaining, in which Lord Keynes laid bare to the United States Treasury the details and extent of Britain's financial commitments and burdens, an agreement was reached under which, subject to ratification by the British Parliament (which took place on December 13) and the American Congress (which took place on July 13, 1946), Britain was to receive a loan of £1,100,000,000 at two per cent interest repayable over fifty years from 1951. Of this total, £162,000,000 was the final settlement of Lend-Lease. Interest

Loan Talks in Washington

CLEARING BRITAIN'S BEACHES

An important task for the Royal Navy and Royal Engineers from 1943 onwards, after the threat of invasion had passed, was the clearing of Britain's beaches of mines and heavy obstructions. Left, an ejector pump on the beach at Great Yarmouth turns over the sand with water jets to locate a mine. Right, Sunday holiday-makers amuse themselves at Southend while removal of defence blocks goes on.   *Photos, Keystone ; Planet News*

was to be cancelled in any year in which Britain's income from home-produced exports should be less than the average for the years 1936-1938. Britain was to ratify the Bretton Woods agreement before the end of 1945 (carried out on December 20), to abolish the sterling area dollar pool, and to support a general reduction of tariffs and other barriers to trade. (*See* also page 3854.)

The Council of the Foreign Ministers of Britain, the United States, the Soviet Union, France and China, set up under

Foreign Ministers Meet

the Berlin agreement, met for the first time in London on September 11. Its immediate task as laid down at Potsdam was "to draw up, with a view to their submission to the United Nations, treaties of peace with Italy, Rumania, Bulgaria, Hungary and Finland, and to propose settlements of territorial questions outstanding on the termination of the war in Europe." At the opening session it was agreed that the five Foreign Ministers should preside in turn at the Council's meetings, and that the Council's terms of reference should be "to continue the necessary preparatory work for the peace settlements and to consider any other matters which may from time to time be referred to it by the Governments who are members of the Council."

The questions of the future of the Italian colonies, and of the Italo-Yugoslav frontier were referred to the Foreign Ministers' deputies for study. The peace treaties with Finland and Rumania were discussed on September 20, that with Bulgaria on the 21st. Complete divergence of view about the Balkan situation between the Soviet Union on the one hand and Britain and the U.S.A. on the other at once became apparent. While the western Allies were not satisfied that the governments in Rumania, Bulgaria, and Hungary represented the majority of the people, the Soviet Union, said Mr. Molotov, unequivocally considered their regimes fully democratic. A French memorandum on Germany was considered on September 28.

But on October 2 a communiqué announced that the conference had ended in deadlock ; not only were there differences on the matters that had been discussed, but differences also on the interpretation to be put upon the terms of the Berlin agreement made a joint communiqué on the work of the Council impossible. Mr. Byrnes, U.S. Secretary of State, summed up the position in a statement made the same day : " On September 22 the Soviet delegation came to feel that treaty discussions should be confined in each case to the signatories of the surrender terms, as contemplated by the first and narrow provision of Article 2, section 3, subsection 2 of the Berlin agreement, rather than under other and broader provisions of the Berlin agreement. The Soviet delegation took the position that the Council should rescind or withdraw its decision of September 11 whereby France and China were invited to participate in all discussions. This would have meant the elimination of China from all discussion of European peace treaties, and the similar elimination of France except in the case of the treaty with Italy." Mr. Bevin said in the House of Commons on October 9, " It seemed to me, as to Mr. Byrnes, that the difference of view with the Soviet delegation, technical though it might appear to be, in reality involved a big question of principle—to what extent are the ' Big Three ' to exclude other nations from the discussion of matters of grave concern to them ? This principle I felt it was incumbent on me to defend."

THE CHANNEL ISLANDS

On May 9, after five years of enemy occupation, the Channel Islands—only British soil overrun by the Germans—were liberated. The surrender was signed at 7.41 a.m., after which a token force of the Royal Artillery went ashore to hoist the Union Jack at St. Peter Port (Guernsey). A relief force of 7,000 arrived on May 12, bringing technicians to restore communications, specialists to assess the needs of the islands' agriculture for machinery, fertilizers, and seeds, and 9,533 tons of supplies, including food for a fortnight, a year's clothing ration, soap (almost entirely lacking during the occupation), medical supplies, coal, and two lorry loads of sterling currency.

The evacuation of the German garrison of 30,000 began on May 13. Next

OPENING OF THE COUNCIL OF FOREIGN MINISTERS

The Council of Foreign Ministers set up under the Berlin agreement met for the first time at Lancaster House, St. James's, London, on September 11, 1945, to discuss treaties of peace with Italy and others of the Axis powers. Below are the Ministers, attended by their experts and advisers : (1) Mr. James A. Byrnes (U.S.A.) ; (2) Mr. Georges Bidault (France) ; (3) Mr. Ernest Bevin (Great Britain) ; (4) Mr. Molotov (U.S.S.R.) ; (5) Dr. Wang Shih-chieh (China).

CABINET'S WARTIME H.Q.

It was disclosed in November 1945 that shortly after the Chamberlain-Hitler talks at Munich in September 1938 construction began of a bomb-proof H.Q. for the Cabinet some 70 feet below ground in Whitehall, to be used in the event of war. The apartments included a 'War Room,' bedrooms for members of the Government, and a 'strong room' for the safe keeping of secret documents. From the 'War Room' (above), hung with maps showing the daily situation on the world fronts, campaigns on four continents were directed. Note the air-conditioning system running along the sides of the walls. Right, the Prime Minister's private room. One of a suite of three occupied by Mr. Churchill and his family, it contained a large-scale map of England. From the large desk in the foreground Mr. Churchill made most of his war broadcasts.

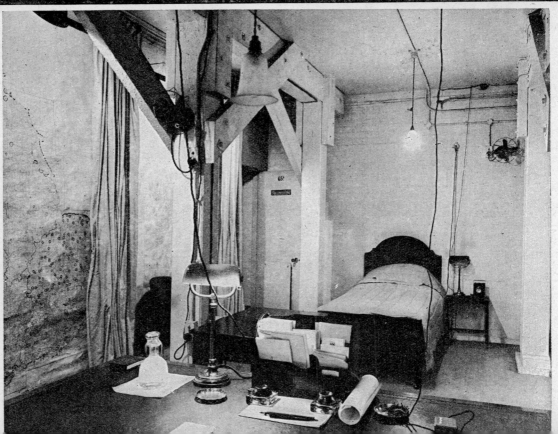

3899   4H³

ATOMIC BOMBS BLAST JAPANESE CITIES

The most horrifying development of the Second Great War was the use of the atomic bomb by the U.S.A.A.F. against Japan in August 1945 (see also page 3847). Two atomic bombs were dropped : the first at Hiroshima (population 320,000) on August 6, the second at Nagasaki (population 260,000) three days later, each causing havoc unprecedented in the history of man. It was officially estimated that at Hiroshima there were 78,150 dead and 13,983 missing. The American Medical Association estimated that there were 40,000 dead at Nagasaki. In addition, some 85,000 in Hiroshima and 75,000 in Nagasaki were left in need of immediate medical care, making a total of over 300,000 casualties caused by the two bombs. Of 580 workers marching across a bridge in Hiroshima, nearly 1½ miles from the centre of the damage, all were burnt (nine died) except three at the rear of the column screened by the eaves of a building. The awe-inspiring smoke-cloud that towered 20,000 feet into the sky three minutes after the bomb had hit Nagasaki is seen above. On the right, devastated Hiroshima, where only steel-framed structures stand

RUINS THAT WERE HIROSHIMA AND NAGASAKI

A British Mission, under the direction of the Chiefs of Staff sent to Japan to investigate the effects of the atomic bombs, spent the month of November 1945 in Hiroshima and Nagasaki. These photographs are reproduced from the report of their mission summarized in page 3847. Above, general view of Hiroshima looking across the centre of damage, the approximate position of which is marked with an arrow. The palace (centre) is 250 ft. and the buildings on the right 500 ft. from the spot on the ground immediately below the explosion of the bomb (which went off in the air).

Below, at Nagasaki, where the centre of damage was to the left, only 300 yards from the bridge.

By permission of His Majesty's Stationery Office

day three hundred displaced persons on Jersey (Spanish Republicans, French and a few Russians) were assembled for repatriation. During the last hopeless months the Germans had been living in indescribable conditions of filth and chaos in requisitioned hotels and houses, wantonly destroying appointments and fittings. Expert reconnaissance of the islands showed that it was probably the most heavily defended area in Europe, and that the Allied Command had been wise in not attempting an attack on the islands : even if successful, it would have destroyed them completely.

Weekly civilian rations during the occupation had been 2 ozs. of meat, 2 pints of milk, 7 ozs. of oatmeal, 5 lb of potatoes, supplemented by swedes and other vegetables and beet syrup. Tobacco had been obtainable at £30 a lb., wood at £50 a ton, wheat at £80 a cwt. second-hand suits and overcoats up to £40, tea at £20 a lb. The general health of the people was fairly good, thanks to the Red Cross parcels which reached Guernsey on December 27, 1943, from Lisbon by the Swedish ship " Vega," and through the retention and diversion by the islanders of undisclosed stocks. During the last part of the occupation the Germans, cut off from all contact with their base, had suffered worse than the local inhabitants, and had been reduced to eating nettles and dandelions, their own horses, cats and dogs, and swedes discarded by the islanders as unfit for cattle.

Mr. Morrison (Home Secretary) arrived at St. Peter Port on May 14 to consult with the States on the future of the islands. His assurance to them that military government would be terminated as soon as it had done its work was carried into effect on August 25, when Lieutenant-General Sir A. E. Grasett was sworn in as Lieutenant-Governor of Jersey, Major-General Neame as

Channel Islanders' Rations

Lieutenant-Governor of Guernsey. The King and Queen visited the liberated islands on June 7.

Speaking in the House of Commons on August 17, Mr. Chuter Ede (Home Secretary in the new Government) gave some account of the history of the war years in the Channel Islands. When British troops were withdrawn on June 19, 1940, the Bailiffs (Mr. Coutanche in Jersey and Mr. Carey in Guernsey) were instructed to stay at their posts and administer the government of the islands to the best of their ability in the interests of the inhabitants. Other officers appointed by the Crown, including Law Officers, were also instructed to remain at their posts. Of the 50,000 inhabitants of Jersey, 10,000 came to England ; of the 40,000 of Guernsey, 18,000. Ten thousand Channel Islanders served in the British armed forces.

The Island States decided to set up a central controlling body to exercise the functions of government. The Germans allowed this body to function, subject to their direction, thus leaving the

THE CHANNEL ISLANDS FREED FROM NAZIDOM

After almost five years of German occupation, the Channel Islands were freed on May 9, 1945. Three days later, crowds assembled outside Elizabeth College, Guernsey (above), used by the enemy as their administrative H.Q., to hear Brigadier A. E. Snow, R.A., commander of the relief forces, read the King's proclamation of greeting. Below, a long line of Nazi prisoners embarks on the way to England. *Photos, P.N.A. ; British Newspaper Pool*

THE KING VISITS LOYAL ULSTER

An important contribution to Britain's war effort—notably in ships, aircraft, linen and agricultural produce—was made by Northern Ireland. Above, in the Commons Chamber of the Parliament at Stormont, Belfast, the King presents decorations at an investiture in July 1945. The Queen and Princess Elizabeth are seated on his right. Left, Belfast's Victory parade on May 16 passes along Donegall-square North. *Photos, Topical Press*

Islands in possession of a large measure of self-government. Information obtained since the liberation showed that the responsible administrators deserved well not only of their fellow islanders, but of Britain for their conduct in a situation which, always difficult, became almost impossible during the last few months of the occupation when the Islands were entirely cut off.

Northern Ireland

Something of what Northern Ireland's loyalty to Great Britain meant was expressed by Mr. Churchill on May 13, 1944, when he said that owing to Mr. de Valera's action in refusing the Allies the use of the southern Irish ports, Britain had only the north-western approach between Ulster and Scotland through which to bring " the means of life and to send out the forces of war." Had it not been for the loyalty of Northern Ireland, " we should have been forced to come to close quarters with Mr. de Valera or perish for ever from the earth."

Northern Ireland did all she could to increase her agricultural production : in 1939, 470,823 acres were under crops ; in 1943, 850,730 acres : an increase of 78 per cent compared with 69 per cent in England and Wales and 46 per cent in Scotland. Flax acreage had increased from 21,194 to 124,536 (the highest since 1870). During the war in Europe, Northern Ireland sent to Britain £3,000,000 worth of fat sheep and cattle, and 20 per cent of home produced eggs. 140 warships and 123 merchant vessels, aggregating 600,000 tons (or 10 per cent of the total United Kingdom merchant shipbuilding), were constructed at Belfast. Nearly 500 tanks, over 500 guns, 14,000 gun barrels and other gun parts, 42,000 carbine machine-guns, about 75,000,000 shells, over 2,000,000 yards of cloth for the Services and 30,000,000 shirts were produced ; 1,500 heavy bombers were built, and some 3,000 aircraft were repaired.

In July 1945 the King and Queen paid a state visit to the country, arriving

in Belfast by air on the 17th. The King, opening Parliament, paid high tribute to the contribution to victory made by the people of Northern Ireland, mentioning specially the hospitality given to the first contingents of American troops to reach the United Kingdom. On the 19th Their Majesties inspected surrendered U-boats lying at Londonderry.

King and Queen Visit Ulster

Following the elections to the United Kingdom Parliament, a meeting of the Nationalists of Tyrone and Fermanagh decided that the Irish Nationalist members for that constituency, Mr. Cunningham and Mr. Mulvey, should take their seats at Westminster, thus reversing the decision of 1935 when the same two men, then also elected members, were asked to abstain from attendance at Westminster, and did so. They took the oath and their seats on August 21. In September Vice-Admiral the Earl of Granville succeeded the Duke of Abercorn as Governor.

END OF THE SECOND GREAT WAR, AUGUST 14, 1945

At midnight B.S.T. on the night of August 14–15, 1945, the Prime Minister, Mr. Clement
R. Attlee, broadcast the news, in the message given below, that Japan had surrendered.
The newly elected House of Commons assembled for the first time next day, August 15
to listen to the King's Speech, extracts from which are also given

Mr. Attlee, Prime Minister of the United Kingdom, announces the end of the Second Great War, August 14, 1945:

JAPAN has to-day surrendered. The last of our enemies is laid low. Here is the text of the Japanese reply to the allied demands :

"With reference to the announcement of August 10 regarding the acceptance of the provisions of the Potsdam declaration and the reply of the Governments of the United States, Great Britain, the Soviet Union, and China sent by Secretary of State Byrnes on the date of August 11, the Japanese Government has the honour to communicate to the Governments of the four Powers as follows :

"(1) His Majesty the Emperor has issued an Imperial rescript regarding Japan's acceptance of the provisions of the Potsdam declaration.

"(2) His Majesty the Emperor is prepared to authorize and insure the signature by his Government and the Imperial General Headquarters of the necessary terms for carrying out the provisions of the Potsdam declaration.

"(3) His Majesty is also prepared to issue commands to the military, naval, and air forces of Japan, and all forces under their control wherever they may be found, to cease all active operations, relinquish all arms, and obey all commands of the allied forces in accordance with the above terms.

(Signed) TOGO."

Let us recall that on December 7, 1941, Japan, whose onslaught China had already resisted for over four years, fell upon the United States of America, who were then not at war, and upon ourselves, who were sorely pressed in our death struggles with Germany and Italy. Taking full advantage of surprise and treachery, Japan's forces quickly overran the territory of ourselves and our allies in the Far East, and at one time it appeared as though they might invade the mainland of Australia and advance into India.

But the tide turned; first slowly and then with ever-increasing speed and violence the mighty forces of the United States and the British Commonwealth and Empire and all their allies, and finally of Russia, were brought to bear. Their resistance has everywhere now been broken.

At this time we should pay tribute to the men of this country, from the Dominions, from India, and the Colonies, to our fleets, armies, and air forces that have fought so well in the arduous campaign, against Japan. Our gratitude goes out to all our splendid allies . . .

We also think especially of the prisoners in Japanese hands, of our friends . . . in Burma and in those colonial territories upon whom the brunt of the Japanese attack fell. We rejoice that their sufferings will soon be at an end . . .

Here at home you have earned a short rest. . . . I have no doubt that to-morrow (Wednesday) and Thursday will everywhere be treated as days of holiday . . . Let all who can relax and enjoy themselves . . . Peace has once again come to the world.

The King's Speech at the Opening of the 38th Parliament of the United Kingdom, August 15, 1945:

THE surrender of Japan has brought to an end six years of warfare which has caused untold loss and misery to the world . . . It is the firm purpose of My Government to work in the closest co-operation with the Governments of My Dominions and in concert with all peace-loving peoples to attain a world of freedom, peace and social justice so that the sacrifices of the war shall not have been in vain.

It has given Me special pleasure to meet the President of the United States on his brief visit to My country after the Conference at Berlin. I have also been glad to express the gratitude of this country to the Supreme Commander of the Allied Expeditionary Force for his inspiring leadership.

My Forces in Europe continue to discharge the duties entailed in the occupation of enemy countries and the repatriation of the many thousands of persons who were deported from their homes by the enemy. My Navy, aided by the Navies of My Allies, is clearing the seas of mines . . .

In the Far East My Ministers will make it their most immediate concern to ensure that all prisoners in Japanese hands are cared for and returned to their homes : . .

My Government will continue the orderly release of men and women from the Armed Forces . . . The arrangements already in operation for the resettlement in civil life of men and women released from the Forces and from war work will be continued and, where necessary, expanded . . .

My Government will take up with energy the tasks of reconverting industry from the purposes of war to those of peace, of expanding our export trade, and of securing by suitable control or by an extension of public ownership that our industries and services shall make their maximum contribution to the national well-being. The orderly solution of these difficult problems will require from all My people efforts comparable in intensity and public spirit to those which have brought us victory . . .

A measure will be laid before you to bring the Bank of England under public ownership. A Bill will also be laid before you to nationalize the coal-mining industry.

My Ministers will organize the resources of the building and manufacturing industries in the most effective way to meet the housing and other essential building requirements of the nation. They will also lay before you proposals . . . to promote the best use of land in the national interest.

You will be asked to approve measures to provide a comprehensive scheme of insurance against industrial injuries, to extend and improve the existing scheme of social insurance and to establish a national health service.

My Ministers will develop to the fullest possible extent the home production of good food . . . and they will keep in being and extend the new food services for the workers and for mothers and children established during the war . . .

Chapter 379

THE ADVENT OF THE ATOMIC BOMB

*Captain Norman Macmillan, M.C., A.F.C., here surveys technical develop-
ments in aero-engine, aircraft and armament design from 1939 to 1945,
demonstrating how power, speed and weight progressively increased. He
records the first operational use of jet-propelled aircraft, and the ever-expanding
use of radar, and concludes his review with a description of the revolutionary
atomic bomb and its appalling effects as evidenced by its use at Hiroshima and
Nagasaki in August 1945. (See colour plate facing page 3862 ; illustrations
in pages 3839, 3850, 3900–01 and 4034 ; and Hist. Doc. No. 309 in page 3847)*

THE Royal Air Force fought the war principally on three famous aero-engines, the Rolls-Royce Merlin, the Bristol Hercules, and the Napier Sabre. The Merlin in 1939 developed 1,030 h.p. at 15,000 feet ; by the time of the Battle of Britain this engine gave 1,300 h.p. at 8,000 feet, an increase of about 350 h.p. at that height. This first advance was largely due to the fuel technologists who had greatly increased the supply of 100 octane petrol. Improved fuel increased the rates of climb of the Spitfire and Hurricane, enabling them to get up to the attacking bombers and fighters more quickly and deal with them on more advantageous terms when encountered. After their earliest mass attacks the Luftwaffe formations came in at greater heights, a change forced upon them by this improved performance of the British interceptors.

R.A.F.'s Three Aero-Engines

The decisive Battle of Britain was fought by the Royal Air Force with all-British equipment on the ground and in the air, with the exception of the fighters' machine guns, which were of American design. American aircraft then delivered to Britain were used only as trainers and in Coastal Command for reconnaissance and bombing.

The Merlin went on developing as a basic engine throughout the war. The Mark 61, with two superchargers and an intercooler, to cool the compressed gas, first saw service in late 1942, and doubled the horse-power of the engine above 20,000 feet. Before the war ended more than 2,000 h.p. was developed by this same basic engine, the Merlin 100 of 1944. Merlin engines were fitted to the Battle, Hurricane, Defiant, Spitfire, Mustang, Fulmar, Barracuda, Whitley, Mosquito, Lancaster, Wellington, Beaufighter, and some Halifaxes.

The Germans did not succeed in producing a two-stage supercharger before the war ended. Instead, they boosted power by injecting methanol-water mixture into the single stage supercharger intake to prevent detonation, and raised the power of an 1,800 h.p. engine to 2,100 h.p. for short periods by this means. When the aircraft reached the maximum supercharged height of its particular engine, this method was valueless. Nitrous oxide (the dentist's " laughing gas ") was therefore injected at greater altitudes to provide more oxygen, and the Junkers Jumo 213E thus gained 418 h.p. at 35,000 feet.

The Bristol Hercules 14-cylinder air-cooled radial entered the war with a power output of 1,340 h.p. Later it gave 1,680 h.p., and finally over 2,000. The Bristol Centaurus 18-cylinder radial first gave 2,500 and later over 2,800 h.p. The Napier Sabre 24-cylinder engine used in the ground strafing Typhoon and the Tempest fighters first developed 2,200 h.p., later 2,400 and finally 3,000. Available engine-power in single units was thus more than doubled in six years of high pressure development, during which fighter speeds rose from the early Hurricane's 335 m.p.h. and the Spitfire's 357 m.p.h. to the 450 m.p.h. of the Spitfire and Mustang models used in 1945. During the battle of the flying bombs a new improved iso-octane fuel, known as 150 grade fuel, was introduced to permit higher power to be taken from piston engines at the low altitudes at which the fighter pilots had to fly to combat the robots.

Engine-Power Trebled

American fighter development was comparable to the British, but Japanese fighter development reached its limit with the 2,000 h.p. Nakajima 18-cylinder radial air-cooled engine, which gave the best Japanese fighter a maximum speed of 420 m.p.h.

Light bomber performance increased from the 256 m.p.h. maximum speed of the Battle to the Mosquito, which could bomb Berlin from Britain at an operational speed of 370 m.p.h. from a height of 30–35,000 feet, a distance and height far beyond the Battle's capacity.

At the beginning of the war the Whitley heavy bomber could carry

'FIDO' CLEARED FOG-BOUND WARTIME AIRFIELDS

One of Britain's most important war inventions was ' Fido,' which cleared airfields of fog with high-powered petroleum burners, thus enabling aircraft to land and take off in otherwise impossible conditions. Invented by the Petroleum Warfare Department and first used in November 1942, it derived its name from the initial letters of ' Fog Investigation Dispersal Operations.' Below, a R.A.F. Lancaster takes off in fog—between two bands of flaming petroleum.

BEWARE MINES!

The Germans in their Baltic seaports issued this poster to warn the inhabitants against R.A.F. sea-mines. 'Beware! Enemy Sea-Mines. Danger to Life,' it read. 'Parachute mines are also dropped from aircraft into rivers and canals. Your life is in danger if you approach or disturb mines which have fallen on land.' *Photo, British Official*

about two tons of bombs to Oslo or Berlin at an operational speed of about 170 m.p.h. The Lancaster raised the load to 10 tons, and the operational speed to about 235 m.p.h. The Super-Fortress could carry up to about eight tons of bombs over the longer striking ranges of the Pacific theatre and operate between 30–35,000 feet at a speed of about 300 m.p.h. Neither the Germans nor the Japanese ever possessed heavy bombers with the characteristics of the Lancaster or of the Super-Fortress.

The war stimulated armaments development. In 1939 the R.A.F. used the 500-lb. bomb as its normal heavy bomb,

Development of H.E. Bombs

but had a 2,000-lb. bomb for use against special targets, such as heavy warships. During the war the largest American bomb weighed 4,000 lb., the German 2,500 kg. (5,500 lb.). R.A.F. bomb development grew steadily from the initiation of the 2,000-lb. parachute bomb to the 4,000-lb., 8,000-lb., and 12,000-lb. blockbusters and the 12,000-lb. and 22,000-lb. streamlined bombs. One Super-Fortress was modified to carry the R.A.F. 12,000-lb. bomb, but the alterations to the structure were not proceeded with in other aircraft of the type.

Great attention was paid by most air forces to incendiary bombs. In 1940 the Luftwaffe tried to burn British towns by dropping considerable quantities of thermite and oil bombs, causing what was currently thought to be great damage, especially when the water supply failed.

The Germans introduced explosive incendiaries to defeat fire-fighting. But nothing the Luftwaffe did compared with the incendiary attacks of the R.A.F. against Germany and those of the U.S.A.A.F. against Japan. The R.A.F. small incendiary and 30-lb. petrol incendiary bombs burned out city after city in Germany, the American 6-lb. petrol jelly bomb caused immense destruction by fire in the more inflammable Japanese cities.

A special mine broke the Ruhr dams (*see* page 2660). The Moehne dam, about 850 yards long, measured 140 feet alike in thickness and in height, and was built of solid concrete. It held back its load of 140,000,000 tons of water by gravity, the force of its own weight. To break such a structure required the destruction of the stable relationship between the dam and the weight of water, and a suitable method was scientifically evolved by Mr. B. Neville Wallis, designer of the dam mines and of the 12,000- and 22,000-lb. streamline bombs. The attack had to be made when the weight of water was at its maximum, and the concrete barrage therefore at its greatest static load, with the water only four feet from the top of the dam. The attacking aircraft had to fly exactly 60 feet above the water at a speed of 232 m.p.h. and release the mines at an exact distance from the dam to prevent them from breaking up at the moment of hitting

Special Mines for Ruhr Dams

the water, and to ensure getting them over the protective net to explode actually against the dam wall 60 feet under the surface. The force of the explosion of these 11 feet diameter mines at this precise depth (which was automatically determined by hydrostatic detonation) imposed such unbalanced stresses on the structure that the dam wall fractured at its base and collapsed. The aircraft's correct height above the reservoir surface and distance from the dam at the moment of release were determined very simply by the focusing of two fixed spotlights on the water's surface, and by triangulation sighting on the dam towers.

Unlike the dam mines, anti-shipping mines were dropped gently into the water by parachute. These mines were cylindrical in shape (for easy stowage in the aircraft) and weighed rather less than one ton. They were detonated by the vessel's magnetic or acoustic fields, and the method of detonation was continually varied to make successful mine-sweeping as difficult as possible. They were effective against both submarines and surface craft. Anti-submarine depth charges weighed about

NEW ALLIED FIRE BOMB

In April 1945 details were released of a new Allied fire bomb. Containing a jellied substance, it burned at 1,400 degrees Fahrenheit, percolating into cracks and crevices which made it hard to extinguish. It was used in the last stages of the war against the defenders of Bordeaux and other French ports. Here, U.S.A. 8th A.F. ordnance men prepare the new bombs.
Photo, Planet News

R.A.F. WIND TUNNEL AT FARNBOROUGH

This enormous wind tunnel for testing models of Britain's fighting aircraft, at the Royal Aircraft Establishment, Farnborough, Hants, contributed to the R.A.F.'s efficiency. Begun in 1938, it could reproduce atmospheric conditions as found in any part of the world. Quarter-size aircraft models, fully rigged and placed on a balance in the interior, were subjected to flying conditions at almost any speed, temperature and altitude. *By permission of H.M. Stationery Office*

in pyrotechnics included marker bombs, sky markers, and photo-flash bombs. Early in the war British night bombers flew singly and lit up their own targets. Accuracy of bombing was poor. The development of pyrotechnics led to the pathfinder method of target location. Marker bombs were the normal 500-lb. bomb case filled with small magnesium cartridges which scattered after the bomb had fallen a certain distance and lit up an area for three minutes. Sky markers were similar but remained suspended at cloud level. Flash bombs for night photography operated automatically when dropped and gave an intense light for one-tenth of a second. The R.A.F. used 1,000,000 candle power cartridges for low altitude, and 200,000,000 candle power flash bombs for greater altitude photography. The U.S.A.A.F. undertook night photography from greater heights, and to photograph the greater area in a single exposure used 700,000,000 candle power flash bombs.

Pyrotechnic Developments

230-lb., and no advantage was to be obtained by increasing the weight of aircraft depth charges, for the lethal hemisphere resulting from the underwater explosion was enlarged but slightly even with great increases in the weight of explosive. Depth charges were hydrostatically detonated to explode at predetermined depths, and much as a bomber attacking a land objective at one period of the war dropped a horizontal "stick" of bombs, the anti-U-boat aircraft could drop a vertical stick of depth charges which would straddle the submarine hemispherically.

Developments in aircraft guns, gun and bomb sights, rocket projectiles are described in Chapter 333. Developments

The only revolutionary aeroplane used operationally by the Allies was the British Gloster Meteor twin-jet fighter. All other Allied aircraft were developments of previously existing types, both in airframe and in prime movers. Britain's initial jet-plane was the Gloster E/28 which first flew in May 1941 with one Whittle unit. The Meteor ap-

The Gloster Meteor

ENEMY RADAR INSTALLATIONS DETECTED

R.A.F. reconnaissance photographs over Cap de la Hague, France, in November 1940 revealed emplacements which had not been there a month earlier. Air Ministry experts called for special low-altitude oblique pictures to be taken which revealed that the Germans were using radar. Right, camera, fitted to the port wing of a Spitfire, used for the low-level 'shots,' one of which is reproduced below.
Photos, British Official

peared in time to take part in the battle of the flying bombs. It was first fitted with Rolls Royce Welland and later with Derwent units, with a speed steadily increasing until with Derwent V units, it flew at 606 m.p.h. in November 1945.

Germany was the only country to fly jet-bombers before the end of the war. One was the Arado 234B light bomber with a top speed of 470 m.p.h. and able to carry 4,000 lb. of bombs. Its successor, the 234C, with four BMW–003 jet units, had a top speed

RADAR'S PART IN A.A. DEFENCE

Radar equipment (see also page 3545) employed by Britain's A.A. crews to assist in the shooting down of flying bombs. Left, 40-mm. Bofors predictor and radar controlled light A.A. gun. Right, mobile searchlight equipped with radar aerials which enabled the beam to find its target automatically.

Photos, British Official

of 540 m.p.h., and was the world's fastest bomber. Junkers had a medium bomber, the Ju.287, with six of these units; it had a crew of three, a maximum bomb load of nearly 10,000 lb., a range of 1,175 miles with three tons of bombs, and a maximum speed of over 530 m.p.h. Only the Arado 234B and the Messerschmitt 262 fighter-bomber flew operationally.

The Germans developed numerous unorthodox air weapons. Rocket development in Germany began privately, early in the 20th century, and attracted official military notice with the advent of Hitler's regime in 1933. Development work continued in Berlin until the Peenemünde research station was set up in 1937-38. Ten rockets (A1 to A10) were designed, but only one, the A4 (known as the V2, *see* Chapter 337) was used in war operations. The first three were short range rockets, leading up to the production of the A4. The A9 was an A4 fitted with wings to increase the range by gliding descent instead of the parabolic curve of the wingless A4. The A10 was intended to convert the A9 into a two-stage rocket, weighing in combination about 100 tons. The A10 was to boost the A9 into the stratosphere, where the fuel-exhausted A10 was to be discarded, leaving the A9 to continue its flight; this rocket, which remained a project, was to have bom-

German Rocket Research

barded New York from Normandy at a range of about 3,000 miles.

Two rocket interceptor aircraft were designed, and one, the Messerschmitt 163, became operational towards the end of 1944. This tailless aeroplane was fitted with a Walter bifuel rocket unit weighing 415 lb. At full power the fuel was consumed in about 4½ minutes, but the aircraft could climb to 40,000 feet in slightly more than three minutes. Its top speed was about 590 m.p.h.

The Natter (Viper) aircraft was propelled into the air at an angle of 75 degrees by two solid fuel rocket assisters which carried it to 5,000 feet. The pilot then continued his climb with a

W.A.A.F. 'GHOST VOICE' UPSET THE LUFTWAFFE

An important part of Britain's struggle against the Luftwaffe was the disturbance of German radio communications. Although this usually consisted in ' jamming ' an enemy signal with a more powerful one of the same frequency, German-speaking members of the W.A.A.F. often broadcast counter-orders. Here, a 'ghost voice' W.A.A.F. sits at the microphone. The gramophone was used for jumbled-voice jamming.

Photo, British Official

BRITAIN'S JET-PROPELLED 'METEOR'

Details of the R.A.F.'s 'Meteor' jet-propelled fighter (below) were disclosed in July 1945. First flown in 1943, it was used against the flying bombs the following year. Powered by two gas jet turbines, its dimensions included : span, 43 feet ; length, 41 feet ; wing area, 374 square feet. It was armed with four 20-mm. Hispano guns. Right, Marshal of the R.A.F. Lord Portal of Hungerford inspects a Derwent jet-unit as fitted to the 'Meteor.' *Photos, British Official; G.P.U.*

Walter rocket unit using liquid bi-fuel. This little aircraft, with 18 feet span wings, was to climb at 37,000 feet a minute and destroy a bomber with its battery of rocket projectiles. The pilot was then ejected, the aircraft broke in two, and the pilot and the rear half containing the rocket unit descended by separate parachutes.

These attempts to intercept Allied bombers by rocket aircraft with almost vertical climbing power indicated all **Radar** too clearly that the **Interception** German warning system was not good enough to enable the normal methods of interception to be used. And it is true that warning intelligence of air attack reached its highest development in the combined work of British scientists and British air staff. In August 1940 a team of British scientists with three service officers went to America to discuss radar. They found that the Americans had radar naval gun ranging, but no radar for detection of air attack, and no airborne

radar. Britain was then far ahead of the rest of the world in the technical development of radar ; America profited by British knowledge, and in turn supplied radar sets to the anti-aircraft guns that shot down a large proportion of the flying bombs in 1944.

British and American bombers used radar sets for navigation, both by signal systems, and by radar echo-signal mapping of the ground flown over, some navigators preferring the H2S method of navigation to any other. H2S enabled blind bombing **Importance of Radar** to be carried out, and eventually made it possible to blind-bomb targets only 500 yards from Allied troops. It was possible for bombers to distinguish friendly from enemy fighters by radar ; and radar, if working, made the identification of friendly aircraft by ground defences simple and certain. Unfortunately, aircraft sometimes returned home with their radar instruments damaged by enemy flak or aircraft gunfire, and some were shot down by naval defences when flying half-crippled and unable to signal. The efficiency of radar-controlled naval anti-aircraft gunfire was in such cases all too tragically demonstrated.

But no other wartime development approached the importance of the atomic bomb, either as a scientific achievement or as a military weapon. Hitherto man had used chemical power, in fire, explosives, fuel. Here was a new source of power, derived from the fission of the inner core of the atom, and not, as in

GERMANY'S JET-PROPELLED BOMBER

Towards the end of the war, the Luftwaffe was flying a new type of jet-propelled aircraft, the Ar 234B light bomber. It could carry up to 4,000 lb. of bombs and had a top speed of about 470 m.p.h. Regarded as a successful design, it was fitted with Junkers-Jumo 004 jet units. The projection above the cockpit is a fairing for the periscopic bombsight and gunsight. (See also illus. in page 3393.) *Photo, British Official*

chemical change, by the alteration of its outer envelope. The atomic bomb derived its energy from the actual disruption of matter. Part of the energy thus released was communicated to the surrounding atmosphere, with a consequent rapid rise of air temperature which caused the expanding air to exert great pressure in a blast wave. Part of the energy took the form of radiation over wavelengths which included infra-red, visible light, ultra violet, X-rays, and probably other rays, covering a range of wavelengths from $\frac{1}{100}$ to $\frac{1}{10000000000}$ cm.

The chemical energy released by the detonation of a normal explosive releases heat locally, but obtains its destructive power from the conversion of the bomb's contents into a gas whose pressure produces a blast wave, similar to but less powerful than that produced by the atomic bomb. The normal bomb does not produce radiation, whose effects on humanity and combustible materials played a major part in the appalling destructiveness of this new weapon.

By 1911 Lord Rutherford had discovered how the atom is constructed, with most of its weight in a nucleus, **British Atomic Research** which carries an immense electric charge. In 1919 he split an atom by shooting a light nucleus at a heavier one, despite their mutually repellant nature. In 1932 Sir James Chadwick discovered the neutron, which has no electric charge, and can therefore be used to bombard the nucleus more easily. Light elements break up into very unequal parts, but in 1938 Professor Hahn of Berlin, a former pupil of Rutherford's, found that atoms of uranium 235 break into two almost equal parts moving at tremendous speed and with the liberation of enormous energy. In splitting, these atoms give off neutrons which attack other atoms and split them in a chain reaction. This process is controllable in pieces of uranium 235 of certain dimensions, which limited the size of the atomic bomb.

Ordinary uranium contains three types of atom of atomic weights 238, 235, and 234, the last two being present only in proportions of 0·7 and 0·006 per cent respectively. The separation of the rare uranium 235 had first to be accomplished in sufficient quantity to produce the material for the atomic explosion on a military scale instead of on that of a laboratory experiment. This was the process which entailed the enormous plants set up in the United States in connexion with the manufacture of the atomic bomb (e.g. *see* illus. in page 3850).

By the summer of 1941 British scientists had reached a stage of development which indicated that an atomic bomb might be produced before the end of the war. On October 11, 1941, President Roosevelt wrote to Mr. Churchill suggesting co-ordinated and joint British and American effort. By the summer of 1942 this joint scientific work had confirmed the earlier British forecasts, and it was decided to build full-scale production plants in the United States, with participation in Canada.

A race had begun between the Allies and Germany for atomic weapons. Heavy water (one part of which is found in 4,000 parts of water) is an essential part of one process for atomic fission. Before the war its manufacture was almost exclusive to Norway, at the Norsk Hydro Company plant at Rjukan. The French had acquired almost the whole world stock—165 litres—from Norsk Hydro just before the German invasion, and Britain obtained this from France before her defeat. But it was recognized that the possession by Germany of this factory was a potential danger to the Allies. Two attempts were made to sabotage the factory, the second successful (*see* page 3202).

Most of the subsequent experimental work on atomic bombs was conducted at Los Alamos in New Mexico. At 5·30 a.m. on July 16, **First Atomic** 1945, at Alamogordo, **Bomb** 160 miles away in the **Exploded** desert, the world's first atomic bomb was exploded on a 100-feet high steel tower. Watchers 20 miles away saw a fire ball far brighter than the sun, and the scrub-covered hills around them were lit up as by the midday sun, then a coloured cloud boiled upward to 40,000 feet. Heavy pressure waves knocked down two men who were outside the control tower 10,000 yards from the explosion. The tower from which the bomb had been suspended was destroyed, the stones on the desert were fused.

At the Berlin Conference of 1945, (*see* Chapter 380) it was decided to use

GERMAN 'VIPERS' WERE NEVER USED

Before the end of the war the Germans were producing a rocket-propelled, piloted missile known as the ' Natter ' ('Viper '). Although never used operationally, it was designed to attack aircraft with cannon, rockets or by ramming. The pilot was able to eject himself mechanically before ramming. Left, a ' Natter ' on its launching-structure, and (right) after its almost vertical take-off.   *Photos, Associated Press*

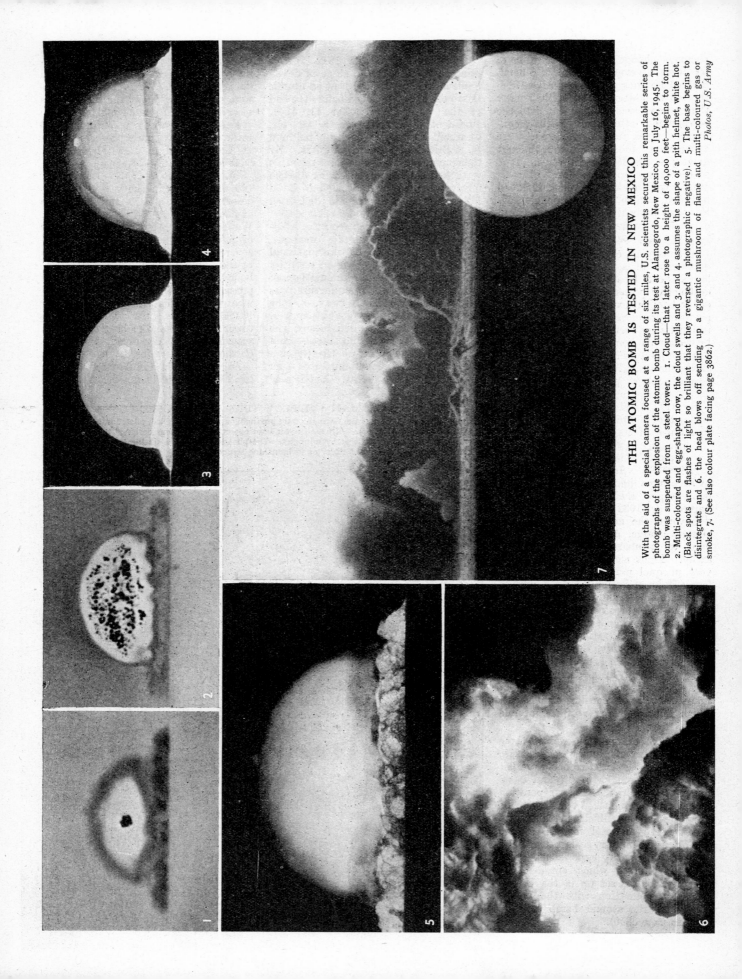

THE ATOMIC BOMB IS TESTED IN NEW MEXICO

With the aid of a special camera focused at a range of six miles, U.S. scientists secured this remarkable series of photographs of the explosion of the atomic bomb during its test at Alamogordo, New Mexico, on July 16, 1945. The bomb was suspended from a steel tower. 1. Cloud—that later rose to a height of 40,000 feet—begins to form. 2. Multi-coloured and egg-shaped now, the cloud swells and 3. and 4. assumes the shape of a pith helmet, white hot. (Black spots are flashes of light so brilliant that they reversed a photographic negative). 5. The base begins to disintegrate and 6. the head blows off sending up a gigantic mushroom of flame and multi-coloured gas or smoke, 7. (See also colour plate facing page 3862.)

Photos, U.S. Army

the atomic bomb against Japan. The first bomb left the United States in the care of Brigadier-General Thomas Farrell nine days before it fell on Hiroshima. Major-General Leslie R. Groves commanded the project and co-ordinated preparations for launching it.

On August 6, 1945, the sirens wailed over the undamaged city of Hiroshima as a single Super-Fortress flying at 30,000 feet approached shortly after eight in the morning. Eye-witnesses on the ground said they saw a blinding white flash above the mercantile quarter. This was followed by a rush of air, a loud rumbling sound, the crashing of disintegrating and falling buildings, settling darkness, and an all-pervading cloud of dust. Innumerable fires sprang up among the city buildings.

Colonel P. W. Tibbets, pilot, and Major Ferebee, bombardier, of the U.S.A.A.F., and Captain W. Parsons, of the U.S. Navy Ordnance service, flying in the aircraft saw a giant mushroom of smoke swirling over the doomed city at a thousand feet.

More than four square miles of Hiroshima were destroyed. At the time of the attack the population was estimated at 320,000, of whom 78,150 died, 13,983 were missing, and some 40,000 were injured. For comparison, in Great Britain, during the whole war, 60,595 civilians, including civil defence workers, were killed, or missing believed killed, including London's total of 30,000. (German V2 rocket bombs discharged against England killed an average of about 2.6 persons each—*see* page 3440.) At Hiroshima, 95 per cent of all who were within a quarter of a mile, 85 per cent of those between a quarter and half a mile of the explosion centre died.

Just after 11 a.m. on August 9, 1945, another atomic bomb was dropped and exploded over the industrial area between the two large Mitsubishi Ordnance plants in the Urakami valley district of Nagasaki. Ground witnesses said they saw three parachutes drop before the fireball flashed. The population of Nagasaki was estimated at just over 260,000, but fewer than 100,000 were exposed to the explosion owing to the shelter given by hills to other parts of the city. Casualty figures given by the American Medical Association in July 1946 were 40,000 dead and 25,000 injured.

In both places city life and industry came to a full stop. Disposal of the dead was a major problem. The only buildings that stood up to the blast within a wide radius were steel-framed heavy concrete structures. Ordinary

load-bearing walls collapsed. Steel-trussed factory buildings and gas-holders were destroyed or distorted. Overhead electric supply, telephone, telegraph, and tramway cables were severely damaged to distances of from half a mile to a mile around the centre of explosion, but underground gas and water pipes were undamaged by the explosion, which was high up in the air.

Flashburn damaged materials, set clothes on fire at distances of a mile and a half, and caused mild burns to human beings at over 2½ miles. Within the central area of intense heat the bodies of human beings left on the asphalt roads whereon they walked, or the polished stone whereon they sat or leaned at the moment of catastrophe, a shadow-like area of unscorched surface. Innumerable fires were caused by indirect means (such as braziers in falling

buildings), aided by the high temperature and dryness of the scorched materials.

Apart from those who died from the explosion, flashburn, and mechanical injuries caused by the destruction of the city, many were burned to death while trapped in blazing buildings. Another major cause of death came from exposure to gamma rays. These killed the human bone marrow, source of cell supply to the blood. Nausea, vomiting, fever, bloody diarrhoea, loss of hair, internal haemorrhage, infection and gangrene brought slow death in from one to eight weeks. Among many who survived there was continuing debilitation. Pregnant women miscarried, aborted or suffered premature births. And the reproductive capacity of both men and women was severely, possibly permanently, damaged.

Casualties at Hiroshima

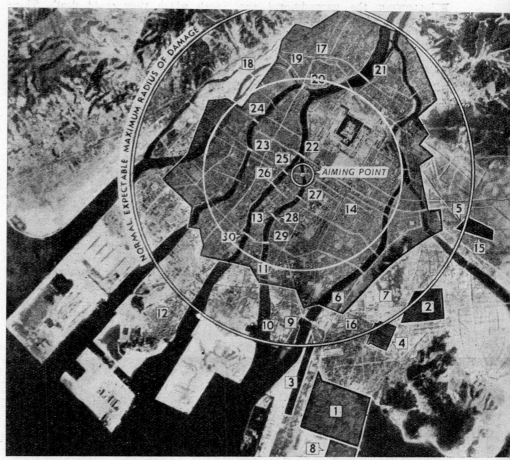

DAMAGED HIROSHIMA AFTER THE ATOMIC BOMB ATTACK

This photographic diagram issued by the U.S.A.A.F. on August 9, 1945, shows the damage done to Hiroshima by the atomic bomb three days earlier. The large circle is 6,330 yards in diameter and shaded areas show devastated sectors. 1. Army transport base, 25% destroyed ; 2. Army ordnance depot ; 3. Army food depot, 35% ; 4. Army clothing depot, 85% ; 5. E. Hiroshima railway station, 30% ; 6. Unidentified industry, 90% ; 7. Sumitono rayon plant, 25% ; 8. Kinkwa rayon mill, 10% ; 9. Toikoku textile mill, 100% ; 10. Power plant ; 11. Oil storage, on fire ; 12. Electric railway power station, 100% ; 13. Electric power generator, 100% ; 14. Telephone offices, 100% ; 15. Gas works, 100% ; 16. Hiroshima railway station, 100% ; 17. Unidentified railway station, 100% ; 18–30 Bridges, most of them unusable through damage.   *Photo, Associated Press*

Chapter 380

GERMANY UNDER ALLIED CONTROL

In Chapter 355, Dr. Frederik Heymann told the history of Germany during the last months of the crumbling Nazi regime, up to the surrender of all German forces on May 8, 1945. Here he continues her history to the end of the year, after her occupation by the Allies. The record is chiefly one of laborious efforts by the Allies to raise her out of the chaos of destruction, wretchedness and hunger into which she had fallen

FOLLOWING the unconditional surrender of the German fighting forces on May 8, 1945 (*see* page 3640 and illus. in pages 3639), Admiral Doenitz, the members of his so-called "Government" (which the Allies had never recognized), and the German High Command were arrested by order of the Supreme Allied Commander on May 23. When troops arrived to arrest him, Admiral von Friedeburg, who signed the German capitulations at Lüneburg (*see* page 3668 and 3671), Rheims (*see* page 3805) and Berlin (*see* page 3651), requested permission to collect some clothes, locked himself into his bathroom, and committed suicide by taking poison.

In all the other countries occupied by the Allies after military victory, there was a central government and a more or less intact administration with which they could deal. There was no such thing in Germany which, after the breakdown of the Nazi regime, was in a state of chaos. Civil administration was completely disrupted; so also were transport, trade, industry and public services. The heads and employees of local authorities, and in particular the Nazis among them, had often fled, and what in many of Germany's larger and medium cities had remained intact through all air attacks—it was little enough—had frequently been destroyed in the last moment by senselessly prolonged resistance.

The picture of prostrate Germany with which the occupying armies were faced was, indeed, quite unbelievable. The state of most of the big cities was incomparably worse than anything seen in London, Bristol or Coventry. There were, of course, differences from one place to another, but a German city of, say, half a million inhabitants which had a third of its buildings and dwellings standing counted as one that had fared comparatively well. Many smaller places, such as Würzburg or Hanau had, except for a few houses on the outskirts, disappeared from the earth. The larger towns of the Rhineland and the Ruhr had suffered worst, but some places in the south-west had suffered hardly less severely.

Most of the countryside—apart from the zones where heavy fighting had occurred—had been hardly touched. But there, too, communications were damaged or destroyed. Railway lines were smashed, road and railway bridges had **Smashed Public Utilities** been demolished in their hundreds, if not thousands, by the retreating German armies right up to the last few days before the surrender, even in places where this demolition could not have the slightest military value. Water, gas, electricity were hardly anywhere in working order. In many places no coal was available. The machinery of food distribution had largely broken down, and here and there the people helped themselves by looting Wehrmacht dumps.

The Allies had expected some sort of guerilla resistance, that was one of the reasons for forbidding private intercourse with Germans by Allied troops, the so-called rule of non-fraternization. There was no such resistance, apart from a very few isolated instances. It soon became clear that it was not German "Wehrwölfe" or any other guerilla groups which had to be feared and fought, but rather the danger of a complete dissolution of the social order—and the probable spread of uncontrollable epidemics as a result.

Thus when on June 5 the Allied Control Council—consisting of Field-Marshal Montgomery, Marshal Zhukov, General Eisenhower and General de Lattre de Tassigny, C.-in-C. respectively of British, Russian, U.S. and French forces of occupation—officially took over the government of Germany,

GERMANS HEAR NEWS OF THEIR DEFEAT

The German people heard the news of their country's unconditional surrender in a broadcast on May 7, 1945, by Count Schwerin von Krosigk, Foreign Minister in Admiral Doenitz's ' Government.' Below, a large crowd gathers in silence outside the Town Hall at Lüneburg, near which the surrender to the 21st Army Group was signed (see page 3666), to hear the news relayed from an Allied loudspeaker. *Photo, British Official*

ALLIES IN BERLIN

At the first meeting of the Allied Control Commission, June 5, 1945: 1. General Eisenhower (U.S.) 2. Left to right, Sir William Strang, political adviser to Field-Marshal Montgomery; Field-Marshal Montgomery (Britain); and Lt.-General Sir R. Weeks. 3. Mr. Vyshinsky, Soviet Foreign Vice-Commissar, and Marshal Zhukov. 4. General de Tassigny (France).

their most urgent task was the re-organization of public life.

This task had actually started long before the final surrender. In Aachen, for instance, the first German city to be

Reorganization Begins

occupied by the Allies in the west, a new municipal administration was at work months before the end of the war. As early as March a German Burgomaster was appointed for Düsseldorf, and in April similar appointments were made in other cities in western Germany, among them Frankfort and Cologne. The Russians, too, appointed German municipal and *Kreis* (county) authorities immediately after taking over eastern Germany.

Before the official end of hostilities the American Army took the first step in re-establishing a wider administration within the area it then occupied. By

the end of May, a German Oberpräsident (title of the head of a province) had been appointed for the Palatinate and Hesse. At the beginning of June,

HITLER'S LAST STAMPS

Last stamps issued by the Nazis on April 22, 1945, ten days before Berlin surrendered, depicted troops of the S.S. and S.A. They were on sale for only two hours as the Russians blew up the post office where they were stored.

similar appointments were made for the Rhineland and for Bavaria. In the latter province, a Roman Catholic politician, Dr. Friedrich Schaeffer, who had been dismissed from his post in 1933 and had been in Dachau, was charged with the task of forming a sort of provisional government for Bavaria with himself as Minister-präsident (Prime Minister). By July 13, little over a month after the end of hostilities, some form of German administration had been installed in about seventy per cent of Germany.

Re-establishment of a working administration was a hard task, mainly because of the difficulty of finding a sufficient number of people who were politically unobjectionable and, at the same time, experienced and efficient enough to do the job, even apart from the material problems that had to be

CHURCHILL IN BERLIN

On July 16, 1945, the day after his arrival in Berlin for the Three Power conference at Potsdam (see page 3919), Mr. Churchill, Britain's Premier, made a long tour of the devastated areas of the city. In the khaki drill uniform of a colonel of the 4th Hussars, he here leaves the shelter in the Chancellery garden where Hitler died. *Photo, G.P.U.*

through the Ruhr to Hanover and from there to Hamburg and Bremen. By the middle of September, some four-fifths of the German railway system within the western zones was working again. (*See* map in page 4033.)

The decision to divide Germany into four zones of occupation was taken at Yalta (*see* page 3563). Territories assigned to the four powers by no means corresponded with the areas of Germany as **Division into Four Zones** they were overrun in the course of military operations. In particular, the line on which the Russian and American Armies met was far to the east of the zonal boundary envisaged at Yalta, and American troops were withdrawn from Saxony and Thuringia to make way for the Russians. The delimitations agreed are shown in the map facing page 4014. Changes took place subsequently, a considerable part of the Russian-occupied area being handed by the Russians to Poland (*see* page 3878 and map in page 3875). The port of Bremen, an American enclave in the British section through which U.S. occupation forces received supplies, was transferred to British control on December 10, though still worked by the Americans. The American zone in Germany joined the American zone in Austria, as did the French zones in the two countries.

Berlin lay in the Russian zone; but it was decided to divide the Reich

tackled. Of these, the most urgent was the restoration of communications and transport. This was as essential for the occupying armies, whose work depended on reliable rail and road transport, as for the German people who without it could not even be fed. The repairing and rebuilding of transport was undertaken with the energy and speed of a war measure, and the American Army had three main lines in working order very shortly after V.E. Day: the line from the French frontier to the Rhine at Mainz; from the Rhine opposite Mainz via Frankfort and Erfurt to Leipzig; and from Frankfort via Nuremberg and Munich to Passau and the Austrian frontier. With equal speed the 21st (British) Army Group restored the main lines of the north-west, mainly those

S.S. MEN FLOODED BERLIN'S UNDERGROUND

The final stages of the battle for Berlin were marked by fierce fighting between the Russians and S.S. troops in the tunnels of the underground railway. On May 4, 1945, S.S. men flooded the Stettiner section of the line, drowning many people sheltering at the time. Above, after the city's fall, workmen at the Anhalter station in an improvised boat, used for recovering the bodies. *Photo, Associated Press*

The last few weeks of the war in Europe saw the overrunning by British and U.S. troops of the notorious concentration camps of Buchenwald, near Weimar, and Belsen, where thousands of prisoners were found dead and dying. 1. A few days after the overrunning of Buchenwald on April 12, 1945, British M.P.s, including Mrs. Mavis Tate, inspect the camp for themselves. The bodies are those of prisoners who had died within the previous 24 hours. 2. These Weimar civilians, forced to inspect the camp by U.S. 3rd Army troops, see the furnaces containing skeletons of the cremated dead.

THIS IS THE SITE OF
THE INFAMOUS BELSEN CONCENTRATION CAMP
Liberated by the British on 15 april 1945

10,000 UNBURIED DEAD WERE FOUND HERE.
ANOTHER 13,000 HAVE SINCE DIED.
ALL OF THEM VICTIMS OF THE
GERMAN NEW ORDER IN EUROPE.
AND AN EXAMPLE OF NAZI KULTUR.

BUCHENWALD AND BELSEN

On April 15, 1945, by arrangement with the Germans made two days earlier, British troops took over the vast typhus-ridden concentration camp at Belsen-Bergen, a few miles N.W. of Celle, where they found evidence of unspeakable crimes. Most of the buildings were burned by Allied military orders on May 21. 3. S.S. men captured at the camp are made to load lorries with bodies of prisoners being taken away for burial. 4. A sign-board which tells its own terrible story. 5. The camp a year later. Graves are marked with the names and nationalities of the dead. Some 13,000 died after being freed.

GERMANY UNDER ALLIED OCCUPATION

By mid-July, 1945, some element of German local civil administration was operating in most of Germany. Germans proved to be untainted with Nazism co-operating with the occupying powers. 1. German civilian given an armlet showing him to be a member of the Military Government police. 2. Berliners wait to be weighed and measured by a British Field Ambulance unit to determine whether they are suffering from malnutrition. 3. In Hanover, a check is made of fire-arms surrendered (by order) to the Military Government.

Photos, British Official ; Planet News

capital into four sectors, its administration as a whole being controlled by the Inter-allied "Komendatura" (a Russian term). Despite the destruction it had undergone through air raids and street fighting, Berlin soon harboured some three and a half millions again.

One of the most difficult problems with which the Allies had to deal was the enormous mass of homeless persons

Moving Masses of Homeless moving across the centre of the continent. There were two main groups : workers who had been brought—many of them by force—from all over Europe into Germany or German-occupied territory by the Nazis, and who numbered more than six millions. Many of them started on their way home as soon as the Nazi regime broke down, and first the Allied armies, later U.N.R.R.A. had to canalize this giant migration, transport, shelter and feed these people on their journey. A minority—still num-

bering tens of thousands—actually did not want to go home, most because they were afraid, for one reason or another, of what would happen to them if they went home, a few because they liked the irresponsibility of life in the U.N.R.R.A. camps, where they were fed and cared for, which sprang up all over Germany —some even on the very sites of Nazi concentration camps.

In these new camps for displaced persons, the inmates had nothing to fear from cruel warders, and they were much better fed than the German population,

but they suffered from the lack of purpose in their lives, and a certain number (mainly Polish) organized themselves into small armed bands which in some parts of Germany terrorized the countryside until stern measures were taken by the Allied military police.

In these camps also lived what were left of the Jewish communities of central and eastern Europe which the Nazis had all but succeeded in annihilating in the gas chambers of their huge extermination camps at Oswiecim (Auschwitz) and Maidanek in Poland

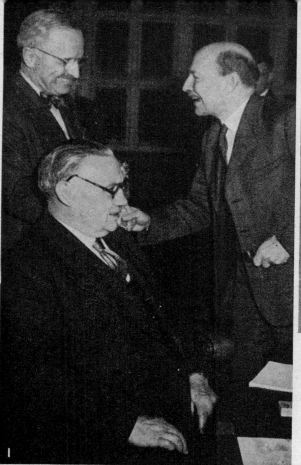

THE BERLIN CONFERENCE, 1945

A conference to determine Germany's future opened on July 17, 1945, at the Cecilienhof Palace, Potsdam, residence of the former German Crown Prince, and concluded on August 1. In its initial stages it was attended by Mr. Winston Churchill, President Truman, and Generalissimo Stalin. On July 25 the conference was suspended to enable the British leaders to return to England to hear the results of the general election. Three days later Mr. C. R. Attlee, new British Premier (who had previously attended the conference at Mr. Churchill's invitation) and Mr. Ernest Bevin, the new Foreign Secretary, flew to Berlin for the final stages. The decisions of the conference (see Historic Document No. 312 in page 3931) were published on August 2. (1) President Truman greets Mr. Attlee; Mr. Bevin in foreground. (2) Stalin talks with Mr. Churchill. (3), the conference in session.

BRITISH FLAG RAISED IN BERLIN

On July 4, 1945, the British 7th Armoured Division, with units of the Grenadier Guards, Devon Regiment, Royal West Kent Regiment and a composite Canadian battalion, under Major-General Louis O. Lyne, entered Berlin to occupy the British sector there. Two days later the Union Jack was formally hoisted (from the highest flagstaff taken from the Berlin Olympic Stadium) at the base of the 1870 Victory Column overlooking the Tiergarten. Silent Germans watched the parade. Here, pipers of the Argyll and Sutherland Highlanders of Canada lead the march past.

BERLINERS WATCH 'DESERT RATS' ENTER THEIR CAPITAL

The British 7th Armoured Division (the famous 'Desert Rats'), with battalions of the Grenadier Guards, Devon Regiment, Royal West Kent Regiment and a composite Canadian battalion, on July 4, 1945, entered Berlin under the command of Major-General Louis O. Lyne, C.B., D.S.O., to take over occupation of the British sector there. This included the Tiergarten, Charlottenburg and Spandau districts. Here, Major-General Lyne takes the salute as the 'Desert Rats' enter a blitzed industrial quarter. Top, Berliners silently look'd on. *Photos, Fox Photos ; Keystone*

BRITAIN'S ARMED FORCES ON PARADE IN BERLIN

The taking over of the British sector in Berlin in July 1945 was marked by impressive military parades attended by Allied Services and other leaders. Above, Mr. Winston Churchill takes the salute at a parade in the Charlottenburger Chaussee on July 21. In front of the saluting-base—on which the British Premier is accompanied by Mr. Anthony Eden, Mr. C. R. Attlee, Field-Marshal Alexander, Field-Marshal Montgomery, General Omar Bradley and Marshal Zhukov—is a contingent of Grenadier Guards. Below, also in the Charlottenburger Chaussee, British armour passes the foot of the 1870 Victory Column during a parade of some 10,000 men of Britain's air, sea and land forces on July 12.

and other concentration camps in Germany. Most of them wanted to get to Palestine. Only a tiny percentage of the German Jews, who had once numbered a quarter of a million, returned to the places from which they had been driven by the Nazis. Measures were taken—most effectively in Bavaria—to restore to Jews the property of which they had been deprived.

Another group of migrants, also numbering many millions, were Germans. In the main they were moving from east to west. This movement started when the Red Army was approaching the frontiers of East Prussia and Silesia. Both those who had sought refuge in the east from Allied bombing in the west and local inhabitants joined

NAZI STAMPS FOR INDIA

So confident of world-conquest was Hitler that he had postage stamps designed and ready to be issued when the Nazis occupied India. These two are from a set of seven ; they depict an Indian woman at her spinning-wheel (left) and a nurse tending a wounded Indian soldier.

the movement which continued growing with the increasing number of people who, frightened by Nazi propaganda, believed the Russians would kill all Germans who fell into their hands. Thus, when the German armies surrendered, there were already masses of Germans in western and southern Germany whose homes had been in the eastern part of the country. But this first wave of refugees was soon followed by a second : the millions of Germans forcibly evacuated by the governments of Poland and Czechoslovakia. Both these immediate neighbours of Germany had suffered through their German

DOENITZ'S FLENSBURG 'GOVERNMENT' IS ARRESTED

By order of the Supreme Commander on May 23, 1945, Admiral Doenitz, second and last Fuehrer of the Reich, his so-called 'Government,' and the German High Command, were arrested at Flensburg and held as prisoners of war. Here are (left to right), Albert Speer, Hitler's Minister of Production ; Grand-Admiral Karl Doenitz ; and Colonel-General Jodl, Chief of German General Staff, after being detained.   *Photo, Associated Press*

minorities. This was particularly true of Czechoslovakia, whose three millions of Sudeten Germans had proved an unending source of trouble and danger to her. The situation in Poland was different. Her pre-war German minority had numbered some 800,000 ; but the inclusion within the proposed frontiers of the new Poland of the " corridor " and of parts of East Prussia, Pomerania, and Silesia (*see* map in page 3875) gave Poland former German territory larger in extent than

Scotland, and with a population of some nine millions. The Poles did not wait for a final settlement, but immediately started ejecting the German population from these areas. It was, indeed, the very method which the Germans themselves had used under the Nazi regime. The resulting misery raised grave doubts in the minds of many people, particularly in England and America. At the Berlin conference of the Big Three, held at Potsdam in July 1945, it **The Berlin Conference, 1945** was decided that, pending the final determination of Poland's western frontier in the peace treaty with Germany, the territory east of the Oder-Neisse line should come under Polish administration at once and cease to be part of the Russian zone of occupation. The Poles (like the Czechoslovaks) were, however, asked to stop wholesale ejection and to use orderly and humane methods so as to make it possible for the Allied administration of the receiving territories of Germany to prepare for the distribution, housing and feeding of those millions of immigrants, most of whom had no means of support.

This was only one, though an important one, of the decisions taken at the Berlin Conference. (For the chief of these decisions, *see* Historic Document 312, page 3931.) Other decisions covered not only the wiping out of all Nazi institutions and the prevention of Nazism and militarism from rising again

THE END OF HEINRICH HIMMLER

Chief of the Gestapo and the S.S., Heinrich Himmler poisoned himself at British 2nd Army H.Q. at Luneburg on May 23, 1945, within 24 hours of being detained at Bemervoerde by Field Security Police. He here lies, wrapped in a blanket, where he fell after swallowing a capsule of cyanide of potassium.   *Photo, British Newspaper Pool*

HITLER'S 'BLACK LIST' OF PROMINENT BRITONS

Discovered in the Berlin H.Q. of the Reich Security Police in September 1945 was a book containing a 'black list' of persons earmarked for arrest in the event of a successful German invasion of Britain. It contained the names of many prominent political leaders, journalists and others. This is a photograph of page 32 of the book, showing the name of Mr. Churchill.

in Germany, but also certain measures of constructive planning for the future of Germany. Organizations to be suppressed included not only the S.S., the S.A., the "Sicherneitsdienst" (special security police), the Gestapo with all its dependent organizations, but also the Wehrmacht with its General Staff, officers corps, military schools, military and crypto-military organizations. All weapons of war, and all installations for the production and maintenance of such weapons, had to be handed over and destroyed. All the political institutions set up by the Nazis were to be abolished, and all special laws intended to cement Nazi power or to discriminate on a racial basis were to be abrogated. Earlier plans aiming at reducing Germany to a purely agrarian state were dropped as they were quite unrealistic, all the more so after the cutting off of the huge, predominantly agricultural areas in the east ; but the size and output of Germany's heavy industries (which, indeed, had been expanded by the Nazis beyond any reasonable peacetime need) were to be strictly limited, though she was to be given a certain freedom in developing industries that would enable her, by exporting consumer goods, to pay for the import of food and necessary raw materials.

Payment of reparations by Germany was also envisaged on a very different basis from that of 1919, when an attempt was made to calculate the complete damage done by Germany and to make her pay a corresponding sum in annual instalments. The 1945 scheme did not attempt any estimate of the money value of the damage done—indeed, in view of the degree of destruction all over Europe, no such estimate could have been made. Instead the Big Three, mainly upon the suggestion of Russia, envisaged German production equipment as the main source from which an effective reparation could be exacted without too much delay. Russia, who was the greatest sufferer among the three big Allies, was authorized to seize

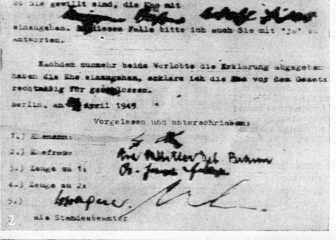

HITLER AND EVA BRAUN

According to British Intelligence experts, Hitler and Eva Braun died in the Reichs-Chancellery in Berlin on April 30, 1945, 24 hours after their marriage. 1. Hitler and Eva—from Eva Braun's personal album. 2. The marriage contract with heavily blotted signatures (discovered in Bavaria). 3. Soviet soldiers indicate the site in Berlin where the bodies of Hitler and his wife are alleged to have been cremated.

Photos, Associated Press ; Keystone

AMONG THE RUINS OF BERLIN

When the German garrison in Berlin surrendered to the Russians on May 2, 1945 (see page 3722), the Reich capital was in ruins. 1. The charred hollow shell that was once the Reichstag. Soviet forces captured it on April 30 after fierce street-fighting (see illus. in page 3729). 2. A British soldier at the entrance to the Reichstag adds his name to those of Russians who had fought their way from Moscow and Stalingrad. 3. Shattered German armoured vehicles in the Court of Honour in the Reichs-Chancellery.

Photos, L.N.A. ; G.P.U ; Keystone

2

WEHRMACHT PRISONERS REACH THE BRITISH ZONE

From all over Europe, remnants of the defeated Wehrmacht trudged home to Germany for demobilization.   1. In the British zone a German girl conscripted for this duty stamps the wrists of P.O.W. to show that their papers are in order.   2. Returning prisoner's bread ration for the journey home.   3. Wehrmacht P.O.W., after delousing, await examination at a clearing station in the British zone.   *Photos, Keystone ; Daily Mirror*

production equipment in the Soviet zone of occupation. Of suitable equipment in the western zones ten per cent was to go to Russia on reparations account and a further fifteen per cent in exchange for food and other material from the Russian zone to the west. Out of Russia's share the claims of Poland, too, were to be met. The claims of all the other powers were to be met out of the production equipment in the western zones not regarded as essential for Germany's peace economy (minus the twenty-five per cent for Russia), and the gold reserves found there. In addition, Germany's foreign assets were to be divided among the Allies.

From Germany's point of view, the most important of the decisions taken at Potsdam was that against the dismemberment of the country (even though more than a year after the conference the administrative bodies to act, notwithstanding the zonal arrangements, for the whole country had not yet been set up).

Among the politically important decisions of the conference was the encouragement given to democratic political parties and to trade unions, neither of which had existed (except underground and in a small way) since the Nazis destroyed them in 1933. This decision followed the actual recognition of political parties in the Russian zone, where the Communist party was allowed to start as early as June 10, three other parties, Christian Democrats, Social Democrats and Liberal Democrats, following a few days later.

Communists and Social Democrats were the legitimate successors of the pre-Hitler parties of the same names ; but the Christian Democrats were only in part successors of the former Centre party : that had been exclusively Roman Catholic, while the Christian Democratic Union claimed to represent all elements with a Christian conviction. It grew in strength, rallying all the non-socialist or anti-socialist groups, while the Liberals had little success. Within the workers' camp, the Social Democrats proved to be stronger than the Communists except in a few places in the Russian zone where they had the backing of the occupying power.

Whilst the Russians admitted parties in their zone with few limitations as to

BREAKING UP THE GERMAN WAR MACHINE

Some 90,000 R.A.F. pilots and crews, comprising 13 Air Disarmament Wings of the British Air Forces of Occupation (formerly 2nd Tactical Air Force) in late 1945 undertook dismantling of the Luftwaffe. Here, on the airfield at Flensburg, cattle graze among former Nazi bombers awaiting destruction.   Left, German warship—typical of many—blasted by Allied bombing at Kiel, where Royal Navy demolition parties completed the work of destruction.   *Photos, British Official ; Keystone*

the range of their activities, in both the British and the American zones the parties were at first allowed only to work as local organizations, though a first conference of Social Democratic representatives of the whole British zone—with guest representatives from Berlin and other zones as well as German Socialist refugees from Britain attending—was permitted to meet at Hanover in September. In the American zone, party organizations for whole states (Länder) were not permitted officially until November, and parties were not permitted in the French zone during 1945.

Restoration of German self-govern-

AN END TO NAZI BOOKS

Eradication of Nazism from education in occupied Germany was an important task of the Allied Military Government. In reopened schools all Nazi textbooks were replaced by others free from Nazi ideology. Here, pupils in Berlin queue to surrender Nazi books to the Principal.

Photo, Keystone

U.N.R.R.A. AT WORK

In a disused convent at Kloster Indersdorf, 25 miles north of Munich, Team 182 of U.N.R.R.A. in July 1945 set up a home for over 200 orphaned and starving children of various nationalities. Above, two officials— an American woman and an Englishman —help some of the children to try on their new outfits. *Photo, Central Press*

ment was, on the other hand, quickest in the U.S. zone. The first important step in this direction was taken on

Some Self-Government Restored September 27, when that zone was formed into three states (Länder), each under purely German administration under overall U.S. supervision : Bavaria, corresponding to its 1933 borders minus Lindau (in French occupation) ; Wurttemberg-Baden, uniting the northern U.S. occupied parts of the two former states of those names ; Hesse-Nassau (including the cities of Frankfort, Wiesbaden and Kassel) with Oberhessen, northern part of the former state of

Hesse, and Rheinhessen (except that part occupied by the French). The Prime Ministers of the three Governments met regularly at Stuttgart to coordinate policy and legislation. Dr. Wilhelm Hoegner (Social Democrat) replaced Dr. Schaeffer as Prime Minister

ROUND-UP IN BERLIN'S 'BLACK MARKET'

Berlin's flourishing 'Black Market' provided a problem for the Allied occupying authorities. On October 14, 1945, British troops, supported by German police, arrested 2,000 people in the Tiergarten. Among those taken were 100 Soviet officers and men, later handed over to the Russians. Here, a British military policeman supervises the German police cordon behind which stand civilians and Soviet soldiers *Photo, Keystone*

PROBLEM OF THE 'D. P.'s'

One of the most urgent tasks facing the Allied Military Government—and later U.N.R.R.A.—in occupied Germany was the care of the homeless, known officially as 'displaced persons.' 1. Displaced persons and ex-prisoners of war of many nationalities west of Berlin crowd a road lined with Soviet 'Stalin' tanks. 2. Lining up for hot food at Berlin's Stettiner station. 3. Home-bound French and Belgian ex-prisoners of war on a German airfield await air transport by Dakotas. 4. On their way from the Soviet to the British zone, these Germans change trains at Friedland.

Photos, British Official; Keystone; G.P.U.

BRITISH BADGES IN GERMANY

On June 4, 1945, Britain, the U.S., Russia and France formally took over governmental control of Germany. Left, shoulder badge of British civilian officer under the Military Government (gold lettering on bottle green). Right, sleeve badge of British members of the Allied Control Commission (yellow letters ' C.C.G '—Control Commission, Germany—on blue cross on red shield).

of Bavaria : Schaeffer had not handled de-nazification satisfactorily, refusing to take measures that would impair the efficiency of Bavarian administration. In this attitude he had to some extent been backed by General George Patton, Commander of the U.S. 3rd Army and Military Governor of Bavaria, who took the view that Germans who had paid only lip-service to Nazism could not be dispensed with immediately if administration was to remain efficient enough to prevent chaos and unnecessary suffering and death. Patton's transfer to the command of the U.S. 15th Army, a headquarters post, was announced on October 2. (He died at Heidelberg on December 21 as the result of a motor accident near Mannheim twelve days previously and was buried at Hamm, Luxemburg.)

This was the most sensational but by no means the only dispute on de-nazification that arose among Allied as well as German authorities. Practice in the four Allied Military Zones, too, differed widely, although there existed a common basic law for all (law No. 8 of the Allied Control Council). The Russians followed, in general, a policy of expediency in that, on the one hand, they were not reluctant to liquidate people whom they deemed dangerous, whilst on the other —particularly in the cultural field— they employed people who were, in the Russian area, useful, even if they were badly compromised by their activities under Hitler.

De-Nazification Problems

A policy based on strict principles was followed by the American authorities. A sweeping purge was carried out in their zone, not only among state employees and holders of public offices of every description, but also in trade and the professions, with a more lenient treatment, owing to the urgent needs of the moment, for the medical profession. Everybody seeking or retaining employ-

ment had to fill up elaborate questionnaires, with high penalties for false statements. People who had become Nazis before 1937 (in which year party pressure, particularly on holders of public offices, greatly increased) were regarded as highly objectionable. In special cases, appeals could be made against dismissals. Later, on the basis of a law proposed by a Communist member of the Bavarian Government and accepted by the Conference of the Prime Ministers and the U.S. Military Government, special courts, consisting entirely of Germans, were set up to deal with de-nazification. To find a sufficient number of people with a clean record proved to be most difficult in building up a new police, a new legal administration, and a new system of education. Yet, as General Joseph T. McNarney (who on November 29 succeeded General Eisenhower as Military Governor of the U.S. zone, and U.S. representative on the Allied Control Council) summed up his policy in a message to the German people, " It is a truism to say that no man is irreplaceable. Germany can and must perform her rehabilitation without the help of those people [the Nazis]."

British policy was on generally similar though somewhat less severe lines. Towards the end of the year, some 50,000 Nazi activists (apart from war criminals) had been arrested in the British zone, compared with twice that number in the American zone. Decisive measures were taken by the British authorities in the field of education, based on Field-Marshal Montgomery's declaration that " No teacher should be left in office whose past could not stand the most searching scrutiny." Elementary schools were opened in the British

zone on October 1 for a million children, part-time elementary instruction was available for another million.

Policy regarding press and other publications was very different in the British zone from that in all other zones. Apart from a newspaper in Aachen which had originally been licensed by the Americans, and a paper in the British sector of Berlin, there were, for a long time, no German-run papers or magazines in the British zone. Papers appearing there, though written in German and employing some Germans on their staff, were entirely under British direction and responsibility. This policy was not modified until after the end of 1945. In the American as well as in the French zone the Germans were given an early opportunity to build up a new democratic press of their own, and in both these zones a considerable number of papers, as well as some magazines, were licensed during the second half of the year, their publishers as well as editors being exclusively German. In the French zone the press remained subject to censorship ; the Americans relied upon careful selection of those admitted to publishing activities, and the threat of the withdrawal of the licence. Twenty-five newspapers (twice weekly except for the Berlin paper) were licensed by the Americans during 1945, some attaining a fair standard of production and content.

Allied Policy Towards the Press

One of the main items reported by the German papers—in very different ways and with very different emphasis—was the trial of the major German war criminals at Nuremberg (*see* Chapter 386), possibly the greatest trial in history.

BRITISH TROOPS ATTEND GERMAN UNIVERSITY

Special facilities were provided for troops of the B.A.O.R. (British Army of the Rhine) who wished to improve their education. Among these, towards the end of 1945, was a month's course at the famous university of Göttingen. Subjects ranged from Art-appreciation, Physics and Biology to French, German and typing. Officers and men, besides members of the A.T.S., attended the same classes. This is a Biology class. *Photo, British Official*

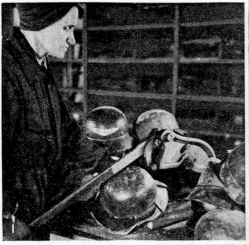

sufficient food, but also to absenteeism arising from their going in search of additional food for their families.

Painfully limited supplies led to a flourishing black market in Germany, as elsewhere in Europe. Cigarettes became a sort of currency, with prices ranging from one to six shillings for a single cigarette. (Highest prices were generally paid in Berlin.)

As the year advanced it became ever more obvious that some of the important provisions of the Berlin Conference were not likely, at least soon, to be implemented. There was hardly any attempt at co-ordination of policy between the occupation authorities of the four zones. The French (who were not present at the Berlin Conference) objected to the setting up of any central German authority and asked for complete separation of the Ruhr from Germany, a demand with which neither Britain nor the U.S.A. agreed: they wanted rather international control of the area within Germany. Even greater differences on how to deal with Germany became apparent between the Western powers and Russia. This lack of unity did not escape the Germans, and wild rumours of imminent war sometimes swept the country. A good many Germans— among them all the Nazis—would have welcomed such a war, but, sobered by experience, were terrified at the thought that Germany might become a battlefield again. Allied differences, indeed, introduced an element of uncertainty which made very much harder the moral, political and economic rehabilitation of Germany.

Effects of Allied Differences

The majority of the German people showed a rather weak interest in these proceedings, as in many other matters of political significance. Still numbed and apathetic, and at the same time suspicious of anything they thought was "propaganda," their whole interest was focused on their individual needs and chance of survival. The problems of shelter, heating and, above all, food occupied their minds. The destruction of the big cities, aggravated by the arrival of millions of refugees from the east, made housing one of the most urgent and, at the same time, most difficult problems. Many of the emergency dwellings (e.g. cellars in bomb shattered houses) were not in any civilized sense habitable in winter, especially with virtually no coal available. Germany is a well forested

Food the Main German Preoccupation

country, and wood minimized the heating problem. To this and to the mildness of the winter of 1945-46, was due, in part at least, the success of the Allied Medical authorities in preventing major epidemics.

The food situation remained tense: during the second half of 1945 the average daily ration in most parts of the British and American zones was increased from 1,000–1,300 calories a day in September to about 1,500 calories towards the end of the year. This standard, however, was not maintained later in the British zone—it had been achieved only by substantial imports (paid for by Britain) of grain and other foods which could not be kept up owing to world shortage. Shortage of food was the key to the shortage of coal, low production by the miners in the Ruhr being due not only to their lack of strength from in-

MAIN DECISIONS OF THE BERLIN CONFERENCE, 1945

Here, in extracts from the text of the report signed in Berlin on August 2, 1945, by Generalissimo J. V. Stalin, President Harry S. Truman, and the Rt. Hon. C. R. Attlee, are the principal decisions taken at the conference to decide on Germany's future which met at Potsdam on July 17 (see pages 3890 and 3923)

Council of Foreign Ministers.

(1) There shall be established a Council composed of the Foreign Ministers of the United Kingdom, the Union of Soviet Socialist Republics, China, France, and the United States. (2) (ii) The first meeting shall be held in London not later than September 1, 1945.

(3) (i) As its immediate important task, the Council shall be authorized to draw up, with a view to their submission to the United Nations, treaties of peace with Italy, Rumania, Bulgaria, Hungary and Finland, and to propose settlements of territorial questions outstanding on the termination of the war in Europe. The Council shall be utilized for the preparation of a peace settlement for Germany, to be accepted by the Government of Germany when a government adequate for the purpose is established. (ii) For the discharge of each of these tasks the Council will be composed of the members representing those States which were signatory to the terms of surrender imposed upon the enemy State concerned. For the purpose of the peace settlement for Italy, France shall be regarded as a signatory to the terms of surrender for Italy. Other members will be invited to participate when matters directly concerning them are under discussion.

Allied Policy Towards Germany.

It is not the intention of the Allies to destroy or enslave the German people.

1. Supreme authority in Germany is exercised, on instructions from their respective Governments, by the commanders-in-chief of the armed forces of the United States of America, the United Kingdom, the Union of Soviet Socialist Republics, and the French Republic, each in his own zone of occupation, and also jointly, in matters affecting Germany as a whole, as members of the Control Council.

2. So far as is practicable, there shall be uniformity of treatment of the German population throughout Germany.

3. The purposes of the occupation of Germany by which the Control Council shall be guided are : (i) The complete disarmament and demilitarization of Germany and the elimination or control of all German industry that could be used for military production. (ii) To convince the German people that they have suffered a total military defeat and that they cannot escape responsibilty for what they have brought on themselves, since their own ruthless warfare and the fanatical Nazi resistance have destroyed German economy and made chaos and suffering inevitable. (iii) To destroy the National Socialist Party and its affiliated and supervised organizations ; to ensure that they are not revived in any form. (iv) To prepare for the eventual reconstruction of German political life on a democratic basis.

9. The administration of affairs in Germany shall be directed towards the decentralization of the political structure and the development of local responsibility. To this end (i) local self-government shall be restored throughout Germany on democratic principles, and in particular through elective councils, as rapidly as is consistent with military security and the purposes of military occupation ; (ii) all democratic political parties with rights of assembly and of public discussion shall be allowed and encouraged throughout Germany ; (iii) representative and elective principles shall be introduced into regional, provincial and state (*Land*) administration as rapidly as may be justified by the application of these principles in local self-government ; (iv) for the time being no central German government shall be established. However, certain essential central German administrative departments, headed by State Secretaries, shall be established, particularly in the fields of finance, transport, communications, foreign trade, and industry.

10. Subject to the necessity of maintaining military security, freedom of speech, Press, and religion shall be permitted. Subject likewise to the maintenance of military security, the formation of free trade unions shall be permitted.

14. During the period of the occupation Germany shall be treated as a single economic unit.

15. Allied controls shall be imposed upon the German economy, but only to the extent necessary (*a*) to carry out programmes of industrial disarmament and demilitarization, of reparations, and of approved exports and imports ; (*b*) to assure the production and maintenance of goods and services required to meet the needs of the occupying forces and displaced persons in Germany, and essential to maintain in Germany average living standards not exceeding the average of the standards of living of all European countries, excluding the United Kingdom and the Union of Soviet Socialist Republics ; (*c*) to ensure in the manner determined by the Control Council the equitable distribution of essential commodities between the several zones, so as to produce a balanced economy throughout Germany and reduce the needs for imports ; (*e*) to control all German public or private scientific bodies, research and experimental institutions, laboratories, etc., connected with economic activities.

19. Payment of reparations should leave enough resources to enable the German people to subsist without external assistance . . . .

German Reparations.

1. Reparation claims of the U.S.S.R. shall be met by removal from the zone of Germany occupied by the U.S.S.R. and from appropriate German external assets. 2. The U.S.S.R. undertakes to settle the reparation claims of Poland from its own share of reparations. 3. The reparation claims of the United States, the United Kingdom, and other countries entitled to reparations shall be met from the western zones and from appropriate German external assets.

[In addition to reparations from the Soviet zone of occupation, the U.S.S.R. was also to receive 15 per cent of capital equipment of certain categories from the western zones in exchange for an equivalent value of agreed commodities, and 10 per cent of such capital equipment without payment.]

Königsberg.

The conference has agreed in principle to the proposal of the Soviet Government concerning the ultimate transfer to the Soviet Union of the city of Königsberg.

War Criminals.

The three Governments reaffirm their intention to bring major war criminals to swift and sure justice.

Poland's Western Frontier.

The three heads of Government reaffirm their opinion that the final delimitation of the western frontier of Poland should await the peace settlement and agree that, pending the final determination of Poland's western frontier, the [area indicated in the map in page 3875] shall be under the administration of the Polish State and for such purposes should not be considered as part of the Soviet zone of occupation in Germany.

Membership of United Nations.

The three Governments will support applications for membership of the United Nations from those States which have remained neutral during the war and which fulfil the qualifications set out [in Article 4 of the Charter of the United Nations]. The three Governments feel bound, however, to make it clear that they would not favour any application for membership by the present Spanish Government.

Transfer of German Populations.

The three Governments recognize that the transfer to Germany of German populations, or elements thereof, remaining in Poland, Czechoslovakia, and Hungary will have to be undertaken. They agree that any transfers that take place should be effected in an orderly and humane manner.

Chapter 381

UNITED NATIONS MEET AT SAN FRANCISCO

*On April 25, 1945, just before the final overthrow of Germany, representatives
of forty-six Allied nations (joined later by four others) met in San Francisco
to draw up the Charter which, it was hoped and believed, would bind its
signatories to abandon war for ever, and to combine in suppressing aggression.
Warmly supported by the United States, the United Nations organization
began life under much better auspices than did the League of Nations*

As Allied armies stood poised on the eastern, western and southern borders of Nazism's central fortress, in February 1945, President Roosevelt, Mr. Churchill and Marshal Stalin with their military advisers held at Yalta in the Crimea (*see* page 3563) the last of their conferences to concert the final Allied onslaught which would bring victory to Europe. At the same time they prepared the foundations for a secure and lasting peace to follow that victory.

The customary communiqué issued at the close of the Crimea Conference included the phrase : " We are resolved

**Decision
to Call U.N.
Conference**

upon the earliest possible establishment with our Allies of a general international organization to maintain peace and security. We believe that this is essential both to prevent aggression and to remove the political, economic and social causes of war through the close and continuing collaboration of all peace-loving people... We have agreed that a

Conference of the United Nations should be called to meet in San Francisco in the United States of America on April 25, 1945, to prepare a Charter of such an organization along the lines proposed at Dumbarton Oaks " (*see* page 3256).

The heterogeneous war-swollen population of San Francisco was compounded of as many racial elements as were represented at the Conference, and the arrival in their midst of Ministers and senior representatives of the old countries from which they or their fathers had come, stirred in San Franciscans many old bonds, half-forgotten in the melting-pot of Americanism which in two or three generations had bred in their city a microcosm of the international harmony to be sought by the Conference for all the world. Thus, though flags were at half-mast for the President whose vision of a world at peace had helped to bring the Conference into being, San Francisco stretched its traditional hospitality to the utmost for the thousands of delegates, experts and staffs of forty-six

nations who towards the end of April made their way by special trains and planes across America or the Pacific.

Taxi-drivers, shop assistants, telephone operators speaking every language of the United Nations were unearthed among the city's divers people and boldly advertised ; hotels which had been forced to ration accommodation ever since San Francisco became the main base of America's vast Pacific war effort agreeably but firmly cleared whole floors and wings ; local Press and radio boomed that San Francisco had at last come into its long-deserved own as the centre of the world's aspirations towards the future. On the highest of the city's many hills a vast concrete cross was for the Conference opening night floodlit in defiance of possible Japanese attack.

In this slightly lurid, hospitable and excitable atmosphere, superimposed on the steady humming war activity of the great naval base and port, delegates from **Nations** Australia, Belgium, **Represented** Bolivia, Brazil, Canada, Chile, China, Colombia, Costa Rica, Cuba, Czechoslovakia, Dominican Republic, Ecuador, Egypt, Ethiopia, France, Greece, Guatemala, Haiti, Honduras, India, Iran (Persia), Iraq, Lebanon, Liberia, Luxemburg, Mexico, Netherlands, New Zealand, Nicaragua, Norway, Panama, Paraguay, Peru, Philippines, Salvador, Saudi Arabia, South Africa, Soviet Union, Syria, Turkey, United Kingdom, United States, Uruguay, Venezuela, and Yugoslavia met on April 25th to talk peace in the splendid halls built by San Franciscans as memorial to their dead in America's former war against Germany. (They were joined during the Conference by four other delegations, from White Russia, the Ukraine, newly liberated Denmark, and Argentina.)

At their first session they heard speeches from the delegation heads of the four convening nations—the Great Powers which were playing the major part in bearing the burden of the war. These speakers, the Foreign Ministers of Britain, China, Russia and the United States, joined in stressing the magnitude and urgency of the task

WHERE THE CONFERENCE WAS HELD

Setting for the first United Nations Conference (April–June, 1945) was the Opera House, San
Francisco. An imposing stone building, it was opened in 1932 and is the only municipally
owned opera house in the U.S. With the Veterans' Building in the adjoining square and a
Memorial Court between, it constitutes the city's memorial to its dead in the First Great War.
The auditorium, where the conference was held, seats 1,106.

EMPIRE LEADERS AT SAN FRANCISCO

At the United Nations Conference which opened at San Francisco on April 25, 1945, a prominent part was played by the British Dominions. Here, Field-Marshal Jan Smuts, 75-year-old Premier of the Union of South Africa, presides over Commission Two which dealt with the powers of the General Assembly of the United Nations. He also drafted the preamble to the Charter. At the rostrum is Dr. Herbert Vere Evatt, Australia's Foreign Minister.

confronting the Conference. Working on the basis of the blueprint drawn up the previous year at Dumbarton Oaks by representatives of only the four great Powers, these delegates from Allied nations of widely varying size, interests and forms of Government, had to agree on a Charter within whose framework of general principle and administrative machinery the sovereign States of the world could in future resolve their differences and disputes and check aggression without again involving the peoples of the earth in war. Theirs might be, as the British Foreign Secretary, Mr. Eden, put it, "the world's last chance" of avoiding "another world conflict which this time might bring utter destruction of civilization in its train." The Great Powers' Foreign Ministers were followed at a series of plenary sessions by the heads of the smaller countries' delegations, each of whom devoted his opening speech to expressing his nation's attitude to the general problems before the Conference and in particular to the Dumbarton Oaks proposals, in whose drafting they had had no share and which many of them sought to modify in the preparation of the final Charter.

"The World's Last Chance"

Although the major storms were ahead, it was at this stage too that there began to appear those differences and wrangles which are inseparable from the work of any so variously-gathered Assembly charged with so great a task. In the behind-the-scenes

organizational preparation for the real work of the Conference—allocation of specific tasks to commissions and committees, selection of chairmen and other officials, and confirmation of credentials—several disputes had arisen and been settled by the end of the Conference's first week of work.

First of these concerned the chairmanship of the plenary sessions of the Conference, Russia's Mr. Molotov challenging the original plan that this should be permanently in the hands of the American Secretary of State, Mr. Stettinius, as senior representative of the host nation. Mr. Molotov proposed, instead, that the chairmanship should rotate among the heads of delegation of the four sponsoring nations, and his suggestion was adopted against opposition by the "Steering Committee" composed of all delegation heads and charged with the general direction of Conference work and the presentation to the full Conference of committee and commission proposals.

Chairmanship of Plenary Sessions

Thorniest of the early problems was the question of admission to the Conference of Argentina, whose government had only very belatedly fulfilled the Crimea qualifications for membership of the United Nations. Perhaps nettled by the Conference's refusal to admit the Provisional Government of Poland pending its modification as proposed at Yalta, Russia strongly opposed the admission of Argentina, and after being outvoted in the Steering Committee, Mr. Molotov brought the issue before a plenary session by proposing that a decision be delayed. Again he was outvoted, though the predominantly anti-Soviet tone of local American opinion swung generally in

INVITING POWERS OF THE CONFERENCE

Sponsoring the San Francisco Conference were Great Britain, the U.S.A., the U.S.S.R. and China. On May 4, 1945, they invited France (who had declined to be one of the inviting powers) to attend on a basis of equality. Above, representing the "Big Four" are (left to right), Lord Halifax, British Ambassador in Washington; Mr. Edward R. Stettinius, U.S. Secretary of State; Mr. Andrei A. Gromyko, Soviet Ambassador to the U.S.; and Dr. V. K. Wellington Koo, China's Ambassador to Great Britain. *Photos, Sport & General*

CONFERENCE STAMP

This was the special postage stamp issued in the U.S. to mark the United Nations Conference at San Francisco, April-June 1945.

the Russian favour on this occasion—chiefly as a result of the effective use he made in debate of the acid opinions expressed of Argentina's government by the late President Roosevelt and his almost universally revered Secretary of State, Cordell Hull, appointed chief adviser to the United States delegation but unable through illness to attend.

Such clashes, combined with the increasingly unspectacular nature of the real work of the Conference following the panoply of the formal opening, awoke a slightly disappointed San Francisco to the fact that this was not, as the city had vaguely expected, a sort of super American-style convention dominated by brass bands and splendid oratory. Instead it was a serious and difficult attempt to solve by discussion a number of the most delicate problems of vital importance to the world's peace. As the Conference entered its second stage—the actual drafting of an agreed Charter by Commissions and their dependent committees meeting in private—it receded almost into the background of the city's normal wartime life.

Crowds no longer embarrassed the security officials by thronging the approaches to the Conference buildings and the lobbies and bars of the delegates' hotels in hopes of a glimpse of, or even a word with, a Foreign Minister or an Arabian prince. San Franciscans saw themselves no longer as ringside spectators at an international circus, but as

unobtrusive hosts to a company of very vital workers.

With this change of attitude there came, also, as the Committees continued to meet through May, a certain impatience and even pessimism about the slowness with which the Charter took shape. As each clause of the Charter worked its way up the necessary chain of approval, from the original drafting committee to the Steering Committee for final presentation to the full Conference, checks inevitably occurred—often from unexpected quarters and at unexpected stages.

Meantime the Nazis had gone down to their final defeat, victory pointing the urgency of the Conference's work and at the same time forcing several of the leading delegates to return to their countries to deal with the pressing problems which followed victory. Among those departing were Mr. Eden and Mr.

BRITAIN AND RUSSIA AT SAN FRANCISCO

As decided at the Crimea Conference (see page 3564), representatives of the United Nations met at San Francisco on April 25, 1945, to set up ' a general international organization to maintain peace and security.' The conference held its final session on June 26 when the Charter was signed (subject to ratification) on behalf of 50 nations. Here, Mr. Molotov addresses the delegates, while (above) Mr. Attlee and Lord Halifax listen to the speeches. *Photos, Fox Photos ; Associated Press*

Molotov, whose absence (especially in the latter case) tended to slow up the unravelling of difficulties. Particularly on the question of the Great Powers' right of veto of action by the organization's Security Council on disputes laid before it, the Soviet delegation proved unable, without reference to Moscow, to agree with other delegations on the interpretation of the decision taken at

Yalta. Since the nature of the whole structure of the world organization and its Charter depended on whether any one Great Power was or was not to have the right to block action by the organization, this delay held up the otherwise almost completed work of the Conference.

Nevertheless, after days of anxious waiting, agreement was reached between the sponsoring Powers, and a proposal laid before the Conference which, in the words of the American Secretary of State, " preserves the principle of unanimity of the five permanent members of the Council [the United Kingdom, China, France, the Soviet Union and the United States] while at the same time assuring freedom of hearing and discussion in the Council before action is taken."

The mere fact, however, that the Great Powers continued to insist on the impossibility of action—peaceful or warlike—by the organization against the opposition of any one of them led to another week of discussion and voting among the delegates. Small nations' representatives, led by Australia's Foreign Minister, Dr. Evatt, expressed opposition to the possible powers of dictatorship over the organization conferred by the arrangement. But in general the smaller countries realized the absolute necessity of Great Power unanimity if world peace was to be preserved, and the proposal was accepted by the Conference—though two delegates (Colombia and Cuba) opposed it and fifteen more (including the Netherlands and New Zealand) abstained from voting as an expression of their opposition in principle.

The spotlight came back to San Francisco as President Truman

Great Power Veto Accepted

flew from Washington to be present at the signing of the United Nations Charter which—in the words of " The Times "—was the fruit of " nine weeks of argument and negotiation and some anxious delays."

The basis of this Charter remained the work done by representatives of Britain, China, Russia and the United States at Dumbarton Oaks in 1944 (*see* page 3256 and illus. in page 3255). But this full meeting of all the United Nations had done two great things. In the first place it had added to and amended the Dumbarton Oaks proposals, and had clarified them in the light of the Crimea agreement on such vital issues as voting procedure in the United Nations Security Council. And in the second it had given the opportunity to every Allied nation, big or small, to contribute its share to the establishment of an organization with the most important purpose in the world—the prevention of war. As President Truman said in his final speech to the delegates on June 26, " This Charter was not the work of any single nation or group of nations, large or small. It was the result of a spirit of give and take, of tolerance for the views and interests of others. It was proof that nations, like men, can state their differences, can face them, and then can find common ground on which to stand. That is the essence of democracy ; that is the essence of keeping the peace in the future."

Fifty nations, comprising more than four-fifths of all the people on earth, had agreed to work together rather than in a spirit of sovereign irresponsibility over a wide range of subjects affecting them all. To quote the Charter's preamble, for the final form of which Field-Marshal Smuts was responsible, " We, the peoples of the United Nations, determined to save succeeding generations from the scourge of war . . . to reaffirm faith in fundamental human rights . . . to establish conditions under which justice can be maintained . . . to promote social progress and better standards of life in larger freedom . . . to practise tolerance and live together in peace with one another as good neighbours . . . to unite our strength to maintain international peace and security . . . have resolved to combine our efforts to accomplish these aims. . ."

First, the Charter established an international organization " based on the principle of the sovereign equality of all its members," who were (at least provisionally) those nations taking part in the Conference. Those members

Fifty Delegates Sign Charter

pledged themselves to settle international disputes by peaceful means and not to threaten or use force against any other State, as well as to give the organization every assistance in any action it might take against States (whether members or not) judged to be acting in a way contrary to the principles of the Charter.

The world organization was to have—apart from its secretariat—five principal organs with functions clearly defined in the Charter. A General Assembly of all member States would discuss any subject within the scope of the Charter, including general questions of international co-operation and specific questions brought before it by any member or by the Security Council. This Council, " the kernel of the new organization," consisted of five permanent members (Britain, China, France, Russia and the United States) and six other nations chosen by the General Assembly for periods of two years each. The Assembly, except in special circumstances, was to meet annually, the Council was to " be so organized as to be able to function continuously." It was designed, in fact, as the executive committee of the organization with delegated power to take any action against threatened or actual aggression, including armed action in which use might be made of forces drawn from member States. In such cases, any State

providing forces would be invited to participate in the Security Council's deliberations.

Action, however, by the provisions of the Charter, would be taken only when seven members of the Security Council, including all the permanent members, voted in its favour. Only if one of these members were party to a dispute would this rule be waived and the member concerned abstain from voting. Otherwise Britain, China, France, Russia or the United States would be in a position individually to check the working of the machinery against herself.

Permanent Members Must Agree

Further power was concentrated in the hands of the " Big Five " by the composition of the Military Staff Committee, to be established " to advise and assist the Security Council on all questions relating to military requirements for the maintenance of international peace and security, the employment and command of forces placed at its disposal, the regulation of armaments, and possible disarmament." The regular members of this committee were the British, Chinese, French, Russian and United States Chiefs of Staff or their representatives. Military leaders of other countries were to be called in only " when the efficient discharge of the Committee's responsibilities requires."

UNITED NATIONS CHARTER IS APPROVED

Climax of the San Francisco Conference was reached on its last day, June 25, 1945, when the plenary session unanimously approved the Charter of the United Nations. Below, chairmen of the fifty delegations rise to their feet to indicate approval of the document. At left, to right of the Norway sign, stands Mr. Gromyko (U.S.S.R.) : at extreme right, beside the Netherlands sign, is Mr E R Stettinius, U.S. Secretary of State. *Photo Spor & General*

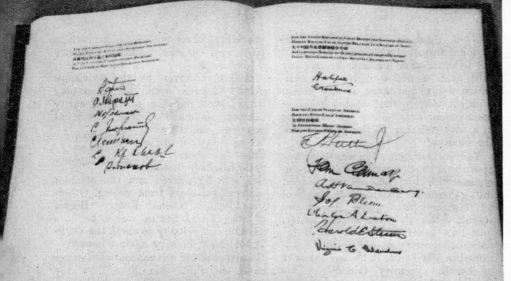

UNITED NATIONS CHARTER

Charter of the United Nations was signed in San Francisco on June 26, 1945, by representatives of the 50 nations then members. Leading signatories for the 'Big Five' were : Lord Halifax (Britain), Mr. Stettinius (U.S.), Mr. Gromyko (U.S.S.R.), Dr. Wellington Koo (China), and Mr. Paul Boncour (France). Above, two pages showing on left the Soviet signatures and on right those of the British and U.S. delegates. Right, book of the Charter.

Photos, Sport & General ; Associated Press

promise draft was reached on this as on other questions.

It covered three classes of territory : areas already mandated to members of the United Nations, areas " which may be detached from enemy States as a result of the Second World War," and areas " voluntarily placed under the system by States responsible for their administration."

A movement early in the Conference to give the Assembly power to bring territories within the system without the consent of the administering State met with heavy opposition from the principal colonial Powers and was shelved.

Two further additions to the old

Just as the Assembly (providing the general base for all the organization's functions) and the Security Council were in effect strengthened developments of the old League of Nations Assembly and Council, so the other three organs set up by the San Francisco Charter were more virile, wider-embracing versions of the specialized sections of the League.

An International Court of Justice, composed of fifteen members of different nationalities, was set up to carry on the

International Court of Justice

international legal authority of the old Hague Court, reinforced by the provision that a State might call on the Security Council to assist it in enforcing a decision given by the Court against another State. Here, again, however, the veto power of the " Big Five " would operate.

Studies, reports and recommendations " with respect to international economic, social, cultural, educational, health and related matters " were entrusted by the Charter to a Social and Economic Council, consisting of eighteen members elected by and acting under the authority of the General Assembly. The specified objectives of the United Nations in this sphere were laid down as the promotion of " higher standards of

living, full employment and conditions of economic and social progress and development," as well as " universal respect for and observance of human rights and fundamental freedoms for all without distinction as to race, language or religion."

Finally, the Charter set up a Trusteeship Council, which in adapted form was to take over the work of the old League Mandates Commission. The terms of reference of this Council were the subject of several heated discussions in the course of the Conference, especially as it was a subject not adumbrated in the Dumbarton Oaks proposals, and the section of the Charter establishing it was a synthesis of several sometimes conflicting memoranda tabled by various delegations.

Finally, after discussion had ranged from the need for military secrecy concerning the administration of small Pacific islands to the relative virtue of the words " self-government " and " independence " as stipulated goals for the administering authority, a com-

mandate system in the new Charter were the provision of special arrangements under the direct control of the Security Council for areas specified as " strategic," and agreement that States administering trustee areas might levy local forces to assist in carrying out their security obligations to the organization.

Thus, in a lengthy document of 111 Articles, every word of which had to be hammered out over the Conference table, the victors of the Second Great War laid down at San Francisco the framework of a body which, they hoped, would ensure that war would never recur. At the final session Lord Halifax of Britain was in the Chair, and when he called for a vote on the adoption of the Charter he asked delegation heads to register their approval by standing in their places, because " this issue upon which we are about to vote is as important as any we shall ever vote on in our lifetime." Fifty men stood, representing some two thousand million seekers after peace.

FIFTY NATIONS SIGNED THE UNITED NATIONS CHARTER AT SAN FRANCISCO

After nine weeks of discussion, the Charter of the United Nations Organization was, on June 26, 1945, signed by the fifty delegations to the San Francisco Conference. The Conference had ended the previous day with the approval of the charter and with speeches from the leading delegates and from President Truman who watched the signing. On June 7 Dr. Manuilsky, the Ukrainian delegate, chairman of the committee charged with naming the Organization, announced that the name had been chosen in homage to President Roosevelt, who first used the phrase to name the Allied wartime coalition (see stamp illustrated in page 3934). 1. Dr. Wellington Koo signs first for China. 2. Lord Halifax for Britain. 3. Mr. E. R. Stettinius for the U.S.A. 4. Mr. Andrei Gromyko for Russia. 5. Mr. Francis Michael Forde for Australia. 6. Mr. Mackenzie King for Canada. 7. Mr. Peter Fraser for New Zealand. 8. Field-Marshal Smuts for South Africa.

Chapter 382

AWARDS AND DECORATIONS OF 1939-45

Nearly two hundred new decorations and medals were issued throughout the world during the period of the Second Great War. Most of the British and Dominion ribbons and certain Allied ones are shown in colour in the plate facing this page. In this chapter details about them are given by Mr. L. F. Guille

THE George Cross and the George Medal of Great Britain were first announced by H.M. King George VI in a broadcast on September 23, 1940 (*see* page 1212 and Hist. Doc. No. 178). Queen Victoria had, of course, named the Victoria Cross after herself, and King Edward VII the Edward Medal (for bravery in industrial accidents) after himself, but this was the first time a Monarch had announced in person to his people the creation of a new decoration. The Cross and Medal (the former ranking second only to the V.C.) are awarded solely for acts of the greatest heroism or of the most conspicuous courage in circumstances of extreme danger, the degree required for the Cross being of a higher standard than for the Medal. When the ribbon of the Cross is worn alone, a small silver replica of the Cross is worn upon it.

Lloyd's War Medal (instituted December 1940) was a distinction which was awarded to those who kept Britain's life line open—the men of the Merchant Service. "Lloyd's"— the world centre of Marine Insurance—

LLOYD'S MEDAL FOR BRAVERY AT SEA
White ribbon with blue stripe near each edge
Courtesy of Lloyd's

made grants of the medal in cases of exceptional bravery in the working of merchant ships or of the saving of lives of their crews. The colours of the ribbon are white with a broad blue stripe near each edge.

When the Airborne troops were formed it was found that in certain cases none of the existing flying decorations fitted their particular cases of heroism, and it was decided, therefore, to extend the award of the Conspicuous Gallantry Medal (a Naval award) to

them. The Airborne Medal is of the same design as the Naval one, but the ribbon has a pale blue (instead of white) centre between dark blue edges.

The Air Efficiency Award (instituted September 1942) is granted to those who have served as Volunteers in the Air Forces of the Empire for a period of ten years, officers and men alike. It is the counterpart of the Royal Naval Volunteer and the Territorial Decorations. The ribbon is dark green with two narrow pale blue stripes in the centre.

To recompense those of the Allied Nations or other foreign subjects who rendered services of eminent character in the cause of freedom and those who displayed gallantry in doing so, H.M. the King created on August 28, 1945, two medals—King George's Medals for Service in the Cause of Freedom—the ribbons of which only had been designed by 1946.

Announcement in 1943 of the institution of two British Campaign Stars, followed in May 1945, by that of six other Stars and a Defence Medal to be awarded for service in the British forces, was the occasion of general approval inasmuch as many of the other Allies had already gone far ahead in this matter. The stars were named to indicate the territory covered. Regulations for these stars, consolidated in May 1945, were further revised in June 1946. Briefly the qualifications for eligibility were as follows :

1939/45 Star. Originally the 1939/43 Star (announced in 1943), the currency of this was in June 1946, prolonged to May 8, 1945, and again (in June 1946) to September 2, 1945. Six months' service in an operational area was required to qualify ; certain exceptions such as Commando raids, Air Crew service of two months and service brought to an end within these periods by death, wounds or other disability also qualified. The granting of an honour or mention was also a qualification. Air crews of fighter aircraft who took part in the Battle of Britain in 1940 wear a special distinction in the form of a gilt rose on the red portion of the ribbon.

Atlantic Star. This award was primarily intended to commemorate the Battle of the Atlantic and was given to those who, also being eligible for the

1939/45 Star, served six months at sea in the Atlantic zone. If the bearer is also qualified for the France and Germany or Air Crew Europe Stars (or both) he wears a silver rose in the centre of the ribbon.

Air Crew Europe Star. Awarded for two months' service and at least one operational sortie over enemy territory, but the 1939/45 Star must first have been earned. A silver rose indicates that the wearer has also qualified for the Atlantic or France/Germany Star.

Africa Star. This Star was granted for operational service of any length in North Africa from the time Italy entered the war (June 10, 1940) to the date when the last enemy resistance in that continent ceased (May 12, 1943). The emblems " 8 " and " 1 " worn on the ribbon indicate service with those respective armies while a silver rose shows closely supporting formations of all three services.

Pacific and Burma Stars. Entry into the operational areas was sufficient to gain one of these stars, while if the wearer also qualifies for the other he adds a silver rose.

Italy, and **France and Germany Stars.** Similar conditions to those above prevail for these stars, but both ribbons can be worn at the same time. The Italy Star was awarded for service from the capture of Pantelleria (June 11, 1943) to May 8, 1945.

The Defence Medal. This was intended to recompense all who—if in the Civil Defence Services—had served for over three years and those also in the armed forces who had served three years at home or more than one year abroad in non-operational areas. This ribbon bears silver laurel leaves if the wearer has been awarded a King's Commendation for Brave Conduct (Civil).

In June 1946 announcement was made of the War Medal, 1939/1945. This was to be granted to all members of the armed forces who served more than 28 days before September 2, 1945. It is upon this ribbon that the Bronze oakleaf for Mention in Despatches and King's Commendation (Air) are worn.

India was specially selected, because of her great area and the diversity of services rendered by her troops, for the award of a separate medal

1939-1945 STAR

AFRICA STAR

ATLANTIC STAR

AIR CREW EUROPE STAR

ITALY STAR

FRANCE & GERMANY STAR

PACIFIC STAR

GEORGE CROSS

WAR MEDAL 1939-1945

DEFENCE MEDAL

CONSPICUOUS GALLANTRY
MEDAL [Air]

GEORGE MEDAL

KING GEORGE'S MEDAL FOR
COURAGE IN THE CAUSE OF FREEDOM

INDIA SERVICE MEDAL
1939-1945

KING GEORGE'S MEDAL FOR
SERVICE IN THE CAUSE OF FREEDOM

BURMA STAR

AFRICA SERVICE MEDAL
(Union of South Africa)

CANADIAN VOLUNTEER
SERVICE MEDAL

CROIX DE GUERRE 1939-1940
(France)

WAR CROSS
(Norway)

WAR COMMEMORATIVE CROSS
(Netherlands)

ORDER OF PATRIOTIC WAR
[1st Class] (U.S.S.R.)

ORDER OF SUVOROV
[1st Class] (U.S.S.R.)

CROSS FOR VALOUR
(Poland)

FLYING CROSS
(Netherlands)

ORDER OF LIBERATION
(France)

MERIT

MILITARY CROSS 1939
(Czechoslovakia)

WAR MEDAL
(Norway)

BRONZE CROSS
(Netherlands)

DISTINGUISHED FLYING CROSS
(Greece)

CANADA MEDAL

DISTINGUISHED FLYING MEDAL
(Greece)

MERCANTILE MARINE MEDAL
(Belgium)

LEGION OF MERIT
(U.S.A.)

AMERICAN CAMPAIGN
(U.S.A.)

DEFENCE SERVICE MEDAL
(U.S.A.)

EUROPEAN—AFRICAN—
MIDDLE EASTERN CAMPAIGN
(U.S.A.)

ASIATIC—PACIFIC
CAMPAIGN
(U.S.A.)

AWARDS AND DECORATIONS OF THE SECOND GREAT WAR

Eight British Campaign awards were approved by H.M. The King during the Second Great War. They were : 1939-45 Star, Africa Star, Atlantic Star, Air Crew Europe Star, Burma Star, France and Germany Star, Italy Star and Pacific Star. (Design of the stars is similar to that of the Burma Star shown here.) Also approved were the War Medal, 1939-45, the India Service Medal, 1939-45, and the Defence Medal. The George Cross and George Medal were instituted on September 23, 1940, primarily to reward acts of gallantry by civilians (men and women), arising out of enemy action, but there is also a small Military Division of the Cross. Ribbons of representative Dominions and Allied awards are also given above.

BADGES OF SHIPS OF THE ROYAL NAVY LOST IN 1944

Represented here are 14 destroyers, 5 minesweepers, 3 cruisers, 2 sloops and the submarine 'Syrtis', all of which were lost during the year 1944. They include the cruiser 'Penelope' (see page 2285)—H.M.S. Pepperpot of the Malta run—and the destroyer 'Janus', veteran of Matapan, which were sunk during the Anzio beach-head operations in January; the destroyers 'Boadicea' and 'Swift', both lost in the Normandy invasion landings in June; and the sloop 'Woodpecker' of 'Walker's Circus' (see page 2854).

From material supplied by H.M. Dockyard, Chatham. By permission of H.M. Stationery Office

BRITISH 2nd   BRITISH 5th   BRITISH 7th (ARMOURED)   BRITISH 11th (ARMOURED)   BRITISH 15th (SCOTTISH)

BRITISH 36th   BRITISH 43rd (WESSEX)   BRITISH 46th   BRITISH 49th   50th (NORTHUMBRIAN)

BRITISH 51st (HIGHLAND)   BRITISH 52nd (LOWLAND)   BRITISH 53rd (WELSH)   BRITISH 56th   BRITISH 78th

GUARDS ARMOURED   4th INDIAN   5th INDIAN   7th INDIAN   8th INDIAN

17th INDIAN   19th INDIAN   20th INDIAN   23rd INDIAN   25th INDIAN

26th INDIAN   44th INDIAN   11th EAST AFRICAN   81st WEST AFRICAN   82nd WEST AFRICAN

DIVISIONAL SIGNS OF THE BRITISH AND INDIAN ARMIES

Distinctive signs for the Divisions of the British Army were used during the war of 1914-1918, and were again employed in the Second Great War. Armies and Corps also had their own insignia (see plate facing page 3483). This selection is representative of the many well-designed 'flashes' worn by British and Indian Divisions whose names frequently occur in the pages of 'The Second Great War', between 1939-1945. Also included are those of the three African Divisions which fought in Burma.

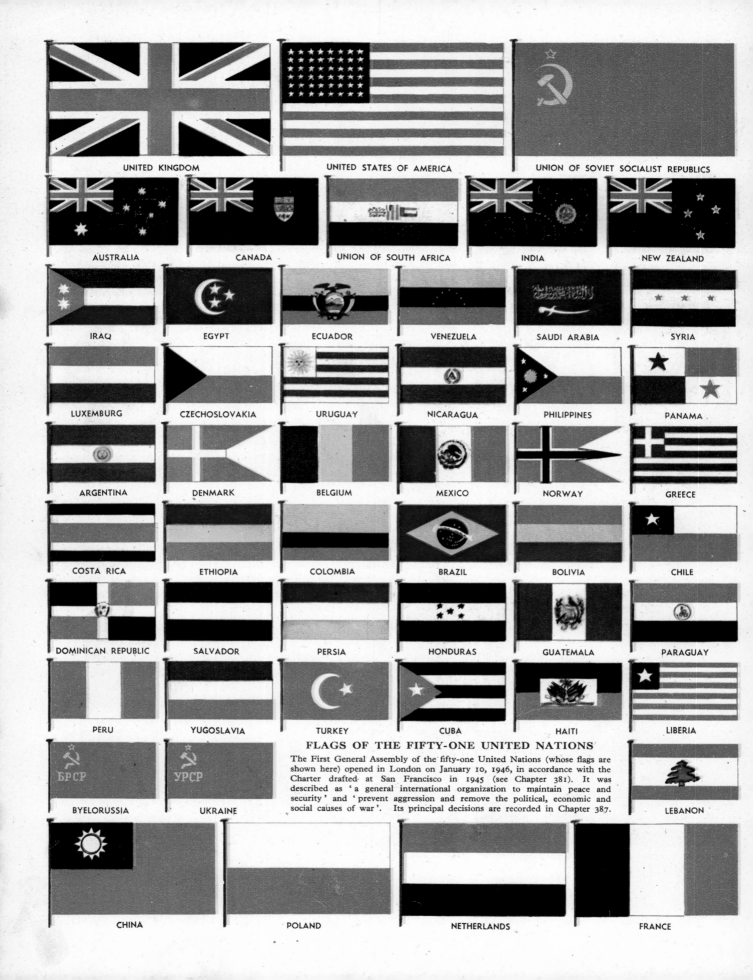

UNITED KINGDOM

UNITED STATES OF AMERICA

UNION OF SOVIET SOCIALIST REPUBLICS

AUSTRALIA

CANADA

UNION OF SOUTH AFRICA

INDIA

NEW ZEALAND

IRAQ

EGYPT

ECUADOR

VENEZUELA

SAUDI ARABIA

SYRIA

LUXEMBURG

CZECHOSLOVAKIA

URUGUAY

NICARAGUA

PHILIPPINES

PANAMA

ARGENTINA

DENMARK

BELGIUM

MEXICO

NORWAY

GREECE

COSTA RICA

ETHIOPIA

COLOMBIA

BRAZIL

BOLIVIA

CHILE

DOMINICAN REPUBLIC

SALVADOR

PERSIA

HONDURAS

GUATEMALA

PARAGUAY

PERU

YUGOSLAVIA

TURKEY

CUBA

HAITI

LIBERIA

BYELORUSSIA

UKRAINE

LEBANON

FLAGS OF THE FIFTY-ONE UNITED NATIONS

The First General Assembly of the fifty-one United Nations (whose flags are shown here) opened in London on January 10, 1946, in accordance with the Charter drafted at San Francisco in 1945 (see Chapter 381). It was described as 'a general international organization to maintain peace and security' and 'prevent aggression and remove the political, economic and social causes of war'. Its principal decisions are recorded in Chapter 387.

CHINA

POLAND

NETHERLANDS

FRANCE

entitled the India Service Medal, 1939/45, which was given to all after three years' non-operational service. It could not be awarded in addition to the Defence Medal. It will be noted that the ribbon colours selected—light blue and dark blue—were those of the two premier Indian Orders, The Star of India and the Indian Empire.

Designs of the various stars were approved in March 1946, and from the example given in the colour plate facing page 3938 it will be seen that they are six pointed, bearing in the centre the Imperial cipher surmounted by a crown with, below, a scroll giving the name of the relative campaign. All eight stars are similar except for the name on the scroll. The metal is a bright coppery colour and a ring is provided for suspension from the ribbon.

The British Dominions created their own medals. The Canada Medal of 1943 was an award for outstanding services to the Dominion and not a campaign medal like the Volunteer Service Medal. The silver maple leaf on the ribbon of the latter represents "overseas" service, those who did not leave Canada wearing the ribbon alone. (See also illus. in page 3734.) The Africa Service Medal is awarded to " all members of the Union Defence Force or other uniformed forces of the Union who attested for service in Africa before May 13, 1943 " (the day the last enemy units in Africa surrendered). Its ribbon shows the orange of the flash which Union troops wore with so much pride in other parts of Africa, together with the green and gold " Springbok " colours. The medal had not been struck by August 1946.

The Belgian Mercantile Marine Medal is an exceedingly handsome piece, being of dark bronze, circular without raised edge, and having on the **Belgian** obverse the Lion of Bel-**Medals** gium and on the reverse the interlaced initials L III. The supporting ring is attached by means of a decorative bow. Belgium, like France, changed the design of the ribbon of its Croix de Guerre, adopting a deep red colour with three narrow green stripes near each edge. After the conclusion of the war five new medals were instituted: The War Commemorative Medal (yellow with black-white-black stripes at each edge) ; the Volunteers Medal (9 dark blue and 8 red stripes) ; the Resistance Medal, black with green edges and two narrow red centre stripes ; and also a Reconnaissance Medal and a Civic Cross.

The Military Cross of Czechoslovakia (instituted in 1939) consists of four barbed arms with, in the centre, a

shield bearing the country's arms. Two swords appear in the angles. Many of these crosses were awarded to British airmen. A Military Medal was also instituted by Czechoslovakia, the ribbon of which is blue with two red stripes in the centre and with red edges. Between the colours is a narrow white stripe. This medal ranks below the Military Cross, though officers and men are eligible for both.

A distinct departure from the conventional is evidenced in the French Order of Liberation. It consists of an oblong " plaque " down the centre of which passes a sword, the hilt bearing a square " ring " for the ribbon. The obverse shows the Cross of Fighting France,

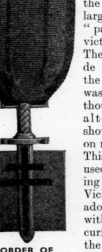

ORDER OF LIBERATION
Green ribbon : black stripes and black edges
Courtesy of J. R. Gaunt, Ltd.

while the back bears the inscription in large Roman letters " patriam servando victoriam tulit." The French Croix de Guerre used in the First Great War was revived in 1939, though with the altered ribbon shown and the dates on reverse changed. This ribbon was used by the Fighting French while the Vichy Government adopted a ribbon with black stripes, curiously enough the same colours as those of the Order of Liberation.

Greece followed the Netherlands and Britain in selecting the diagonal pattern for its Flying award ribbons. The designs were not determined in August 1946. Ribbons of the Greek D.F.C. and D.F.M. are shown in the plate facing page 3938, while white and grey are used in the Greek counterparts of the British Air Force Cross and Medal.

The Flying Cross of the Netherlands is a silver cross pattée bearing a flying eagle on a crowned " garter " worded " Initiative, Courage, Perseverance." The date 1941 appears just above the eagle. The Bronze Cross was instituted by Queen Wilhelmina to reward gallantry or leadership in the presence of the enemy. It could be awarded to all the forces and to civilians, foreigners as well as Dutchmen, and if awarded " with honourable mention " bears a gold crown on the ribbon. Action against the enemy was the criterion for the award of the War Commemorative Cross, each successive engagement being indicated by a bronze star. The cross was awarded

to all participants on the same lines as British campaign stars.

Norway's War Cross was instituted, like its War Medal, in 1941. Both are in bronze, the Cross having three half circles at the end of each arm with the Norwegian Lion on a crowned shield in the centre. It was awarded to both officers and men for conspicuous gallantry. The medal bears King Haakon's effigy below his name HAAKON VII and above the motto ALT FOR NORGE. The reverse has merely the word KRIGSMEDALJE, the Royal cipher and two oak branches. Norway had also a Campaign medal and a Cross and medal for Freedom.

NORWAY WAR CROSS
Red ribbon : blue centre stripe edged with white
Courtesy of Spink & Son

When Poland gained her freedom in 1919 she instituted in 1920 a Cross for Valour which used a purple ribbon with a white stripe near each edge. For the 1939–45 war the Cross was revived and the colours reversed, as shown on the plate facing page 3938. Bars when awarded were indicated by narrow vertical strips of bronze bearing an oakleaf design. Separate medals with ribbons of appropriate colours were awarded to the Army (red and white), Navy (dark blue and white) and Air Force (light blue and white), while the historic capture of Monte Cassino, due largely to the Polish Army in Italy, was commemorated by a ribbon of six bright blue and five red equal stripes.

The United States broke with tradition in instituting in 1942 the Legion of Merit, in four classes. The highest, Chief Commander, has a large, white, five-armed cross which is worn on the left breast. Commanders wear a smaller cross suspended round the neck and the two lower classes are worn on the left breast ; the higher, officer, having a

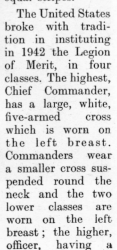

NETHERLANDS FLYING CROSS
White ribbon : orange diagonal stripes
Courtesy of J. R. Gaunt, Ltd.

small gilt model of the cross on the ribbon, legionaries wearing it plain. In undress uniform the various ranks are indicated by emblems on the ribbon ; a small gilt horizontal bar, bearing the same miniature as that for officers, being used by Chief Commanders, the same in silver by Commanders and the miniature alone by officers. It is awarded to the " armed forces of Nations friendly to the United States " (Field-Marshal Viscount Montgomery of Alamein being a Chief Commander) as well as the armed forces of the United States and the Philippines.

American Awards

The American Defence Service Medal was awarded for service " during the limited emergency proclaimed by President Roosevelt on September 8, 1939, or the unlimited emergency proclaimed on May 27, 1941," *i.e.* before Pearl Harbor, December 7, 1941. The campaign ribbons are self explanatory. The American Victory medal ribbon has a centre of red with on either side a miniature Victory ribbon of the First Great War. The occupation of Germany is commemorated by a ribbon half black and half red, with white edges.

After the Revolution in Russia in 1917 decorations were abolished, but it was soon found that even men of Soviet Russia liked to deck themselves with symbols of service and merit, and they were gradually restored. In all, some 50 different orders and medals were available for award by the end of the Second Great War, not to mention numerous " badges " which have no ribbons.

The highest award, the Gold Star, is worn on all occasions, being suspended from a narrow scarlet ribbon. The Order of Suvorov, named after Russia's famous Marshal of Napoleonic times, was granted on much the same terms as the Order of the Bath (Military Division), *i.e.* for the direction of successful operations of bodies of troops varying in size from armies to battalions. The second and third classes of this Order have on their ribbons orange edges to the

HOW THE NAME IS STAMPED

An innovation at the Royal Mint was the employment of women for the making of decorations for the Second Great War. Each medal has the name of the man or woman to whom it has been awarded running round the edge. Here, a woman stamps with a punch the name of the recipient on the rim of a medal.
Photo, ' Illustrated '

green and the third class an additional narrow orange central stripe. The Order of the Patriotic War, however, was given for personal gallantry during the German invasion and was the award for the " Resistance " or guerilla movement.

Other national heroes' names besides Suvorov have been utilized to embellish Soviet orders, amongst them being Kutuzov (another General of the Napoleonic era), Alexander Nevsky (a medieval hero), and Bogdan Khmelnitsky ; Nakhimov and Ushakov, two Admirals, give their names to two Naval orders. There are in all six classes in the three decorations awarded to the Mothers of Russia, the " Heroine Mother," the "Order of the Glory of Motherhood " in three classes and the Medal for Motherhood in two classes. The Soviet Union instituted medals (and struck and distributed them) for the Defence of Leningrad, Stalingrad (*see* illustration in page 2421), Moscow, the Caucasus and the Soviet Arctic, and, when the tide turned, for the Capture of Warsaw, Koenigsberg, Berlin and Vienna and the liberation of Budapest and Prague. Soviet Russian distinctions included also numerous other medals for civilian courage, services to Labour, etc.

Russian Military and Civil Awards

BRITISH CAMPAIGN STARS READY FOR ISSUE

The striking of the Campaign Stars instituted by King George VI for service in the Second Great War was begun at the Royal Mint and the Royal Ordnance Factory early in 1946. Designs for the eight stars—the 1939-1945 Star, Atlantic, Air Crew Europe, Africa, Pacific, Burma, Italy, and France and Germany Stars—were prepared in the Mint where women workers here examine finished awards before packing them.
Photo, P.A.-Reuter

Chapter 383

LATIN AMERICA AT THE END OF THE WAR

*This brief account by Mr. J. C. Metford of events of international significance
in the Latin Americas during 1944 and 1945 shows the continuing growth
of Allied influence and decrease in that of the Axis in those countries. Internal
politics remained as turbulent as ever, and governments new or old were not
notably democratic ; but only in Argentina did the Government continue to
show a strong measure of sympathy with the Axis*

ALARMED at threats to their internal security, Latin American Republics carried out investigations into subversive activities designed to help the Axis. In the first months of 1944 the results of these investigations were made public. It was alleged that Buenos Aires was the centre of Nazi intrigues and this was confirmed when the British authorities in Trinidad revealed that they had arrested Osmar Helmuth, an Argentine of German birth who was on his way to take up consular duties in Spain. The Argentine authorities examined the evidence obtained from him, and on January 25 announced that severe measures would be undertaken to stamp out German espionage in Argentina. Also on January 25, three Germans were arrested in Colombia. On February 5 six Germans were found guilty of espionage in Uruguay and on February 10 Brazil announced the discovery of a spy ring in Porto Alegre. On February 22 the Chilean Government arrested fourteen suspected persons and claimed to have smashed an Axis spy ring organized by Ludwig von Bohlen, former German Air Attaché in Chile. One hundred more arrests were made within the next few days and a short-wave radio transmitter was seized. The Peruvian Government announced that it had deported into the interior German and Japanese subjects who had attempted to seize power and set up a pro-Nazi regime. Although Germany had all along denied interference and espionage in South America, her guilt was proved.

There remained nevertheless the possibility that Germany would attempt to use the notorious instability of South American governments to destroy the solidarity of the Pan-American front against the Axis. For this reason, the Inter-American Committee for Political Defence decided to ask its member nations not to grant recognition to any new government established by force in South America until its anti-Axis stand had been proved. This was a very necessary precaution as, throughout 1944 and 1945, political unrest was prevalent in the Latin-American states.

**Maintaining
Anti-Axis
Front**

Brazil continued her active participation in the war, the Navy on October 11, 1944, assuming entire responsibility for patrolling the South Atlantic. A first contingent of the Air Force left for Europe on January 3, 1944, and others followed. The Brazilian Expeditionary Force (*see* illus. in page 2956) sailed for Italy in May, where it fought with the 5th Army and gave a good account of itself (*see* page 3473 and illus. in page 3467). General Enrico Gaspar Dutra, the War Minister, visited the troops in Italy in the autumn, and went to Great Britain in October, staying for several days in London as the guest of the British Government. Diplomatic relations with the Union of Soviet Socialist Republics were established on April 2, 1945.

BRAZIL

In April 1944, President Vargas promised that after the war the democratic provisions of the constitution of 1937, which had never functioned, would come into force. Nearly a year later, on March 2, 1945, he announced that he intended to surrender his dictatorial powers. Greater freedom was accorded to the Press, and an amnesty was granted to political prisoners. A decree made at the end of April fixed December 2 as the date for the election of a President and Congress, and a few days later compulsory voting for all literate Brazilians, men and women, over 18 was introduced. Dr. Vargas, who had said he would not stand for the presidency again, was compelled by the army chiefs to resign on October 30 on the eve of his fifteenth anniversary in office. In the elections, held as announced on December 2, General Dutra (Social Democratic candidate) was elected President, while the Social Democrats secured forty per cent of the seats in Congress, next largest party being the National Democratic Union with 33 per cent.

Chile established diplomatic relations with Russia on December 11, 1944, at a meeting between the Ambassadors of the two Governments in Washington :

U.S. NAVY FLYING BOATS OVER RIO

From her entry into the war on August 22, 1942, Brazil joined the United States in the naval and air patrolling of the South Atlantic until, on October 11, 1944, she assumed sole responsibility for this task. Below, in February 1944, Mariner flying-boats of the U.S. Navy on patrol fly over the harbour of Rio de Janeiro, capital of Brazil, escorting an Allied convoy.
Photo, Keystone

BRAZIL SIGNS CHARTER
Mr. Pedro Leão Velloso (above), Brazil's Foreign Minister, signs the Charter of the United Nations in the Opera House, San Francisco, at the conclusion of the United Nations Conference there on June 26, 1945. His colleagues on the delegation stand to witness the signature. Brazil ratified acceptance of the Charter on August 31.
Photo, Sport & General

there had been no previous diplomatic contact between the countries since Tsarist days. Chile declared war on Germany and Japan on February 12, 1945.

Argentina's relations with the United States, never particularly cordial, were seriously strained in 1944–45. Historically, culturally and

ARGENTINA economically, Argentina had strong ties with Europe, particularly with France and Great Britain, and the mass of the nation was naturally disposed to favour the European Allies, though some of her leaders were sympathetic to Nazi ideology. Moreover, a self-conscious nationalism, born of the country's material and cultural progress, made her aspire to become the champion of the Latin-American republics against dominance by the United States, whose attempts to weld Latin America into unity of foreign and even domestic policy she steadily resisted.

The revelations of Nazi activities in Argentina which followed Osmar Helmuth's arrest forced the Government's hand, and on January 26, 1944, Argentina broke off relations with Germany and Japan. She severed relations with all Axis satellites on February 4. This led to the overthrow of President Ramirez by some of his former followers. Great Britain and the United States refused to recognize his successor, General Farrell (War Minister under Ramirez), who derived his power from the support of Colonel Peron, formerly Secretary of Labour, now Minister of War, and soon to become Vice-President. Peron had a great deal of popular support because he had sponsored

forward-looking labour legislation, but he was an extreme nationalist, and under his influence the Argentine Government persisted in a tacit policy of non-co-operation with the United Nations. Only Bolivia, Paraguay and Chile recognized General Farrell.

A growing sense of isolation led the Government in October to send a note to Washington proposing the calling of a conference of the Foreign Ministers of the Pan-American Union and the American Republics to consider Argentina's position. This proposal was not accepted, and Argentina thereupon decided to refrain from taking part in meetings of the Pan-American Union. Though she was not represented at the conference of the Union held in Mexico City on February 21, 1945, she was invited to adhere to the Act of Chapultepec (*see* page 3945), drawn up there.

On March 27, a ministerial decree announced the declaration of war on Germany and Japan, and Argentina's acceptance of the Act of Chapultepec. Great Britain and the United States and the other American Republics then resumed diplomatic relations, and although her adherence to the United Nations' cause was after the date set (March 1) at the Crimea Conference by which war must have been declared to entitle a country to an invitation to San Francisco, she was invited to send delegates to the United Nations Conference. Postponement of her admission

to the United Nations was strongly urged at San Francisco by the U.S.S.R.; Mr. Molotov, the Soviet delegate, declaring that " neither the foreign nor the domestic policies of the Argentine regime in this war have met with the United Nations' approval " ; but her immediate admission was voted on April 30 by 31 to 4 (those opposing being the U.S.S.R., Greece, Czechoslovakia and Yugoslavia).

At San Francisco, Argentina had been supported by the United States ; but in June the U.S. Minister in Buenos Aires asserted that the Government was still tolerating pro-Nazi activities, and was not carrying out its obligations under the Act of Chapultepec, with the result that relations between the U.S.A. and

BRAZILIAN FORCES FOUGHT IN EUROPE
Brazilian aircraft served in France with the R.A.F., and the Brazilian Expeditionary Force fought with the 5th Army in Italy from September 1944 till the end of the campaign. (See illus. in page 3467.) Here, Rio de Janeiro turns out, with streamers and confetti, to welcome returning troops in May 1945. Above, member of the Brazilian Expeditionary Force under Major-General Mascarenhas de Morais, disembarks at Naples in July 1944.
Photos, British Official ; Sport & General

U-BOAT SURRENDERS NEAR BUENOS AIRES

At Mar del Plata, near Buenos Aires, the German submarine U 530 surrendered to the Argentine authorities on July 10, 1945 (see page 3504). The commander and crew of 54 were in an advanced state of malnutrition. Here, Argentine sailors man the surrendered U-boat from which the Germans had jettisoned the guns. Right, Captain Otto Wermuth (centre, wearing Iron Cross), with two fellow officers. Above, right, the U-boat putting in at Mar del Plata. *Photos, Associated Press*

Argentina again became strained. The situation was eased when President Farrell appointed a Radical, Dr. Juan Cooke, as Foreign Minister on August 28, with a free hand to co-operate with the United Nations.

President Lopez of Colombia visited the United States in January 1944, and on the 17th signed the Washington Declaration at the White House on behalf of his country. The isolationist party renewed its attacks on his administration. A strike was called to force the President from office, and he resigned; but the Senate rejected his resignation. On July 11 a small military group kidnapped him while he was watching army manoeuvres; but energetic action by the Vice-President Dario Echandia and lack of popular support obliged the rebels to release him in a few hours. The leaders of the attack were sentenced to terms of imprisonment.

COLOMBIA

On July 19, 1945, President Lopez, whose second presidential term would have expired on August 7, 1946, resigned " to pacify the political atmosphere," and was succeeded by his Foreign Minister, Mr. Alberto Camargo, who had represented Colombia at San Francisco.

On May 24, 1944, the Peruvian Government announced that, in pursuance of the treaty concluded at Rio de Janeiro on March 31, 1942, demarcation of the Peru-Ecuador frontier—in dispute for 120 years—had been completed. An agreement embodying the changes was signed by the Ambassadors of Peru and Ecuador at Rio de Janeiro on February 16, 1946.

Peru declared war on Germany and Japan on February 12, 1945.

On May 27, 1944, a revolt broke out in Guayaquil, second largest town of Ecuador. After two days' sharp street fighting, in which tanks were used and about eighty were killed, over a hundred wounded, the rebels gained control of the town and proclaimed their support of Dr. Jose Maria Velasco Ibarra (president for nine months in 1934-35 until driven into exile in Colombia). Simultaneous risings occurred in Quito the capital and other places, and on May 29 President Arroyo del Rio resigned and took refuge in the U.S. Embassy. Two days later, Dr. Ibarra

ARGENTINA BREAKS WITH GERMANY AND JAPAN

The Argentine Foreign Minister, Mr. Alberto Gilbert, on January 26, 1944, signs a decree in Buenos Aires breaking off relations with Germany and Japan. Nine days later Argentina severed relations with all the Axis satellites. As a result of this pro-Allied display, President Ramirez was deposed by some of his former associates, and his War Minister, General Farrell, who was not recognized by Britain or the U.S., was elected in his stead.

INTERNAL POLITICS IN LATIN AMERICA

In spite of Argentina's admission to the United Nations on April 30, 1945, her Government's relations with the U.S. continued to be strained. On September 19 the greatest popular demonstration ever seen in Buenos Aires, organized on a non-party basis by the 'Committee of Democratic Co-ordination,' took place when some 500,000 people called on the Government to resign, acclaiming the U.S. and attacking Colonel Juan Peron (right), the Vice-President, Minister also of War, Labour and Welfare.   Above, the demonstration in front of the Congress building.   Below, Mexico City parade in September 1944 in approval of the imprisonment of leaders of the 'Sinarquiste' pseudo-fascist movement.

reached Quito, where he was enthusiastically received. He took over the Government, and was immediately recognized by the U.S.A. and other American republics. One of his first steps was to recognize the boundary treaty with Peru made in 1942 (*see* page 3943), regarded by many Ecuadorians as derogatory to their country.

It was announced on September 17, 1945, that Ecuador had agreed to lease one of the Galapagos Islands to the United States as a base

ECUADOR for the defence of the Panama Canal, Ecuadorian sovereignty being guaranteed. In return Ecuador received a loan of twenty million dollars to be expended on highway construction, irrigation, and the improvement of port facilities. The United States announced evacuation of the Galapagos Islands wartime bases (established in 1942) on April 6, 1946.

Uruguay declared war on Germany and Japan on February 22, 1945. On March 22, it was announced in Montevideo that in order to maintain meat shipments to Britain the Uruguayan Government had prohibited the export of livestock to neighbouring countries and had introduced domestic meat rationing.

General Isaias Medina, President of Venezuela, visited the United States in January 1944. In an address to a

joint session of Congress on January 20, he confirmed Venezuelan adherence to the United Nations, and said that all Venezuelan resources and raw materials would be placed at the Allies' service.

Venezuela declared war on Germany and Japan on February 16, 1945, and on March 14 established diplomatic relations with the U.S.S.R.

The most important event in Mexico of the years 1944–45 was the conference of the Foreign Ministers of all the member States of the Pan-American Union (except

MEXICO Argentina) which, at Mexico's suggestion, met at Mexico City on February 21, 1945. It reaffirmed the solidarity among the American States in face of any menace of aggression from outside the continent, and drew up the Act of Chapultepec (so called after the Presidential residence in

which the sittings were held), which laid it down that every attack on the integrity or sovereignty of an American State should be considered an act of aggression against all, and that the Republics should consider the conclusion of a treaty, to constitute a regional arrangement within the general international organization outlined at Dumbarton Oaks, whereby any such threat could be met by force if necessary.

The conference also recommended that the Governments represented should consider the creation as soon as possible of an agency composed of representatives of their General Staffs to organize better

military collaboration between them; that the "American system" should be further strengthened by yearly meetings of the Foreign Ministers and four-yearly inter-State conferences; that refuge should be refused to war criminals; that Axis activities within any American jurisdiction should be prevented; and that censorship of press and radio should be removed as soon as possible.

On August 1, 1944, Mexico signed a treaty of friendship with China, after a year's negotiations.

A Mexican Expeditionary Air Force arrived in Manila on May 1, 1945, to fight with, and as part of, the U.S.A. 5th A.F. against Japan. The setting up of a Spanish Republican Government in exile in Mexico City in August 1945 is described in page 3948. On

September 12, 1945, the Mexican Government nationalized all deposits of uranium, actinium, and other radioactive substances (of which a number existed in Mexico).

Other Spanish American Republics establishing or resuming diplomatic relations with the Soviet Union during 1944 and 1945 were Costa Rica (May 11, 1944), Nicaragua (December 17, 1944), Bolivia (March 20, 1945), Guatemala (April 19, 1945), and the Dominican Republic (June 29, 1945).

The Second Great War brought many changes to Latin America. The demand for raw materials and minerals led to the

DEFENCE OF THE CARIBBEAN SEA

Soon after Colombia declared a 'state of belligerency' (see page 2960), General Domingo Espinel, Colombian Chief of Staff, visited General George H. Brett, U.S. Chief of the Caribbean Defence Command, to co-ordinate Colombian with other forces in the area : he is here seen in the gunner's seat of an A.A. gun at an outpost. Left, badges of the Caribbean Defence forces : south area (black sword and cutlass on yellow, with black border), left : north area (black and white sea-horse on khaki with red bar), right. (See also page 2813.) *Photo, Keystone*

exploitation of the natural resources of the continent. Moreover, as supplies of manufactured goods from Europe and United States were largely cut off, many nations were obliged to develop their national industries. Many regions, such as the state of São Paulo in Brazil, became centres for the manufacture of textiles, clothing and machinery. This resulted in a considerable increase in prosperity for some classes, but there was also a steep rise in the cost of living. Much popular discontent was evident, and this provided political leaders with an excuse for overthrowing and attempting to overthrow existing Governments. Nearly all the revolutionaries put forward a programme of extreme nationalism, combined with a promise for the amelioration of the conditions of the working class.

November 1. British warships arrived at Surabaya to evacuate Dutch women and children. British Intelligence decided to presume Hitler dead. Conference of United Nations Educational and Cultural Organization opened in London. U.S. Congress voted $550,000,000 for U.N.R.R.A. New Greek Cabinet formed under Mr. Kanelopoulis.

November 2. Rioting in Cairo and Alexandria and demonstrations in Syria and the Lebanon on the 28th anniversary of the Balfour Declaration ; Lord Gort resigned as High Commissioner in Palestine. Belgian Government published notes on interview between Hitler and King Leopold.

November 3. Lord Wavell saw Pandit Nehru. Bardossy, former Hungarian Prime Minister, found guilty of treason and condemned to be executed.

November 4. French Foreign Minister declared that France would oppose central administration for Germany ; France decided to give Cambodia internal autonomy. Polling in Hungarian general election. Anti-Jewish rioting in Tripoli.

November 5. Dr. van Mook issued declaration of policy of the Netherlands East Indies Government, proposing commonwealth status. Eight Finnish politicians, including ex-President Ryti, arrested on treason charges. Chinese Government forces arriving at Yingkow found Communists in control. Mr. F. J. Burrows appointed Governor of Bengal.

November 6. First session of the French Constituent Assembly held in Paris.

November 7. Soviet-Turkish treaty of friendship and neutrality (denounced by Russia on March 19) expired ; Mr. Byrnes disclosed details of U.S. communication about control of Dardanelles. World air-speed record broken at Herne Bay, Kent, by two British Meteor jet-propelled aircraft averaging over 603 and 606 m.p.h. respectively.

November 8. General Mansergh warned " lawless mob " in Surabaya that they would be disarmed. Announced in Chungking that Government forces were retreating in Hopei province. Lieutenant-General Sir Alan Cunningham appointed High Commissioner for Palestine and Transjordan. Trouble between Royalists and Communists in Bucharest.

November 9. General Mansergh gave 24-hour ultimatum to Indonesians in Surabaya to lay down arms. Mr. Attlee left London for Washington. Reparations Conference opened in Paris.

November 10. Lieutenant - General Wedemeyer, U.S. C.-in-C., China, announced that all U.S. forces would be withdrawn from China by early spring. British forces attacked in Surabaya. Council of Arab League approved common policy on Palestine. U.S. and U.K. recognized Albanian Government on condition that free elections were held at an early date.

November 11. In Washington, Mr. Attlee began talks with President Truman and Mr. Mackenzie King. Polling in Yugoslav general election. Hungarian leaders agreed to form coalition. In London Remembrance Day ceremony at Cenotaph for the first time commemorated the dead of both First and Second Great Wars.

November 12. King Farouk, opening Egyptian Parliament, spoke on Anglo-Egyptian relations and unity of the Nile Valley. China asked Russia for permission to transport Government troops to Manchuria by air to take over as Soviet armies left.

November 13. In Washington, Mr. Attlee addressed joint session of Congress. General de Gaulle unanimously elected head of Government in France. Mr. Bevin announced in House of Commons formation of Anglo-U.S. Committee of Inquiry on Palestine. Shelling by Indonesian-manned guns in Surabaya.

November 14. In Java, new Indonesian cabinet formed under Mr. Sjahrir. Rioting broke out in Tel-Aviv in protest against British proposal for Palestine inquiry. Fierce fighting in Shanhaikwan region of N. China.

November 15. General de Gaulle refused to give Communists any of the " key " portfolios in new French Government. Trial of 40 persons concerned with Dachau concentration camp began at Frankfort. In Budapest, Mr. Zoltan Tildy's coalition Government took over from Hungarian Provisional National Assembly.

November 16. Separatist rebellion broke out in Azerbaijan, N. Persia. Mr. Churchill addressed joint session of Belgian Parliament. Constitution of United Nations Educational, Scientific and Cultural Organization signed in London ; conference concluded. Allied Military Government took over Krupps works at Essen.

November 17. Britain recognized Hungarian Government. Mr. Attlee and Mr. Mackenzie King arrived in Ottawa. U.S. informed Bulgaria that results of forthcoming elections were not likely to be recognized.

November 18. Eleven of the 44 accused in the Belsen trial condemned to death. Insurgents took Mianeh, key railway centre in N. Persia, marching towards Teheran. The liner " Queen Mary " docked at Southampton with 3,459 British ex-prisoners of war from the Far East.

November 19. Announced that Chinese Government forces had taken Shanhaikwan, Manchuria, from the Communists. Government's 80 per cent majority in Bulgarian elections announced. French Assembly confirmed General de Gaulle as head of Government. Mr. Attlee addressed joint session of the Canadian Parliament.

November 20. Learned that Persian forces, en route for Azerbaijan, had been turned back by the Red Army. Nuremberg trial of leading Nazis opened. Greek Regent announced postponement of Greek plebiscite until 1948 ; Mr. Kanelopoulis resigned ; Mr. Sophoulis formed new Cabinet. Announced that all Dutch and Amboinese troops were to be withdrawn from Java.

November 21. General de Gaulle issued names of his Cabinet, with himself as Head of Government and of Armed Forces and Minister of Defence. Sir Alan Cunningham, new High Commissioner arrived in Jerusalem.

November 22. Indonesian nationalists, headed by Mr. Sjahrir and Amir Sjarifudin, refused to attend meeting with Dutch. British arms and ammunition at Adraselain, Palestine, stolen by Jews disguised as R.A.F. men. Rioting in Calcutta as protest against trial of " Indian National Army " officers.

November 23. Final result of Yugoslav elections disclosed 90 per cent for Marshal Tito. U.S. Government asked Russia for information about Red Army action in N. Persia. Allied council reached agreement on Austrian currency plan.

November 24. Preparatory Commission of U.N. held inaugural meeting in London. In Italy, Signor Parri's Government resigned. U.S. Government sent note to Russia proposing that all Soviet, British and U.S. forces in Persia be withdrawn by January 1, 1946. Rationing of all food except sugar ended in U.S. Chinese Government forces claimed capture of Hulutao from Chinese Communists in Manchuria.

November 25. Palestine police stations north of Tel-Aviv blown up by armed Jews. " National Congress of Azerbaijan " demanded autonomy within framework of the Persian State.

November 26. In Palestine, British troops held arms search in Jewish settlement of Shefaim, forced to open fire on Jews at Hogla. Herr Figl's People's Party secured clear majority in Austrian elections held previous day. General MacNarney arrived in Frankfort to succeed General Eisenhower in command of U.S. occupation forces. Chiang Kai-shek created Supreme Economic Council for China.

November 27. Major-General Hurley, U.S. Ambassador in Chungking, resigned. Anton Mussert, Dutch Nazi leader, appeared before special court at The Hague on treason charge. Emperor, opening Diet, urged Japanese to " do your best."

November 28. Russians ordered Chinese Communists to leave Changchung and Mukden ; Chinese Government forces to be flown in. Lieutenant-General Sir Archibald Nye appointed Governor of Madras. Announced that the Böhm and Voss shipyards at Hamburg would be handed over to the Russians.

November 29. Replying to Persian note, Russia declared she would not prevent Persian troops entering Azerbaijan but would have to increase occupation forces in order to maintain peace. Yugoslav Constituent Assembly proclaimed Republic ; King Peter and his family deprived of all rights.

November 30. Bill submitted to French Constituent Assembly for nationalization of Bank of France and four principal deposit banks.

Chapter 384

THE NEUTRALS AND ALLIED VICTORY

With the liberation of Europe from the Nazi menace, the situation in Spain came once more into international prominence. Moves by the Republicans, by General Franco, and the United Nations form the major part of this chapter on the history of the neutral countries of Europe during 1944 and 1945. Other countries covered are Portugal, Sweden, Switzerland, and Eire. For their history in 1943, see Chapter 312

ALL official flags in Portugal were flown at half mast from the announcement of Hitler's death on May 3 until noon on May 4. All German diplomatic and official property was seized on the 6th.

PORTUGAL Twelve days later the Premier, Dr. Salazar, declared that his foreign policy would remain based on the alliance with Britain and friendly relations with the United States. The bases in the Azores granted to Great Britain in 1943 (*see* page 3152) and to the United States were formally returned to Portugal on June 2, 1946.

Internal censorship was removed on October 12, 1945, but as the Press almost unanimously took advantage of this to attack the Government, Dr. Salazar re-imposed it two days later. General elections held on November 18 gave the Government a majority, but as the opposition had in the main boycotted them, the result was not a true index of popular feeling.

The food situation continued difficult, and a drought which did not break until September 7 did great harm to the crops.

At the beginning of February the United States Press published accounts of letters said to have passed between Mr. Churchill and General Franco. Though the text of the letters was not published until September 18, the substantial correctness of the American reports was admitted in London. On November 23, 1944, General Franco had in fact written to Mr. Churchill suggesting that as Spain, the United Kingdom and Germany were the only " virile " powers left in Europe, they should face the " Russian peril " together. Mr. Churchill, replying in mid-January after consulting with President Roosevelt and Mr. Stalin, referred to the British desire for friendly relations with the Spanish people, but dismissed Franco's overtures, and made it clear that there was no question of the British Government supporting the Spanish claim to participate in the peace conference.

SPAIN

Undeterred, General Franco continued his efforts to find favour with the Allies. He released the Italian

cruiser " Attilio Regolo " and four Italian destroyers, held since the Italian surrender. His Foreign Minister, Señor Lequerica, on January 17, told the American Press that Spain had never been anything but neutral—her adherence to the Anti-Comintern Pact had been purely defensive. In March, Franco sent a strong protest to Tokyo demanding an explanation of atrocities against Spanish subjects in the Philippines and the destruction of their property, with an intimation that Spain would cease to safeguard Japanese interests (as she had been doing since Japan entered the war) in countries with which Japan was at war. Breaking off of diplomatic relations was announced on April 12.

On the cease-fire in Europe, Spain broke off all relations with Germany, sequestered German official property, and " froze " all Axis credits in the country. On May 12, however, at a requiem mass for Hitler the Falangists turned up in force.

Meanwhile, at San Francisco, a motion had been adopted making membership of the United Nations open to all peace-loving nations accepting the obligations of the United Nations Charter, but not to defeated Axis Governments or those imposed in any manner by the military forces of the Axis. Señor Quintanilla, delegate for Mexico, the mover of the resolution, made it clear that the second disqualification applied specifically to Falangist Spain. The communiqué issued after the Berlin Conference stated that the three Governments represented at Potsdam (the United Kingdom, the United States, and the Soviet Union) " feel bound to make it clear that they would not favour any application for membership of the United Nations put forward by the present Spanish Government which, having been founded with the support of the Axis Powers, does not, in view of its origin, nature, record and close association with aggressor states, possess the qualification necessary to justify such membership." The Spanish Government rejected as " arbitrary and

Spain and the United Nations

LISBON CELEBRATES V.E. DAY

Portugal's unofficial celebration of the end of the war in Europe included demonstrations with prolonged cheers and the waving of Allied flags outside the British and American embassies in Lisbon. Here, making the ' V ' sign and cheering, crowds cram the street outside the British Embassy. On May 18, 1945, Dr. Salazar, Portugal's Premier, announced that his foreign policy would remain based on friendship with Britain and the United States. *Photo, Associated Press*

SPANISH REPUBLICANS IN EXILE

Following the election of Mr. Martiñez Barrio as President, a new Spanish Government in exile was announced from Mexico on August 30, 1945, with Mr. Jose Giral as Premier. Above, in the front row, stand President Barrio (wearing spectacles) with Mr. Giral. (centre) surrounded by members of his Cabinet. On the same day the regime of President Barrio was recognized by Mexico as the Government of Spain.
Photo, Pictorial Press

Junta de Liberacion, formed in Mexico in November 1943, headed by Martiñez Barrio, President of the last Republican Cortes ; and a small group in London headed by Dr. Negrin, the last Republican Prime Minister.

On January 10, 1945, the Republican Spanish Cortes met for the first time in Mexico. Attempts to unite the Spaniards in exile followed. Dr. Negrin, who arrived in Paris on January 26, secured the support of the Spanish Communist Party in Paris and of the *Junta Nacional*. In mid-August the Cortes met again in Mexico City, Dr. Negrin being present. Diplomatic representatives of the Soviet Union, France, Czechoslovakia, Sweden, Uruguay, Peru, Venezuela, Colombia, Ecuador, and Nicaragua attended. Señor Martiñez Barrio was elected President of the Spanish Republic. Negrin resigned the Premiership, and Barrio asked Dr. José Giral (Prime Minister at the outbreak of the military rebellion in July 1936) to form a new Cabinet. Dr. Negrin and the Communists refused to participate in his Government, but undertook not to oppose it. On August 30, Mexico, which had never recognized Franco, recognized the Barrio-Giral Government as the Government of Spain.

(margin note) Republican Government in Exile

One great success the exiled Spanish Republican Government in Mexico City scored : the resolution against Franco Spain presented by the Mexican delegate at San Francisco and adopted with

unjust " these expressions concerning Spain ; but the prospects of the acceptance of Spain under Franco as a member of the United Nations did not improve.

The relations of Franco Spain with France were complicated by the presence in France of a large body of Spanish exiles, estimated at 130,000, and including more than 10,000 former soldiers of the Republican Army, who were active members of the French Resistance, and in the early part of 1945 were among the forces surrounding German-occupied La Rochelle. After

the liberation of the south of France, an uneasy situation developed along the Spanish frontier. One body of former members of the Spanish Republican Army, variously estimated at from 250 to 800 strong, crossed the border in the Roncal Valley on October 3, 1944, and was repulsed by Spanish frontier troops in six days' fighting. Spanish Republicans also took over the consulates of their country at Perpignan, Marseilles, Toulouse, Pau and Bordeaux, leaving only Paris and Hendaye in the hands of representatives appointed by the *de facto* Government of Spain.

Incidents continued on the frontier until on October 27 units of the Spanish Army opened an offensive near Andorra, and in three days drove the Republicans from the Aran Valley. On October 29, the French Provisional Government ordered Spanish Republicans to quit a zone twelve miles wide along the frontier, and to hand over to the French authorities for return to the Madrid Government the consulates they had seized. In pursuance of the French right to maintain order in Andorra which had existed since the time of Charlemagne, a hundred armed French gendarmes entered Andorra on November 14, and Franco later sent 107 Civil Guards to balance them.

At the beginning of 1945, the Spanish Republicans abroad were divided into three groups : the *Junta Nacional* at Toulouse in France, predominantly Communist, but including also Catholics, Basques and Catalans, and headed by Juan Hernandez, who had been one of the organizers of the Maquis (this body was responsible for the border disturbances in the autumn of 1944) ; the

ROYAL CLAIMANT

Don Juan, pretender to the Spanish throne, on March 22, 1945, handed a note to the Spanish Minister in Berne for transmission to Franco demanding the latter's resignation so as to leave the way open for a restoration of the monarchy which ' alone can provide an effective guarantee for religion, order and liberty.' He is here at his typewriter.

Photo, Associated Press

REPUBLICAN LEADER

Dr. Juan Negrin, last Republican Prime Minister in Spain, whose Government was overthrown in the Spanish Civil War. He fled to London where he continued to lead the section of the Spanish Republicans in exile in England. He went to Mexico in 1945. Before entering politics, he was Professor of Physiology at the University of Madrid.
Photo, Keystone

AT TANGIER

Occupied by Spain since June 1940, Tangier again became an international zone on October 11, 1945, and the sovereign rights of the Sultan of Morocco were re-established. Nations on the Control Committee were: Britain, the U.S., France, Spain, Portugal, Holland and Belgium. Here, the Mendoub (centre), representing the Sultan, arrives on board a French cruiser which also carried Moroccan troops to police the zone.

Photo, New York Times Photos

acclamation was directly traceable to the successful lobbying of four of its members.

Franco's Government was attacked from another direction on March 22, when Don Juan, claimant of the Spanish throne, demanded Franco's resignation

Don Juan Issues a Manifesto

so as to leave the way open for the restoration of the monarchy, and issued a manifesto to the Spanish people suggesting that the monarchy "alone can provide an effective guarantee for religion, order and liberty." This move, however, caused much less stir inside Spain than had been expected. A few Monarchist Ministers and officials withdrew from office, but in general Don Juan's move was felt to be ill-timed. Overtures from Franco to Don Juan made in August met with a rebuff—the Prince resisted any idea of becoming the "inheritor" of the Franco regime.

On May 2, 1945, Laval and his wife, with four other Vichy Ministers, arrived at Barcelona in a Junkers 88 with a German crew. Though requested to leave, he refused to do so, and was interned in the fortress of Montjuich, the Spanish Government refusing to extra-

dite him since he was not classed as a war criminal by the United Nations but was simply wanted by France for trial as a traitor. This brought to a head the hostility felt in France against the Franco regime. Towards the end of May the French Provisional Government sounded Great Britain and America as to the possibility of taking joint action on the Spanish question. But they were not prepared to act against him, though documents covering the period June 1940 to December 1943 captured by their forces in Germany and published on March 4, 1946, provided evidence of Spain's willingness to enter the war on the side of the Axis on condition that Gibraltar, French Morocco and part of Algeria were handed over to her.

The attack by an angry crowd at Chambéry on a trainload of Spaniards, diplomats and others, en route from Switzerland, in the mistaken belief that among them were stragglers from the Blue Division returning home, further strained French-Spanish relations, and on June 21 Spain closed the frontier for three months.

Laval, after ninety days' internment, asked to be allowed to surrender to the United Nations, and on July 31 left an airfield near Barcelona in the same aircraft in which he had arrived.

The penal code of Spain was revised on January 13 to include the death sentence for assaults, and prison terms of 20–30 years for insults and other crimes, against General Franco.

On April 13, eve of the anniversary of the establishment of the Republic

NAZI GOLD IN MADRID

At the Barajas airport, Madrid, in January 1946, a U.S. soldier loads bags of German gold on board an American transport aircraft. The money, £250,000 in all, was turned over to the Allied Control Council in Frankfort, including British and U.S. currency, it had been handed to the Spanish Government by the Nazis in Spain after Germany surrendered.

Photo, Associated Press

in 1931, Franco announced that all political charges pending against Spanish Republicans would be dropped, and that consular officials had been authorized to accept applications from exiles to return. The conditional release

SPAIN CLOSES THE FRONTIER

Relations between France and Franco Spain became increasingly strained after the liberation of southern France, and on June 21, 1945, Franco closed the frontier for three months. Here, at the frontier post at Béhobie-Irun three privileged travellers cross the International Bridge over the Bidassoa River into Spain.

Photo, Associated Press

Sweden sheltered some 48,000 war refugees. Two thousand from Baltic countries taken over by Russia after the war refused to return home, some hunger-striking, others threatening mass-suicide. Left, Balts due for repatriation at Ranneslatt camp, Sweden.

Three Scandinavian premiers met to discuss post-war co-operation at a Trades Union Conference at Stockholm on July 23, 1945. They were (left to right), Mr. Einar Gerhardsen (Norway); Mr. Albin Hansson (Sweden) and Mr. Vilhelm Buhl (Denmark).

The Royal Navy was the first foreign navy to revisit Sweden after the war. Here, the 9,100-ton cruiser H.M.S. 'Birmingham' lies moored behind the still camouflaged Swedish warship 'Sverige,' of 7,000 tons, in Stockholm in early October, 1945.

PEACE MOVES VIA SWEDEN

While on Red Cross duties in Germany, Count Folke Bernadotte, head of the Swedish Red Cross and nephew of King Gustav, met Himmler at Lübeck on April 24, 1945, at the latter's request. Himmler told him that Hitler had only a few days to live and that he (Himmler) was in a position to offer Germany's surrender to Britain and the United States, but not to Russia. He asked that this offer should at once be conveyed to the Allied Powers. Above, Count Bernadotte (left) on arrival in Stockholm on May 1. With him are Mr. Edvin Guenther (centre), Swedish Foreign Minister, and Mr. Axel Bohman, Swedish ambassador to France. Left, crowds celebrate peace in Stockholm.

Photos, Planet; Associated Press, Topical; G.P.U.

of another 2,000 long-term political prisoners was reported on April 22, and of a further 1,032 on August 22. A Bill of Rights, based on the Constitution of 1876, and proclaiming as the guiding principle of the acts of the Spanish State, " respect for the dignity, integrity, and liberty of man " was unanimously approved by the Cortes on July 13. The Falangist salute, hitherto obligatory, was abolished by a decree of September 13. On the other hand, there were numerous fresh arrests of " communists " and others, indicating a state of unrest whose roots lay in economic distress. In 1945 Spain, like Portugal, suffered from drought. For the third year in succession she had a bad harvest, and the exhaustion of her water reserves caused not only actual shortages of water, but also serious cuts in her electricity supplies.

A decree published in Madrid on October 5 vested control of all areas containing radio-active minerals in the Spanish Government—several areas of Spain produce ore containing uranium.

A conference in Paris from August 10–31 of representatives of France, Great Britain, the United States and the Soviet Union called upon the Spanish Government to evacuate the Tangier international zone, occupied by Franco in June 1940 (*see* page 1150). The Spanish Government's acceptance of the Paris decisions was announced on September 19, and international administration of Tangier came into effect once more on October 11.

The help rendered by Sweden to her neighbours grew : on February 3 it was stated that 137,000 Norwegian children in 987 places were being **SWEDEN** given a meal every day at Swedish expense (compared with 500 in 1942 and 115,000 in 1944). In addition, 80,000 meals were being given to old people and 500,000 daily rations to 100 refugee camps in Norway. Including gifts and credits, Sweden's aid to Norway, Denmark, Finland and the Netherlands totalled 3,000,000,000 kroner by June. The help Sweden gave in the form of food meant a cut during the year of the Swedish bread ration by seven per cent (to 167 grammes daily), of the fat ration by twenty per cent, sugar by 5.5 per cent, meat by forty per cent.

On April 29, the Swedish Foreign Office announced that Count Bernadotte, Vice-President of the Swedish Red Cross (who was in Germany in connexion with the repatriation of Swedes living in that country) had been approached by Himmler, who told him that Hitler was a dying man not expected to live more than two or three days, and that he (Himmler) was in a position to offer Germany's capitulation to Great Britain and the United States, but not to Russia, and asked that the Swedish Government should pass on this offer. This was done. In reply, President Truman telegraphed for the three Allies that the only acceptable terms were unconditional surrender to all of them, which message was delivered to Himmler by Count Bernadotte.

On June 18, the Swedish Foreign Office announced that German legations and consulates in Sweden had been sealed and were being held at the disposal of the Allies, while former German diplomats would be handed over if necessary. In a tribute to the Allies in the name of the Swedish people, the Foreign Minister, Professor Oesten Unden admitted on August 16 that the Allied victory had saved Sweden from destruction.

Ten thousand forced foreign workers from Germany, including inmates of Belsen camp, were received in Sweden at the Government's expense for treatment and recuperation. The first contingent left Lübeck on June 25.

Documents discovered in Berlin revealed that early in 1942 Hitler had ordered plans for the invasion of Sweden to be put into effect before that

BRITISH LEAVE TRAINS TRAVEL VIA SWITZERLAND
To shorten the long journey for British forces returning home on leave from Italy, the Swiss Government in July 1945 granted permission for them to travel by train through Swiss territory. Here, at Brig, near Lausanne, a leave train packed with British troops draws into the station.
Photo, Keystone

'STAND DOWN' PARADE OF THE SWISS ARMY
On August 19, 1945, the wartime armed forces of Switzerland held a 'stand down' parade in Berne's Parliament Square. Below, standard bearers march past the Parliament buildings. On the saluting base, from left to right, stand : Mr. Enrico Cleio, Minister of Posts and Railways ; Mr. Carl Kobelt, Minister of War ; President Eduard von Steiger ; and General Henri Guisan, Chief of Staff.
Photo, Keystone

REPERCUSSIONS OF WAR IN SWITZERLAND

1. Allied aircraft which landed on Swiss territory during the war and held at Dübendorf. Of 130 machines, 90 American aircraft were made airworthy and flown back to the U.S. 2. Wooden props that had served to strengthen cellars used as air-raid shelters are sawn up for fuel in Berne. 3. Woman tram-conductor in Basle; as in Britain, women replaced men in Swiss public transport services when man-power was short. 4. Outside Geneva, French rolling-stock, with imports from France, is loaded on a special chassis to be drawn through the town by tram and transferred to the Swiss State Railways system.

3952

year's summer campaign against Russia. The Swedish Government was, however, warned by an unknown civilian, and the invasion was never attempted.

The substitution of English for German as the principal foreign language taught in schools was announced on November 14.

Six Swiss towns along the border were accidentally bombed by American aircraft on February 22, when 18 people were killed, 30 injured. Bombs dropped on Basle and Zürich **SWITZERLAND** on March 4 caused no deaths, but resulted in injuries to a number of people, and twenty fires (twelve of them large) were started in Basle when one of the aircraft, hit by Swiss flak, exploded in the air, scattering its cargo of incendiaries. As a result of these further accidents, it was decided to paint white crosses on roofs, stations and buildings along the entire Swiss frontier. (*See* illustration in page 3158.)

Protests by Mr. Stettinius on behalf of the United States State Department against the continued passage of German war supplies through Switzerland led to a meeting of United States, British, and French representatives with the Swiss authorities and an agreement on March 8 under which trade with Germany was to be reduced to five per cent of 1942 figures, this percentage allowable only

on condition that Germany paid in goods, not gold; Germany was denied facilities for carrying material into and out of north Italy; and the carriage across Switzerland of coal, iron, steel and scrap iron was prohibited. Decrees were made on February 16 and March 3 designed to prevent concealment in Switzerland of German assets and irregular dealings in banknotes.

Complaints made in the spring by the Russians as to the treatment of Russian refugees were investigated by a Swiss-Russian commission which included also a French representative. It found that there was ground for the complaints; but the Swiss authorities pleaded the language difficulty and the indiscipline of some of the 10,000 Russians among the 270,000 refugees who had entered their country. The Soviet members of the commission declared that conditions in the camps had been entirely satisfactory since their arrival.

General Guison resigned his wartime appointment as Commander-in-Chief on June 20, and on August 20 the army ceased to be on an active footing. The Swiss Government revealed on October 4 that it had been fully informed of various German plans of invasion, the danger of which had been most acute in March 1943 when thirty German divisions were massed on the frontier.

When President Roosevelt died, in April 1945, Mr. de Valera not only visited Mr. John Gray, American Minister in Dublin, but **EIRE** also ordered all official flags to be flown at half-mast, and moved the adjournment of the Dail.

On receipt of the news of Hitler's death, Mr. de Valera, accompanied by the Secretary of the Department of External Affairs, called on Dr. Hempel, the German Minister in Dublin, to express his country's condolences. Apart from Portugal, Eire was the only country to take such action. When attacked in the Dail on July 19, Mr. de Valera defended his action as in accordance with established procedure, and said that it implied "no question of approval, disapproval or judgement of any kind."

On May 8, Dr. Hempel called on Mr. de Valera and handed over the German Legation premises. The keys were handed to the American Minister, representing the United Nations, on May 10.

With the abolition of the censorship on May 11 the Press gave Eire on May 12 the first accounts published there of the Nazi terror in Europe, and also of the part played in the war by Irish-

GERMAN LEGATION RADIO
On May 10, 1945, Eire officials handed to Mr. John Gray, U.S. Minister in Dublin, as representing the United Nations, the keys of the German legation there. Above, radio receiver, formerly owned by Dr. Edouard Hempel, German Minister in Dublin, which, with other German legation property, was auctioned in Belfast. *Photo, Keystone*

NEW EIRE PRESIDENT
Mr. Sean T. O'Kelly, Eire's Minister of Finance and Fianna Fail (Government) candidate, was on June 16, 1945, elected President of Eire. He succeeded Dr. Douglas Hyde, the 84-year-old first President, who finished his seven-year term on June 25. Here, Mr. O'Kelly (at table) is inaugurated on June 29 in Dublin Castle. Mr. de Valera stands on his right.
Photo, Keystone

men. The ban on war films was removed at the same time, as well as a number of other emergency restrictions.

The Dail unanimously adopted a proposal made by Mr. de Valera on May 18 to spend £3,000,000 for the relief of distress in Europe, and shiploads of food, clothing and livestock were sent to the Netherlands, France, and Belgium. An Irish team of 25 doctors and 25 nurses went to the Continent to work with U.N.R.R.A.

Demobilization of the armed forces, to be spread over a year, began on November 1. Private motoring was resumed on November 12, late omnibuses ran again in Dublin from November 26.

Mr. de Valera's statement in the Dail on July 11 in answer to a question that Eire was a republic led to a lively debate, but no modification by the Prime Minister of his position.

Mr. Lemass, Minister of Commerce, announced on June 20 that twenty Irish ships, with 138 lives, were lost during the war, sixteen of them through belligerent action.

Chapter 385

THE SECOND GREAT WAR IN RETROSPECT

Contemporaneous military history is inevitably written under the disadvantage of incomplete information, particularly as regards strategical plans, objects aimed at and resources actually available to each of the combatants. All these are carefully guarded secrets. Furthermore it is impossible to know how much the opponents knew of the situation on the other side when they made their plans. But such points are cleared up completely only long afterwards. The Military Editor, Major-General Sir Charles Gwynn, K.C.B., D.S.O., therefore, here reviews the chief strategical situations and decisions of the war in the light of all available but incomplete knowledge

THE Second Great War obviously divided itself into four main phases : (a) the phase of inactivity ; (b) the phase in which the defeat of France made the ultimate survival of the British Commonwealth questionable ; (c) the phase which started with German failure at Moscow and the entry of America into the war, assuring the survival of Britain, though the complete defeat of Germany and Japan was still uncertain ; and (d) the phase which began with the Russian recovery at Stalingrad and Rommel's defeat at Alamein, leading up to ultimate decisive victory over Germany. Once that was achieved final victory over Japan could be foreseen with certainty. The crisis of this period was reached on June 6, 1944, and passed with the break-out from Normandy.

In the first phase the defeat of Poland was inevitable. The Germans, with immense superiority of equipment, a dominating strategic position improved by the occupation of Austria and Czechoslovakia, and holding the initiative, had crushing advantages. The Russian invasion of her eastern provinces eliminated the last possibility of Poland's prolonging the struggle, and neither Britain nor France was in a position to intervene effectively.

In 1946, German generals asserted that the Siegfried line, incomplete and lightly held, could have been broken, **Views of German Generals** but that assertion probably depends on unjustified assumptions regarding France's numerical strength and the state of training and equipment of her army. They assume too that France was prepared to violate the neutrality of Belgium. They also claimed that they looked on the Polish war as an isolated incident and were not associated with Hitler's more ambitious designs ; that they expected that France and Britain, confronted with the *fait accompli* of Poland's defeat, would accept a negotiated peace.

Such statements, if they approximate to truth, may account for the divergent views held by Hitler and his General Staff as to the next step they should take after the conquest of Poland. Hitler appears to have wanted an immediate invasion of the Netherlands. It may also account for the unpreparedness of the Germans to undertake an invasion of Britain when their attack on France had met with complete success.

Although Gamelin was almost certainly well justified in not attempting a major invasion of Germany, in view of the condition of his army and the neutrality of Belgium, his extreme inactivity and obsession with defensive theories cannot be excused. We still do not know what plans, if any, of ultimate offensive action were contemplated by which alone the defeat of Germany could be accomplished, and which alone would have justified the claim that time was on the side of the Allies. We do know the deplorable effects of inactivity on the morale of the French nation and army ; and the establishment of unity of command of the Allied armies, from which so much was hoped, proved merely to have made Lord Gort's task more difficult. General Eisenhower was later to show how effectively unity of command can operate ; but even in his case, unity and energy in the supreme direction of the war effort were essential factors in making unity of command a reality.

How far the invasion of Norway paid Germany in the long run seems doubtful. It certainly added immensely to the tasks of the Royal Navy and the R.A.F., but it involved Germany in numerous disasters and left her in the final phase of the war without the use of a defensive detachment of considerable size. The British immediate attempt to retrieve the situation with untrained and under-equipped troops was apparently one of the consequences of the establishment of unity of command, for Gamelin would not at first agree to the withdrawal of trained troops from France. What troops from France achieved at Narvik suggests

that their earlier employment in the Trondheim region might have met with success.

When the German main offensive started, Gamelin's advance to the Dyle presumably was mainly dictated by the desire to support the Belgians and Dutch and thereby to add to his numerical strength. **Reason for Advance to the Dyle** As a purely strategical move it entailed obvious risks, increased by the fact that he took slow and inadequate measures to defend his flank, and that he retained his main reserve behind the strongest part of the Maginot line. Whether the decision in itself was wrong, or whether it was vitiated by faulty execution, must be left to future historians to decide. It can be noted, however, how curiously the course of action diverged from the passive attitude adopted previously.

The German plan of campaign we now know was not, as in 1914, long prearranged, but was devised during the winter, and was based largely on experiences gained in Poland. It was a bold plan unhampered by scruples ; but it by no means ensured the decisive success it achieved, even granting the German superiority in armaments. Superiority in executive skill and more energetic leadership were the decisive factors.

Having overrun France and having virtually disarmed the British Army, Hitler believed that Britain could not continue the struggle, and by the time he realized that she was still undefeated the opportunity to exploit his success farther had begun to pass. Although preparations for the invasion of England had not been made, it is conceivable that an immediate improvised attempt to secure a bridge-head and cross-Channel airfields might have succeeded. As it was, the plans later made for invasion would seem to have been over-elaborate, and involved the employment of forces for which adequate shipping could not be provided. The Battle of Britain, though undoubtedly a decisive factor, did not cause the

RECONSTRUCTION IN GERMANY

When the Allied Control Council took over the internal government of Germany on June 5, 1945, among its most urgent tasks was the reorganization of public life and the restoration of Germany's shattered communications. Berlin, the capital, was divided into four sectors—British, U.S., Russian and French—its administration as a whole being controlled by the inter-Allied 'Komendatura.' 1. Berlin women, under Soviet direction, forming a 'human chain,' pass along pails of rubble in an effort to clear a badly damaged site. 2. Also in the capital—near the Victory Column in the Tiergarten—hungry Berliners clamour for biscuits being served to them from a Canadian Salvation Army mobile canteen. 3. From a bridge spanning the Kiel Canal, a 'Desert Rat,' formerly of the Berlin garrison, watches a passing merchantman. The famous canal was reopened in June 1945, but was not completely dredged until the end of the year.

Photos, Keystone; G.N.S.

HITLER'S DEFEATED ARMIES RETURN TO THE SHATTERED REICH

An urgent and widespread problem engaging the attention of the Allied Military Government in Germany throughout the autumn and winter of 1945 was the maintenance, disbandment and transport home of several million ex-members of the Wehrmacht taken prisoner as the Allied armies closed in on the defeated Reich. Some had trudged on foot across half Europe, almost all were in rags and in deep dejection. This ragged group back from captivity in Russia was typical of many among Berlin's ruins in the winter of 1945.

Photo, Associated Press

WORLD PEACE ORGANIZATION FOUNDED AT SAN FRANCISCO

The United Nations Conference on International Organization was opened at San Francisco on April 25, 1945 (see Chap. 381) by President Truman, whose inaugural address, broadcast from Washington, is here being relayed to the delegates assembled in the San Francisco Opera House. The conference was attended in its opening stages by representatives of 46 nations. Speeches were made by representatives of the four sponsoring Powers—Mr. E. R. Stettinius (U.S.A.), Mr. Anthony Eden (Britain), Mr. Molotov (U.S.S.R.), and Dr. Soong (China).

Photo, Fox Photos

ITALY'S ONLY AIRCRAFT CARRIER, THE 'AQUILA' (FORMERLY THE LINER 'ROMA')

In October 1940, having no aircraft carriers, Italy began the conversion into one of the turbine passenger-liner 'Roma' (30,816 tons gross), renaming her the 'Aquila.' Her speed as a liner of 21 knots being inadequate, she was re-engined with four sets of Parsons turbines whose combined S.H.P. of 240,000 increased her speed to over 30 knots. A wooden flight-deck 705 feet long was laid over a hangar measuring 500 by 59 feet, divided into four sections by fireproof curtains. There were two lifts measuring 44 by 48 feet. When Italy surrendered in September 1943, the ship was at Genoa ready for sea trials. The Germans at once ceased work on her Here, the 'Roma' lies in Genoa harbour after the war. Note the anti-torpedo nets still draping her side. Photo, Associated Press

immediate abandonment of the invasion project; lack of suitable craft and fear of British naval action were the ultimate reasons for the final dropping of the plan.

It is still difficult to understand why the Germans, with ample forces available, took no immediate steps to stimulate and support Italy's hesitating action in the Middle East. Reinforced and energetically led, Italy would have had ample resources to make the position of Wavell's and Cunningham's small forces virtually hopeless. It would seem that the contempt with which the German General Staff looked on their partner induced them to refuse to become involved in Italian enterprises, and they failed to intervene until Italian potentialities had been immensely reduced by Wavell's and Cunningham's amazingly bold offensive policy. Intervention when it came resulted, as we know, in a fluctuating struggle in which British reverses were experienced; but it involved Germany eventually in a major disaster.

Puzzle of German Failure to Help Italy

Wavell's Libyan and Abyssinian campaigns, amazing achievements in themselves, were to have far-reaching effects. The latter has been criticized as a dispersion of resources, and it contributed to the first reverse suffered at Rommel's hands in Libya. But apart from the blow inflicted on Italian morale and the re-establishment of our prestige in the Middle East, it was fortunate that when Japan entered the war there were no Italian bases in East Africa which Japanese U-boats and cruisers might have used to threaten our communications through the Indian Ocean. That Wavell was able to achieve so much was no doubt due to the bold decision to reinforce him with troops and armaments which could so ill be spared from England. It was one of the greatest decisions of the war.

The decision to intervene in Greece, which could not be strategically justified, invited a serious reverse; but there are occasions when political considerations and points of honour outweigh strategic expediency. Moreover, the Greek adventure had an astonishingly important unforeseen effect. The Luftwaffe was temporarily crippled, German designs in Syria and Iraq were frustrated, and the invasion of Russia was postponed for at least a month, possibly the main cause of Germany's disaster in the winter of 1941-42.

The part taken by Australian, New Zealand and Indian troops in Wavell's campaigns should never be underestimated. It was a wonderful proof of

Empire solidarity, and the contribution made by the Australasian Dominions was all the more altruistic in view of the threatening attitude of Japan even at the time contingents were dispatched.

Hitler's long premeditated and unprovoked attack on Russia was the chief cause of his ultimate defeat. His military advisers undoubtedly looked askance on the undertaking, but were prepared to believe that in a lightning campaign Russia could be reduced to impotence, and that much territory, which would add to the economic self-sufficiency of the Reich,

ALLIED WAR COUNCIL MEETS
On September 22, 1939, the Allied Supreme War Council met in a committee room at Brighton Town Hall. Among those who attended were members of the British Cabinet, Mr. Daladier, the Premier of France, and General Gamelin, Supreme Commander of the Allied Armies. Here, Mr. Neville Chamberlain, the British Premier, and Lord Halifax, Foreign Secretary, leave the building. (See also page 511.)

could be acquired. In spite of warnings, they under-estimated Russian military potentialities, and no doubt believed that mechanized warfare and industrial efficiency had gone far to eliminate the defensive advantages conferred by great spaces and numerical superiority, on which Russia had formerly relied.

Technically, the attack was well planned to give swift results. The main mistake which can be attributed to Hitler's General Staff was failure to

make provision for a winter campaign in case the lightning attack failed to produce expected results. The amazing moral and physical fortitude displayed by the Russians in the face of unparalleled disasters decided the ultimate issue of the war.

Mr. Churchill's immediate acceptance of Russia as an ally, though it may have inspired hopes of early assistance which at the time Britain was in no position to give, may have been an important factor in strengthening Russia's will to resist. The possibility of a simultaneous attack by Japan, on the other hand, weakened Russia's position, although Hitler does not appear to have counted on it, and we now know that Japan was determined to play a lone part and to seize the opportunity to pursue her aggressive designs against Britain and America.

Germany's failure to achieve the expected lightning success involved her army, her main instrument of power, in an entanglement from which it could not break loose, and which brought a series of major disasters; it involved also a suspension of air attack on Britain and imposed an immensely increased strain on German industrial capacity which militated against the full development of the potentialities of her air power; had these been fully developed, it might well have rendered the development of Anglo-American offensive power impracticable.

Von Brauchitsch's failure to take Moscow and Leningrad and the disaster experienced in the winter have been accepted as the decisive turning-point of the war. The Wehrmacht never fully recovered; but that did not deter Hitler from embarking on a fresh and even more dangerous offensive campaign in the summer of 1942. Its initial success was encouraging; but the Russians again evaded complete disaster, and their stubborn defence at Stalingrad and in the Caucasus, coupled with the increasing difficulty the Germans had in maintaining lengthened communications, brought the offensive to a standstill, and involved the Reichswehr in another winter campaign.

Turning-point of the War

Nevertheless, the early autumn of 1942 was the darkest hour for the Allies. Stalingrad was in imminent danger; Rommel, having inflicted on the British in Egypt the heaviest defeat they suffered during the war in an encounter on approximately equal terms, was poised at the approaches to Alexandria; Singapore, Malaya and Burma had been lost and India was threatened. Although Japan's aggression had brought the

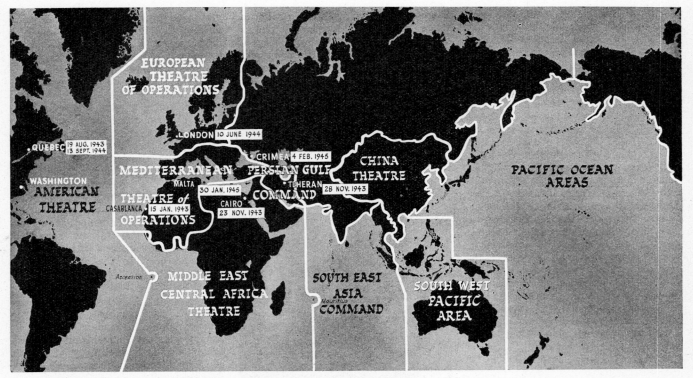

THEATRES OF OPERATIONS IN THE SECOND GREAT WAR

These are the nine operational areas into which the world was divided by the Combined Chiefs of Staff of Britain and the U.S.A. This body was set up after the first war conference of Mr. Churchill and President Roosevelt (held at Washington in December 1941) to implement the decision then taken to pool the resources of Great Britain and the United States in their joint struggle against Germany, Italy and Japan. Places and dates of the periodical conferences of the Combined Chiefs (in a number of cases with their Chiefs of State) are also shown.

Based on the Biennial Report of the Chief-of-Staff of the U.S. Army to the Secretary of War, July 1, 1943–June 30, 1945.

U.S.A. into the war, American recovery from the effects of Pearl Harbor was far from complete. That Japan had suffered heavy naval and air losses in the Coral Sea and Midway Island battles and that the Japanese advance in New Guinea had been stopped by the Australians, leaving communications between the U.S.A. and Australia adequately protected, was the brightest side of the picture. Japanese failure to exploit the Pearl Harbor coup by occupying that vital naval base—which it is now admitted was well within her power if she had been prepared—left the key to the Pacific in American hands, and was a major factor in the rapid growth of America's offensive potentiality.

In the late autumn the crisis passed with the relief of Stalingrad and the battle of El Alamein. From then onwards, in every theatre the Allied counter-offensive began to develop with ever increasing momentum, in spite of occasional checks. Even in the Far East, although it had been wisely decided that Germany had to be defeated before Japan could be dealt with, the counter-offensive began to make progress.

The Russian exploitation of the Stalingrad victory in the subsequent winter campaign was the most striking feature of the Allied recovery, for it was generally held that no large up-to-date army could maintain the momentum of its offensive over any distance exceeding 100 miles under winter conditions. It is now known that the Russians successfully gambled on overcoming the difficulty of maintaining supplies by subsisting largely on those captured from the enemy. The patience with which the Russians had awaited their opportunity at Stalingrad, avoiding the temptation to attack prematurely in view of the desperate situation there, was sure proof of steady nerves ; and the skill with which the counter-offensive developed in successive well timed and well directed blows gave equal proof of the high quality of Russian strategy.

Admittedly Russian victories were largely due to the readiness with which immense, almost reckless, sacrifice of life was accepted—to a degree that Britain with her limited manpower could not have afforded, and from which public opinion both in Britain and the U.S.A. would have recoiled. Nevertheless, it should be recognized that Russian war industries were quite incapable of raising the standard of armament in her huge armies to that which with the western powers led to economy of life, and it should be realized that the Western Allies benefited from Russian determination to succeed at any price. It is understandable that the Russians on their part, especially when the reopening of the western front appeared to hang fire, should have suspected that their allies were shrinking from accepting their full share of sacrifice. Russian lack of experience in the problems of amphibious warfare was an additional source of misunderstanding.

Exploitation of the Alamein victory was no less remarkable. It afforded proof, moreover, that the British Army could produce leaders of outstanding quality, and it was made practicable by the admirable administrative organization and the standard of co-operation between ground and air forces that had been established.

Exploitation of Alamein Victory

Up to this point the Allies, broadly speaking, had been conducting a defensive war, and the R.A.F., in particular in the ever memorable Battle of Britain, had taken its full share ; but it had not as yet had much opportunity of developing its offensive potentialities. This was in part due to unavoidable dispersion of its still limited numerical strength on a great diversity of tasks and in part to some lack of appreciation as to how air power could make its greatest contribution to the war effort. Air power up till then had taken its part in both land and sea operations, but rather by synchronized than integrated action. Moreover, although gallant, and to a degree effective, strategic bombing of enemy sources of power had been conducted, it was found later that results hardly came up to expectation. Attacks had not sufficient weight, and the technique of night bombing had not reached its full development, with the result that a high proportion of bombs dropped failed to find useful targets. The moral effect of attacks had been over-estimated, and the enemy's capacity to make good damage had hardly been realized.

From this time onwards, however, the R.A.F. and the American air forces took an increasing and essential share in the offensive phases of the war, becoming a decisive factor in achieving final victory. Whether Germany might have been brought to her knees by air action alone, as Mr. Churchill at one time suggested was a possibility worth trying, can never be proved, since it was undoubtedly the full development of co-operation between sea, air and land forces that achieved victory before Germany could, with her secret weapons, revolutionize warfare to possibly even a greater extent than had the advent of air power. General Eisenhower and Field-Marshal Montgomery were foremost in recognizing the immense contribution air power could make, and it was an outstanding factor in their strategic and tactical planning and in the conduct of their operations. In naval warfare co-operation developed into integration to an equally marked degree, first in the later stages of the Battle of the Atlantic and ultimately in bringing about the defeat of Japan.

The Anglo-American landing in North Africa induced a response which eventually involved the Germans in the major

Results of Mediterranean War Policy disaster of Tunis, the 8th Army contributing greatly to that result. But it has been argued that the landing in North Africa and the subsequent conquest of Sicily and invasion of Italy were faulty strategy, in that these operations diverted resources from preparations for the reopening of the western front, and because there was no possibility that a decisive attack on Germany could be opened from the south. It has been asserted that, as a consequence, the reopening of the western front was delayed, and that thereby the war was prolonged for a year. Nevertheless, the policy gave important results, and it is hard to see how at the time

3961

more assistance could have been rendered to Russia, or greater damage inflicted on the Axis.

Not the least important consequence of the Mediterranean enterprise was that it gave training and experience to American troops and threw much light on the problems of large scale amphibious operations. It must be remembered, too, that at the time, although the Russians had inflicted a great disaster on the German armies in the winter, it was not till well on in the summer of 1943 that they gave full proof of their offensive power under all conditions, beginning with the battle of the Kursk salient. Even then the Germans had great resources left, strong defences to fall back on and ample room to manoeuvre in retreat. They could undoubtedly, therefore, have produced very powerful forces to counter-attack any forces landed in the west; furthermore, not till 1943 did the air offensive against their war industries begin to become really effective, nor had their oil supplies, the loss of which was such an important factor in their ultimate defeat, been vitally affected. The Italian campaign, weakened by the withdrawal of troops to the west, was in some respects disappointing, but nevertheless it had important diversionary effects; and the complete reopening of the Mediterranean route was an additional result secured by the southern offensive. These are positive reasons to set against the hypothetical results of complete concentration on the western offensive—an adventure in

which, in any case, premature action could not have been risked.

The Russian offensive which started in the Kursk salient was carried on without relaxation in a series of alternating blows till the following spring. It forced the Dnieper line, raised the siege of Leningrad, defeated Manstein's attempt to recover Kiev, and before it ended the whole of the Ukraine had been recovered and the German southern armies had been split in two and forced to retreat in divergent directions. **Russian Gains in Summer of 1943**

1944 saw the beginning of the final phase of the war in Europe, fully described in the Report by the Supreme Commander to the Combined Chiefs of Staff on the Operations in Europe of the Allied Expeditionary Force (H.M. Stationery Office, 2s. 6d.).

In April 1942 Great Britain and the United States decided that plans should be prepared for that great undertaking, and in August 1943 the broad outline of the plan was approved. The Cherbourg peninsula was selected as the point of landing, and May 1, 1944, given as the target date, that being the earliest when climatic conditions would be favourable by which preparations could be completed.

Intensification of the air offensive to secure air superiority and as a "softening" process was ordered in May 1943. In December of that year General Eisenhower was notified that he had been selected as supreme commander, and was given the detailed plans

'OPS' ROOM, WESTERN APPROACHES

In the basement of Derby House, Liverpool (Admiralty H.Q., Western Approaches) was situated throughout the war the nerve centre of the Battle of the Atlantic. Below, the 'Ops' Room, showing the main plot stretching the whole length of the left-hand wall; the disks indicated restricted bombing areas for aircraft of approximately 150 miles radius in those sectors where submarines of the Allied navies were under passage. *Admiralty photograph*

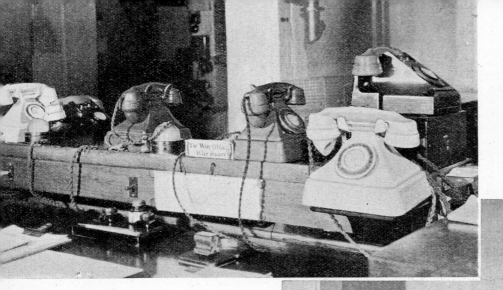

would be made on the Pas de Calais coast. Although Rommel received reinforcements from every other available source, none were drawn from the 15th Army north of the Seine until too late. The Germans also failed completely to foresee the construction of the Mulberry harbour and were convinced that so long as the Allies were denied the use of ports they would be unable to support their armies.

CABINET'S SECRET H.Q.

This battery of secret direct-line telephones connected the British Cabinet's underground H.Q. in Whitehall (see also page 3899) with the War Rooms at the Admiralty, War Office and Air Ministry throughout the war. Right, the fireproof safe—also in this Cabinet wartime nerve-centre—in which secret documents were stored for safety. The maps were used at Yalta and Teheran.

Photos, ' Illustrated'

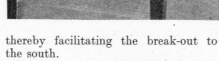

prepared by the staff, though he did not assume command until February. In consultation with General Montgomery, nominated as tactical commander of the early land battles, he insisted on changes in the staff plan which extended the front of assault and raised the strength of the initial landing force from three to five divisions. This entailed the provision of extra landing craft, and the consequent postponement of the landing by a month. It also involved the postponement of the subsidiary landing in southern France (originally intended to be simultaneous with that in Normandy), first to July 10 and later to August 15, when it actually took place.

It was from the first envisaged that after the landing had been effected, and a bridge-head secured (including the port of Cherbourg) **Post-Invasion Plans** that would give room for deployment of sufficient forces, an attempt would be made to break out to the south in order to capture ports in Brittany to which reinforcements and supplies could be shipped direct from America. That would be followed by an advance eastward towards Paris which might bring about a decisive battle between the Loire and the Seine. In the early stages of the invasion it was intended to capture Caen and thus cause the Germans to concentrate in the north for the defence of the Seine crossings and to cover the direct route towards Paris,

thereby facilitating the break-out to the south.

These plans worked out much as designed, though with some delays, partly due to bad weather and partly to the failure to effect the early capture of Caen, which the Germans held with stubbornness as the key to their attempt to seal off the peninsula. This, however, eventually played into Eisenhower's hands, for the enemy expended his strength in resisting Montgomery's persistent attacks and weakened his southern flank. German misappreciation of the problems confronting them was the main cause of their failure to repel the invasion. Rommel, convinced that his coast defences were impregnable, had not provided for defence in depth and, still more important, the German General Staff was obsessed with the belief that the Allied main attempt

The great drive of Lieutenant-General Patton's U.S. 3rd Army (formed on August 1 from four Corps formerly part of the U.S. 1st Army) from Avranches, rapidly cleared the Brittany peninsula, as had been planned, although Brest was stubbornly defended and was so wrecked as to be of small value when finally captured. But Patton, meeting little resistance, also drove eastwards, thus anticipating Eisenhower's programme. The German counter-attack which aimed at cutting his communications at Avranches was not unexpected and was held ; and, being rashly persisted in, led to the development of the fatal Falaise pocket. Too late the Germans drew reinforcements from their 15th Army : these were only added to the bag.

A substantial part of the German armour escaped from the pocket, though with the loss of much equipment ; but the decisive battle between the Loire and the Seine had been fought. Between the rivers, the German 7th Army had been destroyed ; south of the Loire, the German 19th Army was cut off and, weakened, was dealt with by the armies landed in the south and by the Maquis. North of the Seine, the German 15th Army, weakened and disorganized, was in no condition to hold the river line or to prevent the further development of Eisenhower's plans.

Adhering to the conception he had originally formed, Eisenhower decided to advance on a broad front through

Plan for Advance into France

France with his weight on the left, in order to turn the Siegfried line in the north, and to secure a bridge-head across the Maas and Lower Rhine prior to seeking out the enemy in the plains of north Germany and isolating the Ruhr.

Owing to the rapidity of developments, two parts of his original programme had been dropped. The capture of the Brittany ports, now of little significance, was not necessary, and St. Nazaire and Lorient, strongly garrisoned by the enemy, were left to the Maquis to invest. General Patton's rapid thrust eastwards had also rendered it unnecessary to use the airborne army in advance of the original break-out. On the other hand, the rapidity of developments had increased the strain on the Normandy base.

In pursuance of the general plan, during the first half of September Montgomery's 21st Army Group with Lieutenant-General Hodges's U.S. 1st Army swept north-eastwards, the former capturing Antwerp and crossing the Leopold canal before a pause became inevitable in face of increasing resistance and supply difficulties. The latter crossed the Meuse, captured Liége and closed up to the Siegfried Line in the Aachen area. Farther south Patton, thrusting towards Metz, crossed the Meuse and secured bridge-heads on the Moselle, but was also compelled to pause in face of resistance in highly defensible country and supply difficulties.

At this stage with limited port facilities and with road and railway communications heavily damaged by demolitions and Allied bombing, maintenance of supplies was the governing factor. But, still intent on securing a bridge-head across the Lower Rhine before the enemy could recover, Eisenhower approved the project of using his hitherto uncommitted airborne army for the purpose. This airborne operation, although it achieved results of great value, failed in its main object—the establishment of a bridge-head beyond the Rhine. The clearance of the Scheldt estuary was then undertaken, but not till the end of November did Antwerp

become available as a supply port—an essential preliminary to a resumption of the general offensive.

General Eisenhower has been criticized for over-dispersion of his forces by advancing on a broad front, and it has been claimed that a greater measure of concentration, in particular in support of Patton in the Metz region, would have led to a decisive rupture of the Siegfried line and an earlier final decision, or, alternatively, that all transport resources might have been from the first placed at the disposal of the northern thrust.

These are hypothetical claims which cannot be proved, and it seems probable that a greater measure of concentration might, in view of the condition of roads and railways and constant lengthening of distance from the Normandy base, have only increased supply difficulties. Very large forces and immense quantities of material would almost certainly have been required to enable Patton to break through the Siegfried line, and, even if a break-through had been effected, it would have been difficult for the Allied forces to maintain sufficient momentum to prevent the enemy's orderly withdrawal behind the Rhine. Furthermore, failure to engage the enemy on a broad front might have offered him opportunities to concentrate for a disturbing counter-stroke.

Although his advance had been brought to a halt, Eisenhower was determined not to allow static conditions to develop. As soon as the Antwerp base was available, he prepared to launch a

Problem of Rhine Crossing

major offensive designed to secure control of the whole of the west bank of the Rhine. It was hoped and believed that the enemy would accept battle west of the Rhine, and that with his defeat there the very considerable problem of crossing that great obstacle would be eased.

While preparations for the offensive, including preliminary attacks to secure crossings over the Roer River and to gain ground on other parts of the front, were in progress, Rundstedt's Ardennes counter-offensive threw the Allies temporarily on the defensive. The risk of holding this sector of the front lightly had been deliberately taken, to secure greater concentrations for the offensive, and for a few days an admittedly dangerous situation existed. It was, however, quickly restored, and although the Allied offensive had been delayed by over six weeks the enemy was left greatly weakened by his losses, as well as by his transfer of his main armoured reserves to the eastern front.

PLANNING THE OPERATIONS IN ITALY

As C.-in-C., Allied Forces, Italy, General Sir Harold Alexander confers with staff officers at his H.Q. in Italy in March 1944. Standing, left to right, Brigadier-General Lyman L. Lemnitzer, Deputy Chief of Staff ; Lt.-General A. F. Harding, Chief of Staff ; Major-General John K. Cannon, commanding Mediterranean Allied Tactical Air Force and U.S. 12th A.A.F. ; and Major-General Sir Brian H. Robertson, chief of administration and supply.

Photo, United States Information Service

LONDON HEADQUARTERS OF THE 'PHANTOMS'

These innocent-looking pigeon-lofts behind the Guards Memorial in St. James's Park, London, concealed a close-kept British war secret throughout hostilities. They were the headquarters of the 'Phantoms,' known officially as G.H.Q. Liaison Regiment. Task of this highly secret force—personnel of which were dropped behind the enemy lines—was to keep Army, Army Group and Base H.Q. informed, almost minute by minute, of changes in the battle-front situation. Their equipment included specially constructed miniature wireless sets which, besides transmitting messages in code, 'scrambled' them to the extent of unintelligibility complete to all save those at headquarters.   *Photo, Keystone*

The objective of the first phase of the offensive was to capture the ground between the Maas and the Rhine, and thus secure a "line-up" on the latter north of Düsseldorf, in the area where it was proposed the main crossing should take place. Montgomery, whose 21st Army Group still included the U.S. 9th Army, transferred to his command during the Ardennes counter-offensive, was in charge. On the right of the 9th Army General Hodges's U.S. 1st Army was to advance towards Cologne. Farther south, Patton's 3rd Army, which had been drawn into the Ardennes battle, was to fight forward through the Siegfried line and the Eifel region in order in the second phase to join up with the 1st Army on the Rhine north of the Moselle. In the third phase the U.S. 7th Army was to attack the Saar position from the west while Patton struck southwards across the Moselle. Farther south still the French and Americans had already reached the Rhine down to the Swiss frontier.

This programme was carried through almost exactly as designed : not only was the line-up on the Rhine established, but disastrous defeats were inflicted on the enemy, and bridge-heads had unexpectedly been secured across the Rhine at Remagen and south of the Moselle.

In planning to reach the Rhine on a broad front before attempting the main crossing, Eisenhower had aimed at forcing the enemy to disperse his reserves. He was now in an unexpectedly favourable position, and instead of concentrating on his northern drive and carrying out subsidiary operations in his centre and south, he decided to make his principal attack in the centre, with a view to the double envelopment of the Ruhr. This involved the exploitation of the Remagen bridgehead, while at the same time carrying out the deliberately planned crossing in the north.

His plans as thus modified were supremely successful, and with the occupation of the Ruhr and the surrender of the large force within it he had virtually achieved all his original intentions. There remained to be effected, of course, the occupation of much territory, the elimination of other German forces, and junction with the Russians, but deprived of the Ruhr the enemy could not offer any prolonged or co-ordinated resistance.

The amazingly successful landing in Normandy and victory in Italy completed the strategic envelopment of Germany on land. German generals have admitted that with their failure to seal off the Cherbourg peninsula they realized the war was lost. Their sole hope was to get rid of Hitler and make peace with the western Allies, leaving them free to concentrate on staving off the dreaded Russian invasion which, after the disastrous defeat they had suffered in White Russia and the general resumption of the Russian offensive, had become the most imminent danger. By then they had fully recognized that

Hitler's gambling spirit and obstinacy in refusing to contract his commitments had been the chief cause of the desperate situation they were in, but, with the failure of the plot to get rid of him, they seemed to have lost either the courage or the ability to take independent action. Hitler alone, with his faith in secret weapons and in his star, apparently still believed victory might be won, and, failing victory, was determined that Europe should not survive his downfall.

The unrelenting pressure the Allies were by now able to exercise from all directions and their air superiority made the end only a matter of time, but the wounded beast dies hard. The residual power of resistance shown by the Germans on both eastern and western fronts in the autumn and the difficulties the Allies had to overcome in maintaining adequate lines of communication make it improbable that by some different course of action in the West decisive result could have been achieved earlier.

Hitler's extravagant sacrifice of his last reserves, which against all advice he expended in Rundstedt's Ardennes offensive, failed to upset General Eisenhower's plans materially, and probably accelerated the end.

In practice the co-ordination of the final Allied offensive in the east, south and west proved to be admirable. That co-ordination, however, would seem to have resulted less from supreme central direction than from the strategic intuition of the commanders on each of the fronts—for General Eisenhower admits that he was unaware that the Russian Vistula offensive was imminent or of its scale until a few days before his own final offensive was launched, and that he had in fact suspected that the Russian offensive had attained its limit the previous autumn when it reached but could not pass the Vistula.

Once Rundstedt's offensive had been thrown back and Zhukov had reached the Oder the end could not have been long delayed ; but it was accelerated by the orders Hitler issued. His generals had no option but to obey and to fight under the dictates of professional honour rather than those of strategy. Compelled to fight west of the Rhine, they were so decisively defeated that it was impracticable to reorganize for effective defence of that river line. Failure to hold the line of the Oder completed the debacle ; and Hitler's decision to fight it out at Berlin rendered abortive the plans that had been tentatively considered for prolonging the struggle in the southern

Objectives of Rhine Crossing

The End only a Matter of Time

redoubt, even if the Russian thrust into Austria and the advance of the Allied armies in Italy had not rendered the scheme impracticable.

Taking the war as a whole there can be little doubt that Hitler's strategical blunders were the prime cause of German defeat, but unity of purpose established between the Allies, and the tenacity, skill and courage with which their strategical plans were pursued by their three great leaders, was well calculated to lead Hitler into errors and to take full advantage of those he made. Without Russia, complete victory could hardly have been achieved; but it was American resources and the appearance of millions of fresh American troops in the final phases of the war that ensured decisive results. Throughout, the forces of the British Empire in all three elements played an outstanding part; but the Empire's greatest contribution to final victory was its retention of bases and control of communications, without which America could not have brought her potential strength into action.

The Royal Navy and British sea power in all its forms made the main contribution to these results. In combating a *guerre de course* carried out by enemy U-boats, surface raiders, and aircraft, there can, however, be no Trafalgars and it becomes difficult to say where and when decisive effects were achieved. Sea power permeated the whole structure of the British Empire war effort. It was the foundation on which it was built, it was the cement that held it together. It guaranteed the arrival of food and raw materials, without which the nation could not have survived for long nor armed its forces; and it alone made possible the transport of those forces to the theatres in which they were required to operate.

Importance of British Sea Power

Up till the defeat of France, the Royal Navy, with the co-operation of the French Navy, had no great difficulty in carrying out its tasks, despite the reduction of its strength between the wars. But with the loss of French assistance and with the entry of Italy into the war immense and unceasing exertions were demanded from it to the limits of endurance. The Battle of the Atlantic, which had started with the outbreak of war, then became a battle of life or death waged with fluctuating fortune until the surrender of Germany. Fortunately, the Italian Navy never developed its potentialities and allowed itself to be intimidated by Admiral Sir Andrew B. Cunningham's bold offensive policy, nor had the German Navy yet acquired sufficient strength to exploit its opportunity.

But with the outbreak of war in the Pacific and the intensification of operations in the Middle East, further dispersion of naval power became necessary, just at the time the German Navy was becoming most formidable and developing new U-boat tactics and devices. In 1942 and 1943 the Battle of the Atlantic therefore reached its most critical stage, and for a time the entry of America into the war increased rather than diminished the Navy's responsibilities. Not until the U.S.A. was in a position to take a more effective share in the Battle of the Atlantic and until the integration of sea-air power had taken effect, did the battle take a decisively favourable turn.

The Navy's part in amphibious operations also was fundamental.

In Eastern Waters, with limited resources due in part to heavy initial losses, the Navy had a no less exacting task. In the final stages of the

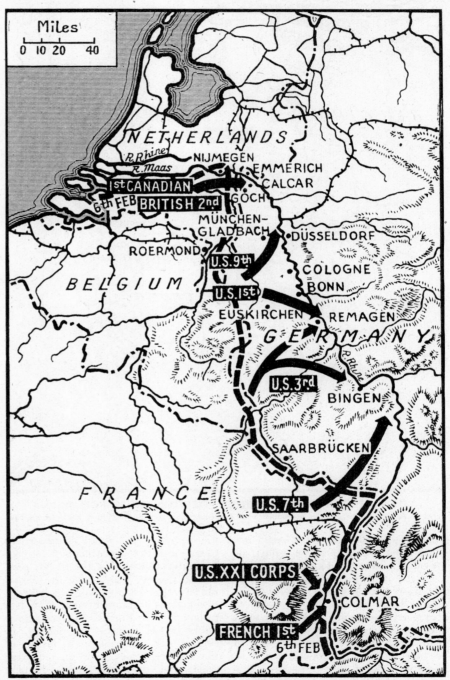

OPERATIONS TO REACH THE RHINE: POSITION ON FEB. 6, 1945
From the Report of the Supreme Commander to the Combined Chiefs of Staff : June 6, 1944–May 8, 1945

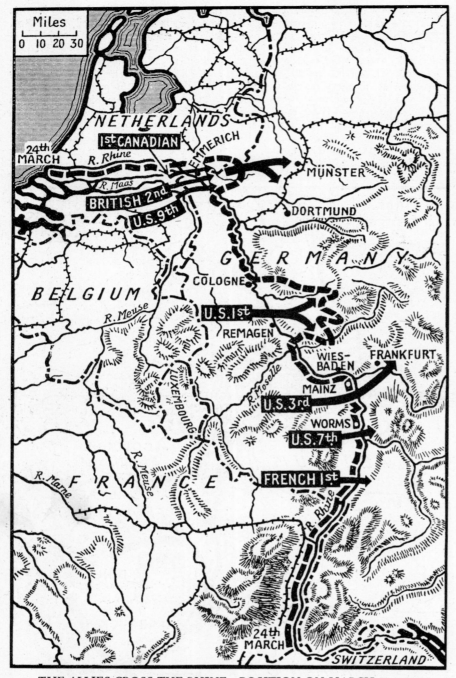

THE ALLIES CROSS THE RHINE: POSITION ON MARCH 24, 1945
From the Report of the Supreme Commander to the Combined Chiefs of Staff : June 6, 1944–May 8, 1945

war in the Pacific, though it could not equal the huge American effort, it provided substantial reinforcement.

Up to 1943 Allied strategy in the Far East was essentially defensive, its objects being to halt further Japanese aggression, safeguard communications between America and Australia, and keep China in the war in order to provide a base for an ultimate air offensive against Japan itself. This strategy involved offensive operations in New Guinea and the Solomon Islands,

the development of air transport to China, and the initiation of a project to link up that part of the Burma road still in Chinese hands with the Assam railway, this last involving the recovery of control of northern Burma. Complete reconquest of Burma was considered impracticable, since the nature of communications through the terrain of the northern frontier prohibited large scale land operations, and shipping could not be made available for an amphibious attack on southern Burma

to secure the port of Rangoon. During 1943, the north Burma operations started. Early in 1944, however, the Japanese offensive, which had the ambitious object of invading India and cutting the Assam railway, threw the Allies on the defensive again. The defence held, and the Japanese invading army was destroyed by a counter-offensive marvellously maintained during the monsoon season. The dry season campaign of 1945, which completed the reconquest of Burma, followed. It was made possible only by the use of air transport on an unprecedented scale.

The liberation of Burma made it possible to employ American-trained Chinese troops to assist China in resisting and defeating a formidable Japanese attack in the spring of 1945, though not **Decisive Theatre in the Far East** before the Japanese had captured the most important air bases from which attacks on Japan might have developed. As a contribution to the final defeat of Japan the reconquest of Burma had therefore lost some of its strategic importance, and the Pacific increasingly became the decisive theatre.

From the first it had been evident that the issue of the war would turn on the control of sea communications, but the problem remained how the Allies were to gain that control in the China Sea and the home waters of Japan, where her navy could, under the protection of shore-based aircraft, await the Allied Fleets operating at immense distances from their main bases. To meet this problem, amphibious operations were planned to secure advanced bases, and the U.S.A. developed to an unprecedented extent the potentialities of sea-air warfare in order to make long-range amphibious operations practicable. Air power had to be employed in a co-operative role and as a long range naval weapon before it could be used as a strategic instrument.

In May 1943 it was decided that offensive operations against Japan should be stepped up, and in August the form they should **Offensive Operations Stepped Up** take was laid down. General MacArthur was directed to continue to extend his operations along the New Guinea coast, with the object of reaching the Philippines by the autumn of 1944. Admiral Nimitz was to secure successively bases in the Gilbert, Marshall and Mariana Islands with a view to securing lodgements in the Ryukyu and Bonin groups which guard Japan's home waters. It was hoped and expected that in the course

PLANNING THE RECONQUEST OF EUROPE

By August 1943 the broad outline of the Anglo-U.S. plan for the invasion of Europe was approved, and the preliminary air offensive had begun. Here, Air Chief Marshal Sir Trafford Leigh Mallory, C.-in-C., Allied Expeditionary Air Force, outlines plans for the paralysis of the German war machine to Allied air chiefs in March 1944. Left to right, Air Marshal R. M. Hill, A.O.C., Air Defence of Great Britain ; Major-General William C. Butler, Deputy C.-in-C., A.E.A.F. ; Air Chief Marshal Leigh Mallory ; Air Vice-Marshal H. Wigglesworth ; Brigadier-General Aubrey C. Strickland ; seated in foreground, Major-General L. H. Brereton, Commanding General, U.S.A. 9th A.F. ; and (extreme right) Air Marshal Sir Arthur Coningham, A.O.C., 2nd Tactical Air Force. Right, Rear-Admiral G. E. Creasy unveils on August 7, 1946, in H.M.S. 'Dryad' (Southwick Park, Fareham, Hants) a commemorative plaque and the wall-map (below) on which Allied leaders watched progress during the Normandy landings on June 6, 1944.

4 K 2

of these amphibious operations the Japanese Fleet might be met and decisively defeated. Both for the support of amphibious operations and to take part in naval engagements provision of carrier-borne aircraft in unprecedented numbers was essential, although as successive bases were secured shore-based aircraft could also take part.

These plans worked out very much as designed, although Japanese detachments resisted amphibious landings of a crushing strength with fanatical courage. By the end of July 1944 MacArthur's American-Australian forces were in control of the whole of New Guinea and the Solomon Islands, and by the same date Admiral Nimitz had reached the Marianas, from which Super-Fortress heavy bombers began the strategic bombing of the Japanese homeland by the end of November.

In October MacArthur, with the co-operation of part of Admiral Nimitz's force, landed on Leyte Island in the Philippines, and the Japanese Fleet, in its attempts to retrieve the situation, met with overwhelming disaster in a sea-air battle, the most decisive naval encounter of the war. In January, by a skilful and bold by-passing manoeuvre, MacArthur landed in the main island of Luzon north of Manila, and by early March the remains of the Japanese garrison **Philippines as Invasion Base** holding out in the less accessible parts of the Philippines were reduced to strategic insignificance. Henceforth Japanese sea communications with the East Indies, Malaya and Burma were almost completely interrupted, while the Philippines provided a place of assembly for the army designed to invade Japan proper.

By this time Super-Fortresses were operating in ever increasing scale from the Marianas ; but it became necessary in February to secure Iwo Jima in the Bonin group, because Japanese aircraft operating from it were intercepting the Super-Fortresses in passage. Its capture enabled the Super-Fortresses to be given fighter escort and provided a landing ground for damaged aircraft on their return flight. There remained, however, the Ryukyus to be taken in order to gain full command of the Formosa Strait and the southern islands of Japan. At the end of March the operation began, but not till June 21 did organized resistance in Okinawa cease, the Japanese in the struggle having lost virtually all the remnants of their navy and a large proportion of their aircraft.

With the European war ended, the air offensive in the East was soon stepped up still further and reached a devastating intensity. Tokyo and other towns were reduced to ruins, while naval forces closed in to bombard ports and coast defences. **Experienced Troops Arrive from Europe** War experienced troops also began to arrive in great numbers from Europe for the army of invasion. The Japanese Emperor, unlike Hitler, had already decided that it was useless to continue the struggle ; it was the military caste in Japan that remained to be convinced of its hopelessness. The use of the atomic bomb in order to save lives that invasion would cost, followed immediately by the Russian declaration of war and invasion of Manchuria, sufficed, however, to bring conviction, and the war ended on August 14, three and a half months after Hitler's death. As in Germany, no fanatical elements of resistance were encountered after the official surrender, and the chief problem that remained was the collection and repatriation of the widely dispersed Japanese army.

ALLIED ADVANCE INTO GERMANY AND ENVELOPMENT OF RUHR
From the Report of the Supreme Commander to the Combined Chiefs of Staff : June 6, 1944–May 8, 1945

December 1. Seventy-six leaders of the Ruhr steel industry arrested by order of Allied Military Government.

December 2. Arab League Council decided to boycott goods manufactured by Jews in Palestine. Polling took place in Albanian elections.

December 3. Britain proposed reduction of all occupying forces in Austria. U.S. State Department announced that Russia had rejected the proposal to withdraw from Persia by January 1, 1946.

December 4. Mr. Sjahrir repeated his Government's readiness to submit Indonesian problem to United Nations Council. Sir Hartley Shawcross opened the British case at the Nuremberg trial. U.S. Senate approved Bill to commit U.S. armed forces to use by Security Council of United Nations.

December 5. General Christison and Dr. van Mook flew to Singapore to confer with Lord Alanbrooke and Lord Louis Mountbatten on military policy in the Netherlands East Indies.

December 6. Arab League replied to Mr. Bevin's Palestine statement. Mr. Attlee announced in the Commons the conclusion of the financial agreement with the United States.

December 7. Announced that the Foreign Ministers of Britain, the U.S. and the U.S.S.R. would meet in Moscow on December 15. General Yamashita sentenced to death as a war criminal in Manila. Bretton Woods Agreement Bill introduced in House of Commons.

December 8. Announced that Allied commander in Java had been fully empowered to restore law and order where necessary. French Foreign Minister informed Britain and America that France would not be bound by any decisions made at a conference to which she was not a party.

December 9. Supreme Allied H.Q. in Tokyo ordered Japanese Government to end the feudal system of land tenure. Mr. de Gasperi formed new Italian Government with representatives of all six former Government parties. Ferenc Szalasi sentenced to death by Budapest People's Court. Three main Austrian parties agreed on the composition of new administration.

December 10. At Calcutta, Lord Wavell, the Viceroy, appealed for goodwill from all leaders ; after interview with the Viceroy, Mr. Gandhi made similar appeal. In House of Commons, Mr. Bevin announced the composition of the Anglo-U.S. Committee of Inquiry on Palestine. Persia appealed to Britain, the U.S. and U.S.S.R. to withdraw troops.

December 11. Mr. Sjahrir declared that Indonesians would resist all British attempts at the forcible restoration of law and order. Arab Higher Committee expressed objection to setting up of the Anglo-U.S. Committee of inquiry on Palestine.

December 12. Allied Commission announced that all Italian territory under Allied Military Government (except areas in dispute) would be restored to Italy about December 31. Announced that Britain's Home Guard would be disbanded on the last day of the year.

December 13. Announced that an agreement had been signed between France and the United Kingdom on joint withdrawal of French and British troops from the Levant. Persian Foreign Minister presented Notes to British, U.S. and U.S.S.R. ambassadors in Teheran demanding the immediate evacuation of their forces. In the House of Commons, the Government motion approving the U.S. Loan was passed by 345 votes to 98 ; Bretton Woods Agreement Bill passed by 314 votes to 50.

December 14. It was announced that the French Government had sent Notes to Britain and the United States requesting an exchange of views on the Franco regime in Spain.

December 15. Making a statement on U.S. policy towards China, President Truman appealed to Communists to disband their army and Generalissimo Chiang Kai-shek to broaden the basis of his Government. Preparatory Commission of the United Nations organization decided that the headquarters of the organization should be in the United States.

December 16. Announced that Tabriz, capital of Persian Azerbaijan, had surrendered to the insurgents ; " Democrat " party in Azerbaijan elected premier and formed " Cabinet." Former Japanese Prime Minister, Prince Konoye, committed suicide. Conference of the Foreign Secretaries of Britain, the U.S. and the U.S.S.R. opened in Moscow.

December 17. Lord Keynes arrived in London from Washington ; spoke in House of Lords debate on the U.S. Loan. In the Canadian House of Commons, Mr. Mackenzie King spoke on the Washington atomic bomb talks.

December 18. Persian Premier declared he would not recognize the Democrat Party's " Government " in Azerbaijan. The House of Lords passed the U.S. Loan Bill by 90 votes to 8.

December 19. It was announced that the British occupation authorities in Germany would control all the coal and heavy industries in the Ruhr as from December 22. The U.S. Government formally accepted the joint responsibility, with Britain, for rescuing interned civilians and disarming the Japanese in Java. Mr. Bevin and Mr. Byrnes saw Mr. Stalin. New Austrian Parliament held its first session ; Dr. Renner called for the return of S. Tyrol.

December 20. Soviet Republic of Georgia claimed districts in the Caucasus and Black Sea areas belonging to Turkey. Dr. Renner unanimously elected President of the Austrian Republic by the Austrian National Assembly. Text of British Coal Industry Nationalization Bill published.

December 21. In the Turkish National Assembly, General Karahekir declared that Turkey must fight if the Soviet claims to the Caucasus and Black Sea areas were pressed. Dr. Figl in his first speech to the new Austrian Parliament called for the immediate return of S. Tyrol. General Patton died in Germany from injuries received in motor accident.

Egyptian Ambassador in London presented Note requesting revision of the 1936 Anglo-Egyptian Treaty.

December 22. Britain and the U.S. recognized the Yugoslav Republic, Britain on condition that Yugoslav international obligations and the rights of British subjects in Yugoslavia were not affected. It was officially stated that the Austrian claim did not involve Trentino.

December 23. In London, the Preparatory Commission of the United Nations organization completed its task. In Moscow, Mr. Stalin received Mr. Byrnes, U.S. Foreign Minister.

December 24. Insurgents converged on Mehabad, strategic point in Azerbaijan. Announced in Canada that all tire-rationing would end there on January 1.

December 25. Broadcast by H.M. the King. General Sir William Slim, former C.-in-C., 14th Army, arrived at Liverpool on board troopship " Georgic " with 5,000 members of the Army and R.A.F. from the Far East.

December 26. The British and U.S. Governments accepted the French suggestion for an exchange of views on the Franco regime in Spain. The French Assembly unanimously approved the Bretton Woods Agreement and the U.S. Export-Import Bank loan ; devaluation of the franc announced at 480 to the pound sterling. Some 250 Jewish immigrants landed illegally in Palestine. Death of Admiral of the Fleet Lord Keyes.

December 27. Mr. Attlee received the Dutch Premier, Dr. Schermerhorn, Dr. van Mook and a Dutch delegation to discuss the situation in the Netherlands East Indies. General Christison announced more active measure against Javanese terrorism, invited co-operation of Mr. Sjahrir and the Amir Sjarifudin. Further bomb outrages at Jerusalem, Haifa and Tel-Aviv caused casualties to British troops and serious damage.

December 28. Statement on Anglo-Dutch discussions issued. Mr. Ben Gurion and Mr. Shertok dissociated the Jewish Agency from the Palestine attacks. Official statement issued on the results of the Moscow conference. Announced that bread rationing in France would be reimposed on January 1.

December 29. Five-Year Commercial Agreement between France and the U.S.S.R. signed in Moscow. British Food Minister Sir Ben Smith, left England for the U.S.

December 30. General MacArthur declared the Four-Power Control Council for Japan " in my opinion not acceptable," but would endeavour to secure the plan's smooth working. Texts of Hitler's personal will and political testament published. King Michael returned to Bucharest after four months' absence.

December 31. Chinese Government announced the conditional acceptance of Communist proposal for " cease-fire " in the civil war. In a New Year message to his people, the Emperor of Japan repudiated the doctrine that he was divine. King Michael broadcast to the people of Rumania.

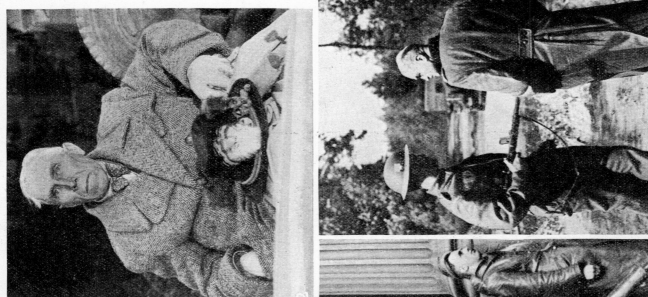

FALLEN LEADERS

1. Dr. Robert Ley, Nazi 'Labour Front' leader, with U.S. parachute troopers who arrested him on May 16, 1945, near Berchtesgaden. He strangled himself on October 25, while awaiting trial at Nuremberg. 2. Franz von Papen, former Reich Chancellor and Ambassador to Turkey, after capture on April 14 by U.S. glider troops near Stockhausen in the Ruhr. Later, he faced trial at Nuremberg. 3. Field-Marshal K. R. G. von Rundstedt, former C.-in-C. in the west, after arrest on May 2, at Bad Tölz, near Munich. 4. Artur von Seyss-Inquart, former Reich Commissioner for the Netherlands, seized by Royal Welch Fusiliers at Hamburg on May 6. 5. Field-Marshal von Blaskowitz, former C.-in-C. in the Netherlands, who surrendered to the Canadians at Appeldoorn, June 5.

Chapter 386

WAR CRIME: A NEW INTERNATIONAL CONCEPTION

*In this chapter the Allied agreements leading up to the indictment and trial
of enemy citizens charged with crimes under international law, the nature of
the crimes charged against them, and the grounds on which the charges were
preferred, are set out. Some account of actual trials is also given*

It is but rarely that an event occurs that can properly be described as of outstanding importance in the history of the human race. The month of August 1945 has some claim, therefore, to be considered unique, for in it there happened two events which history may decide deserve that description.

On August 6 the first atomic bomb used in warfare was dropped at Hiroshima, causing 132,000 casualties, of whom over 90,000 were dead or missing.

On August 8 an agreement was signed between the United Kingdom, the United States, France and Russia containing a Charter declaring for the first time in history that by international law the waging of a war of aggression, the violation of the laws of war, and brutality towards the civilian population even of a State's own nationals are crimes punishable by death, and providing for the trial by an international military tribunal of the military, political and industrial leaders of Germany accused of these acts.

Even had it stood alone, this Charter would have been of outstanding importance, but its significance was increased many times by the realization that with the harnessing of the energy produced by atomic fission another war might well mean the destruction of civilization.

The measures taken to deal with war criminals were very different in the Second Great War from what they were in the First. Then, **After the First Great War** although horrors and atrocities were not lacking—e.g. the treatment of the civilians in Belgium, the executions of Nurse Edith Cavell and Captain Fryatt, and the sinking of hospital ships and of merchant ships such as the "Lusitania,"—no effective steps were ever taken to bring to justice those responsible. Special commissions were set up to make inquiries, and evidence was collected, but events, and mainly the fact that Germany was never occupied, so that the accused could not be seized, made any satisfactory trials impossible. It is interesting to remember that one of these commissions—the Belgian—stated that the atrocities were not isolated acts,

but were premeditated and systematic —an obvious feature in the Second Great War.

By Articles 228–230 of the Treaty of Versailles, Germany undertook to hand over to the Allies persons charged with committing war crimes, to be tried before allied military tribunals, and early in 1920 the Allies delivered lists of those they accused containing nearly 900 names including those of all the greatest men of the war in Germany— Kaiser Wilhelm II, Field Marshals Hindenburg and Ludendorff, Admiral von Tirpitz, the former Chancellor Bethman-Hollweg, the Army Commanders and other famous generals, and most of the Princes. The Kaiser was charged by Article 227 of the Treaty with a "supreme offence against international morality and the sanctity of treaties." He had, however, fled to the Netherlands. The Dutch refused to surrender him to the Allies on the ground that the crime with which he was charged was unknown to Dutch Law and had been created only by the Treaty of Versailles.

That treaty, they contended, attempted to make criminal an act which was not a crime at the time it was done. This "contradicted the very idea of justice."

Many of the other accused were in Germany and could be traced, but the German government pointed out that they could not be surrendered without legislation **Accused Not Surrendered** by the Reichstag, that as many of them were regarded as national heroes no such legislation would ever be passed, and any German government which proposed it would instantly be put out of office.

They made the alternative suggestion that a number of selected cases should be tried before the Supreme Court at Leipzig. This was accepted and 45 cases were selected, the accused being in most cases subordinates. A few convictions were obtained, but the sentences imposed were trivial and the whole proceedings were described by "The Times" as "a travesty of justice," although a careful and fair-minded observer, Mr. Claud Mullins,

NAZI WAR SUSPECTS HELD IN THEIR OWN PRISON

Prisons and concentration camps in Germany which once housed their victims were, after the war, used to hold Nazi suspects awaiting trial. Here, a file of these suspects at the prison-fortress of Hohentubingen, at Rottweil, in occupied Wurtemburg, takes exercise in the yard. Chief of the camp was a Frenchman, Mathias Reger, formerly a prisoner of the Nazis here for 20 months.

PREPARATIONS FOR THE TRIAL OF NAZI LEADERS

Lord Wright, chairman of the United Nations War Crimes Commission, here opens the War Crimes Conference, over which he presided, in the Royal Courts of Justice, London, on May 30, 1945. Below, signing of the Four Powers Agreement on war criminals in Church House, Westminster, on August 8. Left to right, Professor A. N. Trainin and General I. T. Nikitchenko (U.S.S.R.) ; Lord Jowitt (Britain) ; and Mr. Justice Jackson (U.S.).

Photos, G.P.U. ; Topical Press

November 1942 an Edict of the Presidium of the Supreme Soviet of the U.S.S.R. set up a Commission of investigation, declaring that the Hitler Government, the High Command of the German Army, and their accomplices should bear the full measure of criminal and material responsibility for the crimes and material damage done.

A United Nations War Crimes Commission, with Lord Wright as chairman, was set up in London in October 1943 to collect evidence. A declaration made in Moscow in November 1943 by the Foreign Ministers of the United Kingdom, the United States and Russia proclaimed that at the time of any armistice to any government which might be set up in Germany, those German officers and men and members of the Nazi party who had been responsible for or had taken a consenting part in the atrocities, massacres and executions alleged **Moscow Declaration** against them would be sent back to the countries in which their crimes had been committed, to be tried there by the laws of those countries. The major criminals whose offences had no particular geographical location would be punished by the joint decision of the Allied Governments. The declaration was confirmed by the Heads of Government of the United Kingdom, the United States and Soviet Russia at their meeting at Potsdam in 1945 (*see* page 3931).

The Moscow declaration was promptly acted upon in Russia, at Kharkov, where in December 1943 four Germans were convicted and hanged publicly (*see* illus. in page 2935) for the mass extermination of Soviet civilians by gassing.

As the end of the war approached, plans were formulated for the trial of the German leaders as major war criminals, and military tribunals were set up to try minor criminals charged with individual breaches of the laws of war. In the British zone, up to August 31, 1946, out of 442 persons accused 320 had been convicted. For instance, in October 1945, Heinz Eck, the Captain, and four other members of the crew of U-boat 852 were charged with the murder of British and Allied seamen whose ship, the "Peleus,"

was of the opinion that the German judges endeavoured to act fairly.

In the Second Great War, steps were early taken to prevent a repetition of such futility. On October 25, 1941, President Roosevelt and Mr. Churchill both drew attention to the atrocities being committed by the Germans in occupied territory, and Mr. Churchill declared that retribution for these crimes must henceforward take its place among the major purposes of the war. In November 1941 and January 1942 Mr. Molotov circulated among the Powers notes of the atrocities committed by Germans in Russia ; and in

ALLIED JUSTICE FOR BELSEN CRIMINALS

The first mass trial of war criminals opened at Lüneburg, Germany, on September 17, 1945, when 35 former members of the staff of Belsen concentration camp (see illus. in page 3917) were put on trial. President of the Court was Major-General H. P. M. Berney-Ficklin, C.B., M.C. Eleven of the accused—eight men and three women—were sentenced to death on November 18 and executed, among them Josef Kramer, camp commandant, Fritz Klein, camp doctor, and Irma Grese, chief woman warder. 1. The court in session with Kramer on the extreme left in the front row of the dock, and next to him Klein. 2. Irma Grese and Kramer, 'the Beast of Belsen.' 3. The judges' dais.

WAR TRIAL JUDGE

The Rt. Hon. Sir Geoffrey Lawrence, Lord Justice of Appeal, who was appointed on September 28, 1945, as British judge on the International Military Tribunal to try the Nazi war leaders at Nuremberg. He was later chosen as the Tribunal's President. He was born in 1880. *Photo, Illustrated*

had been torpedoed in the Atlantic in March 1944. Most of the crew got on to rafts and wreckage, and the submarine opened fire, killing many of them. At the trial it was stated for the defence that orders had been given to the Captain to destroy all wreckage when a ship was sunk in case its presence should betray the submarine to Allied aircraft. The Captain and two officers were sentenced to death and two other members of the crew were imprisoned.

A German General, Döstler, who had been in command of an Army Corps in Italy, was sentenced to death by an **Death for German General** American military tribunal for having issued an order under which fifteen American Rangers when prisoners of war had been shot, contrary to the Geneva Convention. He pleaded without success the orders of Hitler that all enemy troops captured in commando operations were to be exterminated.

The discovery of the appalling conditions at Belsen, Dachau, and other concentration camps led to the trial and punishment of those responsible.

The trial of the leaders of Nazi Germany opened at Nuremberg on November 20, 1945, before an International Military Tribunal set up under the Charter of August 8, 1945, and comprising the following four members and four alternate members :

For the United Kingdom of Great Britain and Northern Ireland :

THE RT. HON. SIR GEOFFREY LAWRENCE (President) ;

THE HON. SIR WILLIAM NORMAN BIRKETT (alternate member) ;

For the United States of America :

MR. FRANCIS BIDDLE ;

JUDGE JOHN J. PARKER (alternate member) ;

For the French Republic :

M. LE PROFESSEUR DONNEDIEU DE VABRES ;

M. LE CONSEILLER FALCO (alternate member) ;

For the Union of Soviet Socialist Republics :

MAJOR-GENERAL I. T. NIKITCHENKO ;

LIEUTENANT-COLONEL A. F. VOLCH-KOV (alternate member).

The chief prosecuting counsel were : H.M. ATTORNEY-GENERAL, SIR HARTLEY SHAWCROSS, K.C., M.P. (for the United Kingdom of Great Britain and Northern Ireland) ;

MR. JUSTICE ROBERT H. JACKSON (for the United States of America) ;

M. FRANÇOIS DE MENTHON (for the French Republic) ;

GENERAL R. A. RUDENKO (for the Union of Soviet Socialist Republics).

Supreme importance attached to the Charter under which the tribunal was constituted—not, indeed, on account of the punishment that under its provisions might be meted out to the " twenty-odd broken men " sitting in the dock at Nuremberg (for, as Mr. Justice Jackson said, " their personal capacity for evil is forever past "), but in the warning it gave to those who in future might be tempted to wage a war of aggression that this was a crime, and they would do so, in the words of Sir Hartley Shawcross, " with a halter round their necks."

In order that the trial might have this effect, it was not enough that those charged at Nuremberg should be convicted. It was not enough that the whole world should recognize their punishment to be deserved. It must further be universally acknowledged then and in the future that their punishment was according to law. Otherwise Nuremberg would be regarded not as justice but as vengeance—*vae victis*.

The law which made the accused's alleged acts criminal offences could not be the law of the victorious countries for none of the accused was subject to those laws. The Court claimed to be administering international law ; but the Court did not make this law, for it had no power to do so. Its power was limited to deciding whether the accused had committed the acts set out in the indictment. Having so decided, it was bound

by the terms of the Charter to accept that Charter as being correct in law and to hold that these acts were crimes.

Was it then the Charter that made these acts crimes ? The answer is again No. The compilers of the Charter had no power to make any law, for they were not a World Parliament ; nor did they claim any such power. Even if they had had such a power, they would have offended violently against natural justice if they had in 1945 made criminal for the first time acts done by the Germans before that year.

It is a fundamental principle of natural justice that if a man has done an act, however wicked or immoral, which was nevertheless not at the time he did it forbidden and made punishable by law, **A Principle of Natural Justice** he cannot be punished for having done it by a law made at a later time. " Nullum crimen nulla poena sine lege."

The compilers of the Charter could only declare law that was already in existence, and never claimed to do more. The fundamental question therefore was: " Were the acts declared in the Charter to be crimes by international law truly crimes by that law before the Charter was drawn up ? " International lawyers and others in Great Britain were not unanimous in their answer to that question and in their views as to the legality of the trial. On the contrary,

BRITISH PROSECUTOR

It was announced on August 13, 1945, that Sir Hartley Shawcross, K.C., M.P., who had succeeded Sir David Maxwell Fyfe as Attorney-General on the formation of the Labour Government in July 1945, had been appointed chief prosecutor for Britain at the Nuremberg war crimes trial.
Photo, Associated Press

NAZI WAR LEADERS MAKE LAST APPEALS AT NUREMBERG

Twenty-one of the accused in the Nuremberg war crimes trial made their final pleas on August 31, 1946. They were limited to fifteen minutes each. Here, Goering reads his plea into the microphone as Ribbentrop looks on. Field-Marshal Wilhelm Keitel sits impassively on Ribbentrop's left. In the second row, left to right, are Admiral Erich Raeder, Baldur von Schirach, Fritz Sauckel and Colonel-General Alfred Jodl. Goering declared, 'Never did I decree a murder. Never did I decree any cruelty where I had the power and knowledge to prevent it.' *Photo, Associated Press*

IN THE HISTORIC COURT ROOM AT NUREMBERG—

When Lord Justice Lawrence, British President of the International Military Tribunal, opened the war crimes trial at Nuremberg on November 20, 1945, he described it as being ' unique in the history of the jurisprudence of the world ' and ' of supreme importance to millions of people all over the globe.' The trial was held in a sombre panelled court room of the Palace of Justice which had been reconstructed for the occasion. Here, Major Frank B. Wallis (D), one of the American Assistant Trial Counsel, describes how the Nazis acquired power. On the left are the four judges and their deputies, (A) Maj.-Gen. I. T. Nikichenko and Lt.-Col. A. F. Volchkov, Russia; (B) Sir Norman Birkett, Great Britain; (C) Lord Justice Lawrence.

—THE TRIAL OF THE LEADERS OF NAZI GERMANY

The prisoners in the dock on the right are : (E) Goering ; (F) Hess ; (G) Ribbentrop ; (H) Keitel ; (I) Rosenberg ; (J) Frank ; (K) Frick ; (L) Streicher ; (M) Funk ; (N) Schacht ; (O) Doenitz ; (P) Raeder ; (Q) Schirach ; (R) Sauckel ; (S) Jodl ; (T) Papen ; (U) Seyss-Inquart ; (V) Speer ; (W) Neurath ; (X) Fritsche (see page 3979). At a later stage (below), a large chart (see also illus. in page 3981) was displayed demonstrating the distribution of power in the Third Reich among the Nazi Party leaders. On the bench, on the President's left, are (left to right): Mr. Francis Biddle and Judge John J. Parker (U.S.A.) ; and M. le Professeur Donnedieu de Vabres and M. le Conseiller Robert Falco (France).

CASE AGAINST JAPAN'S MAJOR WAR CRIMINALS OPENS AT TOKYO

Prosecution of the leading militarists of Japan by the Far East International Tribunal opened in Tokyo on June 4, 1946. A function of the trial, declared Mr. Joseph Keenan, chief Allied prosecutor, was to establish the fact that there is "such a thing as international law and that a war of aggression is a crime under that law." The defendants included the former Premier, Hideki Tojo, and members of his Cabinet. Above, Tojo (sixth from left in front row of dock) listens intently while Major Ben Blakeney, U.S. Army (standing in front, left) asks the court to adjourn to enable defending counsel to prepare their case. On September 9 Colonel C. D. Wild, liaison officer in South-East Asia, told the tribunal that within two years 16,000 out of 40,000 British prisoners of war had died in Japanese hands.

the trial, although its proceedings were upheld by many of the most eminent lawyers, was considered by some as reminiscent of political treason trials, and as undermining the world's conception of justice. Some attention is therefore given below to the grounds on which the Charter declared certain acts to be crimes.

The accused were 24 in number :

GOERING, Hermann Wilhelm. Supreme Leader of the S.A., Reich Minister for Air, Commander in Chief of the Air Force, member of the Secret Cabinet Council, etc.

RIBBENTROP, Joachim von. Reich Minister for Foreign Affairs, member of the Secret Cabinet Council, etc.

HESS, Rudolf. Deputy to the Führer, member of the Secret Cabinet Council, etc.

KALTENBRUNNER, Ernst. Head of the Reich Main Security Office and Chief of the Security Police and Security Service, etc. (absent at first through illness).

ROSENBERG, Alfred. Editor of the Nazi newspaper " Völkischer Beobachter," Special Delegate for the entire Spiritual and Ideological Training of the Nazi Party, etc.

FRANK, Hans. Reich Commissar for the Co-ordination of Justice, Governor-

GOERING CONSULTS WITH HIS LAWYER

At one time second most powerful personality in Hitler's Reich, Hermann Goering, like other major war criminals on trial at Nuremberg, was granted only the privileges of an ordinary prisoner. Guarded by a U.S. sentry and across the grille, he here discusses the trial with his lawyer, Dr. Otto Stahmer, who reads to him questions which will later be put in court. *Photo, Keystone*

General of the Occupied Polish territories, etc.

BORMANN, Martin. Secretary of the Führer, organizer and head of the Volkssturm, etc. (tried in absence).

FRICK, Wilhelm. Reich Minister of the Interior, Director of the Central Office for all Occupied Territories, etc.

LEY, Robert. Nazi Party Organization Manager, Joint Organizer of the Central Inspection for the Care of Foreign Workers, etc. (Committed suicide in his cell, October 25, 1945.)

SAUCKEL, Fritz. General Plenipotentiary for the Employ-

RIBBENTROP GOES TO COURT

Joachim von Ribbentrop, Hitler's Foreign Minister, enters the specially built walled board-walk between his cell and the Nuremberg court house. It was decided on September 17, 1946, that time and place of any executions following the trial were to be announced only after they had taken place. *Photo, Associated Press*

ment of Labour under the Four Year Plan, etc.

SPEER, Albert. Reich Minister for Armament and Munitions, Chief of the Organization Todt, etc.

FUNK, Walter. Economic Adviser of Hitler, Press Chief of the Reich Government, President of the German Reichsbank, etc.

SCHACHT, Hjalmar. Reich Minister of Economics, President of the German Reichsbank, etc.

PAPEN, Franz von. Reich Chancellor, Ambassador in Vienna, Ambassador in Turkey, etc.

KRUPP, Gustav. Head of Friedrich Krupp A.G., etc. (trial deferred by the tribunal).

NEURATH, Constantin von. Reich Minister of Foreign Affairs, Reich Protector for Bohemia and Moravia, etc.

SCHIRACH, Baldur von. Leader of Youth of the German Reich, etc.

SEYSS-INQUART, Artur. Chancellor of Austria, Deputy Governor-General of the Polish Occupied Territory, Reich Commissar for the Occupied Netherlands, etc.

STREICHER, Julius. Gauleiter of Franconia, Editor-in-Chief of the anti-Semitic newspaper " Der Stürmer," etc.

KEITEL, Wilhelm. Chief of the High Command of the German Armed Forces, Field-Marshal, etc.

JODL, Alfred. Chief of Staff OKW, Colonel-General, etc.

RAEDER, Erich. Commander-in-Chief of the German Navy, Grossadmiral, etc.

DOENITZ, Karl. Commander-in-Chief of the U-boat arm, Grossadmiral, Commander-in-Chief of the German Navy, etc.

FRITZSCHE, Hans. Editor-in-Chief of the official German news agency "Deutsche Nachrichten Büro," Head of the Wireless News Service, etc.

In addition, the following were named as illegal organizations so that under the Charter any person who had been a member of any of these organizations could be tried and punished on that ground alone:

Die Reichsregierung (Reich Cabinet); Das Korps der Politischen Leiter der Nationalsozialistischen Deutschen Arbeiterpartei (Leadership Corps of the Nazi Party); Die Schutzstaffeln der Nationalsozialistischen Deutschen Arbeiterpartei (commonly known as the "SS") and including Der Sicherheits-dienst (commonly known as the "SD") Die Geheime Staatspolizei (Secret State Police, commonly known as the "GESTAPO"); Die Sturmabteilungen der N.S.D.A.P. (commonly known as the "SA"); and the General Staff and High Command of the German Armed Forces.

In the case of the accused persons the acts, declared to be crimes, fell under three heads: (1) Crimes against Peace; (2) War Crimes; (3) Crimes against Humanity.

The indictment against the accused charged them not only with these three offences, but also with the separate offence of participating in a common plan or conspiracy to commit them.

Crimes Against Peace

The planning or waging of an aggressive war was declared a crime because it infringed the common law of the community of nations as contained in and deduced from international treaties and the practice of nations.

A. N. Trainin (*see* illus. in p. 3972) in his "Hitlerite Responsibility under Criminal Law," pointed out that the epoch when nations lived in isolation had passed away. Stable international communion had been created. An infringement of this most important achievement of human society, an infringement of the connexion between states and peoples, is an international crime. International crime, consequently, must be defined as an infringement of the foundations of international communion.

Some support for the view that there is a common law of the community of nations which can be deduced from international treaties was given by Lord Wright **Common Law** in the "Law Quarterly **of Nations** Review" for January 1946. After stating that a treaty or agreement making war illegal binds only the nations who were parties to it, he continues, "But it may be regarded from a different aspect. It is evidence of the acceptance by the civilized nations of the principle that war is an illegal thing. This principle so accepted is entitled to rank as a rule of international law."

Those who demanded that international law should conform to the usual conception of national law, namely a rule enacted by a central law-making authority or a Court, could of course recognize no international law at all, for there was no World Parliament or World Court. Such a conception of law was, however, unduly narrow. Even in English law, what is called common law was originally developed

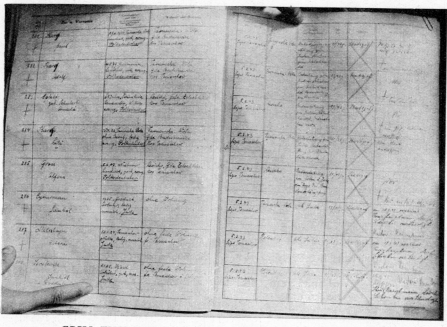

GRIM EVIDENCE AT THE NUREMBERG WAR TRIAL

Among evidence produced for the prosecution at Nuremberg was the register (above) used by the Gestapo in Poland to record the names, offences and fate of arrested persons, the 'crime' of many of whom was simply the fact that they were Jews. A cross on the margin indicated that execution had been carried out. Below, Nazi photograph of Jews being forced from air-raid shelters by S.S. men during the destruction of the Warsaw Ghetto in 1943 (see also illus. in page 2725).

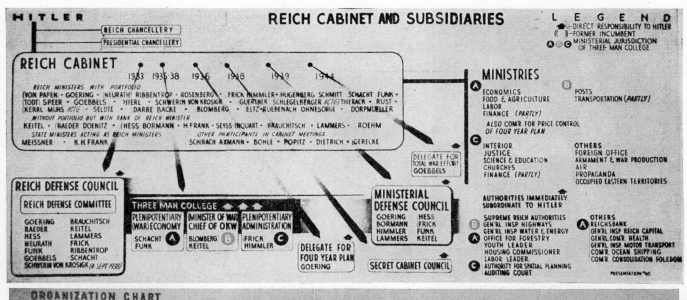

REICH CABINET AND SUBSIDIARIES

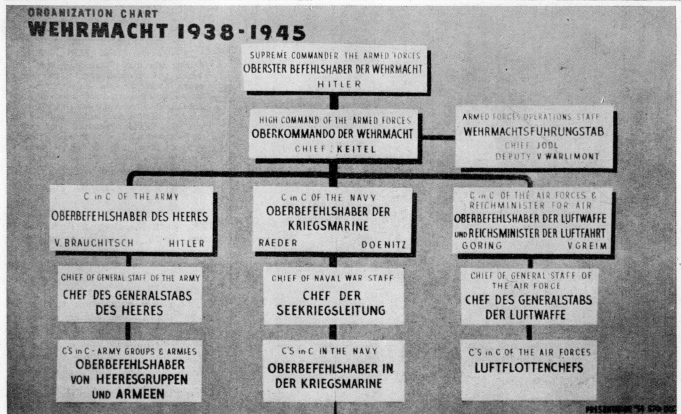

ORGANIZATION CHART

WEHRMACHT 1938-1945

CHARTS SHOWED DISTRIBUTION OF NAZI POWER

Among many significant exhibits at the Nuremberg war trial were these charts. The top one showed in detail the distribution of power, from 1933-1944, among the Nazi leaders, from Hitler downwards. The other showed the organization, from 1938-45, of the entire German armed forces, of which Hitler was also in supreme command. *Photos, G.P.U.*

from local customs which were recognized by the Courts as being common to all parts of the land. There seemed no reason why international law should not develop likewise from the common practice of all civilized states.

At one time war was recognized as a method a state might legitimately employ merely because it considered it was to its advantage to do so. "War is the continuation of politics by other means," wrote Clausewitz. During the 19th and 20th centuries, however, the peoples of the world came more and more

to realize and accept the proposition that war was an evil thing. This changing attitude and the growth of the idea of an international community may be traced in a large number of international treaties designed to prevent war. The first were the Hague Conventions of 1899 and 1907. Neither of these compelled states to submit their disputes to arbitration before going to war, but they did set up machinery for arbitration and for international commissions of inquiry of which states could take advantage if they chose, and this machinery was frequently and effectively used. The Dogger Bank incident

SPARTAN FARE FOR NAZIS

During their trial at Nuremberg, the Nazi leaders had their food served in two special rooms above the court house. They ate from army mess kits, with spoons only, and drank from cups without handles. A typical lunch consisted of bean hash, with bread and cheese, followed by biscuits and coffee. 1. Over his hash, Hess talks to a neighbour. 2. Alfred Jodl (left), former Wehrmacht Chief of Staff, lunches with Wilhelm Keitel, once Chief of the High Command. 3. During an adjournment, accused talk with their counsel.   *Photos, L.N.A.; Planet News*

between Great Britain and Russia in 1904, when the Russian fleet fired on some North Sea fishing vessels under the impression that they were Japanese torpedo boats, was pacifically dealt with under the provisions of these treaties.

The Bryan arbitration treaties between the United States and many foreign countries in 1914 mark a definite advance in that the parties agreed not only to refer their disputes to a permanent international Commission for investigation and report, but also to refrain from going to war until the report of the Commission had been made. The League of Nations, whose formation was included in the settlements following the First Great War, was designed to prevent all further wars.

Arbitration Treaties

Further indications of the changed attitude towards war are found in the provisions designed to limit armaments contained in the Covenant of the League and in various treaties, and even more in treaties (such as the Treaty of Locarno, 1925) by which war is renounced or, in the popular phrase, " outlawed." Overshadowing all agree-

AUSTRIA'S EX-CHANCELLOR

Dr. Kurt von Schuschnigg, Austrian Chancellor (1934-38), who had been held prisoner by the Nazis since the 'Anschluss' of 1938, on arrival at Nuremberg to give evidence at the war crimes trial. He had been rescued from the Praxer Wildsee concentration camp, near the Brenner Pass, by the 5th Army on May 7, 1945. *Photo, Keystone*

ments was the Kellogg-Briand Pact of 1928, the General Treaty for the Renunciation of War, the parties to which solemnly declared that they condemned recourse to war for the solution of international controversies and renounced war as an instrument of national policy. This treaty was ultimately accepted by all the great powers, and in 1939 was binding on more than sixty nations, including Germany.

Besides these general treaties, the right to wage war was, according to Sir Hartley Shawcross at Nuremberg, "further circumscribed

A Thousand Treaties Against War

by a series of treaties numbering—it is an astonishing figure, but it is right—nearly a thousand, of arbitration and conciliation, embracing practically all the nations of the world."

It was contended that the above facts established by 1939 that civilized nations had accepted the principle that war was illegal, and that therefore this principle became part of the common law of the community of nations.

Those who opposed the contention that the acts charged are crimes by international law did so on the following grounds:

(1) Though the Kellogg-Briand Pact and other international treaties made war illegal, they did not make it criminal. This argument overlooks the fact that one of the characteristics which usually distinguish a crime from other illegal acts which are not crimes is that a crime injures in some degree the community as a whole. In this connexion, Lord Wright may be quoted: "War is an evil thing. It is no hyperbole to describe the war of 1939 to be one of the greatest calamities that ever befell the human race. To initiate a war of aggression is not only a crime but the chief of war crimes."

(2) The system of prohibition of war had broken down before 1939 and ceased to be law. For this contention there would at first sight appear to be much support. Between the signing of the Kellogg–Briand Pact and the outbreak of the Second Great War, the Pact was broken eleven times—an average of just over once every year. (Three of these breaches were by Germany, against Austria 1937, Czechoslovakia 1939, Poland 1939, three by Russia against China 1929, Poland 1939, Finland 1939.) But a crime does not become any less criminal because others also have committed crimes, and it was pointed out by Sir Hartley Shawcross at Nuremberg that many of these acts had been denounced as violations of the Pact by the League of Nations, and even if sanctions were not applied as they might have been, "that was a failure of the policeman, not of the law."

War Crimes

Of all the crimes set out in the Charter, war crimes—violations of the laws and customs of war—present the least novelty, as in the past there have been many cases in which military tribunals of one country have tried and convicted nationals of an enemy country for atrocities as violations of the laws and customs of war.

KESSELRING IN WITNESS BOX

Albert Kesselring, one time German C.-in-C. in Italy and the West, gave evidence at Nuremberg. Wearing headphones to enable him to follow the German translation of the proceedings, he here answers accusations put by Mr. Justice Jackson, Chief Prosecuting Counsel for the U.S.A.

Photo, Associated Press

Between the Declaration of St. Petersburg of 1868, which forbade the use of explosive bullets, and the outbreak of the Second Great War, there were some eight further Con-

Conventions Defining War Customs

ventions (the most important of which are the Geneva Conventions of 1906 and 1929, dealing respectively with the treatment of the wounded and of prisoners of war, and the Hague Convention of 1907) containing the laws and customs of war on land.

War crimes were declared to be crimes not only because they infringed one or other of these Conventions, but also because they infringed the "general principles of criminal law as derived from the criminal law of all civilized countries." A novelty was that although some actual perpetrators of war crimes had in the past been tried, this was the first occasion on which the leaders of a nation were charged with crimes committed by persons in subordinate positions.

Crimes against Humanity

The Charter expressly stigmatized as crimes against humanity inhumane acts committed against *any* civilian population *before or during the war;*

or persecutions on political, racial or religious grounds in execution of or in connexion with any crime within the jurisdiction of the Tribunal, whether or not in violation of the domestic law of the country where perpetrated.

That this crime did present some legal difficulty was conceded by Professor Goodhart, Professor of Jurisprudence at Oxford, in the " Juridical Review " for April 1946. It had been generally accepted that international law was not concerned with the way in which a state treated its own nationals. To this, however, there were two answers : in the past states had interfered to protect the nationals of another state against its rulers—e.g. on behalf of Christians in Turkey. Secondly, as Professor Goodhart states, the Charter did not claim that ill-treatment by a state of its own nationals was a crime unless the ill-treatment took place in the execution of one of the crimes already dealt with, in which case it might well be said to affect the international community.

Among other provisions of the Charter which appeared to be innovations was one declaring that the official position of an accused person, whether as Head of State or as a responsible official in a Government Department, should not be considered as freeing him from responsibility.

It further provided that the fact that an accused acted in pursuance of an

U-BOAT OFFICERS TRIED FOR MURDER

The trial of members of a U-boat crew—the U 852—opened at Hamburg on October 17, 1945. They were charged with murdering British and other Allied seamen after their U-boat had sunk the Greek ship ' Peleus ' in the Atlantic on March 13, 1944. Here, Captain Heinz Eck, the commander, who, with two of his officers, was sentenced to death, shakes hands with one of the defence counsel. *Photo, Keystone*

order of his Government or of a superior should not free him from responsibility, but might be considered as a mitigation of his offence.

Hitherto it had been held by some writers on international law, and also in the British " Manual of the Laws and Usages of War on Land " that a soldier charged with committing some breach of the rules of war could escape liability if he could show that he acted on the orders of a superior, and it was the supposed existence of this rule that largely contributed to the failure to punish war criminals after the war of 1914–1918, since it would have led to the charging of all crimes against the Head of the State ; but, under another supposed rule of international law, he as sovereign could claim total immunity. These two rules combined would prevent the punishment of any war criminal except where it could be proved that the act charged was an atrocity committed by an individual without orders.

Former Escape from Liability

The Charter was criticized also on the ground that even if the acts specified in it were crimes by international law, this could not impose any liability on individual nationals of a state for, it was argued, states, not individuals, enter into treaties and are members of the international community and are subject to international law. The liability of individuals under international law was not, however, new, as it had long been recognized that individuals could be punished for breaches of the laws and usages of war committed by them.

" Stern justice will be meted out to all war criminals, including those who have

DEATH FOR THE DESTROYER OF LIDICE

Karl Hermann Frank, who ordered the obliteration of Lidice (see page 2569), came up for trial before a Czechoslovak People's Court in Prague, on March 22, 1946. On May 22 he was publicly hanged in the Pancrac prison, the 5,000 onlookers including (by special invitation) survivors of Lidice. Here, Frank faces his judges in front of the customary crucifix and candles of a Czechoslovak court. *Photo, Keystone*

visited cruelties upon our prisoners," stated the Potsdam Declaration (*see* page 3847), and this declaration was accepted by Japan in the terms of surrender signed on September 3, 1945 (*see* page 3842). By those same terms, the government of Japan passed under the control of the Supreme Allied Commander. In that position General MacArthur on January 16, 1946, issued a proclamation providing

GERMAN GENERALS ON MURDER CHARGE

The trial began at a U.S. court at Dachau (left) on May 16, 1946, of Colonel-General Sepp Dietrich, Generals Fritz Kramer and Hermann Priess, and 71 other German soldiers. They were charged with murdering unarmed U.S. soldiers during the Ardennes counter-offensive of December 1944–January 1945. Above, the defendants in court, with Dietrich (11), sentenced to life imprisonment; Kramer (33), 10 years; and Priess (45), 20 years. Forty-three of the soldiers were hanged.

Photos, Associated Press; New York Times Photos

for the establishment of an International Military Tribunal in Tokyo which was to operate under a Charter issued on April 26, and substantially the same as the Charter of August 8, 1945, under which the German leaders were tried, except that it contained no provision similar to that in the European charter under which the Head of a State is expressly stated to be entitled to no immunity.

Names for membership of the Tribunal were submitted by the signatories to the surrender (*see* illus. in page 3842), and from them General MacArthur selected the following: SIR WILLIAM F. WEBB (Australia), President; JUSTICE E. STUART MCDOUGALL (Canada); JUDGE JU-AO MEI (China); M. HENRI REIMBURGER (France); PROFESSOR BERNARD VICTOR A. ROLING (Netherlands); JUSTICE ERIMA HARVEY NORTHCROFT (New Zealand); JUDGE I. M. ZARYANOV (U.S.S.R.); LORD PATRICK (United Kingdom); MAJOR-GENERAL MYRON C. KRAMER (U.S.A.). Mr. Joseph B. Keenan was appointed to act as Chief U.S. and international prosecutor; Mr. A. S. Comyns Carr, K.C. (assisted by Mr. Christmas Humphreys) as chief British prosecutor; and Mr. Justice Mansfield as chief Australian prosecutor.

The men tried by the Tokyo tribunal, which began its sittings on June 4, 1946, appear in page 3978, and were (front row, left to right): General Kenji DOIHARA, Commander, Special Service Section, Manchuria; General Shunroku HATA, member, Supreme War Council; Koki HIROTA, Premier, 1936; Jiro MINAMI, ex-Privy Councillor; General Hideki TOJO, Premier and War Minister; Takasumi OKA, Chief of Military Affairs Bureau of the Navy, 1940–44; General Yoshijiro UMEZU, Vice-Minister of War; General Sadao ARAKI, member, Supreme War Council; Akira MUTO, Chief of Military Affairs, 1939–42; Naoki HOSHINO, Chief Secretary; Hokonori KAYA, Minister of Finance; Koichi KIDO, Emperor's Chief Confidential Adviser; Heitaro KIMURA, Vice-Minister of War; behind them, left to right, Colonel Kingoro HASHIMOTO, commander of an artillery regiment at the rape of Nanking and the shelling of H.M.S. gunboats "Ladybird" and "Bee"; Kuniaki KOISO, Premier; Admiral Osumi NAGANO, member, Supreme War Council; Hiroshi OSHIMA, Ambassador to Germany, 1938–45; Iwane MATSUI, member, Cabinet Advisory Council, 1938–39; Baron Kiichiro HIRANUMA, Premier, 1939; Shigenori TOGO, Foreign Minister; Mamoru SHIGEMITSU, Foreign Minister; Kenryo SATO, Chief of Military Affairs Bureau, 1942–44; Vice-Admiral Shigetaro SHIMADA, Navy Minister; Toshio SHIRATORI, Ambassador to Italy, 1939; Lieutenant-General Teiichi SUZUKI, Minister without Portfolio under Tojo; Seishiro ITAGAKI, Chief of Staff, Kwangtung Army.

Far Eastern Trials

Meanwhile 239 lesser prisoners had been tried by British military courts between January and July 1946, 98 being sentenced to death, 105 to terms of imprisonment, 36 being acquitted. Also trials before American and Australian Courts involved British victims.

PREPARING THE WAY FOR WORLD ORGANIZATION

The first meeting of the Preparatory Commission of the United Nations was held in Church House, Westminster, on November 24, 1945. All the United Nations were represented on the Commission, which on December 23 finished its work of making provisional arrangements for the first sessions of the General Assembly, the Security Council, and other organs of the United Nations, for the establishment of the Secretariat, and for the convening of the International Court of Justice. Here is the Commission at work, seen from the platform. Above, Mr. Philip Noel-Baker, British Minister of State, addresses the first meeting.

Photos, Barratt's ; Associated Press

Chapter 387

THE UNITED NATIONS HOLD THEIR FIRST ASSEMBLY

The Preparatory Commission of the United Nations, established at the San Francisco Conference in June 1945 to arrange for the first meetings of the General Assembly, the Security Council and other organs, completed its work in just over six months and on January 10, 1946 the first General Assembly was opened at Central Hall, Westminster, by the Rt. Hon. Clement R. Attlee, Prime Minister of Great Britain

WHEN the San Francisco Conference ended in June 1945 the fifty nations represented there had decided to " establish an international organization to be known as the United Nations." In the Charter that they had signed they had laid down the broad principles on which the new organization would work, and they had sketched out roughly its shape ; but there was a great deal more work to be done before the organization could be brought into existence, before the theory of San Francisco could be made practice.

This was foreseen at San Francisco. On the same day that the Charter was signed the delegates of the 50 nations also signed an agreement establishing a Preparatory Commission of the United Nations whose task was to make provisional arrangements for the first sessions of the General Assembly, the Security Council and the other organs of the United Nations. Every Government which had signed the Charter was entitled to be represented on the Commission which was thus, virtually, a skeleton General Assembly.

Six months were to elapse before the work of this Preparatory Commission was completed and it was possible to summon the first General Assembly of the United Nations.

The first stage of the Commission's work was a meeting in London of its Executive Committee in **Preparatory** August 1945. By that **Commission** time the Second Great **in London** War had ended : Japan as well as Germany had capitulated, and a new and vital factor had been introduced into international affairs—the atomic bomb. And to some extent the finer inspiration of the San Francisco Conference seemed to be becoming blunted by many difficulties which were arising after the cessation of hostilities.

It took the Executive Committee nine weeks to hammer out a voluminous report which was virtually a blueprint for the new organization. It took the Preparatory Commission itself another four weeks at a meeting in London which ended just before Christmas 1945 to approve and perfect this document.

During this stage the work was mainly of a technical character and few political issues arose. In the Preparatory Commission most controversy arose over the site of the permanent headquarters of the United Nations. On this, Soviet Russia, still resentful of the fact that she had been expelled from the League of Nations in 1939, led a determined opposition to a return to Geneva, or indeed to the headquarters being in Europe at all. Mr. Noel-Baker, Minister of State and head of the British delegation to the Preparatory Commission, was an equally determined advocate of the need for the new organization to have its home in Europe where it would be in the midst of most of the problems it would have to solve, and where the war-racked countries of Europe could be easily and cheaply represented. This question—an embarrassing one for the United States delegation—almost be-

FIRST U.N. PRESIDENT
Mr. Paul-Henri Spaak, Belgian Minister for Foreign Affairs, who on January 10, 1946 was elected in London first President of the General Assembly of the United Nations. A lawyer by profession and Socialist deputy for Brussels, he had been Foreign Minister in the exiled Belgian Government in London during the war. He was born in 1899.

Photo, Associated Press

came a major issue when Mr. Spaak, the Belgian Foreign Minister, spoke of the danger of having the seat of the United Nations on the territory of one of the Great Powers. Mr. Spaak claimed that the whole structure of the Security Council was based on absolute equilibrium between the five Great Powers, and this equilibrium would be disturbed if, as well as having the privilege of a permanent seat at the Council table, any one of them also had the privilege of having the permanent seat of the organization in its territory.

The final decision to establish the headquarters on the eastern side of the United States (later **Site of** more precisely defined **U.N.** as the Stamford–North **Headquarters** Greenwich area near New York) did not reflect the unanimous opinion of the Commission. The first voting on this important question gave 24 delegates in favour of a site in the United States and 23 in favour of Europe. As Mr. Noel-Baker pointed out, thirteen European countries were not members of the United Nations. Had they been the decision might have been different.

Just before and during the Preparatory Commission's meeting in the autumn of 1945, international affairs had been passing through a difficult stage. The transition from war to peace had given rise, perhaps inevitably, to friction between the Great Powers. The Council of Foreign Ministers meeting in London had broken up almost in disorder : there was disagreement over the situation in many countries in Europe ; Persia was complaining of Russian interference in her northern province of Azerbaijan ; Russia was disgruntled because she had been excluded from the secret of the atomic bomb. In fact, relations were so strained that it was felt that the first meeting of the United Nations General Assembly scheduled for January 1946 might have to be postponed. But after a meeting in Washington between Mr. Attlee, the British Prime Minister, and President Truman (see illus. in page 3855), the Foreign Ministers of the United States, Russia and Great Britain met in

Moscow. There they were able to reach some measure of agreement, including the decision to establish a United Nations Atomic Commission. That the agreement was uneasy was to be revealed later in the Security Council where Mr. Bevin, the British Foreign Secretary, and Mr. Vyshinsky, the Soviet Vice-Commissar for Foreign Affairs, were to become the central figures in a series of brisk actions.

In many ways the structure for the organization which the first General Assembly was to approve was similar to that of the League of Nations. There was to be a General Assembly consisting of all members (the adherence of Poland to the San Francisco Charter had brought the membership up to 51); the key political organ was to be the Security Council consisting of six elected members and the five Great Powers; there was to be a new International Court of Justice, and a Trusteeship Council in place of the former League of Nations' Permanent Mandates Commission. What was entirely new was the Atomic Commission and the creation of an important Economic and Social Council of eighteen members with wide functions and powers to deal with Human Rights, and with international economic, social and cultural, educational, health and related matters.

Organs of the United Nations

And there was one striking difference between the organs and aims of the old League of Nations and those of the United Nations. In the Covenant of the League of Nations, Article 8 was entirely devoted to the need for world-wide disarmament. It was this Article which gave rise to the ill-fated Disarmament Conference which met in Geneva from 1932 to 1934. Disarmament, in fact, was for 15 years one of the most important and controversial items in the League of Nations' programme. In the United Nations Charter there was no word about disarmament, and the subject was never mentioned at the first General Assembly.

Although the structure of the new organization was based very much on that of the League of Nations, there was to be a very striking contrast between the power and authority of the new Security Council and that of the old League Council—the most important difference being that all members of the United Nations were to delegate their powers of action to the Security Council. Thus without consulting the General Assembly these 11 members were to be empowered to commit all other members to any action, including military action, they thought necessary; and the Security Council was to have armed forces at its command for this purpose.

Politically, the main difference was that the permanent members of the Security Council—the United Kingdom, Russia, the United States, France and China—were granted the right of veto. In other words any one of them could prevent action by the Security Council by the simple process of casting an

LONDON'S POSTMARK
The G.P.O. celebrated the London meeting of the United Nations, the Preparatory Commission of which met in 1945, with this special postmark.

adverse vote. This right of veto had been accepted very reluctantly by the smaller Powers: obviously, it created a class of privileged membership, and even the proviso that in certain circumstances a party to a dispute must abstain from voting did not fully satisfy them.

In its voluminous report the Preparatory Commission had recommended that the first General Assembly of the United Nations should be " primarily organizational " and it was strongly hoped that no controversial international issues would be raised while the new organization was finding its feet. But these hopes were not fulfilled.

The General Assembly met in London on January 10, 1946. The British Government had requisitioned the Central Hall at Westminster, and, despite the practical difficulties of the immediate post-war period, every effort was made to house the conference with dignity and appropriate ceremony. The flags of the fifty-one nations fluttered bravely from the building; a smart detachment of Royal Marines provided the Security guards; fleets of cars were placed at the

U.N. General Assembly Meets

PRIME MINISTER WELCOMES THE DELEGATES

Delegates to the first session of the General Assembly of the United Nations in the Central Hall, Westminster, on January 10, 1946, were welcomed by Mr. Clement R. Attlee, the Prime Minister, who here addresses them from the speakers' rostrum. Central figure seated on the platform is Dr. Eduardo Zuleta Angel (Colombia), chairman of the Preparatory Commission and acting chairman of the Assembly. Among the delegates in the front row are those of Saudi Arabia.

Photo, Topical Press

UNITED NATIONS SECURITY COUNCIL MEETS

1. Dr. E. N. van Kleffens, Netherlands Foreign Minister, casts his vote. 2. First meeting of the Security Council. At the table, left to right, Mr. Zygmunt Modzelewski (Poland) ; Mr. Andrei A. Gromyko (Russia) ; Mr. Ernest Bevin (Britain) ; Mr. E. R. Stettinius (U.S.A.) ; Mr. Gladwyn Jebb, Executive Secretary ; Mr. N. J. O. Makin (Australia) in the chair ; Mr. C. de Freitas-Valle (Brazil) ; Dr. Wellington Koo (China) ; Abdul Hamid Badawy Pasha (Egypt) ; Mr. Vincent-Auriol (France) ; Mr. Alfonso Rosenzweig Diaz (Mexico) ; and Dr. E. N. van Kleffens (Netherlands). 3. Left to right, Mr. Andrei Vyshinsky (Russia) ; Sir Alexander Cadogan, Permanent Under Secretary to the Foreign Office ; Mr. Ernest Bevin, British Foreign Secretary ; and Mr. E. R. Stettinius, U.S. delegate, during discussion of the Persian dispute on January 30.

disposal of the delegations, and from a variety of wartime jobs interpreters and translators and experienced *conférenciers* were seconded to provide the administrative staff. Nearly a half of these were former officials of the League of Nations, and many of the delegates themselves brought experience from the League's Secretariat. Eight hundred journalists from every part of the world were accredited to the Assembly, and elaborate arrangements had been made for filming and broadcasting sessions.

On the eve of the opening, H.M. the King gave a State banquet—the first for many years—to the principal delegates in St. James's Palace. Seated on his left was Mr. Paul-Henri Spaak, the Belgian Foreign Minister, who, following the usual custom of preliminary lobbying, had been generally approved as the President for the session.

But one important figure was missing from the gathering of Foreign Ministers and statesmen. Mr. Molotov, the Soviet Commissar for Foreign Affairs, who was to have led the Russian delegation, had created surprise, and because of the earlier difficulties in the Council of Foreign Ministers, some anxiety by announcing that he would not attend the London meetings. His place was to be taken by Mr. Vyshinsky, the Vice-Commissar. For the next week or so this anxiety deepened as Mr. Vyshinsky was reported to be in Sofia, in Moscow, in Berlin: almost anywhere but in London.

However, without waiting for him to arrive, the first General Assembly of the United Nations was formally opened on January 10, 1946, by Mr. Attlee, the British Prime Minister. He closed his opening address with these words : " We who are gathered here today in this ancient home of liberty and order are able to meet together because thousands of brave men and women have suffered and died that we may live. It is for us today, bearing in mind the great sacrifices that have been made, to prove ourselves no less courageous in approaching our great task, no less patient, no less self-sacrificing. We must and will succeed."

Mr. Attlee Opens the Assembly

But on the first day the Soviet delegation gave a foretaste of the vigorous and independent policy which it was to pursue during the next six weeks. With the Ukrainian delegation it intervened to prevent the election of Mr. Spaak as President, and put up a new candidate, Mr. Trygve Lie, the Norwegian Foreign Minister. The intervention was unsuccessful, but it startled the members of the Assembly who had supposed that Mr. Spaak's nomination would be unopposed.

After this unexpected start, the six elected members of the important Security Council — Brazil, Australia, Poland, Egypt, Mexico and the Netherlands—were chosen. The first three were to sit for two years, the others for one year. The representatives of these six countries with those of the five Great Powers were very soon to become the centre of world interest. But for the first week the Assembly was given up to a general debate in which the principal delegates spoke of the magnitude and urgency of the tasks which confronted them.

Statement by Mr. Bevin

An important positive contribution was made by Mr. Ernest Bevin, the British Foreign Secretary, who gave a lead by announcing that the British Government intended to transfer the Mandates which it held over Togoland, the Cameroons and Tanganyika to the United Nations Trusteeship system : and intended to grant independence to Transjordania. The Australian and New Zealand delegates followed with similar declarations concerning their Mandates. Mr. Bidault, the French Foreign Minister, was more reserved about French intentions, and so was the South African delegate.

When, after this general discussion, the General Assembly split up into

UNITED NATIONS ASSEMBLY MEETS IN LONDON

First meeting of the General Assembly of the United Nations was held in the Central Hall, Westminster, from January 10 – February 13, 1946. It was attended by delegates of the 51 nations which had ratified the United Nations' Charter. The Belgian Foreign Minister, Mr. Paul-Henri Spaak, was elected first President. Above, the opening ceremony as seen from the roof: the United Nations emblem is in the top left-hand corner   *Photo, Associated Press*

Committees to carry out its main task of organizing the new organization, it was the Security Council which became the centre of interest. Here events moved swiftly.

Within a week of the establishment of the Security Council, the Persian Government had presented a formal Note drawing the Council's attention to the situation in Persia where, it was alleged, the Soviet forces stationed there by a wartime agreement had interfered with the proper functions of the Persian authorities, and had encouraged the establishment of an autonomous government in Persian Azerbaijan. For the first time the Charter of the United Nations had been invoked and the Persian delegation asked that the Council should recommend the immediate withdrawal of the Russian forces.

By this time the errant Mr. Vyshinsky had arrived in London and within 48 hours there came a swift riposte. Simul-

Russia Accuses Britain

taneously the Russian and Ukrainian delegations presented almost identical complaints to the Council concerning the activities of British troops in two very distant parts of the world. The Soviet Note declared that British forces, then in Greece at the request of the Greek Government, threatened the maintenance of international peace and security. The Ukrainian Note made a similar complaint about the use of British troops which were being employed in Indonesia to disarm and intern the Japanese forces left there, and which had come into armed conflict with Indonesian nationalist extremists.

Whether it was Russian policy to blunt the impact of the Persian appeal, or whether the Soviet Government thought that that appeal had been encouraged by the British Government was not made clear, but " The Times " said quite openly : " The Soviet protest is clearly in the nature of a reprisal, and nothing would have been heard of it but for proceedings elsewhere to which the Soviet Government took exception." Whatever the purpose, the effect of this series of events was to transform what was to have been a " primarily organizational " session into an arena in which Mr. Ernest Bevin and Mr. Vyshinsky exchanged doughty blows, and plainer words were to be spoken at almost every meeting than were exchanged at Geneva during the whole existence of the League of Nations.

These two men—the Briton, a former Trade Union leader who at one time was known as the Dockers' K.C., and the Russian, a lawyer become politician— became the central figures of the dis-

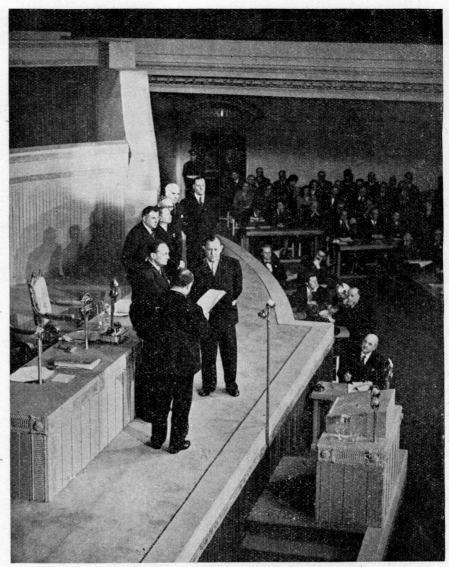

SECRETARY-GENERAL TAKES THE OATH

On February 1, 1946, Mr. Trygve Lie, Norwegian Foreign Minister, was chosen by the General Assembly as Secretary-General of the United Nations. He is here seen (facing the camera) in the Central Hall, Westminster, being sworn in next day by Mr. Paul-Henri Spaak, the President, who reads the oath to him. Mr. Gladwyn Jebb, Executive Secretary, stands between them.

Photo, Topical Press

cussions. Mr. Stettinius, the U.S. delegate, played virtually no part nor did the representatives of the other two Great Powers, Dr. Wellington Koo of China and Mr. Bidault of France. But the most remarkable feature of the handling of these complaints was the bluntness of the new " open diplomacy." Diplomats familiar with the private, discreet, and generally urbane meetings at Geneva listened in consternation as the Foreign Ministers of two of the Great Powers publicly criticized each other and their countries' policies. But not all the delegates were diplomats of the old school—many had played a leading part in resistance movements—and they seemed less concerned about the new form of diplomacy.

The discussion of the Persian appeal was complicated in its early stage by the fact that no sooner had the appeal been lodged than the Persian Government fell, and a new Prime Minister more accept-

Persia's Appeal is Heard

able to Moscow announced that he was prepared to open negotiations with Russia. This made the outcome of the appeal obvious ; but the Council continued with its hearing, and two important factors emerged from the discussions. The first was a decision that any member-country of the United Nations which was not a member of the Security Council was entitled to participate in the Council's deliberations when any complaint it had made, or in

RUSSIAN AND NETHERLANDS DELEGATES

Fifty-one nations were represented at the first meeting of the first General Assembly of the United Nations. Left, Mr. Andrei Vyshinsky, Soviet Vice-Commissar for Foreign Affairs (wearing spectacles), and Dr. Dmitri Manuilsky, Ukrainian Foreign Commissar. Right (left to right), Professor P. S. Gerbrandy, former Dutch Premier ; Professor W. Schermerhorn, Netherlands Prime Minister ; and Dr. E. N. van Kleffens, Netherlands Foreign Minister.

which it was interested, was being considered. The second was a declaration by Mr. Vyshinsky that the Russian Government would regard it as an affront to Russian dignity if the negotiations had to be conducted under the aegis of the Security Council. As a result the outcome of this, the first appeal to the Security Council, was a statement by the President that the Council, having heard the declarations made by the parties, noted that negotiations were to be begun and asked to be informed of the result.

The discussions also revealed weaknesses in the drafting of the Charter, Article 27 of which provides that (1) **Weakness of Drafting in Charter** each member of the Security Council shall have one vote ; (2) decisions of the Security Council on procedural matters shall be made by an affirmative vote of 7 members ; (3) decisions of the Security Council on all other matters shall be made by an affirmative vote of 7 members, including the concurring votes of the permanent members : provided that in decisions under Chapter 6 [Pacific Settlement of Disputes] and under Paragraph 3 of Art. 52 [dealing with regional arrangements] a party to a dispute shall abstain from voting. The Council avoided taking a decision on what precisely differentiated other from procedural matters.

When the question of the British forces in Greece came up it became clear that here was a battle *à l'outrance* between Russia and Britain. Mr.

Vyshinsky declared that the British forces were being used to establish a Right Wing Government in Greece ; that they constituted a threat to international peace and security and that the Council should recommend their immediate withdrawal. Mr. Bevin, to the shocked surprise of the professional diplomats, gave " the lie direct " to Mr. Vyshinsky's accusation that the troops were being used to assist the Right Wing. He assured the Security Council that they would be withdrawn as soon as stability had been restored in Greece, and the Greek Government asked for them to go ; but he demanded that the British troops and the British Government should be acquitted of the charge of menacing international peace.

The British Foreign Minister himself turned to the attack, and accused the Soviet Government of endangering peace by world-wide anti-British propaganda. Mr. Vyshinsky's case was made more difficult by the Greek delegate who insisted that the British troops were in his country at the request of his government, that this was really a matter of Greek sovereignty and that the last thing that Greece wanted was their withdrawal.

After several days—and nights—of meetings, this stage of the Security Council's business ended with declarations by most of the members that they did not consider the presence of British troops in Greece endangered world peace, and the Council took note of the fact that they would be withdrawn as soon as the purpose for which they were

there had been fulfilled. It was another compromise decision ; but the discussions ended on a rather emotional note with Mr. Vyshinsky, Mr. Bevin and Mr. Stettinius, the U.S. delegate, standing with clasped hands while the rest of the Council applauded.

Yet two days later the two main protagonists were at grips again, this time on the Indonesian issue. On this Dr. Manuilsky, the Ukrainian delegate, and **Criticism** Mr. Vyshinsky joined **of Britain** forces in criticizing the use of British troops against what they described as the Indonesian Nationalist Movement, and what Mr. Bevin called extremist Fascist elements which had been armed by the Japanese. Here again the Sovereign power, in this case the Netherlands, spoke of the matter as mainly one of domestic jurisdiction ; and the path to a settlement was smoothed by a declaration from Dr. van Kleffens, the Netherlands Foreign Minister, that negotiations between his government and the Indonesian National Movement were about to begin. Both Russia and the Ukraine pressed for a decision which declared that the British troops were threatening peace, but this the Council refused to give.

There was to be yet another test for the fledgeling Security Council. While these disputes were being heard, the Governments of Syria and the Lebanon had appealed to the Council about the continued presence of French and British troops in their territories. These troops were there largely as a heritage of the war, and, as both the Syrian and Lebanese delegates admitted freely, they were quite satisfied that the British forces would be withdrawn ; they were not so sure about the French. Here again Mr. Vyshinsky's advocacy was

MRS. ROOSEVELT ADDRESSES THE WOMEN DELEGATES

Mrs. Eleanor Roosevelt, widow of President Roosevelt, addressed the first meeting held by the women delegates and advisers to the United Nations conference at Church House, Westminster, on January 4, 1946. On her left is Mrs. Minerva Bernardino, Dominican delegate, and Mrs. E. J. Uralova (White Russia) ; on her right is Miss Ellen Wilkinson, M.P., British Minister of Education. *Photo, Planet News*

exposed himself to what seemed inevitable defeat in the diplomatic field. "The Times" summed up the discussions of the Council in these words :

"The Western Powers have arrived at a clearer understanding of the essentials of Russian foreign policy, which will recognize no interference with its action over the broad borderland of territory **Britain Vindicated** upon which the security of the Soviet Union is held to depend. The Soviet Government on the other hand has received an equally clear intimation that British foreign policy is also founded on clearly determined interests and principles. The vindication of British purposes in the areas of contention discussed by the Council was complete."

While these political issues were being debated so heatedly in the Security Council the Assembly was, more soberly, pressing on with the primarily organizational work. The judges of the International Court of Justice were elected (it was an ironical commentary that when the Court was finally chosen the Assembly had to ask it to give a legal opinion on the legitimacy of the election of the 15th judge). The important post of Secretary-General of the new organization was given to Mr. Trygve Lie, the Norwegian Foreign Minister. The establishment of the Commission on Atomic Energy, to consist of the Security Council together with Canada, when she was not a member of the Council, was approved. The important Economic and Social Council of 18 members was elected and given as one of its major priorities the task of dealing

directed so passionately against Britain and France that Mr. Bidault, the French Foreign Minister, was constrained to accuse him of being " plus royaliste que le roi."

There was to be no compromise this time. A majority of seven members of the Council had adopted a resolution **Majority Decision Accepted** calling for negotiations on the withdrawal of the troops to be begun by F r a n c e, Britain, Syria and the Lebanon. But at this stage Mr. Vyshinsky intervened and exercised his right of veto. Now the veto was intended to be a piece of machinery which would override a majority decision ; but the British and French Foreign Ministers ingeniously turned the tables so that the majority

decision overrode the veto. They both agreed that the Soviet delegate had the right to prevent a formal decision ; but they said the resolution which had been voted clearly showed that the majority of the Council wanted negotiations to be started. They would abide by that decision and begin negotiations.

It was on that note that the first memorable meetings of the Security Council ended. Russian policy had suffered a series of set-backs, and when the Council broke up delegates were still wondering why Mr. Vyshinsky had

MEETING OF UNITED NATIONS MILITARY STAFF

The Military Staff Committee of the United Nations consisting of the Chiefs of Staff (or representatives) of Britain, the U.S.A., the U.S.S.R., France and China, holds its first meeting in London on February 4, 1946. Its function was to advise the Security Council on military matters. Admiral Sir Henry Moore (1) was chairman. Other British representatives are Lieutenant-General Sir Edwin Morris (2) and Air Chief Marshal Sir Guy Garrod (3). *Photo, Topical*

THE KING ENTERTAINS THE UNITED NATIONS

The first State banquet since March 21, 1939—when Mr. Lebrun, then President of France, visited London—was held on January 9, 1946, at St. James's Palace, on the eve of the First General Assembly of the United Nations. At it H.M. the King entertained the delegates to the Assembly. The Diplomatic Corps and nearly all the members of the Cabinet, as well as several ex-Ministers, including Sir John Anderson and Mr. Anthony Eden, were also present. Above, at top table, left to right, Lord Pethick-Lawrence (Secretary for India) ; Dr. Moreno Quintana (Argentina) ; the Earl of Clarendon (the Lord Chamberlain) ; Mr. Manuel Bianchi (Chile) ; the Rt. Hon. Peter Fraser (Premier of New Zealand) ; Dr. de Souza Dantas (Brazil) ; Lord Jowitt (the Lord Chancellor) ; Dr. Eduardo Zuleta Angel (Colombia) ; H.M. the King ; Mr. Paul-Henri Spaak (Belgium) ; Mr. C. R. Attlee (British Premier) ; and Mr. James F. Byrnes (U.S.A.). At the table in the foreground, facing the camera, are, left to right, H. E. Kuzma Kiselev (White Russia) ; Colonel G. Codrington ; H. E. Ato Akilu Hafte-Wolde (Ethiopia) ; the Rt. Hon. Sir Alan Lascelles ; Hamid Bey Frangie (Lebanon) ; the Rt. Hon. George A. Isaacs, Minister of Labour and National Service ; H. E. Eduardo Avilez Ramirez (Nicaragua) ; the Rt. Hon. Anthony Eden.

with the problem of refugees on an international scale. Plans were made for the creation of the Trusteeship Council which was to deal with those territories which had not achieved full self-government. The Military Staff Committee of the Security Council— the representatives of the Chiefs of Staffs of the Five Great Powers— was called together to begin planning the armed forces which were to be the Council's teeth. The first budget for $21,500,000 was voted, and the respective contributions of the various countries assessed.

Gradually, the complicated and closely interlocked structure began to take shape as the experts, the politicians and their advisers, basing themselves partly on the experience of Geneva, partly on the dictates of common sense, built up the machinery of the new organization which to a war-worn world seemed the only hope of a lasting and secure peace.

Occasionally, perhaps, some of these builders cocked an attentive ear to the disputes going on in the Security Council ; but if they did they probably felt more than ever the need for international machinery to deal with international problems and disputes on an international plane. And it was perhaps a timely reminder that the first half of the first General Assembly of the

United Nations should end on a note of grim warning. For on February 13, 1946, the day before the Assembly adjourned, its proceedings were suspended so that the delegates of the Five Great Powers, agreed on this at least, could call attention to the grave shortage of food which threatened the world.

They called for international action to prevent waste and to increase production. Mr. Bevin, who introduced the resolution, said : "This is not a question of a dispute between nations. It is a question of the intervention of Nature itself . . . The period in front of us must be dealt with as a crisis period. In other words it is another war, and we must fight on until we defeat the enemy—Famine !"

Attention Called to Food Shortage

It was with this sombre warning ringing in their ears that the representatives of the 51 nations adjourned until the following autumn. But it was not an adjournment in the usual sense because for the first time since the collapse of the League of Nations they left behind them an international machine which was designed to deal with just such problems as this.

KEEPING CLOSE WATCH ON THE NUREMBERG PRISONERS

Before an International Tribunal at Nuremberg on November 20, 1945, began the public trial of twenty of Germany's major war leaders (see Chapter 386). Those arraigned included Goering, Hess, Ribbentrop, Streicher, Schacht, Papen, Admirals Doenitz and Raeder and Field-Marshal Keitel. President of the Tribunal was Lord Justice Lawrence. This is the main section of the prisoners' block in Nuremberg jail, showing cells occupied by Goering and Hess at extreme right. While awaiting trial, Robert Ley committed suicide on October 25, in spite of the fact that the sentries peered into each prisoner's cell every 30 seconds. *Photo, New York Times.*

FIRST GENERAL ASSEMBLY OF THE UNITED NATIONS MEETS IN WESTMINSTER

An urgent problem facing the organizers of the United Nations meetings in war-damaged London was that of finding a suitable building.   Eventually, the First General Assembly met (from January 10–February 13, 1946) in the Central Hall, Westminster.   Built in 1910, it is the headquarters of the Methodist Church in Britain.   This view from the balcony of the hall during the meeting of the General Assembly shows some of the United Nations' flags.   In the right background lie Central Buildings, whose archway leads to Church House, in Dean's Yard, where the Security Council met.

THIS 'SECRET WEAPON' WAS AIMED AT LONDON

Many of Hitler's 'secret weapons' were put into production too late, and so were never used. Among those discovered by the Allied armies advancing in Normandy in 1944 were these mysterious 400-feet 'gas pipes' dug deep into the Channel cliffs on the French coast. Incapable of either elevation or transverse movement, they were trained directly on London and were designed to fire a sub-calibre, fin-stabilized projectile, 92 inches long. The lateral pipes were to act as booster-chambers to provide additional propelling gases. (See also Chapter 337.)

Photo. Keystone

TROOPS OF THE BRITISH TENTH ARMY LEAVE PERSIA'S CAPITAL

To withstand the threat of a German invasion of Persia through the Caucasus, a separate British Army Command was established in Persia and Iraq in September 1942. Its main tasks were to secure from attack the oil fields and to ensure the transport from the Persian Gulf of supplies to Russia. Main force under the Command was the British 10th Army which included, besides British, Polish, Indian and Iraqi troops. Here, motor vehicles of the Royal Sussex Regiment drive down the Avenue Shah Reza when the 10th Army evacuated Teheran in September–October 1945.

JUSTICE IS DONE UPON GERMAN WAR CRIMINALS

On September 30 and October 1, 1946, at Nuremberg, the International Military Tribunal (*see* Chapter 386), pronounced judgement upon the indicted Nazi leaders. Twelve were found guilty and sentenced to death by hanging ; seven were found guilty and sentenced to terms of imprisonment ranging from ten years to a life term. Three were acquitted and discharged. Vital extracts from the judgement, and individual sentences are given below

THE JUDGEMENT

A common Nazi plan to prepare and wage war had existed. Certain defendants had planned and waged aggressive war against 12 nations.

War crimes had been committed by Germany on the High Seas and in every country occupied by her.

The Germans had also been proved guilty of committing crimes against humanity.

The Leadership Corps of the Nazi party, or a specified group thereof, *was a criminal organization* within the meaning of the Charter of the Tribunal.

The S.S. [the Nazi Black Guard] *was such a criminal organization.*

The Reich Cabinet, as such, could not be declared a criminal organization.

The S.A. [Brown Shirt Storm Troops] was not a criminal organization within the meaning of the Charter.

The German General Staff and High Command was not a criminal organization within the meaning of the Charter.

The Tribunal found that the Nazi leadership *was guilty on all four counts*—conspiracy, crimes against peace, war crimes, and crimes against humanity.

The responsibility could not fall on Hitler alone, but on his military chiefs, his statesmen and those business men who co-operated with him. Such people could not shelter behind official positions to be freed from punishment. Similarly, members of organizations not adjudged criminal can be tried for individual acts.

The war crimes were committed on a scale " never before seen in the history of war," and in particular the persecution of the Jews was a record of consistent and systematic inhumanity on the greatest scale.

INDIVIDUAL DEFENDANTS

GOERING : ' There is nothing to be said in mitigation. Goering was often in deed, and almost always in words and thoughts, second only to his leader. On some specific cases there may be a conflict of evidence, but in terms of the broad outline his own admissions are more than sufficient to be conclusive proof of his guilt. His guilt is unique in its enormity.'

RIBBENTROP : ' He assisted in trying out criminal policies, particularly involving the extermination of the Jews. There is abundant evidence, moreover, that Ribbentrop was in complete sympathy with all the main tenets of the National Socialist creed. His collaboration with Hitler, and his intention in the commission of crimes against peace, war crimes, and crimes against humanity were wholehearted.'

HESS : ' He may have had knowledge of war crimes committed in the east even if he did not participate. The Tribunal, however, did not find that the evidence sufficiently connected Hess with these crimes to sustain a finding of guilt.'

SCHACHT : ' It is clear that Schacht was the central figure in Germany's rearmament programme and that the steps which he took, particularly in the early days of the Nazi regime, were responsible for Nazi Germany's rapid rise as a military power. On the other hand, Schacht, with his intimate knowledge of German finance, was in a peculiarly good position to understand the true significance of Hitler's rearmament, and realized that the economic policy adopted was consistent only with war.'

PAPEN : ' Under the Charter, Papen can be held guilty only if he was a party to the fostering of aggressive war. There is no evidence that he was a party to the plans under which the Austrians were to be the victims of further aggressive action, or even that he participated in plans to occupy Austria by aggressive war itself. It is not established beyond reasonable doubt that this was the purpose of his activities, and therefore the Tribunal cannot prove that he was a party to the common plan under count 1 or that he participated in the aggressive war charged under count 2.'

KEITEL : ' For defence he relies on the fact that he was a soldier and acted under superior orders. Superior orders even given to a soldier cannot be considered in mitigation where crimes so extensive have been committed casually, ruthlessly, and without any military excuse or justification.'

JODL : ' He was the arch-planner of the war and responsible in large measure for the conduct of operations. He was active on the planning against Greece and Yugoslavia and took part in all the conferences preceding the invasion of Russia. Jodl also signed the order to shoot commandos and prisoners of war, the first draft of which was drawn up by his staff. There is little evidence that Jodl was actively connected with the slave labour programme.'

THE VERDICTS AND SENTENCES

The following were found guilty and sentenced to death by hanging :

Hermann Wilhelm Goering. Guilty on all four counts, which were : 1, Common plan or conspiracy to wage aggressive war ; 2, Crimes against peace ; 3, War crimes ; 4, Crimes against humanity.

Joachim Ribbentrop. Guilty on all counts.

Wilhelm Keitel. Guilty on all counts.

Ernst Kaltenbrunner. Guilty on counts 3 and 4.

Alfred Rosenberg. Guilty on all counts.

Hans Frank. Guilty on counts 3 and 4.

Wilhelm Frick. Guilty on counts 2, 3 and 4.

Julius Streicher. Guilty on count 4.

Fritz Sauckel. Guilty on counts 3 and 4.

Alfred Jodl. Guilty on all counts.

Arthur Seyss-Inquart. Guilty on counts 2, 3 and 4

Martin Bormann. Guilty on counts 3 and 4. Bormann was sentenced *in absentia*, since he was not apprehended by the authorities, and there was a strong presumption of his death.

The following accused were found guilty on various counts of the indictment and sentenced to terms of imprisonment :

Rudolf Hess. Guilty on counts 1 and 2. LIFE.

Walter Funk. Guilty on counts 2, 3 and 4. LIFE.

Erich Raeder. Guilty on counts 1, 2 and 3. LIFE.

Baldur Schirach. Guilty on count 4. TWENTY YEARS.

Albert Speer. Guilty on counts 3 and 4. TWENTY YEARS.

Constantin Neurath. Guilty on all counts. FIFTEEN YEARS.

Karl Doenitz. Guilty on counts 2 and 3. TEN YEARS.

Three of the accused were found not guilty on the counts of the indictment with which they were charged. They were therefore discharged.

Hjalmar Schacht. Charged on counts 1 and 2. NOT GUILTY.

Franz von Papen. Charged on counts 1 and 2. NOT GUILTY.

Hans Fritzsche. Charged on counts 1, 3 and 4. NOT GUILTY.

Two other defendants had been indicted : **Robert Ley** and **Gustav Krupp von Bohlen and Halbach.** Ley committed suicide in prison on October 25, 1945. As to Krupp, the Tribunal on Nov. 15, 1945, decided that he could not then be tried, because of his mental and physical condition ; the charges against him were retained for trial thereafter if his physical and mental condition should permit.

DISPATCHES FROM MILITARY COMMANDERS

Outstanding facts from three Reports from Supreme Allied Commanders to the Combined Chiefs of Staff, and fourteen Dispatches from British Commanders to the Secretaries of State for War and Air, all published between May and October 1946. Field-Marshal Lord Gort's Dispatches on the B.E.F. from Sept. 1939 to May 1940 are dealt with in Chapters 147 and 148. Information contained in the Reports of the Chief of Staff of the U.S. Army (July 1943–June 1945), and the Commanding General of the U.S. Army Air Forces (1944), to the Secretary of War is incorporated in the relevant Campaign Chapters of the Second Great War

Maps by courtesy of The Daily Telegraph

ITALIAN CAMPAIGN
JANUARY—MAY 1944

Report by the Supreme Allied Commander, Mediterranean (Field-Marshal Baron Wilson of Libya), to the Combined Chiefs of Staff on the Italian Campaign. (See Chapter 302.)

THE Italian campaign, initiated by General Eisenhower, developed during his three months' direction the features that continued to characterize it: slow, painful advance through difficult terrain against a determined and resourceful enemy. Several small amphibious operations to turn the enemy's flanks were considered—one at Termoli proved encouragingly successful, but a plan to land a small force by sea at Formia in the Gulf of Gaeta had to be cancelled the day before it should have been launched, because the Navy considered it too hazardous an undertaking on account of heavy minelaying by the enemy immediately prior to the intended date of the operation.

ALLIED FORCE HEADQUARTERS
White lettering on blue: red border.

When General Maitland Wilson took over it had become clear that a determined landing behind the enemy's main defence line was "a pressing necessity" in order to obtain passage to Rome. But availability of landing craft was a permanently limiting factor, not only in the Mediterranean, but throughout all the Allied theatres of war. In October 1943, of 90 L.S.T.s operational in the Mediterranean theatre, 68 were due to sail for the United Kingdom almost at once in preparation for the invasion of France; of 201 L.C.T.s, 129 were scheduled to sail to the United Kingdom or India. Difficulties of a similar nature arose over the airborne force to be used: the only suitable team, the 504th Parachute Regiment

of the U.S. 82nd Airborne Division, was due to sail for the United Kingdom early in January to refit and train for the forthcoming invasion of north France.

Permission to retain the 68 L.S.T.s until January 15, 1944 was given; but the date of the proposed landing at Anzio had to be postponed from December 20, 1943, owing to the slowness of the 5th Army's advance. Permission for a further retention of 56 L.S.T.s was obtained, and on January 7 the landing was set for January 22. On January 8 General Alexander met Mr. Churchill at Marrakech (where he was recuperating from an illness), "and means were found to provide the required extra 24 L.S.T.s for the maintenance of the beach-head force until the end of February."

Heavy stores and equipment were

MEDITERRANEAN COMMANDER
Field-Marshal Sir Henry Maitland Wilson, G.C.B., G.B.E., D.S.O., Supreme Allied Commander, Mediterranean Theatre, 1944. From a drawing by Simon Elwes at an Exhibition of South African Middle East War Paintings at the National Portrait Gallery, London, in May 1943.
By kind permission of the artist

loaded in Algiers on eight Liberty ships, to avoid unnecessary congestion in the port of Naples whence the assault task force of 243 vessels, under the command of Admiral Lowry, U.S.N., set sail at 05·00 hours on January 21 under perfect weather conditions. The assault forces, under the command of Major-General Lucas, consisted of some 50,000 U.S. and British troops and more than 5,000 vehicles. The voyage was uneventful and no interception or reconnaissance was made by the enemy. The convoy arrived off Anzio at 00·05 hours on January 22. The port of Anzio was captured before it could be destroyed. Nettuno also was completely in Allied hands in the early afternoon, and before last light the channel had been cleared of mines and the port opened to landing-craft.

Initial opposition was negligible: by midnight on January 22, 90 per cent of personnel and equipment of the assault convoy (36,034 men, 3,069 vehicles and a large quantity of stores) had been put ashore. By 16·00 hours on January 23 the entire British 1st Division and U.S. 3rd Division at assault scales had been landed.

A German Special Order from Hitler captured on January 24 read, "The Gustav Line must be held at all costs for the sake of the political consequences which would follow a completely successful defence. The Führer expects the bitterest struggle for every yard." While implementing this order, Field-Marshal Kesselring built up also a strong counter-attack force to drive the Allies back into the sea and eliminate the threat to Rome. By February 1, the beach-head forces were confronted by the equivalent of five enemy divisions supported by 42 batteries of artillery, Allied thrusts had been blunted and the attack had lost impetus. All parts of the beach-head were under shell fire, and after shelling had destroyed 24 aircraft on the ground, the one Spitfire Squadron was withdrawn, and the

" Hold the Gustav Line "

German U-boats, which had been absent at the time of the landings, were now becoming active.

Stubborn German defence halted the Allied advance all along the Gustav Line. The battle for Cassino had begun ; its capture came after the operations described in this dispatch, the obstacles created by the heavy Allied bombing and shelling of the town proving too difficult to overcome at the moment in face of the enemy's continued obstinate defence of the rubble.

WESTERN EUROPE
JUNE 1944—MAY 1945

Report by the Supreme Commander (General of the Army Dwight D. Eisenhower) to the Combined Chiefs of Staff on the Operations in Europe of the Allied Expeditionary Force. (See Chapters 311, 314, 320, 325, 332, 336, 349, 357, 369)

GENERAL EISENHOWER tells the history of the planning and execution of his West European campaign in considerable and fascinating detail. Here we extract a few of the many fresh facts which his report discloses.

" The chain of Atlantic and Channel ports from Bordeaux to Antwerp was under orders from Hitler himself to fight to the last man and the last round of ammunition," and this led to one notable

SUPREME H.Q. ALLIED EXPEDITIONARY FORCE. *Sword of Liberation on black ; rainbow above with blue field.*

departure from the plan of campaign under which "a primary objective had been the capture of the Brittany ports, through which it was intended to introduce the further divisions from the United States necessary to insure the completion of the German defeat." Instead, "following the collapse of the enemy's west flank at the end of July," Eisenhower decided "to concentrate upon encircling and destroying his forces in Normandy, and to use almost the whole of our available strength in order to attain his object." "Events demonstrated that the decision to throw the maximum weight into the Normandy struggle rather than detach substantial forces to lay siege to the Brittany ports was fully justified. . . . The German armies in Normandy were broken as an effective fighting force, and our way across France was opened."

The initial landing " achieved a degree of tactical surprise for which we had hardly dared to hope," and behind the coastal defences " there was no second-

SUPREME COMMANDER
General of the Army Dwight David Eisenhower, D.S.M. (U.S.), G.C.B. (Hon.), O.M., Order of Suvorov (U.S.S.R.). He was Supreme Allied Commander in the Mediterranean in 1943, and in 1944-45 was Supreme Commander of the Allied Expeditionary Force in Western Europe. This photograph was taken while he inspected the ruins of Bastogne in February 1945.

ary defence line to check our invading armies if they should succeed in penetrating beyond the beach area," so confident was the enemy in the strength of his " Atlantic wall." A similar experience awaited the invader in Germany itself, where " so completely had the Germans relied upon their ability to hold out in the Siegfried Line that east of the Rhine there were no artificial barriers ready to halt our progress other than hastily constructed local defence works."

The German troops which faced the landing parties were composed of men either under 20 or over 45, and " their morale was not of the best : the lavishness of the defences and the concrete protection to their underground living quarters had produced a ' Maginot Line complex,' and having gone below when the bombing began they were not prepared for so prompt a landing when the bombs stopped falling." On the other hand, as the Rhine was approached, despite casualties by then totalling 1,500,000, " German troops continued to put up strong resistance, battling with a stubbornness and Teutonic fury born of the desperate knowledge that they were fighting on their own ' holy soil.' . . ." But their strength was broken, as the Allies had hoped and planned that it should be, before the Rhine was reached, and that barrier, " the greatest natural obstacle with which the Allies had been faced since the landing in France," was breached in

accordance with a plan " basically the same as that envisaged in our long-term plans even before D Day," and with losses that were " fantastically small."

Of the slow realization by the enemy of the nature of the initial landings, General Eisenhower says, " It was not until 16·40 hours that the German 7th Army learned of the Utah seaborne assault, having previously received reassuring reports as to the progress being made against the airborne forces dropped in that area. Meanwhile at noon, the German LXXXIV Corps had optimistically, but prematurely, announced that the attempted landings by the V Corps troops at St. Laurent had been completely smashed. Thanks to such mis-information and to a faulty estimate of the situation, 7th Army decided by the evening of D Day that the landings near the Orne constituted the chief danger in the area so far invaded. . . . This estimate of the situation dominated the enemy's policy, with fatal results, during the ensuing days."

The Supreme Commander's explanation of why Mulberry ' A '—the harbour destined for the use of the Americans—failed to be used is tragic in its simplicity : " By 19 June, the Mulberries were about 90 per cent completed, and over 2,000 tons of stores a day were being handled in the British harbour alone. On that day, 19 June, broke the great storm which at one time seemed certain to bring all our work to disaster. The weather had been unsettled since D Day, but the on-shore gale which now blew up was the worst known in June for 40 years past. The Mulberries took the full force of the mountainous seas driven by the gale . . . The storm continued for four days. . . . To add to our troubles, the enemy's new Oyster mines were activated by the movement of the waters. . . . By 21 June, the Mulberries themselves began to disintegrate, particularly the U.S. installation. . . . Only the blockships saved the situation from becoming one of complete disaster. . . . Some 800 craft were stranded on the beaches. . . . Some 700 were eventually refloated, but the resulting shortage of ferry craft hampered us throughout the summer. Of the Mulberries themselves, that at St. Laurent was so shattered as to be irreparable. The main Phoenix breakwater was broken and the blockships had sunk some ten to twelve feet below their original level."

Among the most interesting points in the report are the references to contact with the Russians. " Our first liaison with Moscow had been effected late in

Tragedy of Mulberry Harbour

1944 when air operations necessitated the establishment of a co-ordinated bomb-line, but . . . up to the end of 1944 I had received no information on matters affecting the Russian grand strategy, although I had expressed my willingness to afford any such information concerning my own overall plans as the Red Army might desire. At Christmas time, however, following upon a message which I sent to the Combined Chiefs of Staff explaining the difficulty with which I was faced in attempting to evolve plans while still ignorant of Russian intentions, President Roosevelt secured from Marshal Stalin his agreement to receive our representative in order to discuss the correlation of our respective efforts in the forthcoming spring. Accordingly, in January, my deputy, Air Chief Marshal Tedder, journeyed to Moscow for this purpose. Marshal Stalin was acquainted with the nature of our own plans, including the timing. He, in turn, responded with a full explanation of the great four-pronged offensive which the Red Army was preparing to launch."

" With the approach of our respective forces from east and west, it was now essential that operations on the two

Russians Told of Plans

fronts should be co-ordinated, and necessary to learn something of the Russians' intentions in order to know best how to exploit such success as our own plan of campaign might achieve. I therefore informed Marshal Stalin of my general plan to strike first in the centre and subsequently to effect a link-up with his forces in the Regensburg–Linz area with a view to neutralizing the Redoubt. Marshal Stalin replied that this scheme coincided entirely with the Russian plans in respect to both the central and southern sectors."

" One of our principal anxieties concerned the mutual identification of our respective forces, both in the air and on the ground. Already, at the beginning of April, our tactical air forces had come into contact and shots had been mistakenly exchanged, and we considered it of the utmost importance that all possible arrangements should be made to insure proper recognition in order to prevent errors and possibly tragic incidents which might result in later recriminations. Following recommendations by the Army Group commanders, a system of recognition signs and signals was eventually arranged by 20 April " and " on 25 April patrols of 273rd Regiment, 69th Division, under V Corps met elements of the Russian 58th Guards Division in the Torgau area."

Considering the slight nature of the relations between eastern and western commanders, the admirable complementary timing of their respective blows seems little short of miraculous.

SOUTHERN FRANCE
AUGUST 1944

Report by the Supreme Allied Commander Mediterranean (Field Marshal Baron Wilson of Libya) to the Combined Chiefs of Staff on the Operations in Southern France. (See Chapter 320)

THE decision to make a major assault on southern France was taken at the conference of Combined Chiefs of Staff held in Cairo late in November 1943, and was subsequently embodied in agreements with Russia reached at the Teheran Conference. To provide the necessary landing-craft to support two assaults on France, the Combined Chiefs of Staff postponed amphibious operations in the Bay of Bengal, tentatively scheduled for 1944 to 1945. On December 6, 1943, the target for operations in both north and south France was set provisionally for the " most suitable date during May 1944."

" The major problem, not only in the Mediterranean, but in every theatre, was the shortage of assault shipping," says General Wilson, and this shortage led in the end to the decision to stage the Mediterranean landings two months after those in Normandy in order that shipping could be released from the north for use in the south.

Amphibious operations against western France, following the breakout into Brittany, or at the head of the Adriatic Sea were proposed as alternatives to the landing in southern France, and General Wilson " recommended from the Mediterranean viewpoint that the strategy best calculated to assist the success of General Eisenhower's operations would be continuation of General Alexander's land advance to the Po Valley and the Ljubljana Gap, with the assistance of amphibious operations against Trieste in September." This plan would " hold out hope of achieving a decisive strategic threat to southern Germany before the end of the year." But General Eisenhower " was firm in his desire for the operation against France, because France was the decisive theatre and additional ports must be acquired for the deployment of reinforcements from the United States in that theatre." General Wilson " was to exercise operational control over the forces after the landings until such time as General Eisenhower was able to assume this responsibility, the date of the transfer to be decided in future conference between us."

Since February 1 the Germans had been building up defences along the entire south coast of France from Cap Benat to Agay Roads, and beach obstacles had been increased. General Wilson asked and obtained additional naval strength, " not because of any significant enemy naval threat, which had been removed once and for all by the surrender of the Italian fleet, but in order to augment our naval fire power against coast defence batteries." Ships and craft of all types to participate in the assault numbered 2,110. Naples was the principal mounting port, but Oran, Taranto and Brindisi were also used. The Airborne Division took off from bases in the Rome area. It overcame all navigational difficulties, and the combined landing casualty figures for parachute and glider troops were roughly 3 per cent.

" The carefully synchronized programme of naval and air bombardment which preceded the assault landings achieved an almost complete neutralization of shore batteries."

Enemy Surprised

Only at one beach, in the St. Raphael area, was there artillery fire serious enough to necessitate the use of an alternative landing beach, although " the enemy was certainly not taken by surprise by the actual fact of an Allied landing ; but his Intelligence was almost totally wrong as to its exact timing and as to the target area," Allied activities " encouraging him to regard Genoa as the most probable objective."

By midday of D plus 1, " the attack was a full day ahead of schedule," and General Wilson's forecast of operations dispatched to the Prime Minister on August 7 predicting the capture of Toulon by September 4, of Marseilles by September 24 proved " unduly pessimistic " : despite the bitter resistance of the German garrisons in both towns, they were in Allied hands during the second week of the invasion. Enemy forces, in fact, had been drawn off from the south by the success of the northern invasion, instead of being drawn off, as originally intended, from the north by the southern invasion.

SOMALILAND, 1939-40

Dispatch submitted to Secretary of State for War on Sept. 12, 1940, by Gen. Sir Archibald P. Wavell, K.C.B., C.M.G., M.C., C.-in-C. Middle East. (See Chapter 108)

FROM 1931 to 1939 the military garrison of British Somaliland numbered 14 British officers, 400 African Askaris, and 150 African reservists. This force, the Somaliland Camel Corps, comprised in 1939 two

Camel Companies (which included two Pony Troops), and one (Nyasaland) Rifle Company. The frontier with Italian-occupied Abyssinia was 750 miles long.

Plans were made for a joint defence, in case of attack by Italy, of British and French Somaliland, but not till May 15, 1940 did the 1st Battalion Northern Rhodesia Regiment of the King's African Rifles reach Berbera; the 2nd Battalion did not arrive until July 12.

It was impossible to obtain funds for defences or roads; not till June 1940 was administrative control of Somali-

Difficulties of Defence

land taken over from the Colonial Office by Middle East Command; and as late as April 1940 Wavell was refused permission to send Intelligence officers over the frontier to obtain information about Italian dispositions. British Somaliland was 2,000 miles from Cairo. There were insufficient aircraft for the many tasks in hand, and often not one to spare for intercommunication; no regular mail service; and letters often took a month to reach Somaliland.

The French armistice resulted in the breakdown of the arrangements for French-British collaboration. General Legentilhomme, in command in French Somaliland, and determined to fight on, was displaced on July 23 by General Germain, sent by the Vichy government by plane, who withdrew French forces from their defensive position in the Pass of Jirre, through which an Italian force estimated at two battalions with 30 motor vehicles advanced.

One Indian battalion (1/2 Punjab Regiment) reached British Somaliland from Aden in the first days of July; the 1st East African Light Battery as well as the 2nd Battalion K.A.R. arrived from Kenya on July 12; the 2nd Battalion the Black Watch arrived on August 7. But superior enemy forces advanced across the frontier at several points, and on August 19 evacuation of British Somaliland was completed by the destruction of the principal Government buildings at Berbera.

CENTRAL NORWAY

Dispatch submitted to Secretary of State for War on May 13, 1940, by Lt.-Gen. H. R. S. Massy, D.S.O., M.C., C.-in-C. North-West Expeditionary Force.
(See Chapter 78)

LIEUTENANT-GENERAL MASSY, appointed C.-in-C. of the Allied forces in Central Norway on April 19, 1940, "exercised this command from his Headquarters in the United Kingdom, as the course of events did not permit the opening of a

* V CORPS
White galley : red cross on sail : on black

Headquarters in Norway." He had as his objects to stop the German advance from Oslo and then to plan a combined operation for the capture of Trondheim.

When General Massy assumed direct control on April 22, Brigadier H. de R. Morgan, D.S.O., with the 148th Infantry Brigade, was in the area south of Trondheim, while Major-General Carton de Wiart, V.C., C.B., C.M.G., D.S.O., was in the Namsos area north of Trondheim in command of Brigadier C. G. Phillips's 146th Infantry Brigade and one demi-brigade of Chasseurs Alpins commanded by General Audet. Major-General B. C. T. Paget, D.S.O., M.C., was selected to command the British forces south of Trondheim: he arrived at Andalsnes on the evening of April 25.

Both Namsos and Andalsnes were being regularly bombed (both were eventually completely destroyed), and the Allied forces north and south of Trondheim had been forced to make withdrawals; but, says General Massy, " should adequate air support be available, I had no reason to suppose that we could not hold our existing positions

* V Corps formed part of N.W.E.F. in Norway, 1940

against the Germans, and at a later date eject them from Trondheim."

The only Allied air support, however, was provided by fighters from H.M.S. " Ark Royal " and " Glorious." On the evening of the 24th, the 263rd Fighter Squadron R.A.F. (18 Gladiators) landed on frozen Lake Lesjaskog, but they were spotted and attacked immediately, and the attempt to establish land-based air support failed.

On April 26 " it became increasingly obvious that in the face of artillery and mortar fire and incessant bombing, to none of which could the Allied troops effectively reply, the German advance could not be stopped. . . . During the afternoon it became evident to me that the chance of our getting any air support which could enable us to compete with the German air menace had vanished. I was convinced that evacuation would therefore be necessary."

The Military Co-ordinating Committee agreed to evacuation, and during the 28th plans were concerted with Admiralty representatives and orders were issued to both General Carton de Wiart and General

Arrangements for Evacuation

Paget. Evacuation of the French was begun on the night of April 28–29. Orders were sent that when Namsos was evacuated a rearguard should fall back on Mosjoen to delay the enemy's advance, another party being sent there by sea; but General de Wiart deemed the land route impossible and no withdrawal by land took place: it was assumed that the Germans could not advance by this route either—an error of judgement, as they made full use of the route, and by May 13 it was " more than likely that we should not be able to hold the place."

In the early hours of April 30, 340, mostly wounded, were embarked on H.M.S. " Fleetwood " from Andalsnes, and at 19.00 hours H.M.S. " Janus " embarked 100 men and two Bofors guns at Namsos and conveyed them to Mosjoen, where they arrived on May 2, having been delayed by dense fog which also prevented ships entering Namsos harbour on May 1. The evacuation of Namsos, however, was successfully carried out on the night of May 2–3, the last ship leaving at 02.20 hours, a total of 5,400 having been embarked. The convoy was continually bombed on its journey across the North Sea. No transport was lost, " but the French destroyer 'Bison' and H.M.S. 'Afridi' were sunk fighting to the end. The losses might well have been far heavier, for there were no air forces supporting the convoy." The force of some 1,700 evacuated from Andalsnes was embarked un-molested, though it had been subjected to a number of "incidents" in its move from Lille-hammer and other positions in the Gudbrandsdal.

Not only had the Allied forces in Central Norway no air cover, but the detailed list of forces allotted to the opera-tions shows that most of the artillery, the medical units, and a large proportion of the R.E. Division which should have been with them were still en route or had not started when it was decided to with-draw the force.

In the light of later events, General Massy's comments on the operation are of special interest: "I have no hesita-tion in saying that a degree of co-operation between the Army and the Air Force, comparable to that which is now the case with Germans, is essential if we are not to remain at a dangerous disadvantage. . . . For this campaign, the expeditionary force headquarters was ordered to form after active opera-tions involving British troops had begun. I cannot stress too strongly the dangers of such improvisation." General Massy listed " certain other require-ments which must be met "—(a) Time for training in amphibian operations ; (b) a suitable training area ; (c) an allotment of landing craft and ships fitted to carry them ; (d) facilities for studying and practising air co-operation, particularly with a fighter and bomber component. (See map in *page 4003*.)

NORTHERN FRANCE
JUNE 1940

Dispatch submitted to Secretary of State for War on June 22, 1940, by Lt.-Gen. Sir Alan Brooke, K.C.B., D.S.O. Commanding II Corps, B.E.F., France. (See Chapters 97, 149)

AFTER the evacuation of the main B.E.F. from Flanders, there re-mained in France the 51st (High-land) Division and the incomplete 1st Armoured Division. These units formed part of IX Corps of the French Tenth Army, then on the line of the Somme. A powerful German offensive of June 5

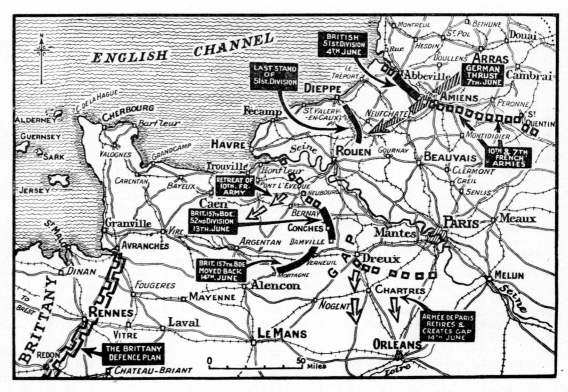

forced the 51st Division, in an exhausted condition after twelve days of continual movement and battle, back fifteen miles to the river Bresle. Another smashing German attack of the 7th split the Tenth Army, cutting off its IX Corps between the Seine estuary and Dieppe, the 51st Division being on the extreme left. On the night of the 8th, the Germans penetrated into Rouen, thus cutting off the 51st Division com-pletely from its proper line of retirement via Rouen.

By June 9 the Germans had es-tablished bridge-heads across the Seine. That day the 52nd (Lowland) Division arrived in France ; one brigade, the 157th, went into the line on the night of June 12–13 to take over an exposed position east of Conches.

On the 13th also Sir Alan Brooke arrived at Le Mans, and at once took command of all British troops in France. He went to French Army Headquarters in Paris, where General Weygand on the 14th told him that the French Army was no longer capable of organized resistance but, in accordance with a decision taken by the Allied Governments, Brittany was to be defended by holding a line across the peninsula in the vicinity of Rennes—a plan Weygand called "romantic." Sir Alan signed instructions for the partici-pation of the B.E.F. in this move ; but on returning to his Headquarters and ringing up the C.I.G.S., he found that neither the C.I.G.S. nor the Prime Minister had heard of such a plan, and

he was told that arrangements were to start for the evacuation of those ele-ments of the B.E.F. not serving with the French Tenth Army ; it was im-pressed on him " that it was most important that everything should be done to ensure good relations between

II CORPS
Red fish on wavy blue bands on white

ourselves and the French, and to avoid, in every possible way, giv-ing the impression that the B.E.F. was deserting them." Later on the 14th the C.I.G.S. informed

Sir Alan that he was no longer under Weygand's orders, and that the B.E.F. was to act as an independent force.

The withdrawal of elements not with the Tenth Army began on June 15 through Brest, St. Malo, Cherbourg, St. Nazaire, Nantes, and La Pallice ; while Sir Alan moved his H.Q. to Vitre, " no known body of troops covering the Le Mans area." Next day, he moved to Redon, thirty miles north of St. Nazaire.

The 157th Brigade was under constant attack from the moment it went into the line. On the 16th the Tenth Army retired on the axis Alençon–Rennes. Co-operation with this movement would have been contrary to instructions given to Lieutenant-General J. H. Marshall-Cornwall (placed on the night of June 14–15 in command of all British troops operating with the French Tenth Army) to withdraw towards Cherbourg, which he ordered his forces to do. The 157th Brigade " was still engaged with the enemy and it was only due to the cool handling and tactical ability of its Brigadier, Sir John Laurie, that it was extricated from its dangerous situation, embussed by midnight on the 16th–17th, moved 200 miles by roads encumbered by columns of troops and refugees and embarked 24 hours later at Cherbourg."

At 13.00 hours on June 17 the C.I.G.S. informed Sir Alan that the B.B.C. had reported that the Pétain Government had asked for an armistice, and that all efforts should be directed to getting personnel away. By 15.30 all communication with London had been cut at Rennes. Sir Alan decided to leave Redon for St. Nazaire, where he went on board the armed trawler H.M.S. " Cambridgeshire," which reached Plymouth at 18.00 hours on June 19. When the last troopship left Cherbourg, at 16.00 hours on the 18th, the Germans were within three miles of the harbour.

BATTLE of BRITAIN

Dispatch submitted to Secretary of State for Air on August 20, 1941, by Air Chief Marshal Sir Hugh C. T. Dowding, G.C.B., G.C.V.O., C.M.G., A.D.C., A.O.C.-in-C. Fighter Command, R.A.F. (See Chapters 110, 114, 115, 119)

AIR CHIEF MARSHAL DOWDING describes the Air Ministry's publication, " The Battle of Britain," as " an admirable account of the Battle for public consumption," but points out two errors, one, the overrating of the Hurricane's speed at 335 instead of 305 m.p.h., of no great importance ; the other much more so : on page 33, it is stated that the " Fighter Squadrons of the Royal Air Force . . . were stronger at the end of the battle than at the beginning." In fact, says Dowding, " the majority of the squadrons had been reduced to the status of training units, and were fit only for operations against unescorted bombers."

Of the four phases of the battle, Air Chief Marshal Dowding says that in the first phase, against convoys and coastal objectives (July 10–August 25), " the amount of physical damage done was not excessive." In the second phase (August 26–September 10) against Fighter aerodromes " Manston, Hawkinge and Lympne, the three advance grounds on which we relied for filling up tanks when a maximum range was required for operations over France, were so heavily attacked that they were temporarily abandoned. . . . Damage done to Fighter aerodromes was serious, and has been generally underestimated. Luckily, the Germans did not realize the success of their efforts, and shifted

their objectives before the cumulative effect of the damage had become apparent to them. . . . By the beginning of September the incidence of casualties became so serious that a fresh squadron would become depleted and exhausted before any of the resting and re-forming squadrons was ready to take its place."

In the third phase (September 11–September 30), the attack on London, " within 24 hours the defences to the south and south-east of London were approximately doubled, and the great increase in the volume of fire was immediately noticed and had a very good effect on public morale . . . . But the main effect was never generally known : on some nights as many as 60 per cent of the raiders approaching London from the south turned back after dropping their bombs in the open country or on the fringe of the barrage."

In the fourth phase (October 1–31), " the main object " was to draw " our Fighters into the air and engage them in circumstances as disadvantageous to us as possible." In that phase, " the apparent ratio of losses in our favour dropped appreciably. I say ' apparent ' because, in fighting at extreme altitudes, fighters often could not see their victims crash, and the percentage reported as Certainly Destroyed was unfairly depressed. . . . Serious as were our difficulties, those of the enemy were worse, and by the end of October the Germans abandoned their attempt to wear down the Fighter Command, and the country was delivered from the threat of immediate invasion."

How remarkable that result was is emphasized by all that Air Chief Marshal Dowding reveals of the inadequacy at that time of identification and tracking of aircraft—radiolocation was in its infancy, and the men of the Observer Corps (later to become the Royal Observer Corps) " constituted the sole means of tracking enemy raids once they had crossed the coast line."

EAST AFRICA
NOV. 1940—JULY 1941

Dispatch submitted to Secretary of State for War on May 21, 1942, by Gen. Sir Archibald P. Wavell, G.C.B., C.M.G., M.C., C.-in-C. Middle East. (See Chapters 163, 164)

THIS dispatch covers reports from Lieutenant-General Sir William Platt, K.C.B., D.S.O. (responsible for operations from the Sudan), from December 1, 1940 to August 26, 1941, and Lieutenant-General Sir Alan Cunningham, K.C.B., D.S.O., M.C. (responsible for operations from Kenya), from November 1, 1940 to April 5, 1941 and April 6 to July 11, 1941.

The reports by General Platt and General Cunningham give detailed accounts of the operations under their command, which cleared the Italians from Italian East Africa except for a pocket of resistance at Gondar (allowed to remain until the following November as it could have no further influence on operations, and Wavell was anxious to transfer troops back to Egypt). The conquest of Italian East Africa was accomplished in four months—from the end of January to the beginning of June. A force of 220,000 men, well found, says General Cunningham, except in a few commodities, was virtually destroyed, with the whole of its equipment.

General Wavell's covering dispatch reveals the background behind these successful campaigns in the field. " During the autumn and winter of 1940–41," he said, " I had to take into account two conflicting policies which were urged on me from different quar-

11th AFRICAN DIV.
Black on White
12th AFRICAN DIV.
White on Black

ters. I was being pressed by the Defence Minister at home to move forces from East Africa to Egypt. . . . General Smuts frequently impressed on me the danger of reducing the forces in East Africa. . . . I resisted proposals to reduce the force in East Africa, at least until we had driven the enemy farther back."

On December 2, 1940, on the eve of the offensive against Marshal Graziani's forces in the Western Desert, General Wavell held a meeting in Cairo at which Generals Platt and Cunningham were present. " The ruling idea in my mind was that the fomentation of the patriot movement in Abyssinia offered with the resources available the best prospect of making the Italian position impossible," says Wavell, who appointed Lieutenant-Colonel O. C. Wingate as staff officer for patriot activities—" his energy and initiative was an important factor in the means by which the patriot movement gained so great an impetus."

" The ultimate pattern of the conquest was a pincer movement on the largest scale, through Eritrea and Somaliland converging on Amba Alagi, combined with a direct thrust through Western Abyssinia by the patriot forces. It looks Teutonic in conception and execution ; but this result was not foreseen in the original plan, but arose gradually through the development of events. It was in fact an improvisation after the British fashion of war rather than a set piece in the German manner.

"General Platt and General Cunningham acted on broad general instructions from me and I made no attempt to control their operations in detail. Success was due mainly to their boldness and skill in execution, the quality of their subordinate commanders and to the dash and endurance of the troops. . . ." In the two months up to the capture of Addis Ababa on April 6, General Cunningham's forces suffered only 500 casualties, of whom under 150 were killed.

The conquest of Abyssinia posed serious problems in the administration of the conquered territory and the security and feeding of the very large Italian civilian population there. A nucleus organization whose formation had been put in train in December 1940 prevented a breakdown in administration ; and apprehensions in regard to Italian civilians proved largely unfounded—the behaviour of the native population to their former conquerors was in general tolerant ; while the food supply was easier than had been expected.

ETHIOPIA, ERITREA AND MADAGASCAR
JULY 1941—JAN. 1943

Dispatch submitted to Secretary of State for War on March 31, 1943, by Lieut.-Gen. Sir William Platt, G.B.E., K.C.B., D.S.O., G.O.C.-in-C. East Africa Command. (See Chapter 225)

BY mid-July 1941 opposition by Italian forces had been almost eliminated, but the maintenance of law and order over more than half a million square miles of conquered territory presented big problems. The country was everywhere armed with rifles, ammunition, grenades, and many automatics, some pumped into Ethiopia from the Sudan to aid the patriots, others issued by the Italians in the unfulfilled hope that they would be used against the British, still others gleaned from deserted battlefields or looted from hidden reserve dumps.

Except in Ethiopia, where the Italians had constructed hundreds of miles of tarred and beautifully graded roads, communications were poor : the four railways between Eritrea and the Zambesi ran from west to east ; save in Uganda and the small island of Zanzibar, there were no roads worthy of the name in the British Colonies, Protectorates and Mandated Territory included in the Command.

EAST AFRICA COMMAND
Crossed machetes on green

With the fall of Gondar, last stronghold in Ethiopia, on November 27, the Italian East African Empire ended. Early in November the Cabinet gave a formal decision for all Italians (numbering some 34,000) to be evacuated from Ethiopia, in accordance with a demand expressed by most Ethiopians from the Emperor downwards. The men were to go as prisoners of war to British East African territories, the women, children and old and infirm men to be repatriated to Italy in Italian ships. Evacuation began in December, although a change of front on the part of the Ethiopians (who went to the length of hiding enemy subjects, so anxious were they to retain their former conquerors for the running of the services the Italians had introduced) and lack of consultation between H.M. Minister, Mr. Howe (who arrived at Addis Ababa in February 1942), and the G.O.C. caused additional difficulties to those already entailed in such an operation.

Japan's entry into the war brought the threat of war to the East African coast. Operations against Ethiopia had caused the Command to face north. It had now to face east. The arrival of coast defence and anti-aircraft units, guns, personnel, and stores began in April 1942.

In response to a War Office request of December 1941, two East African Brigades were selected for service overseas. This was the first time during the war that the employment of East African troops outside Africa had been considered. 21st Brigade embarked at Mombasa early in March 1942 for Ceylon. A brigade also served in Madagascar.

That island remained under Vichy control, and in the first week of May combined forces from Great Britain attacked and occupied Diego Suarez. When by July it became obvious that the Governor-General was unlikely to make the " rapprochement " which had been hoped for, it was decided to undertake further operations. At dusk on September 9 a force arrived from Mombasa just out of sight of land west of Majunga. Neither air nor surface craft had sighted the movement. Shortly after midnight the leading ship of the column of 49 moving in single line ahead dropped anchor. The remainder moved silently to their appointed

stations. A successful landing followed, and by 08.00 hours next day Majunga was in the invaders' hands at a cost of twenty casualties. A rapid advance inland began immediately. Simultaneously with the landing at Majunga, the island of Nosy-Be on the north-west coast was occupied. A party of forty from a Commando unit who landed at Morandava, on the west coast, " by advancing some forty miles inland on their push-bicycles, and by intelligent use of the telephone, created the desired impression that a column of various arms with mechanized transport was advancing on the capital from this place. After 48 hours on land, the diversion was re-embarked." Other landings were made, and troops pushed on towards Tananarive, having to negotiate many road-blocks, but with almost no fighting. They entered the capital on September 23, and were received enthusiastically by all classes of the population.

Some of the officials were unwilling to co-operate with the Allies and were removed, but successors were found and a form of government set up. On October 18 the Governor-General sent a plenipotentiary to negotiate, and hostilities ceased at 14.00 hours on November 5, exactly eight weeks from the day, and 660 miles from the place, of landing at Majunga.

French Somaliland still adhered to the Vichy Government, but after the surrender of Madagascar and the Allied landings in North Africa on November 28, Colonel Raynal and nearly a third

MIDDLE EAST COMMANDERS
General Sir Archibald Percival Wavell, G.C.B., C.M.G., M.C. (right), Allied C.-in-C., Middle East from 1939-41, at an inspection in the Middle East, with Lieutenant-General Sir William Platt, G.B.E., K.C.B. (centre), who was responsible for operations against Abyssinia from the Sudan in 1941 and G.O.C.-in-C., East Africa Command, 1941-45.
War Office Photograph

of the garrison crossed the frontier and announced their adherence to the Allies. On December 26 Colonel Raynal and a Fighting French Force moved into French Somaliland, with strict instructions not to open fire unless first fired on themselves. Two days later the Acting Governor signed an agreement whereby French Somaliland took her place as part of the Fighting French. General Legentilhomme arrived at Jibuti on New Year's Day, 1943, as High Commissioner for French Possessions in the Indian Ocean, and a week later General Platt handed over to him responsibility for the administration of Madagascar, except for the defended area round Diego Suarez.

MIDDLE EAST
AUG. 1939—NOV. 1940

Dispatch submitted to Secretary of State for War on Dec. 10, 1940, by Gen. Sir Archibald P. Wavell, K.C.B., C.M.G., M.C., C.-in-C. Middle East. (See Chapters 108, 130)

AT the outbreak of the war, Middle East Command assumed control over the troops in Egypt, Palestine, Sudan and Cyprus. At that time the fighting forces in the Middle East included no complete formation of any kind ; there were in all 21 battalions of infantry, but only 64 field guns, 48 A.T. guns, and 8 A.A. guns. During the first months of the war, General Wavell was concerned largely with establishing relations with the neighbouring French Commanders in Syria, North Africa, and French Somaliland, and with the military authorities in Turkey. He was allowed to make no preparations against the eventuality of Italy's joining in the war because H.M. Government wanted to avoid doing anything that might impair existing relations with that country.

A few reinforcements, including Australian and New Zealand troops (" magnificent material, but only partially trained and equipped "), arrived between September 1939 and March 1940. A brigade and an air force contingent from South Africa reached Kenya in June—" their quality was extremely high." Southern Rhodesia sent in April " a valuable reinforcement " of 24 officers and 666 men of high quality. Maltese, Cypriots, Mauritians, and Arab and Jewish Palestinians also served in the Middle East forces.

When Italy entered the war (June 10, 1940) there were estimated to be over 215,000 Italian troops in Libya, and over 200,000 in Italian East Africa. Egypt, Sudan, Kenya, British Somaliland adjacent to these countries had

garrisons : Egypt, about 36,000 ; Sudan (1,000-mile frontier with Italian East Africa), about 9,000 ; Kenya (700-mile frontier with Italian East Africa), about 8,500 ; British Somaliland, about 1,475. Palestine, Aden Protectorate, and Cyprus, also liable to attack, had : Palestine, about 27,800 ; Aden, about 2,500 ; Cyprus, about 800. The enemy also had a very considerable numerical advantage in the air. The shortest route by which the Middle East could be reinforced became too precarious ; and 7,000 badly needed reinforcements ready for dispatch in May did not reach the Middle East until the end of August.

After the French accepted the armistice of June 22, General Nogues in North Africa after a little hesitation decided to obey the order to capitulate ; General Mittelhauser in Syria followed suit ; General Legentilhomme in Jibuti (French Somaliland) held out nearly a month, but was unable to induce the colony to continue the struggle.

The foremost defended positions in Egypt were at Mersa Matruh, over 200 miles west of Alexandria and about 120 miles from the Egyptian frontier with Libya. A small British covering force crossed the frontier on the night of June 11–12, capturing Capuzzo and Maddalena on the 14th. An enemy brigade reoccupied Fort Capuzzo, which had been destroyed, but was repulsed before Sollum on the frontier, and the small British force continued to dominate the situation, even after the enemy had been reinforced to a strength of four or five divisions. The enemy crossed the frontier on September 13 on a narrow front along the coast road, and then remained virtually stationary for two months. Published Italian casualties for the period June–mid-September were approximately 3,500 ; British totalled just over 150.

A policy of holding the frontier posts as long as possible was developed in Kenya also, the principal engagement taking place at Moyale, which a company of the King's African Rifles held for several weeks against an Italian force amounting to about a brigade. Not until a second Italian brigade had been brought up was it decided to withdraw the company on July 15. In the Sudan, small mobile forces directed to occupy the principal places on the frontier until attacked by superior forces made several successful raids on Italian frontier posts in the early days of the war, and when finally attacked at Kassala (July 4) and Gallabat (July 6) by greatly superior Italian forces, fought successful delaying actions and inflicted heavy losses on the enemy, who did not follow up his success.

MIDDLE EAST
FEBRUARY—JULY 1941

Dispatch submitted to Secretary of State for War on Sept. 5, 1941, by Gen. Sir Archibald P. Wavell, G.C.B., C.M.G., M.C., C.-in-C. Middle East. (See Chapters 158, 159, 161, 162.)

"IN the six months covered by this dispatch, Middle East was called upon to conduct no fewer than six major campaigns—in Greece, in Cyrenaica, in Crete, in Iraq, in Syria, and in Italian East Africa. During May, five of these were being conducted simultaneously, and there were never less than three on hand at one time. The theatres of these operations were several hundreds of miles apart, in some instances well over a thousand."

In February 1941 the troops available in the Middle East were two armoured, three Australian, one New Zealand and one British Divisions, a Polish Brigade Group, two Indian Divisions (in Eritrea), and one South African and two African Divisions (in East Africa). Of the two armoured divisions, the 7th had been fighting continuously for eight months and was mechanically incapable of further action. The 2nd had arrived from the United Kingdom on January 1, 1941, was two regiments short, and the tanks of two of its regiments were in need of new tracks.

Of the three Australian divisions, the 6th was seasoned and fully equipped. The 7th had had no training as a division and was not fully equipped ; the 9th had only just arrived, was only partially trained, and was very short of equipment. The British 6th was being formed out of battalions in Egypt. The Polish Brigade Group was not fully equipped.

G.H.Q.
MIDDLE EAST
Brown on Black

The maximum force that could be made available for Greece was part of the 2nd Armoured Division, the New Zealand Division, the 6th and 7th Australian Divisions, and the Polish Brigade—virtually all the troops in the Middle East that were fully equipped and fit for operations. But at the time "the Italian armies in Cyrenaica had been so completely defeated that any counter-attack by them could be ruled out for some time to come." Intelligence, however, was weak, and Wavell was unaware that a German Light Armoured Division had begun to land at Tripoli early in February.

It had been understood that the Greek C.-in-C., General Papagos, would withdraw Greek troops from Macedonia, Eastern Thrace and probably Albania (totalling 35 battalions) to the Aliakhmon Line, a short, naturally strong defensive line west of Salonika; but after the Germans entered Bulgaria (March 1) it was found that, apparently for political reasons, he had not done so, " and there was every prospect of the Greek forces being defeated in detail." The difficult nature of the country, the poor communications, and the severe climate in March and April added to the problems confronting the British forces under General Sir H. M. Wilson, whose dispatch to Greece began on March 5. The German attack opened on April 6. By the 20th, the general situation showed that the end of Greek resistance was near. Evacuation began on the night of April 24–25 after the capitulation of the Greek army in the Epirus. The total number of troops sent to Greece was approximately 57,660. Close on 43,000 were safely re-embarked; 27,000 were landed in Crete and the remainder were taken back to Egypt. All guns, transport and equipment other than personal were, however, lost.

Meanwhile the situation in Cyrenaica had been deteriorating. German air attacks made it impossible to use the port of Benghazi, and all supplies to forward troops had to be taken overland from Tobruk, 200 miles away. But from January to April inclusive only 5,865 vehicles (instead of the 3,000 a month promised) arrived; and all 8,000 vehicles sent to Greece were lost in the evacuation.

On March 21 the last Italian detachment left in Cyrenaica (at Jarabub Oasis) was captured. On March 31 the enemy counter-offensive began. General Neame, commanding in Cyrenaica, acting on instructions, fought a delaying action. But the detachment guarding Msus, the principal dump of petrol and supplies for the armoured division, destroyed all the petrol on hearing that the enemy were approaching. The 3rd Armoured Brigade, lacking petrol, was cut off and captured in Derna. H.Q. 2nd Armoured Division (with almost no armoured vehicles) with other

units which had reached Mechili, was attacked in force, and except for " certain parties which showed great determination and resource," was captured; a disaster attributable " mainly to the poor mechanical state of its vehicles, nearly half of which were in the workshops while the remainder were in no condition for a prolonged retreat."

Wavell decided that it was essential to hold Tobruk, both for the large reserves of supplies there and to prevent the enemy from obtaining the use of the port and water supply for his further advance, and he ordered a brigade of the 7th Australian Division to be embarked and sent round to Tobruk, where it arrived on April 7. Some tanks which had been under repair in Tobruk were reinforced with some more tanks from Egypt. A mobile force left outside the defences was driven back to the Egyptian border near Sollum by April 11, and Tobruk was invested.

Until the arrival of Imperial troops from Greece (most of whom were in need of rest and were short of equipment of all kinds), there were three battalions only in Crete, an island about 160 miles long and 40 wide. 16,000 Italian prisoners of war, captured by the Greeks, were under guard on the island. Every effort was made to send stores and material, but a considerable proportion was sunk on the voyage, including about half the field-guns and more than half the engineer stores required for constructing defences.

On May 20 German parachutists estimated to number over 7,000 landed, and though the majority were accounted for, small parties established themselves at various points. The enemy's air strength decided the struggle, for by May 25 " no merchant ships had any chance of survival within 50 miles of the island." Evacuation had to be carried out at night, from beaches reached by rough paths from the high ground above; 14,500 were got out.

" The defence of Crete," says General Wavell, " though unsuccessful, undoubtedly frustrated the enemy plan for future operations by destroying so large a portion of his airborne troops. The total enemy losses were at least 12,000–15,000, of whom a very high proportion were killed. The defence saved in all probability Cyprus, Syria, Iraq and perhaps Tobruk. . . . The Crete fighting may prove a turning-point of the war."

WESTERN DESERT
DEC. 1940—FEB. 1941

Dispatch submitted to Secretary of State for War on June 21, 1941, by Gen. Sir Archibald P. Wavell, G.C.B., C.M.G., M.C., C.-in-C. Middle East. (See Chapters 131, 153)

IN accordance with prearranged policy, little opposition was offered to the Italian advance to Sidi Barrani, and it was not proposed to oppose the enemy in strength until he reached prepared defences at Mersa Matruh. About the middle of October 1940, however, when the enemy had been stationary for a month, General Wavell had decided to attack, believing the morale, training, and equipment of his forces would offset their inferiority in numbers. The invasion of Greece by Italy at the end of October, and the demand for support from Greece, necessitated a delay in the execution of the plan until the beginning of December, but preparations went forward. Dumps of ammunition, water and petrol were established between the British lines at Matruh and the enemy lines, apparently without attracting the enemy's notice. " Several days' **Advance Against Italians** supplies for the whole force were actually stored some 20 to 30 miles in advance of our fortified lines, covered only by our advanced patrols." The plan of attack involved a preliminary movement of some 70 miles for the majority of the troops over open desert. This was to be covered in two marches on successive nights (the whole force being mechanized or motorized), the attack taking place on the early morning following the second night march. The whole force, therefore, had to spend one day in the open desert, within about 30 miles of the enemy, who made no move.

By nightfall of December 10 Sidi Barrani had been captured. By the 15th all enemy troops had been driven out of Egypt. British equipment, notes General Wavell, in particular the Infantry Tanks, Cruiser Tanks and 25-pounders, proved to be excellent. On January 3, 1941, a new attack began. Bardia was secured by the 5th. Early on January 21 Tobruk was entered without resistance. Benghazi surrendered on February 7. (See map.)

" During the two months from December 7 to February 7 the Army of the Nile advanced 500 miles. They had beaten and destroyed an Italian army of four Corps comprising nine divisions and part of a tenth, and had captured 130,000 prisoners, 400 tanks, and 1,290 guns, besides vast quantities of other war material. In these operations we

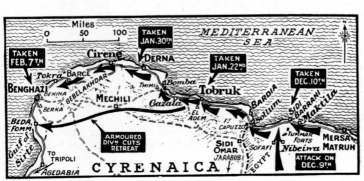

never employed a larger force than two divisions, of which one was armoured. . . . The 7th Armoured Division took part in the operations throughout, at the end of which it was practically reduced to a skeleton. Our casualties amounted to 500 killed, 1,373 wounded, 55 missing only.

"The Army owes much to the Royal Navy, under Admiral Sir Andrew Cunningham, for its support throughout the operation, both in prearranged bombardments of enemy positions previous to the attacks on Sidi Barrani, Bardia and Tobruk, and in answering emergency calls during the actual attacks. . . . The maintenance problems in this quick-moving operation would have been insurmountable without the Navy's assistance in keeping open the sea supply lines."

MIDDLE EAST
JULY—OCTOBER 1941

Dispatch submitted to Secretary of State for War on March 8, 1942, by Gen. Sir Claude J. E. Auchinleck, C.B., C.S.I., D.S.O., O.B.E., A.D.C., C.-in-C. Middle East Forces. (*See Chapter 162*)

"ON taking over command of the Middle East Forces on the 5th July, 1941, I found the general position incomparably better than it had been a year earlier on the collapse of France. This improvement was entirely due to the energy of my predecessor, General Sir Archibald Wavell, and his vigour in seeking out the enemy wherever he was to be found . . . Only in the North had recent events [the enemy occupation of Greece and Crete] made our position more difficult."

The rapidity with which General Wavell's campaigns in Libya, Eritrea, Abyssinia, Greece, Crete, Iraq and Syria had been undertaken with inadequate forces and equipment entailed a comprehensive programme of reorganization, improvisation, re-equipment and training, already in progress when General Auchinleck took over.

Syria was occupied by British and Free French Forces, following the convention signed at Acre on July 14, 1941, by General Wilson and General de Verdillac (representing Vichy France). The garrison in Cyprus was increased, in case of attack through Turkey. Occupation of Iran (Persia) began with the entry of Russian troops from the north and British troops from Iraq on August 25 and was completed on August 28, when the Shah ordered all resistance (little had been offered) to cease. Efforts to concert plans with Turkey in case of an attack on her by Germany came to nothing : "although I believe the

Turks are genuine in their desire to exclude the Germans from their country and to side with us if the situation is favourable, I cannot conceal from myself the possibility of circumstances proving too strong for them, and I am making my plans accordingly."

At a conference at Baghdad on September 26, attended by the C.-in-C. India and General Auchinleck, it was agreed that the Joint Planning Staff, Middle East, should study the problem of defending Persia, Iraq, Palestine and Syria against invasion either through Western Anatolia or the Caucasus or by both routes.

Operations in East Africa were virtually at a standstill. An East African Command established on September 15, 1941, took over control of the area.

In the Western Desert, where the enemy also was reorganizing, as British armoured units were re-equipped and became more numerous, a more offensive policy was gradually adopted. Throughout the summer the enemy devoted much attention to building defences on the frontier between Sollum and Sidi Omar. The defenders of Tobruk, "behaving not as a hardly pressed garrison but as a spirited force ready at any moment to launch an attack," contained an enemy force twice their strength— four Italian divisions and three German battalions—from April until November. The whole Australian garrison except one battalion was got out and replaced by fresh troops in the moonless periods of August, September and October. The service rendered by the Royal Navy, the Fleet Air Arm, and the R.A.F. made it possible to carry out the relief with negligible loss of army personnel, and to maintain the fortress in spite of heavy risks and great difficulties.

IRAQ, SYRIA, PERSIA
APRIL 1941—JAN. 1942

Dispatch submitted to Secretary of State for War on October 18, 1942, by General Sir Archibald P. Wavell, G.C.B., C.M.G., M.C., C.-in-C. India. (*See Chapters 165, 166, 184*)

EVENTS in Iraq in early April 1941 led to the diversion of a convoy, at that time embarking at Karachi for Malaya, to Basra, where it arrived on April 18, evidently greatly to the surprise of Rashid Ali. On April 21 the Iraq Government formally agreed to the arrival of the British troops on condition that no further troops should be landed before those who had already arrived had crossed the frontier out of Iraq. Ancillary troops disembarked at Basra without incident on the 29th.

The first hostile move by the Iraq forces occurred on April 30, when two infantry brigades supported by artillery and some armoured cars began to concentrate round the R.A.F. camp at Habbaniya, training their guns on the camp. A demand for the withdrawal of these troops was refused by the Iraqi Commander, and hostilities broke out on May 2, the R.A.F. station being shelled intermittently until May 5. The camp was also bombed and machine-gunned by the Iraqi Air Force. The R.A.F. bombed the Iraqi positions. In spite of the fact that the aerodrome was often under heavy fire, the R.A.F. during this period evacuated by air to Basra a large number of women and children sent from Baghdad to Habbaniya.

R.A.F. Camp Attacked

By May 3 Iraqi forces had occupied Rutbah, and all refineries and oil installations were in their hands. But on May 6 the British forces at Habbaniya succeeded in clearing the plateau. Iraqi troops were driven from Basra area by May 7. Fallujah was occupied on May 19. On May 12 German aircraft, on May 29 Italian, made their first appearance in Iraq.

Meanwhile, Rashid Ali and many of his principal supporters had fled the country, and the Iraqis asked for an armistice, signed at Baghdad at 15.00 hours on May 31. Mosul was occupied on June 3.

Assistance in the Syrian campaign was then given precedence over all other tasks in Iraq, and on June 22 a force moved to Haditha with orders to capture Abu Kemal, known to be occupied by some French troops and rebel Iraqis. Operations in Syria were completed by July 14.

The attitude of the Iranian (Persian) Government over the expulsion of Axis nationals led to the presentation of an Anglo-Soviet note on August 17. The reply being unsatisfactory, an advance into Persia began on August 25 by sea and overland. As British troops were approaching Ahwaz on the 28th, the news of the Shah's "cease fire" was received. The refinery area was occupied on August 29, and on August 30 troops reached Kermanshah. Russian forces were met at Senna on August 29 and just south of Kazvin on August 31. Russians from the east and west and British from the south entered Teheran on September 17. After a combined British-Russian parade on October 17, the Russians withdrew to Kazvin and Pahlevi, the British to Sultanabad and Hamadan on the 18th.

Work continued on the construction of fortress areas in north Iraq and in Persia throughout the winter. In spite of exceptionally severe conditions, very good progress was made. Work also continued steadily on the development of the main base area at Basra-Shaibo and advanced bases near Baghdad and at Kirkuk and Ahwaz (Persia) ; construction of aerodromes in north Iraq and Persia ; improvement of road, rail and river communications and construction of telegraphic communications in Iraq and Persia ; development of Um Qasr and Bandar Shahpur (Persian Gulf) ports.

INDIA AND BURMA
MARCH–DEC. 1942

Dispatch submitted to Secretary of State for War on September 27, 1943, by Field-Marshal The Viscount Wavell, G.C.B., C.M.G., M.C., A.D.C., C.-in-C. India. (See Chapter 223)

AFTER the fall of Rangoon early in March 1942, when the threat of a Japanese invasion of India became serious, there was in that country no single fully-trained division, troops having been sent abroad since the beginning of the war as quickly as they could be trained. Less than 150 A.A. guns were available to defend Calcutta, India's largest city, instead of the estimated total requirement of 1,500. Instead of the 64 squadrons of aircraft which Wavell considered necessary, there were ten—one of them, at Dinjan, obsolete Audax fighters, six of them in Ceylon. This last concentration proved fortunate, for Japanese carrier-borne aircraft attacked Colombo on April 5, Trincomalee on April 9. The enemy, who suffered considerable losses, did little damage on land ; but a squadron of Blenheims sent to attack his aircraft-carriers was virtually destroyed without accomplishing anything ; and Japanese aircraft sank two 8-inch cruisers "Dorsetshire" and "Cornwall," the aircraft-carrier "Hermes," and some smaller vessels in the waters around Ceylon. "In the Bay of Bengal Japanese light forces and aircraft sank just on 100,000 tons of merchant shipping, dropped a few bombs on Vizagapatam—the first on Indian soil, and caused a panic on the eastern coasts of India. . . . This was India's most dangerous hour ; our Eastern Fleet was powerless to protect Ceylon or eastern India ; and it was becoming increasingly obvious that our small tired force in Burma was unlikely to be able to hold the enemy, while the absence of communications between Assam and Upper Burma [Wavell gives details showing the absence of even one adequate line of communications in north-east India] made it impossible to reinforce it. For-

tunately the enemy naval force withdrew, and no Japanese surface warships have since appeared in Indian waters."

Wavell asked the War Cabinet for help, but he learned that " the Eastern Fleet, instead of being strengthened, was likely to be further reduced for operations in the Mediterranean to provision Malta, that two brigades of the 5th British Division on the way to reinforce India were being diverted for the capture of Madagascar, to which also was being sent an East African brigade which I had been led to expect for Ceylon ; and that the Australian Government was demanding the return to Australia of the two brigades in Ceylon." All these dispositions were made, despite Wavell's protests to the Minister of Defence, but, says Wavell, " Events proved his judgement correct.'

Before any operations could be effected, roads had to be constructed, railways improved and extended. Construction of over 200 airfields was put in hand, the air force was expanded.

An exceptionally heavy monsoon caused extensive flooding north of the Brahmaputra and landslides on the road to Imphal—the sole line of communication with a large part of the force in Burma. "This was followed by the worst malaria epidemic which India had known for many years." "The rebellion organized by Congress was directed especially against our communications in north-east India " and troops equivalent to 58 battalions had to be " used for internal security " instead of continuing their " legitimate work of training and equipping for the dry weather season." Terrorism by the Hurs had to be put down. Some 400,000 civilian refugees from Burma had to be transported and fed—a number marooned at Shingbwiyang for the monsoon period had to be fed by air ; and parties attempting to reach Ledo from Fort Hertz via the Chaukar pass had to be rescued. "General Stilwell himself, the American Chief of Staff to the Generalissimo, had been cut off in Burma and had to make his way on foot to Assam." Several thousands of Chinese troops reached India from Burma.

Brought up to a strength of approximately 30,000 by Chinese flown in from China during October, November and December, they were trained for operations from India into Burma.

Fort Hertz in the extreme north of Burma was reoccupied by air ; and plans for the reconquest of Burma, much on the lines of the actual campaign, were worked out, although Wavell's hopes of mounting seaborne attacks against Akyab and Lower Burma in early 1943 were frustrated.

PERSIA AND IRAQ
AUG. 1942—FEB. 1943

Dispatch submitted to Secretary of State for War on April 8, 1943, by Gen. Sir H. Maitland Wilson, G.B.E., K.C.B., D.S.O., C.-in-C. Persia and Iraq Command. (See Chapters 246, 266)

THE successes gained by the Germans during the summer of 1942 in their South Russian offensive made it necessary to take account of the possibility that they might succeed in occupying the whole of Caucasia, and later undertake an invasion of Persia. Their simultaneous advance into Egypt not only denied to the C.-in-C. Middle East freedom to move forces rapidly from Egypt to Persia (the basis of previous plans for the defence of the latter), but led also to the withdrawal from the British 10th Army of troops, equipment and transport to reinforce the 8th Army in Egypt.

The decision to create in Persia and Iraq a separate Command directly under the War Office was made in August 1942. General Maitland Wilson

PERSIA AND IRAQ COMMAND
Red on royal blue

was appointed C.-in-C., his tasks being (1) to secure at all costs from land and air attack the oilfields and oil installations in Persia and Iraq ; (2) to ensure the transport of supplies to Russia to the maximum extent possible without prejudicing his first task.

"In carrying out my first task," he says, " it would obviously have been preferable for British forces—Army and Royal Air Force—to have given direct assistance to the Russian defence in the Caucasus ; . . . the unwillingness of the Russians rendered such a course impracticable."

There was a shortage of vehicles of all types, and " my capacity to maintain sufficient forces in north Persia was the limiting factor, rather than the availability of forces to the Command.

"The Russian authorities in north Persia were averse from concerted planning, and comprehensive reconnaissance was impossible. . . ."

In the event of attack, the problem would have been to maintain a hold on the only areas offering facilities for airfields between the River Araxes to north and the open country about Kazvin-Teheran-Hamadan on the south.

By November 1942, however, the campaign in Russia and the Allied offensive in North Africa had made a German attack on north Persia virtually impossible at least until the spring.

The defence of northern Iraq was entrusted to the Polish Army in the East, assisted by the Iraqi Army.

In the meantime, aid was going through Persia to Russia. The development of this route began in the autumn of 1941, and any decision to curtail or suspend these supplies, in order to permit the Allied forces to be maintained in their forward operational areas, was felt to be fraught with many difficulties, both political and military, and only to be taken at the last possible moment. In the event, no German attack developed, and the flow of supplies continued unhindered save by the difficulties inherent in the passage across an undeveloped country. The total quantity forwarded from September 1942 to February 1943 inclusive was 245,000 tons, the highest figure in any month being 51,000 tons in February 1943.

N. W. EUROPE
JUNE 1944—MAY 1945

Dispatch submitted to Secretary of State for War on June 1, 1946, by Field-Marshal The Viscount Montgomery of Alamein, G.C.B., D.S.O. (See Chapters 311, 314, 325, 332, 336, 349, 357)

GENERAL MONTGOMERY (as he then was) arrived in England from Italy on January 2, 1944, to begin work on his part in the plans for the assault on the Continent known as Operation OVERLORD. He was to act as Commander-in-Chief of the Allied land forces for the assault, and subsequently until the stage was reached when a complete American Army Group could be deployed on the Continent.

The first part of this dispatch describes the plan that was made, the forces it was decided to employ, and the technical details of the assault. The second part describes the actual assault and the campaign that followed.

A few points of special interest are here extracted. The drop of 6th Airborne Division, just before the landings, was on the whole more scattered than had been planned, " but one repercussion of this was that the enemy was misled about the area and extent of the landings." Heavy seas were running in the Channel during the sea passage, and " it was an outstanding feat on the part of the naval forces that in spite of this every main essential of the plan was carried out as intended."

Montgomery issued orders to the United States 1st Army to capture Cherbourg and clear the Cotentin peninsula of the enemy, he instructed the British 2nd Army to capture Caen by the development of a pincer move-

HEADQUARTERS 21st ARMY GROUP
Gold swords on blue cross on red shield

ment. Enemy resistance in the Caen area was strong. A table shows that while the maximum number of Panzer divisions opposite the Caumont–Cotentin sectors during the period June 15–July 25 was three (on July 20), the minimum number opposite the Caumont–Caen sectors was four on June 15, the maximum 7½ on June 30–July 5 ; maximum tanks engaged on the western sectors were 215 on July 5 ; on the eastern 725 on June 30, with 520 on June 15 as the minimum.

Following the successful breakout in the west, on September 1 the Supreme Commander assumed command and direction of the Army Groups himself, Field-Marshal Montgomery being concerned thenceforth only with the 21st Army Group, that is, the British and Canadian forces with the various Allied contingents serving with them, plus at various times one or more of the American armies.

The eventual mission of the 21st Army Group was the isolation of the Ruhr. The immediate aim of all the Allied armies was to establish bridge-heads over the Rhine throughout its entire length, and to go no farther until Antwerp or Rotterdam was opened.

The airborne battle of Arnhem to secure a bridge-head across the Lower Rhine began on Sunday, September 17 : " had reasonable weather conditions obtained," says Montgomery, " I believe the Arnhem bridge-head would have been established and maintained."

Special amphibious devices enabled troops to operate in flooded Walcheren.

" The battle of the Ardennes was won primarily by the staunch qualities of the American soldier."

" The keynotes of the battle of the Rhineland were the intense and fanatical opposition of the enemy who, as we had hoped, accepted battle west of the Rhine, and secondly the appalling weather conditions. The northern flank of the Reichswald operation was conducted mainly in various types of amphibious vehicles."

By March 27, 1945, the bridge-head over the Rhine was established and next

day the advance to the Elbe began, Montgomery progressively cutting the German east-west lines of communication to the coast and delivering a series of right hooks to round up the enemy, one hook securing Bremen. A manoeuvre for a similar outflanking of Hamburg was under way when the Germans came to negotiate on May 2.

In the course of his summing up, Montgomery says, " The mighty weapon of air power enabled the Army to conduct its operations successfully and with far fewer casualties than would otherwise have been the case." The early stages of the campaign " in plain terms meant the export overseas of a community the size of the population of Birmingham." " Planned operations were never held up even for a single day by any lack of administrative resources." " I am convinced, as a result of experience gained from Alamein to the Baltic, that it is fundamentally unsound to aim at producing one type of tank for co-operation with the infantry and another for the armoured division. We require *one* tank which will do both jobs. I have learnt that the ubiquitous use of armour is a great battle-winning factor." " Nearly two thousand Bailey bridges were erected—some nearly a mile long." " The healing of war wounds has been revolutionized by penicillin."

NORMANDY FRONT
The position on the Normandy front on D day plus 68 (August 13, 1944), showing the pivot on the British left flank at Caen on which swung the whole movement that led to the crossing of the River Seine a week later and the subsequent drive into Belgium.

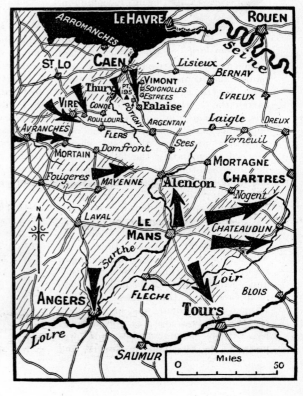

REPORTS ON NAVAL ACTIONS AND TANKS

Here set down are the salient features of the Official Reports on the loss of H.M.S. 'Glorious' off Norway in 1940, the Operations against the 'Scharnhorst,' 'Gneisenau' and 'Prince Eugen' in the English Channel in 1942, and War-time Tank Production. Also included are details of 'Operation Sea-Lion' – the German plan for the invasion of Britain in 1940

Maps by courtesy of The Daily Telegraph

LOSS OF 'GLORIOUS'
JUNE 8, 1940
[Hansard May 8, 1946]. (See Chapter 104)

THE evacuation of Narvik was decided upon on May 24, the very day that British destroyers were evacuating British troops from Boulogne under the guns of the enemy. The forces were to sail in four groups containing in all 13 large transports and a number of storeships. The escort forces consisted of two cruisers (the " Coventry " and the " Southampton "), six destroyers, the " Vindictive " (repair ship) mounting six modern anti-aircraft guns, one sloop, and a number of trawlers.

The aircraft carrier " Glorious " was dispatched from Scapa to Narvik on May 31 to evacuate R.A.F. Gladiator and Hurricane aircraft from Bardufoss

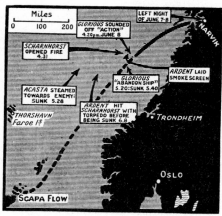

in north Norway. For some months aircraft carriers and other heavy ships had, in the absence of any threat from the German Navy, been proceeding independently across the North Sea without incident. Had the " Glorious " had

Motto : ' The Name Explains Itself '

sufficient fuel, she would have accompanied the second large group of ships from Narvik, as did her sister aircraft carrier the " Ark Royal." The " Glorious," however, was an old ship, whose endurance was limited, and it was consequently necessary that she should proceed immediately the fighters were flown on as otherwise it was calculated she would have insufficient fuel to reach British territory. Two destroyers, " Acasta " and " Ardent," were sent with her as anti-submarine escort.

The " Glorious " shaped course for Scapa at 03.00 hours on June 8, by which time an enemy force consisting of the two battle-cruisers " Scharnhorst " and " Gneisenau " (9 11-inch, 12 5.9-inch each) and the cruiser " Admiral Hipper " (8 8-inch) was in Northern waters. Its presence was not detected by British reconnaissance and was unknown to Flag Officer, Narvik, and

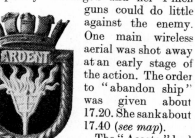

Motto . ' Remember Your Ancestors '

to the C.-in-C. Home Fleet. They had left Kiel on June 4 and passed Bergen about midnight on the 5th. The " Glorious " was proceeding at 17 knots. Only one of five torpedo-spotting-reconnaissance aircraft on board was available for service. No reconnaissance aircraft were up, and none had been up since she parted company from the " Ark Royal." Shortly after 16.00 hours two ships were sighted on the north-west horizon. They were the " Scharnhorst " and the " Gneisenau." About 16.20 action was sounded off. The " Acasta " made for the enemy at high speed, and both destroyers laid a smoke-screen which caused both battle-cruisers to cease fire for some time.

Shortly after the action began, the forward upper hangar of the " Glorious " was hit. A fire started, and was got under control, but it destroyed the Hurricanes and prevented any torpedoes from being got out. A salvo hit the bridge about 17.00 and a heavy shell struck her aft about 17.15. She was completely outranged and her 4-inch guns could do little against the enemy. One main wireless aerial was shot away at an early stage of the action. The order to " abandon ship " was given about 17.20. She sank about 17.40 (*see map*).

The " Acasta " had been sunk about 17.28. The " Ardent,"

however, was still capable of action and as she steered to the south-east fired a four-tube salvo, hitting the " Scharnhorst " with one torpedo abreast of the after 11-inch turret. The " Ardent " was sunk at 18.08. But her single torpedo hit severely damaged the " Scharnhorst," reducing her speed, and the German battle-cruisers abandoned their cruise and made for Trondheim and thus the approaching convoy with its 14,000 troops was saved from attack.

The nearest British warship was the " Devonshire " (cruiser), 80 to 100 miles to westward. No British ship received an intelligible report of the action ; none received any wireless signal. The first news of the loss of the " Glorious " came from a German broadcast on June 9 at 15.00 Heavy loss of life was entailed :

naval losses were 1,474 ; R.A.F., 41. Of the crew of the " Glorious " 38 and of the " Acasta " one were picked up on June 1 by the small Norwegian vessel " Borgund." Five from the " Glorious " and one from the " Ardent " became

Motto : ' Through Fire and Water '

prisoners of war. The motor boat of the " Glorious " could not be floated owing to the heavy list. A large number of men got on to Carley floats but provisions and water had not been provided in all of them, on account of the fire raging in the hangar where the emergency rations were stored. It was very cold (46°) ; there was a sea running (which in the " Acasta " capsized the boats), and within a few hours men were collapsing from exhaustion. One float with 22 officers and men was reduced to four by the morning of the 9th. On that day a British cruiser and destroyers were seen by survivors to the north-west, some five miles off. Aircraft from H.M.S. " Ark Royal " carried out most extensive air reconnaissance during the day, and two passed close over the survivors on rafts in the water, and were seen by those survivors, but it was the tragic fact that these aircraft did not see the rafts.

OPERATION SEA-LION
AUGUST 1940
German Plan for the Invasion of England
(See Hist. Docs. 167, 168: illus. page 1329)

THE plan of Operation Sea-Lion, found in Berlin, was published on September 26, 1945. First, the Luftwaffe was to gain command of the air over southern England and the Channel. Second, both flanks of the Straits of Dover, and the western entrance to the Channel, were to be sealed off by closely concentrated mine barriers. Third, Army Group " A," consisting of the 16th Army (which was to sail from Ostend, Calais, and Boulogne, and land between Margate and Hastings), and the 9th Army (to sail from Dieppe, Le Havre and Caen and land between Brighton and Portsmouth), was to secure beach-heads, airborne troops clearing the exits from the Romney Marshes, the defiles through the South Downs behind Brighton, and other key points in the Brighton area. Army Group " A " having landed, Army Group " B " (consisting of a reinforced 6th Army) was to sail from Cherbourg Peninsula and land west of Bournemouth in Weymouth Bay (*see map*), by which time the Germans presumably anticipated that Army Group " A " would have drawn the central British reserves towards Kent.

Army Group " A's " first main objective was a line from the Thames estuary about Tilbury south-westward through Caterham, Leatherhead and Aldershot to Southampton Water. Army Group " B's " first objective was not set down. The second objective of both groups was a line from Colchester to about Bristol. London was to be encircled and cleared. That achieved, strong mobile forces were to overrun the industrial areas of the Midlands, South Wales, Lancashire, and Yorkshire, and occupy the important ports.

For the assault, the two groups had available eleven infantry and two

mountain divisions (much the same strength as the nine Allied divisions put ashore on June 6, 1944, in Normandy). For exploitation of their beach-heads, they had an armoured force of six tank, two motorized, and one S.S. divisions. In addition, there were to be nine infantry divisions in Army and Army Group reserves, and eight infantry divisions in G.H.Q. reserve, a total of 39 divisions in all.

The Army's specific task was to draw up the operation plan for all units of the first wave ; that of the Navy, to supply transport, using the ships of defeated enemy States. As much heavy artillery as possible was to be used to secure the crossing, and railway artillery was to be brought up opposite Dover to fire on targets on the mainland.

The Luftwaffe failed in the first phase of the operation, with the result that the German High Command continually postponed invasion until the project had to be abandoned.

SCHARNHORST, GNEIS— ENAU & PRINZ EUGEN
FEBRUARY 12, 1942
Report dated March 2, 1942, on the circumstances in which the German battle-cruisers 'Scharnhorst' and 'Gneisenau' and the cruiser 'Prinz Eugen' proceeded from Brest to Germany.
(See Chapter 213)

THE German battle-cruisers "Scharnhorst" and "Gneisenau" were located at Brest on March 28, 1941. The 8-inch gun cruiser "Prinz Eugen" was first seen there in dry dock on June 4. The R.A.F. made a long series of raids on the ships, though none of them suffered damage which would seriously affect its seaworthiness. Enemy destroyers and smaller vessels began to arrive at Brest in January 1942, and on February 11 the afternoon photographic reconnaissance showed that all three heavy units were out of dock. On the other hand, the torpedo booms were in place protecting the ships, which did not suggest a move that night.

The presence of the German battle-cruisers in the Channel was first reported to the Admiralty and Air Ministry shortly before 11.30 on February 12. They must have been out in open water and steaming towards the Straits of Dover for at least 12 hours before H.Q. was notified : how did that happen ?

It was a very dark night ; reliance therefore had to be placed on the ASV. But the ASV of the aircraft on " Stopper " patrol off Brest broke down, and so did that of the aircraft of S.E. patrol next in order, which was ordered to return to base at 21.38 and not replaced

because it was considered that, if the Germans had already come out, patrols farther up Channel would be sure to catch them, and that in any event they would be through the area patrolled by the S.E. patrol before a relief aircraft could arrive. In fact there was no effective reconnaissance between 19.40 and 22.38 on February 11. A daylight patrol on the 12th from Cap Gris Nez to the Somme did notice some small vessels at 08.30, but missed the big ships. No further routine air patrol was flown ; but two fighter reconnaissances sighted at least one of the big ships, and on the report of the second, which saw and recognized the battle-cruisers, action was taken.

It appears probable therefore that the ships slipped through our night patrols owing to the unfortunate breakdown of the ASV in "Stopper" and S.E. patrols, and to the fact that the other patrols just missed them. In the best circumstances, the reliability and efficiency of ASV instruments could not at the time be assessed higher than approximately 50 per cent. The Report states that, having regard to the fact that it was known that the first "Stopper" patrol and the S.E. patrol had failed to function effectively on the night of February 11, it would have been prudent to make a daylight reconnaissance down Channel westward of the Cap Gris Nez–Somme area. It also remarks it would have been prudent to send out an aircraft to replace the aircraft on S.E. patrol as soon as information was received that its ASV was useless.

ASV Failed to Function

The significance was missed of an enemy attempt to jam the RDF screen which began approximately at 09.20 and continued intermittently for about 50 minutes when it became continuous.

The general opinion was that the Germans would make the attempt to run through the Channel by night, and that probability coloured all the actions and arrangements of Coastal Command and the Admiralty. When the authorities were suddenly confronted with the presence of the German ships in daylight, a little to the westward of the Straits, they had little time to organize fighter co-operation for an attack in the Straits.

Against fast, heavily armoured ships the most effective air weapon available was undoubtedly the torpedo bomber, and the provision of a powerful and highly trained striking force of torpedo bombers called for urgent consideration, states the Report. Contrary to expectation, a handful of comparatively slow M.T.B.'s which, owing to the extreme urgency, were unsupported either by motor gunboats or by aircraft, were yet able to get within range and launch their torpedoes against the battle-cruisers, in broad daylight, subsequently withdrawing without loss: this suggested that a greatly increased force of an improved type of M.T.B. would be of the greatest value for offensive action against enemy fighting ships and transports in narrow or coastal waters. The most numerous force employed Bomber Command, played a comparatively ineffective if gallant part in the battle, due in the main to weather conditions; but the evidence showed that Bomber Command was not designed for effective attack on fast moving warships by day. Destroyers stationed at Harwich intercepted a signal at 11.56 and proceeded at top speed in the direction of the rendezvous, but visibility grew steadily worse all day. They did not sight the enemy until 15.43, and though one, the "Worcester," fired a torpedo from a range of 2,400 yards (the others being farther off), no effective hit was scored.

TANK PRODUCTION

Reports by the Select Committee on National Expenditure and Replies by the Government (1942 and 1944)

PRINCIPAL points in the Committee's critical memorandum of August 26, 1942, were, "The decision to go into large scale production of 6-pdr. guns ought to have been balanced by a plan so timed as to produce tanks to carry the guns when they were ready. In fact, time was wasted in working out the tank plan, especially in the stage of design. . . . The story of tanks and six-pounder guns seems to show lack of decisive direction, division of responsibilities as between tanks and guns, and failure to consult manufacturers until a late stage in the work on the design have led to failure to make full use of manufacturing resources in getting timely production of effective weapons. Other examples of similar failure have come to notice in the case of Self-Propelled Artillery. There has been a division of responsibility based apparently on a distinction between a tank carrying a gun (which has been treated as a 'tank') and a gun mounted on a tank chassis (which has been treated as 'self-propelled artillery')."

At the beginning of its second report, dated March 11, 1944, the Committee states, "The general conclusion [of its first report] was that there had been faults in organization which had led to avoidable waste of time, money and material resources. . . . Changes were made in the organization which appeared substantially to satisfy the Committee's recommendations" (*e.g.* that the "responsibility of the War Office and the Ministry of Supply should be more closely 'clamped together'"). The Committee, influenced to make its second report "by the consideration that unfavourable comment was prevalent about tank production," goes on, "On our review of the position, it is impossible to avoid the general impression that, measured in terms of production of tanks fit for current battle requirements, the British manufacturing effort of 1943 has fallen far short of realizing expectations or being fully effective, and has involved what appears to be a wasteful use of national resources." It then goes into detailed criticisms, and in a summing up says: "Whatever their significance, the main facts remain that, apart from the VALENTINE tank in Russia and the limited use of the CHURCHILL in Tunisia, no British tanks during 1943 have been considered worthy of a place in the main battles; that British tanks issued to British troops have gained a bad reputation both for mechanical reliability and fighting arrangements; that British factory workers have seen very large quantities of completed tanks broken up, or parts (finished and half-finished) piling up to be taken away as scrap; and that these things have combined to create a psychological atmosphere about British tanks among all concerned with handling them which must have unfortunate effects and which in our view deserves the urgent attention of the War Cabinet. The past record, in fact, puts the onus of proof very heavily on those who claim that all is now well with the organization for tank production. . . . The new organization has not fully 'made good' and the expectations recorded in the earlier Report have not been fulfilled."

The War Cabinet's reply of August 2, 1944, includes comments from General Montgomery: "In the fighting [in Normandy] to date we have defeated the Germans in battle; and we have had no difficulty in dealing with German armour once we had grasped the problem.

War Cabinet Replies to Committee

In this connexion British armour has played a notable part. We have nothing to fear from the Panther and Tiger tanks; they are unreliable mechanically, and the Panther is very vulnerable from the flanks. Our 17-pdr. gun will go right through them. Provided our tactics are good we can defeat them without difficulty;" and from General Leese: "The Churchills stood up to a lot of punishment from heavy anti-tank guns. Several tanks were hard hit without the crews being injured. They got across some amazingly rough ground" [in the Adolf Hitler Line in Italy]. The Cabinet reply concludes by saying, "Further methods of strengthening such links [between the troops in the battle lines and the design and production organizations] are continually being studied. Officers with recent operational experience are kept in close touch with all stages of development. . . . It is agreed that it would be a national disaster if the country were to fail during the war to build up a first-class organization for producing British Tanks. With the growth of experience in industry and in Government establishments, this objective is being progressively achieved and the Committee need have no fear that every effort is not being exerted towards that end."

'BRITISH ARMOUR PLAYED A NOTABLE PART'

On May 10, 1945—two days after war in Europe had ended—it was disclosed that the British advance across Germany had been led by the 'Comet' (seen above), the fastest and heaviest cruiser tank to date, carrying heavier armour than the 'Cromwell,' a 77-mm. gun and new gun-laying devices. It played a major part in breaking up the German forces between the Rhine and the Elbe.

Photo, New York Times Photos

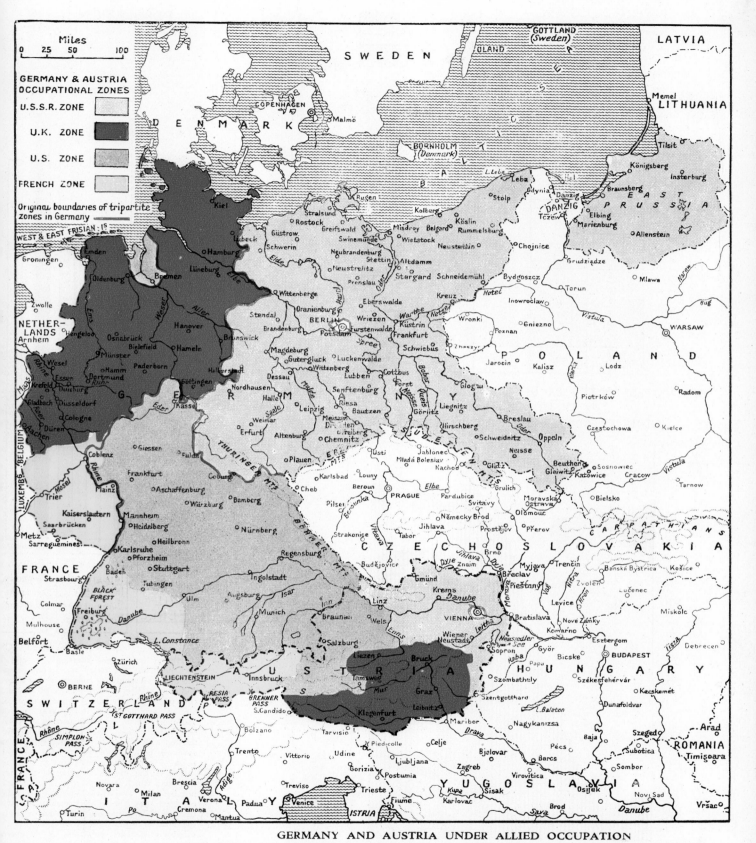

GERMANY AND AUSTRIA UNDER ALLIED OCCUPATION

This official map shows the lines of demarcation of the British, French, American and Russian zones of occupation in Germany and Austria prior to the Berlin Conference, at which Germany east of the Oder and its tributary the west Neisse, and part of East Prussia, were placed under Polish administration (see map in page 3875). The Bremen enclave was transferred to the British authorities on December 10, 1945, the ports of Bremen and Bremerhaven, however, continuing to be operated by the Americans.

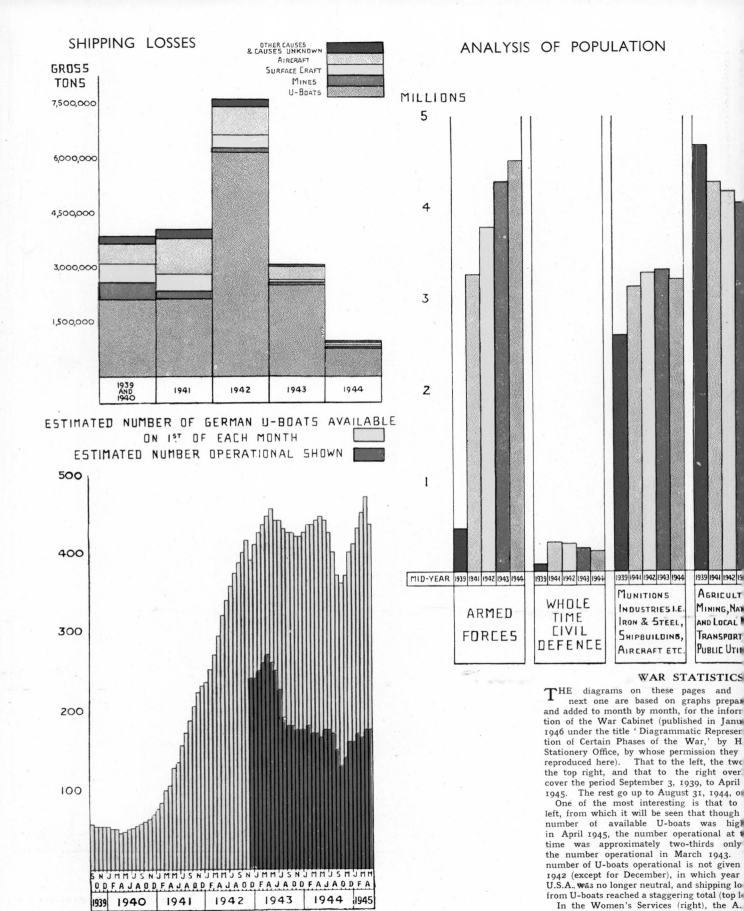

SHIPPING LOSSES

GROSS
TONS

OTHER CAUSES
& CAUSES UNKNOWN
AIRCRAFT
SURFACE CRAFT
MINES
U-BOATS

7,500,000

6,000,000

4,500,000

3,000,000

1,500,000

| 1939 AND 1940 | 1941 | 1942 | 1943 | 1944 |

ESTIMATED NUMBER OF GERMAN U-BOATS AVAILABLE
ON 1ST OF EACH MONTH
ESTIMATED NUMBER OPERATIONAL SHOWN

500

400

300

200

100

S N J M M J S N J M M J S N J M M J S N J M M J S N J M M J S N J M M J S M J M M
O D F A J A O D F A J A O D F A J A O D F A J A O D F A J A O D F A J A O D F A

| 1939 | 1940 | 1941 | 1942 | 1943 | 1944 | 1945 |

ANALYSIS OF POPULATION

MILLIONS

5

4

3

2

1

MID-YEAR | 1939 | 1941 | 1942 | 1943 | 1944

ARMED FORCES

WHOLE TIME CIVIL DEFENCE

MUNITIONS INDUSTRIES I.E. IRON & STEEL, SHIPBUILDING, AIRCRAFT ETC.

AGRICULTURE MINING, NATIONAL AND LOCAL TRANSPORT PUBLIC UTILITIES

WAR STATISTICS

THE diagrams on these pages and
next one are based on graphs prepared
and added to month by month, for the information of the War Cabinet (published in January
1946 under the title 'Diagrammatic Representation of Certain Phases of the War,' by H.M.
Stationery Office, by whose permission they are
reproduced here). That to the left, the two at
the top right, and that to the right over
cover the period September 3, 1939, to April 30,
1945. The rest go up to August 31, 1944, only.

One of the most interesting is that to the
left, from which it will be seen that though the
number of available U-boats was highest
in April 1945, the number operational at that
time was approximately two-thirds only of
the number operational in March 1943. The
number of U-boats operational is not given for
1942 (except for December), in which year the
U.S.A. was no longer neutral, and shipping losses
from U-boats reached a staggering total (top left).

In the Women's Services (right), the A.T.S.
doubled in strength from 1941 to 1942, the peak

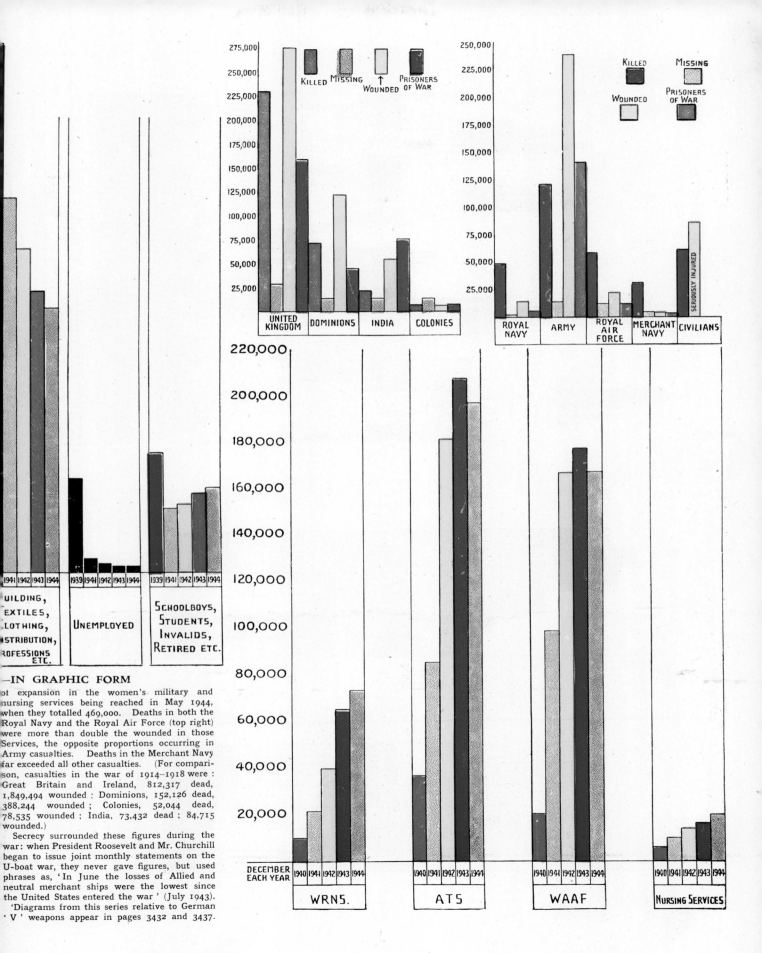

—IN GRAPHIC FORM

of expansion in the women's military and nursing services being reached in May 1944, when they totalled 469,000. Deaths in both the Royal Navy and the Royal Air Force (top right) were more than double the wounded in those Services, the opposite proportions occurring in Army casualties. Deaths in the Merchant Navy far exceeded all other casualties. (For comparison, casualties in the war of 1914–1918 were : Great Britain and Ireland, 812,317 dead, 1,849,494 wounded ; Dominions, 152,126 dead, 388,244 wounded ; Colonies, 52,044 dead, 78,535 wounded : India, 73,432 dead ; 84,715 wounded.)

Secrecy surrounded these figures during the war: when President Roosevelt and Mr. Churchill began to issue joint monthly statements on the U-boat war, they never gave figures, but used phrases as, 'In June the losses of Allied and neutral merchant ships were the lowest since the United States entered the war ' (July 1943). 'Diagrams from this series relative to German ' V ' weapons appear in pages 3432 and 3437.

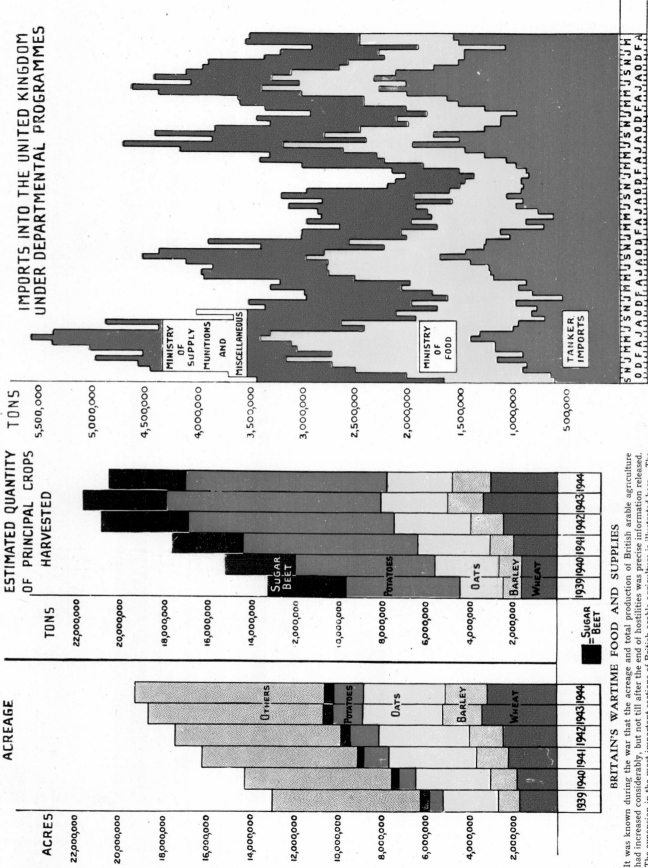

IMPORTS INTO THE UNITED KINGDOM
UNDER DEPARTMENTAL PROGRAMMES

TONS

5,500,000

5,000,000

4,500,000

4,000,000

MINISTRY
OF
SUPPLY
MUNITIONS
AND
MISCELLANEOUS

3,500,000

3,000,000

2,500,000

2,000,000

MINISTRY
OF
FOOD

1,500,000

1,000,000

500,000

TANKER
IMPORTS

1939 1940 1941 1942 1943 1944 1945

ESTIMATED QUANTITY
OF PRINCIPAL CROPS
HARVESTED

TONS

22,000,000

20,000,000

18,000,000

16,000,000

14,000,000

12,000,000

10,000,000

8,000,000

6,000,000

4,000,000

2,000,000

SUGAR
BEET

POTATOES

OATS

BARLEY

WHEAT

1939 1940 1941 1942 1943 1944

= SUGAR
  BEET

ACREAGE

ACRES

22,000,000

20,000,000

18,000,000

16,000,000

14,000,000

12,000,000

10,000,000

8,000,000

6,000,000

4,000,000

2,000,000

OTHERS

POTATOES

OATS

BARLEY

WHEAT

1939 1940 1941 1942 1943 1944

BRITAIN'S WARTIME FOOD AND SUPPLIES

It was known during the war that the acreage and total production of British arable agriculture
had increased considerably, but not till after the end of hostilities was precise information released.
The expansion in the most important sections of British arable agriculture is illustrated here. The
right-hand diagram shows the fluctuations month by month in imports of different categories.
Imports of the Ministry of Food are analysed diagrammatically in page 403i.

GENERAL INDEX

This index is designed to give ready reference to literary and pictorial contents of THE SECOND GREAT WAR
*Page numbers in italics indicate illustrations. Biographical data have been prefixed to entries relating
to outstanding wartime personalities.   In order to clarify reference to items dealing with much-fought-over
regions, approximate dates have been inserted in parentheses. A systematic scheme of cross-reference is embodied.*

C

The part played by women in Britain's war effort

REPLACING MEN

4 examples from Group 2 Industries

Each BLACK symbol represents **10,000** women added
Each WHITE symbol represents **10,000** men withdrawn

AGRICULTURE ETC.

IN
OUT

LOCAL GOVERNMENT SERVICE

IN
OUT

PUBLIC UTILITY SERVICES

IN
OUT

TRANSPORT, SHIPPING AND FISHING

IN
OUT

The total number of men in all branches of Group 2 industries fell by 600,000 and the number of women rose by 800,000

Britain mobilized with all her might

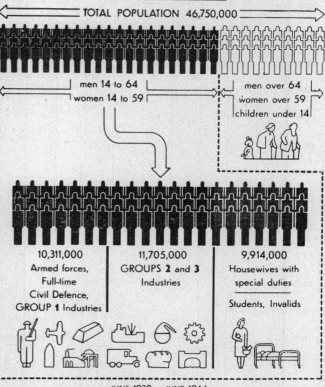

TOTAL POPULATION 46,750,000

men 14 to 64 | men over 64
women 14 to 59 | women over 59 | children under 14

JUNE 1939 — JUNE 1944

DETAILS OF BRITAIN'S WAR EFFORT

These diagrams are from a White Paper issued in Nov. 1944. Group 1 industries include munitions, aircraft, shipbuilding, chemicals and explosives. Group 2, agriculture, mining, Government service, gas, water, transport, food, etc.; Group 3, building, civil engineering, clothing, distributive trades, commerce, and professional services.

Men of the United Kingdom under Arms

'In June of each year'

EACH SYMBOL REPRESENTS **250,000** MEN

1939
1941
1942
1943
1944

Total number of men who have served or are serving

Including the number killed, missing, taken prisoner or released on medical and other grounds, the total during this war is over **5,500,000**

Imports of Foods & Animal Feeding Stuffs into U.K.

(Excluding Imports from Eire)

in thousand tons

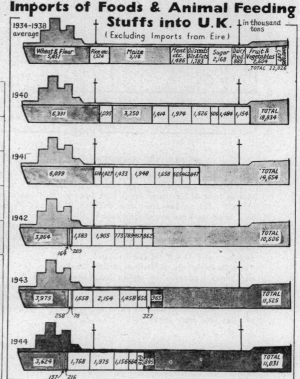

1934-1938 average — Wheat & Flour 5,451 | Rice etc. 1,524 | Maize 5,114 | Meat etc. 1,486 | Oilseeds Oils&Fats 1,783 | Sugar 2,168 | Dairy Prod. 889 | Fruit & Vegetables 2,604 | TOTAL 22,026

1940 — 6,331 | 1,095 | 3,250 | 1,914 | 1,974 | 1,526 | 506 | 484 | 1,154 | TOTAL 18,834

1941 — 6,099 | 514 | 1,027 | 1,433 | 1,948 | 1,658 | 565 | 962 | 847 | TOTAL 14,654

1942 — 3,864 | 164 | 209 | 1,583 | 1,905 | 773 | 789 | 457 | 862 | TOTAL 10,506

1943 — 3,975 | 258 | 78 | 1,658 | 2,154 | 1,458 | 655 | 327 | 963 | TOTAL 11,525

1944 — 3,624 | 137 | 216 | 1,768 | 1,975 | 1,156 | 664 | 969 | 695 | TOTAL 11,031

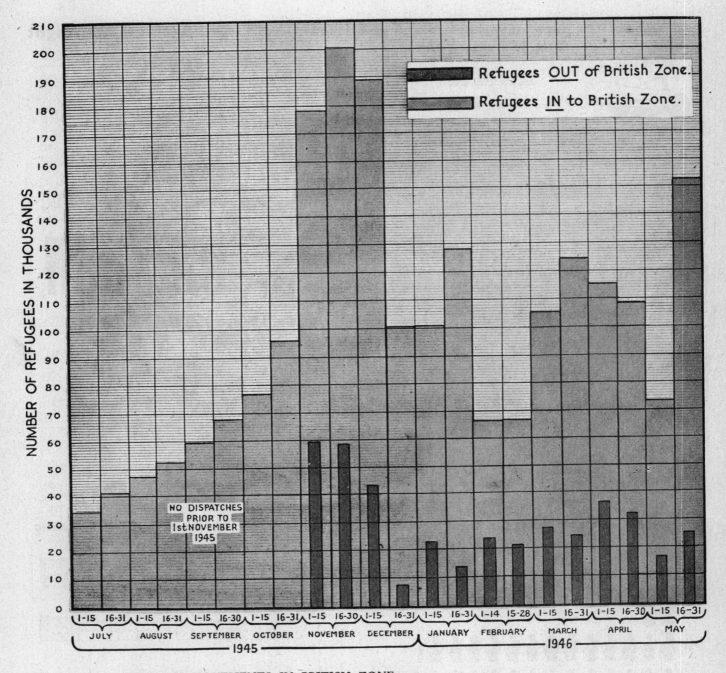

NUMBER OF REFUGEES IN THOUSANDS

Refugees OUT of British Zone.

Refugees IN to British Zone.

NO DISPATCHES PRIOR TO 1st NOVEMBER 1945

| 1-15 | 16-31 | 1-15 | 16-31 | 1-15 | 16-30 | 1-15 | 16-31 | 1-15 | 16-30 | 1-15 | 16-31 | 1-15 | 16-31 | 1-14 | 15-28 | 1-15 | 16-31 | 1-15 | 16-30 | 1-15 | 16-31 |

JULY · AUGUST · SEPTEMBER · OCTOBER · NOVEMBER · DECEMBER · JANUARY · FEBRUARY · MARCH · APRIL · MAY

—— 1945 —— —— 1946 ——

REFUGEE MOVEMENTS IN BRITISH ZONE

THIS diagram—exhibited at the 'Germany Under Control' exhibition in London during June–July 1946—shows the movement of refugees in and out of the British zone of Germany from July 1945 to May 1946. It does not include prisoners of war. The intake from the Russian, U.S., and French zones, and from Austria on a head-for-head exchange basis, totalled 1,603,000. Intake on an other than head-for-head exchange basis totalled 2,324,500, being made up as follows : from Russia, 770,000 ; Poland, 1,500,000 ; Norway, 4,000 ; Denmark, 4,500 : The Netherlands, 800 ; Belgium, 1,200 ; France, 2,000 ; Spain, 16,000 ; United Kingdom, 15,000 ; Empire, 10,000 ; and U.S.A., 1,000.

Those leaving the British zone for the Russian, U.S. and French zones and Austria numbered 1,142,000, of whom 1,046,000 went to the Russian zone. The excess of incoming over outgoing refugees was therefore 1,182,500. The great mass of the 1,500,000 refugees described as from Poland were former inhabitants of the areas east of the Oder placed under Polish administration by decision of the Berlin Conference of 1945 (see page 3931).

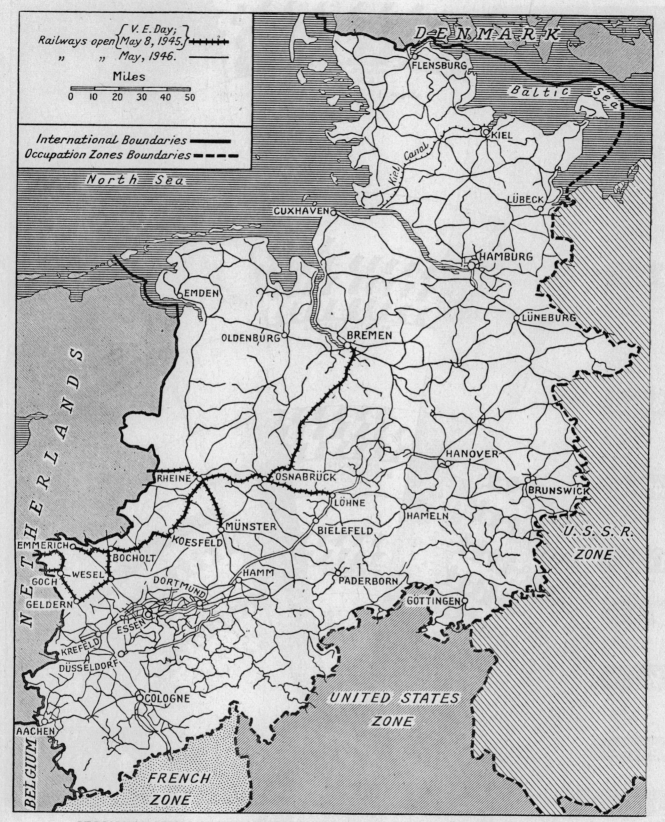

DENMARK

FLENSBURG

Baltic Sea

KIEL

Kiel Canal

LÜBECK

North Sea

CUXHAVEN

HAMBURG

LÜNEBURG

EMDEN

OLDENBURG

BREMEN

HANOVER

BRUNSWICK

RHEINE

OSNABRÜCK

LÖHNE

HAMELN

U. S. S. R. ZONE

MÜNSTER

BIELEFELD

KOESFELD

EMMERICH

BOCHOLT

HAMM

PADERBORN

WESEL

DORTMUND

GOCH

GÖTTINGEN

GELDERN

ESSEN

N E T H E R L A N D S

KREFELD

DÜSSELDORF

COLOGNE

UNITED STATES ZONE

AACHEN

B E L G I U M

FRENCH ZONE

RECONSTRUCTION IN THE BRITISH ZONE OF OCCUPIED GERMANY

In 1939, there were in what became the British zone of Germany 7,588 route miles of railway track. On V.E. Day, only 650 miles were in operation. By December 1945, 7,210 miles were in working order. This map is based on one displayed at the 'Germany Under Control' Exhibition held in London in June–July 1946, another exhibit at which was a specimen of the so-called 'Volkswagen' or 'People's Car,' for which the German people had paid in some £18,000,000 without seeing a car. The companies supposed to make it lay in the British zone, and after the occupation it was put into production for the use of the Control Commission for Germany (British Section).

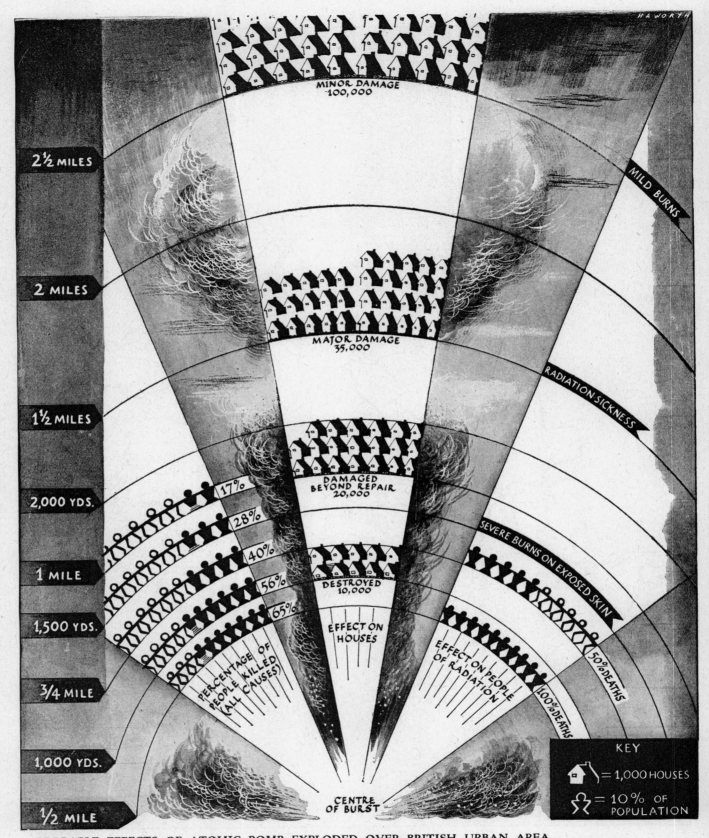

PROBABLE EFFECTS OF ATOMIC BOMB EXPLODED OVER BRITISH URBAN AREA

This diagram, based on a graph reproduced in the report by the British Mission to Japan on 'The Effects of the Atomic Bombs at Hiroshima and Nagasaki' (see page 3847), indicates probable deaths and probable damage to houses which, the experts estimated, would be caused by similar bombs exploded in the air at the same height in an urban area in the British Isles. The probable scale of casualties, remarks the report, would 'make the mere disposal of the dead a major problem.'

Drawn by Haworth

F

H

N

HEART OF THE EMPIRE CELEBRATES FINAL VICTORY

London held its Victory Parade on Saturday June 8, 1946, when the King took the salute from British, Empire and Allied forces in the Mall. The Civil Defence section here swings past the Houses of Parliament into Whitehall.

To face p. 4054   *Direct colour photograph by Pictorial Press*

PEACE Conference of the twenty-one Allied nations, convened to draft treaties with Italy, Rumania, Hungary, Bulgaria, and Finland, began in the Luxembourg Palace in Paris on July 29, 1946. It was formally opened by Mr. Georges Bidault, French Premier and Foreign Minister. Debates at times were stormy and frank to a degree. Dr. Herbert V. Evatt, Australian Minister for External Affairs, provoked much discussion at the first Plenary Session by claiming that the 16 small nations represented in addition to the Big Five—Britain, the U.S.A., the U.S.S.R., France, and China—should have an equal right in making the peace.

After prolonged deliberations which at times threatened to end in deadlock, it was not until August 7 that the Committee on Procedure reached agreement on the methods of voting to be adopted. By 15 votes to 6, it was finally agreed to accept the British compromise amendment whereby all recommendations, whether passed by a simple or a two-thirds majority, should automatically go forward to the Foreign Ministers' Council. On the question of chairmanship the Committee on Procedure on August 2 decided that this office should rotate between the ' Big Five.'

At the opening stages of the Conference the British delegation was led by the Prime Minister, Mr. Clement R. Attlee, in the absence, through illness, of Mr. Ernest Bevin, the Foreign Secretary. Here, Mr. Attlee addresses the Conference on July 30. Above him is Mr. Georges Bidault ; below, some of the team of interpreters.

Photo, Associated Press

To face page 4055

X Y

XE-3 (midget submarine), exploit, 3765, 3771
Xanten, S.L.I. take, *3570*
—Bailey bridge at, *3657*
Yadavindra Regiment, *1424*
Y.A.K.-1, Russian fighter aircraft, *1941*, 1942
Yakhnov, Russians take, 2033, *2036*
Yalta, Russians take, 3134
Yalta Conference, plate f. p. *3558*, *3563*
— —and Poland, 3874
— —and Russia and Japan, 3780
— —and zones of Germany, 3916
Yamamoto, Adm., Japanese C.-in-C., death, 2675, 3288
Yamasaki, Col. Yasuyu, in Attu, 2881
Yamashiro (Japanese battleship), sunk, 3402
Yamashita, Gen. Tomoyukai, death sentence, *3841*
— —demands Bataan surrender, 2092
— —in Leyte, 3270
— —in Malaya, *2041*, *2047*
— —in Philippines, 3743, 3744
Yamato (Japanese battleship), sunk, 3757, 3761, *3762*
Yang Chieh, Gen., in Gibraltar, *3109*
Yangtze R., Chungking on, *2290*, *2304–05*
Yangtze Valley, Japanese offensives in, 1805, 2707
"Yank," U.S. Army newspaper, *2147*
"Yankee Doodle," Eaker's aircraft, *2516*
Yaroslav, Russians take, 3330, 3335
Yarra, H.M.A.S., sunk, 2104
Yartsevo, Russians take, 2827
Yavuz, Turkish cruiser, 722
Yawata, bombed, 3090, 3094, 3285
Ybarnegaray, M. Jean, *1004*, 1009, 1010
—in Pétain's Cabinet, *1167*
"Yellow Peril" (Stearman N2S–2 aircraft), plate fol. p. *2874*
Yellow R., dykes breached, 1996
Yelnya, fighting at, 1835, *1838*, 2826, *2827*
Yemen, and Egypt, 3055
Yenan, Communist government in, 3281, 3775–78
Yenangyaung, captured, 3830
—oilfield destroyed at, 2054, *2056*, *2059*
Yen Kei-shan, Gen., in Shansi, 3777
Yeremenko, Gen. Andrei Ivanovich, *3133*
— —advance on Riga, *3314*
— —in Baltic Republics, 3337, 3341, 3345
— —in Crimea campaign, 3313–35
— —takes Dvinsk, etc., 3330, *3342*
— —takes Nevel, 2919
— —defends Stalingrad, *2413*, 2420
— —summer offensive (1943), 2827
— —and White Russia offensive, 3224
Y Force, Stilwell's, on Salween, 2707
Yingho (gunboat) formerly "Sandpiper," 2295
Yingshan (gunboat) formerly "Gannet," 2295
Yingteh (gunboat), formerly "Falcon," 2295
Yiyang, air raid warning in, *2705*
—civilians return to, *2700*
Ymuiden, demolition at (1940), 826, *845*
Yochow, Japanese base, 2287
Yokohama, Allied generals in, *3836*
—bombed, 3789, 3791, 2125, *2126*
Yokosuka, bombed, 3793
—H.Q. of B.L.F., *3837*
Yomiuri, pictures from, *2299*
Yonai, Adm. Mitsumasa, Japanese Navy Minister, 1475, 1477, 3285
Yontan Airfield, U.S. take, 3754 *3755*
York, H.M.S. and "Artigliere," *1226*
—badge, plate f. p. *1811*
—beached in Suda Bay, *1748*, 1750
York, "Baedeker" raids on, 2115, 2120, *2123*, *2133*
York and Lancs. Regt., in Italy, 2876
Yorkshire, S.S., sunk, *276*, 278
Yorktown, U.S.S., in Coral Sea, *2080*, 2084
—at Midway, *2078*
—sunk, 2085
Young, Sir Mark Aitchison, governor of Hongkong, *1988*, 1989, 1990, 1991, 2104
— —released from internment, *3777*
Young, Maj. Peter, D.S.O., *2407*
Young Communist Party, of Moscow, *1853*
Young Egypt Society, Fascist organization, 3579
Young Spain, march past, *1149*
Yovanovitch, Dr. Slobodan, Yugoslav Premier, 2736
Ypres, Germans take (1940), 885
—liberation (1944), *3251*, *3313*
—Menin Gate, *884* [1521
Yssel Lake, Dutch defence of (1940),
Yssel R., Allies cross (1945), 3663
— —bridge destroyed (1940), *842*
— —as Holland's defence (1940), *292*
— —Nazis bridge (1940), *1552*
Yuan Shih-Kai, Chinese statesman, 1992
Yudenitch, Gen. N. N., Stalin defeats, 2414
Yugoslavia, 123, 557, 571, 762, 763, *1076*, 1866, *3477*, 3869
—Air Force markings, plate f. p. *470*
—in Axis plans, 1587, 1610, 1806, 1809
—ban on King Peter II, 3361
—and Britain, 557, 1613, *3361*
—Bulgaria attacks, 2343
—Chetniks, *1877*, 1878, 1880, 2472, 2573, 3359
—Constituent Assembly, 3871
—coup d'état in, 1866
—flag, plate f. p. *3939*
—frontiers settled by Axis, 2329
—Germany and, 1587, 1610
—German invasion, 1614–22, 1809
—German occupation and rule, 1876–80, 2572
—Govt. in exile, 2736–7
—and Greece, 2577
—and Hungary, 1866, 2339
—and Istria, 3859–61
—"Land Forces, Adriatic," and, 3361
—Mihailovich and Tito, 3359
—Partisans, and Chetniks, 2728, 2737
—post-war problems, 3869
—Regency council, 3361
—Republic set up, 3871
— —federal units, 3362
Yugoslavia (*contd.*)
—Resistance Movement, *2726*, *2727*, 2728–9
—and Russia, *1071*
—Russians enter, *3477*
—Subasich forms Govt., 3361
—Tito as Allied commander, 3359
— —Churchill and, 3360, *3361*
— —Nat. Liberation Army, 3359
— —as Premier, 3869
—and Trieste, 3859–60 *See also* Mihailovich : Tito.
Yui, O. K., Chinese Finance Minister, 3281 [2324
Yukon Territory, Alaska Highway in,
Yumashev, Adm. Ivan, off Japan, 3781
Yunnan, Chinese troops in, *2706*
—land convoy reaches, *3292–93*
—development, 2289
Yunnan-Burma Rly., *2288*
Yussupov M., in Supreme Soviet, *763*
Yuzawa, Michio, Japanese Minister, *2296*, 2899
Ywathitgyi, British at, *3535*

Z

Z5, and Meuse bridges, 1517
Zafrullah Khan, Sir Muhammad, 584, 586, 590, 1734, 1959, 2223
Zagreb, Germans take, 1620
Zahir Shah, K of Afghanistan, 714
Zaimoff, Gen., sentenced to death, 2344
Zakharin, Lt.-Gen., takes Yukhnov, **Zakharov, Col.-Gen. Georgi,** *3222* [*2036*
— —takes Byelostok, *3329*, 3330, 3333
— —takes Ostralenko and Lomza, 3335
— —and White Russia offensive, 3223, 3224, 3226
Zaleski, M. August, Polish Minister, *148*, 149
Zamboanga, Japanese land at, 2094
Zanana Beach, Allies land, 2882
Zangen, Gen. von, and Antwerp 3373
Zanzibar, Sultan of, supports Empire, *197*
—and war charities, *3112*
Zaporozhe, dam destroyed at, *1834*, 1836, 1948
—dam repaired, *3354*
Zara, Allies bomb, 2728 [1084
Zeebrugge, blocked (1940), *917*, 918,
Zeeland, in German invasion, (1940), 1521, *1522*
Zeila, Italians take, 1137, *1138*
Zeitzler Gen., and plot against Hitler, 3168, 3171
Zeke Fighter Aircraft, drop phosphorus bombs, *3093*
Zelenichino, liberated, *2716*
Zero Fighter Aircraft, *2105 2320*
— — —destroyed, New Britain, 3115
— — —down in Kolombangara Is., *3111*
— — —as "suicide planes," *3790*
Zervas, Gen., of E.D.E.S., 2572, 2730
—signs Caserta Agreement, 3358, 3364
Zeven, "tulips" at, *3662*
Zhankoi, Russians take, 3133, 3134
Zhdanov M., in Supreme Soviet, *762*
Zhitomir, fighting at, Russians evacuate 2924, *2925*, 2933, 3075
Zhlobin, Russians take, 3223
ZHUKOV, Marshal Gregory Konstantinovitch (b. 1895). Chief of Russian General Staff and Vice-Commissar for Defence, Feb. 1941. Defeated German offensive, Moscow, 1941;

planned counter-offensive, Stalingrad, 1942; largely responsible partial relief Leningrad, Jan. 1943; promoted Marshal. Commanded 1st Ukrainian Front, Mar. 1944; launched offensive that reached Czechoslovak frontier, Apr. 1945. Commanded Army Group from Vistula to Berlin, Jan.-May 1945. Member Allied Control Commission for Germany, May 1945-April 1946.
— —Allied Control Council, 3914, *3915*
— —in Berlin, *3922*
— —Berlin surrender, 3720–31
— —commands Northern and Central Fronts, 1851, *1852*
— —Chief of Staff, 1821, *1852*
— —Don offensive, 2681
— —and German surrender terms, 3638 *3639*, *3651*
— —saves Moscow, 2162
— —and Oder battle, 3553, *3554*, 3555, 3556, 3559
— —Russian Chief of Staff, 1821, *1852*
— —and Stalingrad relief, 2420, plate f. p. *2495*, 2499, 2500
— —and Ukraine offensive (1944), 3078, 3079, 3082
— —and winter offensive (1942–3), 2711
Zog, King of Albania, country repudiates, 3871
Zietzler, Gen., at Salzburg, 2778
Zilina, fighting at, 3209
Zionism, and Egypt, 3580
—and Iraq, 3582
—Levant and, 3058
Zionists, and Labour Party, 3585
—of Palestine, activities, 2640
—unrest among, 2214
Znamenka, Russians take, 2927
Zouaves, enter Belfort, 3382
—march past of, *620–21*
Zsedenyi, Prof. Bela, President of Hungary, 3326
Zuider Zee, in German invasion (1940), 826, 844, 1521
Zulu, H.M.S., badge, 1454
—sunk, 2388
Zurich, bombs on, 3953
Zutphen, Canadians take, *3663*
Zuzemberk, bombed, *3652*
Zvenigorod, Germans defeated at, 2032
Zveno, Bulgarian Military League, 2798
Zvolen, Russians take, 3623
Zyl, Maj. Gideon Brand van, S. African Gov. Gen., 3741

CORRECTIONS

Page 91. Caption and middle picture: *this photograph is of the* Aircraft Carrier "Glorious," *not the* "Courageous."

Page 806. Air photo. Later officially established that photograph represents Dutch bridges in Maastricht town blown up by Allied sappers. The R.A.F. operation described in caption was carried out against bridges over Albert canal in Belgian territory, two miles outside Maastricht.

Page 1103. Col. 1, lines 1–14, and caption. Later information shows that actual circumstances were these: It was imperative that Surcouf should not run amuck and sink ships in the harbour. Commander Sprague and gallant crew of submarine he was then commanding had difficult task of preventing this. His object was achieved as direct result of well and carefully laid plan being carried out with great courage and determination. It was necessary to force entrance through hatches closed against boarding party. After gaining access to interior of submarine, in course of her capture resistance was encountered which unhappily resulted in Cmdr. Sprague, Lt. Griffiths, an A.B., and one French officer being killed. All other French ships in harbour were dealt with in same way, but any resistance shown was not of such nature as to cause casualties.

Page 1224. Col. 3, line 5 from bottom: *for* Rimmington, *read* Rimington.

Page 1353. Summary in chapter heading, last line: *for* "1941" *read* "1940."

Page 1354. Col. 3, line 7 from bottom: *for* Cavellero *read* Cavallero.

Page 1526. Col. 3, line 10 from bottom, *for* of *read* to.

Page 1756. Expert examination of the photographs which German propaganda alleged were those of the "Bismarck" suggests that in fact they show another German warship—either the "Scharnhorst" or the "Gneisenau."

Page 2197. Col. 3, lines 11, 12 and 13 should read: "War supplies began to roll over the highway in October 1942, but it was not until early in 1943 . . ."

Page 2318. Col. 1, line 12: *delete* "first."

Page 2474. Under date Sept. 2, 1942: *for* Duesseldorf, *read* Karlsruhe.

Page 2539. Col. 1, line 3: *for* has, *read* had.

Page 2582. Col. 2, lines 20–21: *for* "Allied Attack on Oran," *read* "Naval Battle of Casablanca"

Page 2584. Col. 3, lines 4–3 from end: *for* "but only one aircraft-carrier, H.M.S. Eagle. She was sunk on Aug. 11," *read* "and three aircraft-carriers. One, H.M.S. Eagle, was sunk on Aug. 11."

Page 2682. Col. 2, line 6: *for* Feb. 2, *read* Jan. 31.

Page 2692. Col. 3, line 2 of caption: *for* Jan., *read* Oct.

Page 2743. Bottom line of caption: *for* Naysmith, *read* Nasmith.

Page 2753. Col. 1, line 1 of caption: *for* Brigadier, *read* Major-General.

Page 2845. Col. 1, lines 41–2: *for* July 6, *read* July 9.

Page 2848. Col. 2, line 9: *for* Sept. 8, *read* Sept. 3.

Page 2873. Col. 3, line 8: *for* from, *read* to.

Page 2895. Caption, line 3; *for* July 1943, *read* April 1943.

Page 2897. Lower caption, line 1: *for* Dec. 8, *read* Dec. 7.

Page 2901. Col. 3, line 6 from bottom: *for* Order, *read* Ordre.

Page 3001. Lower caption; *transpose names* Gracey *and* Cowan.

Page 3005. Col. 2, last line: *for* Cochrane, *read* Cochran.

Page 3054. Caption, line 5: *for* 1945, *read* 1944.

Page 3150. Col. 1, line 15 from end: *for* "three times as much as expected," *read* "nearly a third more than was expected."

Page 3177. Col. 1, line 2: *for* Barreville-sur-Mer, *read* Barneville-sur-Mer.

Page 3239. Col. 2, line 21: *for* August 12, *read* April 12.

Page 3263. Col. 2, line 13: *for* 2nd, *read* 3rd.

Page 3275. Col. 3, line 3 from end: *for* December 30, *read* December 29.

Page 3322. Col. 1, line 2: *for* August 22, *read* August 20.

Page 3326. Col. 3, last line: *for* December 29, *read* December 28.

Page 3372, *add* under British Units: Army Catering Corps.

Page 3395. Col. 1, caption, line 2: *for* December 11, *read* December 12.

Page 3536. Map: against Cheduba I: *for* Jan. 27, *read* Jan. 26. Under Taungup, *for* March 13, *read* April. 16:

Page 3552. Col. 2, line 8 from end: *for* March 15, *read* March 21.

Page 3588. Col. 1, line 11: *for* Morotai and Halmahera, *read* Morotai in the Halmaheras.

Page 3622. Col. 1, line 10,: *for* south-west, *read* north-west.

Page 3623. Col. 3, line 4: *for* Miskolc, but, *read* Miskolc. But.

Page 3628. *Delete* "R.A.F. attacked Gestapo H.Q., Copenhagen" under March 15.

Page 3777. Lower caption: *for* Sir Charles Shenton Thomas, *read* Sir Thomas Shenton Thomas.

Editor's Epilogue

ONLY by the method of publication which has brought this contemporary chronicle of the Second Great War to completion could a work of its magnitude have been produced by private enterprise. We have seen official histories of one war take so long to gestate that they had not fully issued from the womb of Time before a new and greater war had developed . . . and the course of events in this new war would quickly falsify, perhaps render for ever obsolete, the findings of the learned military and naval experts as set forth in their still incomplete but eminently official record and review of its less grisly predecessor!

In this way the profoundest knowledge of a galaxy of expert contributors, marshalled with sedulous care by a succession of editors through many years, would eventually be entombed in a forbidding array of imposing tomes, at great cost to the taxpayers, few of whom would ever know of the existence of the monumental work. Such official histories are doubtless valuable as quarries of ascertained facts for the historians of a future day, but a contemporary chronicle such as that which has been assembled within the volumes of THE SECOND GREAT WAR claims no sort of relationship to them. It could well be described as The People's History of the First Total World War, 1939–1945—and no less a claim than that, if no higher, its Editor here submits, with the completed work now available for its verification. The title under which it has gone out to the world of readers was first chosen in 1939 as a natural successor to that of *The Great War*, 1914–1918, issued by the same publishers.

AMONG the flood of publications which the outbreak of the War in 1939 called forth—very few of which endured to completion—THE SECOND GREAT WAR stands alone, unique. The success it has already attained offers the completest justification of the serial method of publication. In my introductory note to the first serial number, the reader will find (p. 1, vol. 1) a brief forecast of the editorial plan, and in re-reading that note seven years afterwards, when I have the satisfaction of penning this closing page, I shall venture the statement that we have carried to a successful conclusion that programme which was outlined at a time when, most fortunately, few of the difficulties we were fated to struggle against in the task so enthusiastically entered upon were present in the minds of the Editor and his colleagues, else, indeed, these might well have daunted us.

To enumerate all the obstacles which beset our path of production, especially when our editorial offices and printing works had become storm centres of aerial attack in many of the most devastating visits of the *Luftwaffe*—an early bomb falling plumb in the street in front of the Editor's office, but fortunately doing little damage beyond closing the thoroughfare for five or six months—to recall the hundreds of alarms

and excursions to our underground shelters, which punctuated our laborious days with exciting incidents, would be no more than to describe the daily trials of all toilers " in streaming London's central roar," where siren and falling bomb stressed the roar in a way the poet had scarcely imagined.

But it is worth remembering that the work of producing this contemporary history of the world's most exciting years went forward at the very core of the excitement, not without tremor or apprehension, but with such determination on the part of all concerned that their united labours have brought this vivid pictorial record to completion in a form which derives something from the very enthusiasm and excitement of those days and nights in which its production was achieved. Much that was obtainable in this way and at that time would else have been lost and difficult, if not impossible, to recover in any later effort to arrive at the completeness of text and picture which has here been secured by regularly sustained publication throughout those stirring seven years.

IT has been the privilege of the Editor to carry to their successful conclusion similar pictorial histories of the two greatest wars of modern times, the first in association with the late H. W. Wilson, famous as naval and military critic of the *Daily Mail*, and in the present work he has had the greatly valued co-operation of Maj.-Gen. Sir Charles Gwynn, K.C.B., D.S.O., one of the most scholarly exponents of the military art and a veteran in its practice. On every aspect of the military side of the war his counsel and collaboration have been invaluable, and many of our more important chapters have been written by him. It might be

EDITOR'S EPILOGUE *(Continued)*

said for both of us that, despite the uneasy Peace in which our respective editorial labours are ending and the rash talk of a third world war to be heard everywhere, not the least of our satisfactions is the reasonable hope that such another catastrophe will not come in the years that remain to either of us. But if this were to prove a vain hope, the present writer may at least console himself with the thought that he has now earned his release from the responsibility of making any further addition to the list of war publications which he began in 1914, some mention of which is made below.

To give the reader some idea of the immense total of information which has been accumulated in sequence of time within these volumes of THE SECOND GREAT WAR, I have made the following counts of our contents and will leave these to bear witness to the continuous labours of the editorial staff during the years in which the work has been in production.

DESCRIPTIVE AND CRITICAL TEXT

Three hundred and eighty-seven chapters, making an aggregate of over one and a half million words, wherein are covered critical and descriptive accounts of every campaign, every event of importance by land, sea, or in the air, and a comprehensive review of the social and political conditions obtaining in all countries concerned throughout the War years.

THE DIARY OF EVENTS

A complete day-by-day record of every event of any importance is given at suitable stages throughout the narrative, the total number of pages devoted to the Diary alone being fifty-five.

HISTORIC DOCUMENTS

No fewer than one hundred and sixteen pages comprising three hundred and thirteen separate documents totalling over one hundred and fifty-six thousand words are devoted to a skilful condensation of all the official pronouncements, agreements, pacts, and important speeches of War leaders, from the Chamberlain-Hitler exchanges of August 22 and 23, 1939, on the eve of the War, to the verdict of the Nuremberg trials of Nazi war guilt on September 30

and October 1, 1946. Our whole series of Historic Documents thus forms a continuous digest of the most momentous recorded words in that critical period of time which will change the course of world history for the next thousand years—as Hitler promised the Germans.

THE ILLUSTRATIONS

The pictorial abundance of these volumes is seen in the fact that, counting all varieties of illustrated items, there are upwards of seven thousand five hundred. In the main these are actual photographs of scenes from every theatre of the war, mostly taken at risk of life by accredited official photographers. But they also cover all the historic naval engagements and aerial activities, and include numerous photographs of the leading personages of every country involved in the world-wide conflict.

COLOURED PICTURES

The art of direct photography in colour made considerable progress during the last seven years, and *THE SECOND GREAT WAR* is perhaps the first publication of this kind to have made such use of it in its illustrations. While some hundred and thirty fine art plates containing over six hundred separate subjects printed in full colours add greatly to the attraction of the work as an artistic production, they also enhance its value as a work of reference in reproducing hundreds of ships' badges, Army formation signs, awards and decorations, striking examples of artists' war paintings, and portraits, all in correct natural colours.

MAPS & PLANS OF BATTLE-AREAS

These, of which by far the larger number have been expressly drawn to enable the reader more clearly to follow the narrative, are given as nearly as possible to the text which they were designed to accompany. Their total number exceeds three hundred.

THE GENERAL INDEX

This has been made a leading feature of *THE SECOND GREAT WAR* and runs to great length (120,000 words), with the object of giving the reader the fullest assistance in enabling him to find, with a minimum of delay, any particular event among the many thousands recorded. It is also, in a way, a " Who's Who " of the personalities who have come up to world fame in the course of the conflict, many of whom were previously unknown to the reading public.

*I*t will not be surprising that in the course of the seven years during which the publication of THE SECOND GREAT WAR has been maintained—first on a fortnightly basis before the acute shortage of paper made that inconvenient, and then for over five years as a monthly issue, until in the last year of its production we were able to revert to fortnightly parts—it will not surprise the reader to learn that from a variety of causes many changes had to be made in the editorial and contributing staffs who have assisted the Editor-in-chief. But I have been fortunate in the co-operation of Mr. J. R. Fawcett Thompson, who originally was concerned mainly with the art side of the publication, and from 1943 until its conclusion acted as Associate Editor, and Mr. John St. Denys Reed, who gave skilled service for some four years as an associate editor in charge of text, being eventually succeeded in that capacity, owing to reasons of health, by a very experienced journalist, Miss Irene Clephane. There are others who might be mentioned who rendered some temporary assistance, but it will suffice if I add the name of Mr. Alfred Bell, a veteran of pictorial journalism who has been an active member of our art department from start to finish.

Nor is it out of place to add that the publishers of the serial issue, The Amalgamated Press, Ltd., have a considerable line of war publications to their credit, dating back to the famous *With the Flag to Pretoria* (1900–1), and including *The Great War* (1914–1919, 13 Vols.), *The War Illustrated* (1914–19, 9 Vols.),

World War : A Pictured History (1922, 2 Vols.), *A Popular History of the Great War* (1920, 6 Vols.), *I Was There ! The Human Story of the Great War* (1938–9, 3 Vols.), and *The War Illustrated* (1939–1947, 10 Vols.), the last five named being produced under the present editorship. The Waverley Book Company, in association with The Amalgamated Press, began to issue THE SECOND GREAT WAR in volume form in 1940, and in their hands it has already met with such wide acceptance that its sale promises to eclipse all previous records for any war history first launched in serial form as a contemporary chronicle of events.

THE Editor's chief satisfaction abides in the knowledge that the work of those years of stress and strain devoted to THE SECOND GREAT WAR has produced a collection of pictorial documents that will endure and increase in interest as time goes on, and that readers of a future day will readily find within its literary pages authentic accounts of every happening of importance in those tremendous years when the British Commonwealth and Empire lived through some of her darkest hours to justify the faith of her great leaders in ultimate triumph. Long live the British Commonwealth and Empire !

J A Hammerton

October 1946